# Knight Templar Magazine Biographies

by
Ivan M. Tribe

Edited by
John L. Palmer

Knight Templar Magazine - Biographies

A Cornerstone Book
Published by Cornerstone Book Publishers
An Imprint of Michael Poll Publishing



Cornerstone Book Publishers
New Orleans, LA
www.cornerstonepublishers.com

Cover Design by Michael R. Poll

First Cornerstone Edition - 2014

ISBN: 1613421699
ISBN-13: 978-1-61342-169-7

MADE IN THE USA

## Table of Contents

## Preface and Acknowledgments

In November 1992 I had just completed a book manuscript for the University of Illinois Press when I learned that Roy Acuff, elderly country music star of the *Grand Ole Opry* and long-time Tennessee Mason, had passed to the "celestial lodge above." Having taken note for decades of well-known persons from the pages of history and public life who were brother Masons, I thought that perhaps readers of *Knight Templar* might enjoy reading a brief account of Sir Knight Acuff's life and Masonic background. Receiving a favorable response from then Assistant Editor, Joan Morton, I went forward. From that modest beginning, more articles began to flow from the pen, typewriter, and word processor. Subjects progressed from music figures to movie stars, businessmen, army generals, statesmen, frontiersmen, and other notable persons. Throughout, I tried to concentrate on eminent Masons who had not had much written on them in fraternal journals, believing that there were more Masonic figures who deserved attention than another piece on George Washington, Ben Franklin, Andrew Jackson, or Harry Truman. For that matter, there are still numerous figures out there who deserve our attention such as Robert LaFollette, Jesse Helms, Lyman Lemnitzer, Andrew Mellon, Bart Starr, Tris Speaker, Red Grange, Tony Martin, and Edd Matthews just to mention a few.

As more articles began to appear, compliments from regionally active Sir Knights including Richard Weaver, Don Gardner, and the late George Barkhurst as well as those from my own Athens Commandery No. 15 provided further encouragement. So too did correspondence from such Sir Knights as Joseph Bennett and Norman Lincoln who had themselves demonstrated accomplishment in this form of Masonic biography. Some months ago, Sir Knight John Palmer suggested that these short biographies be collected in book form and Brother Michael R. Poll of Cornerstone Book Publishers concurred, which brings us to the present.

No labor of this magnitude can be exclusively the work of one person. My wife Deanna helped type, retype, and proofread the entire manuscript. Several of the earlier pieces were typed by my student assistants, Abby Goodnite and Shasta Amos. Twenty were put in electronic form by Lady Diane Reeves, wife of my second cousin Sir Knight Virgil Reeves. Another was done by Companion

Robert Fish of Bosworth Council No. 46. Much help with illustrations came from Brother Jacob Bapst of Centreville Lodge No. 371 and Brother John Morris of Brighton Lodge No. 247 (MI). Sir Knight Palmer readied the manuscript for Cornerstone. Most of the original articles benefited from the keen proofreading eye of Sir Knight Roger VanDyke of my own home lodge, Albany No. 723. Brother Bobby Copeland of the Valley of Knoxville and Jerry Douglass of the Valley of Little Rock provided assistance on certain popular culture figures. Numerous persons who either work or volunteer in Grand Lodge offices, Grand York Rite bodies, Scottish Rite Vallies, and Shrine Temples who looked up data in their archives and records deserve my thanks. All of these persons including the aforementioned Morton, Palmer, Poll, and Weaver have earned my gratitude.

Ivan M. Tribe, Ph.D., K.Y.C.H., 33°, K.C.T.
McArthur, Ohio
December 26, 2011

## Foreword

Before I even assumed my duties as managing editor of the *Knight Templar* magazine, I began to get a good deal of advice and "input" from the readers. The number one comment was, "we are sick and tired of stories about dead baseball players." They were, of course, referring to the biographies that the magazine had been publishing for the last fourteen years.

As the Editorial Review Board and I began to formulate policy about what would and would not be published in the *Knight Templar*, we introduced some restrictions on biographical material which would have eliminated many of the previously published biographies. As a result, the number of biographies published in the magazine decreased dramatically for the next two years.

During this time, I began to get inquiries like this: "What happened to the wonderful biographies that you used to publish in the magazine?" Well, you can't please everyone. We are still publishing Dr. Ivan Tribe's biographies at the rate of about two per year. To date, he has had over 90 published in our magazine and I know that he is aspiring to have 100.

Tribe's articles focus primarily on politicians, entertainers, military men, and sports figures who held Masonic membership. You can tell that he has a particular interest in country music, Ohio, and baseball. We hope that this collection of his articles from as far back as 1993 will satisfy the demand to have them re-printed. We have even included a couple that were not printed in the magazine. Sir Knight Tribe has certainly supported the magazine for many years with his work and we publish this book as a tribute to him and his continuing contribution to the success of our magazine.

John L. Palmer
Managing Editor, *Knight Templar* magazine
January 2012

Knight Templar Magazine
Biographies

## Brother A. B. Graham:
*Father of the 4-H Program*

For more than a century the 4-H program has enriched the lives of America's young people. Designed originally for rural youth, the 4-H movement has spread into the cities and to numerous foreign lands. The principal founder of this movement spent much of his later life shepherding and promoting 4-H. He also was a dedicated Mason and spent some seventy years as a member of the order. Albert Belmont Graham had been a township school superintendent in Clark County, Ohio, when he initiated what he first called an Agricultural Experiment Club with thirty members on January 15, 1902. By the time he died fifty-eight years later, millions of boys and girls had claimed membership in 4-H groups.

Albert Belmont Graham was born on a farm in Champaign County, Ohio, on March 13, 1868. His parents, Joseph A. and Esther Reed Graham, had married the year before, and a year and one-half after Albert's birth, the couple had another child, Leticia, nicknamed Lettie. Although the family had been described as "average," Joseph Graham, his brother George, and his cousin William all belonged to Social Lodge No. 217, F. & A.M. in nearby Lena, a lodge that was chartered in 1852. When the children reached school age, both Albert and Lettie walked a half-mile to attend the Carmony one-room school.

Young Albert's youth was severely disrupted on February 2, 1879, when the Graham farm home caught fire and burned to the ground. Joseph Graham suffered injuries during the inferno and died eight days later. The farm had been mortgaged, and Esther Graham was forced to sell it to pay off the debt. With the $1,021.75 left over, she began a new career as a dressmaker in a small home in the nearby village of Lena. The income she received enabled her to rear her two small children in modest circumstances and instill in young Albert a determination to improve his lot in life through additional education.

At seventeen he graduated from Lena-Conover School and the following fall secured a position as teacher at the same Carmony School he himself had attended only a few years earlier. He received a salary of $320 for the first year of teaching and remained at this post for two years.

Aspiring to obtain more schooling for himself, young A. B. Graham enrolled as a full-time student at National Normal University in Lebanon, Ohio, for the 1887-1888 school year. He then returned to Carmony for another term. In the summer of 1889, the young teacher followed in the path of his paternal relatives. On July 11, 1889, he took his Entered Apprentice degree in Social Lodge No. 217. He was passed to the degree of Fellowcraft on August 8, 1889.

According to Graham biographers, Virginia and Robert McCormick, he and a friend aspired to attend Wittenberg College in nearby Springfield. They rented a room and moved to campus, but when the two "discovered that they would not be allowed to attend Masonic meetings in town," they angrily withdrew. Graham "took a train to Columbus" and enrolled at Ohio State University. Over the holiday break on January 2, 1890, A. B. Graham was raised a Master Mason and remained a member for the next seventy years. He also joined the Odd Fellows Lodge in Lena and the Knights of Pythias in nearby St. Paris. Illness soon forced the young student to drop out of O.S.U., but in mid-March he took over as principal of the Lena-Conover School at a monthly salary of seventy dollars. This "pay raise" also enabled him to marry his sweetheart, Maude Lauer, on August 14, 1890. The marriage endured for sixty years until Maude's death and resulted in the birth of five children, one of whom died in infancy.

A. B. Graham spent the remainder of the 1890s as a teacher in various local schools in Champaign, Miami, and Shelby counties. In 1900 he became a full-time superintendent of Clark County, Ohio schools at an annual salary of $675. This system consisted of the one-room variety but some contained two or three rooms. Actually this rural system partly encircled the city of Springfield, a bustling city of 38,000 population with a thriving farm implement industry.

As a teacher and administrator, Graham had become a participant in what was becoming known as the Country Life Movement. As the U.S. became more urbanized and industrialized, many acute observers on the national scene came to believe that rural life had become boring, dull, backward, and stultifying. Farm-reared youth increasingly migrated to the cities to seek industrial work and spend their adult lives in an urban atmosphere, sometimes with negative results. Thus these reformers sought manner and means to revitalize rural living. Concurrently, a back-to-nature movement developed in the cities designed to acquaint urban youth with the "ways of nature" and life in the woods. These movements resulted in the organization of such groups as Junior Audubon societies, the Boy Scouts, the Girl Scouts, and the Camp Fire Girls. Educators pushed such innovations as field trips, classroom libraries, brightly-decorated classrooms, and eventually consolidated school districts. To Graham and his contemporaries, a field trip might range from a simple walk near the school yard to a journey by street car to Ohio State University; each constituted a valuable educational experience.

A. B. Graham's own contribution to the Country Life Movement came in mid-January 1902 when he organized what he termed "Boys' and Girls' Agricultural Experiment Clubs." The children learned how to do soil tests, develop "experimental plots of corn," and "grow flowers from seeds obtained from Congressman (Brother James) Cox." Within ten years Graham's program was attracting state and even national attention. By the fall of 1904, the Dean of the School of Agriculture at Ohio State University reported that there were sixteen clubs with 664 members in ten Ohio counties. Graham's writings and lectures on the program began to have an effect, and the movement spread even more rapidly with a series of articles in a journal called *Agricultural Student.*

In the fall of 1904, A. B. Graham took a teaching position inside of Springfield, but it was only a stopgap job because on April 1, 1905, the Ohio State University Board of Trustees created and named him to the new post of Superintendent of Agricultural Extension at Ohio State at an annual salary of $1,500. In this position Graham made a number of innovations in terms of extension work at Ohio's land-grant college, some of which were later incorporated into the congressional Smith-Lever Act of 1914. This law created the Cooperative Extension Service, a program which several states including Ohio (by the Alsdorf Law) had already enacted. Needless to say, he used this state position to continue promoting the Agriculture Experiment Clubs. After nine years, he left Ohio, resigning on June 24, 1914, to become head of the extension program at the New York School of Agriculture.

Unfortunately Graham's year in New York proved less than satisfactory, primarily because the Empire State's program lacked sufficient organization and proper funding. He quickly became disillusioned but rejected offers to take charge of extension work in Connecticut, South Dakota, and Washington as well as rejecting a return to Ohio. Meanwhile, another offer came from the U. S. Department of Agriculture.

President Wilson signed the Smith-Lever Act on May 8, 1914, creating a federal partnership with state and local governments as the Cooperative Extension Service. A. B. Graham received an offer, which he accepted, to become Administrative Specialist in State Relations Service which allotted funding to states in connection with their own programs.

He retained this status until 1922 when he became the man in charge of Subject Matter Specialists in the Department of Agriculture. After sixteen years in this position, the age seventy mandatory retirement law forced his retirement in March 1938. The veteran educator returned to Columbus, Ohio where he lived for another twenty-two years.

Meanwhile, the youth movement A. B. Graham had started continued growing. Early members in Iowa had used a three-leaf clover with a letter H on each leaf, denoting hands, head, and heart. In 1911 a four-leaf clover with another letter H for "health" was added. In 1918 when the name "4-H Club" came into general use, membership reached a half-million. By 1936 4-H membership totaled over one million for the first time. In 1974 some seven million youth were enrolled in 4-H programs. As 4-H historian Franklin Reck once stated, the program was so big and complex that it could not be claimed by any one man. Others who contributed to the early development included W. B. Otwell, Seaman Knapp, Marie Cromer, O. H. Benson, and Gertrude Warren. Yet Graham must be considered the foremost figure.

As a result, Springfield, Ohio, became the site for issuance of the commemorative stamp honoring the 50$^{th}$ anniversary of 4-H Clubs on January 15, 1952, 50 years after Graham's club had its first meeting. Sir Knight Norman Lincoln was present at the time and recalls that the 84-year-old pioneer figure seemed somewhat confused at the moment when he received the most public honors. Given his advancing age, this seems quite plausible. In the remaining eight years of his life, Brother Graham continued receiving honors including honorary doctorates from both Ohio State University and Marietta College. In 1957 Graham High School in St. Paris, Ohio was named for the aged educator.

A. B. Graham died on January 14, 1960, one day short of the 58th anniversary of the founding of 4-H and 70 years and 12 days after he had been raised in Social Lodge No. 217. Further honors came to him after his death: in 1972 "Great Ohioans" who have had the most influence, and in 1984 he was inducted into the Agricultural Hall of Fame in Bonner Springs, Kansas.

Yet the greatest memorial to Brother Albert Belmont Graham is the 4-H Clubs of America. In 2000 their national office estimated membership at more than six million. Furthermore, 4-H Clubs thrive in many foreign nations as well. His legacy is indeed significant.

**Note**: The best source of information on A. B. Graham is Virginia E. and Robert W. McCormick, *A. B. Graham: Country Schoolmaster and Extension Pioneer* (1984) supplemented by Thomas Wessel and Marilyn Wessel, *4-H: An American Idea, 1900-1980* (1982). The Grand Lodge of Ohio furnished Graham's Masonic record. Sir Knight Norman Lincoln contributed the stamp and his recollection of the 1952 event in Springfield. I also appreciate the Companion (whose name I have forgotten) who a few years ago at an Athens Chapter No. 39 R.A.M. inspection alerted me to Graham's Masonic membership.

July 2002; slightly revised 2011

**Sir Knight Addie Joss:** *The Tragic Story of a Baseball Great*

Just over a century ago a young Wisconsinite emerged as one of baseball's best pitchers. For the next four seasons, he had twenty or more victories, pitched a perfect game, and had a second no-hitter for good measure. John Holway and Bob Carroll in *Total Baseball* called him "the hardest man in history to reach base against." Addie Joss seemed destined to rank with the game's all-time greats and was also a model citizen, excellent family man, skilled sportswriter, and an active member of five Masonic bodies. Then his health went into a tailspin, and he died when barely thirty-one.

Adrian C. Joss was born in Woodland, Wisconsin on April 12, 1880. His father, Jacob Joss, had come to America from Switzerland during the Civil War and initially prospered in the cheese making trade. Addie's mother was the daughter of German immigrants. About 1884, the Joss business fortunes went into decline, probably because Jacob Joss developed a drinking problem which undoubtedly hastened his death in 1890. The boy's widowed mother opened a millinery shop, and young Addie helped her in a variety of ways and played games with other boys in the small town of Juneau. He excelled in baseball, particularly pitching.

Finishing high school at sixteen, Joss taught school. In the spring, he pitched for Wayland Academy and later Sacred Heart College; then he played for local teams in the summer. His blazing fastball attracted widespread attention. Early in 1900, Addie received a letter from the owner of the minor league Toledo Mud Hens offering him a tryout and a salary of $75.00 per month if he made the team.

Addie Joss spent two seasons with the Mud Hens. Pitching in the Inter-State League in 1900, he compiled a 19-16 record. However, with Toledo in a new League, the Western Association, the next year he dominated the circuit, winning 27 games and accumulated 210 strikeouts while walking only 67 batters. Major league owners including Charles Ebbets of the Brooklyn Dodgers tried to buy the young hurler, but Mud Hens owner Charles Strobel refused to sell him. Eventually Joss signed with the relatively new American League team, the Cleveland Bluebirds, when club owner Charles Somers (a member of Tyrian Lodge No. 370 in Cleveland, raised on March 3, 1895) promised to handle any legal wrangling that might result from his departure from the Mud Hens. Ironically, Addie would retain Toledo as his permanent home because his future wife, Lillian Shinavar, hailed from the Glass City.

Addie Joss moved into the starting rotation at Cleveland fairly quickly, posting a 17-13 pitching record including a league-leading five shutouts and a 2.77 earned run average. When the season ended, he married Lillian on October 11, 1902, and then went on a cross-country barnstorming tour. Coming back for a second season with a club now known simply as the Blues, the man often referred to in the press as "the Elongated Twirler" had an 18-13 record for the year. He also had his first bout with illness, missing the entire month of September and undoubtedly missed the opportunity to win twenty games. Recurring health problems plagued him all through 1904, but he still posted a 14-10 record, and his ERA dropped to 1.59.

Charles Somers promised Addie a $500 bonus if he could win twenty games in 1905, and he made an all-out effort to reach that goal since by that time he had a child, son Norman, in addition to a wife to support. Besides, his close friend Napoleon Lajoie had been named player-manager, and the team now known as the "Naps" gave fans hope that the popular second baseman could lift the team out of the general mediocrity they often displayed on the field. The Naps might have reached their goal had Addie not missed several starts in mid-season, and Lajoie missed a month of play after contracting blood-poisoning from a nasty spike wound. Nonetheless, Addie still managed to get his twenty wins, posting a victory in the final game of the season in spite of the Clevelanders committing five errors. He used his bonus to help purchase a home on Fulton Street in Toledo.

The 1906 season started well, and in mid-year, club owner Somers promised an additional $5,000 for team members to divide among themselves if they could bring a pennant to Cleveland. Unfortunately, injuries plagued the team with star third-baseman,

Bill Bradley, shattering his wrist, and others were also out of the lineup for days at a time. At one point, the weak-hitting Joss had to play center field to keep the Naps on the field. In spite of occasional arm trouble and taking a few days off when Lillian gave birth to daughter Ruth Theresa, Addie managed to win 21 games, pitch 9 shutouts, and compile a 1.72 ERA. He earned another $500 bonus. With a wife and two small children at home, Addie showed less interest in post-season barnstorming. Instead he took a position as Sunday Sports Editor for the *Toledo News-Bee*. He proved adept at this job and looked forward to work as a sportswriter when his playing days ended.

During that same winter of 1906-1907, Adrian C. Joss manifested a serious interest in Masonry by petitioning Sanford L. Collins Lodge No. 396 in Toledo. Somewhat surprisingly, by the time he took his degrees, the season had started. Joss was initiated on May 16, 1907; passed on May 28, 1907; and raised on June 25, 1907. Whether he returned to Toledo on these dates or some lodge in Cleveland did courtesy work cannot be determined at this time. What is more certain is that he took his other Masonic work in the off-season. In the York Rite, Joss became a member of Toledo Chapter No. 161, Royal Arch Masons and Toledo Council No. 33, Royal and Select Masters. He took all the chivalric degrees in Toledo Commandery No. 7 on October 9, 1908. Three months later, he took the Scottish Rite degrees in the Valley of Toledo in three days, January 27, 28, and 29, 1909. According to his biographer Scott Longert, Addie took great pride in his "hand-carved sword and ring" (probably a 14° degree AASR ring).

The same winter that Addie Joss petitioned Sanford L. Collins Lodge, he also held out for a $4,000 annual salary, successfully as events would prove. The game's premier pitcher responded to his raise by winning his first ten starts, one of them being a near miss on a no-hitter. He threw two more one-hitters in that season, kept Cleveland in contention through most of the season, and posted his best season at 27-11. He pitched 38 complete games and had a 1.83 ERA. Furthermore, he afterward covered the World Series for the *News-Bee* and the Cleveland *Press,* with the United Press picking up many of his summaries and syndicating them nationwide.

The following season saw the Naps in the thick of the pennant race almost to the end of the season. It also saw Addie Joss pitch what some observers held to be the most perfect mound performance in the history of the game. Near the end of the season on October 2, 1908, Addie retired twenty-seven consecutive batters in defeating the

Chicago White Sox and his rival Ed Walsh in a friendly pitcher's duel. The Naps, however, narrowly lost their opportunity for a World Series. A week later to the day, Joss had the honor of being created a member of the valiant and magnanimous Order of the Temple.

The following season proved disappointing for Cleveland as they dropped to seventh place in the eight team league. Joss had only a 14-13 season. While he still had a most respectable 1.71 ERA, the team didn't score many runs for him. In fact, had it not been for the nineteen wins posted by the recently acquired veteran hurler Sir Knight Cy Young (of St. Bernard Commandery No. 71 in Ohio), the team's slide would have been even worse. Young and Joss had already been friends and became roommates. In 1910, Addie experienced more health problems and went 5-5 for the season but did have a second no hitter among his few victories. On July 25, Joss pitched his last game and went home to rest for the remainder of the season. Little did he know that he would never pitch again in a regular season game. His final won-lost record was 160-97 with a 1.89 ERA.

Joss spent the winter resting and relaxing although he did spend some time greeting friends and customers in the billiard parlor in which he had purchased a half interest. Going to spring training in 1911, Addie hoped to recover his old form, but it was not to be. On April 1, during the trip north, he collapsed on the ball field in Chattanooga. Sent home to Toledo, several physicians examined the ailing pitcher, but by the time his problem was correctly diagnosed as tubercular meningitis, he was near death. In the words of his biographer, "there was no cure and no hope." Sir Knight Adrian C. Joss went to his maker several hours later at about 1:45 A.M. on April 14, 1911.

The city of Toledo gave their adopted son one of the biggest funerals in the Glass City's history. The entire Cleveland team threatened to strike if their game with Detroit was not postponed so the entire squad could attend. League president, Brother Ban Johnson of N.C. Harmony Lodge No. 2 in Cincinnati, first refused but finally relented. A large delegation of fellow Knights Templar accompanied his remains from the Joss home to the Masonic Temple where an honor guard of Sir Knights guarded the casket. Over 15,000 people paid their final respects. Former major league outfielder turned revivalist, Billy Sunday, presided over a service filled with baseball imagery. The event concluded with the Scottish Rite ring ceremony. The Knights took the body to Woodlawn Cemetery where it was laid to rest. It was said to have been "the largest Masonic funeral Toledo had ever seen."

Club owner and Brother Charles Somers took steps to stage a benefit game to raise funds for the family of the club's deceased star. Scheduled for July 24, 1911, a group of baseball all-stars that included such Masonic future Hall of Fame members as "Home Run" Baker, Ty Cobb, and Eddie Collins loaned their talents, and Cobb donated $100 besides. Other donors included two Masons who were National League executives, Brothers Garry Hermann of the Reds and Charles Ebbets of the Dodgers. Even the notoriously tight-fisted Charlie Comiskey of the White Sox chipped in $100. More than $13,000 went to the surprised widow, Lillian Joss. This amount would be roughly equal to a quarter of a million dollars in modern money.

For more than a half-century, Addie Joss, once called "the Swiss Whiz from Wisconsin," was not considered for the Hall of Fame at Cooperstown. Rules required that a player must play in ten major league seasons, and Joss fell short by a year. Finally the rules were changed whereby special exceptions could be made for players whose careers were shortened by death or catastrophic illness. In 1978, Adrian C. Joss was finally made a member of Baseball's Hall of Fame. This was a fitting tribute to a fine man and Mason. Brother Ty Cobb had ranked him with Walter Johnson as the toughest pitcher for him to hit. His roommate and fellow Knight Templar Cy Young was quoted as saying that "I never met a fairer or squarer man than Addie." It seemed like a fitting tribute to a fallen fellow brother.

**Note**: The life of Addie Joss has been chronicled in Scott Longert, "Addie Joss: King of the Pitchers" (Cleveland: Society for American Baseball Research, 1998). Also useful is Michael Coffey, *27 Men Out: Baseball's Perfect Game"* (New York: ATRIA Books, 2004). Also useful is Reed Browning, *Cy Young: A Baseball Life* (University of Massachusetts Press, 2000). The staff at the Grand Lodge of Ohio supplied Brother Joss' blue lodge records while Grand Recorder Richard Palm of the Grand Commandery of Ohio supplied his Knight Templar data as did the staff at the Valley of Toledo AASR. Help with the photographs was supplied by my Rio Grande colleague Sam Wilson, the Western Reserve Historical Society, and Brother Peter Westbere of Guelph, Ontario.

April 2005; slightly revised 2011

## Sir Knight Arthur H. Vandenberg:
*Father of Bipartisan Foreign Policy*

Arthur H. Vandenberg died more than a half-century ago and seems largely to be a forgotten figure, yet in the last quarter century of his life, Vandenberg was a major player on the American political scene. In the early years of the "Cold War," this Senator from Michigan ranked behind only the president and the secretary of state in formulating America's reaction to new challenges in the post-war world.

Arthur Hendrick Vandenberg was born in Grand Rapids, Michigan on March 22, 1884. His parents, Aaron and Alpha Hendrick Vandenberg of Dutch and Anglo-Saxon backgrounds, had migrated to the Wolverine State from the Mohawk Valley of New York. Alpha's father had been a delegate to the 1860 Republican National Convention that nominated Abraham Lincoln for president. Aaron Vandenberg had been in the harness business until his establishment went under in the Panic of 1893. Arthur's mother opened a boarding house, and the only son worked at selling vegetables and newspapers, delivering shoes from warehouse to freight yard, and running a lemonade stand. Remaining in school, he became known for his oratory and debate skills, becoming a strong admirer of Alexander Hamilton. At fifteen he is said to have set his sights on success in business after which he wished to become a United States Senator. Not many persons set their goals so high that early in life, but the teenager from Grand Rapids turned out to be amazingly accurate.

At sixteen young Arthur graduated from high school at the top of his class and went to work in a local cracker factory. A few months later, his boss fired him for skipping work to watch a parade for—soon to be Brother—Theodore Roosevelt, the GOP candidate for vice president. He then took a lowly job for the Grand Rapids *Herald*, a position which probably enabled him to watch parades as part of his work. In the fall of 1901, he entered the University of Michigan but left college after a year, returning to the *Herald.* Arthur also wrote short stories for such magazines as *Collier's* and *Lippincott's* and once spent a year in New York City with *Collier's*, again returning to Grand Rapids. In his newspaper work, the young journalist got to know some prominent regional political figures, in particular Brother and Congressman William Alden Smith of York Lodge No. 410 in Grand Rapids.

In 1906 Smith was elected for the first of two terms to the United States Senate. He also purchased the *Herald* and promoted Arthur Vandenberg to the post of managing editor. At the age of 22, the young college dropout had advanced to a ranking position in journalism. The depression that followed the Panic of 1893 had strengthened the family's commitment to the Republican Party. According to one apocryphal story, Aaron Vandenberg's deathbed wish had been for Arthur to always remain a faithful Republican. Simultaneous with his newspaper job, the young editor served on the Grand Rapids Charter Commission and at 32 was chair of the state GOP convention. During World War I, the ever eloquent speaker helped raise money for Liberty Loan Bond drives. By the time he reached the age of 36, he was helping write speeches for presidential candidate Warren G. Harding. Continuing a writing career outside of his newspaper work, Vandenberg wrote three books, two of them about his favorite among the founding fathers, Alexander Hamilton.

Shortly after taking over the reigns at the *Herald,* Arthur Vandenberg also became a Mason. On May 8, 1907, he was raised in Grand River Lodge No. 34 in Grand Rapids. He subsequently joined York Rite bodies in Grand Rapids including Columbian Chapter No. 132, R.A.M. and DeMolay Commandery No. 5. He completed the Scottish Rite degrees in DeWitt Clinton Consistory of the Valley of Grand Rapids and became a Noble of Saladin Shrine Temple in Grand Rapids. Later in life he received the 33°. He also held membership in the Masonic Country Club of Grand Rapids. His other fraternal memberships included the Benevolent and Protective Order of Elks, the Woodmen, and during his short stay in college, Delta Upsilon fraternity.

On March 23, 1928, Michigan Democrat Senator, Brother Woodbridge N. Ferris of Big Rapids Lodge No. 171, died and the state's Republican governor appointed Arthur Vandenberg to fill out his term. The new lawmaker soon made a name for himself as an advocate of congressional reapportionment (Michigan was under-represented at the time), and as a result, Vandenberg was elected to a full six-year term by a landslide in November of 1928. In 1934, he became one of the few Republican survivors of a Democratic landslide to win a second six-year term. He won additional terms in 1940 and 1946, dying in the fifth year of his fourth term. By the early thirties he was considered among the leading Republican senators. However, this group was a rather small one through much of that New Deal-dominated decade. In that period Vandenberg was ranked among the Senate's isolationist bloc. He served on the Nye Committee and not only helped steer the Neutrality Acts through Congress but in 1939 vigorously opposed their repeal.

In regard to domestic New Deal legislation, the Michigan Senator compiled a mixed record. He voted for creation of the Securities and Exchange Commission and the Federal Deposit Insurance Corporation. He also voted for the Social Security Act of 1935. He opposed the Tennessee Valley Authority Act, the National Industrial Recovery Act, the Agricultural Adjustment Act, the Wagner Act, the Wage and Hours Act, and the Florida Ship Canal. He also opposed the Burke-Wadsworth Selective Service Act of 1940 remarking, "Say what you please...something precious goes out of the American way of life and something sinister takes its place under conscription." Yet his isolationist position was beginning to totter. Within weeks he began calling himself an "insulationist," urging all aid to the allies short of war.

In 1940 some support for an Arthur Vandenberg GOP presidential nomination developed, but the surprise rise of Wendell Willkie of Coventry Lodge No. 665 in Akron, Ohio, to prominence doomed whatever hopes his supporters may have had. Although mentioned as a candidate in 1944 and 1948, he lost out to Governor and Brother Thomas Dewey of Kane Lodge No. 454 of New York. Ever the faithful party man, Vandenberg supported the Republican nominee in each election campaign. He served as a principal foreign-policy advisor to Dewey in the 1948 campaign.

Although he had been considered a leading figure in the Senate and in his party since the early thirties, Arthur Vandenberg's stature as a statesman of major rank emerged in January 1945 when he announced that there would be no Republican opposition to the U.S. joining the United Nations. Welcoming this new support from Republicans in foreign policy, Franklin D. Roosevelt appointed the

Michigander to the San Francisco Conference that April, which subsequently drew up the U.N. Charter. In April 1946—by which time Harry Truman was President—Vandenberg accompanied Secretary of State, Brother and Sir Knight James F. Byrnes (of Spartan Lodge No. 70 and Spartanburg Commandery No. 3, both in South Carolina), to the Meeting of Foreign Ministers in Paris, France in what the *New York Times* called an act of "bipartisan unity and…high level statesmanship."

All of this action served America well, because with a Republican takeover of Congress in 1947, unity on the foreign-policy front reigned supreme as American-Soviet relations worsened steadily in that period. As Chairman of the Senate Foreign Relations Committee, Vandenberg played a key role in obtaining congressional support for the Truman Doctrine and the appropriation of the funding of aid to Greece and Turkey which carried it out. As an associate of Secretary of State George C. Marshall at the Rio de Janeiro Conference in August 1947, Under Secretary for Latin American Affairs Summer Welles credited "Vandenberg for saving the Inter-American system." Despite some dissatisfaction with parts of the treaties ending World War II with former German allies Italy, Bulgaria, Romania, and Hungary, the senator supported ratification since failure to approve meant "greater confusion [and] greater chaos."

Perhaps Vandenberg's greatest achievement came with his lining up of bipartisan support for the European Recovery Program (otherwise known as the Marshall Plan) and the funding to carry out this first massive foreign-aid mission. The success of this plan and the strong economy soon manifested in Western Europe led to other aid programs in the coming years, some of them not so rewarding. After Truman won a four-year term as president and the Democrats recaptured the control of Congress in November 1948, Vandenberg lost his chairmanship and returned to minority status, but he maintained correctly that "the elections would have no effect on the country's bipartisan foreign policy." Or at least they did not until the coalition collapsed in the late sixties tensions concerning the Viet Nam conflict, but by this time, Arthur Vandenberg had long been deceased.

By 1950 Arthur Vandenberg's health had begun to decline. He did not complete his last term in the Senate as he passed away on March 28, 1951, a few days after his 67th birthday. His second wife (his first wife died in 1916) and three children survived him. However, his greatest achievement, the bipartisan foreign policy that guided

America through the tense days of the Cold War in the late forties, remained as a hallmark of his statesmanship. Together with other Masonic Brothers such as James Byrnes, George Marshall, and Harry Truman, he helped forge an America that has stood tall in the world for more than sixty years.

**Note**: Arthur Vandenberg's life is outlined in two entries in *Current Biography* in 1940 and 1948. For his key speeches and writings, see Arthur H. Vandenberg, Jr., editor, *The Private Papers of Senator Vandenberg* (1952). His Masonic record is in William R. Denslow, *10,000 Famous Freemasons* IV(1961).

August 2002; slightly revised 2011

## Brother Audie Leon Murphy:
*From War Hero to Movie Star*

A poor lad from a Texas sharecropper family, grade school dropout, orphaned at sixteen, goes off to war and becomes an acclaimed military hero who then goes on to win fame and fortune in Hollywood—it sounds like the impossible, yet for Audie Murphy it happened. However, if Murphy were alive today, he would no doubt reluctantly concede that it did not happen often.

Audie Leon Murphy was born near Kingston in Hunt County, Texas, on June 20, 1924. Although his family was financially poor, his direct ancestors had compiled fine military records in the American Revolution, the War of 1812, and the Civil War. Other kinfolk had fought in the Texas Revolution and World War I. Besides Audie, two more brothers saw World War II action.

The young Audie Murphy faced a hard scrabble existence. As a song lyric reads, "Daylight to dark, work's never done, Lord have mercy on a sharecropper's son." The story goes that Audie learned to be a crack shot because the family depended on his hunting for much of their meat supply, and money for bullets was so scarce that a missed shot meant no food on the table.

In 1936, Emmett Murphy deserted his family. Audie quit school and went to work full time as a farm hand. He did whatever had to be done to keep the rest of the family together. Then when he was sixteen, his mother, Josie Bell Murphy, died. Audie, the oldest child at home, faced up to the dilemma of placing the younger children in an orphanage and going to work in the county seat at a combination grocery-service station. When World War II came along, he initially tried to enlist in the Marines but was rejected for being underweight. Finally, at eighteen, the U. S. Army took him as an infantryman (or boy).

After some months of training at Camp Wolters, Texas, and Fort Meade, Maryland, Private Murphy arrived in Casablanca, Morocco, in February of 1943, assigned to Company B, 1st Battalion, and 15th Infantry Regiment of the 3rd Infantry Division. Although Murphy saw little combat action in North Africa, his unit more than made up for it when the campaigns in Sicily and Italy began. Later he also experienced the war close up in the invasion of Southern France and finally inside Germany.

Audie related his experiences and account of the war in the classic autobiography, *To Hell and Back* (New York: Henry Holt and Co., 1949). Modestly told, you would hardly know from reading the text that Murphy had emerged from the conflict as the most renowned citizen soldier of his era. Audie earned more medals than anyone else in the army during that war including three Purple Hearts for actions on September 15, 1944; October 26, 1944; and January 25, 1945. His Medal of Honor resulted from actions in France on January 26, 1945. By this time he had become a second lieutenant and commanded Company B. His citation concluded that Murphy's indomitable courage and his refusal to give an inch of ground saved his company from possible encirclement and destruction, enabling it to hold the woods which had been the enemy's objective. Audie's original postwar objective had been to go to West Point, but his service-related injuries prevented it. He did, however, fulfill his promise to get his younger siblings out of the orphanage and purchased a home for older sister Corrinne so that she could help rear the children.

Audie Murphy's wartime heroics landed his photo on the cover of the July 16, 1945, issue of *Life.* Among those who saw his picture was film star James Cagney who thought the young soldier had Hollywood potential. Audie, in fact, came to California and stayed for several weeks, but as no offers were forthcoming, he departed. Later he returned, and his luck changed. In the meantime, he experienced a triumphant homecoming in his honor held at Farmersville, Texas and an Audie Murphy Day at Ebbets Field in Brooklyn. He also made a return trip to Europe at the behest of the United States Army.

Finally, a Hollywood deal came through. Audie landed a small part in an Alan Ladd-Donna Reed Paramount film titled *Beyond Glory.* In this offering, he played the part of a West Point cadet. Murphy had another small role in another picture, *Texas, Brooklyn, and Heaven.* His movie career seemed to be going nowhere until the fall of 1948 when he landed a major role in *Bad Boy,* an Allied Artist feature in which he played a juvenile delinquent who is rehabilitated at a place called "Boy's Ranch" in Texas.

Finally, Murphy's career in Hollywood zoomed upward. So did his romantic life as he had begun to court and on January 8, 1949, married a young star named Wanda Hendrix whose petite-ness matched Audie's perpetual youthfulness. Universal International offered him a seven-year contract at $2,500 weekly, and he moved into the starring role in *The Kid From Texas*, another film in a long list of movies about Billy the Kid. He then co-starred with Wanda in another western titled *Sierra.* However, by the time the picture was released in June of 1950, the couple's marriage was headed for the divorce courts in the manner of many show business linkages.

After another western titled *Kansas Raiders* in which he portrayed Jesse James, Audie, on loan to M.G.M., starred as Henry Fleming in *The Red Badge of Courage,* an adaptation of Stephen Crane's Civil War novel. More than his previous films, this boosted his stature as an actor. As one critic wrote, "Audie Murphy gives a sensitive performance, wonderfully conveying . . . the fall . . . of a man in combat." Universal followed this success by placing their star in eight consecutive westerns, the most notable being *Destry*, the third Hollywood rendition of Max Brand's famed novel, *Destry Rides Again.* Meanwhile, on April 23, 1951, Audie married again to Pamela Archer, a former airline stewardess. This union endured and produced two children, Terry and James (nicknamed Skipper), on March 14, 1952, and March 23, 1954, respectively.

By 1954, one could conclude that Audie had achieved stardom, albeit he was being increasingly typecast in westerns. That fall he began filming his own story, *To Hell and Back,* which turned out to be Universal's biggest hit up to that time. Premiering in August 1955 in four Texas cities, the film quickly set attendance records and grossed some ten million dollars in its initial theatrical release. He also made ten percent of the net profits on the picture which totaled up to some $387,000 through October 1966. Prior to the release of his film autobiography, Murphy starred in a boxing picture titled *The World in His Corner* with Barbara Rush. However, the public seemed to prefer their hero either in westerns or war movies (or a combination of both). He did a different type of western in *Walk the Proud Land*, the story of Apache Indian agent, John P. Clum, who pioneered in encouraging self-government on reservations. A military comedy, *Joe Butterfly*, set in postwar Japan represented Murphy's only effort in a humorous mode although several of his westerns had their lighter moments.

Meanwhile, Audie Leon Murphy had begun his Masonic journeys by joining North Hollywood Lodge No. 542. He was initiated an Entered Apprentice on February 14, 1955; passed to the degree of Fellowcraft on April 4, 1955; and was raised a Master Mason on June 27, 1955. On May 14, 1956, he became a plural member of Heritage Lodge No. 764, also in North Hollywood. He retained membership for the rest of his life.

Murphy had purchased a home in Dallas in the early fifties although he never lived in it on a regular basis. He did continue his Masonic endeavors there, completing his Scottish Rite degrees in Dallas on November 14, 1957. In October 1965, he received the KCCH and less than two months before his death moved his Scottish Rite membership to the Valley of Long Beach, California (more than two decades later he was posthumously made a 33°, the only person in history other than John Philip Sousa to be so honored).

Audie Murphy's movie career continued to move forward in the later fifties as the older B pictures faded into the past and "adult westerns" dominated the television screens. The former war hero ranked among the few remaining cowboy film stars. Among his more memorable efforts from this period are *The Guns of Fort Petticoat* with Kathryn Grant Crosby, *Night Passage* in which he co-starred with the late James Stewart, and *The Wild and the Innocent* where he portrayed a backwoods trapper who pursued dance hall queen Joanne Dru and was in turn pursued by teen star Sandra Dee who eventually got her man. Murphy also had a brief fling with television adult westerns in 1961 by starring in a series about the introduction of more modern police methods in Denver. Titled *Whispering Smith,* the series was short-lived despite good reviews on the NBC Network.

Although his TV series did not endure, Audie Murphy's motion picture career continued to do well through the mid-sixties. The decade began with the release of *Hell Bent for Leather* in February of 1960 that also starred Felicia Farr and Stephen McNally. He also continued to do non-westerns such as another World War II drama *Battle at Bloody Beach* (1961) and one of foreign intrigue *Trunk to Cairo* (1965). However, cowboy films remained his main bread and butter. Among his more notable pictures from this time included *Posse from Hell* (1960), *Six Black Horses* (1962), *Gunfight at Comanche Creek* (1963), and *Bullet for a Badman* (1964). A Murphy film that might be of some interest to Masons, *Gunpoint* (1965), featured two other noted members of the fraternity, Edgar Buchanan and Royal Dano, in strong support roles.

Murphy also made something of a name for himself as a songwriter. Roy Clark, Eddy Arnold, and Jimmy Dean were among those who recorded his efforts. His best-known composition, co-authored with Scott Turner, was "Shutters and Boards," which made the Pop Top 30 for Jerry Wallace in 1963 and the Country Top 30 for Slim Whitman in 1970.

From 1965, Audie Murphy's movie career began to fade. He made a pair of films for Columbia, *The Texican* (1966) and *40 Guns to Apache Pass* (1967), the former of which was made in Spain. In 1969, he tried his hand at production in *A Time for Dying* in which Budd Boetticher directed and Audie had a smaller dramatic role, but it remained unfinished at the time of his death.

Audie Murphy died in a plane crash on May 28, 1971, near Galax, Virginia. Some days elapsed before the bodies were recovered. He was buried in Arlington National Cemetery on June 7, 1971. Future President George H. W. Bush was numbered among those who attended his funeral. For some years it was reported that only John Kennedy's gravesite had more visitors. Two years later in 1973, his country honored him by naming the Audie L. Murphy Memorial Veteran's Hospital in San Antonio for him. In 1996, his movie contributions received recognition with his induction into the "Hall of Great Western Performers" at the National Cowboy Hall of Fame in Oklahoma City. His pictures have been regularly shown on TV and several are available on video cassette and DVD. Like Sergeant Alvin York from World War I, Audie Leon Murphy became the personification of the heroic citizen soldier. On top of these achievements, Brother Murphy needs to be remembered as one of the most distinguished Masons of his generation.

**Note:** There are two biographies of Audie Murphy, both now out of print: Harold B. Simpson, *Audie Murphy: American Soldier* (1975) and Sue Gossett, *The Films and Career of Audie Murphy* (1996). For his Masonic record, I am indebted to Grand Secretary of the Grand Lodge of Ohio, David Dresser, and to John Cooper II, Grand Secretary of the Grand Lodge of California, and staff member Eileen M. Irby. His Scottish Rite record was researched by Joan Sansbury, Librarian at the House of the Temple. Student aide Abby Goodnite Ehman typed the original version. One may also wish to consult the Audie Murphy Research Foundation at 18008 Saratoga Way, Suite 516, Santa Clarita, California 91351.

October 1998; slightly revised 2011

## Sir Knight Barry Goldwater:
*Champion of Old Fashioned Liberty*

In the annals of American presidential elections, the losing candidate sometimes has nearly as much influence on the national scene as does the winner. Among those who have lost these elections are several Masons: DeWitt Clinton, Stephen Douglas, William Jennings Bryan, and Thomas Dewey. More recent Masons who failed to win a White House term include Hubert Humphrey, George McGovern, Gerald Ford, and Robert Dole. Over the past half century, Sir Knight Barry Morris Goldwater took one of the worst beatings ever in the 1964 presidential sweepstakes, losing some forty-four states. Yet in a retrospective eulogy appearing in "The Weekly Standard" on June 15, 1998, columnist David Frum wrote, "Despite his crushing 1964 defeat, Barry Goldwater exerted more influence on American politics than any other losing major-party nominee of the twentieth century."

Barry Morris Goldwater was born in Phoenix, Arizona Territory on January 1, 1909. The Goldwater family had originally been Jewish political refugees from Eastern Europe who made their way first to the more liberal Western Europe and then to America in 1852 and "gold rush" California. Grandfather Michael Goldwater and his brother Joe dabbled in business as saloon keepers, freighters, and finally as merchants in Prescott, Arizona, and other desert boom towns. Eventually their business centered on stores in Prescott, Tucson, and finally Phoenix. Barry's father, Baron, ran the store in Phoenix from 1896 and in 1907 married a nurse from Nebraska named Josephine Williams. The future senator was their first child. Later they had another boy, Robert, in 1910 and a girl, Carolyn, in 1912.

Baron Goldwater always remained something of a distant and private person, and Josephine, known as "Mun," reared the children. As Barry later recalled, she took them on camping trips all over the new state. Another strong influence on Barry was his more extroverted uncle Morris Goldwater who had been a legislator, vice president of the Arizona Constitutional Convention, active Democrat, and an avid Mason. Morris had served as Grand Master of the Grand Lodge of Arizona and in similar positions in both the Grand Chapter and Grand Council. A photograph also shows him wearing a Past Commander's jewel, and according to his nephew, he was considered to be among the founders of the Eastern Star in that state. The family had become Episcopalians by that time. In matters of politics, however, Barry followed his mother's leanings, a lady he described as "a staunch Republican."

After a lackluster freshman year in high school, the Goldwaters sent young Barry to Staunton Military Academy in Virginia where he learned self-discipline. After graduation, he enrolled at the University of Arizona in the fall of 1928. Following his father's unexpected death on March 6, 1929, the youth dropped out of college and entered the family business. The manager, Sam Wilson, placed him in most of the store's individual departments so he could learn all aspects of the business first hand and view the operation from the lower rungs of the economic ladder. Barry also received the same beginning salary as other employees, $15.00 per week.

During those early years in the family business, the future senator and spokesman for modern conservatism also became a Mason. On May 12, 1931, he became an Entered Apprentice in Arizona Lodge No. 2 in Phoenix. Goldwater was passed to the degree of Fellowcraft two weeks later on May 26 and on June 23, 1931, was raised a Master Mason. Nearly eight years later, on May 8, 9, and 10, 1939, he took the Scottish Rite Degrees in Tucson. His AASR record gives his occupation as "dry goods merchant." He also became a Noble of El Zaribah Shrine Temple in Phoenix.

During the remainder of the thirties, Barry Goldwater took over the management of the Phoenix store, learned to pilot planes, and courted a Muncie, Indiana girl, Margaret (Peggy) Johnson, whose family wintered in Phoenix. The couple married in 1934 and subsequently had four children. Goldwater took little active interest in politics but developed a strong personal animosity toward the New Deal which he viewed as excessively interfering in economic activity. He became especially exasperated at the policies of the National Recovery Administration.

During World War II, Goldwater entered military service, spending most of his time in the Air Transport Service. Although regretting that he never got to be a combat pilot, he did perform significant roles. Initially, Barry helped train other pilots and later transported supplies to India and other locales. After his discharge in November of 1945, he was asked to form an Air National Guard unit in Arizona and spent many years in the Air Force Reserves, eventually becoming a major general.

Back in the civilian world, Goldwater returned to a Phoenix that had really begun to boom. He took an increasing interest in civic affairs. By 1949 this concern prompted him to seek and win a seat on the city council. The following year he assisted Howard Pyle in his successful quest for the Arizona governorship, an event that many observers view as being the beginning of traditionally Democratic Arizona's evolution into a two-party state. In 1952 the Arizona GOP not only re-elected Pyle to a second term in office and carried their Eisenhower-led presidential ticket but also narrowly elected by a margin of 6,725 votes a United States senator in the personage of Councilman Barry Goldwater. The latter's victory, which all pundits agreed had resulted from Eisenhower's coat-tails, proved all the sweeter for Republicans as Goldwater had defeated Senate Majority Leader Ernest McFarland (a member of Pinal Lodge No. 30 in Casa Grande).

After his first year as a freshman senator, Goldwater became something of a party maverick, often taking more conservative positions than President Eisenhower's moderate stance. With the death of Senator Robert A. Taft in mid-1953, Goldwater increasingly became the spokesman for the party's right flank, particularly after November of 1958 when such GOP "Old Guard" members as John Bricker and William Knowland met with defeat. Goldwater himself had been targeted for defeat both by Democrats and organized labor that year, but he handily won a second term by again defeating Ernest McFarland, this time by a comfortable 56% - 44% (35,000) margin.

Early in 1960, Goldwater's book, *The Conscience of a Conservative,* first appeared in print. This brief volume remained available for years and is credited by many with launching the "new conservatism" that has had considerable political impact on the American scene over the next four decades. It also launched a 1960 presidential "boomlet" for the outspoken Arizonan who withdrew moments after his nomination at the GOP national convention. With its plea for a smaller federal government, a tough stand against Communism, and championing of state's rights and laissez faire economics, *The Conscience of a Conservative* influenced a generation of young conservative American thinkers who did not share their more numerous colleagues' infatuation for the New Frontier and its successor, the "Great Society." A second book, *Why Not Victory?* (1963), concentrated on foreign policy and Cold War issues.

Although he had no personal enthusiasm for a run, Barry Goldwater finally yielded to supporter demands that he seek the presidency in 1964. The mainstream media disdained the Goldwater brand of conservatism, and the "Eastern Establishment Republicans" who generally gravitated around New York Governor Nelson Rockefeller worked hard to prevent his nomination. Although unsuccessful in the short run, they undoubtedly weakened his appeal in the general election. Despite a memorable nominating speech by Brother and Senator Everett Dirksen of Illinois, Goldwater came out of the convention as "damaged goods" and as the standard bearer of a badly-divided Republican Party. The opposition party then piled on him unmercifully, branding him as a warmonger, racist, and reactionary who might well destroy the world in a nuclear holocaust. In retrospect, it seems unlikely that any Republican could have defeated Lyndon Johnson in 1964. Goldwater carried but six states, amassing some 27 million votes while Johnson got roughly 41 million. The electoral count was 486 to 52. Still, in taking defeat with dignity, coupled with the subsequent disenchantment with LBJ's Viet Nam policy and the failure of many Great Society programs to meet their expectations, Goldwater eventually saw many of his positions vindicated. In addition, his candidacy brought many new enthusiasts into the Republican Party, some of whom still treasure their Goldwater dolls, Goldwater soft drink cans, and political badges.

After four years of private life back in Arizona, Barry Goldwater again ran for a senate seat. Brother Carl Hayden (of Tempe Lodge No. 15), who had been in Congress since Arizona had become a state and in the Senate since 1927, chose to retire. In the meantime, Goldwater, who had always been an avid ham radio operator, had set up a system whereby he aided soldiers in Viet Nam to relay messages to loved ones back in the states. In his comeback bid, Goldwater bested former Hayden assistant Roy Elson for the position, winning by a comfortable 58% margin. This time he remained in the Senate for three more full terms before retiring, making his total service in that august body a total of five six-year terms. He retired on January 3, 1987.

Perhaps the most difficult and courageous moments in Senator Goldwater's entire public career came in early August of 1974 when he went to the White House on a somber mission with Brothers Hugh Scott of Pennsylvania (Hiram Lodge No. 81) and John Rhodes of Arizona (Oriental Lodge No. 25) for a private meeting with President Richard Nixon to inform him that his chances of acquittal in an impeachment trial were virtually non-existent. The next day Nixon resigned. It proved to be a difficult time for the American people, but Goldwater, who had been a prior defender of Nixon, handled himself with honor, dignity, and character. With the passage of time, however, Barry became more critical of Nixon. In 1976, the Arizona senator faced a difficult decision, but he ultimately chose to support Brother Gerald Ford for president over the man who in many respects had become his political protégé, former California Governor Ronald Reagan who had been one of his most effective backers in 1964.

In 1980, the Senator won his fifth and last senate term by emerging with a narrow victory over a younger challenger named Bill Schultz. It had been his closest race since his narrow 1952 victory, and this convinced the 71-year-old lawmaker that he should retire after that term. Nonetheless, he played a key role in the Senate during those final six years, taking considerable satisfaction in many aspects of the Reagan presidency. While Ronald Reagan's views generally coincided with his own, Barry Goldwater could still manifest that degree of independence which always characterized him. In general, one could say that the Senator's opinions had mellowed somewhat over time.

Through the years, several Masonic honors came to the noted Arizonan. On October 23, 1959, Barry Goldwater received the 33°, having been elected to receive both that and the KCCH three days earlier. From 1965 to 1995, he held a plural membership in Red Rock Memorial Lodge No. 63 in Sedona, Arizona. On April 22, 1978, Goldwater was honored by having a York Rite class named for him, one in which he was the primary candidate. His congressional friend, John Rhodes, was also a member of that class. On that day, Barry Morris Goldwater became a member of Scottsdale Chapter No. 18, Scottsdale Council No. 11, and was knighted in Scottsdale Commandery No. 12. Given his uncle's affinity for the York Rite bodies, one feels certain that Morris Goldwater would have been proud. In retirement the former Senator received his fifty year Scottish Rite pin in 1989 and his sixty-year pin from Arizona Lodge No. 2 in 1992.

Personal tragedy came to the Senator in 1985 when his wife of fifty-one years passed away. Retiring to his home "Be-Nun-I-Kin" (a Navajo name) in 1987, the elder statesman continued to make the newspapers now and then with the kind of feisty remarks that had long characterized his makeup. He also taught an occasional class at Arizona State University in nearby Tempe. In 1992, he married a second time to a lady named Susan Wechsler. On May 29, 1998, at the age of eighty-nine, Barry Goldwater passed to the "celestial lodge above."

In retrospect, Barry Goldwater lived long enough to see many of his once unpopular political positions vindicated. Columnist Michael Barone outlined many of these in an op-ed piece entitled "The Last Laugh" in the memorial issue of *The Weekly Standard* (June 15, 1998). By that time he had won the respect of many of his former critics while continuing to enjoy the respect—most of the time—of the conservative following he had once led. While continuing to be no stranger to controversy, both friend and foe would probably have agreed by 1998 that Sir Knight Barry Goldwater was "an American original."

**Note**: Several biographies of Barry Goldwater exist. Those with the best historical perspective are Robert Alan Goldberg, *Barry Goldwater* (1995) and Peter Iverson, *Barry Goldwater: Native American* (1997). Also useful are his earlier autobiography *With No Apologies* (1979) and the later *Goldwater* (1988). For his Masonic records, I am indebted to Robert Henderson, Grand Secretary of the Grand Lodge of Arizona; Paul Dorre, Secretary of Arizona Lodge No. 2; Gilbert Eno, Grand Recorder of the Arizona York Rite bodies; and Joan Sansbury, Librarian of the AASR, SJ, of The House of the Temple, Washington DC.

September 1998; slightly revised 2011

**Brother Bill McKechnie:**
*Baseball Hall of Fame Manager and Fifty-Year Mason*

Nobody ever accused Bill McKechnie of being a great baseball player. He was good enough to make the major leagues but was average at best. However, as a manager he was atypically outstanding. Lee Allen, the baseball historian of a generation earlier, described the man called the "Deacon" as a "wily ascetic . . . shrewd handler of men and a genius at getting the most out of pitchers." In his years as a manager in the National League, he managed to bring in four pennant winners and two world championships. When one considers that many—if not most—of his managing years were spent with cash-strapped franchises, his achievements seem even more remarkable. On top of all that, McKechnie spent more than fifty years as a Mason.

William Boyd McKechnie was born of Scottish ancestry in Wilkinsburg, Pennsylvania, on August 7, 1886. His parents, Archibald and Mary Murray McKechnie, had immigrated to the Upper Ohio Valley from the greater Glasgow area. It was said of young Bill that he inherited from his parents the typical Scottish characteristics of being "dour, thrifty, and canny." Like many American youth, especially those in the greater Pittsburgh area, McKechnie fell in love with baseball. After some semi-pro experiences, he entered the minors in 1906 via the Washington franchise in the Pennsylvania-Ohio-Maryland League, a Class D loop with teams extending from Zanesville, Ohio, to Cumberland, Maryland, with most of the teams in the Keystone State. His major league baseball career began in 1907 when the near-his-hometown Pittsburgh Pirates called him up in late summer to play third base. He made his debut with the Bucs on September 8. It was hardly a spectacular beginning. Bill appeared in three games, getting one hit in eight times at the plate for a .125 average.

Over the next five years, McKechnie divided his time between the Pirates, Canton of the Ohio-Pennsylvania League (where he played regularly and hit a respectable .274), and St. Paul of the American Association. His best year with Pittsburgh came in 1911 when he hit .227, appearing in 104 games. Not long afterward he went briefly to the Boston Braves and on to the New York Highlanders, then managed by Frank Chance, once famed as the "peerless leader" of the Chicago Cubs. By this time Bill was gaining a reputation as one of the shrewdest baseball men around in spite of his limited talents as a player. Fred Lieb, a Mason and one of the best-known baseball writers, is alleged to have asked the manager why he kept a .134 hitter like McKechnie next to him on the bench. Chance replied "because Bill McKechnie has more brains than the rest of this dumb club put together."

In the meantime, the young Scotsman married Berlyn Bien in 1911. She passed away in 1957. The McKechnies had four children including Bill, Jr. who went into the business side of baseball and served in various capacities including director of the Cincinnati Reds farm system and president of the Pacific Coast League from 1968 until 1973. He also became a Mason. The other children were James, Beatrice, and Carol.

In 1914, William Boyd McKechnie joined Orient Lodge No. 590 in Wilkinsburg, ironically giving his occupation as "salesman," which must have been his off-season job. He received his degrees on May 26, 1914, November 17, 1914, and December 20, 1914. He also belonged to the Scottish Rite, joining the Valley of Pittsburgh in November of 1915. His other Masonic affiliations included Syria Shrine Temple in Pittsburgh and Pittsburgh Court No. 2 of the Royal Order of Jesters. On February 2, 1940, he received the 33° by special dispensation in Pittsburgh. On June 2, 1964, he received his fifty-year pin from the Grand Lodge of Pennsylvania. Known for his regular attendance and choir membership in the local Methodist church, he earned the nickname "Deacon."

McKechnie soon got the opportunity to play regularly when a new major league, "the outlaw" Federal League, entered the picture. Bill joined the Indianapolis club and experienced his best season as a player, playing regularly at third base, compiling a .304 average in 149 games and chalking up 47 stolen bases. The team was loaded with talent. Five players hit over .300 with Benny Kauff as their top star, and another future Hall of Fame member Edd Roush led the way to a first-place finish. Nonetheless, the club lost money, and the owner transferred the franchise to Newark, New Jersey in 1915.

McKechnie hit only .257, but in mid-season he got his first shot as a manager. His team compiled a winning record, but he proved unable to lift the team out of fifth place. Nonetheless, his reputation as being baseball-smart continued to grow and improve. With the demise of the Federal League, Bill returned to the Nationals with the New York Giants.

A Giant for slightly more than half a season, McKechnie, along with Edd Roush and Christy Mathewson, were traded to the Cincinnati Reds on July 20, 1916. The latter became the Reds manager and Bill continued in his familiar role as a utility infielder. By 1918, he was back with the Pirates where he experienced one of his better seasons, hitting .255. Closing out his major league career with the Bucs in 1920 with a .216 average in 46 games, Bill had one more year as a player hitting .321 with Minneapolis of the American Association. He came back to Pittsburgh as a coach in 1922. When Manager, George Gibson, had problems maintaining discipline, he resigned, and McKechnie became the Pirate skipper. The stern Scotsman had more success despite the antics of such rowdy players as Rabbit Maranville and Moses Yellowhorse, bringing the team in for a third place finish. Two more similar seasons followed, and then in 1925, the Pirates won their first pennant since 1909. With future Hall of Famers like Max Carey, Harold "Pie" Traynor (also a Mason), and Hazen "Kiki" Cuyler, the Pirates also took the World Series over the Washington Senators.

The 1926 season proved a disappointment for both McKechnie and Pirate fans. Much of the problem resulted from a feud between star player, Max Carey, and former Pirate manager and club Vice President, Fred Clarke. Carey was released on waivers to Brooklyn on August 18. The team slipped to third, and Bill's "contract was not renewed for 1927." He closed his career as Pirate manager with 409 victories against 293 defeats. Needing a job, the Wilkinsburg native signed with the world champion St. Louis Cardinals as a coach for 1927.

The Redbirds slipped to second place under new manager Bob O'Farrell, and the front office elevated McKechnie to become manager in 1928. Bill led the Cards to another pennant but lost the World Series to the virtually unstoppable New York Yankees. Club owner Sam Breadon sent McKechnie to Rochester and brought in Red Wing manager Billy Southworth to St. Louis. However, Southworth was not ready for the big time yet, and by July, the owner brought McKechnie back to St. Louis to finish the season. This time Breadon admitted his error and offered the Deacon a two-year contract. In essence Bill said "thanks but no thanks" and signed a longer management contract with the Boston Braves.

Although Brother McKechnie's eight-year tenure in Boston did not bring any pennants to Braves Field, the manager received numerous positive marks for doing as well as he could with what he had. The franchise tended to be both cash-strapped and talent limited during those depression-wracked years. At his best, the Deacon provided Beantown fans with three winning seasons and another break-even year. At his worst, the 1935 Braves team had one of the poorest seasons in National League history winning 38 and losing 115 (being just slightly worse than the 1961 New York Mets). It was his only managing job in the majors where his teams had overall losing records, and many considered him a virtual miracle worker for doing as well as he did. In 1936, the new owner renamed the team the Boston Bees, but it did not bring about substantial improvement. Bill received Manager of the Year honors in 1937 just for bringing in a winning record (79-73) and a fifth-place finish.

After the expiration of his last contract with the Boston Bees, Bill McKechnie received several managerial offers but accepted that of the Cincinnati Reds. The latter franchise had also endured hard times during the depression years, but some seeds of improvement had already been sown. Local business tycoon Brother Powel Crosley had bought the bankrupt club in 1933 and hired Brother Larry McPhail to run it. After finishing in the cellar for four consecutive years, the team had climbed to sixth and fifth in 1935 and 1936 but fell back to the bottom in 1937. They had a nucleus of a better team, however, with solid performers like Ernie Lombardi, Paul Derringer, Frank McCormick, and Ival Goodman. McKechnie induced Crosley to buy pitcher (and Brother) Bucky Walters from the Phillies in mid-season, and he went on to win eleven games for the Reds. Johnny VanderMeer pitched a pair of back-to-back no-hitters in raising the Reds to fourth place, finishing only six games out of first. As Reds historian, Lee Allen, recalled, "Writers tabbed the Reds as the team of the future."

The future came to pass in 1939 and 1940. Walters and Derringer were at their peak, winning a total of 50 games the first year and 42 in the second, while rookie Junior Thompson proved to be an able starter. Billy Werber held down third base while Lonnie Frey and Billy Myers patrolled the middle of the infield, and Harry Craft gave the Reds their best center fielder since Edd Roush. In 1940, McKechnie found a fourth able starter in veteran Jim Turner who had won twenty games as a thirty-four year-old rookie in Boston for the Scotsman in 1937. The Yankees humiliated the Reds in the 1939 World Series, but in 1940, the boys from Cincinnati defeated Detroit in a seven-game series and became the champions of baseball. Derringer and Walters won two games each in that series.

While the Reds were at their peak in those years, one might take note that Masonic influence was strong. Club owner Powel Crosley belonged to College Hill Lodge No. 641. In addition to manager McKechnie, coaches Hank Gowdy and Jimmy Wilson both held membership in the fraternity. Team members who were or eventually became Masons included Bucky Walters, Bill Werber, Billy Myers, and Junior Thompson.

The 1941 Reds fell to third place, and then World War II and the aging process took a toll on the squad. The team remained in the first division through 1944, managing to finish a distant second in 1944. The next two years were even worse as the 1945 team dropped to seventh (61-93), and only the 1935 Braves lost more games among McKechnie teams. The first post-war Reds squad was only slightly better, and with the fans demanding a new manager, Bill was dropped. It did not help; his successors did worse, and there was no winning home team at Crosley Field until 1956. Brother McKechnie's career in the national pastime continued as a coach with the Cleveland Indians from 1947 until 1949 and with the Boston Red Sox in 1952 and 1953.

Thereafter, he retired to Bradenton, Florida where the Pittsburgh Pirate spring training ballpark was named McKechnie Field in their former manager's honor. In 1962, as the only manager ever to win pennants for three separate franchises, Brother McKechnie was elected to the Baseball Hall of Fame. He died on October 29, 1965, "due to complications caused by a lingering illness of leukemia and virus pneumonia." His services were held in the Trinity Methodist Church in Bradenton on November 1 with many baseball dignitaries in attendance. Burial took place in Manasota Memorial Park in Oneco, Florida. Election to the Cincinnati Reds Hall of Fame took place in 1967.

Brother Bill McKechnie is remembered as one of the best National League managers. His teams won four pennants and two World Series. All of the teams he managed had winning records except for the Boston Braves, and his work there was considered a tribute to what a good skipper can do with a weak team. According to the *Baseball Encyclopedia*, Bill McKechnie stood only five feet, nine inches tall; his obituary in the Scottish Rite records quoted a long-time friend as saying he was "a humble but great man, a devoted husband, and an ardent believer in prayer," but as a man and as a Mason, he stood much taller.

**Note:** Bill McKechnie lacks an adequate biographer, but much information may be gleaned from the histories of teams that he managed. Among the best are Brian Mulligan, *The 1940 Cincinnati Reds* (McFarland, 2005) and Lee Allen, *The Cincinnati Reds* (Putnam, 1948). Others include Frederick Lieb's two classics, *The Pittsburgh Pirates* (Putnam, 1948) and *St. Louis Cardinals: The Story of a Great Baseball Club* (Putnam, 1944); and Harold Kaese, *The Boston Braves* (Putnam, 1948). For McKechnie's Masonic records, I am indebted to the staff at the Grand Lodge of Pennsylvania and to the Ancient Accepted Scottish Rite, NMJ. Thanks also to Sir Knight Roger E. VanDyke for his careful proofreading.

August 2009; slightly revised 2011

## **Brother Bob Baker**: *A Nearly Forgotten Hollywood Singing Cowboy*

While Bob Baker never quite attained the level of fame of such Masonic movie singing cowboys as Gene Autry and Roy Rogers or the action heroes typified by Tom Mix and Buck Jones, he nonetheless managed to leave his boot prints on the pages of western film history. As Universal Pictures' first singing cowboy, Baker actually had the distinction of beating out Roy Rogers for this position a few months before the latter signed with Republic. Although his period of stardom was relatively brief, he did make the top ten western star listings in 1939. Bob also had real life experience, not only as a working cowboy, but also as a law officer. Finally, he joined a Masonic Lodge at an earlier age than any of his fellow movie cowboys with the exception of Gene Autry.

Baker was born with the name Stanley Leland Weed in Forest City, Iowa on November 8, 1910, the son of salesman Guy Weed and his wife Ethel. The Weeds had another son Robert and three daughters: Miriam, Margaret, and Gretchen. When Gretchen encountered health problems, the Weed family physicians advised the family to relocate to a drier climate. As a result, in 1924 the Weeds migrated to a small town near Denver and then in 1926 to Arizona. Young Stanley adapted to the wide open spaces rather easily and soon went to work as a ranch hand. He also acquired the nickname "Tumble," soon stopped using his first name Stanley, and began signing his name Leland Weed. "Tumble" also worked as a guide for a dude ranch and plied the rodeo circuit. In 1929 Weed joined the U.S. Calvary.

During his five years as a soldier, Leland was stationed in Fort Bliss, Texas where he learned to sing and play the guitar. Peacetime army duty in the early thirties was not so strenuous as to prevent Weed from having a regular radio program at KTSM in El Paso. Back in civilian life, he went to work as a guide at the Grand Canyon. There he met Evelyn McCauly, and the two married on September 17, 1935. The couple subsequently had three sons; Kenneth, Tom, and Walter; as well as a daughter, Barbara.

Some weeks after his marriage, "Tumble" Weed became serious about a career as a radio singer and took such a position at WLS Chicago. There he had his own 15-minute daily program and also appeared on a morning show, *Smile-A-While,* and on the Saturday night *National Barn Dance.* Gene Autry had already gone from WLS to Hollywood, and comedians Pat Buttram and Max Terhuue soon followed. Weed did too, except that after a year in Chicago, he returned first to Arizona and his old job at the Grand Canyon. When word came that Universal Studios wanted a singing cowboy, Tumble's mother contacted him and arranged for an audition. Other contenders for the job included Leonard Slye (later known as Roy Rogers) and Stuart Hamblen (both later members of Hollywood Lodge No. 355). Weed won the contract, and studio officials wanted to call him "Tex Baker" but eventually settled for "Bob Baker." His first film, *Courage of the West,* came out late in 1937 to favorable reviews.

Bob Baker starred in a dozen pictures. In five of them, Marjorie Reynolds, who was known in later years as the wife of Chester Riley in the TV sitcom *The Life of Riley,* was his leading lady and added a bit of romance to the films. Other leading ladies included Constance Moore, Joan Barclay, Dorothy Fay (who later became the wife of Sir Knight Tex Ritter), and Marjorie Bell who went on to win greater fame as dancer, "Marge Champion." Sidekicks included Fuzzy Knight, Hal Taliaferro, and George Cleveland, later famous as "Gramps" on TV's *Lassie.*

Midway through his period as a film hero, Bob Baker (under his real name) became a Mason in El Sereno Lodge No. 588 in Los Angeles. As Leland Weed he was initiated an Entered Apprentice on July 12, 1938. A heavy filming schedule delayed his advancement for several weeks, but on October 31, 1938, while filming a stage coach runaway scene, the vehicle wrecked and the star suffered injuries that sidelined him for a time. Baker took advantage of the lull to be passed a Fellowcraft on November 15, 1938, and to be raised to the sublime degree of Master Mason on November 29, 1938. He remained a member of El Sereno until 1948 when he took a demit and affiliated with an Arizona Lodge.

After recovering, Baker completed the filming of *The Phantom Stage*. He then found himself demoted to the level of co-star with Fuzzy Knight in a series of Johnny Mack Brown films at Universal. According to most reports, Bob was not happy with this situation and was hoping for a contract with another studio when Uncle Sam recalled him to active duty as part of the pre-World War II defense buildup. The army discharged him on January 16, 1941, and Leland Weed joined the police force in Flagstaff, Arizona.

In February 1942, Bob Baker went back to Hollywood and over the next two years had small parts in other pictures, most notably the 1942 Universal serial, *Overland Mail,* and the 1943 Monogram Trail Blazer feature, *Wild Horse Stampede.* His last film appearance came in a 1944 Hopalong Cassidy film, *Mystery Man*. After that, Bob sold his trained horse Apache to Monte Montana and returned to Flagstaff and the police force. During that time—in 1948—he affiliated with Flagstaff Lodge No. 7. He remained a member of that body until his death except for a brief time period when he was dues delinquent. He had remained in the Army Reserves and in 1950 and 1951 spent a third stint on active duty in the Korean War. Returning again to Flagstaff, Leland T. Weed resumed his position as a police officer where he remained until 1954.

During lulls between films back in 1939 and 1940, Bob had become proficient in leather craft and saddle making and had thereafter supplemented his income thusly. In 1954 he moved to Wickenberg and opened his own saddle shop which he operated until 1957. At that time, Tumble joined the staff at Beaver Creek Guest Ranch. In 1959 he opened another saddle shop in Camp Verde, Arizona. He pursued this trade for a decade, but in 1969 he suffered the first of three heart attacks and experienced severe heart problems for the rest of his life. By 1972 he was retired and had sold his shop. Baker apparently was quite good at his craft. One-time leading lady, Jennifer Holt, reported that some of her husband's most prized leather collectibles had been handcrafted by Bob Baker.

Leland T. Weed (alias Bob Baker) died in the Whipple V.A. Hospital at Prescott on August 30, 1975. The Brethren of Flagstaff Lodge conducted Masonic services on September 3 and the Fort Verde Chapter of the D.A.V. conducted graveside rites the following day. Evelyn Weed outlived her husband by eighteen years, passing away on July 12, 1993, fifty-five years to the day after Bob had first knelt at the altar as an Entered Apprentice. Some years earlier, she described her husband thusly, "Tumble was an honest, loving, friendly, proud, outgoing man who was self-motivated and would do without to help a friend in need." In conclusion, although his period of stardom may have been short, Brother Bob Baker nonetheless managed to distinguish himself as a man and as a Mason.

**Note**: In writing this article, I appreciate the counsel and research work of Brother Bobby J. Copeland in *The Bob Baker Story* (1998). Thanks also to the Grand Lodge of Arizona for supplying his Masonic record. Although Baker made no commercial recordings, a cassette of songs from his movie soundtracks is available.

October 2001; slightly revised 2011

## Sir Knight Robert Joseph Dole:
*Twentieth Century Statesman*

Throughout the twentieth century, many noted members of the United States Senate have also been Masons. Politically they range from some of the most liberal—for example, Hubert Humphrey and George McGovern—to some of the most conservative like John Bricker and Jesse Helms. They have included such respective party stalwarts as Democrat Robert Byrd and Republican Everett Dirksen as well as political mavericks typified by Robert LaFollette, George Norris, and Burton Wheeler. Seated comfortably near the center, albeit slightly to the right, in this panorama of statesmen is a man who occupied center stage for nearly twenty-eight years. Like the other aforementioned Senate notables, it has not been Robert Dole's destiny to attain the highest office in the land. Yet like the Senate giants of the nineteenth century—Clay, Calhoun, and Webster—Sir Knight Dole may be as remembered by posterity as they have been, while lesser figures who occupied the White House such as Tyler, Fillmore, and Pierce are largely forgotten.

Like many Americans who have attained national stature, Robert Joseph Dole came from modest albeit honorable beginnings. Born in Russell, Kansas, on July 22, 1923, to Doran R. and Bina Talbott Dole, Bob grew up a typical Midwestern small town youth. Like many Great Depression era families, the Doles struggled with the hard times that characterized the thirties. Doran Dole advanced from running an egg and cream station to managing a grain elevator. Mrs. Dole was a Singer sewing machine sales agent. When a minor oil boom hit Russell, the family rented rooms in their home to oilfield workers and moved into the basement. Young Bob had a paper route and then worked in a local drugstore. He also displayed an interest in high school sports, competing in football, basketball, and track.

Following graduation in the spring of 1941, Bob entered the University of Kansas with intentions of studying medicine.

American entry into World War II in December of 1941 changed the course of millions of lives. After finishing his second year of college, Bob Dole enlisted in the United States Army. He became a member of the 10th Mountain Division and saw extensive combat duty in Italy. While leading an attack on a German machine gun unit in the Po Valley on April 14, 1945, parts of an exploding shell hit Lieutenant Dole.

His combat duty ended suddenly and the young officer now began his fight for life. His right shoulder was virtually gone, some neck and spinal vertebrae were fractured, and several slivers of metal penetrated his body. Three years of hospital rehabilitation followed, including three major operations. Slowly the wounded soldier recovered the ability to stand, walk, and use his left arm and hand. During his period of recovery, Dole met and married Phyllis Holden, a young physiotherapist who had helped with his recovery. When Bob re-entered college, Phyllis took lecture notes for him until he learned to write with his left hand. The couple later had a daughter, Robin. Their marriage, however, ended in January 1972. In 1975, he married again to Elizabeth Hanford of Raleigh, North Carolina, who would eventually serve in a cabinet post and in the United States Senate.

Discharged from the Army in 1948 with the rank of Captain, Bob Dole now displayed a determination to return to college and pursue a career in law. Taking advantage of the GI Bill, he briefly attended the University of Arizona and benefited from Tucson's healthful climate. Returning to Kansas, Dole completed a B. A. degree at Washburn University in Topeka. He then entered its law school.

In 1950, the twenty-seven year old Dole made his initial entry into politics when he became a candidate for the Kansas legislature. Although his forebears had been Democrats, Bob Dole chose to cast his political future with the GOP which has generally been the dominant party in the Sunflower State. Elected to a two-year term in November 1950 while still a student, the young legislator completed his law degree, graduating magna cum laude in 1952. With his law license in hand, Bob Dole returned to Russell that fall where he was elected County Attorney, a part-time position that also permitted him to pursue a private practice. He held this office for four two-year terms.

During this eight-year residence in Russell, Bob Dole participated in a variety of community and service groups. He joined the Kiwanis Club, Trinity Methodist Church, the Benevolent and Protective Order of Elks, and several veterans' organizations. He also petitioned Russell Lodge No. 177, Free and Accepted Masons. Bob was subsequently initiated an Entered Apprentice on April 19, 1955; passed to the degree of Fellowcraft on June 7; and was raised a Master Mason on September 20, 1955. Seeking additional light in Masonry, Dole completed the Scottish Rite degrees in the Valley of Salina on December 10, 1966, and the York Rite in Aleppo Commandery No. 31 in Hays, Kansas. He also became a Noble at Isis Shrine Temple in Salina. During his later years in Washington, the Senator served on the advisory committee for national affairs of the Masonic Service Association. In the seventies, Dole received the KCCH on October 15, 1971, and on November 15, 1975, the 33° in the Ancient Accepted Scottish Rite, Southern Jurisdiction.

After eight years as prosecutor in Russell County, Bob Dole decided to seek a seat in Congress. His district, which covered virtually the western half of the state, was a large one, but he managed to win both the primary and general elections and went on to serve eight years before moving to the Senate. During his years in the House, Dole served on the Agriculture Committee where he became a spokesman for Kansas wheat farmers. He also became a strong critic of liberal policies. A popular speaker on the GOP dinner circuit, Sir Knight Dole spoke at a Lincoln Day dinner in McArthur, Ohio on March 21, 1964, in company with local Congressman and Brother Homer E. "Pete" Abele of Delta Lodge No. 207 and Jackson Commandery No. 53. It was this writer's pleasure to meet and shake hands with the gentleman from Kansas that evening.

When veteran Senator and Brother Frank Carlson announced his retirement early in 1968, Congressman Dole stood for the seat, winning sixty-eight per cent of the vote in the primary, followed by another relatively easy sixty per cent victory in November. In the Senate, Dole gained an early reputation as a strong supporter and defender of Nixon Administration policies. This led to his subsequent elevation to the position of chairman of the Republican National Committee. However, when the Watergate scandal ultimately led to the demise of the Nixon presidency, Dole narrowly managed to win a second Senate term in 1974. An anti-Nixon backlash nearly ended his career as he squeezed out a thin victory of a less than two percent margin. His third, fourth, and fifth terms were won easily, and his Senate stature grew accordingly.

During his long tenure in Washington, the aggressive, youthful congressman mellowed somewhat as he became more of a coalition and consensus builder. With a Republican president and a Democratic Congress, Dole realized that in order to accomplish their goals, the GOP must build some bridges to the opposition. While toning down some of the old partisan fire, a more moderate and more effective Senator emerged. Ironically, when the GOP came to control the Senate in 1981, some of the younger firebrands sometimes viewed Bob as being too willing to compromise.

After 1974, Bob Dole became something of a spokesman for the Ford Administration, and in 1976 President and Brother Gerald Ford selected him as his running mate. Republicans had not yet fully recovered from the Watergate imbroglio, and the primary challenge of former California governor Reagan had also been decisive. Trailing Democratic nominee Jimmy Carter by double digits at convention time, the Ford-Dole forces took the offensive with Dole firing most of the salvos. In spite of some costly errors, they closed most of the gap by November and provided the American people with the tightest electoral count since 1916 (until 2000). By sweeping most of the western states, the final total stood at 297 to 240. A change of 10,000 votes in Ohio and 15,000 in Mississippi would have given them the victory.

Dole's narrow loss of the vice presidency did not diminish his Senate stature, and he soon emerged as a prominent critic of the Carter administration while making efforts to remold his image as a "conservative with compassion." Although successful to a degree, it was not enough to propel him to the top level of GOP presidential hopefuls in 1980, and he withdrew after the New Hampshire primary to seek and win a third term in the Senate. The victory of Ronald Reagan that November provided coattails of sufficient length to give Republicans a majority in the upper house for the first time since 1954. Bob Dole became chairman of the Senate Finance Committee.

In his new role, Senator Dole played a leading part in the passage of two major bills, the Economic Recovery Tax Act of 1981 and the Tax Equity and Fiscal Responsibility Act of 1982. He also proved to be a key player in the preservation of the Food Stamp program, extension of the Voting Rights Act, the Social Security bailout of 1983, plus legislation making Martin Luther King, Jr.'s birthday a national holiday. Dole also became known as a champion of legislation on behalf of the handicapped. After the retirement of

Howard Baker, Bob Dole became the GOP leader in the Senate, a position he held for eleven and one-half years (majority leader, 1985-86, 1995-96; minority leader 1987-94), until he relinquished the post to Brother Trent Lott of Mississippi, a member of Pascagoula Lodge No. 419.

In 1988, Robert Dole mounted another presidential challenge with a much stronger organization than in 1980. He scored an impressive win in Iowa but stumbled in New Hampshire and afterward when Vice President George Bush put together an impressive string of victories that left Dole and the other major challenger, Brother Jack Kemp (of Fraternal Lodge No. 625 in Hamburg, NY), far behind. Like the team player that he had always been, Dole continued to serve as a major spokesman for the Bush administration, and Elizabeth Dole who had earlier served as Secretary of Transportation on the Reagan team became Secretary of Labor (until resigning to head the Red Cross).

The GOP Congressional victories in November of 1994 again elevated Bob Dole to Senate Majority Leader and made him an early favorite for his party's presidential nomination. After a rocky start in the 1996 primaries, the Senator pulled off several major wins that left challengers Lamar Alexander, Patrick Buchanan, and Steve Forbes out of the running. Some Buchanan supporters in particular seemed to reflect a touch of anti-Masonic sentiment, one being quoted on NPR that he would have a hard time voting for a 33rd degree Mason. Nonetheless, Dole chose another one in Brother Jack Kemp 33° (in 1998) for a running mate, making the announcement prior to the convention and also choosing to retire from the Senate in mid-summer to give full attention to his campaign. Some pundits saw the ticket as an unlikely pair since Kemp had been a champion of "supply-side" economics that Dole neither particularly warmed up to nor really understood; their differences otherwise tend to be minute.

The Dole-Kemp "All Masonic" ticket ended up winning nineteen states for a total of 159 electoral votes. They won back three states the GOP had lost in 1992—Colorado, Georgia, and Montana—but lost Republican-leaning Florida and Arizona, probably because of the so-called "Mediscare." Rightly or wrongly, many voters viewed incumbent President Clinton as having co-opted many of the positions normally taken by Republicans. Nonetheless, Sir Knight Dole accepted his defeat with grace and has appeared on national TV in such roles as a guest on David Letterman's show and a commercial for Visa

Card, donating the proceeds to charity. He also made two subsequent appearances on the cover of *Knight Templar* Magazine.

In conclusion, while Robert Joseph Dole may have fallen short of his presidential quest, his life represents a symbol of triumph over adversity. The small-town Kansan, whose broken and wounded body lay at death's door on that Italian battlefield in mid-April 1945, made a remarkable comeback. He could have opted to spend the rest of his life drawing a disability pension and swapping war stories with other veterans in some American Legion hall out on the Great Plains. Instead he chose to give the people of Kansas a decade of dedicated public service and the American people nearly thirty-six years of like dedication in the halls of Congress. On January 17, 1997, his opponent, President William Clinton rewarded him with the Presidential Medal of Freedom. To borrow a phrase from the title of Brother John Wayne's most celebrated motion picture, Sir Knight Bob Dole has and continues to display "True Grit."

**Note**: The Grand Lodge of Kansas through M. W. Brother David Dresser, Grand Secretary of Ohio supplied Dole's blue lodge records, as did the Library staff of the Scottish Rite, SJ his Scottish Rite Records. See also the article by J. E. Behrens, "Our Templar Senators," in the October 1977 issue of *Knight Templar*, pp. 7-12. His autobiography, *One Soldier's Story: A Memoir*, was released in 2005 by Harper-Collins. The portrait photo came from the late Bro. Frank Cremeans of Morning Dawn Lodge No. 7, member of the 104th Congress.

May 1997; slightly revised 2011

## Bob Evans:
### *Mr. "Down on the Farm" and Sixty-Year Mason*

In the past generation, one of the more pleasing signs for hungry travelers along the highways and interstates of Middle America has been that of a Bob Evans Restaurant. These operations once described by an insider as "family-style eating establishments" have made the name of an Appalachian Ohio farmer of Welsh extraction a household word throughout much of the nation. For a fellow whose original dream consisted of having his own farm, Evans came a long way. Lesser known was the fact that Bob was a Master Mason for some sixty-seven years as well as a sixty-year member of Aladdin Shrine Temple.

Bob was born Robert Lewis Evans in Wood County, Ohio on May 30, 1918. His parents, Stanley and Elizabeth Lewis Evans, were both products of the Welsh immigrant community that had flourished for several decades in rural Gallia and Jackson Counties of hilly southeastern Ohio. Surnames like Davis, Evans, Jones, and Lewis still abound on area mailboxes. Stanley and Elizabeth had married three years earlier, and the former worked at various jobs in Cincinnati and elsewhere, struggling to support a growing family.

In 1924 when Bob was nearly six, Stanley got the opportunity to enter the grocery business with an older brother back in his native area in the Ohio River town of Gallipolis, the county seat of his Gallia County homeland. Growing up in Gallipolis, young Bob Evans attended the local schools, worked in his dad's store, played baseball with his peers, took care of the backlot henhouse, sold *Literary Digest* subscriptions, and labored as a newspaper carrier for the *Columbus Dispatch.* The Evans Grocery Stores expanded into a chain of sixteen outlets in neighboring towns.

Bob's father sent him first to Greenbriar Military School and then to Ohio State University. By this time, the adolescent youth aspired to a career in veterinary medicine, but an eye injury forced him to drop out of college after two years.

Returning to Gallipolis, Bob went to work for the Evans Packing Company, another business his father and uncles had initiated. He also began courting Jewell Waters whose family had moved to Gallia County from Morganton, North Carolina, in 1937. The pair married in June of 1940 and subsequently became the parents of six children.

Masonry and matrimony struck young Evans at nearly the same time. He took the Entered Apprentice degree at Morning Dawn Lodge No. 7 in Gallipolis, Ohio on June 11, 1940. He was passed on August 13, 1940, and Raised to the sublime degree of Master Mason on September 10, 1940. Bob later became a member of the Ancient Accepted Scottish Rite, Valley of Columbus, and a Noble of Aladdin Shrine Temple in Columbus, Ohio, on May 2, 1947.

Many, if not most, of the men in the Evans clan have been active Masons including Bob's father Stanley. Several have been members of Patriot Lodge No. 496 in the hamlet of Patriot which is one of the smallest communities to have sustained an active lodge for well over a century. Bob's cousin, Ben R. Evans, was likely the most active Mason in the family, having served as Grand Master of the Grand Lodge of Ohio in 1966-1967.

After World War II military service, Bob returned to Gallipolis and opened his first restaurant. With a continuing interest in agriculture and conservation combined with a desire to rear his children on a farm, Bob and Jewell purchased the now famous Homestead Farm on the outskirts of Rio Grande (it had previously been operated by Rio Grande College). The children learned the virtues of rural living and participated in 4-H programs. Meanwhile, Evans worked to perfect his recipe for sausage and opened a second restaurant nearby on U. S. Highway 35.

From these modest beginnings, the sausage business expanded to the point where it was marketed in twelve states by 1980, and the "eating establishments" by 1994 had increased to 297 under the Bob Evans name and to over 500 by 2010. For a time they also operated several Owens Family Restaurants in Texas and also Cantina del Rio that served Mexican style food but discontinued both by 2006. A more successful subsidiary, Mimi's Café, acquired in 2004, operates more than 100 establishments, primarily in California. This gave Bob Evans Farms Incorporated some 600 plus outlets, covering much of the United States. Their commercials with the familiar "Down on the Farm" slogan have familiarized Americans everywhere with the man, the sausage, and a menu of fine food.

In addition to his business affairs, Evans also pursued numerous other activities, many of them related to agriculture and soil conservation. These efforts resulted in his becoming the recipient of such awards as Soil Conservationist of the year and Wildlife Habitat Conservationist of the Year. In 1977, Governor and Brother James A. Rhodes presented him with the Governor's Award which is given yearly to a selected few prominent Ohioans of high achievement.

The Evans interest in education also manifested itself in many ways. Bob served for several years from 1967 as a member of the Board of Trustees of Rio Grande College. Then in 1978, Governor Rhodes appointed him to the Ohio Board of Regents. He assisted the late Brother Wayne White of Waterloo Lodge No. 536 in securing funding for the Ohio Appalachian Center for Higher Education to encourage more college attendance in the region and was a long-time supporter of 4-H youth programs.

One of Bob's preferred activities for several decades came in his support for the projects of the Southeast Ohio Regional Council. This organization worked to encourage both private and public development of the region. It manifested major efforts in promoting highway expansions and improvements.

Always interested in politics, he generally supported Republican causes and ideas. In 1994, Bob took special pride in serving as general chair in the successful campaign of his friend and fellow Morning Dawn Lodge member, Frank A. Cremeans (Raised June 12, 1970), to the United States Congress. Since Cremeans had little experience and minimal name recognition outside his immediate area, the TV commercials Bob did on Frank's behalf played a major role in his victory. Cremeans served but one term and has since passed away.

Each fall on the second weekend in October, the Bob Evans Farm Festival attracts tens of thousands of visitors to the Homestead near Rio Grande. There city dwellers and country folk alike can see demonstrations of many of the older crafts and skills associated with rural living. They can also hear traditional American music played by such masters of their trade as the old-time oriented Briarhoppers (in the 1990s), the newer bluegrass of the Rarely Herd or Doyle Lawson and Quicksilver, or even the sounds of Jerry Weaver's Goodtime Jazz Band. Through the nineties, attendees would often be greeted by Bob

Evans himself or even have their grandchildren pose for a photo with the man who in many respects became the personification of what is both good and successful about rural America.

Although Bob Evans largely retired from day-to-day operations of Bob Evans Farms, Inc. in 1986, he remained quite active into the 21st century. One of his later efforts consisted of pushing for year-round grazing as a means of revitalizing agriculture and perhaps the salvation of family farms in Appalachian Ohio. His fifty year pin in Morning Dawn Lodge was presented in 1991 and on September 23, 1997, he received the 33°. He had transferred his Scottish Rite membership to the Valley of Cincinnati some years earlier. Whether promoting farm activities, regional development, Shrine charities, improved education, or GOP candidates, it remained a safe bet that Bob Evans would be in there doing his share of whatever project he tackled.

It was a long trek from delivering newspapers on Second Avenue in Gallipolis to having his name on a chain of five hundred restaurants and making "down on the farm" a household phrase. With a major amount of grit and determination, Brother Bob Evans managed to do just that by the time of his death on June 21, 2007.

**Note**: Bob Evans himself and Sir Knight Gordon Fisher, the Secretary of Morning Dawn Lodge, provided much of the information for this article along with material on the Evans Family in *Gallia County, Ohio: People in History to 1980* (Taylor Pub. Co., 1980). Since Bob Evans' death his daughter Robbin Evans wrote an affectionate biography with Mike Harden, *A Bountiful Heart: The Life of Bob Evans* (2008).

October 1995; slightly revised 2011

## Brother Robert T. Secrest:
*The Muskingum Valley Conservative Democrat*

The Muskingum Valley of eastern Ohio has contributed its share of political legends to the American scene ranging from Rufus Putnam who helped found the Grand Lodge of Ohio to 1950s Governor and Supreme Court Judge, C. William O'Neill. Within the last century, probably none could match the success of a moderate to conservative Democrat named Robert Secrest who served ten terms in the United States Congress and an additional ten years in the Ohio Legislature. He managed to do this in an area generally dominated by Republicans. A Mason for sixty-six years, Brother Bob had his share of admirers and critics, but in his locale, he could claim almost everyone as a friend. Secrest's political rivals within Republican ranks also included a considerable number of Masonic Brothers, some of whom were also his friends.

Robert Thompson Secrest was born in Noble County just outside Senecaville, Ohio, on January 22, 1904. His parents were Ralph and Amelia Thompson Secrest; the former was a farmer and was also employed as a coal miner at various times. Bob lived a typical life of rural youth—attending school, working as a farm laborer, and even toiling some in the mines. When he finished high school, Bob went to Muskingum College in New Concord (later famous as the hometown of astronaut Brother and Senator John Glenn who was only a baby when Secrest started his higher education). The future congressman earned an A.B. degree in 1926 and expected to spend his working life as a school teacher. He had, in fact, a brief experience as a teacher at the one-room Opperman School in 1922. After another brief pedagogical fling at the junior high in the county seat of Cambridge, he became high school principal in his hometown of Senecaville, a post he held for five years.

Robert Secrest began his Masonic journey when he was initiated an Entered Apprentice on January 11, 1928, in Point Pleasant Lodge No. 360 in nearby Pleasant City (Senecaville had no lodge). He was passed to the degree of Fellowcraft on February 8 and raised a Master Mason on March 28, 1928. He retained membership there for the next sixty-six years. Becoming very much a joiner, he also belonged to the Odd Fellows, Elks, Eagles, and Patrons of Husbandry (Grange). On November 28, 1929, the young principal married Virginia Bowden who bore the affectionate nickname "Dutch." The marriage resulted in two daughters, Nancy Anne and Mary Jane, and a son Robert T. Secrest, Jr.; Virginia Secrest passed away on August 10, 1990. Bob and Virginia both belonged to the Eastern Star in Pleasant City, and both were also members of the Presbyterian Church.

Bob Secrest entered politics seemingly as an afterthought. When Noble County's representative to the Ohio House, H. D. Hune, decided not to seek another term in 1928, he persuaded the young school principal to run for the office. That turned out to be a very poor time for a Democrat to begin a political career, as Republicans swept nearly everything in Ohio that year from Herbert Hoover to Governor Myers Cooper and most of the legislators. Secrest, whose opponent S. W. Burlingame said that he was too young for the job, made a close bid, losing only by 3, 249 to 3, 513. Two years later, it was a different story with the country falling into the Great Depression and the GOP on the defensive. This time Secrest won, defeating Burlingame by a comfortable margin, 4,184 to 2,692. By all accounts, Secrest was always a strong and skillful campaigner.

The Ohio Legislature was not a full-time job, and Bob Secrest moved to another teaching job as head of the Murray City Schools in Hocking County. Meanwhile Brother Secrest challenged a seven-term incumbent congressman, Republican C. Ellis Moore, in the six-county Fifteenth Congressional District. The Great Depression made things difficult for Republicans everywhere, and Secrest rode into office on Franklin Roosevelt's coat-tails, 50,313 to 38,113, a margin of 12,200 votes. One of the winner's major campaign points was to champion the early release of the World War I Veteran's Bonus, a hot issue at the time. He never taught school again and served in Congress for nearly a decade, resigning to enter the United States Navy on August 3, 1942.

The Fifteenth District, normally Republican, had its challenges. In both 1934 and 1936 he faced strong competition from another educator-politician, Kenneth C. Ray of Morgan County, a member of Clemente Amitie Lodge No. 285. The two had served together in the Ohio House and were, in fact, close friends. Ray's son John, a retired physician in Zanesville, recalled that the two often campaigned together. As Secrest frequently had car trouble, Ray often drove him to public appearances. Ray carried Morgan County both times but came up short in the whole district by respective margins of 8,772 and 11,210. Ken Ray later enjoyed a distinguished career as an educational appointee, serving as head of the Ohio school system in the Bricker Administration (1939-1945), as a federal administrator under Eisenhower, and as a faculty member at Ohio University; but he never bested Bob Secrest in an election. The year 1938 saw a strong GOP comeback at the polls, and Secrest faced another challenge from Percy W. Griffiths, a former Marietta College football coach, auto dealer, mayor, and member of American Union Lodge No. 1. Griffiths ran especially well in Muskingum County but came up 3,670 votes behind Secrest. In 1940, Brother Bob coasted to easy victory in his fifth consecutive term. During his years in Congress, his major accomplishment came in successful efforts to make the Muskingum River Conservancy program a reality, particularly Lake Seneca.

The coming of World War II changed the Secrest focus. He resigned from Congress on August 3, 1942, and entered the United States Navy during which time he served in England, North Africa, Italy, and the Pacific, rising to the rank of Commander. For fifteen months his duties included serving on the staff of Admiral Chester Nimitz. Discharged on February 28, 1946, he soon entered the race for his old seat in Congress.

Meanwhile the Fifteenth District had returned to the GOP fold. With Secrest in military service, Percy Griffiths had captured the seat in both 1942 and 1944, and in 1946 he sought a third term. Dissatisfaction with the Truman Administration peaked that fall; it was not a good year for Democrats, even for a returning war hero. Griffiths won the race by 4,405 votes, with Secrest winning only Noble County by 246 and losing what was increasingly considered his home county of Guernsey by twenty-two. Two years later, however, a different situation existed, and Secrest recaptured his old seat by a margin of 10,281 with Griffiths carrying only Morgan County. After Bob won easily in 1950, Brother Griffiths made a last challenge in 1952, but Bob had become entrenched, and even the popularity of Eisenhower did little for the Marietta man as Secrest won by a 27, 947 margin in an enlarged district that now included Perry County. By this time, Veteran's Affairs had become his major specialty. He maintained active connections with the American Legion, Veterans of Foreign Wars, and other veterans' groups long after he had retired from politics.

Brother Secrest continued his Masonic sojourn. In the fall of 1953, he took the Scottish Rite work in the Valley of Cambridge through the 18°. As Cambridge did not confer the Consistory degrees until 1955, he did not become a 32° Mason until September 8, 1958, in Guernsey Consistory. Secrest subsequently became a member of Aladdin Shrine Temple in Columbus. On January 3, 1973, he received an honorary membership in Summerfield Lodge No. 425. On September 28, 1977, he received the 33° in Pittsburgh. Brother Bob once wrote that "since my career has been a mobile one," he never held any offices in his Blue Lodge, but it has been noted that he often spoke at various Masonic functions.

Although he now occupied a safe seat, Robert T. Secrest took on a new challenge when President Eisenhower appointed him to the Federal Trade Commission; he resigned on September 26, 1954. A Perry County Democrat, Max Underwood (son of Mell Underwood of New Lexington Lodge No. 250 who had been a congressional colleague of Secrest), replaced him. However, Republicans again took the 15th District with a new face, two-term Guernsey County State Representative, Brother John Earl Henderson (33° at the Valley of Cambridge in 1966). Henderson served three terms and retired, after which Brother Tom V. Moorehead of Zanesville, a long-time GOP state senator, narrowly took the seat in 1960.

Brother Secrest's term on the FTC expired at the end of 1961, and the Guernsey County man was appointed Director of Commerce in the cabinet of Ohio Governor Mike DiSalle. When William Rider resigned as the Democratic 15th District Congressional nominee in mid-1962, local Democrats designated Bob as his replacement. Back in his favorite role of campaigning again, Bob bucked a Republican trend and took the seat from Moorehead by a narrow plurality of 3,761 votes.

In 1964, Secrest won his biggest Congressional victory by defeating former Washington County prosecuting attorney, Randall Metcalf (of American Union Lodge No. 1 and the Marietta York Rite Bodies), in a landslide vote of 62,438 to 31,803, sweeping every county in the district. Ironically, Metcalf's father, Brother Verner Metcalf, had been a popular state senator in the thirties and later an Appellate Court Judge (and District Deputy Grand Master) in many of the same counties as the Secrest district.

Unfortunately, that would be Secrest's last victorious congressional race. A court-ordered redistricting led to the abolition of the old 15th District and placed it in the Columbus area where Brother Chalmers P. Wylie held the seat for another generation. Meanwhile, Guernsey County became part of the 17th District which had been held for sixteen years by another popular incumbent, the articulate conservative Republican, John M. Ashbrook (of Center Lodge No. 86 in Johnstown, Ohio). In another ironic twist, Ashbrook's father, Brother William A. Ashbrook, had been an anti-New Deal conservative Democratic Congressman prior to his death on January 1, 1940; he and Secrest were colleagues. While Secrest had been the most conservative Democrat in the Ohio Congressional delegation, he still looked like a liberal to the younger Ashbrook. Secrest did well in familiar counties like Guernsey and Muskingum, but most of the battle was fought on Ashbrook turf, and the latter prevailed by a margin of 14,101 votes.

The Secrest career had hardly ended as he came back in 1968 as a candidate for the state senate. Former rival Tom Moorehead had been chosen for a two-year term in 1966, and Secrest challenged him for a full four-year term. Bob made Moorehead's comeback a short one by beating him by 30,798 votes. Moorehead was probably ready for retirement at age seventy, but Secrest must have given the veteran lawmaker nightmares. Bob Secrest went on to serve a second term in the state senate, winning his last victory in 1972 over the little-known Clyde C. Hardesty by a vote of 82,830 to 40,147—his only two-to-one victory in a series of contests that began forty-four years earlier.

Robert T. Secrest retired at the end of his term in 1976. With his retirement, his Senate district went back into Republican hands as Brother Sam Speck of New Concord (a 1988 Valley of Cambridge 33°) easily defeated his Democratic opponent. Secrest and Speck must have enjoyed a good relationship because when "Dutch" Secrest died in 1990, Speck helped with the service at her funeral. During his half century in politics, Brother Bob had won so many honors that it would double the length of this article just to list them.

Robert Thompson Secrest lived in retirement until his death on May 15, 1994. During his latter years he was widely regarded as an elder statesman in the Muskingum Valley. When he received his fifty-year pin in Point Pleasant Lodge, Brother Glenn Arnold, highly active Scottish and York Rite Mason, was honored to be asked to present it. Unlike many well-known Masons, Brother Secrest did leave some written comments on the fraternity which are quoted herein: "The lessons learned in Masonry transcend into everyday life. Its philosophy fits into one's own life and forms the basic rules and conduct we should each live with. Everything should have its basis in good words and deeds. Early and often attendance in lodge helped and still does today, to formulate and reinforce our beliefs. Masonry has a tremendous positive influence on everyone it comes in contact with, either directly or indirectly, and cannot help but have an uplifting effect on the lives it touches."

Much of the world may have forgotten the highly-successful state and national legislator who became a legend in the Muskingum Valley, but his name lives on in that region. The Secrest Auditorium in Zanesville, the Robert T. Secrest Senior Citizen Center in Senecaville, and a life-size statue in front of the courthouse in Cambridge all serve as reminders of the Democrat who became a legend in an area generally dominated by Republicans, many of whom also held him in high esteem. As a man and as a Mason, he stood tall.

**Note**: No biography exists of Brother Secrest, but this sketch has been put together with Congressional directories, election statistics, material supplied by Brother Chad Simpson of the staff of the Grand Lodge of Ohio, recollections from my own memory and a file of documents held by the Valley of Cambridge, A.A.S.R. and made available by Sir Knight E. Glenn Arnold, Emeritus Secretary of the Valley of Cambridge.

December 2003; slightly revised 2011

**Sir Knight Ernest Borgnine**: *Oscar Winning Actor and Advocate for Freemasonry*

Between Warner Baxter in 1929 and John Wayne in 1970, a total of five Masons have won the Academy Award for best actor in a motion picture. By far the most active Brother in this hallowed group is the 1955 winner Ernest Borgnine. While not holding lodge office "per se," he has served in a variety of roles as a spokesperson for Masonic charities and also been a tireless advocate for the fraternity. In his screen career Brother Ernie is neither the legendary figure nor the matinee idol such as Brother Clark Gable, but he has established a solid celluloid persona for six decades, a rare feat in his own unique manner.

Born in Hamden, Connecticut on January 24, 1917, to Italian immigrant parents, Ermes Effron Borgnino (later Anglicized to Ernest Borgnine) had a fairly normal childhood with one exception. At the age of two, his mother took him and returned to Italy, coming back to the United States in 1924. In his boyhood, the youth joined the Boy Scouts and had a part in a high school play. Not long after completing high school in New Haven, Ernest enlisted in the United States Navy. Discharged in mid-1941, he returned to the Navy after Pearl Harbor and ultimately spent a total of ten years in military service as a gunner's mate and chief petty officer.

Out of the Navy, Borgnine's mother suggested that he take up acting on the basis of his "strong personality." Under the G. I. Bill, he enrolled at the Randall School of Dramatic Art in Hartford for six months. Borgnine opted not to go to Yale since they had so many degree requirements far removed from theater. Instead he sought practical experience and went to Abingdon, Virginia and its somewhat renowned Barter Theater, where for the next five years he did everything from driving a truck and painting scenery to walk-on parts and eventually lead roles. Certainly his best experience for Barter was as a cast member of Shakespeare's *Hamlet,* touring Denmark and Germany, mostly on military bases. He also had parts in such productions as *State of the Union* and the Tennessee Williams play *The Glass Menagerie.*

During his years in Virginia, Ernest Borgnine also became a Mason. Initial interest came from his father who had been a Scottish Rite member. Next came his affection for Abingdon and its friendly people and atmosphere recalling that, "I grew to love the town and all it offered." One day he went to the print shop to pick up some show posters where the owner Elmo Vaughn was a Mason. Ernest told him that his father was a Mason and asked him about joining. Vaughn smiled but said nothing. Later, after asking a third time he received a petition. He says "I didn't learn 'til later that in those days you had to ask three times." Borgnine took his Entered Apprentice degree on July 7, 1948. Several months later on April 25, 1949, he was passed to the degree of Fellowcraft and after another week, raised a Master Mason on May 2, 1949. Even after moving on to Broadway and Hollywood, Brother Borgnine kept his membership in Abingdon Lodge No. 48.

Before permanently settling in California, Ernest Borgnine made a few appearances in Broadway theater productions. His first role came as a male nurse in *Harvey.* Other stage roles followed in *Born Yesterday* and *Mrs. McThing,* playing a gangster in the latter. This led the actor to frequently being typecast as a villain when he moved to California in 1951. After a couple of small bit parts, he landed a larger job in *From Here to Eternity* as the brutal army sergeant "Fatso" Judson who administers a fatal beating to Frank Sinatra. While landing him high marks for his acting, Borgnine also received death threats for those who took his film treatment of a legendary screen favorite seriously.

Although Brother Borgnine's stature as an actor was increasing, the film that really elevated him to star status came in 1955 with his Oscar winning title role in *Marty,* a tender love story in which lonely but plain people meet and fall in love. *Marty* also won the best picture award. Marty Pilletti, a rather portly and homely but good-hearted Bronx butcher, was portrayed to perfection by Brother Ernie who demonstrated tremendous versatility. Film critic Bosley Crowther wrote in *The New York Times* calling his work "a performance that burns into the mind." A more modest Borgnine gave much of the credit for the film's success to writer Paddy Chayefsky whom he described as a master of "kitchen sink realism." In the year following his Oscar winning film, Borgnine continued to handle such varying roles as an Amish farmer in *Violent Saturday*, a rancher in *Jubal* with Brother Glenn Ford, a fight promoter in *The Square Jungle*, and a harried husband in *The Catered Affair* with Bette Davis and Debbie Reynolds, who played his wife and daughter, respectively.

In the 1958 western *The Badlanders*, Borgnine and Alan Ladd portrayed two ex-convicts who got revenge by robbing a crooked mine owner who had wrongfully got them sent to Yuma Prison. One of the film's female stars, Hispanic actress Katy Jurado, subsequently became Ernest's second wife (he had an earlier marriage to a Navy nurse). Key parts in military and action dramas became his forte as roles like that of Marty Pilletti did not often come along in Hollywood. As a result, he continued in a wide variety of character parts in television as well as motion pictures. For instance, he guested on the initial episode of the long-running adult western *Wagon Train* in September 1957 as "Willy Moran," a former Union soldier struggling to recover from a battle with alcoholism.

Although widely known as an actor, Brother Borgnine probably gained his greatest fame as star of the TV hit comedy *McHale's Navy* from 1962 until 1966. As the "gruff but lovable" Lieutenant Commander Quinton McHale, Borgnine became a familiar figure in millions of American living rooms. Like most military sitcoms, *McHale's Navy* bore little resemblance to reality. As one critic argued, the United States would not have won World War II if McHale and his inept crew had been typical. Still audiences loved him and servicemen also took him to heart, and he became one of their favorites, no doubt wishing that his character had been their own commanding officer. Injured veterans fondly recall his many visits to military hospitals. For example, my predecessor as Commander of Athens Commandery No. 15, Ken Jones, treasures his memory of Borgnine's visit when he was in Bethesda Naval Hospital recovering from injuries sustained in Viet Nam.

During his *McHale's Navy* days—no longer traveling as much to exotic film locales in foreign lands—Brother Ernest Borgnine became more active in Masonic work. He completed his Scottish Rite degrees in the Valley of Los Angeles on March 14, 1964. On June 6 of the same year he became a Noble at Al Malaikah Shrine Temple. The next year on February 4, 1965, Borgnine became a dual member of

Hollywood Lodge No. 355. However, his Masonic work was not yet finished.

More Scottish Rite honors came in later years. In 1979, Ernie received the K.C.C.H. and the 33° in 1983 and the Grand Cross in 1991. He took his York Rite Degrees in July 1985 in Long Beach Chapter No. 84 Royal Arch Masons, Long Beach Council No. 26 Royal and Select Masters, and ultimately was knighted in Long Beach Commandery No. 40, Knights Templar, on July 28, 1985. He is a life member of all of these bodies.

Not merely content with just being a "celebrity Mason," Brother Borgnine has become a public advocate for Masonic bodies. Typical of his comments is found in a 2007 article titled "Mouth to Ear" in *Masons of Texas:* "As I've advanced in Masonry, I have found we are an elite group of people who believe in God, country, family, and neighbours [sic]. We work hard to help our fellowman; and through our charitable work, such as support for the Childhood Language Disorders Centers, we have made it possible to help many children grow into good American citizens. We should always be proud of the order which we belong to [sic]. Where in all the world do you find so many great men and Brothers who have helped the whole wide world? But—we are hiding our light under a bushel basket." In 2000, Sir Knight Borgnine was the recipient of the Grand Encampment National Award.

In practicing what he preaches, Brother Ernie has served as honorary chair of the Scottish Ritecare Program. Between 1972 and 2002 he marched several times in a Shrine unit as the "Grand Clown" in the Great Circus Parade in Milwaukee. He was also honorary chairman of a program to support the Scottish Rite Childhood Language Center in Richmond, Virginia. In non-Masonic charity work on behalf of veterans, he served in 1996 as chairman of the National Salute to Hospitalized Veterans and traveled throughout the country making numerous visitations.

Although *McHale's Navy* lasted through four seasons (138 episodes) plus re-runs, Borgnine was hardly ready for retirement. He continued appearing with regularity in both lead and support roles, both in major films and prime-time television. Listing all of this activity would be both exhausting and time consuming, so only a few of the highlights will be mentioned here. Motion pictures include *Pay or Die* (1960) in which he played the martyred New York Police Detective Joseph Petrosino who was among the first to investigate the Mafia; *Go Naked in the World* (1961) with Gina Lollobrigida; *The Dirty Dozen* (1967) with Lee Marvin and Charles Bronson; and three made for TV sequels — *The Legend of Lylah Claire* (1968) with Kim Novak, *The Wild Bunch* (1969) with William Holden, and *Hannie Caulder* (1971) with Raquel Welch.

In made for television movies, the more memorable titles included a western *The Trackers* (1971) with Julie Adams and Sammy Davis, Jr.; *Legend in Granite* (1973) in which he portrayed football legend Vince Lombardi; and more recently the lead role in a holiday season family effort, *A Grandpa for Christmas* (2007). Guest spots in major dramas included one of the most memorable episodes of *Little House on the Prairie* (1974) and the final two episodes of *ER* in 2009, which netted him an Emmy nomination. He did a voice part in the cartoon series *All Dogs Go to Heaven* and another in *Sponge Bob Square-Pants.* From 1984 to 1986, he had a second prime-time adventure series *Airwolf* (55 episodes) with Jan Michael Vincent and a lesser but regular role as "Manny the Doorman" in *The Single Guy* (23 episodes) from 1995 to 1997. Although seventy-eight when this series started, it was reported that Sir Knight Ernie was the first to arrive on the set, the last to leave, and generally had the most fun.

On his ninetieth birthday in January 2007, Brother Borgnine was honored with a dinner in West Hollywood. Attendees included his wife, the former Tova Traesnaes, other family members, his buddy from the "McHale" era, Tim Conway; Bo Hopkins; Burt Young; two notable leading ladies from earlier days, Debbie Reynolds and Connie Stevens; and a number of others. Miss Stevens, fondly remembered as the star of the *Hawaiian Eye* TV series and such youth films as *Parish* and *Susan Slade,* interviewed at the 2011 film fair in Winston-Salem, North Carolina, had only positive comments about Borgnine whom she described as a "wonderful person."

Active until his death on July 8, 2012, Brother Ernie reminisced to a London reporter in May 2009 for *The Scotsman* with a touch of humor concerning his long film career, "I've died onscreen almost thirty times, I've been shot, stabbed, kicked, punched through barroom doors . . . pushed in front of moving subway trains, devoured by rats and a giant mutated fish, blown up in spaceships, melted down into a Technicolor puddle, jumped into a snake pit, and I perished from thirst in the Sahara Desert. I bounced around [in a] capsized ocean liner, beat Frank Sinatra to death, impaled Lee Marvin with a pitchfork, and had my way with Raquel Welch."

Honors also continue to be accumulated by the senior actor. In January 2011, the Screen Actors Guild presented him with their Life Achievement Award. Some opposition arose from younger generation members who have found fault with his occasional politically incorrect comments, but it mattered not to Brother Borgnine who *The Scottish Rite Journal* pointed out was the only Mason besides the late Ill. Brother Red Skelton to receive this recognition. On May 7, 2011, the Valley of Long Beach held a dinner in which they named their theater in the Scottish Rite Temple after the acclaimed actor with Ill. Brother Norm Crosby presiding.

In reviewing and concluding this survey of the career of this noted Mason, it seems relevant to close with one of his own quotes, "I speak out loud about Masonry to everyone! I'm proud of the fact that I belong to an organization that made me a better American, Christian, husband, and neighbour [sic]; and all it took was a little self-determination by going foot-to-foot . . . and mouth to ear."

**Note**: Material for this article comes from the 1956 article on Ernest Borgnine in *Current Biography*, a variety of motion picture and Masonic websites including articles by Blake Bowden in *Masons of Texas* and in February 2011, *The Pennsylvania Freemason*. His book *Ernie: The Autobiography* (2008) is an honest survey of Borgnine's life and thoughts about his films, directors, and associates but has only one passing reference to Masonry. I especially appreciate the assistance of the staffs at the Grand Lodges of Virginia and California, the Grand York Rite bodies of California, the Valley of Los Angeles, and Al Malaikah Shrine.

May 2012; updated post-mortem

**Brother Brad Paisley**: *Contemporary Country Music Star*

Modern Masons often look to the past for examples of successful persons in their fields of endeavor. In the field of music for instance, such figures as John Philip Sousa and Lauritz Melchior are often cited. In more vernacular forms of the art, one might choose such persons as Tony Martin, Jimmie Rodgers, Roy Acuff, or Gene Autry. A contemporary member of the Craft, who is currently making a name for himself is Brother Brad Paisley, a "Grand Ole Opry" star and multiple Country Music Association award winner. His songs are especially effective in striking a chord with what one critic called "snapshots of everyday life, and life lived with a smile."

Brad Douglas Paisley was born in Glen Dale, West Virginia, on October 28, 1972. Glen Dale is a town along the Ohio River a few miles south of Wheeling, long famed as the home of radio station WWVA and "Jamboree, U.S.A." (1933-2005). It is a program often considered second only to Nashville's "Grand Ole Opry"as a live country music show. The story goes that when the child was about four, his grandfather asked him what his favorite type of music was, but the youngster was not quite sure what he meant, so when grandpa told him his favorite type was country, the boy agreed with the older man. When Brad was eight his grandfather gave him a guitar, and from this modest beginning a career and stardom was born. A few years later Brad formed a band and began to play for local events such as churches and Rotary clubs, composing a song called "Born on Christmas Day," which became a ticket to a performance on "Jamboree, U.S.A." He soon became a virtual regular. This provided him with an opportunity to mingle with the better-known guest stars who had come to dominate the program.

After finishing high school, Brad entered college at nearby West Liberty, but after a couple of years, transferred to Belmont University in Nashville which had an increasingly noted Music Business program. Receiving an ASCAP scholarship, he interned there, graduated in 1995, and wrote a couple of hit songs for other artists. In the latter part of 1998, he signed a contract with Arista Records.

Meanwhile, Brad began his Masonic life. His father, Douglas Paisley, has been an active member of Marshall Union Lodge No. 8 in Moundsville as well as the Scottish Rite and Shrine. Brad joined Hiram Lodge No. 7 in Franklin, Tennessee where Little Jimmy Dickens was a newly raised Mason (also home lodge of PGM John Palmer, *Knight Templar* magazine editor). Brother Paisley received his degrees on June 2, September 1, and October 27, 1998. Later he joined Osiris Shrine Temple back in Wheeling where his dad was also a member. On October 28, 2006, he took the Scottish Rite degrees in Washington, D.C. His keyboardist, Kendal Marcy, also received the 32°, and mentor Jimmy Dickens was made a KCCH. Brad affiliated with the Valley of Nashville.

Paisley's first song hit, the title cut from his first compact disc, "Who Needs Pictures," reached number twelve on the *Billboard* charts, first appearing on February 6, 1999. Two other cuts from that project, "He Didn't Have to Be" and "We Danced," reached the top. On February 17, 2001, Paisley became a regular cast member of the "Grand Ole Opry." West Virginia-born Country Music Hall of Fame member, Little Jimmy Dickens, has been a particular mentor.

Brother Paisley's second album, released in 2001, titled "Part II" contained five hits, but the only one to make it to number one, "I'm Gonna Miss Her (the Fishin' Song)," remained there for two weeks in July 2002. On the charts for seventy weeks, the disc was certified platinum in August 2002.

Somehow in a busy touring schedule, Brad Paisley managed to find time to pursue a personal life. He made an acquaintance with Hollywood actress Kimberly Williams, star of the remake of "Father of the Bride" who had also appeared in one of his music videos. After a nine month engagement, the pair married on March 15, 2003, at Stauffer Chapel located on the campus of Pepperdine University in California. The couple maintains two homes, one in Franklin, Tennessee and another in the Golden State at Malibu. They have two sons, William and Jasper, born in 2007 and 2009 respectively.

A third Paisley disc bore the unromantic title "Mud on the Tires" and featured a cover picture of the artist in one of his white stage costumes splattered with mud. Nonetheless, the song of the same name reached number one and another song "Whiskey Lullaby," a duet with country-bluegrass songstress Alison Krauss, won the Country Music Association's Musical Event of the Year Award. Two other songs from the album made the top ten listings and it was certified double platinum.

Brad Paisley's musical successes continued. His fourth disc, "Time Well Wasted," won the album of the year award in 2006. Its fifteen songs included a duet with Dolly Parton and another with Alan Jackson. The fifth one appropriately titled "5th Gear," released in 2007, included four songs that reached number one. It also helped the West Virginian win the CMA Male Vocalist of the Year Award, a prize repeated in 2008 and 2009. In 2010, Brad won the top award, CMA Entertainer of the Year. He won his first Grammy in 2007 for his instrumental "Throttleneck." Through mid-2011, he had nineteen number one hits. The most recent one, "Remind Me," is a duet with reigning country queen, the appealing former 2005 American Idol winner, Carrie Underwood.

An earlier characteristic of country music artists was the practice of either including a sacred song or two on their albums or doing exclusively gospel discs on occasion. This trend has largely ended in recent years. Paisley, however, has revived the older trend by cutting such numbers as "In the Garden," "The Old Rugged Cross," "Farther Along," and "The Unclouded Day," all long-time favorites with country fans.

In July 2009, Brother Paisley performed at the White House. For at least three times, he has served as co-host of the CMA Awards Program on Prime-Time Network TV, most recently in November 2011, again with Carrie Underwood. It is sometimes said that about seven years at the top is about as long as current country stars remain, but for Brother Paisley who enjoyed his first number one hit in 1999 and is still having them in 2011, it seems likely that he will experience a greater degree of star longevity.

Note: Since Brother Paisley is still rather young, much of the readily available printed information is often of a "fanzine" nature. However, a short sketch is in *Grand Ole Opry Picture History* (2001) and on his website: www.bradpaisley.com. For his Masonic record, thanks go to the staff at the Grand Lodge of Tennessee, the Secretary of Osiris Shrine Temple, the staff at the House of the Temple, and that of Scottish Rite Valleys of Nashville and Wheeling.

April 2006; revised 2011

## **Sir Knight Branch Rickey**: *The Man Who Changed Baseball the Most*

Many if not most of the great Masonic baseball players have had their careers profiled on these pages. Ty Cobb, Christy Mathewson, Rogers Hornsby, and Cy Young are just a few of the diamond heroes who have been chronicled in *Knight Templar.* Branch Rickey was a mediocre player with a .239 lifetime batting average and compiled a losing record in more than a thousand games as a manager (.473). Yet as a general manager and franchise executive, he may well have had more positive influence than any other individual player. Brother Wesley Branch Rickey—through his development of the "farm system," racial integration of the game, advocacy of continental expansion, and a number of lesser innovations—did much to make the sport what it has become today.

Wesley Branch Rickey was born near Little California (later renamed Stockdale) in Pike County, Ohio, on December 20, 1881, the middle of three sons of Frank and Emily Brown Rickey. The Rickey's were a struggling farm family who learned the virtues of hard work raising corn, sorghum, hogs, and cattle on their hilly acreage. Although Frank's family had been of the Free Will Baptist faith, he gravitated toward Emily's Methodist Protestant church, naming their son for the founder of that denomination. In 1883, the family moved to Duck Run in Scioto County which later gained minor fame as the boyhood home of movie cowboy (and Sir Knight) Roy Rogers. In 1892, they made their final move to another small farm at the edge of the village of Lucasville. Since Rickey had two cousins with the first name of Wesley, he stopped using this name at the age of twelve and became known simply as "Branch." By this time he had also met Jane Moulton, the daughter of Chandler Moulton, a local merchant, politician,

Mason, and member of Calvary Commandery No. 13 in nearby Portsmouth, Ohio. In 1906, Jane and Branch were married, a union that would endure for fifty-nine years and result in six children.

The Rickeys may not have had much wealth, but they were strong advocates of education, and Branch's older brother Orla obtained a teaching certificate first, and Branch soon followed him into that profession. Orla also introduced his sibling to baseball when the elder came home from his first teaching job in the spring of 1895. The brothers became dedicated Cincinnati Reds fans, and as Orla (also a Mason) was a fair left-handed pitcher, Branch became a catcher. Branch passed his exam for teaching and taught two years at Turkey Run School, a community some fourteen miles from Lucasville. Before reaching his twentieth birthday, Rickey had completed his teaching experience and entered Ohio Wesleyan University in Delaware, Ohio in September 1901.

At OWU, Branch played football, basketball, and baseball and did well in his studies. In the summer of 1902, he played baseball for a semi-pro team and lost his amateur status with the Ohio Wesleyan nine. However, he became the team coach and continued to play other sports. One of the more defining moments in Rickey's life was his observation of the discrimination that his African-American first baseman had to endure. It would later play a major role in Branch's career. After his graduation, he began catching for Dallas in the Texas League. Before entering professional ranks, he made a commitment to his mother that he would neither play baseball nor even enter the ballpark on the Sabbath, a promise that he zealously kept for sixty years. When Dallas sold his contract to the Cincinnati Reds without telling Manager Joe Kelly, the latter was infuriated, and Red's team owner Garry Herrmann (a Mason) was more understanding, but nonetheless returned Rickey and his contract to Dallas. In the fall, he coached football and taught at Allegheny College.

Later the Chicago White Sox purchased Rickey's contract and then traded him to the St. Louis Browns where he made his major league debut with the Browns on June 16, 1905, going hitless in three trips to the plate. Meanwhile, Branch returned to Allegheny College and vowed that the following year would be his last in baseball, and his prime interest was in securing money for law school. Engaged to marry Jane on June 1, 1906, he took a few days off from baseball and came home to Lucasville where he took his Entered Apprentice degree in Lucasville Lodge No. 465 on May 31, 1906, and married his betrothed the following morning. The honeymoon consisted of rejoining the team on an eastern road trip. As events turned out, Rickey had his best year as a player batting .284 in sixty-one games. He also went back to Allegheny College in Pennsylvania and left the Browns in September prior to the season's end. He decided against leaving baseball, but events the following year would soon bring his playing career to an end. While under contract to the New York Highlanders, he had a miserable year at the plate. His batting average dropped to .182, but even worse, his throwing arm went dead, and after thirteen runners stole bases on him in a single game, he knew it was over.

Deciding to enter law school, he worked for the YMCA at OWU through the winter of 1907-1908 and gave temperance lectures throughout Ohio during the summer and into the fall. He also campaigned for William Howard Taft for President and found time to complete his Masonic work, being passed a Fellowcraft on July 9, 1908, and raised to the sublime degree of Master Mason on August 10, 1908. He remained a member of Lucasville Lodge until 1920 when he dimitted to a Missouri Lodge, having had residence in St. Louis since 1913. Diagnosed with tuberculosis that winter, he spent several months in a sanitarium in the Adirondacks.

In 1909, Branch Rickey entered law school at the University of Michigan and was graduated in 1911. He also coached the Wolverines baseball team in the spring. He and two other Ohio Wesleyan alumni started a law practice, but business was so poor that he returned to Ann Arbor in the spring of 1912 to coach the Michigan nine. In the summer of 1912, the new owner of the St. Louis Browns offered him a job with the organization. By August 1913, he had become the Brownie's manager. The St. Louis American League team was not very successful, but Rickey lifted them from seventh to fifth place in 1914. The next year they fell back to sixth but acquired the man who would became their greatest player in George Sisler (who later became a Mason).

When Phil Ball became Browns owner in 1916, Rickey was removed as field manager but was retained as general manager. The two apparently did not care for one another personally (although ironically, both later belonged to the same blue lodge). After that season, Rickey was hired to become President-General Manager of the St. Louis National League team, the Cardinals. Neither team in the River City had been particularly competitive, but in time, the Ohio native would build the Cards into a real powerhouse. World War I intervened in which Rickey spent several months in military service with the rank of major, instructing soldiers in how to cope with the challenges of mustard gas. Back in St. Louis, he took over the field manager's job but relinquished the club's presidency to Sam Breadon, a wealthy auto retailer. In 1920, Rickey must have felt sufficiently settled in St. Louis that he demitted from Lucasville Lodge and affiliated with Tuscan Lodge No. 360 on March 15, 1921. Other members of this lodge at one time or another included Phil Ball, owner of the Browns, and two members of the Spink Family of *The Sporting News* fame. Branch retained membership there for twenty-three years before transferring again by demitting on June 20, 1944, and affiliating with Montauk Lodge No. 286 in Brooklyn on October 2, 1946. Not long after departure from the Dodger organization, he demitted from Montauk Lodge on May 16, 1951, affiliating with Bellefield Lodge No. 680 in Pittsburgh, Pennsylvania on November 9, 1951. He retained his membership there for the rest of his life. According to his entries in *Who's Who in America* in the 1960s, Rickey was identified as a member of the Scottish Rite, Knights Templar, and Shrine, but the location of these memberships is not mentioned except for taking his York Rite work in Ohio.

However, the information available from "Proceedings" in Ohio is that Rickey joined Mt. Vernon Chapter No. 23 R. A. M. and Solomon Council No. 79, probably in late 1916. Branch's brother Frank also joined those bodies. A brochure obtained by Sir Knight Tim Martin suggests that Rickey and four others from Lucasville Lodge were slated to receive the Chivalric Orders on December 26 and 29, 1916. Grand Commandery of Ohio records give the dates for Branch's degree dates as April 23, 1917 for Red Cross and Malta, and April 27, 1917 for the Order of the Temple, all in Calvary Commandery No. 13 in Portsmouth. It would appear that he missed the December dates and made them up the following April. Two other candidates in December 1916 were named Moulton, likely in-laws. Rickey's membership in Calvary Commandery ceased in July 1933. His further York Rite memberships remain unknown at this time.

By 1921, Rickey had piloted the Cardinals to a third place finish, and their first real superstar had come of age in the person of Rogers Hornsby who won the first of six straight batting titles in 1920. During the early twenties, Branch Rickey developed one of the greatest innovations yet known to the National Game—what became known as the "Farm System." The Cardinals either owned controlling shares or had established working agreements with a number of minor league teams. They held tryout camps all over the country supervised by Rickey's staff of scouts, signed promising players, and optioned them to these minor league teams where their development was closely watched and promoted as they progressed. The more significant "higher" minor league teams over the next twenty or so years included the Rochester Red Wings in the International League, Columbus Red Birds in the American Association, and Houston Buffaloes in the Texas League. There were numerous others in the "lower" minors. By 1940, the St. Louis farm system included thirty-two clubs owned outright and another eight with which they had working agreements. As Cardinal teams won pennants in 1926, 1928, 1930, 1931, 1934, 1942, 1943, 1944, and 1946, the overwhelming majority of their talent pool came from their farm system. Since this setup produced more good players than the Cardinals could use, they sold or traded the excess to other teams at a handsome profit. Despite critics, other franchises soon began to develop their own farm systems, although never as complex as the Cardinals in the Rickey era and for a few years thereafter.

In 1925, Branch Rickey relinquished managing the Cardinals but still remained as General Manager through 1942. Bringing six league championships and three World Series winners to a franchise that had once been considered a perennial loser made "The Mahatma," as he was becoming known, one of the game's top executives. An often overlooked characteristic of Cardinal strength in this period was the sizable number of other Masons within the Rickey stable of players, coaches, and minor league managers in this period. They included such figures as Rogers Hornsby, Frank Frisch, Rip Collins, Billy Southworth, Taylor Douthitt, Bill McKechnie, Clyde Sukeforth, Estel Crabtree, Burt Shotton, Les Bell, and Pepper Martin. Yet tension was brewing within the top echelons of St. Louis management. Sam Breadon wanted more control and resented the high ($75,000) salary that the General Manager commanded.

Rickey left the Cardinals at the end of the 1942 season but soon got an opportunity to build another ball club as Larry McPhail had left the Dodger organization to join the war effort and suggested Rickey to become General Manager of the Brooklyn franchise. "The Mahatma" soon set out to do for Flatbush what he done for the Cardinal organization. He worked to build up a Dodger farm system and generally strengthened the so-called Bums. Rickey's leadership brought two pennants to Ebbets Field, two second place finishes, and three thirds. Only in 1944 could a season be termed a failure. Ironically, the Cardinal franchise, still essentially based on the "house that Rickey built," continued as Brooklyn's chief rival in this period under the field leadership of Billy Southworth and Eddie Dyer.

Branch Rickey's main contribution to the game in this era was the racial integration of the long segregated system. Rickey came from anti-slavery forebears and had remembered the treatment Charles Thomas had faced as a player for Ohio Wesleyan more than four decades earlier. He knew that it would take a very special person to break the color barrier. Branch found such a person in Jackie Robinson, an all-around athlete capable of keeping his temper under control in the face of adverse racial taunts and jeers. After a year at Montreal in the International League, Robinson was deemed ready and experienced an outstanding year while enduring a wave of poor treatment. Once the barrier was broken, other African-Americans had succeeded in the game including such other Rickey discoveries as Roy Campanella, Don Newcombe, Dan Bankhead, and Joe Black. It took a decade for every team to have an African-American on their squad, but Rickey's great experiment became a true American success story. Before he died, Jackie Robinson was alleged to have said that Rickey had done more than anyone other than Abraham Lincoln to elevate his race.

Branch Rickey's Dodger teams in this era were a colorful bunch and among the more remembered by Brooklyn fans. They included such personalities as Duke Snider, Gil Hodges, and Pee Wee Reese in addition to the aforementioned African-American super stars. Carl Erskine and Bobby Bragan rank among the more significant Masonic players of that era, but those on the sidelines contributing to Brooklyn success in those times must take into account such figures as Burt Shotton, Clyde Sukeforth, Jake Pitler, and Branch Rickey, Jr. The latter had been raised in Baldwin Lodge No. 1047 in Baldwin, New York in 1948 and later affiliated in 1960 with Fox Chapel Lodge No. 784 in Sharpsburg, Pennsylvania where he remained until his death the next year.

Despite his achievements in Brooklyn, a power struggle for control of the franchise had begun to shape up between Rickey and rival stockholder, Walter O'Malley. To make a long story short, Rickey lost the battle, but the Dodgers continued to do well, largely with the teams that he had developed. Meanwhile Branch was soon hired on November 3, 1950, by an old friend, John Galbreath (of University Lodge No. 631 in Columbus, Ohio), as General Manager of the Pittsburgh Pirates. The Bucs were badly in need of rebuilding, and the challenge would be one of his most difficult.

Under Rickey's front office direction, the initial conclusion would be that his five years at the helm were a failure, as the Pirates finished seventh once and in the cellar four times in a row. The 1952 version of the Bucs would be remembered as one of the worst in modern history. Yet a closer look reveals that the core of the Pittsburgh championship team of 1960 either came up through Rickey's farm system, had been retained and further developed under Rickey, or drafted out of the Dodger organization by him, such as Roberto Clemente and Elroy Face. As in prior times, a number of these persons were Masons (e. g. Fred Haney, Bob Friend, and Dick Groat) as were such front office figures as Tom Johnson and Rickey's successor, Joe Brown.

After 1955, Branch Rickey's Pirate connections were relatively minimal, but as demonstrated above, much of the later Pirate success virtually had his initials all over it. In 1959, he began to conceive an idea for a third major league—the Continental. While this operation never got off the ground, it influenced the expansion moves of the other two leagues and thus served a significant purpose. In 1960, Rickey moved back to St. Louis and to a secondary position in the Cardinal organization. Although his main job was to provide advice, it was seldom solicited and even less often followed. As Rickey biographer Murray Polner demonstrates, it mostly made two key figures in the front office—Bing Devine and Richard Meyer— feel more insecure. But the truth was that "the Mahatma" was beginning to age more rapidly. Branch Jr. died in 1961, and Rickey himself began to fail. During a speech at Columbia, Missouri on November 13, 1965, he collapsed and soon lapsed into a coma. Death came on December 9, 1965. At his funeral, Jackie Robinson praised what Rickey had done. Ultimately, his remains were interred in the Rush Township Cemetery overlooking the Scioto Valley, about three miles from his boyhood home in Lucasville, where Jane (who died in 1970), his parents, brothers, and three of his children also rest.

In his time, Brother Branch Rickey ranked as one of the major figures in both sport and society. In addition to his aforementioned accomplishments, he can be accredited with such innovations as sliding pits, team air travel, batting cages, batting helmets, and promoting knothole gangs. Masons everywhere should revere him not only for his achievements, but also as one who exemplified the highest tenets of our profession: brotherly love, relief and truth.

**Note:** The major biography of Branch Rickey is Murray Polner, *Branch Rickey* (1982). Also important is John C. Chalberg, *Rickey & Robinson* (2000). For his Masonic record, I am indebted to George O. Braatz of the Grand Lodge of Ohio, Ron Miller and Sandy Clark of the Grand Lodge of Missouri, Thomas Savini of the Livingston Library of the Grand Lodge of New York, and Glenys A. Waldman, Librarian at the Archives and Library at the Grand Lodge of Pennsylvania in Philadelphia. For Commandery information, I am indebted to S. K. Tim Martin and Richard Palm.

February 2007, slightly revised 2011

**Brother Buck Jones:**
*Cowboy Film Star of Both the Silent and the Sound Eras*

In his authoritative book on motion picture cowboy stars, *Saddle Aces of the Cinema,* Buck Rainey describes actor Buck Jones as "An Idol Nonpareil." Sir Knight Norman Lincoln, a knowledgeable motion picture expert in his own right, recalls Buck Jones as the first western picture hero his mother took him to see in a Richmond, Indiana theater and that Jones left a vivid impression on his memory. Considering that seventy-two years have elapsed since "old Buck" met his untimely death in a fire, the man must have exhibited a lingering charisma.

Certainly this silver screen cowboy surpassed his contemporaries in one respect: Jones managed to achieve major stardom in both silent and sound pictures. Whereas Tom Mix, William S. Hart, and Fred Thompson achieved great success in silent flicks, they either did not appear in talkies or were considered near failures in them. Tim McCoy, Hoot Gibson, and Ken Maynard did better, but they never approached the level of stardom they had experienced earlier. Jones, however, excelled in both.

Buck Jones began life as Charles Frederick Gebhart (sometimes spelled as Gebhard or Gebhardt) in Vincennes, Indiana, on December 12, 1891. Truth is somewhat difficult to separate from the fiction dreamed up by studio publicists when one researches the lives of movie personalities, and the story is that Gebhart's family moved to Red Rock, Oklahoma, when Buck was quite young. Thus did the future star learn the basic features of cowboy and ranch life in his childhood. It now seems more likely that the future star spent most of his youth at various locations in the Hoosier State; however, he did learn a great deal about how to handle horses.

About 1907, an attack of "wanderlust" struck the teenager and he enlisted in the U.S. Army where he remained until October 1913. During two hitches in the military, Charles spent some time along the Mexican border and in the Philippines where he sustained a leg wound. Recovering, he again enlisted and achieved the rank of sergeant; however, he left the army when thwarted in his desires to become a pilot, being instead relegated to the role of a mechanic.

Unemployed in Texas City, Texas, that October, young Gebhart took a job with the Miller Brothers' 101 Ranch Wild West Show helping take care of the horses. His skills as a rider and bronco buster, however, soon elevated him to star attraction status. The following year when the 101 Ranch played New York City, Charles met an equally talented young equestrienne named Odille Osborne. On August 11, 1915, the attractive couple married in a show ring in Lima, Ohio. Their marriage endured. In 1918, daughter Maxine was born.

During World War I, Gebhart worked as a horse breaker in Chicago, taming steeds for the cavalry at various times for the British, French, and American armies. As hostilities wound downward, he and Odille returned to the circus life, riding first with Gollmar Brothers and then the famed Ringlings. By the end of 1918, Charles and Odille traveled to California. With a baby on the way, the couple hoped to find a more settled life in the emerging motion picture industry.

People skilled with horses always seemed to be in demand around the sets of western films in Hollywood. After playing bit parts in longer Tom Mix pictures and with Franklin Farnum in a series of two-reelers, studio head William Fox decided to elevate Charles Gebhart to star status, first as "Charles Jones" and then as "Buck Jones." Fox's original scheme had been to groom Jones for stardom as a way to keep his number one cowboy—Tom Mix—from becoming too independent; however, it soon developed, according to Rainey, that "Fox had a second goldmine in Buck Jones."

The original contract for Jones had called for a weekly salary of $150.00 (a very good wage for 1920), but by the time of his last contract with Fox, Buck's weekly earnings had climbed to $3,500.00. During his eight years with Fox (1920-1928), Jones starred in sixty-two pictures, mostly but not exclusively westerns. For instance, one his most heralded dramatic roles came in 1925 when he was cast as star in the eight-reel picture, *Lazybones,* with Madge Bellamy and Virginia Marshall. Meanwhile, back in 1922, Jones obtained his prize horse, Silver, who thereafter appeared in most of his films, sometimes sharing screen credits with Buck. According to Buck Rainey, much of Jones' favor with westerns fans derived from the fact that his portrayals represented a compromise between the "austere" realism of William S. Hart and the "flamboyant" showmanship associated with the films of Tom Mix.

During the height of his career as a silent movie star, Buck Jones under his real name petitioned Henry S. Orme Lodge No. 458 in Los Angeles. Initiated an Entered Apprentice on January 17, 1924, he was passed to the degree of Fellowcraft on February 16, 1924. Five days later on February 21, the brethren raised Charles F. Gebhart to the degree of Mater Mason. Several other significant western film personalities also belonged to this Blue Lodge including an older character actor, Roy Stewart; sidekick, Raymond Hatton; and leading man, Richard Dix. Film directors Scott Dunlap and Lambert Hillyer also ranked among the Orme membership. Somewhat later, Buck also became an active member of the 233 Club, a Masonic group made up of persons in the film industry. On August 18, 1926, Jones and Roy Stewart led a group of western actors in a parade unit of the club in which more than one thousand members marched down Hollywood Boulevard. Richard Dix also belonged to the 233 Club as did such Masonic cowboy stars as Tom Mix, Raymond Hatton, Hoot Gibson, and Harry Carey.

Buck left Fox Film Studios in 1928 and formed his own production company. He soon turned out an airplane movie titled *The Big Hop,* but the venture failed and wound up costing Jones a great deal of money. So, too, did a circus which he subsequently formed in an effort to recover his earlier losses.

Fortunately he was saved from poverty when his agent landed him a new deal with Columbia Pictures. By now, sound had taken the industry by storm, and although Buck Jones would never again command a salary of $3,500.00 per week, he became quite successful in talking pictures to a much greater degree than his contemporaries. Through some thirty-five starring roles at Columbia and twenty-two at Universal plus four Universal serials, he managed to maintain his star status throughout the depression decade. Muriel Evans ranked as Buck's favored leading lady in this era, and many critics consider the 1932 Columbia offering, *White Eagle,* with Barbara Weeks, Ward Bond, and Jim Thorpe to rank as his best single feature.

In 1936, Buck Jones ranked as the top western star in the *Motion Picture Herald* poll. Thereafter, Gene Autry took over the top spot and held it until he entered the service in World War II. However, Jones held on to third place for two more years and then dropped to the eighth position in 1939.

The rise of the singing cowboys; Autry, Roy Rogers, and Tex Ritter; offered a new form of competition to the older action stars who also faced the challenge of younger rivals such as Charles Starrett, William Boyd (slightly younger), Bill Elliott, John Wayne, and Johnny Mack Brown. When Buck's contract with Columbia expired at the end of 1938, studio officials did not renew it.

As a freelancer, Buck made a non-western for Paramount about an aging prize fighter, *Unmarried.* He probably hit his career nadir when he played a villainous role as a corrupt sheriff in *Wagons Westward*, a Republic feature in which both he and Silver died. Shortly afterward, however, his progress rebounded. Initially, he made two successful serials. The first, *White Eagle* (remake of his 1932 classic), for Columbia, proved that he still had box office appeal. And the second, Universal's *Riders of Death Valley*, in which he co-starred with former Warner Brothers' singing cowboy, Dick Foran, did even better. One of the support players in the latter film, Noah Beery, Jr., had recently become Jones' son-in-law having married Buck and Odille's only daughter, Maxine, on March 30, 1940.

The popularity of the aforementioned serials induced a Monogram Pictures producer and fellow Lodge Brother, Scott Dunlap, to co-star Buck and two other western film veterans in a new "trio" series called the *Rough Riders.* Tim McCoy (reputedly a Mason) and sidekick, Raymond Hatton, rounded out the threesome. The series proved successful through eight features made between July 1941 and October 1942 when McCoy left the series to reenter military service. Monogram made one final film with Rex Bell replacing McCoy. Studio officials announced their intentions of giving Jones his own series again with the crusty Hatton as his sidekick. First, however, Buck went on a bond selling drive and publicity tour. With war again raging, Hollywood stars did their part for the Allied cause by participating in such fund-raising efforts.

In Boston on November 28, friends held a dinner in Buck's honor at the Cocoanut Grove. Unfortunately, Jones became one of the 491 victims of one of the most tragic fires in American history, passing into the sunset on November 30, 1942. According to Mrs. Jones, Buck managed to initially escape the blaze, but went back into the inferno to search for Brother Scott Dunlap. A few weeks later his last picture *Dawn on the Great Divide* was released in theaters.

In his fifty-one years, Brother Charles Frederick Gebhart, who became famous to millions of western movie buffs as Buck Jones, exemplified the highest tenets of his profession. Like the late Brother Roy Rogers, Brother Jones endeavored to be a proper role model for the millions of youth who idolized him. Critics generally agree that he exhibited more acting talents than most of his contemporaries and that he always rendered his best effort.

Quoting again for one final time his biographer, Buck Rainey, said of Jones that he "loved the genre that made him a star and was loyal to it...the recognition of his contributions to western films is still ever-growing. Time only magnifies his memory." In his chosen field of endeavor, Buck Jones proved himself a standout figure, both as a man and as a Mason.

**Note**: One seeking to learn more about Buck Jones may wish to consult his two-volume biography published by World of Yesterday and authored by Buck Rainey, *The Life and Films of Buck Jones: The Silent Era* and *The Life and Films of Buck Jones: The Sound Era.* For a condensed treatment, see the chapter on Jones in Buck Rainey, *Saddle Aces of the Cinema* (A.S. Barnes & Co., 1980). A newer source is the chapter by R. Philip Loy, "Buck Jones: An Old Time Cowboy" in Gary A. Yoggy, editor, *Back in the Saddle: Essays on Western Film and Television Actors* (McFarland & Co., 1998). For his Masonic record, I appreciate the efforts of Brother Harold Hand, Secretary of South Pasadena Lodge No. 290, which merged with Henry S. Orme Lodge some years ago. I also appreciate the encouragement and suggestions of Sir Knight Norman K. Lincoln of Eaton, Ohio and the research on the 233 Club, done some years ago by the late Companion Jerry Erickson.

March 2000; slightly revised 2011

## Sir Knight Burl Ives: *Actor and Folk Singer*

Through the middle half of the 20th century, Burl Ives constituted one of the most versatile figures in the world of American entertainment. Starting his professional career as a folk singer, the burly, bearded Ives went on to win acclaim as an actor on both the stage and screen and recorded hits in both the popular and country fields, all without abandoning his original vocation. Like another well-known Hollywood personality, John Wayne, Burl came to Masonry later in life, but also like the Duke, his presence in the fraternity came at a time when the order began experiencing decline. Therefore, his membership and honors proved not only rewarding to himself but added considerable prestige to the various organizations.

Born with the lengthy sobriquet of Burl Icle Ivanhoe Ives in Jasper County, Illinois, on June 14, 1909, the future star spent his first years in a tenant farm family. His parents, Frank and Cordella White Ives, came from pioneer stock, and singing played a major role in their social life. As time passed, Frank Ives studied engineering and bought into a small construction business in Newton, Illinois where the family improved their economic standing. Burl attended high school in Newton where he was graduated in 1927, having been fullback on the football team.

That fall Burl Ives entered Eastern Illinois State Teachers College in Charleston intending to major in physical education and coach football. On December 5, 1927, he also (like John Wayne) became a member of the International Order of DeMolay. In school Ives continued to display a strong interest in athletics and music, but he demonstrated moderate indifference toward the more academic aspects of college. In 1930 Ives dropped out and trying to cure a case of depression "wanderlust," bummed around the U. S. and Canada. He supported this vagabond lifestyle by earning a few dollars singing, playing, and doing occasional odd jobs. Along the way he added many traditional songs to the vast repertoire of folk numbers he first began amassing from his grandmother in childhood.

Burl stopped at Indiana State University in Terre Haute long enough to finish college. While there, he earned some extra dollars as a radio singer and a drugstore clerk. Advised by Clara Lyon, a singing teacher, to continue his training in New York City, Ives went to the Metropolis where he settled in at the International House and continued to sustain his existence through odd jobs, some of them musical in nature. In 1937 he enrolled in courses at New York University, studying theater and music, although folk songs remained his principal interest. Booking agents continued to tell him that they had no interest in "hillbilly acts."

In the summer of 1938, Ives obtained some paying work as a character actor at the Rockbridge Theater in Carmel, New York, appearing in such plays as *Ah Wilderness!*, *Flight*, and *Pocahontas Preferred.* On Broadway he starred in a short-lived comedy, *The Boys from Syracuse.* He also landed a four-month engagement at the Village Vanguard Night Club. In 1939 he had a role in the touring company of a Rodgers and Hart musical, *I Married an Angel*, and on Broadway in *Heavenly Express.* He also appeared on network radio and eventually landed a regular CBS program of folk songs, *The Wayfaring Stranger*, giving him a nickname he would retain throughout his singing career. About this time, Burl also began recording for the Columbia label.

Just as Ives had begun to achieve success in his fields, World War II intervened. Drafted into the army in April 1942, he still managed to remain mostly in theater and radio. He had a role in Irving Berlin's *This Is the Army* and a radio program, *G. I. Jive* for Armed Forces Radio. Discharged in October 1943, he continued entertaining soldiers and introduced Broadway songwriter Frank Loesser's ballad tribute to the common infantry man, *Rodger Young*, to a national audience.

In more civilian-related endeavors, Burl played a long night club engagement at Café Society Uptown and in a new Broadway folk song musical, *Sing Out Sweet Land.* The latter won him the Donaldson Award as the best supporting actor on Broadway for 1944-45. In Hollywood that same year, he debuted in a new adaptation of the Will James novel, *Smokey*, about a horse, and the Disney picture, *So Dear To My Heart* (1948), among others. In the writing and publishing field, his autobiography *Wayfaring Stranger* (McGraw-Hill) appeared in 1948. He followed it up over the next seven years with four books that were essentially folk song and ballad collections.

Back on Broadway in 1954, Ives played the role of Captain Andy in a revival of the Jerome Kern Classic, *Show Boat*. The following March he first appeared as Big Daddy, the crusty plantation owner diagnosed with terminal cancer (called a "spastic colon"), in the classic Tennessee Williams' drama, *Cat on a Hot Tin Roof*. Burl so made the role his own that he repeated it in the 1958 MGM film version that also starred Elizabeth Taylor and Paul Newman. The next year his portrayal of the feuding cattle king in *The Big Country* won him an Oscar as the best actor in a supporting role. In a sense, this latter role seemed to be a replay of Big Daddy in a western setting rather than in the plantation South. His Oscar to the contrary notwithstanding, the Big Daddy part will go down as the most remembered Ives' film role among his 32 screen credits.

Burl Ives also remained a recording artist of considerable renown. His folk song albums, *The Wayfaring Stranger* and *Return of the Wayfaring Stranger*, remained in the Columbia catalog for years. During the sixties he recorded several albums for Decca, many of them new songs aimed at the Billboard charts in both the country and pop fields. His greatest success came in 1963 with "A Little Bitty Tear" which made number two in country and number nine in pop. Other good songs for Burl included "(It's My) Funny Way of Laughin'," "Call Me Mr. In Between," and "Mary Ann Regrets." In all, Ives turned out several albums for Decca in this period and landed on the country charts nine times and in the "pop top forty" ten times.

Ironically, Burl Ives did not experience as much success in television. In 1957 he appeared as a panelist on a show, *High-Low,* and in 1965 starred in a short-lived sit com, *O. K. Crackerby*. His best effort came as attorney Walter Nichols in *Lawyers* from 1969 to 1972. He also had some good roles in dramas shown on *Playhouse 90* and as a guest on *Daniel Boone* and *Alias Smith and Jones.*

On the personal side, Ives married twice. He wed his first wife, Helen Ehrlich, in 1945. They subsequently had a son Alexander. In 1971 Burl married Dorothy Koster, who survived him.

Burl Ives had cut down on his entertainment activity by the time he became serious about Masonry. As told by Brother Julian Endsley in an article in *The Scottish Rite Journal,* Burl began thinking seriously about becoming a Mason when he studied the script of a movie version of 1776 and he considered the role of Benjamin Franklin. Gaining an awareness of Franklin's strong Masonic ties reminded him of the Masonic and Eastern Star memberships that most of his family held back in Illinois and of his own DeMolay background. When he moved to Santa Barbara in 1975, he petitioned Magnolia Lodge No 242 in August and received the Entered Apprentice degree on September 5, 1975. Passed to the degree of Fellowcraft several weeks later, brother Endsley had the honor of raising Ives to the sublime degree of Master Mason on the night of February 10, 1976. Endsley recalled that during the refreshment period following the meeting Burl simply became "one of the boys" and even helped the assisting DeMolay youth by pouring coffee and giving each the DeMolay handshake.

Not much time elapsed before Burl Ives sought additional light in Masonry. He completed the Scottish Rite degrees in the Valley of Santa Barbara on May 21, 1977, and became a Noble of Al Malaikah Shrine Temple in Los Angeles on November 5, 1977. He took the York Rite the following spring. He was exalted a Royal Arch Mason in Corinthian Chapter No 51 on April 8, 1978; was greeted in Ventura Council No 15, Cryptic Masons on April 14, 1978; and was Knighted in St. Omer Commandery No. 30 on April 15, 1978. When he moved to Anacortes, Washington, he took a dual membership in the Valley of Bellingham. Receiving additional honors from the A.A.S.R., he was invested a KCCH on October 21, 1985 and coroneted a 33° on October 21, 1987. He received the Grand Cross in 1993.

Brother Ives had not totally retired from his profession when he became a Mason. Some of his later pictures included *Just You and Me, Kid* (1979) with old-timer George Burns and teen star Brooke Shields and *Earthbound* (1981), a science fiction film.

By the time of his relocation to Washington State, Brother Ives had pretty much retired from entertainment. He and his second wife Dorothy lived quietly until his passing on April 14, 1995, two months prior to what would have been his 86th birthday. His widow subsequently donated much of his memorabilia to the Scottish Rite, and it is housed today in a special Burl Ives room. Above all else, this collection demonstrates the pride that Sir Knight Ives manifested in his Masonic membership. By the same token, Masons the world over can take pride in knowing that the famed "Wayfaring Stranger" became one of their own.

**Note**: Brief sketches of Burl Ives' life can be found in his entry in *Current Biography* for 1946 and 1960. For his Masonic record, see Julian E. Endsley, "The Masonic Progress of Burl Icle Ives, 33°, Grand Cross," in *The Scottish Rite Journal*: 105: 10, October, 1977, pp. 18-22. Thanks to Shasta Amos for manuscript preparation.

February 2001; slightly revised 2011

## Brother Burton Mossman:
*Arizona Ranger and Western Cattle Baron*

Thanks to motion pictures, television, and action-paced novels, Americans have developed a mythology of the American West. This myth includes images of hard-riding, quick-on-the-draw, tough-as-nails cowboys, law officers, and outlaws who played out their real life roles in the closing years of the frontier. While many of these portraits are either fictional or greatly exaggerated, some, however, do have a considerable basis of fact behind them. One such frontier cowboy and lawman is the subject of this sketch. Burt Mossman went to New Mexico as a youth, worked his way from cowhand to ranch boss, organized and led the Arizona Rangers, and finally became a big time "cattle king." Moreover, for sixty-four of his eighty-nine years, Mossman was a Mason.

Burton Charles Mossman was born near Aurora, Illinois, the son of a Marietta, Ohio-born Union Army veteran. When Burton reached the age of six, his father moved the family to Lake City, Minnesota. In 1882 the Mossmans moved again to New Mexico Territory.

At seventeen, young Burton went to work as a ranch hand. In those days he had a reputation of being somewhat quarrelsome and prone to getting into fights. As he matured, he learned to better control his "hair-trigger" temper. At twenty, the young cowhand went to work for a cattleman named Warren Carpenter who owned the Bar-A-Bar Ranch. At that time, western cattle traders were trying to recover from the drought of 1886 and the hard winter that followed it. In spite of a reduction in the beef supply, prices remained low. Then in August 1888, Warren Carpenter died from being struck by lightning in a thunderstorm. The deceased's brother, Andy Carpenter, made Burton foreman of the ranch. At twenty-one, he had the responsibility of looking after 8,000 head of cattle. As drought conditions continued for three years, the young foreman had his hands full just keeping the herds alive.

In 1891 Burton Mossman decided to become a Mason. He petitioned Western Star Lodge No. 14 in Chloride, New Mexico. This lodge no longer exists and Chloride no longer has a post office. He received his Entered Apprentice degree on December 19, 1891; was passed a Fellow craft on April 28, 1892; and was Raised a Master Mason on July 15, 1892. The following year, Burt took a new job as manager of another ranch in the Bloody Basin country along the Verde River in Arizona. Accordingly, on April 21, 1894, he demitted from Western Star Lodge and later affiliated with Winslow Lodge No. 13 (June 12, 1900) in Winslow, Arizona.

The company that Mossman worked for in the Bloody Basin, Thatcher Brothers and Bloom, wanted to liquidate their herds and recover as much of their losses as possible. It took the manager some time, but he eventually succeeded in selling most of the livestock and coming out not only with losses paid but actually turning a profit for them. After this experience, the thirty-year-old ranch foreman relaxed in Phoenix for only two or three weeks; then he received another, even more challenging job offer. The president of the Aztec Land and Cattle Company (known as the "Hash Knife") had purchased more than a million acres of railroad land-grant property in northern Arizona, south of the Santa Fe tracks for eighty miles south and west of Holbrook. Since the alternate sections belonging to the U.S. government were under the company's indirect control, the business controlled ranch land larger than either the state of Delaware or Rhode Island. In fourteen years, the corporations never paid any dividends to their stockholders. The ranch had the reputation of having employees and cowhands that helped themselves to the parent company's herds. Burton's biographer, Frazier Hunt, stated that managing the "Hash Knife" brand constituted the "toughest, biggest, deadliest, and the most thrilling ranch job in America" and Mossman "took it."

The Aztec Company owned around 50,000 head of cattle and 2,000 horses, but Burt knew that to succeed he would not only have to stop the cattle rustling but get the culprits convicted. Mossman obtained a deputy sheriff's commission, and Navajo County Sheriff Frank Wattson supplied him with another deputy. Within a few weeks, eleven rustlers were in jail awaiting trial. When a jury eventually brought in convictions, conditions began to look up for the Hash Knife outfit.

In spite of the improvements Mossman's management brought to the Aztec Land and Cattle Company, the board of directors decided in1900 to liquidate the Hash Knife assets. Most other corporate ranch efforts had already ended. Burt felt disappointed, but again he had held up his end, and his reputation as a ranch boss remained quite good. He went to Phoenix and talked with copper tycoon, Bill Green, who considered purchasing Colonel Henry Hooker's Sierra Bonita Ranch in Graham County and hiring Mossman as manager, but the deal never materialized, and Burt went into partnership in a butchering business in the booming copper camp of Bisbee. Soon, however, the former ranch manager answered a request from territorial governor, Nathan O. Murphy.

Murphy wanted to create a state police force to combat lawlessness throughout Arizona. The group would be patterned after the Texas Rangers. The legislature passed the bill on March 21, 1901, creating the Arizona Rangers. The group would consist of fourteen men—one captain, one sergeant, and a dozen privates. The governor wanted Burton Mossman to head this agency. The latter reluctantly agreed to take the position for a year providing that he could pick his men and name his successor. "Cap" Mossman began his duties on August 30, had his subordinates chosen by mid-October, and set up headquarters in Bisbee. Meanwhile, he demitted from Winslow Lodge on July 9, 1901, and on February 6, 1902, he affiliated with Perfect Ashlar Lodge No. 12 in Bisbee.

Tragedy soon struck the Rangers when privates Carlos Tafolla and Bill Maxwell were killed in a shoot-out with rustlers. All through the year that "Cap' Mossman led the Rangers, the war on rustlers continued. Arizona's most wanted outlaw, Augustin Chacon who was part Apache but mostly Mexican, managed to avoid capture. Operating from a sanctuary in Sonora, Chacon continued to commit crimes in Arizona. Burt determined to bring the noted outlaw to justice and arranged amnesty for a pair of shady characters—Burt Alvord and Billy Stiles—who would lure Chacon to a spot near the border where the Ranger leader would capture him. Alvord indeed accompanied the wanted man to a spring sixteen miles into Sonora where Mossman and Stiles (temporarily a Ranger) met them. On September 4 they arrested the culprit and brought him back to Arizona. Technically, the capture had been made four days after Mossman's commission expired and in a place where he had no authority, but Chacon was tried in Solomonville, Graham County, and hanged on a gallows that had been built for him in 1897. When the noose tightened on the outlaw's neck on November 22, 1902, the man who brought him in was vacationing in New York City. Thomas Rynning, a former Rough Rider, replaced him as Ranger captain. Under the latter and his successor, Harry Wheeler, the force was expanded to twenty-six men until the legislature abolished the Arizona Rangers in 1909.

After his New York vacation, Cap Mossman (this nickname from his Ranger days would remain with him) returned to ranching. In partnership with Colonel Green and B.A. Packard, who became a banker in Douglas, Arizona, they went into business, holding leases in the Pecos River country in New Mexico and in South Dakota. Burt kept busy for many years in this business but took time out in 1905 to marry Grace Colburn, the daughter of a fellow rancher. The couple had two children, Burton, Jr. (nicknamed Billy), and a daughter Mary. Unfortunately, Grace died when Mary was only nine days old. Cap determined to rear his "little family" by himself and did so.

Eventually Mossman organized his ranch holdings into a corporation, the Diamond A, and went into the sheep business in addition to his long-time infatuation with cattle. In 1925 he married a second time to Ruth Scrader who was twenty-five years his junior. Although holding on to his Dakota leases into the mid-thirties, Cap settled permanently in Roswell, New Mexico in 1918. He had demitted from Perfect Ashlar Lodge on November 7, 1912, but once his residence became fixed, he affiliated with Roswell Lodge No. 18 in 1921 and remained a faithful member until his death thirty-five years later. He also joined either the York Rite or Scottish Rite bodies and became a Noble of the Mystic Shrine as well (no dates or location available, however).

Both honors and tragedy stalked Cap Mossman in his later years. In 1941 he was inducted into the Cattleman's Hall of Fame at the Saddle and Sirloin Club in Chicago. Two years later, his pilot son, Major Billy Mossman, died in Europe when his plane was shot down. Finally in 1944 at seventy-seven, he disposed of his Diamond A Ranch and retired to a comfortable home in Roswell. Crippled with arthritis in his last years, the old pioneer died September 5, 1956.

Somehow the movie and television producers have missed out on turning Brother Mossman's exciting life into a major motion picture or western series. Yet they have not totally neglected him. In 1954 while Burt still lived, the TV program *Stories of the Century* had an episode titled "Augustin Chacon" in which the hero, a railroad detective named Clark (played by Jim Davis), captured the notorious border outlaw. More important, in October 1963 *Death Valley Days* had a segment entitled "Measure of a Man" wherein Cap Mossman, played by Rory Calhoun, captures the murderous bandit Chacun [sic], played by screen villain Michael Pate, and he is brought to justice.

In his long life, Brother Burton Mossman made two major contributions to the history of the West. As organizer and first captain of the Arizona Rangers, he set that territory on the path of law and order that paved the way for statehood. Second, in his long career in the ranch business, he advanced from lowly cowhand to cattle king. Burt is summed up by his biographer, Frazier Hunt, who stated: "Quite unconsciously, he had become the leader and spokesman of the range men of the West. His wits, his incisive mind, and his fearlessness made his the true voice of cowmen everywhere."

**Note**: Although the Burton Mossman life story appears in many books about Western legends, the most useful sources are the anecdotal biography by Frazier Hunt, *Cap Mossman: Last of the Great Cowmen* (Hastings House, 1951) and the definitive history by Bill O'Neal, *The Arizona Rangers* (Eakin Press, 1987). For his Masonic records, I am indebted to the staff of the Grand Lodge of New Mexico and Robert Henderson, former Grand Secretary of the Grand Lodge of Arizona. Thanks also to Shasta Amos for preparing the original manuscript.

September 2000; slightly revised 2011

**Brother Carl Thomas Curtis:**
*Nebraska's Watchdog of the Treasury*

Throughout the twentieth century, hundreds of individuals, including numerous Masons, have held seats in the United States Senate. While perhaps a majority make only a minimal impact on the national scene and leave little impression after their departure, others distinguished themselves as leaders. They may have been either Democrats or Republicans by party affiliation, and their philosophical leanings range from very liberal to hardcore conservative. The subject of this sketch, Brother Carl T. Curtis, spent most of his forty House and Senate years in the minority. Yet he earned a wide degree of respect throughout the period from both friends and foes for honor and integrity while being an unyielding opponent of big government, big labor, and big deficits. However, his most significant legacy is probably as "father of the Individual Retirement Account (IRA) Law."

Carl Thomas Curtis was born in Kearney County, Nebraska, on March 15, 1905. His grandfather, Swedish immigrant Carl Svenson, had met a girl named Mary Johnson aboard ship, and they married after arrival in America. Svenson changed his name to Charles Curtis and worked for a half-century as a blacksmith. His father, Frank Curtis, had a small farm and worked as a custodian in the courthouse at the county seat of Minden. Later, young Carl would begin his public service career in that same courthouse as a county attorney.

Curtis grew up on his father's farm near Minden, learning about hard work at an early age and learning the "three Rs" at the local one-room school that his father had helped build. Later, he went to a larger school in town. The family also attended lectures on the local Chautauqua circuit. History became Carl's favorite subject. At Minden High School, he was a member of the football and debate teams; he graduated in 1923. Afterward, he taught school for a year in nearby Danville and then entered Nebraska Wesleyan University.

When his mother suffered a stroke, he returned home without ever receiving his degree.

Carl resumed teaching at rural high schools in Kearney County and then became an elementary principal in Minden. During his teaching days, he set his heart on the legal profession. At that time in Nebraska, one could still study law on one's own or with a practicing attorney. Curtis did this for three years, took his bar exams, and got his legal license in January 1930. The following year, he was married to Lois Atwater of Minden, and the couple subsequently adopted two children.

During his years as a young barrister, Carl Thomas Curtis began his long affiliation with Masonry. Petitioning Minden Lodge No. 127, he was accepted and received his Entered Apprentice degree on March 21, 1934. Passed to Fellowcraft on April 25, he was raised a Master Mason on September 26, 1934. A dozen years later he completed the Scottish Rite degrees in the Valley of Hastings on October 25, 1946 and became a Noble of Tehama Shrine Temple. In addition to his Masonic connections, Curtis became an Odd Fellow, an Elk, a member of Phi Delta Phi Legal Fraternity, and the Pi Kappa Delta Forensic Fraternity. On October 27, 1955, he received the KCCH and the 33° on December 12, 1959.

Young lawyers in smaller counties, then and still, get practical experience and build up their reputations by serving as county attorney or prosecuting attorney. Carl Curtis followed that route, winning his first election in 1930. Ironically, he began his career as a Democrat. Years later he reflected, "I wasn't a good Democrat." Even then he "admired the intellectual integrity and the principles of Herbert Hoover."

Nonetheless, he served his first four years in office as a Democrat during the early years of the New Deal. By 1936, Curtis threw his support behind Sir Knight Alfred Landon (of Fortitude Lodge No. 107 and St. Bernard Commandery No. 10 in Independence, Kansas) for president. According to his biographer, Regis Courtemanche, the Nebraska lawyer "proclaimed himself a Republican." At the time, this may have seemed politically suicidal since this was a time when the Cornhusker State's leading statesman, George Norris, termed himself an Independent Republican and supported most of President Franklin Roosevelt's policies.

Yet Carl Curtis was undeterred. In 1938 he entered the Republican primary for the Fourth Nebraska Congressional District. To again quote Courtemanche, "He had no rich friends, no private fortune, and no political organization." Of course, as an eight-year practicing lawyer, he was not a total unknown. As Curtis himself said, he had only a deep seated conviction that the "course charted. . . by the New Deal was basically wrong." Still, he had to overcome two primary opponents, both of whom he defeated in August and then faced incumbent Democrat Charles G. Binderup who also came from Minden, voted in the same precinct, and attended the same Presbyterian Church. Above all else, the GOP challenger crusaded for flood control on the Republican River. Floods had devastated the Republican Valley in 1935, and Binderup had crusaded for this project too with the Public Works Administration, but to date his pleas had not resulted in action. Curtis vowed to push harder for the project, and voters apparently took his promises to heart because in November he defeated Binderup by more than 16,000 votes.

Brother Curtis took office and immediately began to push for Republican River flood control but shifted his focus to the US Army Corps of Engineers and Bureau of Reclamation. Other Nebraska congressmen worked on this effort too, including Norris, but Curtis gave a renewed emphasis to the project. His efforts turned out to be successful. Even though slowed down by World War II, the Republican Valley, and in fact the entire Missouri Valley flood control endeavors eventually became a reality. His success in this area probably goes a long way to explain his popularity with constituents. In 1940 he won easy re-election and ultimately served eight terms in the House.

Nebraska voters had largely been isolationists in the immediate pre-war period, and Curtis, like Norris, reflected their viewpoint. He opposed Lend-Lease and continued to identify with the anti-war movement until Pearl Harbor, but then he became an enthusiastic supporter of all efforts to produce victory. He especially took a position of opposition to labor disputes that might interfere with the cause of winning the war. However, his main thrust always remained with domestic issues.

Perhaps the most notable actions of Congressman Curtis dealt with his policy making in the area of Social Security legislation. During the first two years of the Eisenhower administration, he chaired the sub-committee that eventually put together the Social Security Act of 1954. His goals were to make the system as universal in coverage as possible to maintain "fiscal soundness." Throughout his subsequent twenty-four years in the Senate, he continued to strive for those goals.

In 1954, Carl Curtis ran for and was elected to the United States Senate. During his many years there, he introduced a constitutional amendment requiring a balanced budget—several times in fact—and also advocated giving the president line-item veto power in order to reduce and control federal expenditures. He became one of the best known of what would later be termed "deficit hawks." Continuing in this role during the turbulent sixties, he opposed most of the New Deal-Great Society measures as fiscally unsound. In 1972, he opposed a 20% increase in Social Security on the grounds that such a large increase was more than the system could bear. Only four senators had the courage to oppose it, and Curtis was the only one up for re-election. Many seniors criticized the aging Nebraskan for this act, particularly since he had always been known as a friend of Social Security. He managed to win a fourth term but by a smaller margin than ever before—roughly 36,000 votes or 53%. As historian Regis Courtemanche commented, "The populace does not strew garlands along the path of financial responsibility." However, the problems that the Social Security system began to face in the early 1980s and thereafter more than justified Curtis' view that the 1972 increase had been extravagant. One can say in retrospect that as the cost of entitlement programs have increased in ways that their original supporters had not imagined; much of the Curtis reluctance to support them has been vindicated.

Carl Curtis became known not simply for being one opposed to what he considered excessive government spending even though he termed his combination biography-autobiography, *Forty Years Against the Tide.* Perhaps his principal positive legacy outside of the Missouri Basin flood control and irrigation project was his long-time championing and eventual success as the main advocate of the Individual Retirement Account (IRA). The Nebraska Senator first began to push for this plan in 1959, and it took fourteen years to get it adopted. Selling powerful Democrat Brother Russell Long on the idea took some time, but it eventually succeeded in 1973. The act was amended and enlarged in 1981, two years after Curtis had retired.

As one of the most unabashed conservatives in the Senate, Brother Curtis came to be a close friend of the more colorful and charismatic Brother Barry Goldwater of Arizona. Accordingly, Goldwater appointed Curtis as his floor manager at the GOP National Convention in 1964 that nominated him. Brother Everett Dirksen gave the nominating speech. While the Nebraskan has generally been praised as doing a good job for his fellow senator at the convention, in retrospect probably nothing would have made Goldwater a winning candidate in November. Curtis did believe, however, that Goldwater could have done better if the people running his general election campaign had been more competent.

Relating a full history of Carl Curtis' forty years in Congress would encompass more space than would be wise in a brief article of this nature. Therefore, it would seem best to mention only a few of the highlights of his many faceted career. He served on the committees that investigated both the Billie Sol Estes and Bobby Baker scandals, convinced that the majority party did its best to prevent any leads that might go to the White House since many in the minority believed that Lyndon Johnson would be implicated.

Brother Carl T. Curtis chose not to seek another Senate term in 1978 and retired on January 3, 1979, having spent a combined total of forty years in the House and Senate. While elated at the election of Ronald Reagan to the presidency in 1980, he seemed to have no regrets about leaving the Senate when he did. In 1982, his devotional book, *To Remind,* was published (Curtis was a devout Presbyterian), and in 1983, he returned to Nebraska where he and his second wife Mildred (Lois had died in 1970 and he remarried in 1972) made their home in the Cornhusker state capital of Lincoln. His autobiography, *Forty Years Against the Tide: Congress and the Welfare State,* written with the help of Professor Regis Courtemanche of Long Island University, came out in 1986.

More than sixty-five years after he became a Mason in Minden and more than sixty years after he had first set foot in Congress, Brother Carl Curtis passed to the celestial lodge above on January 24, 2000. He had been his home state's reigning elder statesman for more than twenty years. While he and Nebraska's other statesman of stature, Brother George Norris, represented different political traditions, they still managed to complement each other in many respects, and both earned much respect.

**Note:** The principal source of information on Brother Curtis is the aforementioned *Forty Years Against the Tide: Congress and the Welfare State* (1986) and the two sketches in *Current Biography.* For his Masonic record I am indebted to the staff at the Grand Lodge of Nebraska and of the Scottish Rite to Brother John Boettjer, former managing editor of *The Scottish Rite Journal.*

September 2003, slightly revised 2011

**Brother Cecil H. Underwood:** *The Youngest and the Oldest Governor*

Twentieth century America has had many noted state governors who were also Masons. They have ranged from such figures as Kentucky's A. B. "Happy" Chandler, who became baseball commissioner, to Louisiana's Jimmie Davis who became a member of the Country Music Hall of Fame. George Wallace and James Rhodes both set records for serving a total of sixteen years in their respective states of Alabama and Ohio. One man, Cecil Harland Underwood of West Virginia, held the unusual distinction of being both his state's youngest and oldest governor with a thirty-six year lapse between terms. Back in 1957, he became the nation's youngest governor at thirty-four, and on his seventy-fourth birthday, he became governor-elect of the Mountain State for a second time.

Cecil Underwood was born in Joseph Mill, Tyler County, West Virginia, on November 5, 1922. His parents, Silas and Della Forrester Underwood, operated a family farm. Young Cecil received plenty of agricultural work experience at home, particularly during the Great Depression when his father took cash paying jobs away from home. He attended elementary school in a one-room rural locale. In high school at the county seat of Middlebourne, the youth participated in such activities as the speech club and the Future Farmers of America. As a senior he became a member of the National Honor Society and graduated fifth in his class in 1940. He also delivered the Gettysburg Address at a local Lincoln Day dinner which paved the way for his later entry into politics.

The young farm youth received a tuition scholarship to Salem College where he managed to graduate in three years. He majored in political science, speech, and history while minoring in biology. A busy student, Underwood also had a part-time job, participated in debates, and served as president of his senior class. Cecil served briefly in the Army Reserves but was discharged because of an abnormal heart beat.

Following graduation, Cecil Underwood took a position as a high school biology teacher in St. Mary's, West Virginia where he spent three years. Meanwhile, he also embarked on his entry into politics by successfully seeking a seat in the lower house of the West Virginia legislature as a Republican. He went on to serve six consecutive terms in the House of Delegates, becoming minority floor leader from 1949. Since being a legislator in West Virginia ranked only as a part-time position (at a $500.00 annual salary), Cecil left his teaching job to become an assistant to the president at Marietta College just across the river in Ohio. Although this job had flexible hours that provided time to attend legislative sessions, it also involved recruiting students, alumni fund raising, helping with student activities, and coaching the debate team. In 1950, he accepted the vice-presidency of Salem College where he performed somewhat similar duties plus being in charge of public relations.

Cecil H. Underwood began his Masonic journey on March 16, 1954, when he received his Entered Apprentice degree in Phoenix Lodge No. 73 in Sistersville. Advancing quickly, he was passed on April 6, 1954, and raised a Master Mason on May 28, 1954. Three years later in his first term as governor, Underwood completed the Scottish Rite degrees in John W. Morris Consistory in the Valley of Charleston on August 24, 1957. He became a Noble of Beni Kedem Shrine Temple on May 15, 1959. During his second term as governor, on October 6, 1997, he received the KCCH and the 33° in 1999. Not exclusively Masonic, Brother Underwood was also a member of the Benevolent and Protective Order of Elks.

Although the Republican Party had been strong in West Virginia from 1896 through 1929, the impact of the Great Depression and the decline of the coal industry had left the GOP in a weakened condition. However, by the mid-1950s, time seemed right for a modest comeback. During the controversial administration of then governor William Marland, the Democrats had been torn by schism—one of their Senators, Brother Harley Kilgore, had died and the usual unifier, Brother Matthew M. Neely, had begun to slow down from advancing age. Furthermore, the incumbent President Dwight Eisenhower's popularity cut across party lines. All this plus his own broad appeal combined to give Cecil Underwood atypical appeal for a Republican in a strong Democratic state. As a result, the young minority leader made a strong candidate, and with some help from the Eisenhower coattail effect, Brother Cecil H. Underwood was propelled into the statehouse by a 63,000 vote majority—440,502 to 377,121.

As governor, Underwood proved to be both a capable and honest chief executive. In his first year in office, he enjoyed a fairly harmonious relationship with the legislature despite strong Democratic majorities. Thereafter, partisanship became increasingly strong as Democrats sought to rebound from their 1956 losses, and with the economy in recession during much of 1958, their chances did indeed improve. Another 16,000 coal mining jobs went by the wayside between 1955 and 1961. While Underwood neither started nor could he alter this long-time economic trend, it did not bode well for his political success in the short run.

Nonetheless, history looked kindly on Cecil's initial term in the State Capital. As the Mountain State's pre-eminent historian, Otis K. Rice, phrased it, "When Underwood left office, there was general agreement that he had given the state dignified and responsible leadership. He was held in high esteem . . . in both the state and nation, and his political future seemed bright." Delays occurred in Brother Underwood's political future, however. With his term as governor expiring in January 1961, Cecil sought a seat in the U. S. Senate but lost to the incumbent, Jennings Randolph. In 1964 he made his first effort to regain the state house but lost to Brother Hulett C. Smith by some 77,000 votes. In 1968 he lost the GOP primary to Arch Moore who went on to become the first West Virginia governor to serve two consecutive terms (prior to 1968 West Virginia governors could not succeed themselves). After Moore left office, Cecil again sought the statehouse but lost badly to the immensely wealthy John D. Rockefeller IV.

Although Cecil Underwood had no political successes for decades he did manage to prosper in the private sector. He held positions with such firms as Island Creek Coal and Monsanto Chemical. From 1972 to 1975 he served as president of Bethany College in the West Virginia "northern panhandle." As a volunteer, he served as a trustee of his alma mater Salem College and on the state boards of the Cancer Society and the Boy Scouts. From 1960 through 1988, he was a delegate at every Republican National Convention each year except 1968.

In 1996, at an age when most politicians think seriously about retirement, Cecil Underwood decided to make one final run for the statehouse. As in 1956, disarray among Democrats worked to the advantage of badly outnumbered Republicans. In 1992, State Senator Charlotte Pritt had run a close primary race, nearly defeating incumbent governor Gaston Caperton. When Pritt won nomination narrowly in 1996, many of the old Capertonites and friends of the defeated Joe Manchin distanced themselves from Pritt who was viewed as too liberal. Taking advantage of the split, Underwood won a second term by 36,000 votes.

Although Bill Clinton easily carried West Virginia in 1996, reducing the Underwood victory margin, seven additional state senators and five house Republicans rode into office along with Underwood, although Democrats still had strong majorities in both houses of the legislature. As Governor, Underwood stressed technology and education along with West Virginia's constant need for highway improvements. The Democrat legislature usually scaled back his requests, but he did have some successes and fulfilled the duties of the office with the quiet dignity that had become his trademark.

At the age of seventy-eight in 2000, Cecil Underwood hoped to become the second West Virginian to hold the office for three terms, but it was not to be. In a fairly close election, he lost out to the much younger congressman Bob Wise by less than 19,000 votes. In January 2001, he finally retired. Meeting him in 2006, he signed a picture for me with the caption, "Thanks for the article" (referring to the magazine version of this piece) and mentioned that he had been recovering from a stroke. He passed to the "celestial lodge above" on November 24, 2008, a man who had left a considerable legacy of honorable service behind. In retrospect, it would seem unlikely that his feat of serving his state as governor in two separate eras will be duplicated often. Also few are likely to have experienced being both the nation's youngest and oldest governor in the same lifetime.

**Note**: I wish to express my appreciation to the staff of Grand Lodge of West Virginia, Ms. Joan Sansbury of the Scottish Rite Library in Washington D. C., and the Secretary of Beni Kedem Shrine Temple for the data on Governor Underwood's Masonic Records. Thanks also to Robert Fish, KCCH, Valley of Charleston.

February 1999, slightly revised 2011

## Sir Knight Charles Warren Fairbanks:
*Hoosier State Vice President*

The states of Virginia and Ohio have sometimes used the nickname "Mother of Presidents" because so many of the nation's chief executives have come from those locales. If the nickname "Mother of Vice Presidents" existed, both New York and Indiana could lay some claim to the title. The reason for this circumstance requires an understanding of presidential and Electoral College politics and the key role of certain swing states in national elections. For instance in the 1880s, New York and Indiana determined the winner in every one of the three elections held in that decade. The candidate who carried those states won the presidency. It was that simple! From the Civil War to World War I, Empire and Hoosier State men—along with Ohioans—dominated major party tickets. In this less than chaotic mixture, men such as our subject, Charles Fairbanks, for a time occupied a place in the center of the stage.

Charles Warren Fairbanks was born in Union County, Ohio on May 11, 1852, the son of a farmer-wagon maker, Loriston Fairbanks. His mother, Mary Smith Fairbanks, pursued the avocation of temperance activist when she could escape from the farm kitchen. Charles grew up as a typical farm boy during a time when many—perhaps a majority of Buckeye State dwellers—saw the Republican Party as the savior of the Union. They viewed the GOP as having cleansed the nation of the sin of slavery and then pursued policies that were causing America to grow into an economic giant by means of sound money and a protective tariff that encouraged industrialization and agricultural expansion that created employment for the masses of the citizenry. The Fairbanks family received enough of these bountiful gifts that they could send young Charles to Ohio

Wesleyan from whence he received a degree in 1874 and then to Cleveland Law College which he completed a few months later.

The young law student married Cornelia Cole on October 6, 1874, and the newlyweds went to housekeeping in Indianapolis where Charles practiced law, usually as an attorney for railroad corporations. His law firm was successful, and Fairbanks invested part of his fortune in newspapers. At one time he held the controlling interest in both *The Indianapolis News* and *The Indianapolis Journal.* He also indulged in a great deal of Republican politics, supporting the failed efforts of fellow Hoosier, Walter Q. Gresham, for president in 1884 (Gresham later jumped the political fence, endorsed Grover Cleveland in 1892, and became Secretary of State).

In 1892, Fairbanks, who had been rebuilding the Indiana GOP after the Democratic landslide of 1890, met Ohio Governor and Sir Knight William McKinley and harnessed his own political fortune to that of the rising Republican star and his financial backer-campaign manager Mark Hanna. In 1896, Charles Fairbanks delivered the keynote address at the Republican National Convention in St. Louis and then delivered the Indiana delegation to McKinley. In the fall election, he played a key role in McKinley's victory in the Hoosier State and a GOP takeover in the legislature. The grateful lawmakers then sent their party leader to Washington, rewarding him with a full six-year term in the United States Senate.

According to his most astute biographer, the late William T. Hull, "Fairbanks' Senate career proved competent if unspectacular." He generally voted with the administration on most issues and demonstrated himself sufficiently congenial and honorable to win the respect of his Senate colleagues. The Senator spoke out strongly for limiting immigration and requiring literacy of those who were admitted. When Fairbanks served on the Alaska-Canada Boundary Commission, he won sufficient respect and admiration from the local populace of the territory that they named one of their new settlements after him. A part of his old, radical Republican youth surfaced when during the Spanish-American War he stuck up for African-American units' rights to have black officers. Thanks to his position on this issue, Indiana became the first state to have integrated militia units. His calm demeanor and tall, dignified stance gave him the appearance of a true statesman, and some people began to see him as potential presidential material at some future point.

Fairbanks' political fortune suffered a mild setback with the sudden rise of Theodore Roosevelt to prominence following President

McKinley's unfortunate assassination. Moreover, he now had a rival within Hoosier GOP ranks with the coming of young Albert J. Beveridge (of Oriental Lodge No. 500 in Indianapolis) to the Senate in 1899. A more reform-oriented brand of Republican was coming to the forefront. Whereas McKinley had been closer to Fairbanks, Teddy Roosevelt saw Beveridge as one of his key supporters of "progressive" legislation in the Senate.

Nonetheless, Roosevelt acceded to Fairbanks as a running mate in 1904, partly because he needed an "old guard" Midwesterner to balance the ticket. Fairbanks not only filled the bill but proved to be an aggressive campaigner who carried much of the traveling and speaking tours that fall. The President adopted what in future years would become known as a "rose garden" strategy, where the incumbent let the vice presidential candidate do the heavy campaigning and he remained "above the fray" of hard politics. The Democrats boasted a competent ticket but one that has been described by historians as rather "lifeless." New York Judge and Brother Alton B. Parker (of Kingston Lodge No. 10) and West Virginia octogenarian Brother Henry G. Davis (of Elkins Lodge No. 108) provided an unexciting opposition, and the Roosevelt-Fairbanks ticket swept to an easy, electoral victory of 336 to 140. Democrats carried only the so-called "Solid South" as the old Confederacy had become known. This victory gave Republicans their strongest majority in thirty years and set the stage for more progressive reforms.

The tickets of both parties had been almost all-Masonic ones in 1904, and that was about to change. The Grand Lodge of Indiana made Charles Warren Fairbanks a Mason "at sight" on December 27, 1904 when he received all three degrees and affiliated with Oriental Lodge No. 500 (the same as rival Albert Beveridge) in Indianapolis. Like Teddy Roosevelt, he became a member of the order while Vice President-elect. Unlike T. R., Fairbanks continued his Masonic journeys far beyond the Blue Lodge. He was exalted a Royal Arch Mason in Keystone Chapter No. 6 on March 20, 1905, and knighted in Raper Commandery No. 1 on June 26, 1905. On November 8, he completed the Scottish Rite degrees in the Valley of Indianapolis. One and a half years later he became a member of Murat Shrine Temple in Indianapolis.

Unlike some celebrities who are made Masons "at sight" and are never seen in a lodge again, Fairbanks appears to have been fairly active and quite enthusiastic about his membership. According to William R. Denslow, "During his life, he is recorded as a visitor of lodges from coast to coast." Among public Masonic functions, he participated in laying the cornerstone at a new federal building in Flint, Michigan and on October 29, 1906, he became an honorary member of American Union Lodge No. 1 in Marietta, Ohio. In one of his pronouncements on the fraternity, he said, "I am a firm believer in the virtue of Masonry. . .The foundation principles of the organization are everlastingly sound."

As Vice President, Fairbanks also took his role as presiding officer of the Senate seriously unlike some veeps who let others fill their role. In fact, he still considered himself to be more a part of the legislative branch than of the executive. Oddly enough he never had the opportunity to break a tie vote. Despite his growing identity with the old guard conservatives, he helped gain passage of some key laws of the Roosevelt era including the Hepburn Act to regulate railroads, the Pure Food and Drug Acts, and the Employer's Liability Act in the District of Columbia. He also helped in the passage of the Aldrich-Vreeland Act and shared the President's enthusiasm for conservation measures (perhaps one of the few passions they shared other than Masonry), but he also cooperated with the "old guard" such as Brothers Nelson Aldrich and Joe Cannon in seeing that Square Deal bills they strongly opposed never got out of committee. Meanwhile, Senator Albert Beveridge had become the Hoosier favorite in the White House, and Fairbanks received no support from TR as a presidential nominee in 1908. To paraphrase a well known song of the era, when his term ended, Fairbanks found himself "Back Home in Indiana."

In Indianapolis, Charles Fairbanks remained moderately active in politics and stumped occasionally for Republican candidates. After the disastrous GOP split of 1912, he preached a message of renewed party unity, and perhaps for that reason, his name cropped up again as a vice presidential possibility. However, he emphatically stated, "My name must not be considered for Vice President and if it is presented, I wish it withdrawn." Nonetheless, when actually nominated in 1916, he dutifully accepted and with Charles Evans Hughes, participated in a campaign that came close to victory. It was the only race in which two Indianans opposed each other on the second slot. By a 277 to 254 count, Fairbanks lost out to another enthusiastic Mason, Sir Knight Thomas Riley Marshall of Fort Wayne.

After this last political race, Fairbanks again retired to Indianapolis and conservation activities. Ever the faithful patriot, when the United States entered World War I, in the name of national unity he visited army camps to encourage the soldiers and did his part to assist with Liberty Loan drives. However, he did not live to see victory and armistice as he passed away on June 14, 1918. His old running mate and sometimes nemesis Teddy Roosevelt outlived him by just a few months.

Like the majority of former vice presidents, Sir Knight Charles Warren Fairbanks is largely forgotten today, although his name lives on in the Alaskan city that has grown to a population of over 30,000, second in the state in size. As a Senator and Vice President, he ranks as better than some, lesser than others. To again quote the late William Hull, "Fairbanks was neither a great orator, nor a brilliant political thinker. He succeeded by mastering the intricacies of the Senate" and "was skilled in the arts of political management and compromise." His talents "were far less useful in presidential politics." He managed to reach the number two spot in the American ship of state, but in an era dominated by such Masons as Teddy Roosevelt, Robert LaFollette, William Howard Taft, William McKinley, and his Indiana rival Albert J. Beveridge, "his political skills were not sufficient to allow him to escape the shadows of those men."

**Notes**: The best evaluation of Fairbanks is the chapter by William T. Hull, "Charles Warren Fairbanks," in Mark O. Hatfield et al., *Vice Presidents of the United States* (1997). Less reputable books on Vice Presidents such as Sol Barzman, *Madmen and Geniuses* (1974) and Steve Tally, *Bland Ambition,* (1992) are more interested in making "light humor" about the office than in serious history. His Masonic history is in William R. Denslow, *10,000 Famous Freemasons*, II (1958).

November 2002; slightly revised 2011

## Brother Charles Goodnight: *Texas Cattle King and Western Trail Maker*

In the annals of the Trans-Mississippi cattle business, the name of Charles Goodnight ranks among the most prominent. A native of Illinois, Goodnight began raising cows in Texas for market after the Civil War and within a generation had become one of the industry giants. In addition, he lived to the ripe old age of ninety-three and saw the frontier tamed. The Colonel as he became known also spent some sixty-six of those years as a Mason.

Charles Goodnight was born in Macoupin County, Illinois, on March 5, 1836. His paternal great-grandfather, Michael Goodnight, had come to Virginia from Germany roughly a century before. His descendants became part of the westward movement. Goodnight's father, also named Charles, died in 1841, and his mother, Charlotte Collier, remarried to Hiram Daugherty. At the age of nine, while Texas was still an independent republic, the youth moved with his mother and stepfather, older brother, and two younger sisters to Milam County in what soon became the Lone Star State.

In 1855, Charles began a junket to California but halted his trip when he reached the Brazos and initiated his first venture into livestock raising in Palo Pinto County. As he built up a small herd, Goodnight also spent time as a Texas Ranger, keeping Indians at bay during the Civil War years. One of his first biographers, Dane Coolidge, stated that as a Northerner by birth, Charles did not wish to fight against his own people and so served Texas by guarding against and sometimes fighting Comanches rather than Yankees.

The young rancher was in fact doing just that as early as December 18, 1860, when he participated in the Pease River fight under the direction of Captain John J. Cureton. It was said that Goodnight spent about four years in the Ranger service, which at that time was more of a volunteer militia group than the state law enforcement agency that it became after 1874. The young frontiersman became especially adept at open plains country scouting.

During the Civil War years, Charles Goodnight began his long affiliation with Masonry. Due in part to likely gaps in the files of the Grand Lodge of Texas, his record is somewhat spotty, albeit voluminous. The future cattle baron took his degrees in Jacksboro Lodge No. 238 in Jacksboro. He was initiated on June 6, 1863; passed on July 4, 1863; and raised on August 2, 1863. The following year he appears as Senior Steward in Belknap Lodge No. 274. On March 24, 1866, he affiliated with Phoenix Lodge No. 275 in Weatherford. Goodnight demitted from Phoenix on February 27, 1869. There is no record of his withdrawing or being suspended from any of these bodies, although it seems possible that this may have happened. He may also have held membership in a Colorado lodge as he lived in Pueblo off and on for several years. He does not appear in Texas Grand Lodge files again until May 1910.

It was during his time of membership in Phoenix Lodge that some of the most memorable incidents in Goodnight's life took place. By the time the war ended, Texas was in a sense "cattle poor," with plenty of cows but little market for them. Back in 1859, Oliver Loving (ca. 1812-1867) had driven Texas cattle to the Denver area to market them in the mining areas. In 1866 Goodnight and Loving formed a partnership to drive about a thousand cattle to Fort Sumner, New Mexico, where the federal government was buying beef at decent prices to feed some 11,000 reservation Indians and to supply western forts.

From Young County, Texas to Fort Sumner was a dangerous journey of 600 miles. However, through a series of difficulties and hardships, including one junket of ninety miles without water, they made it. They marketed the cattle for eight cents a pound on the hoof.

The following spring, the pair gathered some 2,500 cattle and went up the trail again. They had problems with the Comanches, lost some 400 head to the Indians, and Loving suffered wounds which eventually cost him his life. However, once the cattle were sold Goodnight fulfilled his partner's dying wish that his body be returned to Weatherford, Texas for burial with Masonic rites. Several scholars including Joe Bennett believe that the Masonic ties of the two men made Goodnight determined to carry out his commitment to Loving. According to Dane Coolidge, Goodnight also delivered some $40,000 to Loving's estate (a figure that seems too high for the times to this writer).

Meanwhile in the coming years, some 250,000 cattle would be driven up the Goodnight-Loving Trail which ultimately extended into Colorado. It was said that for some sixty years thereafter, the cattle baron always referred to Oliver Loving as his "old pardner." He also kept his portrait hanging over the mantelpiece of his home.

Brother Goodnight continued in the cattle business until 1871, sometimes in partnership with John Chisum, until he had accumulated a small fortune. He then settled in Pueblo, Colorado, for a time and invested his profits. On July 26, 1870, he had surrendered his bachelorhood and married Mary Ann Dyer, usually known as Molly. Most of his wealth vanished when the Panic of 1873 hit.

Ordinary men might have become discouraged, but not Charles Goodnight who saw opportunity back in Texas. Since he knew the cattle business about as well as anyone, the rancher took his remaining herd of 1,600 head and in 1875 drove them to the Palo Duro Canyon country in the Texas Panhandle. He also met an affluent Irish immigrant named John Adair who owned a brokerage firm in Denver. With a $12,000 investment from Adair and his own experience, the two formed a partnership as the JA Ranch in June 1877. Initially Goodnight simply managed the firm at a $2,500 annual salary and a third interest. Eventually the Goodnight-Adair partnership had a ranch of some 600,000 acres, leased about that much more land, and ran nearly 100,000 head of cattle.

The JA Ranch practiced progressive agriculture, importing Durham, Hereford, and Angus cattle to improve the quality of their stock. Goodnight also preserved a small herd of bison and attempted to create a new breed by crossing them with cows which he termed the "cattalo." However, his plan did not succeed as the hybrid proved infertile (like a mule), but he kept experimenting with the cattalo until well up in old age. Nonetheless he did receive credit for helping save the American bison from extinction.

Like other cattlemen, Goodnight had trouble with rustlers. He once warned Texas Ranger Captain George Arrington that if the rangers could not solve the problem, he would personally take about seventy-five men and take care of the rustling on his own. It has been said that the thievery stopped. To again quote Dane Coolidge, "the old colonel hated a cow thief and he put the fear into many a black heart." In 1881 the cattle king took the lead in helping form the Panhandle Stockmen's Association. Combating rustlers became one of the major goals of this organization.

John Adair died in St. Louis on May 14, 1885, and in 1887, the ranch was divided with the widow Cornelia Adair taking her share and becoming a "Cattle Queen" in her own right. Charles Goodnight continued with his smaller 140,000 acre operation until he sold out in 1890. At only fifty-four he could not stay retired for long. He continued ranching on a smaller basis and remained an authority on the cattle industry as a business. He also invested in some mining properties in Mexico

Charles Goodnight as he aged gained a reputation as a crusty old pioneer who sometimes bordered on the eccentric. He disallowed drinking and gambling among the cowhands on his ranch; however, his principal battle was against the relatively harmless pastime of mumblety-peg which he opposed passionately. At one point he even tried to get the Stockman's Association to ban mumblety-peg on all the ranches in the group. A heavy cigar smoker, it had been said that he was sometimes known to smoke a box of fifty in a single day. However, as folklorist J. Frank Dobie wrote, quoting a man named Lester Sheffy, "under [his] gruff exterior [he had] a heart as gentle and kind as any man ever possessed."

On May 28, 1910, Charles Goodnight affiliated with Goodnight Lodge No 1015 in Goodnight, Texas. This was in the small town near his ranch that had been named for him and his membership remained constant throughout his remaining years. Unfortunately, Goodnight Lodge no longer exists.

The cattle king also dabbled in philanthropy. Although not a formal church member, Brother Goodnight contributed money to build two churches. He also funded in 1898 a private school known as Goodnight College which was converted to a public high school in 1918.

Widowed at the age of ninety, it seemed that the old cattle baron had nothing else to do but wait for the grim reaper to come. However, he soon struck up a correspondence with a younger unrelated woman named Corrine Goodnight. The two met and subsequently married on his birthday, March 5, 1927, and she provided the old pioneer with considerable comfort in his last years. Age finally caught up with him, and he died in Tucson, Arizona on December 12, 1929, at the age of ninety-three.

Charles Goodnight seems likely to be remembered as one of the most important of the so called "cattle kings." Others may have had bigger ranches or made more money, but the Illinois-born frontiersmen did well at both. Biographer J. Evetts Haley called him "the most representative cowman the West has known." The more flamboyant Dane Coolidge termed the Colonel "the greatest trail-maker in Texas—a man who left his mark on the West." J. Frank Dobie wrote, "He made a deeper imprint on the Great Plains than any other man who has lived there." In 1993 the U. S. Postal Service honored him with a stamp in its "Legends of the West" series, the only cattle baron to be included but not the only Mason as Kit Carson and Buffalo Bill Cody also had their portraits on the sheet. Like them, Charles Goodnight stood high in the annals of the American frontier.

**Biographical note:** The definitive book on Charles Goodnight is J. Evetts Haley, *Charles Goodnight: Cowman and Plainsman* (1936). Other books with chapters include Dane Coolidge, *Fighting Men of the West* (1931); Dee Brown, *Trail Driving Days* (1952); J. Frank Dobie, *Cow People* (1964); and Lewis Atherton, *The Cattle Kings* (1964). I also appreciate the advice and council of Sir Knight Joseph Bennett and the staff at the Grand Lodge of Texas.

October 2005, slightly revised 2011

## Sir Knight Charles Grosvenor:
*President McKinley's Man in Congress*

Political figures from the so-called "Gilded Age" have often been dismissed by later generations as bearded, boring old men who fought endless battles over equally dull issues such as tariff rates, soft money versus hard money, and pension bills. While it is true that many of those individuals from the 1870-1900 period sported long beards and mustaches, they frequently also exhibited dynamic, complex personalities. Such a person was Sir Knight Charles H. Grosvenor, a Civil War hero, a twenty-year member of Congress especially influential during the McKinley presidency, and a sixty-year Mason at the time of his death. Known sometimes as "the Sage of Athens" in his Ohio hometown, Grosvenor's fascinating life story follows.

Charles Henry Grosvenor was born in Pomfret, Connecticut on September 20, 1833, the son of Peter and Ann Chase Grosvenor. The paternal line descended from John Grosvenor who died in Roxbury, Massachusetts, in 1690. Grandfather Thomas Grosvenor had been a colonel in the Continental army and later served as a circuit judge. Peter Grosvenor had been a militia major during the War of 1812. At the age of five, Charles Grosvenor moved to Athens County, Ohio, and settled in Rome Township.

Although the Grosvenors had a distinguished bloodline, whatever wealth the family may have once possessed appears to have been exhausted by the time young Charles reached his teens. A local historian writing in 1883 described young Charles Grosvenor's education: "Our subject received his rudimentary education in the district (one room) schools of Athens County, and being thrown out upon his own resources at an early age, he was obliged to teach school, tend store, and work on a farm in order to obtain means to further pursue his studies. In his private study he was assisted by his mother, an amiable and intelligent lady. . . ."

When Grosvenor began his private studies in law, he did so under the tutelage of Lot L. Smith, a former Athens County Prosecuting Attorney and State Senator,who belonged to Paramuthia Lodge No. 25. Ironically, Smith held firmly to Jacksonian Democratic views while Grosvenor was on his way to becoming a fervent Republican. Apparently it was during this time that twenty-three-year old Charles petitioned Bartlett Lodge, U. D. (later No. 293) which lay just across the line in Washington County, not far from the family farm. Accepted, the young law student received his Entered Apprentice degree on April 11, 1857, passed as a Fellowcraft on August 8, and was raised a Master Mason on September 5, 1857. Since Bartlett Lodge No. 293 received its charter that October, the Brethren counted young Charles Grosvenor among their charter members.

That same year, the young reader passed his bar exams. Since minimal opportunity for lawyers existed in rural areas outside of county seats, Charlie moved into Athens and formed a law partnership with Samuel S. Knowles, another Mason. He also applied for affiliation with Paramuthia Lodge and was admitted on June 22, 1858. Later that same year he married Samantha Stewart. She was the grand-daughter of Daniel Stewart, another Mason in whose store young Grosvenor had once clerked. The marriage was apparently a happy one, but Samantha died eight years later, leaving a young daughter.

Like others of his generation, Charles Grosvenor joined the Union Army soon after the War of the Rebellion started and was elected a major in the 18th Ohio Volunteer Infantry. He became a regimental commander from November 1864. Breveted a Brigadier General in March 1865, Grosvenor played a heroic role in the Battle of Nashville in mid-December 1864, and two weeks later he participated in the capture of Decatur, Alabama. He had earlier participated in such major battles as Stone's River (Murfreesboro) and Chickamauga. Brother and General George Thomas wrote that, "Grosvenor has served under my command since November 1862 and has on occasions performed his duties with intelligence and zeal" in endorsing the Ohioan's successful promotion to full colonel. The brevet rank, however, remained sufficient for Charles Grosvenor to be known as "General" for the rest of his life.

Back in civilian status from October 1865, the General soon formed a new law partnership (Knowles had moved to Marietta) with Joseph M. Dana, who at one time or another held numerous local offices and also served as presiding officer of all the Athens Masonic bodies except the Commandery. Grosvenor also joined all of the local York Rite bodies, Athens Chapter No. 39, R.A.M.; Athens Council No. 15, R.&S.M.; and Athens Commandery No 15, K.T. Perhaps because of his years in military service, Sir Knight Grosvenor showed a preference for Chivalric Masonry and served two years as Eminent Commander, 1877 and 1878. Meanwhile after a year as a widower, in 1867 Grosvenor married again, this time to Louise Currier, the daughter of former Judge Ebenezer Currier. Ironically, decades earlier the Currier family had been leaders in the county's anti-Masonic movement.

As his law practice became more established and successful, the barrister took an increasingly active interest in politics. He had been a Republican presidential elector for U. S. Grant in 1872. The next year, he won election to the Athens County seat in the legislature. Re-elected in 1875, his colleagues in Columbus chose him to be Speaker of the House. By 1879, his oratorical prowess had won the General sufficient reputation that he stumped widely in the state of Maine on behalf of the GOP ticket. In 1880 he served as a presidential elector for James Garfield. Joseph Dana died in 1881, and Grosvenor obtained a new law partner in Evan Jones. In addition, he had a second law partnership in Pomeroy as Grosvenor and Vorhes.

In 1884, the General won his first of three consecutive terms in Congress. Since Democrats controlled the House and Grover Cleveland the Presidency until 1889, the "Sage of Athens" had little to show for his first two terms, but with a GOP Congress and Benjamin Harrison in the White House, the 1889-1890 legislative session accomplished a great deal. Long term incumbencies were not common in Southern Ohio during the Gilded Age, and Grosvenor lost his bid for a fourth term when the Republican nomination went to another Masonic brevetted brigadier, William Enochs of Ironton's Lawrence Lodge No. 198.

Redistricting in 1892 paved the way for a Grosvenor comeback. He then went on to serve seven more terms before being retired again in the 1906 nominating convention to a younger Republican, Brother Albert Douglas of Chillicothe. In those days, Ohio Republicans were factionalized with one group centering on Marc Hanna, John Sherman, and Brother William McKinley. The other centered on former Governor Joseph Foraker and future Governor Asa Bushnell, both Masons as well. Grosvenor allied himself with the Hanna-McKinley faction. Usually the two factions reached an accommodation and Republicans remained strong and united in the Buckeye State through a difficult era.

The election of Sir Knight McKinley to the White House in November 1896 placed Grosvenor in a strong position. The congressman tended to be more conservative than the President but generally ranked among his more reliable allies in the House, helping to steer such key legislation as the Dingley Tariff through Congress. Grosvenor also generally championed the President's foreign policy in Congress but seemed especially valuable in dispensing political advice. The two could sometimes differ, however, as in 1900 when McKinley chose Brother Theodore Roosevelt as a running mate over the General's favorite Brother Jonathan Dolliver of Iowa. After McKinley's assassination, Grosvenor authored an affectionate biography of the martyred leader.

Some notion of Grosvenor's stature in his day may be gleaned from his travels on the Chautauqua circuit. He and a leading Democrat, Brother Champ Clark of Missouri (Perseverance Lodge No. 92), would debate the leading issues of the day, often quite furiously, on the stump on their touring schedules. Yet they often dined and traveled together as friends and Brothers when not on the rostrum. Clark in his autobiography (he later became Speaker of the House and experienced a near miss of the presidency at the 1912 Democratic Convention) describes Grosvenor as a worthy opponent.

Charles Grosvenor's influence in Congress began to erode in the Teddy Roosevelt era in part because advancing age was taking a toll on his energy and health. In 1906, nearing seventy-three, Brother Albert Douglas bested him for the nomination. As he neared retirement, Congress voted funding for a new post office building in Athens. Returning to law practice in his hometown, the old General played a role in helping the soon-to-be Brother William Howard Taft in securing the 1908 presidential nomination and later served on the Chickamauga Battlefield Commission.

In 1910 when the Athens Masonic Bodies dedicated a new temple, General Grosvenor gave a public address on Masonry to the assembled throng. Seven years later "the Sage of Athens" died at the age of eighty-four, sixty years after he had been raised in Bartlett Lodge and a decade after his retirement from Congress. He had a Knight Templar service.

Although nationally he is forgotten except to a handful of scholars of the McKinley era, his name lives on in his adopted hometown. Athens has a Grosvenor Street, Ohio University has a Grosvenor Hall, and two of the railroads that served the city intersected at Grosvenor Crossing which was controlled by a Grosvenor Tower. For some years, the nearby mining town of Sugar Creek had the post office name of Grosvenor before being changed to Poston. In his day, few people in his part of America had a greater impact than Sir Knight Charles Henry Grosvenor.

**Note**: There is no biography of Sir Knight Grosvenor, but his life can be pieced together from several local histories. For his Masonic Records, I appreciated the help of Sir Knights Clayton Smith, Roger Van Dyke and Roger Wiseman, all of Athens Commandery No. 15. Abby Goodnite Ehman typed the original article.

January 1999; slightly revised 2011.

**Brother Charles Sawyer:**
*President Truman's "Conservative Democrat"*

While the Masonic connections of Brother and Sir Knight Harry S. Truman are well-known to many of the readers of this magazine, those Masons among his key subordinates have often been overlooked. For instance, several cabinet members in the Truman era also wore the square and compass including State Department heads, James Byrnes and George Marshall; Treasury Secretaries, Fred Vinson and John Snyder; Attorney General Tom Clark; and Agriculture Secretary Clinton Anderson. Another Mason is the subject of this sketch: self-styled "conservative Democrat," Brother Charles Sawyer, who held the office of Secretary of Commerce.

Charles A. Sawyer was born in Cincinnati, Ohio on February 10, 1887. His parents were both New England born teachers; his father, Edward Sawyer, was from Maine and his mother from Connecticut. The family, according to Charles, were thrifty folk with a strong "belief in the old-fashioned virtues." The Sawyers eventually settled in the suburb of Madisonville, but each summer the family returned to Maine for a long vacation spent mostly in the small community of Ingall's Station. Charles recalled that, although not poor, the Sawyers spent virtually no money except for necessities and the annual trip to Maine. Charles had to do odd jobs to earn spending money.

After finishing high school in 1905, Sawyer matriculated to Oberlin where he completed a bachelor's degree in three years. In the spring of 1908, Charles delivered the nominating speech at Oberlin's mock Republican Convention for the future GOP nominee, William Howard Taft, a fellow Cincinnati man who also soon became a member of Kilwining Lodge No. 356 in the Queen City. Initially Sawyer and a friend had planned to purchase a small newspaper in South Dakota, but their aspirations collapsed when the old owner found a cash purchaser.

With no job prospects in mind, Charles Sawyer decided to accept a scholarship at the University of Cincinnati Law School. Ironically, until then he had not thought of law as a profession and had received the scholarship because he happened to be the only Oberlin senior from Cincinnati; however, the young college graduate took to legal studies like the proverbial "duck takes to water." He had to support himself by sales jobs in the summer and teaching night school classes for twelve dollars a week.

Shortly after returning to the Cincinnati area, young Charles Sawyer became a Mason. He took his Entered Apprentice degree in Madisonville Lodge No. 419 on August 29, 1908; was passed a Fellowcraft on September 30, 1908; and was raised to the sublime degree of Master Mason on November 5, 1908. Brother Sawyer remained a faithful (if not particularly active) member of Madisonville Lodge for more than seventy years. On February 21 and 23, 1917, he took the Scottish Rite work in the Valley of Cincinnati. He received the 33° on September 28, 1966.

Even before finishing law school, Sawyer plunged into local politics by trying to keep Madisonville from being annexed by Cincinnati. While losing on this issue, he had better luck when he ran for city council in the fall of 1911 as a Democrat in a Republican city. Reformer Henry T. Hunt was in the process of finishing off the remnants of the Cox machine in the Queen City, and Sawyer became what was then the youngest councilman in the city's history. Two years later he won a second term without the benefit of Hunt's coattails for Hunt suffered defeat.

In 1912 Sawyer attended his first of many Democrat National Conventions. In 1915 the two-term councilman was asked by leaders of his party to run for mayor. However, Sawyer was soundly defeated by a vote of 57,414 for Republican George Pushton to his own 35,144. The loser did manage to take some consolation in the fact that he ran 4,000 votes ahead of his party's ticket.

In 1917-1918 he, along with some 3,000,000 other Americans, joined the army for service in World War I. During this period in 1918, he married Margaret Johnson. The couple eventually became the parents of five children.

Returning from the war, his law firm became increasingly influential. He gained such clients as William Proctor of the Proctor and Gamble Company and Powell Crosley of manufacturing and WLW radio fame. Sometime later Sawyer became a major stockholder in the Cincinnati Reds with Brother Crosley as club president and Brother Lee McPhail as General Manager. The new management eventually brought National League championships to Crosley Field in 1939 and 1940 although the club had been in bankruptcy when they took control. In fact, Sawyer had invested in many other enterprises during the twenties, but luckily he managed to sell off many before the crash of 1929. One of the few interests he retained was that of the *Lancaster Eagle-Gazette*, a southeast Ohio newspaper of some renown.

Except for some casual political work, Charles Sawyer had been largely inactive in politics during the twenties, but in 1930, local Democrats persuaded him to run for Congress. The depression had given new life to the Democrats by 1930, but the lawyer lost a close race to Brother William Hess by only 566 votes. He had much greater success in 1932 when he was elected Lieutenant Governor on a state ticket headed by incumbent Governor, Brother George White (of American Union Lodge No. 1), by more than 89,000 votes.

By this time Brother Sawyer had by his own admission abandoned his one-time progressive stance and had become a conservative. Nonetheless, he remained loyal to both the New Deal and the Fair Deal. Under the *Ohio Constitution*, lieutenant governors have few duties other than replacing the chief executive and presiding over the state senate. Since that body was equally divided between Democrats and Republicans, this proved more interesting than usual. Most issues, however, did not follow strict party line votes.

In 1934, Brother Sawyer threw his hat in the ring to succeed outgoing Governor White but lost a close primary battle to former congressman, Brother Martin L. Davey (of Rockton Lodge No. 316), who won the November election. Davey soon proved to be an unpredictable party maverick who quarreled with virtually everyone in the Roosevelt administration, especially Harry Hopkins. However, with Mrs. Sawyer fighting what proved to be a fatal battle with cancer, Charles stayed out of the 1936 race. Davey narrowly won a second term over GOP hopeful, Brother John Bricker (of Mt. Sterling Lodge No. 269).

In 1938 when Davey sought a third term, Sawyer was ready. In his own words, he "had thrown down the gauntlet." A bitter primary contest followed in which Sawyer won by about 30,000 votes; however, the resulting party split paved the way for Republican resurgence in which Brother Bricker won. This proved to be Sawyer's last quest for elective office (but not Davey's). Sawyer did take some satisfaction in helping restore some dignity to Buckeye State politics. For that matter, his career in public service was still in its early stages.

As Ohio's Democratic National Committeeman, Charles Sawyer helped Brother Franklin Roosevelt carry Ohio for the third time in 1940. In 1942 he married a second time to Elizabeth de Veyrac, a lady whom Sawyer had known as a child. She had also lived in Belgium for several years, a factor that became highly significant when President Roosevelt persuaded him to accept an appointment as Ambassador to Belgium and Minister to Luxembourg in the late summer of 1944. The fourteen months Sawyer spent in this position probably ranked as the most crucial time in the history of Belgian-American relations. With World War II coming to a close and the future of Western Europe in doubt, Sawyer's success in that sensitive position brought him diplomatic acclaim as the best Ambassador to that county since Brand Whitlock.

In 1946 Charles Sawyer returned to Cincinnati, but two years later in April 1948, President Truman appointed him Secretary of Commerce succeeding Averill Harriman. He served in this position until Truman left office in January of 1953. This job proved to be the zenith of Brother Sawyer's frequently interrupted career in public service. Several issues dominated the department in those years including internal security, the 1950 census, complex issues concerning the Dollar Steamship Lines, and the controversial steel strike issue of 1952. Perhaps the most significant long-range contribution was Brother Sawyer's efforts supporting the construction of the St. Lawrence Seaway.

When Brother Truman left office, Charles Sawyer returned to Cincinnati and private life. His last regular contribution to public life came with service on the Hoover Commission. Sawyer's efforts here concerned foreign aid and the waste and misuse of these funds; however, like other efforts to reduce government power and inefficiency, little resulted from the commission's recommendations. After a failed move to assist Vice President Barkley in 1952, he stopped active participation in politics, attending his last Democratic National Convention as a guest in 1956. As a volunteer, he led Community Chest drives in the Queen City for some years and in 1956 became a senior partner in the prestigious law firm of Taft, Stettinius, and Hollister.

In 1958 he received his fifty-year pin from the Grand Lodge of Ohio and in 1968 his sixty-year pin. That same year his autobiography, *Concerns of a Conservative Democrat*, came out from the Southern Illinois University Press. He lived on for another decade, passing away on April 7, 1979, at the age of ninety-two. In his long life, Brother Sawyer rose from modest beginnings to enjoy a career of business, legal, and civic achievement. In his era he ranked among the most prominent Masons in public life and he deserves to be remembered as such.

**Note:** The major source of information on Charles Sawyer is his *Concerns of a Conservative Democrat* (1968) supplemented by a 1948 entry in *Current Biography.* For his Masonic record, I am indebted to David Dresser, Grand Secretary of the Grand Lodge of Ohio. For his AASR records, thanks are extended to Jack DeVise of the Valley of Cincinnati.

September 2001; slightly revised 2011

## **Brother Chris Madsen:** *Masonic Marshal of the Oklahoma Frontier*

Over a period of several years, Sir Knight Joseph Bennett authored numerous articles in various Masonic magazines detailing the Masonic backgrounds of several noted Texas Rangers and New Mexico law officers in the Trans-Mississippi frontier. Other regions in the Old West also had officers who wore stars on their chests and the square and compasses on their lapels, fingers, or watch chains. Among them were Arizona Ranger leader Burton Mossman, Wyoming sheriff Frank Canton, and the subject of this sketch, Christian Madsen, who helped tame the Oklahoma frontier in the waning years of the nineteenth century and after.

Madsen came to this country from Denmark, and like many old-time frontier characters, he became something of a tall tale-teller in his old age. Some of these yarns included spending time in the Danish army as a teenager and somewhat later a stint in the French Foreign Legion. More recent research indicates that he was something of a ne'er-do-well, vagrant, and jailbird in his homeland. What is certain is that Christian Madsen was born on the Danish Island of Funen on February 25, 1851, and that he came to the United States in January of 1876 and within days enlisted in the United States Cavalry.

Madsen spent fifteen years in the cavalry and compiled an honorable if not an especially distinguished record. He left his shady past behind him except for an 1881 incident in Wyoming Territory where he and some army buddies apparently shot some livestock belonging to a civilian; perhaps it was a little prank that got out of hand. Among other incidents, Chris is supposed to have witnessed the famous fight in which Sir Knight Buffalo Bill Cody killed the young Cheyenne warrior, Yellow Hand, on July 17, 1876 (labeled by the press as "the first scalp for Custer"). He also participated in two additional conflicts with Indians; the Battle of Slim Buttes, Dakota Territory in September of 1876 and Milk Creek, Colorado on October 5, 1879.

Madsen re-enlisted in January 1881 while stationed at Fort Laramie and in January 1886 at Fort Supply, Indian Territory. He also spent some of his army years at Fort Riley, Kansas and Fort Reno, Indian Territory. In 1886, he was promoted to quartermaster sergeant. Early in 1888, Chris married Margaret or "Maggie" Morris. The couple had two children, Christian Reno and Marion, who married Frank Derr. Maggie, however, contracted tuberculosis and died in May of 1898. Although Chris remained in the army until January of 1891, he filed a homestead claim in 1889 during the first Oklahoma land rush, selecting a quarter section some seven miles from the newly founded town of El Reno in Canadian County.

When he left the army at nearly forty years of age, Chris apparently intended to farm his homestead claim, but another occupation soon beckoned. Before the month had expired, he accepted an appointment from U.S. Marshal William Grimes as a deputy. While El Reno would be his residence for the next several decades, his law enforcement duties sometimes kept him away from home for weeks and even months at a time. It was at El Reno Lodge No. 50, A.F. & A.M., that Christian Madsen took his Masonic degrees. He was initiated an Entered Apprentice on April 8, 1895; was passed to the degree of Fellowcraft on July 15; and was raised to the sublime degree of Master Mason on September 16, 1895. He retained his membership there for the next forty-nine years.

In the 1890s, Oklahoma Territory and the neighboring Indian Territory harbored an amazing number of outlaw bands of which the Daltons and the Doolin gang ranked as the most notorious. Other bandits of note included Ned Christie, Ben Cravens, Al Jennings, the Bill Cook gang, and the Rufus Buck gang. Three law officers in particular—Chris Madsen, Henry A. "Heck" Thomas, and William Tilghman—earned fame as the "Three Guardsmen" who did the most to bring law and order out of this chaos. Additional well known officers of the region included Frank Canton, Bud Ledbetter, and James Masterson. Of these, Madsen, Canton, and probably Tilghman were Masons.

Chris Madsen became a deputy U.S. marshal shortly after he left the army in January of 1891 and remained in this job at various posts for the next twenty-five years. During his early months on the job, the Danish-born deputy worked primarily as a jailer or guard, but early in 1892, he was involved in a crisis that involved serving court injunctions upon [homestead] lot jumpers. Chris performed especially well in the El Reno area, almost single-handedly "trying to keep down trouble." As a reward, he was promoted to the position of chief deputy and put on a monthly salary of $250.00. (Deputies were normally paid only on a fee system in those days.) By that time, residents of the territory had become alarmed about the robberies attributed to the Dalton gang, and the law—including Madsen—spent quite a bit of time trying to capture them. Ironically, when the outlaws over-extended themselves on October 5, 1892, by trying to rob two banks at once in Coffeyville, Kansas, an impromptu party of armed citizens ended their careers on short notice. Bob and Grat Dalton, along with two gang members, were killed, and young Emmet Dalton survived his wounds to serve a long prison sentence.

Madsen and the other officers soon found themselves busy chasing other outlaws including Tulsa Jack Blake, Bill Dalton, Dick Yeager (alias Zip Wyatt), Oliver Yantis, and George "Red Buck" Waightman. Eventually all of these desperadoes were captured and imprisoned or killed. Chris missed out on some of the action when he found himself transferred to the Kansas City office for a period extending from July of 1896 until the end of 1897. During this time, Deputy Heck Thomas killed Bill Doolin. Finally, Madsen the lawman received a transfer to Ardmore, Indian Territory, which was nearer home. It came at an opportune time for Maggie Madsen's health was in rapid decline, and she died on May 2, 1898.

Maggie's death occurred the day after the opening battle at Manila Bay in the Spanish-American War. Before the month ended, Chris found himself back in the cavalry as a quartermaster sergeant in the Rough Riders. The war proved to be a short one, and Chris got no closer to Cuba than Tampa, Florida (not all the Rough Riders got into combat). After a brief illness (according to one report Madsen lost so much weight during this second tour of duty that his children failed to recognize him when he came home), Chris reported for work at the U.S. Marshal's office for the Southern District of Indian Territory in Ardmore. Much of his time was spent at the office in nearby Paul's Valley. He continued as a field deputy until 1902. After that, most of his remaining career in law enforcement was spent as an office deputy. Considering that he was past fifty years of age by that time and generally described as being only 5 feet, 7 inches in height and weighing 200 or more pounds, this seems to make a great deal of sense.

Actually by this time, much the Marshal's duties tended to be routine. Serving court papers, transferring prisoners, arresting vagrants, an occasional apprehension of horse thieves, whiskey sellers, and gamblers had become the typical work of the law officers and staff. In 1906, Chris was transferred back to Guthrie, much nearer his farm at El Reno. In that year, the U.S. Marshal position became vacant, and Chris hoped for the appointment. However, President Teddy Roosevelt appointed a more flamboyant frontier character, "Catch 'Em Alive Jack" Abernathy, although Madsen was retained as chief deputy. Abernathy, whose renown derived from his ability to capture wolves and coyotes with his bare hands, proved to be a total disaster and an incompetent in a position of responsibility. At the end of 1910, Attorney General Wickersham finally forced his resignation, and for the first three months of 1911, Chris, who had been doing Abernathy's work, held the position of U. S. Marshal. The veteran chief deputy again hoped for the permanent appointment, but no matter how competent and well-liked he might be in Guthrie, he seemingly had little pull in Washington, and a man named William S. Cade got the job, again retaining Chris as chief deputy.

During those years in Guthrie, Chris Madsen took additional Masonic work in the Guthrie Scottish Rite bodies beginning in 1911. Whether time conflicts or lack of funds slowed his progress cannot now be determined, but he did not receive the 32° until 1914. Meanwhile, his one-time fellow officer, Heck Thomas, had fallen upon hard times and ill health since losing out as Lawton police chief in 1909. Chris tried to help his old friend and secured him some part-time work as a deputy. By 1912 the man once known as a "terror to outlaws" was reduced to hoping for a state appointment as deputy game warden. When even this failed to come through, "he just seemed to give up." Thomas died virtually penniless on August 15, 1912. The second "guardsmen" Bill Tilghman died in the line of duty as marshal in Cromwell, Oklahoma, in 1924, leaving his widow deeply in debt and Madsen as the surviving member of the famous threesome.

Brother Chris had continued on as the chief deputy at the marshal's office in Guthrie until November 1913. The new marshal from the incoming Wilson administration demoted the aging Republican back to mere deputy status. In 1916, they replaced him altogether with a Democrat, and Chris went back to his farm at El Reno. After a few months in March of 1917, he secured a bookkeeping job as auditor for the Tulsa Police Department until August of 1918 when another change of politics sent the old guardsman back to his El Reno homestead once again. Fortunately, by this time Madsen had been able to draw a small pension from his military service as a veteran of the Indian Wars. When Warren Harding became president, Chris applied for the U.S. Marshal's position again, but at the age of seventy, he apparently received little consideration. Nonetheless, the aging frontiersman continued to hold part-time or temporary jobs for several more years. These included guard duty at an Oklahoma City branch of the Federal Reserve Bank, a special investigator on call from the governor's office, and acting superintendent at the Union Soldier's Home. He also sometimes acted as a bailiff at the Federal Court.

In his old age, Chris also traveled a bit on special occasions where he received recognition as a survivor of bygone frontier days. For instance in 1934, He journeyed to Nebraska where he and an elderly Sioux (Lakota) Indian named White Buffalo posed at the unveiling of a monument marking the site of the Buffalo Bill-Yellow Hand encounter. Three years later Madsen went to Houston where he posed for pictures with former outlaw Al Jennings and E. D. Nix who had been U.S. Marshal of Oklahoma Territory during part of Grover Cleveland's second term. (Ironically, Nix had been removed for malfeasance in office, but that didn't stop him from taking much of the credit for the outlaw cleanup that started before he came into office and ended after his departure.) In 1941, Chris went to Hollywood and visited the movie lots where he met up-and-coming motion picture hero (and later Sir Knight) Roy Rogers. The previous year, Chris had been elected to the Oklahoma Hall of Fame, an event that must have pleased him a great deal. Mostly, however, Madsen's favorite pastime seems to have been spinning big yarns to naïve young newspaper reporters about his role in the nation's history—many of them self-contradictory.

Late in 1943 Chris broke his hip and his condition worsened. On January 4, 1944, he was admitted to the Masonic Home in Guthrie and died five days later, six weeks short of his ninety-third birthday. According to his biographer, Homer Croy, he received the Rose Croix Rites at his funeral held at the Guthrie Scottish Rite Temple. He was buried beside his long deceased wife Maggie at the Frisco Cemetery in Yukon, Oklahoma. Son Reno and daughter Marion survived him, and both lived to ripe old ages themselves. Son-in-law Frank Derr served the Scottish Rite bodies in Guthrie as Secretary for many years. If Brother Madsen's real-life achievements were somewhat less than he made them out to be in old age, they were still sufficient to rate him a significant place in the history of the American West. In addition, he more than made up in service to his adopted homeland whatever shortcomings he had demonstrated in a reckless youth.

**Note**: The standard Madsen biography by Homer Croy, *Trigger Marshal: The Story of Chris Madsen* (1958) needs to be balanced with the revisionist study by Nancy Samuelson, *Shoot from the Lip: The Lives, Legends, and Lies of the Three Guardsmen of Oklahoma* (1998). For researching Madsen's Masonic and Masonic Home record, I appreciate the help of Brother Jim Tresner of Guthrie, Oklahoma.

October 1999; slightly revised 2011

## Sir Knight Clyde Beatty: *King of the Lion Tamers*

For some three decades, Clyde Raymond Beatty was known as one of America's biggest circus attractions. His reputation as the most famous lion tamer (Beatty himself preferred to be known as an "animal trainer") in modern history would seem to be unchallenged. In his prime, Beatty fearlessly entered a cage with as many as forty lions and tigers at a time with only a chair, a whip, and a pistol that shot blanks. Through a radio adventure series and movie serials, his name became a household word to millions who were never fortunate enough to see him on the stage or in the ring.

Sir Knight Beatty's life also personified the American dream of one who went from rags-to-riches, the type of youth who filled the pages of Horatio Alger Junior's inspirational novels. Clyde Beatty was born in Bainbridge, Ohio on June 10, 1903 (or perhaps 1902), the son of Margaret Beatty. Later, his mother married, and young Clyde had four younger half-sisters and a half-brother. As he grew up, the youth became no more than an average student in the classroom, but he developed a deep love for the outdoors and activities that helped put food on the table such as hunting and fishing. Like many other youth of his era, Beatty earned money by selling newspapers in Bainbridge and along with his younger sisters kept a number of pets.

At the age of nineteen, "Buster" Beatty left Bainbridge via the D.T.& I. Railroad on August 16, 1921, for Washington Court House and joined a show under the "Big Top"—to be more specific, Howe's Great London Circus. Entry level positions with the circus frequently paid no more than room and board, but they did provide opportunities to learn while performing such unpleasant tasks as cleaning animal cages, assembling and dismantling tents, feeding animals, and carrying water. For the dedicated and career-minded youth, it also meant a great deal of hands-on experience.

By 1922 Beatty was tending a hippopotamus for Gollmar Brothers (actually the same show under a different name), and the next year he had a polar bear act. By 1925, he had settled on the form of animal training that would make him a legend, to-wit working with the "big cats." He studied their behavioral patterns both from reading and learning from experienced trainers such as John "Chubby" Guilfoyle and Peter Taylor.

Despite the fact that Clyde Beatty used a whip and a blank-shooting pistol in his lion and tiger training act, he was generally affectionate toward them. The pistol shots were more to scare the big cats and the whip seldom touched them. According to a lengthy biographical piece in *Timeline* by Danny Fulks (Professor Emeritus at Marshall University), "he learned to keep his animals well fed, groomed, and healthy by veterinarians. He learned what spooked them, how they communicated with one another, how males related to females, how they played, and what made them happy. He liked his cats fresh from the jungles, and within the constraints of their lives in captivity, kept them free from curiosity seekers, other trainers, and naïve cage boys who might taunt them. He trained them to submit to his commands using limited physical forces and relying upon behaviorism—traditional carrot-and-stick techniques. He petted his animals when they seemed to ask for it, used his whip to stroke their whiskers in an affectionate manner, and returned to his cage after his act to show his appreciation." Clyde Beatty's initial years of "big top" stardom were spent with the Hagenbeck-Wallace Wild Animal Circus (1925-1934) when by 1930 their publicity posters referred to him as "Capt. Beatty" who presents in sensational exhibit at one time 40 ferocious kings of the jungle."

The next year, he hooked up—temporarily—with Ringling Brothers, Barnum and Bailey and took his death-defying act to Madison Square Garden in New York City. During the cold season, Beatty worked on new acts, toiled as a technical advisor on a Tarzan movie, and in 1933 played himself in a motion picture called *The Big Cage.* The following year he starred again in a twelve-chapter Mascot serial, *The Lost Jungle*, that co-starred Cecilia Parker and Mickey Rooney.

The bosses at Ringling reportedly began complaining that Beatty's movies might be hurting attendance at his live circus appearances. The man billed as the "World's Greatest Animal Trainer" accepted a better offer and joined the Cole Brothers Circus. The downside of this switch was that all the "Big Cats" that Beatty used in the circus and both movies were the property of Ringling Brothers. Accordingly, Clyde had to train a whole new corps of lions and tigers, but he opened on schedule to an enthusiastic crowd at the Chicago Coliseum during the third week of April and had even actually used the same ones in February at the Detroit Shrine Circus.

The following winter Beatty made another serial for Republic, a fifteen-chapter play, *Darkest Africa*, later retitled *King of Jungleland*. A featured young actor in this series, Manuel King, received second billing as the "World's Youngest Wild Animal Trainer." Back in the circus, Clyde commanded a salary of $3,500 weekly in season despite the Great Depression. He did product endorsements for items ranging from Eveready batteries to Studebaker automobiles, with the latter company furnishing him a new vehicle. Stories (probably fictional) about his adventures with lions appeared in Big Little Books (four titles) and as featured portions of *Crackajack Funnies* and *Super Comics*. In addition, a single special 25-cent edition of *The Action-Packed Adventures of Clyde Beatty* appeared in October of 1953.

Despite his ability to handle the big cats better than anyone before or since, Beatty managed to survive several close calls with death. In 1926 a five-hundred-pound lion attacked him and he had to be dragged from the cage by an assistant. In January of 1932 when he turned his back on a lion named Nero (who ironically had once rescued Clyde from an attack by two tigers), the beast sank a fang into his leg and infection developed. But after treatments, Beatty still opened in New York on schedule.

While touring as a circus act remained his principal occupation, Clyde occasionally diversified his activity. In 1939 he spent the summer at the Pier in Atlantic City and operated a "jungle zoo" in Rochester, New York, for a season. From 1939 until 1945, Beatty and his wife, Harriett Evans (his second marriage in 1933), operated a zoo in Ft. Lauderdale, Florida. It eventually closed, following complaints from nearby residents concerning occasional loud noises. Perhaps most significant, he starred in a thrice weekly radio adventure series on the Mutual Broadcasting System during the early fifties sponsored by Kellogg's cereal (was Tony the Tiger involved?). As an author he collaborated on three books: *The Big Cage* (1933 with Edward Anthony), *Jungle Performers* (1941 with Earl Wilson), and finally *Facing the Big Cats: My World of Lions and Tigers* (1965 with Edward Anthony) which appeared just prior to his death.

With the end of World War II, the renowned lion tamer purchased a previously existing circus and renamed it the Clyde

Beatty Circus. He sold that one after a season and bought a larger one with partner Arthur Concello, also named the Clyde Beatty Circus. He eventually became sole owner and kept it in operation with himself as the star attraction until the operation went bankrupt in 1956. He then went back to working for others until 1959 when he became part of the Clyde Beatty-Cole Brothers Circus. He continued touring into the early sixties. The circus as a form of American entertainment began to decline in the later fifties and early sixties, and Beatty was beginning to get older, but he kept going.

Outside the circus, Beatty also had other show business ventures. In 1949, he had returned to Hollywood and made a popular film with the comedy team of Bud Abbott (a Mason) and Lou Costello titled *Africa Screams*, the cast of which also included Frank Buck, known for his own adventures with wild animals. In 1954, Clyde co-starred with detective novelist Mickey Spillane and veteran actor Pat O'Brien in a mystery with a circus setting, *Ring of Fear*. While he never had a TV show of his own, Beatty did make some appearances on the small screen, displaying his talents on the Ed Sullivan Show, among others.

Not long afterward, Clyde Raymond Beatty became a Mason. Under a special dispensation, he received his Blue Lodge degrees in Craftsman Lodge No. 521 in Detroit, Michigan on February 10, 1956 (during the Detroit Shrine Circus). A little over two years later, he received his Royal Arch degree in Monroe Chapter No. 1 on November 22, 1958, and was knighted in Damascus Commandery No. 42 on November 24, 1958. He immediately became a Noble of Moslem Shrine Temple in Detroit. The latter has some significance, because Beatty gave one of his last stellar performances at the Detroit Shrine Circus in February of 1963.

Aging began to take some toll on the man who had long plied his unusual trade. Harriett had died of heart problems in 1950, and the circus as an institution seemed to be on the decline. In 1964, Clyde began losing energy and went to see a doctor who diagnosed his problem as cancer. After an operation, he tried to come back again in 1965, but the old strength was gone. He went to his west coast home in Ventura, California. He died a few weeks later on July 19, 1965, at the age of sixty-two. Among the mourners at his funeral were his co-stars and friends from *Ring of Fear*, Patrick O'Brien and Mickey Spillane. He was survived by his third wife, Jane; their son, Clyde, Jr.; and a daughter, Joyce, by his first wife.

Although Brother Beatty's Masonic career lasted for only a little more than nine years, he exemplified the view of those in the order who stress that one should do their best in their chosen vocation. Clyde Raymond Beatty may have had an atypical occupation, but none can doubt that he was the best at what he did.

**Note**: A brief biography is Danny Fulks, "Bainbridge Ohio's Cat Man: Clyde Raymond Beatty" in *Timeline,* July-August 2002, pp. 2-20. One may also wish to consult Beatty's own books delineated in the text. For his Masonic records I am indebted to the staff at the Grand Lodge of Michigan as well as William R. Denslow, *10,000 Famous Freemasons, IV* (1961), p. 371. I also appreciate the assistance of Bro. David Price of Nashville who is the ultimate Clyde Beatty authority.

May 2003; revised 2011, 2012

**Brother Dave Thomas:**
*An Old-Fashioned, Modern Day Success*

The contemporary, conventional wisdom is that Horatio Alger type rags-to-riches success stories just don't happen anymore. According to historians, they did not happen very often in Alger's time either. However, "rags-to-riches" did become reality for a few in the 19th century and this continued through the 20th for a small number of folks. One of the best current examples of a poor boy who worked hard and gained wealth and fame is R. David Thomas of Wendy's Old Fashioned Hamburgers. He also became a familiar face to Americans via his appearances in the company's television commercials.

Thomas, who was adopted as an infant, experienced a difficult childhood, dropped out of school at sixteen, and became a millionaire before reaching forty. Born in Atlantic City, New Jersey, on July 2, 1932, Rex David Thomas took the name of the Michigan couple, Rex and Auleva Sinclair Thomas, who adopted him when he was six weeks old. Auleva died when Dave was five, so he was reared largely by Rex Thomas who lived the life of an itinerant construction worker. It could hardly be described as a happy or stable childhood. Some constancy derived from summers spent on the Michigan farm of his grandmother, Minnie Sinclair, who provided Dave with some sense of security and the virtues of hard work.

As the virtual poster person for adoption in recent years, Thomas conceded that while his own experience as an adoptee fell short of the ideal, he still believed it was much better than life in an orphanage. Since the Thomas family often struggled to make ends meet, the youth began holding part-time jobs from the age of twelve. He did everything from delivering groceries to being a soda fountain jerk and a restaurant busboy.

In 1947 the Thomas family moved to Fort Wayne, Indiana where Dave worked as a busboy in a Hobby House restaurant, quitting high school in his sophomore year to work there full time. It was later surmised that since David and Rex Thomas frequently ate in cheap eateries, the youth developed a fascination for food service and a desire to own his own place. Rex Thomas prepared to move again in 1949, but Dave chose to remain in Fort Wayne. When the Korean War broke out in 1950, young Thomas enlisted in the army where he went to cooking school at Fort Benning, Georgia. As a staff sergeant and cook at a military base in Germany, he supervised the feeding of some 2,000 soldiers and learned "important skills about the big picture of feeding a lot of people." Back in Fort Wayne as a civilian in 1953, Thomas went back to Hobby House as a $35.00 a week short-order cook.

On May 21, 1954, R. David Thomas married Lorraine Buskirk, another Hobby House worker. The couple subsequently had five children: Pam, Ken, Molly, Melinda (nicknamed Wendy), and Lori. David remained with Hobby House, becoming assistant manager at the Hobby Ranch House with Barbecue in the mid-fifties.

In 1959 Rex David Thomas joined Sol D. Bayliss Lodge No. 359 in Fort Wayne. He received his Entered Apprentice degree on April 13, 1959; was passed to the degree of Fellow Craft a week later on April 20, 1959; and was raised a Master Mason on May 25, 1959. Two years later in mid-November 1961, Thomas took the Scottish Rite degrees in the Valley of Fort Wayne. At that time his occupation was listed as "Vice-President, Hobby House."

The following year, Dave Thomas received his "opportunity." In Alger novels, the rags-to-riches hero always found true success because he capitalized on his opportunity when it came. Phil Clauss, his boss and mentor at Hobby House, had acquired four failing Kentucky Fried Chicken franchises in Columbus, Ohio. If Thomas could turn these restaurants around—with business sense—Clauss would transfer 45% of the ownership to him. Dave accepted the challenge, moved to Columbus, and succeeded, making a strong, positive impression on Colonel (and Brother) Harland Sanders in the process.

After expanding the business, in 1968, Thomas sold his shares of ownership in the K.F.C. franchises back to the parent corporation for more than a million dollars. He then joined Kentucky Fried Chicken in a management position but soon resigned after a disagreement with new owner, John Y. Brown. No doubt another reason for Thomas' departure from the fried chicken business was his plans to launch his own company.

Dave's idea was to open a hamburger business that would be sufficiently different from other competitors by using fresh ground beef (cut in squares) instead of frozen meat. He named Wendy's Old Fashioned Hamburgers for his then eight-year-old daughter. The first Wendy's restaurant opened on East Broad Street in Columbus, Ohio, on November 15, 1969. According to an article in the *Columbus Dispatch,* Brother Thomas did not initially intend to start a major chain, but he planned only two or three restaurants in Columbus that would enable him and his family to live in relative comfort.

However, as sometimes happens, success builds upon success, and in 1972 a Wendy's opened in Marion, Ohio, and in 1973, Indianapolis became the site of the first out-of-state franchise. After that, Wendy's grew by leaps and bounds, and in a 100-month period, 1,000 new restaurants opened for business. By 1984 the phrase "Where's the beef?" had become so famous from TV commercials that Walter Mondale adopted it as a slogan in his 1984 primary campaign for the presidency. It worked better in his quest for the nomination than in the fall 1984 contest in which he suffered a record electoral defeat. By the end of the 20th century, there were some 5,600 Wendy's outlets worldwide, many of them in foreign countries.

In 1982 R. David Thomas resigned as CEO at Wendy's to assume a less active role as senior chairman. Initially this move seemed successful, but when business began to slump later in the decade, a new CEO, James Near, accepted the job in 1989 only on the condition that Thomas resume a "guiding role" in the firm. His appearances in the corporation's television commercials seem to have been especially effective in creating a positive image for Wendy's, and they have also made the name and face of Dave Thomas among the most recognizable on the American scene.

Meanwhile, the congenial business executive became a Noble of Aladdin Shrine Temple of Columbus, Ohio, on September 21, 1990. When Thomas moved to Fort Lauderdale, Florida, he moved his Scottish Rite membership to Miami on December 18, 1991. Soon after, he received in succession the KCCH on November 13, 1993, the 33° on November 25, 1995, and the Grand Cross on October 3, 1997. Since 1995, he had a dual membership in both Miami and Ft. Wayne.

Brother Thomas also distinguished himself in the field of philanthropy. In 1992 he started the Dave Thomas Foundation for Adoption "to help raise awareness about these [orphaned] children, to educate the public about the benefits of adoption, to make adoption more affordable by helping the public and private sectors initiate innovative programs, and to cut the red tape from the process." He urged other corporate officials to start adoption programs and crusaded for Congress to enact tax credit laws for adoptive parents. Outside his foundation efforts, Thomas served on the boards of St. Jude's Hospital in Memphis and Children's Hospital in Columbus. As a high school dropout, Thomas also expended considerable effort to urge youth to remain in school. Practicing what he preached, the senior executive obtained his GED from Coconut Creek High School in 1993 where his amazed classmates voted him most likely to succeed.

Dave Thomas also became an author of some note. He started with *Dave's Way: A New Approach to Old Fashioned Success* in 1991. Three years later, he came up with *Well Done: Dave's Secret Recipe for Everyday Success*. His last effort a "how-to" book, *Franchising for Dummies,* appeared late in the summer of 2000.

By the time of his death at age sixty-nine on January 8, 2002, Brother Dave Thomas could have looked back over a life of triumph over numerous challenges. As a dedicated Mason for more than forty years, he was never backward about expressing his thoughts on the fraternity: "I'm proud to be a Mason. I believe Freemasonry is the cornerstone of America today. It brings good people together for a common cause—helping others."

**Note**: The best sources of information on R. David Thomas are his aforementioned books. For his Masonic record, I am indebted to Max Carpenter of the Grand Lodge of Indiana and Hans Sheridan of the Valley of Fort Wayne. Thanks also to the staff of Aladdin Shrine Temple in Columbus, Ohio.

May 2001; slightly revised 2011

**Brother Dean Elmer Hess**: *War Hero, Humanitarian and Sixty-year Mason*

In retrospect, looking back at the incidents which won Brother Dean Hess a degree of fame, one would almost have to conclude that it could happen only to an American. That a man trained to be a minister becomes a minister, has a popular motion picture made recounting his life story, and then retires from the Air Force to become a high school teacher sounds almost like fiction, yet for Colonel Hess, it has seemed like an almost natural progression and simple career. To top it all, Dean Hess has been a Mason for more than fifty years.

Dean Elmer Hess was born on December 6, 1917, in Marietta, Ohio. His father Lemuel Hess worked as an electrician and belonged to Harmar Lodge No. 390, serving that body as master in 1947, and he also was an Eminent Commander of Marietta Commandery No. 50. An older brother, George Hess, recently deceased, served as Master of American Union Lodge No. 1 the same years his father was Master of Harmar Lodge, and he held membership in the Marietta York Rite Bodies. The Hess family also had another brother Tom and a sister Ethel. When Dean was almost ten, Brother Charles Lindbergh piloted the *Spirit of St. Louis* from New York to Paris and sparked the youngster with a lifetime interest in aviation.

The Hess Family all belonged to the Christian Church although only the children attended services regularly. Young Dean developed a strong interest in religion and was especially influenced by an affable young minister named Robert Updegraff. Dean began to take charge of the youth services in his own church and also began to serve as a guest youth minister in other area churches.

When Dean finished high school, he worked at a service station to earn money so he could attend Marietta College. Dean also met Mary Lorentz from the neighboring village of Lowell. Although he managed to save only $86 for education that summer, Hess entered Marietta College anyway. Continuing to work at the gas pumps to remain in school, Dean admitted that he often fell asleep from exhaustion. Nonetheless, he managed to graduate in June of 1941. Ordained as a minister in the Christian Church, Hess took a job at Republic Steel in Cleveland to pay off his college debts and support his preaching habit at three small rural churches. He was still doing this when the bombs fell at Pearl Harbor on December 7, 1941.

Dean Hess had taken some pilot training courses at an airfield near Parkersburg, West Virginia, during his college days at Marietta. Although he had earlier applied for a chaplain's commission, Hess made the decision soon after Pearl Harbor that he would enter the Army Air Force and train to become a combat pilot. He attended training schools at Maxwell Field and at Napier Field, both in Alabama. When he graduated from flight school in September 1942, his parents came down for the ceremony, and on the same day, he and Mary Lorentz were married.

Dean Hess remained at Napier Field in Dothan, Alabama, though 1943. He took his Entered Apprentice Degree on February 12, 1943, in Harmar Lodge No. 390 in Marietta (presumably on a visit back home). On October 22, 1943, Mary gave birth to the first of what would eventually be three Hess children.

Finally in 1944, Hess got his orders to go to Europe. Between October 1944 and May 1945, the young pilot flew 62 missions and rose to the rank of major. Although he expected to be transferred to the Pacific, the use of the atomic bombs brought the war to a quick end. Back in Marietta, Hess took his Fellowcraft Degree on December 3, 1945, and was raised to the sublime degree of Master Mason on January 7, 1946. A month later, the 28-year-old pilot received his military discharge.

Like many other World War II veterans, Dean Elmer Hess decided that he needed additional education and entered graduate school at Ohio University in Athens to study history. Although somewhat embarrassed by the publicity he received in the "Ohio Alumnus" magazine as the "flying fighting parson," Brother Hess labored diligently on his graduate program, finishing his M.A. thesis on labor reform in Great Britain. His work was under the direction of the late Doctor Carl Gustavson (also a former professor of this writer). Enrolling at Ohio State University, Hess hoped to earn a doctorate in history and ultimately teach in a seminary. However, with the "Cold

War" in full swing, he was recalled to active duty in the Air Force, being initially assigned to officer procurement.

In April 1950, Dean Hess received orders to go to Japan as an information officer. Two months later, the Korean War broke out, and again his life was changed. Transferred to Taegu Air Base, his first duty was to train South Korean pilots. Later, however, he flew some 250 combat missions. On September 27, 1950, Hess arrived at Yongdungpo Airfield near Seoul. There he began the other phase of his career and the one that provided him with his greatest humanitarian achievement.

Like all wars, the Korean conflict created thousands of orphans and displaced children. Hess and others began to spend their spare moments when not on duty, attempting to find food and shelter for these hapless waifs. When the North Korean-Chinese "volunteer" counteroffensive threatened the security of Seoul, Lieutenant Colonel Hess prevailed upon General Earle Partridge, commanding officer of the $5^{th}$ Air Force, who furnished some fifteen C-54 airplanes. Organizing an airlift known as Operation Kiddy Car, they evacuated hundreds of children from the metropolitan area of Seoul to Cheju Island where the South Korean government provided an abandoned agricultural school to house the orphans.

Some believe that Brother Hess' humanitarian instincts had been shaped by his accidental bombing of an elementary school in Germany during World War II. Perhaps this is the case, but one cannot help but think that he had strong convictions in this area anyway. After all, not only did he possess strong Christian values, but he had additional teachings in the area of "Brotherly Love, Relief, and Truth!"

Operation Kiddy Car turned out to be only the beginning of Brother Hess' efforts on behalf of the Cheju Island orphans. While the island may have offered a degree of security from the ravages of war, the children still suffered from illness, wounds, injuries, and above all else starvation. Hess continued to expend all of his spare moments on behalf of the children, donating much of his own pay, soliciting funds from fellow soldiers, encouraging contributions from the United States, and prevailing upon the military establishment, the CARE program, and the South Korean government to do more. Finally, with the help of Madame Syngman Rhee, wife of the South Korean President, one of her old friends, a Buddhist lady by the name of Mrs. On Soon Whang, took charge of the orphanage.

Mrs. Whang had been trained in modern social work in England, and her own son had apparently been killed by the Communists in her absence. She was in her early fifties and "threw herself into the work with wholesouled intensity." According to Hess, she "reflected...strong, patient character, and great warmth."

Mrs. Whang had her work cut out for her. Two hundred of the children died in the first three months from inadequate food and medicine. Those who survived generally had little to eat but "rice soup" (rice and hot water). Water had to be carried from a mile away. Whooping cough proved fatal to many. Slowly but surely, conditions improved. Mary Hess, back in Marietta, collected funds, toys, clothing, and other supplies. So did the wives of other state-side soldiers. When Hess returned to the U.S., he continued efforts on behalf of the Cheju Island orphanage. In his first year, the Colonel raised $10,000 through speaking engagements and other appearances. He also organized a nonprofit corporation, Hope, Incorporated, to assist war orphans. Most significant, Brother Hess wrote his autobiography *Battle Hymn* (1956) which called attention to the problem. Universal-International bought the movie rights and war correspondent, Quentin Reynolds, authored a widely read article: "The Battle Hymn of Dean Hess" in the February 1957 issue of *Reader's Digest.*

The Reynolds' article and the motion picture version of *Battle Hymn* probably did more than anything else to publicize the efforts of Colonel Hess and the needs of the Cheju Island orphanage. Rock Hudson, then at the zenith of his popularity as a leading man, portrayed Hess with Martha Hyer as the dedicated wife. Anna Kashfi as Mrs. Whang was much younger than the real person she portrayed and contrary to the movie, she did not die in an air raid. The film was well received and for a time made the name of Dean Hess a household word.

Colonel Hess remained in the Air Force. After retirement in 1969, he taught high school for five years. In 1975 he returned to Cheju Island and also visited the Korean Air Force Academy which he had helped found. Now in his 94th year, Brother Hess and his wife Mary live quietly in the Dayton suburb of Huber Heights, Ohio, near Wright-Patterson Air Force Base and the Air Force Museum.

In an article in the *Journal American Aviation Historical Society*, Hess said, "I do have regrets for the necessity of war; remorse that I, representing mankind, do not have an alternative; and compassion for all who suffer the onslaught of war—including the enemy. What would happen to our Christian principles in the hands of an aggressor that has no sensitivity toward the sanctity of life? Perhaps there will be a better day; until then we will not have the absolute choice of right or wrong. We can only pray for the wisdom to distinguish and choose the lesser of two evils."

On October 27, 1995, Hess received his fifty-year pin from Harmar Lodge and the Grand Lodge of Ohio. The late Sir Knight Richard Dennis, a former Grand Commander, and Sir Knight Earl Gifford, Grand Secretary of the Grand Chapter of Ohio, both members of Harmar Lodge, had fond memories of Brother Hess and his family in Marietta. Sir Knight Gifford recalled that Mary Hess' ill health kept Brother Hess away from Marietta at the time of the presentation.

Marietta has a historic past and in the 20th century had produced its share of local heroes including two Masonic Ohio governors (George White and C. William O'Neill, both of American Union Lodge). None have stood taller in achievement than the well-decorated and awarded Brother Dean Elmer Hess, Col. USAF retired, minister, humanitarian, and sixty-year Mason.

While duty on faraway fronts may have prevented his regular participation in the affairs of Harmar Lodge, his actions in both war and peacetime exemplified the highest ideals of the fraternity. In his autobiography, Brother Hess did not discuss his Masonic connections except that he closed it with the familiar phrase with which this essay will also close, "So mote it be."

**Note**: The major source of information on Brother Hess is his autobiography, *Battle Hymn* Rev. Ed. (1987), supplemented by the 1957 entry in *Current Biography* and an April 1947 article in *The Ohio Alumnus*. For his Masonic Record, I am indebted to Grand Secretary of the Grand Lodge of Ohio, David Dresser, and to Harmar Lodge members Richard Dennis, Earl Gifford, H. Lee Hadley, and Andrew Young and indirectly to Brother George Hess. For the use of the photographs, I owe a debt of thanks to Clark St. John of the Buckeye Aviation Book Company, Box 974, Reynoldsburg, Ohio 43068.

March 2001; slightly revised 2011

**Sir Knight Earl Warren:** *From Golden State Grand Master to Governor and Chief Justice*

In the middle decades of the twentieth century, no well-known American Mason was more celebrated than Harry S. Truman who rose from haberdasher to Missouri Grand Master, Senator, Vice President, and ultimately President. Not far behind Brother Truman in terms of impact was Sir Knight Earl Warren who also served as a Grand Master, state Attorney General, Governor, and Chief Justice of the U. S. Supreme Court. Both men came from modest origins, joined lodges before they were thirty, and joined the military during World War I, but in other respects—except that both men ran for Vice President—their careers took different paths. Assuming that the Truman story is better known, this article examines the life and career of Sir Knight Warren.

Earl Warren was born in Los Angeles on March 19, 1891, the son of Scandinavian immigrants. His father labored for the Southern Pacific Railroad and had once lost his job through participation in labor disputes. The S.P. came under frequent criticism from political reformers for its corporate and near monopolistic power. Although the young Warren later worked as a "call boy" for that company, he became a critic of that firm and tied his early political wagon to that of Progressive-Republican Sir Knight Hiram Johnson (see article in *Knight Templar,* October 2004). At home, Earl's parents who had moved to Bakersfield, taught him the values of temperance, hard work, self-sacrifice, and education.

Earl Warren left Bakersfield in 1908 to attend the University of California at Berkeley. Upon receiving his B. A. in 1912, he entered law school from which he graduated in 1914. While in law school, the student exhibited a maverick streak by working part-time for a legal firm in violation of rules and by refusing to speak in class. Warren argued that passing the exams was sufficient. Earl passed the tests but found "lawyering" to be a disappointment, so when the U. S. entered World War I, he joined the army and rose to the rank of first lieutenant by the time of his discharge on December 18, 1918.

Following a short visit with his family, the young veteran went to Oakland where he took a $7.00 a day job as a court clerk. Over the next few months, he took his blue lodge degrees in Sequoyah Lodge No. 349. Raised to the sublime degree of Master Mason on November 1, 1919, Warren joined the Scottish Rite in Oakland that same December. He held offices in Sequoyah Lodge from 1922 and served as Master in 1928. As a Noble of Aahmes Shrine Temple in Oakland, he served as Potentate in 1933. However, his most notable fraternal service came later.

When Brother Warren first became a Mason, he worked as a deputy city attorney for the city of Oakland and the following year became a deputy Alameda County attorney. While in this position, he courted and married in 1925 a young widow, Nina Palmquist Meyers, who had a son. The Warrens subsequently had five additional children. After the Alameda County Attorney resigned, Earl Warren received the appointment to fill out his term and in the fall of 1926 won election to the first of three full four-year terms to the office.

During his twelve years as a prosecutor, Brother Warren earned a reputation for fighting crime and corruption second to none in the entire country. Hard work, honesty, and encouragement of scientific law enforcement became his by-words. Critics might have added ruthlessness to those words as well. His successful prosecutions included that of Alameda County Sheriff, several deputies, prostitution rings, gambling, and other activities associated with organized crime. Warren also pushed hard for better training of police officers and more scientific study of evidence. The prosecutor came down relentlessly on labor radicals, a recurring issue in California, dating from the early years of the century. Such was Brother Earl's acclaim that according to a biographical sketch by scholar Paul Finkelman, "by the mid-1930s, Warren was probably the best-known district attorney in the United States with a reputation that far exceeded the prestige or power of his office." Concurrently, across the continent in the same decade another young prosecutor, Brother Thomas Dewey (of Kane Lodge No. 454 in NYC), was also making a name for himself as a crime fighter. Later they would become presidential-nominee rivals and in 1948, running mates.

Meanwhile, Earl Warren's Masonic career continued unabated. Between 1928 and 1933, he served on a variety of Grand Lodge committees. Elected Senior Grand Warden in 1933, he moved up to Deputy Grand Master in 1934 and thence to Grand Master in 1935. During his term in office, membership in the Grand Lodge numbered about 128,000. As Grand Master, he endeavored to visit smaller lodges in more remote parts of the state and also in Hawaii which was under the jurisdiction of California at the time. He reported warm welcomes wherever he went. He took a strong position against gambling within lodges which may have been his most remembered stand. Taking note of the rise of totalitarian governments abroad in Italy, Germany, Russia, and Japan as part of his annual message, Warren noted prophetically: "They rarely call these autocracies by the same name but . . . they are the same thing in that they are the opposite of free government and human liberty becomes dead. When free government dies, Masonry dies with it, and in all of these countries today, their lodge rooms are dark, their property has been confiscated, our brethren are persecuted for their beliefs, and all men are denied the freedom of speech, of assemblage, of the press, and of religion—these rights, which to Americans . . . are the very essence of life itself. In all of these countries we now find war or frantic preparations for war . . . and as such to plant the heel of ruthless government upon the chests of their weaker neighbors. . . . Let us love it and cherish [our freedom] as we do few other things and let us pledge . . . Masonry to its principles as strongly as did our brethren who did so much to bring it [the USA] into being."

With his term as Grand Master drawing to a close, Warren continued to be an active Mason. At some point, he joined Oakland Chapter No. 36, Royal Arch Masons; Oakland Commandery No. 11, Knights Templar; and St. Phillip Conclave No. 23, Red Cross of Constantine. In 1938 he served as Master of Rose Croix and in 1945 after he had become governor of the Golden State as presiding officer of the Lodge of Perfection. By that time, he had already been coroneted with the 33° AASR (SJ) on December 23, 1941.

Meanwhile in 1938, Brother Warren sought and won election as California Attorney General. Under the unique California system of cross-filing, he actually won in the Republican, Democratic, and Progressive primaries. With such strength, he won a roughly 4 to 1 victory in the fall election over a hapless opponent named Karl Kegley. As the state's chief law officer, he continued to vigorously combat organized crime, political corruption, and vice activity. Warren also opposed alien ideologies of both left and right. After the attack on Pearl Harbor, he strongly favored the federal internment of Japanese-Americans. In later years, after his retirement, Warren conceded that this action had been "regrettable."

In 1942, Brother Earl Warren challenged incumbent Democrat Governor Culbert Olson of whom he had been a frequent critic. The candidate won the GOP primary easily and even took nearly 45% of the Democratic vote, making him a comfortable winner (57%) in November. He went on to be elected governor three times, serving over ten years in the office. As the Golden State's chief executive, Brother Warren generally followed a moderate path in the style of his early idol, Hiram Johnson. In retrospect, some of his moderation seems odd. For instance, during the "McCarthy era," he opposed loyalty oaths for University of California professors, but favored them for other state employees, signing such a bill into law.

Following Warren's overwhelming victory for a second term, presidential rumors soon followed for the popular governor of the second largest state. Losing out to New York's Tom Dewey, he accepted the second spot on the ticket. In a spirited four-way contest in which all the presidential candidates were Masons (as well as two of the Vice Presidential nominees), the Republican early lead faded, but the GOP made their best showing since 1928, garnering 189 electoral votes in losing to Truman and taking back such states as New York and Pennsylvania that had been in the FDR camp.

In 1950, Brother Warren easily won a third term and again had presidential ideas but like the other GOP hopefuls had little chance against Dwight D. Eisenhower. The retired general won an easy victory and promised Warren "the first vacancy on the Supreme Court." When Chief Justice Fred M. Vinson of Apperson Lodge No. 195 in Louisa, Kentucky died on September 8, 1953, the President chose Warren within days as an interim appointment. He then won Senate confirmation on March 1, 1954.

Earl Warren came to the court at a crucial time. The case of "Brown v. Board of Education of Topeka" concerning racially segregated schools had come up for consideration. In a decision that still stirs emotions in some circles, Sir Knight Warren managed to steer a potentially divided Court into making a unanimous decision. At the same time, the Chief Justice realized that it would take some time to be fully implemented. As a result, "all deliberate speed" could sometimes be what seemed rather slow. In many parts of the Deep South, nearly two decades elapsed before school integration became a reality.

The era of what became known as "the Warren Court" (1953-1969) were years of rapid social and economic change in American society. The "Brown" case turned out to be the first of many decisions that carried more than a spark of controversy. Several of these involved providing increased protection for the rights of the accused. For instance "Mapp v. Ohio" (1961) threw out evidence obtained without a warrant, "Gideon v. Wainwright" (1963) required courts to appoint defense attorneys for accused felons who could not afford lawyers, and "Miranda v. Arizona" (1966) forced police to inform persons being arrested of their rights. In the words of historian George B. Tindall, such decisions upset numerous "middle class Americans who resented . . . the federal government's excessive protection of the 'undeserving.'" During the sixties, the ultraconservative John Birch Society began placing numerous "Impeach Earl Warren" billboards across the fruited plain.

Other decisions also led to sweeping changes in society. "Engel v. Vitale" *(1962)* banned state-sanctioned school prayer. "Loving v. Virginia" (1967) struck down a law that forbid inter-racial marriages. "Griswold v. Connecticut" (1965) struck down state laws that banned use of birth control devices or pills that created precedent for several later cases based on "a right to privacy." In "Baker v. Carr" (1962) and "Reynolds v. Sims" (1964), the Court first declared that state legislative districts not based strictly on population were unconstitutional and in the second mandated the "one man one vote principle." Sir Knight Warren himself considered "Baker v. Carr" his most significant case.

With advancing age, Brother Warren chose to retire from the Supreme Court in June 1969. After leaving the Court he lectured, gave public speeches, and wrote his memoirs. He passed to "the celestial lodge above" on July 9, 1974. His widow lived a full century, dying in 1993.

In retrospect, Sir Knight Earl Warren's judicial legacy, while increasingly accepted as part of the American mainstream, remains controversial in many circles. Few would argue that he ranks second only to Brother John Marshall as the most important Chief Justice. Ironically, as Governor he was seen as a uniter, but as what many called "the Super Chief," he was a divider. However, in many respects it seems ironic that a man who in his personal life exemplified the old fashioned American virtues did so much—for better or worse—to alter and change them.

**Note**: Those who wish further examination of Sir Knight Earl Warren and his life may want to consult his own *The Memoirs of Earl Warren* (1977); G. Edward White, Earl Warren: *A Public Life* (1982); and Lucas A. Powe, Jr., *The Warren Court and American Politics* (2000). For his Masonic records I am indebted to Bro. Adam Kendall of the Henry Wilson Coil Library and Museum of Freemasonry at the Grand Lodge of California in San Francisco, a 2003 article in *The California Freemason* and William R. Denslow, *10,000 Famous Freemasons* (1961), Vol. IV, pp. 297-298.

February 2010; slightly revised 2011

**Brother Edd Roush:**
*The Pride of Redland Field*

Not many major league baseball players could say that they hit .320 or better for ten straight years. One of those who accomplished that feat was Edd Roush of the Cincinnati Reds. An Indiana farm boy whose career spanned some eighteen years in the big time and who made it into Baseball's Hall of Fame in 1962, Roush was also a Mason for seventy-one years. The teams he played on at the time also had several members of the fraternity.

Edd J. Roush was a lifelong resident of Oakland City, Indiana, where he was born on May 8, 1893. The Roushs were originally Palatinate Germans who migrated to America in 1735 where many of the second generation settled on both sides of the Ohio Valley counties of Meigs and Gallia in Ohio and Mason and Jackson in [West] Virginia. Others scattered farther down the river, including southern Indiana. Edd and his twin brother Fred were the only children of William C. Roush who had been a pretty good semi-pro baseballer himself, dating back to the 1880s. However, by the time the sons came along, William Roush owned and operated a dairy farm just outside of Oakland City. Edd and Fred learned to play baseball while taking breaks from their farm labors when "the horse got hot" and needed a rest.

Local towns in much of Middle America had baseball teams. About 1909 when one of the players for the hometown Oakland City Walk-Overs failed to appear, Edd got his chance to play, got two hits, and became a regular. After a dispute in 1911, he left the hometown team and played for Princeton, twelve miles distant. Midway through 1912, still another move led to his becoming a full-fledged professional when he signed with the minor league team of Evansville. Playing in forty-one games, the teenager batted .284. A natural lefthander, he had earlier learned to throw with either hand. When he went professional, he finally got a left-handed glove.

Edd Roush began the 1913 season with Evansville, but sporting a .317 batting average, the Chicago White Sox purchased his contract, and he made his major league debut on August 20, 1913. After getting only one hit in the American League, the Sox sent him to Lincoln, Nebraska for the balance of the season. Roush began looking for greener pastures.

He found them in the newly organized Federal League whose promoters claimed major league status. Even though major league executives threatened to ban players who joined the new outfit, Edd Roush signed a contract at $225 monthly with Indianapolis. This team ended up winning a close pennant race, primarily on the strength of a super season by Benny Kauff who led the league in batting average, runs, hits, doubles, and stolen bases. Roush played in only seventy-four games, but hit a respectable .333. However, the team lost money, peddled Kauff to the Brooklyn Feds, and shifted the franchise to Newark, New Jersey. This gave Edd a chance to play regularly, and he hit a respectable .298. The Federal League folded after only two seasons, but some of the best players, including Kauff, Roush, and Newark player-manager, Bill McKechnie, all went to the New York Giants. Baseball historians have considered Roush to have been the best young player to come out of the Federal League.

Edd Roush clearly was unhappy as a Giant, partly because of his dislike of New York, and even more by his antipathy for John McGraw and his managerial style. As a result, he was delighted when Bill McKechnie (of Orient Lodge No 590 in Wilkinsburg, Pennsylvania), Christy Mathewson (of Architect Lodge No. 519 in New York City), and he were traded to Cincinnati on July 20, 1916. Mathewson was a fading star and wanted a chance to manage. He was surprised to find out that McGraw had told Matty that he should put Roush in the Reds outfield regularly. The Hoosier responded by batting .289 for the remainder of the season.

That winter, Edd Roush became a Mason, joining Oakland City Lodge No. 467. He was initiated an Entered Apprentice on February 9, 1917; passed to the degree of Fellowcraft on February 20; and raised a Master Mason on March 1, 1917. He would remain a member of this lodge for the rest of his life, a total of seventy-one years, and be a seasonally active one for the remainder of his playing days. Having married Essie May Swallow back in April of 1914, the Roushs also became parents that year as their only daughter Mary

Evelyn was born in August of 1917.

That same year would also inaugurate Roush's "golden decade" on the playing field as he led the National League in batting with a .341 average, living up to McGraw's expectations. With their new manager, the once lowly Reds experienced their first winning season since 1909. In 1918, they rose to third place—with Roush batting .333—in a season cut short by World War I. There were a couple of dark spots. Matty had problems with Hal Chase, later termed "baseball's biggest crook," and accused "Prince Hal" of throwing games, and Matty himself entered military service in August leaving third baseman Heinie Groh to finish out the season. Matty incurred health problems that subsequently shortened his life. Still the Reds had hopes for 1919.

With club owner August "Garry" Herrmann unable to make contact with his manager in the winter of 1918-1919, he hired former Phillies manager Pat Moran in his place. The Reds, largely with the team that Mathewson had put together, won both the National League championship and the World Series. Roush again led the league with a .321 average. It has been pointed out that a high proportion of this team already was or would become Masons. Brother Edd Roush anchored the outfield, flanked by Greasy Neale on one side (of Mt. Olivet Lodge No. 3 in Parkersburg, West Virginia) and Rube Bressler (of Kilwining Lodge No. 356 in Cincinnati) on the other. Pat Duncan (of Trowel Lodge No. 132 in Jackson, Ohio) came up to help out in the last month of the season. The infield had Jake Daubert (of Reliance Lodge No. 776 in Brooklyn, New York) at first; Larry Kopf (of Centennial Lodge No. 118 in New Britain, Connecticut) at shortstop; and Heinie Groh (of E. T. Carson Lodge No. 598 in Cincinnati) at third. Ivy Wingo (of Norcross Lodge No. 228 in Georgia) split the catching chores, and one of the starting pitchers was Ray Fisher (of Union Lodge No. 2 in Middlebury, Vermont). While going all the way to the World Championship, their victory would always be somewhat tainted by the Black Sox scandal. Roush contended that the Reds would have won anyway and some baseball historians have concurred, although of course the truth can never be known.

Edd Roush continued to play good ball all through the early twenties. The Reds won no more pennants, although they managed to stay competitive in every season except 1921 when they fell to sixth place. The Hoosier center fielder gained a reputation for his individualism. He hated spring training and found ways to avoid it, usually by not signing his contract until the start of the season. Edd argued that he stayed in shape by hunting in the off-season. Some of his holdouts were more serious. Once he missed the first three weeks of the season and in 1922 held out until July 23, playing in only forty-six games that year, and in 1930, back with the Giants, he held out the entire year.

Manager Pat Moran died before the 1924 season, and the Reds hired Jack Hendricks to replace him. Roush considered his new boss a novice at baseball knowledge who also showed favoritism to the Catholics on the squad. Finally they had words (as Roush recalled in an interview with baseball historian Eugene Murdock): "The backbone of this ballclub are [sic] all Masons and you don't hear anybody say a . . . word about the Masons do you? We don't brag about it."

Roush had a point. At that time, those who already were or soon would be Masons included pitching aces Eppa Rixey (Kilwinning No. 356 in Cincinnati), Carl Mays (Canyon City No. 34 in Oregon), reliever Jake May (Wendell No. 565 in North Carolina), catcher "Bubbles" Hargrave (Trinne No. 190 in St. Paul, Minnesota), infielders Sammy Bohne (Lincoln No. 470 in San Francisco) and Hugh Critz (Greenwood No. 135 in Mississippi), and outfielder Curt Walker (Beeville No. 261 in Texas). After that, conditions improved although Roush still never cared much for Hendricks. So it was no surprise that when his three-year contract expired after the 1926 season, he was traded back to the New York Giants. Although unhappy, he blamed neither club President Garry Herrmann ("he was all right, he was a Shriner") nor his son-in-law Sid Weil.

As Giant property, Edd Roush wasn't sure he could play for John McGraw, but they finally agreed on a three-year contract at $70,000. The Little Napoleon had mellowed somewhat and left him alone, and Roush gave him two good years hitting .304 in 1927 and .324 in 1929. Plagued with injuries in 1928, he missed most of the season and hit only .252. Despite his good season in 1929, Charles Stoneham wanted to cut his salary (by either $7,500 or $10,000 depending on the sources), and Edd became a whole season holdout. He pretty much intended to retire, but finally agreed to play one more season for the Reds who had nearly hit bottom. Sid Weil had gotten control of the club and thought Roush could help the club by boosting morale and attendance. After the Giants gave him a release, he came back to Redland Field for a final season, patrolling the outfield with two other Masonic ballplayers, Estel Crabtree (Philodorian No. 157

in Nelsonville, Ohio) and Taylor Douthitt (Yerba Buena No. 403 in Oakland, California). Nothing helped much. Reds attendance continued to decline, and they finished in the cellar for the first time since 1914. Edd Roush went back to Oakland City and stayed retired.

Cincinnati baseball fortunes continued to decline until Sid Weil lost control of the club after the 1933 season. Larry McPhail (Cumberland Lodge No. 8 in Nashville) came in as General Manager, local magnate Powel Crosley (College Hill No. 641 in Cincinnati) bought the club to keep them in the Queen City, and a slow rebuilding process began. The revitalization picked up steam when Brother Bill McKechnie, who had first come to Cincinnati in the trade that brought Roush to the Reds, came in as manager in 1938. He brought Hank Gowdy (York No. 563 in Columbus) with him from Boston as coach and persuaded Roush to come back as the other coach. Edd retired again after that one year, but the rejuvenated Reds first climbed to fourth place and then had two championship seasons.

Meanwhile back in Oakland City, Edd Roush and Essie enjoyed their retirement and lived comfortably. Edd, who had never been a lavish spender, invested his earnings from his hard-fought contracted salaries in such stocks as General Motors and Proctor and Gamble. They became involved in a variety of civic and local affairs from their comfortable home on Main Street. Ironically, Roush, who had never liked spring training, spent more and more of his retirement time in Florida during the cold season and was in fact in Bradenton when he died on March 21, 1988. In the meantime, honors came to the retired star. He entered the Reds Hall of Fame in 1960, the Baseball Hall of Fame in Cooperstown in 1962, and was selected for the All-Time Reds All-Star team in 1969. The memory of his achievements in Redland Field may have faded somewhat by the rise of "The Big Red Machine" of the mid-seventies, but that could not totally erase the man remembered as the team's greatest player in the first half of the twentieth century.

***Note:*** The best biographical data on Edd Roush comes from the chapter on him in Lawrence S. Ritter, *The Glory of Their Times* (Vintage Books, 1985), pp. 218-230, and Eugene Murdock, *Baseball Between the Wars* (Meckler Pub., 1992), pp. 115-154. For photos and Masonic records, I am indebted to S. K. Peter Westbere of Guelph, Ontario. Thanks also to S. K. Norman Lincoln of Eaton, Ohio who alerted me to the large number of Cincinnati Reds Masons in this era.

August 2005; slightly revised 2011

**Eddy Arnold:**
*"The Tennessee Plowboy," Superb Singer, and Sixty-Year Mason*

When Joel Whitburn compiled his authoritative reference work, *Top Country Singles, 1944-2005* (2006), one vocalist had far outpaced all of his near rivals for solo hits. In a period extending over some fifty years and spanning some six separate decades, Eddy Arnold chalked up 146 charted hits in *Billboard* magazine, some thirty of which also ranked in the top one hundred pop listings as well. Viewed from almost any vantage point, the career of the man once known as "The Tennessee Plowboy" was remarkable.

As his nickname suggests, Arnold came from honorable yet humble origins. Born Richard Edward Arnold in Chester County, Tennessee, on May 15, 1918, the youth lost his father at eleven. In the next few months, the surviving members of the family lost their farm and saw their possessions auctioned to pay creditors. The Arnolds endured the Great Depression as sharecroppers on their former land, and Eddy came by his subtitle honestly. Yearning for a better way of life, the youngster learned to sing and play guitar, hoping it would provide him with a means of advancement.

Success as an entertainer did not come easily or quickly, however. In 1935, Eddy and a fiddler friend named Howard "Speedy" McNatt started a radio program at WTJS in Jackson, Tennessee. By evenings they played in clubs, often for no more than fifty cents or a dollar per night. The pair soon moved to radio spots in larger locales such as Memphis and St. Louis, but financial prosperity still eluded them. Arnold finally got a chance to move modestly up the ladder of success when Pee Wee King and his manager J. L. Frank hired Eddy as a vocalist with their established country and western band, the Golden West Cowboys, based at WSM radio in Nashville, where they were featured on the popular jamboree, the *Grand Ole Opry*.

The coming of World War II brought a revival of the economy that had skipped America in the 1930s, and the popularity of country music also soared since common folk could again afford to buy more records and tickets to shows. In the meantime, Eddy met a soda fountain clerk named Sally Gayhart in Louisville, and they married in November 1941 (subsequently parenting two children). Some two years later, the Tennessee Plowboy asked for and received his own show at WSM, and a little later his own spot on the *Opry*.

It was in this period that Arnold followed his friends Pee Wee King and Roy Acuff into Masonry. He was raised in East Nashville Lodge No. 560 on March 21, 1944, exactly a month after Acuff. Later that spring, in May and June, the threesome took the Scottish Rite and Shrine together, all in Nashville.

In the meantime, Eddy's solo career took off with a bang. He soon rivaled Acuff as the *Opry*'s most popular star, and he signed with RCA Victor Records. However, he had to wait until the first Petrillo ban against the recording industry had ended to schedule his first session in December of 1944. Arnold's initial release on Bluebird was a tear-jerker titled "Mommy, Please Stay Home with Me" backed with a war theme, "Mother's Prayer." A somewhat later release "Each Minute Seems a Million Years" marked his first entry on the *Billboard* charts in June of 1945. Unlike the mountain-styled vocals of Roy Acuff or the honky-tonk approach of Ernest Tubb, Eddy Arnold started a penchant for country crooners that would in many respects during the coming years help to narrow the gap between what had once been derisively termed "hillbilly" and pre-rock and roll popular music. Arnold's hits like "I'll Hold You in My Heart," "Bouquet of Roses," "Anytime," and "Just a Little Lovin' Will Go a Long Way," collectively, spent well over a year at the number one position. From November 1, 1947, through November 13, 1948, Arnold's songs exclusively topped the country charts.

The Tennessee Plowboy left the *Grand Ole Opry* in 1948 to pursue other entertainment ventures. He made two films for Columbia, *Feudin' Rhythm* in 1949 and *Hoedown* in 1950. Like Roy Acuff's movies, these pictures were light on plot and heavy on songs, but country fans liked them. Eddy also did network radio programs, and in the early fifties he moved into brief flurries on network television as a summer replacement for Perry Como on CBS for two months in 1952 and for four months on NBC in 1954. In 1956, he had a more elaborate program on ABC that ran from April to November for thirty minutes in prime time.

Meanwhile, Arnold continued to roll out the hit records on RCA Victor. Between the end of 1948 and the end of 1955, he had fourteen more number one hits of which "Cattle Call" may have been the most memorable. Certainly, it is the one most identified with him. His original version of the song had been done for Bluebird at his very first 1944 session. Another thirty-four of Eddy's songs made the top ten through 1956.

The decade from 1956 provided something of a downturn in the Arnold career while many entertainers would call a similar period for them a peak. The musical revolution associated with the rise of rock and roll made a heavy impact on the entertainment world in those years, although in retrospect it is clear that Brother Arnold weathered this era quite well. For instance, he had hit records in every year except for 1958 and 1960, placing some seventeen more numbers on the charts. The most memorable of them were probably his interpretations of the Rex Griffin ballad composition "Just Call Me Lonesome" and Jimmie Driftwood's saga of a remarkable horse, "The Tennessee Stud."

The mid-sixties witnessed a strong revival of Eddy Arnold's popularity. In the spring of 1965, he had his first number one hit in nearly a decade with "What's He Doing in My World," which also placed on the pop charts. That fall, "Make the World Go Away" also went to the top and to number six in pop. Five more songs went to number one in the next three years. Eddy's concerts in these years reflected his new prestige as he filled large municipal auditoriums in major cities and appeared on many prime-time TV network variety shows. Often he was backed by an orchestra that provided more of a popular music sound which continued to broaden the appeal of country music. Among the honors heaped upon the one-time Tennessee Plowboy were election to the Country Music Hall of Fame in 1966 (the fourth living member to be inducted and also the fourth Mason after Jimmie Rodgers, Roy Acuff, and Tex Ritter) and the Country Music Association's Entertainer of the Year in 1967. According to those close to Arnold, it was his achievements from the late sixties in which he took the most pride.

Although Brother Arnold had no more number one hits after 1968, his songs continued to appear regularly on the charts for another fifteen years. He left RCA Victor in 1973 and signed with M.G.M., but after three years, he returned to his old firm. In 1980, he scored a pair of top ten songs with "Let's Get It While the Gettin's Good" and "That's What I Get for Loving You." His last appearance on the

*Billboard* Charts with RCA came in 1983 with a modest effort called "The Blues Don't Care Who's Got 'Em." By that time, according to one report, Arnold had sold some seventy-five million records, ranking him second only to Elvis Presley among Victor artists.

In later years, Eddy Arnold pretty much—although not totally—retired from his long musical career. He did a tour of several cities in the fall of 1993, including Wheeling, West Virginia, where this writer witnessed a sell-out concert to an appreciative audience that demonstrated that he still had the touch. At that time, RCA released a two compact disc set entitled "Last of the Love Song Singers," which was also how he was billed on the tour (apparently "Tennessee Plowboy" by then sounded too countrified). One of the discs labeled "now" contained newly recorded material, while the other simply called "then" sampled a few of his hits from past years. This, however, did not constitute his musical swan song. That came in 1999 when he made a duet with contemporary star, LeAnn Rimes, which consisted of a new release of his old favorite "Cattle Call" which peaked at number eighteen on the charts, thus providing the octogenarian vocalist with hits in six different decades

In addition to his membership in East Nashville Lodge, and the Shrine, Brother Arnold joined the Nashville Scottish Rite in November of 1944. He was invested with the KCCH in October of 1983, he received his 50 year pin in 1994, and was coroneted a 33rd Degree in October of 1997. The Scottish Rite class in April of 2011 in Nashville was named in his honor. Given the accomplishments that Eddy Arnold achieved in his lifetime as a giant in the world of entertainment, Masons everywhere could take pride in the honors bestowed upon him. A modest man himself, Eddy once commented to a biographer that his private life was rather ordinary. He said, "I'm just an average human being that can sing." Brother Arnold was a week short of his ninetieth birthday when he passed away on May 8, 2008.

**Note**: For those wishing to learn more about Eddy Arnold, he wrote an autobiography that is long out of print titled *It's a Long Way from Chester County* (Hewitt House, 1969). After this article first appeared, two good biographies came out in 1997: Don Cusic, *Eddy Arnold: I'll Hold You in My Heart* (Rutledge Hill Press) and Michael Streissguth, *Eddy Arnold: Pioneer of the Nashville Sound* (Schirmer Books). His Masonic data was obtained through Sir Knight Ray Huffines who served in the mid-nineties as Secretary of East Nashville Lodge and Nashville Lodge and Editor John Palmer.

August 1995; slightly revised 2011

## Brother Elliot Richardson: *Quadruple Cabinet Member*

Over more than two centuries, numerous Masons from Henry Knox and Edmund Randolph to Dan Glickman and Tommy Thompson have sat in presidential cabinets. In fact, every administration through 2008 has had at least one Mason in the cabinet. Only one person, however, has held four cabinet posts. That person was Brother Elliot Richardson of Joseph Webb Lodge in Boston. During the decade of the 1970s, he—at one time or another—headed the departments of Commerce, Defense, Justice, and Health, Education and Welfare.

Elliot Lee Richardson was born in Boston, Massachusetts, on July 20, 1920. His father was a well-known physician and professor at Harvard Medical School. The Richardsons were established in the Boston area as attorneys, bankers, and doctors. Elliot—it was said—decided to enter politics at an early age. He graduated cum laude from Harvard in 1941, but after a brief sojourn at the Harvard Law School, he entered military service where he soon became a lieutenant in the Fourth Infantry Division. As a soldier, the young Harvard alumnus compiled an enviable record, participating in the D-Day Landing at Normandy, earning a Bronze Star and two Purple Hearts.

After the war, Elliot returned to the Law School where he served a stint as editor of the *Harvard Law Review*. After receiving his law degree (cum laude, again) in 1947, Richardson clerked for the noted Judge Learned Hand in 1947-1948 and then for even more noted Supreme Court Justice, Felix Frankfurter, in 1948-1949. Frankfurter thought Richardson so talented that four years later he suggested Richardson for the presidency of Harvard.

In 1949 Elliot Richardson took a position with a Boston law firm and remained there until 1953 when joined the staff of

Massachusetts' Republican U.S. Senator and Sir Knight, Leverett Saltonstall (St. Bernard Commandery in Boston). After a year in this job, he returned to the Boston law firm of Ropes, Gray, Best, Collidge, and Rugg, but in 1957 he came back to Washington when President Dwight D. Eisenhower appointed him Assistant Secretary of Health, Education and Welfare for Legislation. During the two years Richardson held this position, he did the yeoman's work of writing the National Defense Education Act that the administration designed as a reaction to the Russian launching of Sputnik to upgrade the quality of American secondary education. (I was a beneficiary of this act as a participant in a 1968 graduate summer program at the University of Dayton.) Between April and July 1958 he served as acting head of the Department following the departure of Marion B. Folsom. In 1959 Richardson returned to Massachusetts as U.S. Attorney. There he secured the conviction of textile manufacturer, Bernard Goldfine, whose gifts to former New Hampshire Governor and White House Chief of Staff, Sir Knight Sherman Adams, had embarrassed the Eisenhower Administration.

With the advent of the Kennedy Administration, Elliot Richardson resumed private life and his old law firm now known as Ropes and Gray. In 1962 he sought the office of Massachusetts Attorney General but sustained a primary loss to Edward Brooke, another rising star on the GOP political horizon. Two years later his luck improved as he was elected Lieutenant Governor. With the cooperation of Governor John Volpe, he also took an active role as coordinator of Massachusetts' education, health and welfare programs, heading a task force that helped with passage of the Mental Health Act.

With Edward Brooke successfully running for the U.S. Senate and Republicans enjoying a good year in 1966, Richardson followed his earlier victory by winning the state attorney general post. As the state's chief law enforcement officer, he concentrated on developing consumer protection and crime prevention legislation. He took the lead in prosecuting consumer fraud and unfair trade practices in the courts.

Elliot Richardson joined Joseph Webb Lodge in Boston, being initiated an Entered Apprentice on April 3, 1968. He was subsequently passed to Fellowcraft on May 2, and raised a Master Mason on June 5, 1968. Eleven years later he completed Scottish Rite degrees on December 8, 1979. He received the 33° on September 30, 1981.

The election of Richard Nixon as President in November of 1968 brought Richardson back to Washington, initially as Under Secretary of State. Former Attorney General William P. Rogers, the newly appointed head of the State Department, had been much impressed with Elliot's work in the Eisenhower Administration and wanted him as his "alter ego." Although he had virtually no experience in foreign policy, Richardson soon demonstrated himself to be an active participant in major international conferences in Paris, Helsinki, and Brussels. Ironically both Richardson and Rogers found themselves overshadowed by National Security Advisor, Henry Kissinger. Nonetheless, the two established a close working relationship, and many hailed the Under Secretary's efforts to introduce administrative reforms into the unwieldy foreign affairs bureaucracy.

In June of 1970, President Nixon appointed Elliot Richardson to be Secretary of Health, Education, and Welfare, replacing Robert H. Finch. As a former assistant in that department in the Eisenhower Administration, Richardson seemed like the ideal person to take over an agency torn by dissension, disorder, inefficiency, and demoralization. He managed to reorganize a department that had grown to become one of the largest government agencies by reducing bureaucratic red tape and restoring morale and order. In keeping with the administration's "New Federalism," he made the Family Assistance Plan the centerpiece of departmental policy. Unfortunately, the F.A.P. as it became known won approval in the House but stalled in the Senate. In later years many observers labeled it one of the best plans the administration developed and analysts lamented its failure to become law.

With Nixon winning a second term in 1972, some shuffling went on in the cabinet, and in early January of 1973, the President named Richardson as Secretary of Defense, replacing the retiring Brother Melvin Laird (the other Mason in the Nixon cabinet). As events concerning the Watergate Scandal unfolded, Nixon decided that Richardson was needed more in the Justice Department. The President secured the resignation of Attorney General Richard Kleindienst and asked the Massachusetts lawyer to replace him. Brother Richardson was asked to take the post in part because the mainstream media viewed him as the epitome of the Eastern Establishment Liberal Republican and had more confidence in him than in someone viewed as a Nixon political crony. The new Attorney General, for his part, insisted that the President had received a strong mandate in November of 1972, should show that he had nothing to hide from special prosecutor Archibald Cox, and should cooperate fully with him.

Elliot Richardson's career as head of the Justice Department came to a quick end on October 20, 1973, when the President asked him to remove Cox. Richardson, having made the commitment at his Senate confirmation hearing that he would not interfere with Cox in any way, chose to resign instead. This promulgated what has become known as the "Saturday Night Massacre" which resulted in the firing of both Assistant Attorney General William Ruckelshaus and Prosecutor Cox. It accelerated the downfall of the Nixon presidency, culminating in the President's resignation in August of 1974. Nixon biographer, Stephen Ambrose, pointed out that Nixon was legally correct in dismissing Cox who had overstepped his bounds, but that it was politically unwise. Actually Richardson was perhaps the only one to come out of the incident with honor unscathed.

After Nixon's presidency came to an end, President and Brother Gerald Ford called Elliot Richardson back into government service. Ford appointed him Ambassador to the United Kingdom, serving from March of 1975 until January of 1976 and then Secretary of Commerce from January of 1976 until January of 1977. When Ford and Richardson left office in January of 1977, the latter had become and remains the only man in American history to have held four cabinet posts.

Richardson also served in the Carter Administration as head of the U.S. delegation to the third U.N. Conference on the Law of the Sea. Ironically, he held this relatively low profile government post longer than any of the other cabinet posts in which he had served. Thereafter, his government service was confined to such short-term positions as observer to elections in Nicaragua, as representative of the President at the Multilateral Assistance Initiative in the Philippines, and as a member of a U.N. humanitarian mission to Iraq following the Gulf War in 1991. In 1984, he sought public office again seeking a U.S. Senate seat from Massachusetts but failed to survive the primary.

In between, Richardson worked in the Washington office of a New York law firm and wrote books such as *The Creative Balance* (1976) and *Reflections of a Radical Moderate* (1996). In private life, Elliot Richardson had married Ann Hazard in 1952, a Radcliffe College graduate. They became the parents of three children: Henry, Nancy, and Michael. Brother Richardson, a Unitarian, passed to the celestial lodge above on December 31, 1999, leaving behind a unique achievement as the only person to have held four cabinet posts. Although some might disagree with his unbounded capacity for "radical moderation," none could deny that he served his nation with administrative efficiency, honor, and integrity.

**Note**: The best sources of ready information on Elliot Richardson are his 1971 sketch in *Current Biography* and his own aforementioned books. For his Masonic records, I am indebted to the staff at the Grand Lodge of Massachusetts and the Valley of Boston, AASR, NMJ.

October 2002; slightly revised 2011

## **Brother Eppa Rixey:** *Hall of Fame Southpaw Pitcher*

The winningest left-handed pitcher in National League baseball history is Warren Spahn who toiled for many years for the Boston and Milwaukee Braves prior to ending his career with the New York Mets. In the American League, Sir Knight "Gettysburg" Eddie Plank who spent most of his playing days with Connie Mack's old Philadelphia Athletics holds the honor. Both Spahn and Plank won more than three hundred games. In between these two individuals, another southpaw hurler chalked up enough wins to make the Hall of Fame while often taking the mound with second division clubs. Until the advent of Spahn, Eppa Rixey held the National League record for victories by lefthanders. This is his story.

Eppa Rixey was also the first Virginia native to earn Hall of Fame honors. Born in Culpepper on May 3, 1891, Eppa Rixey, Jr. was the son of a local banker. The Rixey family had originally come from Italy where their name had been spelled "Riccia." By the time of Eppa's birth, it had long been Anglicized. The fourth child in a family of six, Eppa moved with his parents to Charlottesville when he was ten. After completing high school, he entered the University of Virginia from whence he was graduated in 1912 with a major in chemistry. Growing to the impressive height of six feet five inches, the lanky lefty became the mainstay of the Cavalier's baseball pitching staff and also proved to be a standout in the then relatively new sport of basketball. Charles Rigler, a major league umpire who worked as a coach at Virginia, thought Rixey had a promising career in the majors and arranged for a contract for the young lefty with the Philadelphia Phillies. The whole incident led to a ban on umpires scouting for professional teams, but it launched Eppa's career although neither he nor Rigler ever received the promised $2000 cash bonus for signing. Rixey had initially not wanted a baseball career, preferring to pursue work as a chemist, but fearing an economic downturn and wanting to help his brother with college expenses, he journeyed to the City of Brotherly Love.

Eppa Rixey became one of the first baseball players to go directly from the college campus to the majors. He made his major league debut on June 21, 1912, and pitching for a fifth place team in his rookie year, had a respectable if unspectacular 10-10 record with a 2.50 earned run average. In the off seasons, the young pitcher completed a master's degree in chemistry back in Charlottesville. One winter he taught Latin at Episcopal High School in Washington, D. C. Atypically well educated for a major league ballplayer, he proved to be something of a "Renaissance man" who enjoyed writing poetry in his spare moments.

In his second year with the Phils, Rixey had a 9-5 record, but his third year proved to be a disaster, going 2-11 while his ERA climbed to 4.37. However, 1915 showed improvement for both Eppa (2.39 ERA) and the Phils, who took their first ever pennant. Scholars of the game credit his comeback to new team manager Patrick Moran who had a reputation as a skillful handler of young pitchers. Still the Virginia lefty had a losing record (11-12), and his performance lagged behind that of Phillie ace Grover Cleveland Alexander (31-10, 1.22 ERA), Erskine Mayer (21-15), and Al Demaree (14-11). In the World Series, Rixey relieved Mayer in the third inning of the fifth game and took the loss, giving up an uncharacteristic two home runs in the eighth inning. Doing better at the plate, he actually went one for two. Sadly, this was his only opportunity to play in the Fall Classic.

Under Moran's tutelage, Eppa came onto his own in 1916 with a 22-10 season and a 1.85 ERA. The team actually won more games that year than in 1915 but lost out to Brooklyn in the pennant race. Rixey propelled his team into first place by winning the first game of a doubleheader over the Brooklyn Robins on September 30, but Alex lost the second game, and that was as close as Philadelphia got. The Phils fell back into the second division in 1917, and Eppa led the league in losses with 21, despite a good earned-run average. The following year saw Rixey in military service with the Chemical Warfare Division. This unit—in retrospect—seems to have been a haven for Masonic ball players including Ty Cobb, Christy Mathewson, and Branch Rickey, although Rixey was not yet a member of the Craft. Back with the Phillies, Eppa seemed to have lost his touch, experiencing two consecutive poor seasons with a team that sank into the league cellar both times. It has been reported that the tall Virginian did not hit it off well with Manager Gavvy Cravath. In fact, after eight seasons in Philadelphia, Rixey had an 86-103 won-lost record, not exactly what could be considered Hall of Fame material. As a result, he was happy to be traded to Cincinnati on January 22, 1921, where he could again be guided by Pat Moran.

Eppa Rixey not only found his niche in the Queen City, but it became his home for the rest of his life. Over the next five years, the tall southpaw blossomed into one of the league's premier hurlers winning one hundred games over the next five years including three twenty-win seasons, and never less than fifteen. Only once did his ERA go over 3.00, and that was in 1922, the year that he experienced a career high twenty-five wins. Perhaps his keenest achievement—in 1921—was allowing only one home run in 301 innings pitched. Known as something of a playboy during his early years in town, he soon settled down and as Jan Finkel, who wrote an authoritative sketch on him, said, "enriched his community."

Perhaps his settling down was related to his petitioning Kilwinning Lodge No. 356 in 1922 when he received his Entered Apprentice degree on August 30, 1922. His other two degrees took place that winter as he was passed a Fellowcraft on December 27, 1922, and raised a Master Mason on January 31, 1923. Fellow lodge members included his long-time roommate Raymond "Rube" Bressler and Ex-President, Chief Justice William Howard Taft. He remained a member of Kilwinning Lodge for twenty-five years. Another factor in Rixey's change was his October 29, 1924, marriage to Dorothy Meyers in suburban Terrace Park's St. Thomas Church. The Rixeys subsequently had two children, Eppa III and Ann. In the off season, Eppa worked for his father-in-law's insurance business of which he ultimately became the owner. In more recent years, this has been operated by Eppa Rixey IV as the Eppa Rixey Insurance Agency.

As a pitcher, Rixey was apparently a master at fooling hitters. His roomie Bressler later related to baseball historian Lawrence Ritter that Rixey had once told him that when he was behind on hitters, they invariably expected him to throw a fastball, but that he never did. Rixey, it was said, struck out few batters and walked even fewer. Known as a mild-mannered gentleman most of the time, he could really get angry at himself when he made costly mistakes on the mound and would take it out afterwards on the furniture in the clubhouse. He took the good-natured and not so good-natured kidding from team mates and rival players about his Southern background with grace. Nicknamed "Jeptha" by sportswriters because it rhymed with Eppa, he learned to accept it, but never really liked it.

Following the death of his favorite manager Pat Moran in March of 1924, Rixey had an off-year that season, going only 15-14 but bounced back to win 21 in 1925. Although his best days were behind, he still managed to turn in credible pitching for the rest of the decade, although as the Reds fell into the second division, his effectiveness also declined. In 1930, he went 9-13 and had a 5.10 ERA, the worst of his career. With the Reds mired in the league cellar in his last three years, Eppa became a spot starter and accumulated fifteen wins and the same number of losses. He closed with 266 wins and 251, losses often playing for mediocre and weak teams in the second division that scored few runs. A better examination of Rixey's quality pitching might be his career ERA of 3.15 which compares favorably with contemporary Hall of Fame hurlers as Jess Haines, Ted Lyons, Herb Pennock, and Red Ruffing, all of whom had better won-lost percentages.

After his 6-3 record in 1933, Eppa Rixey hung up his glove and spikes, announcing his retirement just prior to spring training on February 16, 1934. Concentrating on the family insurance business, he prospered and eventually passed it on to his descendants. Some years after his retirement, he visited the Hall of Fame in Cooperstown and humorously wrote postcards back to Cincinnati saying "I finally made it!" When Warren Spahn broke his record on September 26, 1959, for the most wins by a National League lefthander, Eppa told the press that he was glad his record had been broken because people had forgotten that he had earlier set it. That recollection may have got him into the Reds Hall of Fame that same year. He still holds the post-1900 record for the most wins by a Cincinnati pitcher with 179. Four years later on January 27, 1963, he was selected for the bigger Hall of Fame in upstate New York. With characteristic modesty, he told reporters, "They're really scraping the bottom of the barrel, aren't they?" Sadly, he suffered a fatal heart attack a month and a day later on February 28, before his induction. He was buried in Greenlawn Cemetery in suburban Milford, Ohio. The bad news for Eppa Rixey, as John B. Holway and Bob Carroll stated in the second edition of *Total Baseball* (1991), was "he seldom pitched for teams that were likely to make him a household name at World Series time." The good news for the tall Virginia gentleman was that he made it into the Baseball Hall of Fame anyway.

**Note:** The principal sources for the life of Eppa Rixey are the sketch by Jan Finkel on the SABR website and the uncredited sketch on BaseballLibrary.com, plus various histories of the Cincinnati Reds. His baseball records are in *Total Baseball* (1991); Masonic Records were furnished by George O. Braatz, Grand Secretary of the Grand Lodge of Ohio. The portrait came from my University of Rio Grande colleague, Prof. Samuel Wilson.

May 2008; slightly revised 2011

**Sir Knight Ernest King**: *World War II Fleet Admiral*

The Second World War provided America with some of its finest hours both as a nation and as a people. Freemasons in this same era also provided Americans with some of their most notable leaders including Presidents Roosevelt and Truman; Army commanders typified by Generals Arnold, Bradley, MacArthur, and Marshall; and the subject of this sketch, Fleet Admiral Ernest Joseph King. Described by military historian Mark M. Boatner III as "brilliant" and "irascible," Brother and Sir Knight King served as Chief of Naval Operations throughout most of the conflict.

Ernest King was born in Lorain, Ohio on November 23, 1878, the son of an Irish immigrant, James Clydesdale King, who had migrated to America prior to the Civil War, and Elizabeth Keam King. A grandfather on his mother's side had been a sawyer in the Royal Navy dockyard at Plymouth, England which may have prompted young Ernest's interest in a naval career. In addition, an article in the *Youth's Companion,* the leading juvenile magazine of the day, also stimulated his interest in the sea. According to one story, inspired by an old sailor who lived nearby, he almost ran away and went to sea at the age of seven.

In September of 1897 at eighteen and having recently graduated from Lorain High School, King entered the U.S. Naval Academy at Annapolis as a cadet. According to one story, his railway mechanic father furnished him with a return pass on which to get back home if he changed his mind, but the ticket remained unused. When Congress declared war on Spain in April 1898, the teenage student saw temporary duty aboard the *U.S.S. San Francisco.* The war soon ended and young King returned to Annapolis and continued his studies, graduating on June 7, 1901 and ranking fourth in a class of sixty-seven.

Two years at sea followed on the *U.S.S. Eagle* after which Ernest King received his commission as an Ensign. During the Russo-Japanese War, the young officer served on the *U.S.S. Cincinnati*, a "protected Cruiser," observing the first major conflict of the new century. Promoted to Lieutenant on June 7, 1906, King served a two-year stint as an instructor at the Naval Academy. Meanwhile back on October 10, 1905, he had married Martha Egerton of Baltimore, Maryland, in West Point, New York. In their fifty-year marriage, the Kings reared six children, five of them girls.

After a third year at Annapolis as a member of the academy's Executive Staff, King returned to sea duty for three years beginning with a year as an Aide on the *U.S.S. Minnesota.* Promoted to Lieutenant Commander on July 1, 1913, the rising officer received his first command post on April 30, 1914, on the *U.S.S. Terry.* The *"Terry"* was involved in the occupation of the Mexican port city of Vera Cruz and led to the future Admiral's becoming a recipient of the Mexican Service Medal. This assignment proved to be brief, because in less than three months, he became commander of the destroyer *U.S.S. Cassin.* In 1916 he joined the staff of Admiral Henry T. Mayo, a member of Burlington Lodge No.100 in Vermont, who became Admiral of the Atlantic Fleet during World War I. Promoted twice during the conflict, King became a Commander in July of 1917 and a Captain in September of 1918. According to historian Boatner, this experience of working closely with the Navy's top Admiral provided King "valuable insight into the problems of high command within an alliance and taught him leadership principles he would use thereafter, how to decentralize authority and develop initiative among subordinates while maintaining strong control at the top."

After the war, Captain King returned to Annapolis until mid-1921 when he took control of a refrigerator ship, the *U.S.S. Bridge,* for some fifteen months. Since German submarines had provided the Allies with some of their biggest challenges in the World War, it was hardly surprising that the naval establishment manifested considerable interest in this field of operations. Captain King was no exception, and after a lesser assignment dealing with U-boats, he became commanding officer of the Submarine Base at New London, Connecticut. A pair of disasters took place in the later twenties both of which inspired topical ballads that enhanced King's reputation for efficiency. The first occurred when the *S-51* sank off Block Island on September 25, 1925, with a loss of forty lives. The Captain received the Distinguished Service Medal for directing salvage. On December 17, 1927, another tragedy struck with the sinking of the *S-4* near Provincetown, Massachusetts with thirty-seven fatalities. Although King had been elsewhere by that time, he was again placed in charge of the salvage operation and succeeded in raising the ship, winning a Gold Star for his efforts.

In mid-1926 King's assignment had changed when he became commander of the *U.S.S. Wright*, what was then termed an "aircraft tender" (later known as an aircraft carrier). At forty-eight, he began rigorous rounds of flight training at Pensacola, Florida and became a pilot in May of 1927, afterward returning to the "*Wright.*" However, he was soon appointed Commander of the Naval Air Station at Norfolk, Virginia. Then it was back to sea for more than two years at the helm of the *U.S.S. Lexington*.

In April of 1933, Ernest King was promoted to Rear Admiral and also became chief of the U.S. Navy Bureau of Aeronautics. During his three years in this position, the Admiral advocated shifting of emphasis from battleship reliance toward aircraft carriers. Also during those years, Ernest Joseph King became a Mason. A petitioner to George C. Whiting Lodge in the District of Columbia, the Admiral received his degrees on June 25, July 25, and September 12, 1935. Known as a "stickler for form" in the Navy, King seems to have been much more relaxed in lodge meetings which he attended frequently. According to one source, in the lodge he was content simply to be "one of the boys," and many of his Brothers never realized that he was a high-ranking Navy officer. This attitude continued when he was transferred to California and promoted to Vice Admiral and where he took the Capitular degrees in Darius Chapter No. 143 in San Diego on June 17, July 8, and August 26, 1938. The following year on July 12 and July 19, 1939, Admiral King received the Chivalric Orders in Holyrood Commandery No. 32 in Berea, Ohio (suburban Cleveland), near his hometown of Lorain. World War II interrupted further Masonic activity, but after the conflict in 1946, he became a Noble of Al Koran Shrine Temple in Cleveland.

Back in Washington, D.C., King was appointed to full Admiral and named Commander-in-Chief of the Atlantic Fleet on February 1, 1941. In August, the Admiral accompanied President Roosevelt to the Atlantic Charter Conference. Then Pearl Harbor happened, followed by public and congressional clamoring for scapegoats. Admiral Harold Stark was "out" and Admiral Ernest King was "in"—Commander-in-Chief or as it was termed "COMINCH." In March, Sir Knight King also held the title, Chief of Naval Operations. As with the Atlantic Charter Conference, King participated in many of the major strategy sessions including Casablanca, Cairo, and Yalta.

As a top leader in the "greatest generation" who also faced great challenges, Admiral King did his part to win the victory. Yet he did not do so without controversy. King's gruff exterior alienated many of his contemporaries, and British officers considered him, rightly or wrongly, an "Anglophobe." One critic remarked that he was "the most even tempered person in the . . . Navy . . . angry 100% of the time." Even FDR, with whom the Admiral generally enjoyed good relations, allegedly described King as "a man who shaves with a blow torch." King himself was reported to have said at the beginning of American entry that "when the shooting starts, they call for the (expletive) of the (expletive)." Others complained that King was overly obsessed with the prestige associated with his high rank. Somewhat concerned about his bald head, he was always photographed wearing a cap, yet he was congenial with civilians, especially ladies, and is described as an excellent dancer. He also manifested kindness and patience toward children.

Generally speaking, King aroused British ire by advocating that more Allied resources be allocated to the Pacific Theater. Conditions often led him to alter his positions, circumstances not unusual in challenging military conflicts. King did enjoy a harmonious relationship with Secretary of the Navy, Brother Frank Knox (of Bethel Lodge No 358 in Michigan). In the final analysis, one must conclude that nothing succeeds like success, and in this category King came out a big winner.

On December 17, 1944, Ernest King became the second American to hold the rank of Fleet Admiral (the first was William Leahy, with Chester Nimitz third, and finally William Halsey in November 1945). The war moved toward Allied victory in September 1945. The harmonious relationship with Navy Secretary Knox ended with Knox's death in April of 1944, and King feuded with his successor, James Forrestal. King had the satisfaction of seeing Nimitz named as his replacement by President Truman over Forrestal's objection.

In retirement, Ernest King resided in Washington, D.C. He did serve as an advisor to the Defense Department after Forrestal was no longer involved. He also wrote and published his memoirs, *Fleet Admiral King*, in 1952. Eventually his health began to fail, and he spent his last days in the Naval Hospital at Portsmouth, New Hampshire. He died there on June 26, 1956, and was buried in Annapolis. In addition to a Navy funeral, George C. Whiting Lodge No. 22 held Masonic services. Martha King lived on until 1969. Of their children, three of the daughters—often referred to as "the King boys"—married army officers, and only one married a naval officer. Ernest King, Jr. followed his father to Annapolis and a Navy career.

**Note:** The most complete life story of Sir Knight King is Thomas B. Buell, *Master of Sea Power: A Biography of Fleet Admiral Ernest J. King* (1995). A shorter sketch is found in *Current Biography* (1942) which is, of course, incomplete. Useful sketches of King and many of his contemporaries are in Mark M. Boatner III's, *The Biographical Dictionary of World War II* (1996). On King as a Mason is Brother R. A. Lord's, *Ernest Joseph King Fleet Admiral* at www.masonicworld.com. A shorter version can be found in William R. Denslow, *10,000 Famous Freemasons, III* (1959). The photograph is from the US Naval Historical Center website.

January 2008, slightly revised 2011

## Brother Ernest Shackleton:
*Antarctic Explorer and Survivor*

In past generations, Americans and Europeans generally held polar explorers in high esteem. Those who endured great hardship won wide acclaim for their achievements, sometimes giving their lives in the process of their quest for fame. Among those who devoted their energies to such endeavors were a number of Masons, both American and British, including Nathaniel Palmer, Elisha Kent Kane, Robert Peary, Robert Falcon Scott, Admiral Richard E. Byrd, and the subject of this sketch, Sir Ernest Shackleton. While he discovered neither the North nor the South Pole, his exploits in the Antarctic rank as some of the major accomplishments of the age, particularly his 1914-1916 expedition where his name and character became virtually synonymous with the ship, *Endurance,* that bore him and his men to the far south.

Ernest Henry Shackleton was born at Kildea in County Kildare, Ireland, on February 15, 1874, to a farmer-physician father whose ancestors hailed originally from Yorkshire, England and an Irish mother. In 1884, the Shackletons moved to suburban London. In 1887, young Ernest became a student at Dulwich College. He seems to have been somewhat indifferent to academics, and his teachers held him up as an example only after he became famous. Shackleton dropped out of school in 1890 and joined the Merchant Navy, making his first voyage from Liverpool to Valparaiso, Chile aboard the *Hoghton Tower.* He made other journeys in the next few years, becoming certified as a First Mate in 1896 and as a Master two years later. Somewhat later, he gained a commission as a Lieutenant in the Royal Naval Reserve. During this time, he served on two voyages that transported soldiers and supplies to Cape Town in the Boer War. That 1890 trip around Cape Horn always stuck in his mind and whetted his sense of adventure. He later told a journalist that "I felt strangely drawn to the mysterious south."

Ernest Shackleton's pathway to international fame and "the mysterious south" began when he joined the *Discovery* expedition organized by the Royal Geographical Society and led by Robert Falcon Scott, a navy officer and member of Drury Lane Lodge 2127 in London. In fact, prior to the group's departure, Shackleton took his Entered Apprentice degree on July 9, 1901, in Navy Lodge No. 2612, also in London. Several years would pass before he took additional Masonic work.

Antarctic expeditions were a dangerous business. A legend concerning the *Discovery* voyage is that a 1901 recruiting advertisement in the *Times of London* read, "Men wanted for hazardous journey. Small wages. Bitter cold. Long months of winter. Constant danger. Safe return doubtful. Honour and recognition in case of success." The trip of 1901-1902 fulfilled many of these promises although most members survived. While Scott, Shackleton, and a Dr. Edward Wilson journeyed overland to a new record of 82° 17'S latitude on December 31, 1902, they were still four hundred sixty-three nautical miles from the South Pole. Ernest became seriously ill with scurvy, and Scott had him sent back home. Back in England, Shackleton married Emily Dorman on April 9, 1904. Emily had been a friend of Ernest's sister whom he had first met in 1897 after returning from a sea voyage to Japan. The marriage resulted in three children—Raymond, Edward, and Cecil—but was characterized by long separations in which Emily often had to support herself and the children. Hoping to return to the Antarctic, Shackleton worked for *Royal Magazine* as a journalist and secretary of the Royal Scottish Geographical Society. The following year, the thirty-one year old explorer made an unsuccessful attempt for political office, "standing" for a seat in the House of Commons from Dundee, Scotland. Soon after, he began to work at securing financial support for another trip to the "far South." Much of the monetary help Shackleton needed was provided by a Glasgow industrialist named William Beardmore. A grateful Shackleton subsequently named a newly-discovered mountain range and glacier after his chief benefactor.

This journey which commenced in August of 1907 became known to history as "the Nimrod Expedition" and provided Ernest Shackleton with the "honor and recognition" he had so desperately sought. New innovations used by these explorers included the use of an automobile and Manchurian ponies as beasts of burden, but they proved of limited value. The leader's three goals included the exploration of that portion of Antarctica known as King Edward VII Land, reaching the South Pole, and reaching the Magnetic South Pole. All of the objectives were accomplished except for that of reaching the South Pole. Since Shackleton divided them into three groups, the trio of Douglas Mawson, Edgeworth David, and A. F. Mackay reached the Magnetic Pole in January of 1909, enduring considerable hardship in the process. The exploratory group among other things ascended Mt. Erebus, the active volcano on Ross Island.

Shackleton's group included Frank Wild, Eric Marshall, and Jameson Adams. On their unsuccessful quest to reach the Pole, the foursome managed to cross the Trans-Antarctic Mountain Range and became the first humans to set foot on the South Polar Plateau. Stretched almost to the breaking point, they reached 88° 23'S latitude on January 9, 1909, a new record but still ninety-seven miles short of the Pole. Fearing death and disaster if they tried to go further, they wisely returned to their base. Returning to England, they were nonetheless treated like heroes for their valiant effort. Shackleton was knighted for his efforts and basked in the glory of having led a party farther south than anyone had ever gone. His book, *The Heart of the Antarctic,* won him further acclaim. Of his failure to reach his main goal, he is said to have philosophically remarked, "Better a live donkey than a dead lion." He received additional Masonic light, being passed a Fellowcraft on November 2, 1911, and raised a Master Mason on May 30, 1913, both in Guild of Freemen Lodge No. 3525. According to a very well-researched article by Leon Zeldis, Shackleton remained a member of both Guild of Freemen Lodge and Navy Lodge for the rest of his life.

During these years back in England, other polar explorers reached the long-sought destination of 90° S. The Norwegian Roald Amundson arrived late in 1911, followed five weeks later on January 18, 1912, by Shackleton's sometimes friend sometimes rival Bro. Robert Falcon Scott who unfortunately perished with his companions on the return back to his base. Ernest Shackleton now sought a new goal, crossing the southern continent from the Weddell Sea to the Ross Sea. Seeking new financial supporters, he found three in the persons of Sir James Caird, well-to-do jute manufacturing tycoon and Member of Parliament, Dudley Docker, and Stancomb Wills. All three had lifeboats named in their honor. The principal ship was the well-named

*Endurance.* By now Greenland sled dogs had been established as the most successful animal companions for Antarctic exploration, and English schoolchildren were said to have raised the money to buy and train them with participating schools getting a dog named for their school. A second ship, the *Aurora,* met Shackleton on the Ross Sea side of the continent. World War I was just starting in early August 1914 as the twenty-eight voyagers prepared to depart England, but Winston Churchill, first Lord of the Admiralty, told Shackleton to "proceed" as he had originally planned.

The *Endurance* reached the Weddell Sea in January of 1915 after an earlier two-day stop at the whaling station on the island of South Georgia. The weather in 1914 was exceptionally cold in the Antarctic, and by January 18, 1915, the ship was surrounded by ice floes and soon became trapped, frozen into an ice floe at 76° 34'S. Under normal conditions, they were only a one-day journey from their proposed land base at Vahsel Bay. For two hundred eighty-one days, this situation continued, although the ice floe shifted several hundred miles in the process. The men occupied themselves with a variety of work and activities, initially supplementing their food supply with seal and penguin, but then in September, conditions became worse. Temperatures became colder, the water beneath the ship began to freeze, and on October 23, crushed it "beyond all hope of ever being righted." But as Shackleton further noted in his journal, their supplies were saved and "we are alive and well, and we have stores and equipment for the task that lies before us." The task before them had now become survival. Against overwhelming odds, they succeeded.

The immediate goal of Shackleton and his men was to reach Paulet Island some three hundred forty-six miles away where they knew that a cache of supplies existed that had been left by a 1902 expedition (frozen food preservation did have some positives in Antarctic trips). They also had three lifeboats which they could drag across the ice and use them in the chilly waters whenever they had the opportunity. After considerable hardships and near brushes with death, the weary sojourners reached Elephant Island in the South Shetlands on April 12, 1916. They had made land on a barren island, but real safety still eluded them. Shackleton decided that he and five others would take the largest life boat, the *James Caird,* and attempt to reach the whaling station on South Georgia, an eight hundred mile journey.

Brother Frank Wild, the second in command and an Australian, remained behind with the others with instructions to move to Deception Island if Shackleton had not returned by a certain date. After seventeen days and surviving storms in an open boat, the *James Caird* made landing but some one hundred thirty miles by sea from the whaling station, so he and two others went over the rocky hillside of South Georgia to the station, and a rescue party soon went out and picked up the other three. Relieving those twenty-two men back on Elephant Island still remained a daunting task. Chartering a small whaler from South Georgia proved impossible as Elephant Island was now blocked by ice floes and the rescue ship could only get within seventy miles of the men. Shackleton then went to Port Stanley in the Falklands and appealed for help, but his only immediate offer for aid came from Uruguay who sent out a small fishing ship. It too was forced to turn back thirty miles from its destination. Journeying now to Punta Arenas, Chile, a third rescue effort via the *Emma* had to turn back when that ship was damaged by an iceberg. Finally, a fourth attempt to reach Elephant Island on a ship called the *Yelcho* under the command of a Chilean navy officer and Mason named Luis Pardo (of Aurora Lodge No. 6 in Valparaiso) managed to reach the island on August 30, 1916, and rescue the castaways who had survived their own share of hardships—including one pair of amputated toes—for one hundred five days on the island and were down to their last four days of food rations. Back in Punta Arenas, on September 4, the outside world that had heard nothing of the Shackleton Expedition since October of 1914 soon learned of their incredible but successful struggle in that all members of the party had survived.

Shackleton's new goal was to learn the fate of the *Aurora* and its crew that was to meet him on the Ross Sea side of Antarctica. However, first he, together with Brothers Luis Pardo, Frank Wild, and Dr. A. McIlroy (the ship surgeon and the other Mason on the expedition) were honored on September 30, 1916, at a special meeting of Lodge of Harmony No. 1411 under English charter in Valparaiso. Shackleton was escorted to the East and honored for his achievements. Some forty-four members and eighty-five visitors from other English-speaking and Chilean lodges attended this historic meeting. Brother Luis Pardo, the Chilean connection in the historic rescue, was promoted by the navy for his heroic efforts and eventually spent four years in Liverpool, England as a Consul, dying in 1935.

Leaving Chile for New Zealand, Ernest Shackleton learned in December of 1916 that many of the personnel from the *Aurora* expedition were stranded in the Ross Sea region. This group was not as lucky as those who had sailed on the *Endurance* as all of this party did not survive. Nonetheless, the intrepid leader did what he could, and to make a long story short, the survivors were on their way to Wellington by February of 1917. By May, Shackleton was back in England, and World War I continued to rage.

With his health increasingly shaky, the adventurous explorer still wanted to get into military action, but was instead sent on a diplomatic mission to South America in hopes of persuading Argentina and Chile to abandon neutrality and join the allies. This proved an utter failure. Shackleton then became involved in an effort to establish a British presence on the Island of Spitzbergen, a property of neutral Norway. His Masonic brothers from the *Endurance,* Frank Wild and Dr. McIlroy, were also in on the plan. In the Norwegian town of Tromso, Shackleton experienced what McIlroy assumed was a heart attack, but "the Boss" would not undress so his physician friend could examine him. Nonetheless, he had to return to London, and Wild took over the expedition. It was Shackleton's first trip north of the Arctic Circle. He soon returned in October of 1918, however, as part of a British force bound for Murmansk where he held the position of "Staff Officer in Charge of Arctic Equipment," a glorified term for storekeeper. Three weeks after his arrival in Murmansk the Great War ended, and the Allies were now in opposition to the Bolsheviks who were trying to solidify their control of Russia. In a letter home, Shackleton had some prophetic and astute comments about the evils of Bolshevism, but he was drinking heavily and his health continued to decline. By March of 1919, he was back in London and demobilized after five months of service. Although hoping for another polar expedition, the symbol of British endurance was now virtually broken financially and lecturing twice a day about the *Endurance* Expedition. His last book simply *titled South: The Story of Shackleton's Last Expedition* (1919) sold well, but he had signed over royalties to pay debts.

Despite his deteriorating health, Shackleton still planned a return to Antarctica. This time his goal was to circumnavigate the continent. A wealthy old friend from school days, John Q. Rowett, came forth with finances. Several veterans from earlier journeys joined him, and a ship renamed the *Quest* was outfitted for the journey. Leaving England on September 17, 1921, the ship was not a good one and had to be repaired en-route more than once. The leader was also frequently ill. The *Quest* reached South Georgia on January 4, 1922. Later that night the noted explorer, old before his time, had another heart attack and died in the early morning hours on the fifth. Comrades were transporting his remains back to England, but when his widow got the news, she asked that his body be returned to South Georgia. She wrote that "His spirit had no place in England . . . if he had a home on earth, it must be among the mystic crags and glaciers of the island in the Southern Ocean which had meant so much to him." Receiving the word at Montevideo, Uruguay, they returned him to South Georgia where he lies in the cemetery at the whaling station at Grytviken.

In his day, Shackleton was celebrated as one the great explorers of the age. Largely forgotten for a time, interest in his exploits revived a few years ago when documentary films about his adventures revived interest in the man. Although he never discovered the South Pole, he did contribute much knowledge of Antarctica through his expeditions. His cool leadership in the face of the adversity encountered during the *Endurance* episode revealed an extraordinary talent for "grace under pressure." Members of the fraternity worldwide can take pride in the determination and skill that Brother Ernest Shackleton exhibited during his lifetime.

**Note**: Books about Shackleton are numerous. The most detailed is Roland Huntford, *Shackleton* (1996) while Caroline Alexander, *The Endurance: Shackleton's Legendary Antarctic Expedition* (1998) is also quite good. His own accounts have been reprinted. Internet searchers can benefit from the biography at http://www.south-pole.com). Of particular interest to Masons is Leon Zeldis, *Sir Ernest Shackleton and Luis Pardo: Two Masons Joined by Fate and Heroism,* at the Freemasonry in Israel website. His Masonic record is also on the website of the Grand Lodge of British Columbia and the Yukon.

March 2008; slightly revised 2011

**Brother Everett M. Dirksen:** *Orator and Senator from the Heartland*

One of the pleasures of coming of age politically conservative in the late fifties and early sixties consisted of seeing and hearing Senate Minority leader Everett Dirksen with some frequency on news broadcasts. Known in some circles by such nicknames as "the Wizard of Ooze," the Illinois statesman spoke with a voice that seemed unique in mid-twentieth century politics. One newsman described him as having "tonsils marinated in honey." Whether one agreed or disagreed with his position, opinion remained virtually unanimous that Dirksen was an extraordinary orator. Through sixteen years in the U.S. House and nearly nineteen in the Senate, Brother Dirksen also was acclaimed a major statesman by the mid-sixties and since his death.

The Everett McKinley Dirksen story began with his birth on January 4, 1896, in Pekin, Illinois. His parents, Johann Frederick and Antje Conrady Dirksen, were German immigrants and loyal Republicans as can be illustrated by the names they gave their sons: Benjamin Harrison Dirksen, Thomas Reed Dirksen, and Everett McKinley Dirksen with the only question being, who was "Everett?" Johann Dirksen worked as a decorator for a buggy and carriage manufacturer until he suffered a stroke when Everett and twin brother Thomas were five. After that, Mrs. Dirksen kept the family together by gardening and raising livestock, selling for cash what the family themselves did not eat. The other brothers became high school dropouts, but Dirksen continued with his education, graduating in 1914. Next to his senior yearbook picture, the newly coined term "bigworditis" appeared. A high school friend once said he "must have swallowed a dictionary." In retrospect, both characterizations seemed prophetic.

Dirksen spent that summer working long hours in a corn refinery for $54.00 per month. He spent a few spare moments in an amateur theater group. When his mother suggested that Everett take a short vacation and visit an older half-brother in Minnesota, he did, and while there, the youth decided to attend the University of Minnesota. He worked at a variety of part-time jobs to help pay his way and had little time for extracurricular activity other than debate. In 1916 Dirksen did some work for GOP presidential candidate, Charles Evans Hughes, and a local congressional candidate, Brother Ernest Lundeen (of Minneapolis Lodge No. 19). He also met Brother William Jennings Bryan, a man whose oratory he admired, although not his politics. After the election, as the country moved in the direction of entering World War I, Dirksen joined the army on his 21st birthday, January 4, 1917. Sent first to Camp Custer, Michigan; second to Camp Jackson, South Carolina; and then to France, young Everett came home in October of 1919, uncertain as to what to do with the remainder of his life. After a few months of indecision, during which time he even temporarily occupied the pulpit in his local Reformed Church, he entered the bakery business with his brothers Ben and Thomas.

When not delivering bread, Everett Dirksen continued his interest in amateur theater and also wrote plays and short stories. He became quite active in the American Legion and became District Commander in 1926. In 1927 Everett married Louella Carver. Their only child, the late Danice Joy Dirksen, born in 1929, grew up to become the wife of Howard Baker, Jr., the one-time Tennessee Senator.

Everett McKinley Dirksen made his initial entry into politics in 1927 when he successfully sought a seat on the Pekin City Commission. As finance commissioner, he felt a degree of satisfaction, but he began to set his sights on higher office. In 1930 he challenged incumbent congressman Brother William E. Hull of Peoria (Temple Lodge No. 46) in the Republican primary. Although initially unsuccessful, he vowed to try again in 1932.

Meanwhile Dirksen joined Pekin Lodge No. 29, A.F. & A.M. Initiated an Entered Apprentice on March 3, 1931; passed to the degree of Fellowcraft on July 9, 1931; and Raised to the sublime degree of Master Mason on July 23, 1931, Dirksen gave his occupation as "baker" on his petition. That fall he took part of the Scottish Rite degrees in Peoria and completed them in 1932.

In the 1932 primary, Brother Dirksen again challenged Brother Hull, and this time the outcome was different as Everett won the narrow victory. Although Republicans found themselves on the defensive in 1932, Dirksen carried his six-county district by some 23,000 votes, about the same margin that Brother Franklin D. Roosevelt carried it in the presidential sweepstakes. As lawmakers struggled with the problems of the Great Depression and widely debated the merits of the New Deal, Dirksen displayed a degree of independence by supporting some of FDR's programs while opposing others. With the passing of time however, he increasingly identified with the New Deal critics, concerned with the mounting national debt and the growing concentration of power at the federal level. Still, he could display considerable independence at times. In foreign policy he began as an isolationist, opposing lend-lease in the spring of 1941, but he was gradually moving toward preparedness by that fall. Consistently re-elected, Dirksen served eight consecutive terms in the United States House.

By the midpoint of World War II, Dirksen had become a national figure within the GOP circles. In 1944 he enjoyed an unsuccessful presidential boomlet designed to make him a vice-presidential nominee in case John Bricker would not accept the second spot on the ticket, but Bricker did accept. With the GOP takeover of Congress in 1946, Dirksen gained a committee chairmanship and increased prestige. However, eye problems in 1947 and 1948 led him to announce his retirement from Congress and that he would not seek another term in 1948. He did campaign extensively for Dewey and Warren that fall although he became increasingly skeptical—and correctly so—about their chances of victory. Back in Illinois he rested his eyes, devoted himself to gardening (he became known as "Mr. Marigold"), and pondered a Senate race in 1950, if his health permitted it.

Illinois Republicans had taken it on the chin badly in 1948 with the election of Democrats Adlai Stevenson and Paul Douglas to respective statehouse and Senate seats. Hope for a GOP comeback centered on efforts to defeat Democrat incumbent, Scott Lucas, from his Senate chair. Brother Dirksen, sufficiently recovered, finally decided to run, knowing that he must walk a fine line to gain full support from both the conservative old-guard and the more moderate factions within party ranks. With the help of Louella and Joy, the Three Musketeers as he termed them, Everett jumped into the race in full force. The campaign was a hard fought one, but Brother Dirksen came out the winner. Although he never discussed his Masonic membership in his posthumously published autobiography, *The Education of a Senator* (1998), he did discuss that he addressed "the Grand Chapter of the Order of the Eastern Star…in Chicago…because I was a member of our local Chapter." He went on to relate how many of them organized informal groups of volunteers in his campaign. He uses this circumstance to illustrate the power of women in organization. When the votes were tallied, Dirksen won by some 294,000 votes. He won again in 1956, 1962, and 1968 but passed away in the first year of his fourth term.

During his early years in the Senate, Dirksen identified with the Taft segment of the Republican Party, sometimes referred to as the "old guard," many of whom had been pre-World War II isolationists. Some still were. This group included many other Masons including Homer Capehart and William Jenner of Indiana, Bourke Hickenlooper of Iowa, Carl Curtis and Roman Hruska of Nebraska, Milton Young of North Dakota, Karl Mundt of South Dakota, and John Bricker of Ohio. Since most identified with the Taft campaign of 1952, they tended to be initially uncomfortable with some of the "modern Republicanism" typified by the new Eisenhower administration. Most however, managed to accommodate, particularly after the death of Taft in July 1953 and the excesses of Wisconsin Senator, Joe McCarthy. After Taft's demise, Brother William Knowland of California (Oak Grove Lodge No. 215) became GOP Senate leader, and Dirksen became Republican Whip. Knowland's retirement after 1958 elevated Dirksen to the top Republican in the Senate. He held this position until his death.

Already renowned for his speaking skills, Brother Dirksen took time to serve the Grand Lodge of Illinois as Grand Orator in 1953-1954. On September 29, 1954, he received the 33°, A.A.S.R., N.M.J. The Winter 1965 issue of the *Royal Arch Mason* identified him as a Royal Arch Mason "who always carries his Chapter Penny," but no further details are available on York Rite membership.

The defining moment in Senator Dirksen's elevation to the rank of major statesman probably occurred when he helped President Lyndon Johnson secure sufficient votes to get the Civil Rights Bill of 1964 through Congress. At almost the same time, he displayed his commitment to conservatism by giving the nominating speech for Senator Barry Goldwater at the Republican National Convention. As a strong—albeit unfanatical—anti-Communist, Dirksen also provided support for Johnson's increasingly controversial Vietnam policy at a time when some of the more liberal Democrats, typified by brothers George McGovern and Wayne Morse along with Robert Kennedy, were deserting the course. On most spending issues, Dirksen remained staunchly conservative, concerned about budget deficits and the escalating costs of social programs that a later generation would term "entitlements."

By the mid-sixties, "the Wizard of Ooze" had become a folk hero, an able statesman and effective leader of the loyal opposition. Capitol Records signed him to a contract in 1966 and his single release "Gallant Men" became a charted hit on both the pop and country listings in 1967. The album was primarily made up of patriotic readings and recitations.

From 1967, advancing age began to slow the Senate Minority Leader down a little, and he suffered such infirmities as a broken hip. He still took delight in helping young senators like Brother John Tower of Texas (Iowa Park Lodge No. 713) and his son-in-law Howard Baker, Jr., learn the tactics of statecraft. Tower says in his autobiography that Dirksen often presided over what he termed a "Twilight Lodge," an informal gathering of Senate comrades who would swap stories and perhaps have a little nip. The Texan recalls that Everett advised him to "learn to be a senator." One did this by "keeping quiet, listening, and observing until one had been there for a while."

Frank A. Mackaman, a Dirksen scholar, thinks that Everett Dirksen's influence actually eroded when Richard Nixon moved into the White House. This derived in part from the fact that the Illinoisan had so perfected the role of opposition leader that he found readjustment difficult. Then too, his health was slipping faster than he thought. Shortly after the congressional recess of mid-August 1969, he entered the hospital for removal of a malignant tumor on his right lung. Although he came through the operation, later complications led to further decline and he expired on September 7, 1969. An era had ended.

An outpouring of grief from the national leadership followed. Friends and foes alike paid tribute to Brother Dirksen. The tribute paid to him by then President Nixon probably defined his legacy as well as any when he said, "His impact and influence on the nation was greater than that of most Presidents in our history."

**Note:** The major source for this sketch is the Dirksen autobiography, *The Education of a Senator* (University of Illinois Press, 1998), plus the lengthy introduction by Frank H. Mackaman. Other useful works are E. L. and F. H. Schapsmeier, *Dirksen of Illinois: Senatorial Statesman* (University of Illinois Press, 1985), and Louella Carver Dirksen, *The Honorable Mr. Marigold: My Life with Everett Dirksen* (Doubleday, 1972). The Grand Lodge of Illinois supplied his Masonic record and Miss Shasta Dawn Amos prepared the manuscript. Photograph is courtesy of the Dirksen Congressional Center, 301 South Fourth Street, Pekin, Illinois 61554-4219.

April 2000; slightly revised 2011

**Brother Frank Canton:** *The Mediocre Outlaw Who Became a Legendary Frontier Lawman*

The annals of the American West are filled with legendary characters. Some earned their status through deeds of courage and daring while others did not. Some fought Indians, outlaws, or the elements of raw nature to earn their place in history, although a few typified by Jesse James and Billy the Kid were what some people might call social bandits. The subject of this sketch was an outlaw who fled the Texas legal system and then spent the rest of his life as a law officer in such far-flung locales as Wyoming, Alaska, and Oklahoma. Brother Frank Melvin Canton never became as famous as Wyatt Earp, Wild Bill Hickok, or Bat Masterson, but his career in law enforcement not only lasted longer than the others but held equal significance. Also like the others, Canton often found himself embroiled in controversy.

Frank Canton was born Josiah Horner on September 15, 1849. Of Virginia origin, the family of John Horner and his second wife Mary Jane Clemmons, lived in Henry County, Indiana at the time. A restless family that came to number nine children, the Horners lived in Ozark, Missouri in 1862 when John and an older son joined the Confederate Army. John Horner died, probably in a Yankee prison early in 1865, and the following year, surviving family members settled in Denton County, Texas, where an older married sister had earlier moved.

Young Joe Horner, as Josiah became known, worked at farming and a variety of odd jobs over the next few years, mostly as a cowboy. He helped tend the herds of an aging rancher named Christopher Carter. One exception came in April 1868 when he participated in a cattle drive for one Jerry Burnett who sent 1,500 head of longhorns to the railhead at Abilene, Kansas. Burk Burnett, a nineteen-year-old son of the owner, made the drive, too, and the pair became life-long friends.

In 1873, Joe Horner had his first scrape with the law. Taking horses from Indians, although illegal, was often "winked at" by Anglo-American Texans; both Comanches and whites engaged in purloining horses from each other. He also experienced altercations with Negro soldiers in a Texas where many of the locals still resented symbols of reconstruction. On January 10, 1876, he participated in a bank robbery in the town of Comanche where three members of the "Horner Gang" took $5,500. At some point Joe also took part in a stage robbery, subsequently claiming that he only held the horses for the other robbers. Whichever, he was caught, broke jail in San Antonio twice, but was eventually tried and sentenced to the prison in Huntsville where he was a "guest of the state" from May 5, 1877 until August 4, 1879 when he took flight from a work crew and as they say "lit out for greener pastures." As Robert K. DeArment, his biographer states, "a man calling himself Frank M. Canton, would spend the remainder of his days trying to eradicate the memory of Joe Horner forever."

Greener pastures in this fugitive's case turned out to be Wyoming where he adopted a new name, "Frank Canton," and began a new life, mostly as a law officer. By late 1879 or early 1980, "he was working as a cowboy," but had apparently decided "to align himself with those who held the levers of power." Before the end of 1881, he had become a deputy sheriff in Johnson County, and the following year, he won election as sheriff. Ferreting out cattle rustlers became Canton's specialty, and in between official positions, he often worked as a range detective or inspector for the Wyoming Stock Grower's Association. Horse stealing constituted another serious crime. During the two terms he held office, Canton and his deputies captured a number of noted outlaws, most spectacularly a leader of a gang of horse thieves known as Teton Jackson (real name Harvey Gleason). Over his four years as sheriff, Canton sent thirteen convicted horse heisters to the Illinois State Prison and six cattle rustlers to the pen as well. He also hanged one convicted killer known as Bill Booth (real name John Owens) who had crushed the skull of an elderly German immigrant. Some idea of Canton's standing in law enforcement in September of 1885 may be gleaned from the comment in Bancroft's *History* "Mr. Canton stands very high," adding that he "is a man of iron nerve and a typical frontiersman."

Romance and marriage also entered Canton's life during the mid-eighties. He courted Anna May Wilkerson, the daughter of an area ranch foreman, and they married on January 20, 1885. Frank's bride was not quite eighteen, but the marriage was a happy one (despite the groom's frequent absences from home) and resulted in two daughters, Helen who died at age six and Ruby who outlived her father.

Frank Canton decided not to seek a third term as sheriff of Johnson County, in part because of the changing nature of the local populace. As increasing numbers of homesteaders and small ranchers moved into the area, tension between the two groups was growing. Big ranchers, rightly or wrongly, considered many if not most of these newcomers to be cattle rustlers who stole cattle from their more affluent neighbors. Sympathy for the big ranchers began to decline and convictions were more difficult to obtain. Canton's feelings favored the so-called cattle barons, and the lesser folk considered him their tool. While nineteen horse and cattle thieves were sent to prison during Canton's time in office, only five were put away by his successors. These mounting tensions eventually culminated in the infamous Johnson County War in which Frank Canton was a major player.

After Frank's term ended, the Canton Family moved to their own ranch, and he began building his own herd. However, he was soon back to work as a range detective for the Wyoming Stock Grower's Association. In this capacity, he soon made enemies of those who saw themselves as leaders of the small rancher faction including Nathan Champion, Nick Ray, and John Tisdale. The latter was murdered on December 1, 1891, and Canton was believed to be the one who dispatched him. Canton left the area for a time, but was back by April of 1892 to take part in the so-called "invasion" of Johnson County in which an "army" of some fifty hired gunmen in the employ of the big ranchers endeavored without much success to exterminate the small ranchers, some of whom may have been "rustlers" in the usual definition of the term. They did succeed in killing Champion and Ray, but ultimately the "invaders" yielded to superior forces. Ultimately, Canton and his cohorts were acquitted in some instances and charges were dropped in others. The ranchers who had employed him supplied legal support enabling him to be represented by Willis Van Devanter (of Acacia Lodge No. 11 in Cheyenne), probably the best lawyer in the state and who later served twenty-seven years on the United States Supreme Court. Events associated with the Johnson

County War remain controversial, and while many people believed Canton guilty, the truth will likely never be known with certainty.

Leaving Wyoming, the former sheriff and detective worked briefly, managing a meat packing plant in Nebraska but soon relocated to Oklahoma Territory where he took a position as a deputy sheriff in Pawnee, working under an old acquaintance from Texas named Frank Lake. During this time, Canton endeavored to square accounts for his past crimes and after some efforts revealed to Governor James S. Hogg of Texas that he was the wanted man from 1879, Joe Horner. On July 17, 1894, the governor signed a pardon for Horner's prior transgressions. The Territory had its share of outlaws, and Canton pursued many of them and caught some. He also held a commission as a Deputy United States Marshal. Among the lawless was one Bill (or Bee) Dunn and his brothers, petty outlaws who sometimes served as informers for other marshals including Bill Tilghman and Heck Thomas. Deputy Canton killed Bee Dunn in a gunfight at Pawnee on November 13, 1896. As a nearby person who took cover put it, "I knew [when I heard the shot] who had been killed. Canton . . . was faster on the draw."

Just when and where Frank Canton became a Mason is uncertain, possibly in Wyoming or during his short stay in Nebraska. However, it is certain that he affiliated with Pawnee Lodge No. 82 on May 1, 1897. Apparently his homicidal handling of Dunn a few months earlier did not seem detrimental to his reputation among the local brethren. Over the next thirty years, he held membership in three different Oklahoma lodges. At the end of 1906, he demitted from Pawnee Lodge and the next month affiliated with Grayhorse No. 124 in nearby Fairfax where he resided for a time. After retirement in 1922, Canton demitted again and affiliated with Edmond Lodge No. 37 in Edmond where the Cantons lived with their daughter who was a librarian at Central State College.

Since Canton was a Democrat, with William McKinley becoming president, he was dismissed from his federal position. However, he did secure another commission in far distant Alaska Territory and left Pawnee at the end of July. Canton encountered many problems and frustrations during his two adventurous years in Alaska, partly because of the poor communication problems, mostly in the winter. Frank's biographer Robert K. DeArment gives two examples of how the marshal took his Masonic responsibilities seriously while in the frozen north. During a visit to Dawson in the Yukon Territory, a

Mason named Frank Hertz died and Canton not only helped bury him, but also boxed up the man's belongings and sent them back to his relatives in Pennsylvania. Another Mason, Paul Dinslee, died from typhoid fever on a boat in the Yukon River, and Canton had the Captain take the body ashore and with twenty-eight other Masons he gathered from the passengers, conducted Masonic rites prior to burial. To the best of the marshal's knowledge it was the first Masonic funeral ever held in the Yukon River Valley.

In October of 1899, Frank Canton met his wife and daughter in Wyoming where they had been staying with her parents during his absence in Alaska. Needing income, he toyed with the idea of pursuing train robbers, as the Butch Cassidy gang had recently attacked a Union Pacific train at Wilcox, Wyoming, which offered big rewards. As neither the railroad nor the Pinkerton Agency would cover his expenses while in pursuit, his plan fell through, and he returned to Pawnee County, Oklahoma, as a deputy sheriff. Later he worked in a similar capacity in Comanche County at Lawton. Briefly, he held another appointment as a Deputy United States Marshal. Then in 1907, when Oklahoma attained statehood, he received the most prestigious position of his life, that of Adjutant General.

Although Frank Canton had not a single day of actual military experience, he now held the rank of Brigadier General in the Oklahoma National Guard, a position he held through three governors for nearly nine years. In addition to organizing the guard units and lobbying with the legislature, General Canton led the state's sharp-shooting team to the national competition at Camp Perry, Ohio in 1908. The commander himself won first prize in a pistol shooting contest, hitting the bull's eye with every shot at twenty-five yards. This demonstrated that the old gunfighter had not lost his touch at the age of fifty-nine.

Retiring on July 1, 1916, several weeks short of his sixty-seventh birthday, Canton took another job as a detective with a livestock association. However, the aging lawman stated to a reporter, "I don't go to the hills and the sticks, the caves and the canyons and underbrush like I did as a young man. My duties are to assist the county attorney in prosecutions after our field men and sheriffs have rounded up the men charged with cattle stealing." He also worked on an autobiography which was published three years after his death as *Frontier Trails.* As one critic wrote, it was as interesting for what he left out as for what he included. Eventually, he retired on a small pension, and he and Annie lived with their daughter in Edmond until he died on September 27, 1927, at the age of seventy-eight.

Frank Canton was buried with full military and Masonic rites. Daughter Ruby died in 1928. The widow Canton, active in both her church and the Eastern Star, survived working for some years as a visitor's guide at the Oklahoma Historical Society before dying in the Masonic Home in Guthrie on September 3, 1948. Canton's life, like that of many people, was "checkered with good and evil." Although controversial, one would probably conclude that his strengths outnumbered his weaknesses. As Sir Knight Joe Bennett chose to quote in his evaluation of Dallas Stoudenmire (another Masonic gunfighter) from one line in a funeral service, "Let us cast around his foibles the broad mantle of a Mason's charity."

**Note**: By far the best source of information on Canton is Robert K. DeArment, *Alias Frank Canton* (Norman: University of Oklahoma Press, 1996) although his own *Frontier Trails* (1930 and 1966) makes interesting if incomplete reading. Books on the Johnson County War such as D. F. Baber, *The Longest Rope* (1959) and Helena Huntington Smith, *The War on Powder River* (1966) offer a somewhat different perspective. For his Oklahoma Masonic records, I am indebted to the staff of the Grand Lodge in that state. Anyone who can identify Frank Canton's original lodge would be deeply appreciated.

September 2006; slightly revised 2011

**Sir Knight Gene Autry**:
*The Original Singing Cowboy*

Over the past few years, this writer has presented a series of articles concerning singers who are members of the Country Music Hall of Fame and who are Masons. Probably the best known, most successful, and perhaps the most influential is Gene Autry. He started his career as a telegrapher on the Frisco Railroad and spent many later years as the multi-millionaire owner of the Los Angeles Angels baseball team. However, during the in-between era of 1930-1960, this same Autry earned his premier fame as a radio and recording star and became the man who first made the singing motion picture cowboy an American cultural symbol.

The original singing cowboy was born Orvon Gene Autry in Tioga, Texas on September 29, 1907, the eldest son of Delbert and Elnora Ozmont Autry. The elder Autry dealt in livestock and horseflesh while Gene's mother instilled in him a love of singing and music. The youngster paid $8.00 for his first guitar—obtained at age twelve—and soon found himself helping out at community and neighborhood entertainments.

Rather than aspiring to become either a cowboy or an entertainer, the young Gene Autry looked to the railroad and knowledge of the Morse code as the key to his economic future. It did not take the fifteen-year-old boy long to finagle a $35.00 a month part-time job at the local depot, and by 1927, he had turned into a full-fledged $150.00 per month telegrapher. In Oklahoma in those years, this was a position that had both local prestige and a steady income. That same summer, a chance happening in the form of a visit by the nationally-known humorist, Brother Will Rogers (of Claremore Lodge No. 53), changed the young telegrapher's career outlook. Rogers came in to send a telegram and took note of Autry's singing and guitar playing to pass the time. The older man suggested that Gene might benefit by a singing job on radio or for recordings. It took a couple of years for Autry to get serious about a musical career. In the meantime, he went to New York for a tryout where it was suggested that he get more experience. This prompted him to obtain a small program at KVOO radio in Tulsa while he continued with his railroad position.

Orvon Gene Autry still worked as a telegrapher when he petitioned Catoosa Lodge No. 185 in Catoosa, Oklahoma, a stop on the Frisco main line fourteen miles out of Tulsa. The future star received his Entered Apprentice degree on June 6, 1929; was passed to the degree of Fellowcraft on July 4; and was raised to the sublime degree of Master Mason on August 2, 1929 (not 1927 as has been reported in earlier publications). Some years later, Gene continued his Masonic work, but in the meantime his career went through some changes.

Autry went back to New York in the fall of 1929 to pursue a recording contract. With the help of two Oklahomans who had started to record earlier, Johnny and Frankie Marvin, he finally secured a session with the Victor Talking Machine Company and had his first successful one on October 9, 1929. Another railroader named Jimmy Long who had accompanied him to go to New York joined him in a pair of duets: "My Alabama Home" and "I'm Always Dreaming of You." The Marvin boys provided instrumental accompaniment, and Frankie did a bit of yodeling. Frankie Marvin would thereafter play steel guitar on many of Gene's recordings, but Autry soon learned to do his own yodeling. Jimmy Long often sang duet on many of his early recordings including his big hit of 1932, "That Silver Haired Daddy of Mine." Gene subsequently married Long's niece, Ina Mae Spivey.

In his early days, Autry did sessions for several companies such as Grey Gull, Gennett, OKeh, and Victor, but eventually he contracted to record exclusively for Art Satherly of the American Record Corporation, the precursor of Columbia. In those early days as a recording artist, Gene covered the songs of Victor's leading country star, Jimmie Rodgers (also a Mason), and did numerous other songs in the white blues style. He also sang some topical numbers such as "The Death of Mother Jones" and "The Gangster's Warning."

In 1930, Gene secured a radio position at WLS in Chicago. There he became a star on the *National Barn Dance* live audience show and had another program of his own as well. The success of "That Silver Haired Daddy of Mine," recorded on October 29, 1931, propelled the twenty-four-year-old former telegrapher to the front ranks of country recording artists. The next few years saw Autry assume more and more of a cowboy image that had not been particularly strong in his earlier days on record and radio. Sears, Roebuck, and Company began marketing a Gene Autry "Roundup" guitar that sold thousands of copies. His recordings by 1933 and 1934 contained a higher proportion of songs with cowboy and western themes.

In 1934, a motion picture career beckoned. Ken Maynard (also reputed to have been a Mason) had sung an occasional song in his movies from 1930 onward, and Gene made an early appearance in one of his 1934 films, *In Old Santa Fe,* followed by a science-fiction-western serial, *The Phantom Empire*. Both met with sufficient popularity for producer Herbert Yates to decide to introduce a new type of western hero to movie fans, the singing cowboy.

Yates and his newly-formed Republic Pictures Corporation released *Tumbling Tumbleweeds* in September of 1935 and the singing cowboy fad caught on quickly. Republic cameras ground out three more Autry films by the end of the year, and rival corporations sought out other singing cowboys—Dick Foran, Tex Ritter, Bob Baker, Smith Ballew, James Newill, and Jack Randall—among others. Ironically, the only singing cowboy whose popularity ever came to seriously rival Autry was the one Republic signed to keep Gene from becoming too independent at contract renewal time, Roy Rogers. It is generally agreed among film historians that the arrival of Autry on the scene gave cowboy movies a much-needed shot in the arm as some of the older stars had begun to slip in fan appeal, and the singing cowboys helped give B-Westerns a whole new lease on life.

Gene Autry's tough negotiating position at contract time constituted but one indication of the tremendous popularity he enjoyed in the 1936-1942 era. In 1936, he only ranked behind Brother Charles "Buck" Jones (of Henry S. Orme Lodge No. 458 in L A.) and George O'Brien in esteem among western stars, and from 1937 he held the number one spot. For three of those years he ranked among the top ten movie stars in the entire industry. In addition to his forty-eight starring films for Republic, Autry starred in another film on loan for Twentieth Century Fox, continued to have hit records, and in 1939 inaugurated his CBS network radio program *Melody Ranch* which ran for seventeen years. Among his hit records in the late thirties were such Hispanic-flavored songs as "South of the Border (Down Mexico Way)," "Mexicali Rose," and the number which became his long-time theme "Back in the Saddle Again." His films typically included not only adventure and music but a generous dose of comedy usually supplied by Smiley "Frog Millhouse" Burnette. Except for the Fox film *Shooting High,* Gene became virtually the only star of his time to use his own name for the character he played. In 1941, he became a comic book hero when Fawcett and later Dell initiated a series that continued for eighteen years.

It was during his early years as a Hollywood star that Brother Autry took additional Masonic work. He joined the Valley of Long Beach, receiving the 32° on April 2, 1938. Shortly afterward he joined Al Malaikah Shrine Temple in Los Angeles. Some decades later he joined the York Rite bodies back in Oklahoma.

The original singing cowboy's popularity continued unabated until July 1942 when he chose to enter military service. Although promised a commission, Autry wound up getting his promotions the hard way before becoming a pilot in the Air Transport Service. Gene flew cargo planes in locales as far apart as North Africa, the China-Burma-India Theater, and points in between. Discharged in the late summer of 1945, the western hero returned to Hollywood to resume his movie career. His radio program had continued and he managed to squeeze in at least one recording session every year except 1943. Although Roy Rogers had moved into the top spot among B-western stars, Gene held on to number two for as long as the polls continued to be taken.

He soon became embroiled in another squabble with Republic Studios and Herbert Yates. After only five more films for Republic, Autry moved to Columbia and finished his movie career there. Gene made thirty-two films in his series at Columbia which began with *The Last Roundup* in November of 1947 and continued through *Last of the Pony Riders* in November of 1953. Pat Buttram, who had been a regular on the radio series, served as comic sidekick in several of the films although Smiley Burnette returned for the final six pictures. The late Gail Davis, who later starred in her own *Annie Oakley* TV series, was his leading lady in many of these films.

In this period, Autry had his biggest record hit, a children's Christmas song, "Rudolph, the Red Nosed Reindeer," which, although first introduced in 1949, still ranks as one of the all-time best sellers. Not far behind was another holiday favorite, "Frosty the Snowman." In addition, he also had a million-seller with the Easter season favorite "Peter Cottontail." Meanwhile, he also kept recording for the adult market. Gene remained with Columbia through 1957 and later recorded for Challenge, a company he owned.

By the early fifties it had become increasingly obvious that television was becoming a major factor in the entertainment world and that the B-westerns were beginning to fade in fan appeal. Gene Autry moved into the newer medium while still making movies and formed Flying A Productions. Between 1950 and 1956, he made 104 thirty-minute TV shows supported by Pat Buttram and Gail Davis. In addition, Flying A created four other TV westerns: *Annie Oakley* starred Ms. Davis and is historically significant as the first western with a female lead; *The Range Rider* starred Jack Mahoney and helped elevate this one-time stunt man to movie stardom; *Buffalo Bill, Jr.* starred Dick Jones and had another well-known character actor and Mason, Harry "Pappy" Cheshire, in a support role; and *The Adventures of Champion* featured Gene's long-time faithful horse. Unlike Roy Rogers' faithful steed Trigger, there were actually three different horses that were Champion at various times. In 1964, Gene revived the *Melody Ranch* program for local television, and although he seldom appeared on it, most of the old gang from network radio days was there including Pat Buttram, Johnny Bond, Carl Cottner, and Frankie Marvin.

Gene himself played fewer and fewer live shows in this period and engaged in a variety of business pursuits, having wisely invested his earnings from his years as a top star. Since the early sixties, one of his business efforts gained him fame as a business executive. After the Dodgers relocated from Brooklyn to Los Angeles, the American League reacted by expanding to ten teams including a new one on the West Coast. The Los Angeles Angels with Autry as chief executive took their name from the old Pacific Coast League team and in fact played the 1961 season in the old PCL Park, Wrigley Field. Like most expansion franchises, the Angels, who from 1965 played in Anaheim as the California Angels (and more recently as the Los Angeles Angels of Anaheim), took their share of defeats in the early years, but Gene invested in the Angels, and they eventually gained respectability on the diamond. They found good pitchers, first with Dean Chance and then Hall of Fame strikeout king Nolan Ryan. While a World Series victory did not come to the Angels until 2002, four years after Gene's death, they did win three division titles before he relinquished control in 1996.

Even after he had largely left the entertainment world by the time he reached his senior years, numerous honors and recognition still came his way. In 1969 he was inducted into the Country Music Hall of Fame and in 1972 into the National Cowboy Hall of Fame. Back in 1941, the citizens of Berwyn, Oklahoma had renamed their town Gene Autry in his honor. As Pat Buttram jokingly put it, "Mr. Artery [sic] used to ride off into the sunset, now he owns it." In the later eighties, Gene, Pat, and sometimes his second wife, Jackie, (Ina Autry died in 1980) hosted the re-running of many of his old films on the Nashville Network. He also opened a class-act museum, the Gene Autry Western Heritage Center in Los Angeles, ably directed by Joanne Hale, the wife of another cowboy star, Monte Hale.

Numerous Masonic honors also came his way. Gene was already a fifty-year blue lodge member when he received the KCCH on October 15, 1979. Then on December 17, 1983, he received the 33°, in July of 1988, his fifty-year pin from the Scottish Rite, and also the Grand Cross somewhat later. Meanwhile back on October 6, 1973, by special arrangement, he took the York Rite Degrees in Guthrie, Oklahoma, as part of a special one-day class, becoming a member of Tulsa Chapter No. 52, Royal Arch Masons; Tulsa Council No. 22; and Trinity Commandery No. 20, Knights Templar in Tulsa.

Gene Autry passed away on October 2, 1998, outliving his movie rival Roy Rogers by only a few months. He had earlier joked that when he died he planned to take his money with him. Widow Jackie Autry has accordingly been quoted as saying "Before he was buried, I put a check in his pocket for 320 million dollars." To date, the check has not been cashed.

During his life, Gene had said some fine things in public concerning the Fraternity to which he had belonged for one year less than seventy years. His most appropriate remark comes from an article in the June 1997 issue of *The Scottish Rite Journal*: "Fortunately for me, I was accepted into Masonry when I was 21. . . . It has been a most rewarding experience. . . . I advise all young men to take the first step in Masonry as soon as they become eligible. Throughout my life, I have been inspired and guided by the lessons of Freemasonry. I fervently wish more people could understand and appreciate how idealistic and impressive these lessons are! What a wonderful world this would be if everyone practiced the idealism of Freemasonry."

**Note**: Those wishing to learn more about Gene Autry may consult his autobiography, *Back in the Saddle* with Mickey Herskowitz (1978). Since the initial publication of this article two newer quality books are Don Cusic, *Gene Autry: His Life and Career* (2007) and Holly George-Warren, *Public Cowboy*

*No. 1: The Life and Times of Gene Autry* (2007). For his Masonic records I am indebted to the staff at the Grand Lodge and Grand Commandery of Oklahoma and Joan Kleinknecht Sansbury of the Scottish Rite Library and Museum in Washington, D. C.

January 1998; slightly revised 2011

## Brother Gerald Rudolph Ford, Jr.: *The Most Recent Masonic President*

For those of us who have been around for a while, it hardly seems like more than three decades have elapsed since the most recent of the fourteen confirmed Master Mason Presidents left office. To be sure there have been Masons on national major party tickets since then (Robert Dole, Lloyd Bentsen, and Jack Kemp), but only Ford sat in the Oval Office as the occupant. Coming to the presidency at a difficult time in the country's history and under what are still unique circumstances, Brother Ford fulfilled the executive's job with courage and restored its dignity.

Gerald Ford began life in a distant locale from the places where his name would forever be etched on the pages of history. He was born Leslie Lynch King, Jr. on July 13, 1913, in Omaha, Nebraska. However, the King marriage soon disintegrated and the young mother, Dorothy Gardner King, took her baby son back to her parent's home in Grand Rapids, Michigan, where she subsequently met and married Gerald Rudolf Ford who adopted her young son and changed his name (the adoptee later changed the spelling of his middle name). The elder Ford owned a paint and varnish company. At various times he served as Kent County Republican chairman and held memberships in the Elks, Masons, and Shrine. Dorothy Gardner Ford was active in a number of local community and civic groups. Jerry described his adoptive father as a "man of impeccable integrity who exerted the strongest influence on my life." As for his mother, she was a "selfless" and caring lady. He recalled seeing his biological father only twice, once at age seventeen when he gave him $25 and once when he was in law school.

As Gerald Ford grew into adolescence, he developed into a stellar athlete and became an Eagle Scout. He graduated from Grand

Rapids South High School in 1931 and received a football scholarship to attend the University of Michigan. With the country mired down in the Great Depression and since money was scarce, Ford held a variety of part-time jobs to help with expenses. The future president has been described as generally a B student who earned four A grades as an undergraduate.

Jerry Ford played center on the second team on the offensive Wolverine line on undefeated teams as a sophomore and junior. As a starter in his senior year, he was voted Most Valuable Player on the 1934 squad from Ann Arbor. He also played in the East-West Shrine Game in San Francisco and also in the College All-Star game against the Chicago Bears. As a Delta Kappa Epsilon fraternity member, he did dishes to help cover expenses. Upon graduation in 1935, he received professional offers from both the Detroit Lions and Green Bay Packers, but he chose instead to go to Yale Law School.

At Yale, Ford helped coach football and boxing to assist in paying his way. Finally admitted into the law program in 1938, the future president's classmates included such notables as future Supreme Court Justice Potter Stewart (of Lafayette Lodge No. 81 in Cincinnati) and future Secretary of State Cyrus Vance. Dabbling in the political issues of the day, the law student supported the presidential hopes of Brother Wendell Willkie (of Coventry Lodge No. 655 in Akron) and joined the isolationist-oriented America First Committee. However, like his political hero, Senator and Sir Knight Arthur Vandenberg, Ford's views began to change in the next several months. Graduating from law school in January 1941, Jerry returned to Grand Rapids to study for the Michigan bar exams which he passed in June. Thereafter he formed a law partnership with Philip A. Buchen which ended when Ford joined the US Navy several weeks after the Japanese attack on Pearl Harbor.

Serving in the navy from April 1942 to February 1946, Jerry Ford rose in rank from Ensign to Lieutenant Commander. He first worked as a physical-fitness instructor, but in 1943, he requested sea duty and received assignment to the "USS Monterey," a light aircraft carrier. His ship took part in most of the major battles in the Pacific including assaults on Wake Island, and Okinawa and the recapture of the Philippines. The young officer earned ten battle stars and survived a typhoon. After hostilities concluded, Ford spent the remainder of his navy duty at the base in Glenview, Illinois.

After the war, Jerry Ford resumed his law practice with another firm—Butterfield, Keeney, and Amberg—back in his hometown of Grand Rapids. He quickly became a member of such veteran groups as the American Legion, Veterans of Foreign Wars, and AMVETS. Ford also began to take a more serious interest in politics, particularly the local congressional seat then held by Bartel J. Jonkman, a staunch isolationist and vocal critic of Senator and Sir Knight Arthur Vandenberg, the newly-converted internationalist and the political figure Ford probably admired most. He entered the 1948 primary against the incumbent and managed to win by more than 9,000 votes. That November, the young veteran won what was generally considered a safe seat for Republicans by a margin of more than 28,000 votes.

During the year prior to his election to Congress, Ford began a serious romance with thirty-year old Elizabeth (Betty) Ann Bloomer Warren. They married on October 15, 1948, at Grace Episcopal Church in Grand Rapids in the midst of his congressional campaign. The couple subsequently had four children: Michael, Jack, Steven, and Susan. Mrs. Ford became known for her frank honesty and sometimes independent views.

Soon after Gerald Ford entered Congress, he began his Masonic journey by petitioning Malta Lodge No. 465 in Grand Rapids. He received his Entered Apprentice Degree on July 14, 1949. A year and a half ensued before he was passed to the degree of Fellowcraft on April 20, 1951. As a courtesy to Malta Lodge, his raising to the sublime degree of Master Mason took place in Columbia Lodge No. 3 in Washington, DC, on May 18, 1951. He remained a member of Malta Lodge until it merged with Doric Lodge No. 342 in Grand Rapids where he became numbered among the 50-year members. Ford completed his Scottish Rite degrees in the Valley of Grand Rapids on October 17, 1957 and received the 33° on September 26, 1962. In 1959 he became a Noble of Saladin Shrine Temple, and he also joined Court No. 11, Royal Order of Jesters. Like such notables as Ernest Borgnine, Roy Clark, Glenn Ford, and Jack Kemp, he appeared in various public service ads on behalf of Shrine Hospitals. In the York Rite, he was said to have become a companion in the Chapter and Council, but seems not to have found time to take the Chivalric degrees.

Gerald Ford went on to be elected to his congressional seat a total of thirteen times, always by at least 60% of the popular vote. During this time, he established himself as a moderate conservative in domestic politics and like his mentor Vandenberg, a supporter of internationalism and bipartisan foreign policy. He set as his ultimate goal the attaining of the position of Speaker of the House, an objective that seemed increasingly remote given the solid majorities that House Democrats commanded between 1955 and 1995. However, he did attain the position of House Minority Leader in 1965 and worked tirelessly on behalf of GOP congressional candidates. It was in this capacity that this writer twice met Brother Ford in the late sixties when he spoke on behalf of 10th District Congressman Clarence Miller. While as Minority Leader Ford made few enemies, President Johnson complained that he had "spent too much time playing football without a helmet." In defense of his integrity, a Democratic colleague, Martha Griffiths, said in 1974 that she "never knew Mr. Ford to make a dishonest statement nor a statement part-true and part-false." Philosophically, Ford's political position bore considerable resemblance to that of Richard Nixon but without the negative character aspects accredited to Nixon.

After winning his thirteenth term in 1972, Gerald Ford concluded that he would never become Speaker and decided to retire after one more term (when Nixon's second term would presumably terminate). Fate, however, dealt him a different hand. Although the Watergate Scandal dominated much of the headlines during 1973, a separate investigation led to the resignation of Vice President Spiro T. Agnew in October. A new Constitutional Amendment provided for filling the vacancy through presidential appointment with congressional consent. According to well-founded rumors, Nixon himself would ideally have preferred former Texas governor and then recently retired Treasury Secretary John Connally, but he wanted to maintain party unity by avoiding such ideological figures as Ronald Reagan and Nelson Rockefeller, so he chose Ford, a middle-of-the-road person certain to win easy confirmation. Gerald Ford won Senate approval 92-3 and House approval 387-35. Sworn in on December 6, 1973, the man from Grand Rapids served just eight months in the number two position.

The deepening fallout from Watergate and the subsequent "cover-up" as virtually everyone is aware eventually engulfed the Nixon White House. Facing impeachment, the President resigned effective at noon on August 9, 1974. Ford took the oath of office a few seconds later and the nation had its 38th chief executive and 14th Masonic president. In spite of high tensions engendered by the trauma, Ford enjoyed relatively high poll ratings until issuing the Nixon pardon in December; an act which was unpopular in many circles at the time but undoubtedly was the best way to bring closure to an emotionally divisive issue.

Ford came to the presidency at one of the most tension-filled times of anyone who ascended to the Oval Office on short notice. Congress was not in session when Brother Andrew Johnson replaced Abe Lincoln. Despite the still-raging World War II, Brother Harry Truman had a friendly congress until January 1947. Ford had an unfriendly congress, and the Nixon pardon guaranteed him one of the shortest political "honeymoons" on record. Congress became even less friendly after the pardon, and the Republican minority became even smaller after the November 1974 elections. Moreover, Republicans in Congress were increasingly divided between moderate and conservative factions. Within the cabinet, a feud between Secretary of State Kissinger and Secretary of Defense Schlesinger made life difficult for the President. In retrospect, that he managed to accomplish anything in his nearly two and one-half year tenure seems remarkable.

During his time in the White House, Ford battled inflation with limited success, secured the release of American sailors from the "Mayaguez," and did his best to cool the emotional tensions that still smoldered from the traumas associated with Viet Nam and Watergate. The task he faced was a difficult one. The United States also celebrated two hundred years of independence on July 4, 1976, with national spirits much restored. Ford's own evaluation in a 1988 interview with historian John Robert Greene is one that few could argue with today; he said that he "left the White House in better shape than when I took it over."

In the bicentennial year of 1976, Ford faced challenges on both ends of the political spectrum, and in reflection he admits that he underestimated both. A primary challenge from former California Governor Ronald Reagan almost succeeded and hampered Republicans as they went into the general election. In the fall, a nearly unknown former Georgia Governor, Jimmy Carter, (in an early 1975 appearance on *What's My Line,* no panelist could guess who Carter was or what he did) squeezed out a narrow victory. Ford erred in underestimating both.

In his autobiography, *A Time to Heal,* Brother Ford conceded that he viewed the smiling Georgian as a "flash in the pan" who had "little more going for him than a winning smile." Time, of course, has vindicated much of Ford's initial assessment, but in 1976 the voters turned to Carter as the outsider who could bring a fresh approach to national problems. Still, in spite of the dark cloud of the Nixon pardon hanging over his head, a hostile press that viewed him negatively, and a major gaffe concerning Poland in the debate over foreign policy,

Ford almost won. In an electoral vote of 297 for Carter and 241 for Ford, analysts have pointed out that a shift of 8,000 votes in the states of Ohio and Hawaii, narrowly won by Carter, would have changed the outcome of the race.

Ford retired and generally proved to be a former president with grace and style. He briefly considered running in 1980, but ultimately chose not to enter the fray. He also chose not to be a vice presidential running mate in 1980. He did take on the role of elder statesman but unlike some former occupants of the White House, did not seek the limelight. Passing the age of ninety, Brother Ford demonstrated himself as one of healthiest and longest living emeritus White House occupants.

While Gerald Rudolph Ford will not be remembered as one of the nation's greatest leaders, he certainly made himself a place in history as one who did his part to heal a troubled land in turbulent times. Circumstances "bequeathed to" him a situation that all but made it impossible for Ford to establish a "Presidency" before he took the reins of power. A hostile Congress and disunity within his own minority party further complicated matters. Yet, as his biographer John Robert Greene concludes, "as a moral leader Ford surpassed the examples of every President" in the two decades that followed Eisenhower. This atypical man and Mason from Grand Rapids, Michigan once remarked, "If I'm remembered it will probably be for healing the land." That said, Brother Ford accomplished this feat better than he could have imagined in 1977. By the time of his death on December 26, 2006 at the age of ninety-three, most of the nation agreed. He served the country well.

**Note**: The best book on Gerald Ford is John Robert Greene, *The Presidency of Gerald Ford* (1995). His autobiography, *A Time to Heal* (1979) is also worth reading. For the details of his Masonic Record, I appreciate the help of the staff at the Grand Lodge of Michigan, the Valley of Grand Rapids, Saladin Shrine Temple, and the brief note in *Masonic Americana, I* 3rd Edition, p.3.

February 2003, slightly revised 2011

**Brother Glenn Ford:**
*Hollywood Leading Man*

In 1958, *The Motion Picture Herald*'s annual poll named Glenn Ford the top ranking box office star in America. From 1946 well into the 1970s, Ford was counted among the more durable male stars on the Hollywood scene, noted in the words of the British film critic Leslie Halliwell as adept at [portraying] tortured heroes. In those years Ford starred not only in rugged he-man westerns, but he effectively played shady underworld characters, crooked policemen, and sensitive school teachers. Less well known is the fact that Ford was a Mason for more than fifty years and a Shriner for more than a quarter century.

Born Gwyllyn Samuel Newton Ford in Quebec on May 1, 1916, the only child of Newton and Hannah Ford had some distinguished persons in his family tree. Sir John MacDonald, his Father's uncle, was the first prime minister of Canada (and a longtime member of St. John's Lodge in Kingston, Ontario), and another relative was United States President Martin Van Buren. The family owned a paper mill in Glenford, Ontario, and young Gwyllyn Ford spent his early years there. Later he dropped his Welsh first name and borrowed the name of the town of his childhood as a professional name as Gwyllyn proved a bit too complex for American theater goers. Ford has been quoted as saying his ambition to be an actor dated from a local stage role he had at age four which required him to eat a large quantity of chocolate candy.

When Ford reached the age of seven, his parents moved to Santa Monica, California. There the youngster attended public schools, graduating in 1934 from Santa Monica High School where he had excelled in English and had competed in several varsity athletic teams. His parents did not object to an acting career, but they did insist that he learn a trade in case acting did not work out. Ford had already begun to work in a variety of amateur theatrical groups as both a stage manager and an actor. In 1938 he took a part in the play *Soliloquy*, but it failed after three days in New York, and the young aspiring actor returned to California on borrowed train fare.

Finally, in 1939 Glenn Ford's luck changed as he landed a major role in a minor film, *Heaven with a Barbed Wire Fence*. Soon afterward he signed a contract with Columbia Pictures, and good roles followed in the westerns *Texas* (1941) with William Holden; *The Desperadoes* (1943) with Randolph Scott; and a comedy, *Go West Young Lady*, (1941) with Ann Miller and Penny Singleton of Blondie Bumstead fame. Glenn had a smaller role in *The Lady In Question* (1940) with Rita Hayworth, the first of five films in which the two appeared together; they eventually ranked as one of screenland's great romantic teams.

Prior to the release of *The Desperadoes*, Glenn enlisted in the United States Marines on December 13, 1942. He served for the duration of the war. During his years in military service—on October 23, 1943—Ford married actress Eleanor Powell who is often remembered as the most acclaimed dancer in motion picture history. The marriage lasted until 1959 and produced a son Peter with whom Ford made his home in later years. Three later marriages proved to be of short duration.

Following his wartime duty, Glenn Ford returned to Hollywood and soon emerged as one of the top stars of the postwar generation. Two films in 1946 that did much to elevate his reputation were *A Stolen Life* with Bette Davis and *Gilda*, the picture that perhaps more than any other established Rita Hayworth as one of the silver screen's all-time sex symbols. As "Johnny Farrell," the casino manager and former lover of Gilda who wins her away from her rich gangster husband, George MacCready, Ford created one of the film's more memorable characters.

Other films in the immediate postwar years that helped enhance Ford's reputation as a versatile actor included *Framed* (1947) with Janis Carter, *The Return of October* (1948) with up-and-coming starlet Terry Moore, and *The Loves of Carmen* (1948) in which he was miscast as a bullfighter but was again matched with Rita Hayworth. He also continued to make successful westerns, not always in heroic roles. For instance, in *The Man from Colorado* (1948) he played a power-crazed judge who comes to a bad end. However, he fared better in *The Redhead and the Cowboy* (1951) with Rhonda Fleming and overcame accusations of cowardliness in *The Man from the Alamo* (1952) with

Julia (later Julie) Adams. Another film from that era, *The Secret of Convict Lake* (1951), paired him with Gene Tierney.

In 1954 Glenn Ford became a member of Palisades Lodge No. 637, F. & A. M., in Santa Monica. He was initiated an Entered Apprentice on March 23, was passed to the degree of Fellowcraft on July 20, and was raised to the sublime degree of Master Mason on November 9, 1954. On June 27, 1957, he became a plural member of Riviera Lodge No. 780 in Pacific Palisades. In 1987 Palisades Lodge merged with Santa Monica Lodge No. 307. Some years later on May 6, 1972, Brother Ford took the Scottish Rite degrees in the Valley of Los Angeles and the following week on May 12 he became a Noble of Al Malaikah Temple, AAONMS.

Meanwhile Ford remained quite active in the motion picture industry for the remainder of the decade. Many critics responded favorably to his parts in the "Film Noir" classics, *The Big Heat* (1953) and *Human Desire* (1954). Others preferred his role opposite Eleanor Parker in *Interrupted Melody* (1955) or what some considered the high point of his career as the troubled teacher combating juvenile delinquency and school violence in *The Blackboard Jungle* (1955), or with Donna Reed as concerned parents of a kidnapped child in *Ransom* (1956). *Affair in Trinidad* (1952) reunited Ford with Rita Hayworth while *It Started with a Kiss* (1959) and *The Gazebo* (1960) paired him with Debbie Reynolds, the reigning Hollywood sweetheart and the girl-next-door of the Eisenhower Era.

Some of Glenn Ford's most memorable roles in the fifties continued to be in westerns, *The Fastest Gun Alive* (1956) saw Ford and his wife Jeanne Crain trying to live down his reputation as a gunfighter but being forced into a showdown with the villainous Broderick Crawford. In *3:10 to Yuma* (1957), regarded as a classic, Ford played "an amiable but deadly scoundrel" being transported to prison by failing farmer Van Heflin and playing "mind games" with his guard. Other Ford westerns included the title role in *The Sheepman* (1958), a tough trail boss in *The Cowboy* (1958), and as the central figure in a remake of Edna Ferber's epic novel, *Cimarron* (1960). The latter is said to be Glenn's own favorite among his many starring efforts.

In 1961 Glenn Ford had one of his more memorable and unusual roles as "Dude Conway" in *Pocketful of Miracles* in which he is part of a group that helps bag lady, "Apple Annie" (Bette Davis), by temporarily upgrading her status when her daughter—played by a young Ann Margret—pays a surprise visit. In *The Courtship of Eddie's*

*Father* (1963), he plays a widower whose young son works at playing matchmaker with Shirley Jones as the aspiring step-mom. Other Ford films of the sixties include *Experiment in Terror* (1962) with Lee Remick and *Dear Heart* (1964) with Geraldine Page. One of several westerns was *Smith* (1968) in which he is a white farmer who tries to defend his Indian neighbors. He also made a final film with Rita Hayworth.

Meanwhile, outside of his screen career, Ford acquired something of a reputation as a Hollywood Mr. Do-It Yourself. While waiting for his break as an actor, he had supplemented his income by installing windows and shingling roofs. In later years, Glenn installed his own plumbing, wired his home, and put in the air-conditioning system. According to his 1959 entry in *Current Biography*, the actor was then passing on these skills to adolescent son Peter.

With fewer motion pictures being made in the seventies, Brother Ford turned increasingly to television as did more and more Hollywood people with the passing of time. His principal entry into the small screen division came in 1971-1972. *Cade's County* dealt with a modern sheriff coping with the challenges of law enforcement in a large western county. He also played the same role in a TV movie *Marshal of Madrid* (1972). He did another short-lived series in 1975, *The Family Holvak*, where Glenn portrayed a minister in the South during the Great Depression. In fact, many of Ford's later films consisted of the "made for television" variety such as *The Disappearance of Flight 412* (1974) or in such mini-series as Louis L'Amour's *The Sacketts* (1979).

Nonetheless, he still had some good moments in movies for theater release. Among these was *Santee* (1972), in which he plays a mean bounty hunter out to avenge the death of his ten-year old son. British-born Dana Wynter had the leading lady role. In the first big-budget *Superman* (1978), Glenn played the part of Jonathon Kent who adopts the baby from doomed planet Krypton and rears him as Clark Kent.

Glenn Ford slowed down considerably after 1981. Except for a brief flurry of 1989-1991 activity, he pretty much retired. He played a sheriff in *Casablanca Express* (1989) and had a supporting role in *Border Shootout* (1990). During the mid-nineties, he made some headlines when he was victimized by someone who tried to cheat him out of a considerable sum of money. In poor health from the late nineties, he made his home with son Peter and his family. Boyd Magers, who edits *Western Clippings*, a newsletter that keeps up with the activity of aging western stars, reported that Ford celebrated his

83rd birthday in May 1999 and reminisced about one of his favorite mementos, a gun presented to him some years earlier by John Wayne. He also reported that Ford almost never left the house.

In his retirement Brother Glenn Ford could look back over a long and satisfying career as a film star until his death on August 30, 2006. He may not have reached the legendary status of Brother John Wayne, but in his lengthy career as a leading man, Masons everywhere can recall Glenn Ford as one of the best in his profession during the post-World War II generation.

**Note**: This biographical sketch has been put together from a variety of film encyclopedias as well as Ford's entry in the 1959 edition of *Current Biography*. He did author an autobiography entitled *Glenn Ford, R.F.D. Beverly Hills* (1970), which may be available in some libraries. For his Masonic record, I am indebted to the staff of the Grand Lodge of California and Al Malaikah Shrine Temple. Mrs. Joan Sansbury, librarian at the AASR.,S.J., supplied his Scottish Rite record. I also appreciate the information furnished by Mr. Boyd Magers of Albuquerque, New Mexico.

August 2000; slightly revised 2011

**Brother Grandpa Jones:** *Country Music Legend and Freemason*

For more than sixty-five years, Louis Marshall Jones proved himself both an enduring and an endearing figure on the American music scene. A native of Kentucky, Jones spent his adolescent years in Akron, Ohio, where he became a radio entertainer prior to his sixteenth birthday, playing and singing the songs that were traditional in Southern rural culture. After a long apprenticeship on various radio stations—large and small—he came to Nashville and the *Grand Ole Opry* in 1946 where he became a fixture. Beginning in 1969, he found TV stardom on the popular *Hee Haw* show for another twenty-three years. Ironically, this man who had become known to millions as "Grandpa" Jones since 1935 did not actually become a grandfather until his last years.

Born near Niagara in Henderson County on October 20, 1913, Marshall Jones came from a family of tobacco farmers and carpenters. He was the youngest in a family of ten children and spent most of his childhood in the country except for a year in Evansville, Indiana. In 1954, he recalled an incident from his youth when a crew of sawmill workers left an old guitar at the Jones house and the youth learned a few chords on it. Not long afterward his brother found an old guitar in a junk store for seventy-five cents and brought it home. Thereafter, young Jones improved his guitar skills, learned to sing a few old numbers, and heard more songs on radio and records.

In 1928, the Jones family followed an older brother to Akron, Ohio. The city was then becoming the rubber capital of the world and a virtual magnet to which thousands of Southern and mountain folks found industrial work. Marshall Jones adjusted quickly to the new environment, and in March of 1929, won a talent contest sponsored by Wendell Hall, then nationally renowned as the "Red Headed Music Maker."

This modest beginning led to regular appearances on local radio. He made friendships with other musicians such as the aspiring harmonica player, Joe Troyan (known on stage as Bashful Harmonica Joe), and two veteran recording artists, Warren "Cap" Caplinger and Andy Patterson. Soon Jones was earning some fourteen dollars weekly and gaining a reputation as "the young singer of old songs," which wasn't bad for a fellow still in high school (until 1932) and the country in a deepening depression.

In the fall of 1932, these musicians and two others became the Pine Ridge String Band, appearing on the *Lum and Abner Show* from WTAM Cleveland which was then carried on over forty-four stations. This program was becoming one of radio's most enduring hits running for more than a quarter century. (Its stars, Chester "Lum" Lauck and Norris "Abner" Goff, were both longtime members of Dallas Lodge No. 128 in Mena, Arkansas.)

After Lum and Abner moved their radio base to Chicago in 1934, Jones and Troyan worked clubs around Akron until March 1935 when they became support musicians for the famed "Kentucky Mountain Boy," Bradley Kincaid. It was during this period that twenty-two year-old Marshall Jones became "Grandpa" Jones, partly because he could be rather grumpy on mornings following an inadequate amount of sleep and partly because he always sounded like a much older man. Attempting to look the part on stage, he donned a drooping false mustache and a costume characterized by old-fashioned glasses, suspenders, and boots. Grandpa eventually aged into his stage persona and grew a real mustache, but he continued favoring the original stage clothing that became a virtual trademark until his death.

By early 1937, Grandpa Jones decided to go on his own and landed a spot on the *World's Original Jamboree* from WWVA in Wheeling, West Virginia. There he met a lady five-string banjo picker known as Cousin Emmy (Carver). She taught him the fundamentals of that instrument. As the years went by, Grandpa came to be even more identified with the old-time banjo than with the guitar.

Grandpa spent most of the next five years alternating between radio jobs in Hartford, Connecticut and Fairmont, Charleston, and Wheeling, West Virginia. In November 1938, he married Eulalia Losher, the niece of his one-time associate Andy Patterson. Thirteen months later the couple had a daughter Marsha, but the marriage later became a casualty of World War II. Grandpa also formed a band called the Grandsons, but despite his regional radio popularity, he had yet to become a recording artist.

This would change however, after Jones came to WLW Cincinnati in 1942. The next year, a local businessman named Syd Nathan started King Records. Grandpa not only became one of King's most significant artists in the eight years (1943-1951, 1956) he spent with them, but most of his best-known songs first appeared on King such as "Old Rattler," "Mountain Dew," "Eight More Miles to Louisville," "Fifteen Cents Is All I've Got," and "Tragic Romance."

He is best remembered today for lyrics that took a humorous look at rural life. However, many of Grandpa's earlier efforts were heart songs typified by "Are There Tears Behind Your Smile" or sad tear-jerkers such as "Send Me Your Address from Heaven." He also waxed a few duets with Merle Travis under the pseudonym "Sheppard Brothers" and many gospel quartets as lead vocalist in the Brown's Ferry Four.

Early in 1944, Grandpa Jones enlisted in the army and eventually went to Germany where he served as both an MP and an assistant cook. With a few other soldiers, he also formed a musical group called the Munich Mountaineers and had a daily program on the Armed Forces Network for five months. Discharged from the army on January 6, 1946, Marshall returned to the United States. His marriage had disintegrated by the time he got home, and Cincinnati did not seem the same since many of his close associates like Merle Travis and the Delmore Brothers had moved elsewhere,.so Jones, too, sought greener pastures.

He soon found a new spot at WSM Nashville, Tennessee, where he made his debut at the *Grand Ole Opry* on March 16, 1946. He began romancing Ramona Riggins, an Indiana girl he had first met in Cincinnati where she had worked with Sunshine Sue's Rock Creek Rangers. Grandpa and Ramona married in mid-October of 1946; the marriage endured for more than fifty-one years and resulted in three children. Ramona proved to be not only a good wife and mother but played an excellent mandolin, bass, and fiddle and sang harmony on their duet songs.

Grandpa Jones endured as an *Opry* star for a half-century with two brief exceptions (1951-52 and 1956-59) when he was based in Richmond and Washington, D. C., respectively. His recording career also continued through the decades. From 1952 through 1955, his material appeared on RCA Victor where he made thirty-two solo efforts and also made a few duets with hillbilly comedy queen Minnie Pearl. After a brief return to King, he spent three years with Decca where his entire output was released on a 1992 compact disc in the MCA Hall of Fame Series. In 1960, he began a long-time relationship with Monument Records that resulted in his biggest solo hit, a revival of the old Jimmie Rodgers classic (a member of Bluebonnet Lodge No. 1219 in San Antonio at the time of his death), "T for Texas," in 1962. In addition to a thematic album of Rodgers' yodeling songs, Grandpa also turned out a fine album of old-time folk songs and a gospel quartet tribute to the Brown's Ferry Four. Ramona assisted her husband on many of his recordings and personal appearances but not all of them as she also spent time at home caring for the younger Jones children Eloise, Mark, and Alisa.

During this period, Grandpa Jones took his initial plunge into Masonry receiving the Entered Apprentice degree in Greenbrier Lodge No. 753 in Greenbrier Tennessee on February 16, 1960. The irregular work schedules of musicians who tour extensively for their livelihood can sometimes slow one's progress in the order, and such was the case with Marshall Jones. However, when George McCormick, a member of John B. Garrett Lodge No. 711 in Nashville, started working with Grandpa on the road, he helped him with his proficiency work. Accordingly, Brother Jones was passed to the degree of Fellowcraft on March 19, 1973, and raised a Master Mason on October 15, 1973. After June 1983, he also held a dual membership in Blue Mountain Lodge No. 202 in Mountain View, Arkansas. Although never an officer, he apparently took his membership seriously, attended meetings whenever schedules permitted and made occasional visits to Goodlettsville Lodge No. 271 in suburban Nashville. By the time he reached his early eighties, his hearing began to fail and he stopped attending and experienced problems singing as well.

Meanwhile, as *Hee Haw*'s popularity reached soaring heights through the 1970s, Jones became more popular than ever. He sang and played the banjo, participated in numerous comedy skits, and sometimes with Ramona's support even got to display such rare talents as playing cowbells, a trick he apparently learned from old-time vaudeville artist Lennie Aleshire who had worked with him on radio in Fairmont, West Virginia. He also re-created the quartet sound of the Brown's Ferry Four as part of the Hee Haw Gospel Quartet, whose membership at various times included Buck Owens, Roy Clark,

Kenny Price, and Joe Babcock. In all, *Hee Haw* did much to enhance the status of Grandpa Jones as a legendary country music figure.

In the late seventies, Grandpa began to record for the CMH label of Los Angeles. Over a period of several years, he cut four double albums for this firm that included some of the best traditional country music then available. Ramona and the children helped out on several of these efforts as did George McCormick. A fifth double album made with Merle Travis and the team of Rose Lee and Joe Maphis—called the *Farm and Home Hour*—successfully attempted to re-create the flavor of old-time country radio.

In 1978, Grandpa Jones received the pinnacle of recognition within his profession when he was inducted into the Country Music Hall of Fame. In a sense, this was somewhat unusual because although he had a long recording and performing career and turned out many favorites—even classics—only two were ever classed as hits. However, in another sense few performers in any field have enjoyed as long a level of popularity or had more friends and fans. Seemingly he was loved by all.

Even with his lasting fame, he continued to perform. As his children grew up, they too displayed a knack for music that they often showcased at the dinner theater the family built in Mountain View, Arkansas in 1980. Older daughter Marsha played the autoharp, Eloise sang, Mark played several instruments, and Alisa gained mastery of the hammered dulcimer, a rare primitive forerunner of the piano. When Grandpa was not on the road, the entire family entertained at the dinner theater, and when he went on tour, Ramona, Mark, and Alisa held down the fort.

For eleven years from 1979, the entire family (minus Marsha) made their home in Mountain View, and Grandpa commuted to Nashville for his musical commitments there. After the 1989 tourist season ended, they leased out the theater, which later burned, and returned to their former home between Goodlettsville and Greenbrier, Tennessee. However, they continued to return to Mountain View two or three times each summer. In 1984, Grandpa's autobiography, *Everybody's Grandpa: Fifty Years behind the Mike,* came off the presses and stands as one of the best books of its kind.

After that, Grandpa and his long-time musical associate Brother George McCormick continued to work the *Opry* and tour on a limited basis. As he became older, hearing impairment took some toll on his singing and playing but fans often seemed not to mind.

On January 3, 1998, he did his usual stint at the *Opry*, but less than two hours later suffered a massive stroke and never really recovered. As daughter Alisa told it, the family maintained a constant vigil (except for older daughter Marsha who herself died a few days after the stroke) until the man sometimes called "Everybody's Grandpa" passed away on February 19, 1998. Brother Jones had lived a full life and is remembered as one of the best at what he did.

**Note**: The best source on Grandpa Jones is his own book, *Everybody's Grandpa* (1984). After his death Ramona Jones also wrote her own story as *Make Music While You Can* (1999). Masonic information was obtained through Brother George McCormick of Cookeville Lodge No. 266 and Brothers Charles Williamson and Ed Suter, Secretaries of their respective Lodges in Goodlettsville and Greenbrier.

January 1997; slightly revised 2011

**Brother Hank Locklin**:
*Pioneer of the Nashville Sound and "Grand Ole Opry" Star*

Roughly a half-century ago, country music record producers in Nashville began to develop a smoother, more appealing style that found a wider popularity with listeners. This studio creation of men like Chet Atkins, Owen Bradley, and Don Law soon became known as the "Nashville Sound." The late Jim Reeves perhaps ranked as the biggest music star to benefit from this change. Close behind was another veteran country vocalist who hailed from the piney woods region of the Florida Panhandle. This is the story of Brother Hank Locklin who spent more than half of his ninety-one years as a member of Red Rock Lodge No. 96 in Munson, Florida.

Lawrence Hankins Locklin was born in the tiny community of McLellan in Santa Rosa County, Florida, on February 15, 1918. His father, Lawrence Locklin, had been a railroader turned farmer, and his mother played piano in a local church where the boy first heard music. At the age of eight, a school bus ran over his left leg, and during a long, painful recovery he learned to play the guitar. Later the youth went to high school in Munson and played basketball, but dropped out prior to graduation. Over the next several years, Hank worked at a variety of laboring jobs including the WPA but mostly in the shipyards at Mobile, Alabama, dabbling in music on a part-time basis. Meanwhile in April of 1938, he married Willa Jean Murphy, a union that lasted thirty-one years and produced three children.

Locklin entered military service briefly during World War II, being discharged when physicians learned that his old injury had left him with one leg shorter than the other. As the war wound downward, Hank at the age of nearly twenty-seven opted for a full-time musical job as guitarist with Jimmy Swan and his Blue Sky Playboys. From this job, he worked in bands in Shreveport, Louisiana; Hot Springs, Arkansas; and finally, Houston, Texas. He was not yet a leader but mostly played guitar and sang on occasion. By 1948, he had emerged as leader of a band called the Rocky Mountain Playboys and made his first recording on the local Gold Star label. The next year, Hank Locklin signed with Four Star Records and had his first hit with an original number "The Same Sweet Girl" which reached number eight on the country charts. Ironically, by mid-1949, Eddy Arnold, three months younger than Locklin but who had got a much earlier start, had already racked up some twenty-three hits.

Hank continued to work in Texas and record on Four Star (a few sides were leased to Decca) through 1954. Among his more notable songs was "Send Me the Pillow That You Dream On" which he would later record again for RCA Victor, becoming one of the first Nashville Sound major hits. In 1953 "Let Me Be the One" went on to become his first number one hit, spending three weeks atop the *Billboard* charts in late December and early January 1954. Its success led to Hank's obtaining a contract with RCA Victor records, his first session for the larger company taking place on May 30, 1955.

Hank Locklin's earliest RCA recordings made little impact, but that began to change when Chet Atkins replaced Steve Sholes as producer. A cover of the George Jones song "Why Baby Why" made a brief appearance in the charts in 1956. Then with his song "Geisha Girl" in 1957, true stardom beckoned. Along with the Bobby Helms hit "Fraulein," it ushered in a fad of songs concerning "foreign love," a subject with which many former American servicemen could identify. Hank recorded a whole album of such numbers that stands as one of the earlier concept albums in country music history and led to a revival of interest in such past classics as "Lili Marlene," "Filipino Baby," "Mexicali Rose," and "When Irish Eyes Are Smiling." The latter of these helped make Locklin popular in the "Emerald Isle." In 1963 he recorded another concept album of Irish songs and made several tours of Ireland where he remained in demand for several decades. The musicians on Hank's records during those years included several people who created the Nashville Sound including lead guitarist Grady Martin (a member of Dillahunty Lodge No. 112 in Lewisburg, Tennessee) and pianist Floyd Cramer who went on to become a solo recording star on the strength of his work on Locklin's records. Both "Geisha Girl" and "Fraulein" came from the pen of Lawton Williams, a Texas songwriter and longtime friend. Over the years Hank would record many of Lawton's compositions.

For Hank Locklin, "Geisha Girl" proved to be the first of a string of major hits that included the new recording of "Send Me the

Pillow That You Dream On," "It's a Little More Like Heaven," "Happy Birthday to Me," and "Happy Journey." In the midst of those successes came the defining song of his career, "Please Help Me I'm Falling" in 1960 which spent fourteen weeks at number one and a total of thirty-six weeks on the *Billboard* country charts. It also reached number eight on the pop charts and was a top ten hit in the United Kingdom. All of these demonstrated the crossover appeal and success that the architects of the Nashville Sound had anticipated.

Meanwhile, Locklin had continued to make his home in Houston and also appeared as a regular on *The Big D Jamboree,* a popular live audience rival of the *Grand Ole Opry* which broadcast from KRLD in Dallas. Ultimately, he returned to the Florida community of his birth and operated a 350 acre beef cattle ranch that he called the "Singing L" when not on tour. In November 1960 he joined the cast of the *Grand Ole Opry* but still commuted from his Florida home to Nashville. WSM announcer and deejay Ralph Emery bestowed the honorary title "Mayor of McLellan" on Hank with many fans never realizing that McLellan is too small to have a city government.

It was after his return to Florida that Lawrence Hankins Locklin began his Masonic journey. Petitioning Red Rock Lodge No. 96 in Munson and gaining approval, Hank was initiated an Entered Apprentice on May 25, 1962. Passed to the degree of Fellowcraft three months later on August 28, Locklin was raised a Master Mason on October 17, 1962. He completed the Scottish Rite degrees in Nashville on September 30, 1968 and was created a noble of Hadji Shrine Temple in Pensacola on October 12, 1968. The "Mayor of McLellan" received his Twenty-Five Year Award and Forty Year Awards from the Grand Lodge of Florida in 1987 and 2002, respectively. Perhaps it was not just a coincidence that he became a Mason in roughly the same time period that he recorded a tribute album to the most celebrated Masonic figure with a long-time *Grand Ole Opry* connection, Sir Knight Roy Acuff.

While Hank Locklin continued to have mid-level hits regularly through 1971, he also did more concept albums with success. These included tribute albums to Eddy Arnold and Hank Williams, a collection of country standards from earlier years, the aforementioned *Irish Songs, Country Style,* and a salute to the Country Music Hall of Fame and its members. The title song from the latter album, "Country Hall of Fame" in 1968 became his final big hit.

Brother Locklin's string of hits began to run out in the early seventies. His last chart appearance came in the spring of 1971 with

"She's as Close as I Can Get to Loving You" which peaked at number sixty-one. RCA released his final album, *The Mayor of McLellan, Florida,* in 1972 but continued with singles until 1974. Hank signed with MGM and had three singles and an album that, although musically sound, produced no hits. A stint with Plantation Records in the later seventies yielded more numbers but with similar results. Thereafter, he continued to record sporadically with his last effort being a gospel compact disc with the help of several well-known figures on the Southern Gospel circuit. Hank also continued to tour in both the United States and Europe with seemingly perpetual popularity in Ireland.

With the passing of years, Locklin became less active. In 1970 he married again—to Anita Crooks, and the couple had a son, Adam. At the age of sixty-six the "Mayor of McLellan" moved a few miles northward to Brewton, Alabama, still playing the *Opry* several times a year. Getting together with living musicians with whom he had played in the forties, he did some shows in the immediate area. Observers marveled at the quality of his voice which remained remarkably constant even as he aged into his eighties. In 2001, when he again recorded another album, he told a reporter for the *Birmingham News,* "The Lord gave me a good voice and I can still sing." Bear Family Records of Germany released two boxed sets containing all 186 of the recordings he made through 1964, and RCA reissued his best and biggest numbers in their *Legends* Series.

The hand of time catches up to all of us sooner or later. Hank's "By the Grace of God: The Gospel Album" at age eighty-eight in 2006 proved to be his last. On September 8, 2007, he made what would prove to be his final *Grand Ole Opry* appearance. Hank lived a full life and experienced a musical career that spanned more than six decades despite a late start. Brother Lawrence Hankins Locklin passed away a year and a half later on March 8, 2009, his destiny fulfilled.

**Note**: The best biographical and discographical data on Hank Locklin is found in the two respective booklets by the late Otto Kitsinger and Kevin Coffey that accompany his Bear Family boxed sets. My own first writing on Locklin is his entry in *Definitive Country: The Ultimate Encyclopedia of Country Music and Its Performers* (New York: Perigee Books, 1995), p. 477. His Masonic records were provided by the Grand Lodge of Florida, the Scottish Rite in Nashville and the Hadji Shrine Temple in Pensacola.

Hitherto unpublished

**Brother Hank Thompson**:
*From Making Music to Making History*

Among the many innovators in the evolution of country and western music during the forties, fifties, and sixties, few had a more long-range impact than a soft-spoken gentleman from Texas named Henry William Thompson. Combining the honky-tonk sound popularized by Ernest Tubb and Hank Williams with the big band, western swing music associated with Bob Wills, Hank Thompson led an aggregation called the Brazos Valley Boys that made numerous musical inroads during the quarter century following World War II.

Lesser known is the fact that Hank entered Masonry shortly after he came of age and although his constant traveling precluded heavy participation in the usual Masonic activities, his group played for so many Shrine functions over the years that he became an honorary member of several Temples throughout the entire country.

Henry William Thompson was born near Waco, Texas on September 3, 1925, and grew up the son of a railroader-auto mechanic. He exhibited an early interest in making music and initially learned on the harmonica, a skill that the youngster successfully demonstrated in local talent shows. However, when he saw singing cowboy hero and long-time member of Catoosa Lodge No. 185 in Oklahoma in a live concert, young Hank added singing with guitar to his developing prowess. Soon he had a Saturday morning job at a local theater and in 1942 added a radio program on station WACO where he became known as "Hank, the Hired Hand."

Following completion of high school early in 1943, Thompson, along with thousands of other young men, entered military service by joining the United States Navy. He served as a radio technician until the end of the war and spent brief stints attending Princeton, Southern Methodist, and the University of Texas.

However, he soon returned to his initial love, radio entertaining, when he took a job at newly opened KWTX in Waco in the summer of 1946. In August, Hank had his first recording session when he went to Dallas and cut "Whoa, Sailor" and "Swing Wide Your Gate of Love" for the small independent Globe label. A few months later, he waxed four more sides for Blue Bonnet.

During this same period when Thompson was initiating a career that would make him a major figure in his chosen field of music, he was also beginning his Masonic experiences. Shortly after his twenty-first birthday, Hank received his Entered Apprentice Degree in George N. Denton Lodge No. 24 in Waco. In December 1946, Henry William Thompson was raised to the sublime degree of Master Mason. He continued his Masonic education in the York Rite Bodies of Waco in the early months of 1947. Hank explained his preference for the York Rite in practical terms for one in his occupation. A country-western musician's best work opportunities took place on weekends and one could take Chapter and Commandery work on week nights.

Thompson also joined the local Karem Shrine Temple in the spring of 1947, but as their ceremonial interfered with a lucrative show date, he actually "walked the sands" in the spring class at Arabia Temple in Houston as a courtesy to the Nobles in Waco.

Meanwhile, Hank Thompson's musical star continued to rise. At the suggestion of another singing cowboy star, Tex Ritter (member of Metropolitan Lodge No. 646 in Los Angeles), Hank signed a contract with Capitol Records, making his first recordings late in 1947. His first hit, "Humpty Dumpty Heart," peaked at number two, spending thirty-eight weeks on the charts beginning in late January 1948 but failed to displace Brother Eddy Arnold's "Anytime" at the top. Through the end of the forties, eight more of his songs made the *Billboard* listings.

In 1949, Thompson spent a few months at the *Grand Ole Opry* in Nashville and had several moderate hits, but it was his recording of "The Wild Side of Life" made on December 11, 1951, that would propel the young Texan into the ranks of musical legend. The song had been a minor hit for Jimmy Heap's Melody Masters on Imperial Records a few months earlier, having been co-written by that group's piano player, Arlie Carter. Hank's rendition became one of the all-time country classics with its memorable chorus line, "I didn't know

God made honky-tonk angels." The lyrics addressed a real social problem—the increased instability of home-life and marriages in the faster-paced life styles of post-World War II America—and hit home with tens of thousands of working class citizens. The song hit number one on the *Billboard* charts in May 1952 and remained there for fifteen weeks. It spent a total of seven months on the listings, climbed to twenty-seven on the pop charts, and became a certified million seller.

The success of "The Wild Side of Life" altered the course of country music history in ways that Hank could not have foretold when he first recorded the song. For instance, it quickly spawned a lyrical answer, "It Wasn't God Who Made Honky-Tonk Angels," that launched country songstress Kitty Wells on the road to becoming the first female superstar in what had generally been a male dominated field. Her achievement, in turn, led to other country girl singers receiving contracts on major record labels.

In fact, Hank himself, who was always ready to help upcoming talents, assisted three of the best of the new wave of vocalists. In 1953, he helped Jean Shepard secure her first contract with Capitol. The following year, he did the same for young Wanda Jackson, who was initially contracted to Decca and then Capitol. He played a lesser role in aiding Wanda's friend, Norma Jean (Beasler), who would subsequently have a string of hit records on RCA Victor.

Meanwhile, Hank and the Brazos Valley Boys shifted their home base to Oklahoma City where they enjoyed a top-rated TV show for several years while continuing to tour extensively and work at the local Trianon Ballroom in between times. He also continued to turn out hit records including "Yesterday's Girl," "Blackboard of My Heart," Honky-Tonk Girl," Wake Up Irene," and "Rub-a-Dub-Dub." In the later fifties he cut a few numbers with a rockabilly flavor such as "Rockin' in the Congo" and "Squaws Along the Yukon" but then came back to his old sound with "A Six Pack To Go," "Hangover Tavern," and a revival of Jack Guthrie's classic song from 1945, "Oklahoma Hills." For fourteen years in a row (1952-1966), the Brazos Valley Boys were ranked as the nation's leading western band.

During those years, Thompson and his band entertained at many Shrine Temples. Noble Hank was made an honorary member of several including Anchorage, Denver, Longview, Oklahoma City, Trenton, and Tulsa. He decided to join the Scottish Rite and was accepted to receive the degrees in Oklahoma City, but he never did find the time to take the work. He did, however, join one more

Masonic-related group in 1985 when he became a member of the Tulsa Court of the Royal Order of Jesters.

Hank Thompson broke up his bigger band in the later 1960s, working most often as a solo vocalist while continuing to record first for Warner Brothers and then on Dot for eleven years. He had some additional hits, most notably "Where Is the Circus" in 1966, "The Older the Violin, the Sweeter the Music," and "Who Left the Door to Heaven Open," both in 1974. Hank remained a fixture on the charts through 1983, chalking up a total of seventy-nine hits.

However, the eighteen years Thompson spent on Capitol with his band, sometimes numbering as many as eleven members, would be those that highlighted his talents at their best. In 1989, his long years of musical quality were rewarded when he was elected to the Country Music Hall of Fame.

While Hank Thompson's place in country music history remained secure, he continued to be the modest relaxed gentleman who persisted into his seventies in giving his loyal fans the opportunity to see him. In the late 1990s, he still played about a hundred dates yearly from his home in Roanoke, Texas, a few miles from Fort Worth. By the time of his death on November 6, 2007, both he and the fraternity could take just pride in Brother Thompson's achievements to the American music scene.

**Note**: Brother Hank Thompson himself furnished much of the information for this article including the portrait photograph.

September 1996; slightly revised 2011

## Brother Henry Harley "Hap" Arnold:
*Creator of the Modern Air Force*

Of the few American military figures to attain the five-star rank or higher, Henry Harley Arnold is probably the least known today. Yet more than the others, Arnold seems to be the man most responsible for changing the nature of warfare. His belief in the growing significance of air power and implementation thereof proved not only prophetic but played a key role in the Allied victory of World War II. When the Air Force became a separate branch of the Defense Department, Arnold, although officially retired, became their ranking general. Despite his position, rank, and importance in the history of aviation, Brother Arnold remains less known today than either Brother Charles Lindbergh or one of his predecessors, the court-martialed air power advocate of the twenties, General Billy Mitchell.

Henry Harley Arnold was born in Gladwyne, Pennsylvania on June 25, 1886. The Arnold family had something of a citizen soldier tradition as his ancestors had fought in both the American Revolution and the Civil War. Herbert Arnold, his humorless father, had been an army physician in the invasion of Puerto Rico during the Spanish-American War and remained in the Pennsylvania National Guard while his mother, Ann Harley, came from a Pennsylvania Dutch background. Hap grew up in Ardmore, Pennsylvania, and manifested an early interest in a military career. In 1903 at seventeen, he secured a West Point appointment and entered the United States Military Academy in July of 1903. As a cadet, he generally performed in the average range, graduating 66$^{th}$ in a class of 111 in 1907. Hoping for a cavalry assignment, he felt disappointed at being placed in the infantry. However, he accepted it and was sent to Fort McKinley in the Philippines.

Little did either the young lieutenant or his superiors know at the time that events were occurring that would change both his life and the military establishment forever. The year that Arnold entered West Point, two brothers who operated a bicycle shop in Dayton, Ohio, built and flew the first airplane for a distance of 120 feet. The year that he graduated from the Academy, the Army Signal Corps began taking an interest in aeronautics. Shortly after he returned from the Philippines to take an assignment at Governor's Island, New York, Wilbur Wright and Glenn Curtiss made their historic flight demonstrations. Soon afterward, the Army purchased three planes from Wright and two from Curtiss. Hap Arnold and Thomas Milling were accepted as volunteers to receive training as the first army pilots. The two went to Dayton, Ohio where they not only learned to fly the planes but learned virtually everything known about them at the time. In June 1911, Arnold went to College Park, Maryland, where he became a flight instructor.

Over the next several years, Hap Arnold had numerous assignments in various locales including another tour of duty in the Philippines. In the fall of 1916, he received a promotion to Captain and in July 1920 to Major. Ironically, as a man who craved action, when the United States entered World War I, Arnold, according to his biographer Dik A. Daso, "hoped to obtain a command of a flying squadron bound for Europe, but he was destined to remain in Washington as a non-combat staff officer." In those years, the future Army Air Force commander started a family, marrying Eleanor Pool (usually known as "Bee" or "Beadle") on September 10, 1913. The marriage ultimately resulted in four children and endured for the life of the participants, although it did become strained at times as was often the case with career service people.

Major Arnold spent the period from 1919 to August 1924 in California where he served with other officers who also played key roles in the development of air power including Brother James Doolittle, Ira Eaker, and Carl Spaatz. He also had made the acquaintance of Billy Mitchell with whom he shared many ideas, but as Daso states, he also learned from Mitchell "how not to tackle political problems." While Mitchell virtually martyred himself, Arnold was "exiled" to Fort Riley, Kansas. He remained in the service and continued his advocacy of air power inside the system, a strategy that eventually triumphed.

In Kansas from March 1926 until June 1929 as the senior air instructor at Riley, Arnold also wrote a series of six juvenile books about an aviator named "Bill Bruce" (a name taken from his middle son). During those years he also became a Mason. Henry Harley

Arnold was raised in Union Lodge No. 7 in Junction City, Kansas, on November 3, 1927. A year and a half later, he completed the Scottish Rite degrees in Army Consistory in the Valley of Fort Leavenworth on April 11, 1929. Sixteen years later when his name had become a household word, General Arnold received the 33° on October 19, 1945. General Doolittle received the 33° at the same time. At the time of his AASR work, Hap was attending the General Service School at Leavenworth. After completing this school, he was assigned to the Fairfield Air Depot near Dayton, Ohio. He took command of this important air research center on June 25, 1929.

Two years later in February, he received a promotion to lieutenant colonel. That fall, he became commanding officer at March Field near Los Angeles. He remained there until January 1936 when he became Assistant Chief of the Army Air Corps. Hap served under Brother Oscar Westover. Unfortunately, Major General Westover died in a tragic air crash on September 21, 1938. Eight days later, H. H. "Hap" Arnold found himself appointed by President Roosevelt as Commanding Officer of the Army Air Corps. Already holding the temporary rank of Brigadier General, he also became a Major General the same month.

Arnold assumed his position at a time when war clouds were gathering in both the Far East and Europe. The Japanese had launched their war against China in 1937, and the Munich Conference had dominated the news the week of his appointment. Ideas like those of Billy Mitchell were no longer considered crazy and within a few years were counted as prophetic. The budget cuts of 1933 and 1934 had halted in 1935, and the budget began to slowly increase in 1936. From the time Arnold took command in September of 1938 until his death in January 1950, the general kept "technological change and its impact upon airpower at the forefront of his . . . efforts." With the reorganization of the War Department in June of 1941 he became chief of the Army Air Forces. By that time, air defense preparation had reached major proportions, particularly after the fall of France in June of 1940. Several months of witnessing the German blitzkrieg had made the need painfully obvious to even a tightfisted Congress.

Once the war began for the United States in December of 1941, time became a major factor. General Arnold had earlier called for a 50,000-plane air force that would take eighteen months to construct and two years to properly train the personnel, considered impossible by many critics. But with the determination of an American public and the General's direction, it became a virtual reality. Along with Secretary of War Henry Stimson, Navy Secretary Brother Frank Knox, General and Brother George Marshall, presidential advisor Harry Hopkins, Admirals Harold Stark, and Sir Knight Ernest King, Hap became part of the "war fighting brain trust for the next five years." As the war progressed, Arnold attained a third star on December 15, 1941; a fourth on March 19, 1943; and a fifth on December 21, 1944.

As commander of the Army Air Force, Hap Arnold's responsibilities seemed virtually insurmountable. Planning and implementing daylight bombing missions took top priority, and providing air support for the ground forces came in a close second. Arnold discussed his other work as follows: "Air power is a composite of airplane, air crews, maintenance crews, air bases, air supply, and sufficient replacements in both planes and crews to maintain a constant fighting strength, regardless of what losses may be inflicted by the enemy." He also knew that there were times when public relations were important. Perhaps the best known of these was carrying out the dramatic air raid—led by Jimmy Doolittle—over Tokyo on April 18, 1942. While the successful raid "accomplished little in the way of physical damage to the enemy, it boosted allied morale in unquantifiable ways." Doolittle (a member of Hollenbeck Lodge No 319 since August 16, 1918), who had once been disciplined by Arnold, received the Medal of Honor for his action and eventually became a three-star general.

A catalog of Arnold's activities during the war would be lengthy but serve little purpose here. He continued, as had Mitchell, to work toward an independent air force as a branch of the military. His grueling war-time schedule did take a toll on his health. He experienced his first serious heart problem in May 1943. Not long after receiving his fifth star in January 1945, he suffered a heart attack. This disabled him until mid-March. Nonetheless, he continued on duty until June 30, 1946 when he officially retired. Finally, on September 18, 1947, his goal of a separate air force became a reality, although the navy continued to have an air contingent.

Hap and Bee Arnold had purchased a small ranch near Sonoma, California as a retirement residence. Health problems continued to plague his declining years although he managed to make a few trips back East, part of them to receive a variety of honors. He worked on his memoirs which saw publication as *Global Mission* by Harper & Brothers in 1949. His condition continued to decline, and he passed away on January 15, 1950. He received a full military funeral in Washington on January 19 and was buried in Arlington. More than a half century after his death, Brother H. H. Arnold's legacy seems assured. To him, more than to any other individual, belongs credit for making the United States the dominant air power.

**Note**: The most up-to-date work on Brother Arnold is Dik Alan Daso, *Hap Arnold and the Evolution of American Airpower* (2000). For his Masonic background, see William R. Denslow, *10,000 Famous Freemasons,* I, p. 31 (1957).

August 2006, slightly revised 2011

**Brother Heinie Groh**:
*The Bottle Bat Man and Fifty Year Mason*

To the degree that Henry Knight Groh is remembered by baseball fans today, it is usually for his unusual shaped bat that resembled a milk bottle with a slender elongated handle. However, Groh was much more than that, being one of the best fielding and hitting third basemen of his generation. In addition, "Heinie" (as most German-Americans named Henry were nicknamed in that era) was a fifty-two year member of E. T. Carson Lodge No. 598 in his adopted hometown of Cincinnati.

Henry Knight Groh was born in Rochester, New York, on September 18, 1889. As a youngster, Henry and his older brother, Lewis, both developed a serious interest in baseball, and both eventually played in the big time, although Lew only got into two games with Connie Mack's Philadelphia Athletics in 1919. Rochester was a hot baseball town, being a stalwart in the International League from 1899 until 1962, albeit the city didn't really experience its best days until the team became the crown jewel in Branch Rickey's vast St. Louis Cardinal farm system from 1928. When Heinie finished high school, he was about to enter the University of Rochester when fate intervened, and in 1908 he accepted an offer to play shortstop with Oshkosh in the Wisconsin-Illinois League. He later recalled that his parents thought he would be back home in less than a month, but the youth stayed for the rest of the season. While Groh did well in the field, he batted a lackluster .161.

Heinie Groh was bitten by the "baseball bug" and was determined to improve his skills with the bat. As he later told baseball historian Lawrence Ritter, "I kept practicing and practicing at it and the next year I hit about .285, and the year after that I made it to .300 [actually .297]." For the 1911 season, he played first for Decatur in the "Three I" League until July when the New York Giants purchased his contract and assigned him to Buffalo where he hit .333, and the Giants brought him up to the parent club in 1912.

Groh made his major league debut as a pinch hitter for the Giants on April 12, 1912. Umpire Bill Klem thought New York manager John McGraw was playing a joke on him by sending the pint-sized infielder into the game, but Heinie had the last laugh by hitting a single. Still, he didn't play much that year, getting into only twenty-seven games and batting a respectable .271. In that first year, he did get a custom bat made for himself at McGraw's suggestion with a thick barrel for maximum contact with the ball, but with a thin handle that he could best grip with his small fingers and hands. Thus the bottle bat became Groh's trademark for the remainder of his career.

The next major event in the young infielder's career came in May of 1913 when he was traded to the Cincinnati Reds. This provided him with the opportunity to play regularly, and in 117 appearances he became a fixture at second base and hit .282. In fact, for the rest of his time with the Reds, that would be his lowest average except for an off-year in 1916 when he dropped to .265. In 1915, he was switched to third base and proved especially adept at fielding bunts in an era when the "hot corner" was just that.

In 1916, Henry Knight Groh became a member of E. T. Carson Lodge, being initiated an Entered Apprentice on January 14 and passed to the degree of Fellowcraft on February 11. Spring training intervened at that point, but not for long as he was raised to the sublime degree of Master Mason on April 14, 1916. Heinie went on to receive his Fifty Year Award in 1966.

In mid-July 1916, the Reds and Giants engaged in one of the games more unusual trades. Club President Garry Herrmann traded Cincinnati manager Buck Herzog and others to the Giants for fading one-time pitching superstar Christy Matthewson and others. Matty then became the Reds manager. Whether the latter would have become a great manager had not World War I intervened is hard to say, but in 1917 and 1918, the Reds, did post-winning records for the first time in several years. Heinie led the league in hits in 1917, in doubles both of those years, and in runs scored in 1918. When Mathewson entered military service in August, Groh served as interim manager, winning seven victories in the final ten games of that shortened season.

In 1919, the Reds, paced by team captain Groh and center fielder Brother Edd Roush who had .310 and .321 seasons, respectively, struck pay dirt. The team brought home both the National League pennant and a World Series victory to Redland Field. The latter would forever be tainted by the Black Sox scandal that unraveled the next year. However, both Groh and Roush maintained to their dying day that the Reds would have won anyway. Masonic membership on that team was high, since other members of the squad included Jake Daubert at first base, Larry Kopf at short, catcher Ivy Wingo, pitcher Ray Fisher, and outfielders Earle Neale, Rube Bressler, and Pat Duncan in addition to Roush, Groh, and club President Garry Herrmann. As team captain, Henry K. Groh received the winning team's share of the World Series money—$117,157.35—from which each player received a full share of $5,207.01.

The 1920 edition of the Reds slumped to third, and Heinie's average dropped to .298 although Roush surged to .339. This circumstance may have been a contributing factor in both of the team stars becoming holdouts in the spring of 1921. Groh signed on June 1 only after being promised that he would immediately be traded back to the Giants. Then Commissioner Landis voided the trade but finally approved it in December. As a result, the little third baseman played in only ninety-seven games in his last year as a Red and hit only .231.

Back with John McGraw's team in the Polo Grounds, the 5' 8" third baseman had only a mediocre season at the plate, but the Giants had a good year, coming in seven games ahead of the Reds for league honors and trouncing the Yankees in the World Series. However, that Series provided Groh with some of the finest moments of his career. While the Reds had won in 1919, Heinie's own performance had been unspectacular. His play in this all New York classic was among the best ever. He made a total of nine hits, scored four runs, knocked in two, and had a .474 average (just ahead of Frank Frisch's .471). The story goes that he was so proud of his performance that he had the number 474 on his Ohio license plate for the remainder of his life.

Groh spent two more years as a regular at the "hot corner" for McGraw's Giants. Unlike his friend and brother Edd Roush who cared little for the belligerent and controversial Giant skipper, Heinie respected and got along with the man. He also continued as a solid performer in the Giant lineup hitting .290 and .281 in those years. Late in the 1924 season, he sustained a knee injury and had to be replaced in the World Series by young Fred Lindstrom who had the misfortune of having a ground ball take a bad bounce over his head and pave the way for an unexpected Washington Senator world championship. Heinie had a pinch hit single in his only plate appearance.

Heinie Groh's knee injury continued to plague him, and he saw only limited action with the Giants in the next two years as Fred Lindstrom took over third base chores. McGraw released the veteran player in 1926. Former major leaguers often continued for several years in the minors in that era. Signed by the Toledo Mud Hens, he held down third base for much of that season batting .304 in 104 games. Heinie went back to his old hometown of Rochester where he also hit above .300 and found himself back in the big time in the latter part of 1927 when the Pittsburgh Pirates called him up toward the end of the season. He made his last appearance in a big league uniform as a pinch hitter in the 1927 series. Overall, the little German-American had a .292 lifetime batting average. Returning to the minors, he managed and played part-time for Charlotte in the South Atlantic League in 1928, for Hartford in the Eastern League in 1929, and finally for Canton in 1930. Playing on a part-time basis, he continued to bat in excess of .300 each year.

After managing in the minors and doing some scouting, Heinie Groh returned to Cincinnati where he made his home in the off-season and worked as a cashier at River Downs Race Track near the Queen City until he retired. He participated in old-timer events and was enshrined in the Cincinnati Reds Hall of Fame in 1963. In 1966, he received his fifty-year pin from E. T. Carson Lodge, passing away on August 22, 1968. Numerous advocates still favor his enshrinement in Cooperstown.

**Note**: A prime source of information regarding Groh is the chapter in Lawrence S. Ritter, *The Glory of Their Times* (Vintage Books, 1985) and various books on the Cincinnati Reds, especially Greg Rhodes and John Snyder, *Redleg Journal* (Road West Pub., 2000). For the data on his Masonic records, thanks to George Braatz, PGM and Grand Secretary of the Grand Lodge of Ohio. Thanks also to S. K Norman Lincoln of the York Rite bodies in Eaton, Ohio for assistance with photos and a variety of internet data including the SABR website bio of Groh by Sean Lahman; I appreciate the help of Bro. Jake Bapst of Centerville Lodge No. 371 in Thurman, Ohio.

May 2007; slightly revised 2011

**Brother Henry M. Jackson:**
*The Ultimate Cold War Liberal!*

In the post-World War II generation, a high degree of inter-party cooperation developed between Democrats and Republicans in the field of what became known as "Bipartisan Foreign Policy." The latter largely grew out of cooperation between liberal President, Brother Harry S. Truman, and a conservative Senate leader, Brother Arthur Vandenburg, in their support of the Marshall Plan. This foreign assistance program was successfully designed to restructure a war-torn Western Europe and simultaneously serve as a bulwark against a potentially expansionist Soviet Union. Politicians who supported liberal domestic programs while equally backing a strong anti-Communist foreign policy agenda became known as "Cold War liberals." One of the strongest among this group was Brother Henry M. Jackson of Washington State who toiled for thirty years in the United States Senate as a "staunch cold warrior." One of the tragedies of Jackson's life was that he did not live to see the downfall of the Old Soviet Union.

Henry Martin Jackson was born in the lumber mill town of Everett, Washington, on May 31, 1912. He came from a Norwegian ethnic background, and Henry's father had Anglicized the family name from Gresseth. The elder Jackson worked his way up the economic ladder from laborer to independent contractor and secretary of a local of the Plasterers and Cement Masons Union. As a youngster, a sister gave Henry the nickname "Scoop" which he retained through life. He sold newspapers and later worked summers in a local sawmill. Young Henry also belonged to DeMolay.

After graduation from high school in 1930, young Jackson went to Stanford University for a short time but then returned to his home state and the University of Washington. He obtained a BA in

1934 and a law degree in 1935. He briefly worked for the F.E.R.A. until passing his bar exams when he joined a local law firm. In 1938 Jackson ran for Snohomish County prosecuting attorney. He defeated the Democratic incumbent in the spring primary and won an easy victory in the fall. Scoop soon earned something of a Puritanical reputation with a crusade against bawdy houses, speakeasies, and bordellos. In 1940 he decided to run for Congress when the House member from his district opted to run for a Senate seat. Jackson ran first in a primary field of five and won the seat in November on the coattails of F.D.R's third-term victory.

Meanwhile, Henry Martin Jackson began his Masonic journey by petitioning Everett Lodge No. 137 on March 13, 1939. Scoop took the Entered Apprentice degree on April 1, 1939; was Passed on July 24, 1939; and Raised a Master Mason on October 16, 1939. The following year, he completed the Scottish Rite degrees on December 18, 1940.

As a member of Congress, Henry Jackson served the Second District of Washington for twelve years. He spent much of 1943 and the early part of 1944 in the United States Army but retained his House seat. In 1944 President Roosevelt recalled "uniformed members of Congress" to Washington and "Scoop" received his military discharge.

During his years in Congress, Jackson earned high marks in his district for promoting defense industries, championing public power projects, and supporting organized labor. His popularity can be best illustrated by the fact that he was virtually the only Democrat in the Pacific Northwest to survive the GOP landslide of 1946, an election that saw him defeat a perpetual opponent named Payson Peterson. Throughout most of his career in Washington, Jackson styled himself a Truman Democrat.

In 1952 Jackson gave up his relatively safe House seat to challenge incumbent GOP Senator, Harry P. Cain, described by one historian as an "archconservative." Trends favored Republicans that year, as the party of the elephant was riding on a tidal wave of the popularity of their presidential nominee, General Dwight D. Eisenhower. However, Scoop Jackson bucked the odds and became one of only two Democrats to defeat a sitting Republican senator. Jackson bested Cain by a vote of 595,675 to 460,884. Ironically, both candidates accused the other of being soft on Communism.

Early in his Senate career, Henry Jackson first gained national attention by his increasing dissatisfaction with the methods of

Wisconsin's anti-Communist zealot Joe McCarthy's censure. A grateful party leadership rewarded Scoop with the kind of committee assignments most beneficial to a Pacific Northwest Senator—Interior and Insular Affairs, Armed Services, and Atomic Energy. As the fifties came to an end, Jackson expressed increasing concern that the Eisenhower Administration's fiscal concern with balancing the budget was creating a "missile gap."

As a supporter of Senator John F. Kennedy in the 1960 presidential race, Henry Jackson became chairman of the Democratic National Committee and campaigned hard for the Kennedy-Johnson ticket. Helping to secure a narrow victory for his team further enhanced Scoop's prestige within the party ranks although he seems to have become disenchanted with the Kennedys. He opposed creation of the Arms Control and Disarmament Agency in 1961 and supported the 1963 Nuclear Test Ban Treaty with considerable reluctance. However, he continued to support opposition to North Vietnamese aggression in Southeast Asia.

As cracks appeared in the armor of bipartisan foreign policy in the latter half of the sixties, Henry Jackson remained firmly in the camp of the staunch opponents of Communism. While increasingly at odds with the "dove" faction in his own party on foreign policy issues, Scoop Jackson remained firmly in the liberal camp on civil rights issues, although he ultimately opposed forced busing to bring about school integration. He also gained a reputation as a strong supporter of the rights of American Indians, particularly as Chair of the Interior and Insular Affairs Committee. A supporter of most New Frontier and Great Society programs, Jackson also distinguished himself as a strong supporter of Israel from 1948 until his death. In 1974 the Jewish Heritage Society named the Washington Senator as their Man of the Year. Throughout the seventies Jackson expressed concerns for the plight of Soviet Jews.

Although Jackson remained a strong Democrat, Richard Nixon, when he became President, offered him the post of Secretary of Defense, but the senator declined out of fears that he might become a scapegoat for the failure of others. The position ultimately went to House member, Brother Melvin Laird of Wisconsin. Nonetheless, he continued as a leader of Democratic "Hawks" and supported the bombing of North Vietnam and the mining of Haiphong Harbor.

In 1972 Henry Jackson decided to seek the Democratic presidential nomination, becoming especially critical of "dove" leader,

Brother George McGovern of South Dakota. However, he found himself running behind flamboyant Southerner, Brother George C. Wallace of Alabama, in efforts to court conservative Democrats. He dropped out of the race after his best showing was a third place finish of 13.5% in the Florida primary.

McGovern's drastic defeat in November led the Democrats in search of a more centrist candidate in 1976, and Jackson appeared poised to give the nomination his best shot. Jackson looked impressive in Massachusetts and Georgia. Once again, however, Scoop lost out to a Southern moderate, the "Georgia Peanut Man," Jimmy Carter. Jackson, the team player, in June 1976 endorsed Carter who had defeated him in the Pennsylvania primary.

In spite of his apparent lack of charisma in pursuit of the presidency, Jackson continued to retain favor with the citizenry in his home state. Seeking a fourth term in 1970, anti-war liberals mounted a strong effort to defeat Jackson in the primary. Scoop however, buried his leftist opponent by winning 84% of the Democratic vote. In November he also took 84% of the total vote. In 1976 the veteran solon easily won a fifth term, racking up a 71% victory.

Conservation constituted another policy area where Henry Jackson distinguished himself. In 1969 he became the first elected official to win the Sierra Club's John Muir Award. The following year he was the National Wildlife Federation's Legislator of the Year. Insisting on balance between economics and environmental issues, he supported such programs as the Supersonic Transport plane (SST), the Alaska Oil Pipeline, and offshore oil drilling.

The late seventies proved to be frustrating times for the Everett Washington statesman. His increasing unhappiness with the Carter Administration became increasingly obvious with the passing of time. National security issues lay at the heart of Jackson's dissent. Back in 1972 he had supported the Strategic Arms Limitations Treaty (S.A.L.T) I only after securing an amendment guaranteeing United States parity in future dealings with the U.S.S.R. The S.A.L.T. II Treaty, negotiated in 1979 and initially signed by Carter and Brezhnev, was totally unacceptable to Jackson who denounced it as appeasement in its purest form. Scoop also quarreled with the administration over their energy policies.

Henry Jackson did achieve some Masonic honors during the 1970s. On October 18, 1971, he was awarded the KCCH. Seven years later on November 12, 1978, he received the 33° from the Ancient Accepted Scottish Rite, Southern Masonic Jurisdiction.

In 1980 Henry Jackson distanced himself from the Carter Administration. As a result, President-elect Ronald Reagan appointed him to chair his transition team. Republicans took over the Senate, and with the new Chair of the Senate Armed Services Committee, Texas Brother John Tower (of Iowa Park Lodge No. 713), and former Chair, Brother John Stennis of Mississippi, Jackson set about to rebuild America's defenses. They had already achieved much of their goal when Jackson, who had been reelected to a sixth term in 1982, died from a heart attack on September 1, 1983.

He had been in Congress for more than forty-two years, more than thirty-one of them in the Senate. As Senator Tower, who was as conservative on domestic issues as Jackson had been liberal, recalled in his memoirs, "Scoop's untimely death...cost me a good friend...based on mutual and strongly held convictions.... By the time of Scoop's death, his legacy was priceless: strength and peace."

On the personal side, Brother Henry Jackson remained a bachelor until 1961 when the forty-nine-year-old Senator married Helen Hardin. They subsequently had two children, Anna and Peter. The Jacksons were Presbyterians and lived a fairly quiet life at their two houses (in Everett and in the Spring Valley section of Washington, D. C.). Their children attended public schools in the District of Columbia.

There were many men who made notable contributions to American statecraft during the Cold War Era. They range from Presidents Harry Truman to George Bush and from Senators Arthur Vandenberg to Richard Lugar. Certainly one of the figures who played a significant role throughout much of this period and who never wavered in his commitment to the concept of "peace through strength" was Brother Henry Martin Jackson of Everett, Washington.

**Note**: Sketches of Henry Jackson appear in the 1953 and 1979 editions of *Current Biography* and have been supplemented by other contemporary histories and accounts. For his Masonic record, I am indebted to the staff of the Grand Lodge of Washington and to Mrs. Joan Sansbury, Librarian of the A.A.S.R., S.M.J., in Washington, DC. Many of Senator Jackson's ideas can be gleaned from his book *Fact, Fiction, and National Security* (New York: McFadden Books, 1964). I am indebted to Ohio's Senior Senator in Washington, Michael DeWine, and the United States Senate Historical office. Thanks also to Shasta Dawn Amos for preparing the original typescript.

December 2000; slightly revised 2011

**Sir Knight Hiram Johnson:**
*Reform Governor, Isolationist Senator, and Father of California Recall*

The excitement engendered by the California Recall Election of October 7, 2003, should provide Americans in general and Golden State residents in particular cause to remember Hiram Warren Johnson who became one of the nation's key political figures during the first half of the twentieth century. From 1910 until his death thirty-five years later, Sir Knight and Brother Johnson—a maverick Republican—held center stage much of the time. He first gained fame as a reform governor in California after his election in 1910 and went on to become the Bull Moose Party's candidate for Vice President on a ticket with Brother Theodore Roosevelt in 1912, the only time a third party ever took second place in a national election. As a successful United States Senate candidate in 1916, he may have indirectly cost Charles Evans Hughes the Presidency, and by turning down a vice presidential nomination in 1920, probably cost himself the White House. Never afraid to take controversial positions, Johnson is almost as known for his isolationist foreign policy as for his earlier image as a reformer. A fifty-six year Mason, Brother Johnson was one of the most memorable figures of his era.

Hiram Warren Johnson was born in Sacramento on September 2, 1866, the son of Grove and Annie Johnson. Grove Johnson was one of the California capital city's best-known and most successful attorneys who served one term in Congress and several times in the state legislature. Ironically, when young Hiram became seriously involved in politics, he staunchly opposed the power of the Southern Pacific Railroad while his father represented the S. P. and was considered one of their prime defenders. Hiram attended the local schools and after finishing high school, worked briefly as a court stenographer before going to the University of California. He dropped out of college in his junior year when he married Minnie McNeal at age twenty.

The young college dropout passed his bar exams in 1888, and both Hiram Johnson and his older brother Albert went into their father's law firm. During his first full year as an attorney, Hiram Warren Johnson became a member of Washington Lodge No. 20 in Sacramento. He was initiated on March 21, 1889; passed on April 11, 1889; and raised to the sublime degree of Master Mason on May 9, 1889. He remained a member of Washington Lodge until his death. As a York Rite member, he joined Sacramento Chapter No. 3, Royal Arch Masons and Sacramento Commandery No. 2, Knights Templar. A futile search for his degree dates by current Recorder Jon Humphreys turned up nothing beyond his being in good standing at the time of his death, but it seems likely to have been either during the period after he was raised or during the time he was governor, because he resided in San Francisco from 1902 onward except while he was in the State House.

Johnson practiced law with his father and brother for several years and became known as a courtroom attorney of quality. Hiram's first real experience in politics came in 1892 when he and Albert managed their father's winning campaign for Congress. However, when the time came for a second term, the sons refused to help, because Grove Johnson had not been independent of the rail interests. They in turn formed their own law firm, and for several years, father and sons were estranged. At one point, Grove Johnson reportedly called them his "two chief enemies . . . Hiram, full of egotism . . . and Albert, full of booze." The brothers then successfully supported reformer George Clark for mayor, and Hiram became city attorney. During this period, he further established his reputation as a reformer by cleaning up the vice and gambling interests in the city.

In 1902, the Johnson Brothers moved their law practice to San Francisco where Hiram joined Islam Shrine Temple and became "one of the best jury lawyers on the Pacific Coast." He also became closely identified with the reform wing of the Republican Party and a disciple on the national scene of President Theodore Roosevelt (of Matinecock Lodge No. 806 in Oyster Bay, N. Y.). The reformers organized a group known as the Lincoln-Roosevelt League as a vehicle to promote reform and what came to be termed the "progressive" movement within GOP ranks. Events in San Francisco would soon give a strong boost to their cause.

Federal attorney Francis Heney was in the course of prosecuting a number of city officials in connection with bribery and corruption, most notably San Francisco "political boss," Abraham Ruef. At a moment filled with drama on November 13, 1908, a man whose convict past had caused him to be rejected as a juror shot Heney and later took his own life in his jail cell. Although Heney eventually recovered, Johnson took over the prosecution and secured Ruef's conviction. The case made Johnson a household name in the Golden State and a favorite in the 1910 race for governor. He toured California in a little red auto with one son driving the car and another ringing a cowbell to announce the candidate's arrival. He promised clean government, numerous reforms, and a pledge to get the Southern Pacific Railroad out of the state's politics. He triumphed over four opponents in the primary, getting 101,000 votes to his nearest rival's 55,000 but had a closer call in the general election, winning over Democrat Theodore Bell by 177,000 to 155,000.

The heart of Governor Johnson's reforms—other than to reduce the influence of the Southern Pacific—was embodied in a series of state constitutional amendments submitted to the electorate in 1911. Among them was "recall." Removing public officials before the expiration of their term of office had been approved in other locales beginning with the Los Angeles City Charter of 1903 and the state of Oregon in 1908. The most controversial aspect of the California plan came in the fact that it included judges; even some advocates opposed this portion on the grounds that it would subject judicial decisions to public whim. However, the recall amendment passed by more than a three to one margin while items considered much less controversial today including initiative and woman suffrage barely passed. On the strength of his achievements in the Golden State, Teddy Roosevelt chose Johnson as his running mate on the Progressive Party "Bull Moose" ticket in 1912. The Roosevelt-Johnson team carried six states with 88 electoral votes and 27% of the popular vote nationwide, the only time a third party ever came in second place. The Bull Moose ticket narrowly carried California by a plurality of fewer than 200 votes.

Elected to a second term as Governor on the Progressive ticket, Johnson pulled more than 460,000 votes to the regular Republican John Fredericks' 271,000 and Democrat John Curtin's 116,000. He continued reform programs but became increasingly drawn to national issues. As Teddy Roosevelt returned to the Republican Party, it eventually dawned on Johnson that the Progressive Party was dying, and he too came back to the GOP ranks but remained a party maverick. In 1916, Hiram Johnson announced for the U. S. Senate. Elected easily, some blamed him for the defeat of Republican presidential nominee Charles Evans Hughes who lost California and the White House by only 4,000 votes. However, as historian George Mowry has suggested, it seems more likely that women voters' support for Wilson ranked as the major factor. It is also true that Johnson's support for Hughes was less enthusiastic than it could have been.

Johnson held the Senate seat for the rest of his life. He was re-elected in 1922, 1928, 1934, and 1940. By his last term, California voters, by virtue of their open primary, actually nominated the old reformer warhorse not only on the Republican ticket, but also on the Democratic and Progressive party lines as well, although he got more GOP votes.

It would hardly be surprising to learn that Johnson continued his maverick ways throughout his Senate career. In 1920, Sir Knight Warren Harding offered him the vice presidential nomination, but Sir Knight Johnson rejected it, thus missing his best chance for the White House when Harding died in office in 1923. The Californian did challenge Calvin Coolidge in 1924 but failed to gain the nomination. During the Hoover administration, Johnson opposed Herbert Hoover's policies most of the time. Offered a cabinet post by Franklin Roosevelt in 1933, he refused it but did support enough of the New Deal to win an endorsement from FDR in 1934 when he received his largest majority yet. However, he soon fell out with Roosevelt.

During his Senate career, Hiram Johnson became best known for isolationist views on foreign policy. He began this position shortly after entering the Senate in 1917 by voting against American entry into World War I. After the conflict ended, he was one of the two or three most important of the "Irreconcilables" who opposed the Treaty of Versailles and American membership in the League of Nations. In the words of historian Robert H. Ferrell, Johnson held to the viewpoint that the United States should continue "abstention from international political commitments," maintaining the freedom to act in her own best interests. During the twenties, he steadfastly opposed the United States joining the World Court, and one of the primary reasons for his break with FDR was his negative views toward the reciprocal trade treaties that the State Department negotiated in the era when Cordell Hull ran foreign affairs. In the pre-World War II period, he opposed any type of aid to the allies and in 1940 provided enthusiastic support for Wendell Willkie, the first time he had been really enthusiastic about any Republican contender since the days of Teddy Roosevelt. Willkie's later internationalism must have disappointed him greatly. Johnson did vote for a Declaration of War following the Japanese attack on Pearl Harbor, but opposed using any National Guard troops outside of the Western Hemisphere. One of his last efforts in the Senate was in opposition to the United States joining the United Nations. He announced his position from his deathbed and shortly afterward passed to the celestial lodge above on August 6, 1945.

Hiram Johnson's career was indeed an odd mixture. His enemies on the right considered him a "revolutionary," while those on the left called him "reactionary." He made numerous miscalculations and too frequently displayed more concern with personalities than with issues and principles. While the "special interests" he fought in 1910 are different from those of more recent times, they can still create problems for the broad spectrum of the public. When one looks at either the difficulties of Californians in recent years or at the failure of the United Nations to do anything but pass meaningless resolutions and then do nothing to enforce them, one suspects that if Sir Knight Hiram Johnson were alive today, he would probably be saying "I could have told you so."

**Note**: For a serious look at Hiram Johnson, see George E. Mowry, *The California Progressives* (1951) and Ralph Stone, *The Irreconcilables* (1970). See also his 1941 entry in *Current Biography*. For his Masonic record, I am indebted to the staff at the Grand Lodge of California and the Grand York Rite Bodies of California. Although his search proved fruitless, that of Jon Humphreys, Secretary of the Sacramento York Rite Bodies, was more than commendable.

October 2004; slightly revised 2011

**Brother Honus Wagner:**
*The Greatest Pittsburgh Pirate*

When the first five names were announced for entry into Baseball's Hall of Fame on February 2, 1936, three of the inductees were Masons. Ty Cobb and Christy Mathewson enjoyed careers that have already been discussed in this journal. The third was a modest German-American nicknamed the "Flying Dutchman" who hailed from an industrial town near Pittsburgh—John Peter "Honus" Wagner—who by consensus at the time was considered the greatest shortstop who ever played the game. An outstanding hitter as well, Wagner batted .300 or better for seventeen consecutive years and won eight batting titles in that era. Described by authoritative baseball historian Charles Alexander as "homely, ungainly, [and] beer-bellied," Wagner hardly looked like the All-American athlete, but one could scarcely argue with his achievements.

Johannes (John in English) Peter Wagner was born in Mansfield, Pennsylvania on February 24, 1874. His parents, Peter and Catherine Wagner, had migrated from a village on the Rhine River in 1866. The family also included three older boys as well as one younger boy and a younger girl. John attended both public school and a Lutheran school until the age of twelve. Then he went to work in the coal mines with his father. What spare moments the youth and two of his older brothers had was taken up by baseball. After four years in the mines, he got a chance to become an apprentice barber to his oldest brother. This provided him with more opportunity to play ball in the warmer months and to hunt wild game in the winter. Brother Al and John soon developed local reputations as good ball players and exhibited their skills for a number of area teams throughout the early 1890s.

From mid-1893, the United States experienced several years of economic depression, and Charlie Wagner's barber shop ranked among the casualties. Al and John opted for a professional baseball career, signing contracts with the Steubenville club in the Inter-State League. The precarious economy also took its toll on minor league baseball teams. After a month, the Steubenville franchise shifted to Akron and folded a week later. He moved to the Mansfield, Ohio club, and that team also became defunct on June 14. Wagner contracted with Adrian in the Michigan State League, but homesickness drove him back to Pennsylvania in July. After a few days, he went to Warren, Ohio in the Iron and Oil League where Al Wagner had gone when John signed with Mansfield. The next year, he signed to play for Paterson, New Jersey, in the Atlantic League, playing a year and a half for Ed Barrow (1869-1953) who later became more famous as the long-time General Manager for the New York Yankees. In this locale, he first gained the nickname "Honus" which derived from "Hannis," an abbreviation of Johannes, his German birth name. Young Wagner did outstanding play for all of the teams, but there was no stability except for Paterson. In mid-July of 1897, Barrow sold his contract to Louisville, then a franchise in the twelve-team National League.

In two and one-half years with Louisville, Honus Wagner quickly proved himself to be one of the better players in the National League, hitting .338 for that half-season and following it up with .305 and .336 in 1898 and 1899 respectively. Playing mostly at second base and in the outfield, he also demonstrated adeptness as a base runner, and in an era when home runs were few and far between, he hit ten in 1898. However, his team was mired in the second division of a twelve-team league finishing eleventh once and ninth twice. After the 1899 season, the Louisville and Pittsburgh clubs merged as the league reduced its teams from twelve to eight. Louisville owner Barney Dreyfus bought the Pirates, and Honus Wagner now played for a Pittsburgh team only ten miles from his home in Carnegie. Several of the key Louisville players also came to the Pirates including manager-outfielder Fred Clarke, infielder Tommy Leach, and pitcher Deacon Phillippe. Together with established Pittsburgh stars such as outfielder Clarence "Ginger" Beaumont (a member of Temple Lodge No. 96 in Waterford, Wisconsin), along with pitchers Jess Tannehill and Jack Chesbro, the club rose to second place. Wagner led the way with a brisk .381, taking his first league batting title.

The first decade of the new century proved to be the glory years of the Pirates as they won four National League pennants and the World Series in 1909 (the Cubs also won four and the Giants two).

Tannehill and Chesbro jumped to the American League, but newly acquired pitchers like Vic Willis and Charles "Babe" Adams (a member of Bethany Lodge No. 97 in Missouri) more than took up the slack. Beaumont led the league in batting in 1902, and Wagner won a total of eight through 1911, never hitting less than .320. Honus had played several positions in his earlier years, but by 1903 he had more or less settled in permanently at shortstop. The World Series triumph over Detroit in 1909 was especially satisfying as it gave the Bucs the opportunity to avenge an earlier 1903 series loss at the hands of the Boston Pilgrims (later known as Red Sox).

Honus Wagner won his last batting title, hitting .334 in 1911 and afterward began to slow down. He slacked to .324 and .300 in the next two years, and while he continued to play more or less on a regular basis through 1916, he dropped to a low of .252 in 1915 and played more often at first base in 1916. He did not sign in 1917 until June and then hit only .265 in seventy-four games. The Flying Dutchman had reached the end of the road as a major league player, but his life was far from over.

Throughout most of his playing days, the notoriously shy John Peter Wagner had not been much involved in romance, preferring such male-oriented activities as basketball, hunting, fishing, or hoisting a cool beer with friends when not on the diamond. At age forty, he began to quietly court a Crafton girl named Bessie Smith, some seventeen years his junior. Finally in late December 1916, the twosome married and began planning a new home on Beechwood Avenue in Carnegie. Over the next several years, the couple had three daughters, one of whom died in infancy.

When Honus Wagner retired, he held a number of National League baseball records including 3,418 hits; most batting titles, 8; most at bats, 10,427; and most doubles, 651. He ranked high in other categories, too, including stolen bases and triples. He ended with a lifetime batting average of .327 and stood almost alone as the league's greatest player prior to World War II. While many of his career totals have since been passed by others, he still ranks as the best ever in Pittsburgh although Roberto Clemente might have surpassed his totals if he had not died in a tragic plane crash.

Although retired as an active major league player, Honus still barnstormed with different teams for years, hunted, fished, made some investments including a sporting goods store, and generally enjoyed life. A member of the Carnegie Lodge of Benevolent and

Protective Order of Elks since 1903, he also became a Mason. On March 17, 1919, he was initiated an Entered Apprentice in Centennial Lodge No. 544 in Carnegie. Passed a Fellowcraft on April 21, he was raised to the sublime degree of Master Mason on May 19, 1919, before a record crowd of over 700 brethren. It was said to have been the largest crowd of Masons ever assembled in that city. Wagner held a life membership for over thirty-six years until his death.

Wagner's comfortable existence continued throughout much of the 1920s, but as the decade wore on, it began to wear thin in the economic sphere. An unsuccessful run for Allegheny County Sheriff followed by the failure of his sporting goods business and some investments going sour did serious damage to his financial stability. By 1932 he faced difficult straits. Two brother Masons ultimately came to his rescue—long-time New York sportswriter Fred Lieb of Lodge No. 882 in New York and Bill Benswanger of Lodge No. 45 in Pittsburgh, the son-in-law of former Pirate owner Barney Dreyfuss. Lieb reminded readers of Wagner's loyalty to the National League in the early years of the century when the American League was grabbing up many of the senior loop's best players. Benswanger, then current president of the Bucs, secured him a coaching job beginning with spring training in 1933. After sixteen years, Honus was back in a Pirate uniform. In addition to his coaching duties, the hitherto modest and often taciturn Wagner developed some skills as an after dinner speaker in the immediate area, entertaining both youngsters and adults with stories, some true and some tall tales, from his baseball days. Wagner also helped train younger players, especially Arky Vaughn who, like his mentor, eventually became a Hall of Fame shortstop. In 1936, Honus became one of the initial five Hall of Fame selectees and was among those inducted at the 1939 dedication ceremonies. Helping train and inspire younger Pirates proved highly satisfying to the now aging Flying Dutchman.

Honus Wagner held a coaching position for eighteen years until age seventy-seven. In 1952, new front office man Brother Branch Rickey gave him a choice between a new contract and a pension for life. Having become increasingly infirm, missing spring training since 1948, and sometimes not feeling up to road trips, the aging legend accepted the pension. In April 1955, his life-size statue was unveiled in Pittsburgh. As it turned out, Wagner made his last public appearance at the dedication. Thereafter confined to his home, he died on December 6, 1955.

Honus Wagner tends to be remembered more than many baseball legends from a century ago. One reason is because one of his baseball cards is considered the rarest and most treasured of its kind. Another is because baseball-fan couples in Pittsburgh sometimes have their weddings adjacent to his statue. A third derives from the popular motion picture from 2003, *The Winning Season*, a fantasy film in the *Field of Dreams* mode in which Wagner figures prominently. The Pittsburgh Pirates have had many Masons on their teams over the years including not only several aforementioned Wagner teammates but also such figures as Wilber Cooper, Glenn Wright, Gus Suhr, Paul and Lloyd Waner, and younger living legends typified by Bob Friend, Dick Groat, and Bill Virdon. None quite have the stature of the Flying Dutchman. As a man and a Mason, like many others in the fraternity, Brother John Peter Wagner exemplified the highest tenets of his profession.

**Note**: Honus Wagner is the subject of two biographies: William Hageman, *Honus: The Life and Times of a Baseball Hero* (Sagamore, 1994) and Dennis & Jeanene DeValeria, *Honus Wagner: A Biography* (Henry Holt, 1995), both of which mention his Masonry. Also useful is David Finoli & Bill Ranier, *The Pittsburgh Pirates Encyclopedia* (Sports Publishing LLC, 2003). His Masonic Record is in William R. Denslow, *10,000 Famous Freemasons IV* (*Royal Arch Mason*, 1961), pp. 285-6. In addition I am indebted to Brother Jake Bapst and Brother Barry Thompson, both of Centerville (Ohio) Lodge No. 371, the former who helped in securing photos and the latter who alerted me to *The Winning Season* motion picture.

Previously unpublished

## Sir Knight Hubert Horatio Humphrey:
*"Trail Blazer for Civil Rights and Social Justice"*

Today Americans recall Hubert H. Humphrey as Lyndon Johnson's vice president and as an unsuccessful presidential candidate. Yet in his lifetime Humphrey was a great deal more significant as one of the country's most influential and constructive Senators. Considered an ultra-liberal in his earlier days, he often moderated and compromised his positions when faced with hard reality. While Humphrey championed numerous welfare state social programs, he also reminded the beneficiaries of them that they ultimately had moral responsibilities for their behavior. In the long run, he probably should be remembered for what author Jules Witcover termed an effective "trail blazer for civil rights and social justice."

Hubert Horatio Humphrey, Junior was born in Wallace, South Dakota, on May 27, 1911, the son of a small town druggist and Christine Sannes Humphrey, a lady of Norwegian ancestors.
In 1915 the family took over a pharmacy in the village of Doland, South Dakota where young Hubie spent his formative years. The twenties were not particularly good times for the Dakotas as their farmers enjoyed much less prosperity than the rest of the nation and local businesses like that of the Humphrey drug store depended upon them for their own livelihood.

Despite Hubert's relatively comfortable youth, the shadow of hard times remained ever present. Both banks in Doland failed in 1927, and conditions became worse. After finishing high school in 1929 at the head of a class of twenty, Humphrey received a scholarship to the University of Minnesota and put in two years of college.

Meanwhile, as the Great Depression worsened, the elder Humphrey relocated his business to the larger town of Huron and needed his son to come home and work in the store. Hubert came back to the family pharmacy where he remained until 1937 (except for a five-month hitch at a pharmacy school in 1933). The store managed to survive—barely—, and the young druggist bided his time until he could afford to return to college. During this period he courted and married Muriel Buck, their wedding taking place on September 3, 1936. The Humphreys eventually became the parents of four children.

By the time Hubert Humphrey had returned to college, the New Deal was in full swing and as his family's political philosophy already reflected a combination of "Prairie Populism" and Wilsonian Internationalism, he now absorbed into his point of view the New Deal and what was at the time perceived as the radicalism of the third party Minnesota Farmer-Labor Movement championed by Brothers Floyd B. Olson of Hennepin Lodge No. 4 and Elmer Benson of Appleton Lodge No. 137.

In 1939 Hubert completed his degree in political science and went on to Louisiana State University where he acquired a master's degree the following year. Back in Minnesota he began teaching at the University of Minnesota and also began work on a doctorate which he never completed. His government service began in 1941 when he took an administrative position with the W.P.A. followed by another job with the War Manpower Commission which included teaching classes at McAlester College.

At age thirty-two Humphrey made his first plunge into electoral politics when he sought to become mayor of Minneapolis; however, he lost the race to incumbent Marvin Kline by some 4,900 votes. The following year, the aspiring politician participated in a project that had a great bearing on the future course of Minnesota politics—a merger of regular Democrats with the Farmer-Labor Party, a move that paved the way for much of his own later political successes in the Gopher State. In a second run for mayor of Minneapolis in 1945, Humphrey outpaced Kline in votes by roughly 84,000 to 54,000. He received near unanimous support from organized labor and promised New Deal type reforms for the city.

During Hubert Humphrey's first year as mayor of Minneapolis, he became a member of Cataract Lodge No. 2 in that city. (It now has gone suburban in Richfield). He received his Entered Apprentice degree on November 13, 1946. He was passed to the degree of Fellowcraft on December 7 and was raised a Master Mason on December 18, 1946. He held membership in this lodge for nearly 32 years. Brother Humphrey continued his Masonic journey in the local

York Rite bodies completing them with his knighting in Darius Commandery No. 7. He also became a Noble of Zuhrah Temple of the Shrine.

In 1947, Mayor Humphrey easily coasted to a second term and set his sights on the Senate seat held by Joseph Ball, a maverick Republican who had supported FDR over Tom Dewey in 1944. Again, labor support and the unified D.F.L. Party were crucial in his chances for victory. He also made national waves in the summer of 1948 with the introduction of a strong civil rights plank in the national party platform. Once adopted, this plank may have lured some of the Henry Wallace liberals back into the Democratic fold, but mostly it had the negative result of threatening to destroy the party's Southern base as it precipitated the "Dixiecrat' revolt and the third party candidacy of Strom Thurmond. This schism in particular threatened to take enough electoral votes away from Truman to hand an easy victory to Republican Thomas Dewey.

In a four-way contest in which all of the major party candidates were Masons (Dewey, Thurmond, Truman, and Wallace), Truman fought back hard to win a come-from-behind victory. In Minnesota, Hubert H. Humphrey took 59% of the vote and became the first Democrat to win a Senate seat from the Gopher State since 1901. In his early months as a Senator, the exuberant young lawmaker displayed a tendency to "ruffle the feathers" of older more experienced solons. An example of this came in his failed attempt to abolish the Joint Committee on the Reduction of Nonessential Federal Expenditures as a needless federal expense which alienated its powerful chairman, Senator Harry F. Byrd of Virginia (a member of Hiram Lodge No. 21 in Winchester).

However, with the passing of time, the man from Minnesota learned—partly with the help of Texan Lyndon Johnson—to choose his battles more selectively and with more wisdom. Still, he remained one of the Senate's most outspoken liberals throughout the Eisenhower era. Reelected easily in 1954, he soon became one of the Senate's "inner circle." In 1956 Humphrey "campaigned vigorously" for the vice presidential slot but lost out to Tennessee Senator, Estes Kefauver (of Chattanooga Lodge No. 199). In 1960, HHH threw his hat into the Democratic presidential sweepstakes but lost out in a string of primaries to the better financed and more charismatic John F. Kennedy.

Nonetheless, after Kennedy took office, Humphrey, ever the faithful team member, sponsored or co-sponsored several New

Frontier and Great Society measures. These included bills that created the Peace Corps, the Jobs Corps, the Food Stamp Program (an extension of the Food for Peace Program), and the 1964 Civil Rights Act. He also helped secure ratification of the 1963 Limited Nuclear Test Ban Treaty.

Perhaps because of Humphrey's role as a "faithful scout" of the New Frontier, President Lyndon B. Johnson chose him as a running mate in 1964. During this time, the candidate made some effort to moderate his ultra-liberal image, announcing that while he retained his old goals, he was now willing to take a more incremental approach. Campaigning hard for the Johnson-Humphrey ticket, the nominee's party overwhelmed the Goldwater-Miller forces of the GOP in a popular and Electoral College landslide obtaining a still unsurpassed 61% of the vote.

According to one biographer, Lyndon Johnson had hated the vice president job because it left him "powerless" while Hubert Humphrey "relished" it because of the "national podium it offered." Certainly HHH took the job seriously and became a zealous spokesman for Great Society programs including the 1965 Voting Rights Act, Model Cities, Medicare, creation of the Department of Housing and Urban Development, the Office of Economic Opportunity, and the Headstart Program. He also lobbied heavily for increased funding of previously existing social programs.

Yet as the "great society" predicted by the implementation of these expenditures failed to materialize and both Congress and the White House became tighter with the purse strings, Humphrey found the vice presidency increasingly frustrating. He also became a spokesman for the Administration's Vietnam policy. As dissatisfaction with the conflict grew, Humphrey increasingly had his doubts about the wisdom of it. Yet he could not break with the Johnson team. When he took the position in 1965, he was quoted as saying, "I did not become vice president with Lyndon Johnson to cause him trouble."

LBJ's withdrawal from the race on March 31, 1968, opened the door for Humphrey's nomination, but unlike such rivals as Eugene McCarthy, Robert Kennedy, and later George McGovern who had the freedom to distance themselves from the administration, Humphrey could not. Bobby Kennedy's assassination guaranteed Hubert the nomination, but Democrats came away from their 1968 Chicago convention badly split. By contrast, the once divided GOP was fairly solid for Richard Nixon although George Wallace threatened to take votes away from both candidates in the no longer solid South and perhaps in the North as well. Nonetheless, Humphrey "fought the good fight," but he could not quite overcome the lead that the Nixon forces had accumulated. Hubert Humphrey finished the race just over half a million votes behind Nixon and accumulated 191 electoral votes to Nixon's 301 and Wallace's 46.

Some have argued that had Humphrey broken with Johnson, he might have nosed out a victory; however, a close analysis of this theory demonstrates that it does not hold water. Distancing himself from LBJ would almost certainly have cost Humphrey his narrow win in Texas, and it is doubtful that he could have made this up elsewhere, let alone picked up additional states.

January 1969 found the retiring Vice President out of public office for the first time since 1945. However, he did not remain out of the public eye for long. The retirement of Eugene McCarthy from the Senate opened up a place for him as Minnesota's junior Senator, and in November 1970 the Gopher State electorate sent Humphrey back to the Capitol. He remained there until his death and while he was an important member, his hopes for the presidency had virtually vanished. He entered the Democratic race again in both 1972 and 1976, but as the pundits said "the times had passed him by."

The man once considered too liberal had by now become too identified with the "establishment." The young liberals who took control of the party in 1972 favored Brother George McGovern as their choice to run for the White House while the more hawkish minority threw their support to Brother Henry Jackson of Washington State.

In 1976, a tired Humphrey tried again, but outsider Jimmy Carter won the nod, and the less liberal Democrats again favored Henry Jackson. Bills he sponsored in Congress such as the Humphrey-Hawkins Full Employment and National Growth Act which eventually passed in 1978 obviously did not produce the desired results. Nonetheless, Hubert Humphrey continued his tireless efforts in the Senate even while his health and indeed, his life, slowly ebbed away. Sir Knight and Senator Humphrey died on January 13, 1978. It was ironic that Hubert Humphrey, once considered too liberal eventually came to be thought of as excessively establishment. A close analysis of his career suggests that he usually put his causes ahead of his own personal ambition.

Biographer Carl Solberg described Humphrey as a deal maker and an advocate; as an effective Vice President and Senator. He called

Hubert "a terrific fighter but no killer." A panel of journalists, perhaps in part reflecting their own philosophy, once named him as the most effective Senator of the 1925-1975 half century. Another admirer called him "the premier lawmaker of his generation." Today, Masons can remember Brother and Sir Knight Humphrey as one who "fought the good fight" and stood his ground for those causes in which he believed. They may not agree with his causes, but they can hardly question either his integrity or his zeal.

**Note**: Those who want to learn more about Hubert Horatio Humphrey may wish to read the thorough biography by Carl Solberg, *Hubert Humphrey: A Biography* (1984). A more personal approach may be found in Edgar Berman, *Hubert: The Triumph and Tragedy of the Humphrey I Knew* (1979) while Allen H. Ryskind, *Hubert: An Unauthorized Biography of the Vice President* (1969) is highly critical from a conservative viewpoint. A sound but brief account is the chapter in Mark O. Hatfield, et al.: *Vice Presidents of the United States, 1789-1993* (1997, pp. 465-477.) The Grand Lodge of Minnesota furnished his Masonic record.

March 2002; slightly revised 2011

## Sir Knight Hugo Black:
*Thirty-Four Years on the Supreme Court, Sixty-Four Year Mason*

As of 2007, three of the longest-serving judges on the U.S. Supreme Court, John Marshall, William O. Douglas, and the subject of this sketch, Hugo Lafayette Black, have been Masons. Marshall and Black each spent thirty-four years on the federal bench while Douglas was there for thirty-five. Several other Masons with long years of court service include Joseph Story, John McLean, Stephen Field, Willis Van Devanter, and Potter Stewart. The years encompassing Sir Knight Black's tenure, 1937-1971, coincided with one of the most significant decades and decisions of the twentieth century.

Hugo Lafayette Black was born near Harlan in Clay County, Alabama on February 27, 1886. At the age of five, his parents, William and Martha Toland Black, moved into the county seat of Ashland where they operated a general store. He attended school at what he once described as a "primitive sort of academy" known as Ashland College. An older brother, Orlando Black, had become a physician and Hugo was also slated for a career in medicine at the Birmingham Medical School. However, after a year, he changed his mind and switched to law school at the University of Alabama. He graduated with an L.L.B. in 1906 at the ripe old age of twenty! He returned to Ashland and opened a law office over a store, but Ashland was the seat of a small rural county and the clients few. Like a lot of young aspiring professionals, youthful barrister Black joined the local Masonic lodge, Ashland Lodge No. 356. Barely of lawful age, he received his Entered Apprentice degree on March 23, 1907. On April 12, 1907, lodge brethren passed him to the degree of Fellowcraft, and two weeks later, Hugo Black was raised to the sublime degree of Master Mason.

In his law practice, business remained minimal, and shortly thereafter, the store and law office went up in flames. Lawyer Black used the fire as an excuse to move his legal practice to the growing southern metropolis of Birmingham, the industrial capital of the Deep South. He also moved his lodge membership to Birmingham Temple No. 636 on January 16, 1908, where it would remain for the rest of his life.

Lawyering paid better in Birmingham, and Black was elected a police court judge in 1910. After four years, he became Jefferson County Solicitor. During the next 2 ½ years that he held this position, Black continued with additional Masonic work. In the York Rite, he joined Mineral City Chapter No. 101, Royal Arch Masons. Brother Black was advanced to the honorary degree of Mark Master and inducted into the Oriental Chair of Past Master on May 13, 1915, received and acknowledged as a Most Excellent Master on May 27, and exalted a Royal Arch Mason on June 2, 1915. That fall he took the Cryptic degrees in Woodlawn Council No. 71, R. &S.M. A year passed before he became a Knight Templar, taking all the Chivalric orders on October 13, 1916, in Cyrene Commandery No. 10. At some point, he also joined the Scottish Rite bodies in Birmingham and became a Noble of Zamora Shrine Temple. Described as "a great joiner"" Black belonged to numerous fraternal groups and seems to have been most active as a Knight of Pythias where he served a term as Grand Chancellor of the Alabama K. of P. Some years later, one of his fraternal memberships would come back as a major embarrassment.

When the U.S. entered World War I in April 1917, Hugo Black answered the call. He became a captain in the 81st Field Artillery stationed first at Fort Oglethorpe, Georgia, and then at Chattanooga, Tennessee. After his discharge, the young attorney entered private practice and prospered. One observer termed him the master of the "soft question that provokes the wrathful answer." Labor law and personal injury cases became his specialties. In 1921, he married Josephine Patterson Foster. The couple became the parents of three children—Hugo, Sterling, and Josephine. After thirty years of marriage, Josephine Foster Black, died, and in 1957 Black married Elizabeth DeMeritte.

In 1921, lawyer Black defended a prominent Ku Klux Klan member accused of shooting and killing a prominent Birmingham Catholic. At the trial, Black allegedly sought to discredit Catholic prosecution witnesses by appealing to anti-Catholic prejudices among jurors. His client was acquitted, but the lawyer became somewhat tainted as anti-Catholic. He also joined the KKK himself, becoming a member of Robert E. Lee Klan No. 1 in Birmingham from 1923 until 1925. In 1926, he addressed a large Klan meeting. This association with the Klan, however brief and inconsequential it may or may not have been at the time, later came back to haunt him.

In 1926, veteran two-term Senator Oscar Underwood, a member of Birmingham Fraternal Lodge No. 384, decided to retire. Hugo Black filed for the seat and won a tough primary besting three opponents. His support ranged from the labor unions to the Ku Kluxers. Some scholars believe that the Klan support may have been crucial in providing him with the winning margin. With a weak Alabama GOP offering little more than token opposition, Black cruised to a nearly 81% landslide victory in November. He won a second term in 1932, garnering some 86.3% of the vote.

As a Senator, Black first turned to the Muscle Shoals controversy where he joined forces with maverick Republican George Norris as a proponent of public power at that site. He gained national attention for his efforts, investigating a perceived scandal in awarding air mail contracts which ultimately led to the Black-McKellar Air Mail Act of 1934. With the national victory of FDR and the coming of the New Deal, Black generally showed himself to be a loyal New Dealer, although he opposed the National Recovery Act (NRA) and correctly pointed to some of the problems that ultimately helped put its ambitious program on the scrap heap of history. He also became an enthusiastic proponent of wage and hour labor legislation. Generally speaking, he gained the most prominence from his participation on various Senate Investigation panels and committees. He also enthusiastically supported FDR's failed Supreme Court Reform plan, bitterly denounced by conservatives as the "court packing" bill. Perhaps for this reason, on August 12, 1937, the President nominated him for the Supreme Court, replacing the retiring Brother Willis Van Devanter of Acacia Lodge No. 11 in Wyoming and one of the sharpest conservatives on the High Court.

Unanimous confirmation of Senators to the Federal Bench had long been the custom in the Senate. However, Hugo Black ran into unexpected difficulty. Criticism came from both parties, primarily for two reasons. Some of his biggest critics were fellow Masons. Republican stalwart Warren Austin of Vermont raised the issue of eligibility since Black had recently voted to increase salaries of Federal Judges. A more serious question raised by Democratic Senators

Edward Burke of Nebraska and Royal Copeland of New York concerned the Ku Klux Klan membership. The unanimous approval Black had sought went down the drain, but Hugo Black ultimately won confirmation by a comfortable vote of 63 to 13.

Observers thought Judge Black might have kept a low profile in his early months on the bench, but that was not to be the case. In his first eight months on the Court, he handed down thirteen dissenting opinions which were hailed by the "New Republic," but met with frequent criticism by columnist Marquis Childs. In time, the controversies surrounding Black faded somewhat as other liberal justices joined him on the High Court such as Felix Frankfurter and Brother William O. Douglas, although he still dissented a great deal. Generally speaking, Black demonstrated nearly consistent devotion to defense of free speech and civil liberties. In the 1944 case of "Korematsu vs. United States," he wrote the majority opinion sustaining arrest of a Japanese-American who resisted internment. As the civil rights movement gained strength, Black nearly always stood on the side of African-Americans in such cases, a position that often placed him in opposition with his former Caucasian constituents back in Alabama. In fact, Hugo Black, Jr. ultimately chose to leave his home state. The senior Black did however dissent in the ruling that declared state poll taxes unconstitutional.

During the years associated with the liberal decisions associated with "the Warren Court," Black generally sided with the liberal majority. These included the several cases involving the separation of church and state. He also formed part of the majority in the "Miranda" decision which required persons to be informed of their rights prior to their arrest.

Yet on other cases, Black's opinions seemed more in line with conservative positions. For instance, he did not oppose capital punishment. Furthermore, he did not believe that non-speech actions connected with "free speech" were constitutionally protected. Numerous examples to support this belief can be cited. Even though a protester was entitled to free speech on government property in "Adderley vs. Florida" (1966), Black held that this did not immunize him from prosecution for trespassing. Dissenting in the case of "Tinker vs. Des Moines" (1969), he disagreed with the majority view that the wearing of armbands was protected under the free speech clause. Black wrote "While I have always believed that under the First and Fourteenth Amendments neither the State nor the Federal

Government had the authority to regulate or censor the content of speech, I have never believed that any person has a right to give speeches or engage in demonstrations where he pleases and when he pleases." Likewise he did not believe that flag burning or profanity printed on jackets constituted free speech. He argued that the latter "was mainly conduct and little speech." In general, the Judge found the civil disobedience and protest marches that characterized the late sixties as highly unsettling and that they undercut the fabric of democracy and society.

Justice Black also dissented in the landmark case of "Griswold v. Connecticut" (1965). He wrote "I like my privacy as well as the next man," but "unlike my brethren, I am simply unable to find a constitutional right to it." This was the decision that marked the Court's move in the direction of a "right to privacy" that ultimately led to the controversial "Roe vs. Wade" (1973) judgment. (Black was retired and deceased by the time this case came to the Court in 1973.) Black had held to the judicial philosophy that if the *Constitution* guaranteed a protection, all well and good. He did not, however, believe in granting constitutional protection if there was no such meaning in the document. In this circumstance, many legal scholars today would classify Black in what has become known as the "originalist" school. To use his own words, he held that judges ought to "support the Constitution as written, not as revised by the Supreme Court from time to time."

At the age of eighty-five, Judge Black entered Bethesda Medical Hospital on August 28, 1971. He resigned from the Supreme Court ten days later and died on September 25, 1971. Over a career that encompassed forty-six years of significant national service, Sir Knight Hugo Lafayette Black had made his mark as a Senator and Associate Justice. Subsequently laid to rest in Arlington National Cemetery, he was later honored with his picture on a 1986 stamp and by having a new Federal Courthouse in Birmingham named for him. Men and Masons can take pride in his achievements.

**Note**: There are several biographies of Justice Black, but the best for general readers is probably Tony Allen Freyer, *Hugo L. Black and the Dilemma of American Liberalism* (1990). For his Masonic records, I am indebted to W. Bro Jerry Underwood, PGM of the Grand Lodge of Alabama and Sir Knight Hiram O. Williams, Jr. of the Alabama Grand York Rite Bodies.

December 2007; slightly revised 2011

**Brother Jack French Kemp:**
*From Football Hero to Congress and Cabinet*

While Masonic membership has declined in the last four decades both among the general population and among those in higher echelons of public service, numerous Brethren within the Fraternity still held prominent positions on the American scene. In 1996, two of these individuals sought the nation's highest offices. Although the presidential and vice presidential quest of Brothers Bob Dole and Jack Kemp fell short of success, both men have exemplified the highest traditions of public service with their lengthy and significant careers.

The junior member of this team, Jack French Kemp was born in Los Angeles, California, on July 13, 1935. Jack ranked as the third of four sons of Paul and Frances Pope Kemp, his father being the owner of a small trucking firm. As a youngster, the son worked part-time for his dad's firm while attending Fairfax High School. His major interest, however, tended to be football, and he became known as an excellent quarterback. Somewhat physically small, Kemp enrolled at Occidental College. In later years, he recalled, "I wasn't big enough to go to USC (University of Southern California) or UCLA (University of California at Los Angeles)," nonetheless, displaying grit and determination, he added, "but I was going to play football" and "I was going to play pro football."

Academically, Jack Kemp, who majored in physical education and minored in history, described himself as only an average student. However, on the gridiron his star shone brilliantly, and in 1956 he became the nation's leading small college quarterback gaining special attention for his accuracy in passing. Occidental doesn't turn out many professional football players, but Kemp made a significantly sufficient impression to be a seventeenth round Detroit Lions draft choice in 1957.

Early efforts to make it in the National Football League must have been frustrating for the aspiring youngster. Joining the Lions after his June 1957 graduation as their third string quarterback, he was released before the regular season started. Signed by the Pittsburgh Steelers, Jack saw limited action in five games that fall before again receiving his walking papers. After spending 1958 on active duty in the U. S. Army during which time he married Joanne Main, Kemp had a brief fling with the Canadian Football League's Calgary Stampeders in 1959; he was also briefly the property of both the New York Giants and the San Francisco 49ers. In 1960, the newly-formed American Football League, presided over by former war hero and South Dakota Governor and Brother Joe Foss of Minnehaha Lodge No. 5 in Sioux Falls, provided a new lease on life for Jack Kemp. Signed by the Los Angeles Chargers, the twenty-five year old quarterback led the League in 211 pass completions for 3,018 yards and twenty touchdowns. The team moved to San Diego in 1961, and Jack had another fine season, but injuries sidelined him through most of 1962.

Picked up by the Buffalo Bills from the waiver lists, Kemp enjoyed his best years in the mid-sixties. His passing skills led the Bills to three straight division titles and AFL championships in both 1964 and 1965. The latter season saw the strong-armed quarterback at his peak as Jack was named the AFL player of the year and most valuable player in the league championship game where he led Buffalo to a 23-0 victory over his former Charger teammates.

Jack Kemp spent four more years with the Bills, but injuries plagued his later years in football. These included two fractured ankles and shoulders, a broken knee, and several concussions. Retiring after the 1969 season, Kemp then held the career league record for passing attempts, completed passes, and yards gained in passing. The Buffalo management retired his number 15 jersey. Off the field, Jack had served as president of the Players' Association, helping his peers get good work contracts. For a year after leaving the gridiron, the one-time pass thrower spent a year as a PR officer for the Marine Midland Bank of Buffalo, New York. Meanwhile, the Kemp family—grown to include four children—settled in the Buffalo suburb of Hamburg.

In 1970, local Republicans sought out Kemp as a congressional candidate in the 39$^{th}$ District. As one party leader said, "We were looking for an attractive, articulate, forthright, aggressive man," and "finding Jack Kemp was like finding the Holy Grail." Although he had the advantage of his celebrity name, the newly retired footballer was not a political novice having prior participation in campaigns for Governors' Rockefeller in New York and Reagan in California as well as the presidential quests of both Barry Goldwater and Richard Nixon. Furthermore, Jack had taken graduate courses in political science at Long Beach State and began some rigorous self-study in economic history. He would later describe the study as "a road-to-Damascus-like experience." Certainly it came in handy later in the decade when Kemp became a major congressional spokesman for "supply side" economics.

Jack Kemp won his first congressional race in a district comprised largely of the suburban portions of Erie County by a relatively modest 51.6% of the vote. Thereafter, in an enlarged 38th District, voters returned the former gridiron hero by margins in excess of 70%. In 1978 Jack enjoyed the luxury of running unopposed. Although he maintained a fairly low profile outside his district in his early years on Capitol Hill, he was increasingly in the national spotlight by the later seventies.

During his first term in Congress, Jack French Kemp petitioned Fraternal Lodge No. 625 in Hamburg, receiving his Entered Apprentice degree on February 25, 1971. Congressional duties, heavy scheduling of public appearances, and popularity on the GOP speaking circuit undoubtedly slowed his progress in the order, but on December 6, 1974, Kemp was passed to the degree of Fellowcraft. On May 31, 1975, the Brethren raised him to the sublime degree of Master Mason. A decade later, on October 26, 1985, Jack completed the Scottish Rite degrees in the Valley of Buffalo. In late September of 1988, Brother Kemp received the 33° in Grand Rapids, Michigan. Meanwhile, he had been made a Noble "at sight" at Ismailia Shrine Temple in Buffalo on December 14, 1985. Together with former President Gerald Ford, singer Roy Clark, and actors Glenn Ford and Ernest Borgnine, Jack appeared in ads on behalf of Shrine hospitals.

By the later seventies, Jack Kemp had begun to emerge as a major figure on the American political scene. In 1978, he became known as co-sponsor of the Kemp-Roth Bill, a broad ranging plan for tax reductions to stimulate the stagnant economy. Although it failed to pass Congress, a modified Kemp-Roth plan became part of the GOP platform in 1980. It became a key feature of the Reagan administration's economic program and many economists have identified it as the main catalyst for the so-called "seven good years" of economic recovery that began in 1983.

Through the eighties, Jack Kemp's national stature increased, and many young conservatives saw him as the logical heir to the

Regan mantle, given his knack for defining conservatism in positive terminology. In 1988, he gave up his safe seat in Congress to seek the White House but generally ran third behind the better-known Vice President George Bush and GOP Senate leader and fellow Mason, Bob Dole. Nonetheless, his championing of such proposals as "free enterprise zones" in inner cities and the sale of public housing projects to occupants as a way to promote pride in home ownership made him a natural choice for Secretary of Housing and Urban Development in the Bush administration. Kemp served four years with honor and dignity in the Cabinet. Unfortunately, his ideas met with a chilly reception in a Congress still oriented toward "big government" and some skepticism among those in his own party who had other priorities.

When the Bush presidency ended after the 1992 election, many pollsters and pundits expected Jack Kemp to be the GOP standard bearer in 1996. In fact, delegates at the 1992 convention gave him a plurality of their votes in a straw poll conducted at the time. However, Jack and former Secretary of Education William Bennett threw their energy into the Empower America Foundation, a think tank that promoted positive conservative ideas and values. In 1995, to the disappointment of many of his followers, he decided not to seek the presidency in 1996. The following July, however, Jack did accept the vice presidential nod from Brother and Sir Knight Robert Dole who had secured a majority of convention delegates in the spring primaries. His selection added some spark to the Republican ticket. While the fall campaign proved unsuccessful, the Dole-Kemp ticket attracted more than thirty-seven million popular supporters and carried nineteen states for a total of 159 electoral votes.

In addition to the aforementioned endeavors, Jack Kemp wrote two books: *An American Renaissance: A Strategy for the 1980s* in 1979 and more recently *The American Idea: Ending the Limits on Growth."* Numerous honors were bestowed upon him over the years. Of the four Kemp children, all have names that begin with the letter "J" like their parents: Jeffrey, Jennifer, Judith, and James. Jeff, the elder son, graduated from Dartmouth and has also carved a career in professional football. In matters of religion, the Kemps were Presbyterians.

After his last political race, Jack Kemp continued an active life with Empower America. He remained a popular orator on the speaking circuit as an admired public figure. In football, statecraft, and politics he fought the good fight. It came as something of a shock to his many admirers when it was announced in January of 2009 that he had terminal cancer. Both supporters and even critics of Brother Jack French Kemp mourned his passing on May 2, 2009.

**Note**: Brother Kemp's Masonic records were furnished by Sir Knight Wilfred J. Salisbury, Secretary of Fraternal Lodge No. 625. The late Brother Frank A. Cremeans of Morning Dawn Lodge No. 7 in Gallipolis, Ohio supplied the portrait photo in the waning days of his term in the 104th Congress.

June 1997; slightly revised 2011

## Brother James A. Rhodes:
*The "Taxpayer's Governor and Fifty Year Mason*

When one thinks of longevity among twentieth century political figures, names such as Robert Byrd, Strom Thurmond, and Jamie Whitten—all Masons—come to mind. Governors of states usually do not last so long, partly because of term limits and partly because it is more difficult for them to delegate blame than it is for legislators who usually share collective rather than individual responsibility for their mistakes. Nonetheless, a few governors have exhibited considerable staying power with one of the most durable being James A. Rhodes of Ohio who spent a total of sixteen years at the helm of the Buckeye State. Early in his first term, Rhodes earned the sobriquet "the Taxpayer's Governor" in a favorable biography. In retrospect, it seems likely that is how future generations will remember the coal miner's son who rose from humble origins to the State House.

James Allen Rhodes was born in the mining town of Coalton in Jackson County, Ohio on September 13, 1909, the only son of James and Susan Howe Rhodes. Like many of the mining and farming people of that area, the family had a generous strain of Welsh ethnic stock in their roots. About 1916, the elder Rhodes survived a mine accident only to die in the 1918 flu epidemic, and the distraught mother took her three children to the larger city of Springfield. Young Jim helped support his mother and sisters by working a variety of odd jobs. He managed to play sports and remain in high school until his graduation, but he sometimes took less than a full course load so he could also keep working. As a result, he had passed his twentieth birthday before obtaining his high school diploma in the spring of 1930.

Determined to attend college, Rhodes came to Columbus and enrolled at Ohio State University in the fall of 1930. He also took a part-time job as clerk for state legislator Grant Ward. Within a year, Ward staked the youth in a small restaurant business. This venture soon occupied so much of Jim's time that he dropped out of school, never to return.

As a young businessman, James Rhodes continued to manifest an interest in recreational youth programs. He founded a Knot Hole Gang which raised money to pay for youth admissions to Columbus Red Bird games (Triple A Farm Club of the St. Louis Cardinals). He also showed interest in local Republican activity, becoming a precinct committeeman in 1933. This combination of volunteerism and grassroots politics together with practical business experience provided a foundation for his later endeavors.

The future governor's first actual public position followed his election to the Columbus Board of Education in November 1937. Two years later, the city's electorate chose him to fill an unexpired term as city auditor. For the next thirty consecutive years, Rhodes was in public service to either his city or state. In 1941, he married Helen Rawlins and the couple subsequently had three daughters.

After being elected auditor for a full term in 1941, he served just half of it when the voters sent him to the Columbus Mayor's office in November of 1943. Known initially as the "Boy Mayor," he soon became known as the "boy's mayor" because of the continued combination of volunteer efforts with increased public funding. His continued youth work included organizing a junior police group and a zoo support organization. Following the initial publication of this article in *Knight Templar,* this writer received a letter from an older Sir Knight in a distant state who related an account of his youth in Columbus and getting into some trouble and how Mayor Rhodes had given him a serious one-on-one talk in the mayor's office that had quite likely saved him from a life of crime. He still harbored gratitude for the man who helped him get his "head on straight," to use a well worn phrase.

As a part of Rhodes' interest in youth athletics, he was elected president of the Ohio branch of the Amateur Athletic Union in 1940. From 1947 to 1949, he served as president of the national A.A.U. In the public sphere, Rhodes succeeded in enlarging the budget for the city's recreation department from $34,000 to $200,000. The juvenile delinquency rate was cut in half, and the mayor's efforts were considered a success. He was, in fact, so recognized when he won not only the Helms Foundation Award but also the Silver Keystone Award from the Boy's Clubs of America.

It was during his years as mayor that James Rhodes became interested in Masonry. He had become a member of the Kiwanis Club and the Benevolent and Protective Order of Elks prior to petitioning Neoacacia Lodge No. 595. He was Raised on November 1, 1950, and two years later took the Scottish Rite degrees in the Valley of Columbus. Subsequently, he also became a Noble in Aladdin Shrine Temple. Many years later on September 30, 1981, Brother Rhodes received the 33° in Philadelphia.

After nearly nine years as mayor of Ohio's capital city, the state's voters elected Jim Rhodes state auditor when he defeated sixteen-year incumbent Joe Ferguson by more than 319,000 votes. An initial run for governor in 1954 fell short as he failed to unseat popular Democrat incumbent Frank Lausche. However, he remained secure in the state auditor's post winning two additional terms by wide margins.

In 1962, however, the political wind blew in the Rhodes direction. Incumbent Democrat Michael DiSalle had pushed for an unpopular tax hike and had been tainted by scandal. Running on a platform which promised to hold the line on taxes and promote private sector job growth, Rhodes won a resounding and unprecedented 555,000 vote victory and carried the entire GOP ticket into office including several other Masons such as Lietenant Governor John W. Brown, Secretary of State Ted W. Brown, Attorney General William Saxbe, and Chief Justice of the Supreme Court Kingsley A. Taft who defeated another distinguished Mason, long-time incumbent Carl V. Weygandt. Masons in the Ohio government were quite prominent in the 1960s including both House Speaker Roger Cloud and Senate leader C. Stanley Mechem.

Although any governor of a large state is never going to have total success, Jim Rhodes came closer than most. His commitment to maintain the status quo on taxes while encouraging economic growth by attracting new industry and promoting expansion of older ones worked pretty well. He had promised 200,000 new private sector jobs and eventually added 330,000. An extensive construction program in highway and state facilities benefited not only state residents but also business and labor in the building trades. He also promoted every county's having its own airport or easy access to one with most still existing today. Before the end of his first year in office, the economy-minded governor attracted the attention of a Pulitzer Prize winning journalist Edward J. Mowery who authored an all-too-brief biography titled *James Allen Rhodes: Taxpayer's Governor* (New York, 1963). Jim's accomplishments caused him to beat his own record of 1962 by winning a second term in 1966 by a margin of 703,000 votes.

In his second term, the governor undertook an expansion of the education system. At the higher level, the municipal universities of Akron, Cincinnati, and Toledo were all converted into state institutions. Private colleges in Cleveland and Youngstown were transformed and expanded into full-fledged state universities, and a wholly new Wright State University emerged from what had once been a joint branch of Ohio State University and Miami University. In addition, a whole new system of vocational high schools and community-technical colleges evolved from Rhodes' plans. Through a penny increase in the sales tax, more money also went into the public schools. As in the first term, a cooperative Republican legislature enacted most of the governor's proposals.

However, all in the late sixties did not come up roses either. Many of the building programs had been funded by increasing the state's bonded indebtedness, and voters grew increasingly uneasy about further bond issues. In addition, anti-war protests caused student unrest in Ohio as elsewhere, ultimately culminating in the 1970 tragedy at Kent State University that left four students dead. The latter may have contributed to the governor's narrow loss in the 1970 primary contest for the United States Senate.

Nonetheless, the next four years paved the way for a successful Rhodes comeback. Democratic Governor John J. Gilligan not only raised taxes sharply but displayed a degree of abrasiveness in crucial moments that turned off much of the electorate. Even so, the Watergate scandals had left Republicans in a down-spirited mood. Jim Rhodes, however, kept plugging away at the Gilligan lead. On election night after two networks called the election for Gilligan, Rhodes conceded defeat and went to bed. At 3:30 AM, his daughter awakened him with the news that he had moved into the lead. Asked by a reporter why he had conceded prematurely, the sleepy governor-elect is alleged to have replied, "[honest] Concession is good for the soul."

By a narrow margin of 11,488 votes, James Allen Rhodes had won an unprecedented third four-year term. In 1978, he followed with a fourth term when he emerged victorious over Richard Celeste by a margin of some 48,000 votes. Midway through his last year in office, Rhodes made history by surpassing Arthur Fenner of Rhode Island who served 15 ½ years before dying in 1805 as the longest-serving state governor ever. Brother George Wallace of Alabama would later tie the record, both serving a total of sixteen years.

The last two Rhodes' terms did not go as smoothly as the first two. Democrat control of the legislature made things difficult, but a sluggish economy made it even tougher. After some initial sparring, Rhodes managed to forge a working relationship with long-time Democrat House Speaker, Vernal Riffe of Scioto County (another 33° Mason), and the two eventually became friends. Rhodes and Riffe would often praise one another in public and not all for show either. The booming economy of the mid-sixties ran into problems in the early seventies as Ohio was quickly becoming part of the "rust belt." As authoritative journalist Lee Leonard phrased it, "much of his second eight years was spent marking time trying to keep the state afloat," but "in fairness, he had some successes in industrial development, and some of his programs took root years later."

James A. Rhodes retired from office in 1983 with a record sixteen years as governor. Although later tied, it does not appear likely that his record will be surpassed in the immediate future. (As of 2006, there were five governors including Rhodes who were tied for the longest serving.) Jim ran again at age seventy-seven in 1986 when he sought a fifth term. However, the old magic was gone and he did not even come close. In retrospect, even many of his close friends and supporters thought he should have remained in retirement. Nevertheless, he still held considerable respect as an elder statesman, and the margin of his 1966 victory remained a record until surpassed in 1994 by his last lieutenant governor and protégé, George Voinovich, for whom he had campaigned tirelessly and successfully in 1990. An early investor in Wendy's International, Inc. (whose CEO Brother Dave Thomas has become a household name in recent years), the octogenarian former governor still came to his office regularly in late mornings. He died a few months after his ninety-first birthday on March 4, 2001.

James Rhodes was named an honorary trustee at Rio Grande College/University of Rio Grande from 1953. Some years ago when the College's Board proposed naming their new student center in Rhodes' honor, he objected, but they named it after him anyway in spite of his modesty. A few examples of honoring the former governor are a major state office building in downtown Columbus known as the Rhodes Tower, the James A. Rhodes Appalachian Highway which traverses southern Ohio from state line to state line, and Rhodes College in Lima. While it would be an overstatement to call Brother Jim Rhodes universally loved by all Ohioans, it appears safe to say that the man, first known in 1963 as the "taxpayer's governor," will be long remembered as an all-time booster for Ohio and its products.

**Note**: Appreciation is expressed to the staff at the Grand Lodge of Ohio and the A.A.S.R.,Valley of Columbus for their help. The best biographical data on Governor Rhodes are the two entries in the 1949 and 1976 editions of *Current Biography.* For the best look at his gubernatorial career, see the two relevant chapters in Alexander P. Lamis, editor, *Ohio Politics* (Kent State University Press, 1994), by Richard C. Zimmerman and Lee Leonard, respectively. After this article was published, Byrl Shoemaker, another Valley of Columbus 33° and one who helped develop Rhodes' vocational and technical school plans, wrote *Ohio's Greatest Governor: Politician of the Century* (Orange Frazer Press, 2005), an affectionate biography and memoir.

August 1997; slightly revised 2011

## Sir Knight James F. Byrnes: *New Deal Senate Leader and Cold Warrior*

In the crucial decades that spanned American history from the time of William Howard Taft through the early years of the Eisenhower presidency, Sir Knight James Francis Byrnes occupied key positions in the United States Government. During that time, his public service included experience in both houses of Congress, a stint on the United States Supreme Court, a key civilian appointment during World War II, Secretary of State, and finally Governor of South Carolina. In those same years, his philosophy identified with the Southern Progressives and New Dealers, but eventually his innate conservatism led him toward an independent stance and finally to the endorsing of GOP presidential contenders during the sixties as a respected elder statesman. Described as "a small, wiry, neatly made man . . . with an expression of quizzical geniality," Byrnes spent sixty-one years as a Mason, fifty-five of them as a Knight Templar.

Few American statesmen sprouted from more humble beginnings than Byrnes whose grandparents had been poor Irish Catholic immigrants who came to America during the great migrations associated with the potato famines of the 1840s. Born in Charleston, South Carolina on May 2, 1882, James Francis Byrnes came into the world a few months after his father had died and his mother, Elizabeth McSweeny Byrnes, virtually penniless, managed to survive as a dressmaker. Her young son had to quit school at the age of fourteen and go to work. He became a clerk in the law office of Mordecai and Gadsden but with the help of Benjamin Rutledge was able to continue his education on an informal basis. From there he advanced to the position of a court stenographer in 1900, moving to Aiken where he continued to study during his free time and finally, at the age of twenty-one, passed his bar exams. He still had to work as a court stenographer for a time.

On May 2, 1906, Jimmy Byrnes' birthday also became his wedding day when he married Maude Busch in St. Thaddeus Episcopal Church in Aiken. Although born and reared a Catholic, he had been attending the Episcopal Church since his move inland, and he subsequently became an Anglican. Remembering his origins and respecting his devout mother, he never became anti-Catholic in the manner of many Southern politicians. In 1908, he became a district solicitor or prosecuting attorney. Two years later he challenged the incumbent member of Congress in the Second District and won in a run-off primary. In the next forty-plus years, Byrnes lost only one election.

James Francis Byrnes became a Mason during the months before the next Congress went into session. On January 12, 1911, he was raised in Aiken Lodge No. 156. Later that year, Byrnes completed his Chapter degrees at Kadoshlayah Chapter No. 41, Royal Arch Masons also in Aiken. Five years elapsed before he was knighted in Columbia Commandery No. 2 on October 20, 1916, and he later affiliated with Aiken Commandery No. 14. In 1920 he joined Aiken Council No. 23 Royal and Select Masters. In later years when he relocated his law practice to the growing Piedmont city of Spartanburg, he moved his memberships there, first affiliating with Spartan Lodge No. 70 on July 5, 1926. Over the next several years his York Rite affiliation came to be in Chicora Chapter No. 23, Blake Council No. 19, and Spartanburg Commandery No. 3. Byrnes also belonged to the Shrine, Odd Fellows, and Knights of Pythias.

Jimmy Byrnes went on to serve seven terms in the House. During that time, he served on the Pujo Committee that investigated the banking practices of the J. P. Morgan Syndicate, urged the formation of the Roads Committee, and worked behind the scenes to make an impression on party leaders. By the time the United States entered World War I, Byrnes held a key position on the Appropriations Committee. Over the next few months, he formed close friendships with Assistant Navy Secretary, Brother Franklin D. Roosevelt, and financier Bernard Baruch, two associations that would serve him well in future years. On both domestic and foreign policy, Byrnes identified himself with those of President Wilson. After the Republicans regained control of Congress and the rejection of the Versailles Treaty and the League of Nations, some of the South Carolinian's influence declined, and in 1924 he decided to seek a Senate seat.

Byrnes suffered defeat in the primary, losing out to Cole Blease, one of the most colorful of the Southern demagogue politicians of that generation who attacked Byrnes for his childhood, Catholic background. After his defeat, the former Congressman relocated to Spartanburg where he built up a successful law practice and waited for an opportunity for a rematch with Blease whose blatant racism included advocacy of lynching. Byrnes saw himself as a moderate on racial issues, and while he did not challenge the "Southern way of life," he never based his campaigns on the Blease brand of race hatred that appealed to many poor whites. Byrnes thought that what Southerners needed most was more economic opportunity and less appeal to emotion.

In 1930 his opportunity came. Blease's anti-black ravings made less sense, and Byrnes' brand of Wilsonian progressivism made more sense in an era where Palmetto State residents were feeling the effects of the Great Depression. In addition, Jimmy Byrnes received considerable financial help from his old friend Bernard Baruch whom Blease had alienated with his brand of anti-Semitism. Byrnes won the primary by 2,500 votes and was unopposed by any Republican in November. The new junior senator from South Carolina went to Washington in December of 1931 and formed close friendships with other influential senators in the "Southern bloc" that included such luminaries as Carter Glass of Virginia, Pat Harrison of Mississippi, and Joe Robinson of Arkansas—all fellow Masons—who became men of considerable stature with the soon-to-be-coming of a Democratic congressional majority, the presidency of Franklin Roosevelt, and the New Deal. In the 1932 national election, Byrnes allied himself with the forces of FDR early in the year.

During the early years of the New Deal, Byrnes became one of the nation's most influential senators. As a champion and advocate of reform legislation and depression combating agencies that formed the core of congressional action of the 1933-1937 era, the freshman senator gained a reputation as being highly effective. Among other achievements, he served as floor manager of the bill to create the Works Progress Administration (WPA).

From 1937 Byrnes' innate conservatism began slowly to be manifested. It first began to show in disputes about the amount of WPA funding and increased with the President's Supreme Court reform and White House support for sit-down strikes. Through these issues, Byrnes supported the President's position with some reluctance. However, when Joe Robinson died and FDR threw his support in the July contest to Alben Barkley over Pat Harrison to succeed him as Senate Majority leader, in the former's one vote margin of victory to become Robinson's successor, Byrnes found himself in the minority. He also remained aloof from FDR's efforts to "purge" conservative Democrats in the 1938 primary season.

Nonetheless, Byrnes swallowed his pride and backed FDR for a third term in 1940, although he was disappointed when the President chose Brother Henry Wallace instead of him as a running mate. Despite his growing disenchantment with New Deal liberalism, Byrnes supported Roosevelt's foreign policy in opposition to isolationist sentiment. In the spring of 1941, he helped steer the *Lend-Lease Bill* through the Senate by a vote of Sixty to thirty-one. By this time, liberals held a solid majority of the United States Supreme Court, and with the retirement of James McReynolds from the Supreme Court, FDR expressed a willingness to appoint a more conservative southerner. As a result, Senator Byrnes received the nod in spite of opposition from both the CIO and the NAACP. He was confirmed unanimously in mid-1941. Byrnes served on the Court until October of 1942. His decisions generally demonstrated a moderate viewpoint, taking a liberal perspective on some cases and conservative on others.

Still, rumors had it that Jimmy was bored with his appointment. With World War II now raging, Byrnes jumped at the opportunity to take a newly-created civilian administrative post. As a result, he became Director of the Office of Economic Stabilization on October 15, 1942. In May of 1943, Byrnes became head of the Office of War Mobilization. In these roles, the former Justice became unofficially known as "the Assistant President," a nickname that reflected his overall significance, but this apparently rankled FDR somewhat. By this time, Byrnes hoped for the vice presidency in 1944, as opposition to Henry Wallace was becoming rampant, especially among the more conservative elements of the New Deal coalition. However, he proved unacceptable to the CIO and the NAACP, and the Senator and Brother Harry Truman received the nod. Again Byrnes played the part of loyalist to the President and the ticket. After he was also passed over for Secretary of State in November 1944, the "Assistant President" determined that he would retire from his post as soon as the defeat of the Germans became a certainty. His resignation became effective on April 2, 1945. Before leaving that position, Byrnes did serve as part of the United States delegation to the Yalta Conference in February of 1945. Jimmy and Maude Byrnes left Washington on April 7, 1945, to return to their home in Spartanburg.

Less than a week later, Franklin D. Roosevelt was dead. Within hours of hearing the news, the new President Harry Truman requested him to come back Washington. Byrnes left the following morning.

On the way back from attending the Roosevelt funeral in Hyde Park, New York, Truman told Byrnes that he wanted him to be his Secretary of State. Byrnes accepted, but did request that the President delay the appointment for several weeks out of respect for the current occupant, Edward Stettinius, Jr., who had replaced Cordell Hull. At this time Byrnes also told Truman about the top-secret atomic bomb project.

Byrnes took up his duties in the State Department on July 8, 1945. Within a week, he and the President were on the way to Germany for the meetings at Potsdam, the last of the great World War II conferences. For the first six months of his tenure as head of foreign affairs, "patience and firmness" became Byrnes' slogan in his dealings with the increasingly difficult Soviets while hoping that the two powers could continue some spirit of their wartime cooperation. However, after the Moscow meetings of December 1945, President Truman believed that Byrnes had been somewhat too patient and insufficiently firm in his meetings with Molotov and Stalin. As a result, Truman urged Byrnes to take a tougher line in his dealings with them stating that "I'm tired of babying the Soviets." Following his stern admonition—and probably his own inclinations as well—James Byrnes became more of what would be termed a "Cold Warrior." In his last four major conferences, one in London and three in Paris, Byrnes took a firmer stand in negotiations with the Soviets. He also decided to retire from the job, doing so in January of 1947 after one and one-half years in the position. Later that year his well-received book, *Speaking Frankly,* described his experiences in the foreign policy field.

After his resignation, the Byrnes' relationship with Truman suffered a serious decline. The 1948 Democratic platform took a strong stand in favor of civil rights for African Americans which made many Southerners uncomfortable to say the least. While Byrnes took no part in the Dixiecrat revolt of that year, he did not endorse Truman either. He did, however, decide to run for governor of South Carolina in 1950. As the barriers associated with segregation had begun to fall, Byrnes defended the long-established order of southern life, but he did advocate equality of education funding for both races. Jimmy Byrnes wanted to avoid the type of racism that had been associated with such past South Carolina politicians as Cole Blease, Cotton Ed Smith, and Pitchfork Ben Tillman, and saw himself occupying a middle ground between that and the integrationists. In this respect, his position was not unlike that of Louisiana's Jimmy Davis. In his private life, Byrnes was known for his kindly treatment of African-Americans, and he helped fund numerous scholarships for poor children of both races. Byrnes won the race, served four years as governor, and retired from public office early in 1955.

While Byrnes never formally left the Democratic Party, he did help lead the way to a two-party system in the once "Solid South." In 1952 he introduced Dwight Eisenhower on the steps of the state capital and led a move for an "Independents for Eisenhower" slate of delegates from South Carolina that obtained some 46% of the vote. (The GOP slate of Ike's electors got almost another 3%.) In 1960, 1964, and 1968, Byrnes endorsed GOP presidential candidates Nixon (twice) and Goldwater. He also approved Strom Thurmond's party switch of 1964. During Nixon's first term, Byrnes' health declined, and he died on April 9, 1972, a few weeks short of his ninetieth birthday. During his long career in public service, he held numerous elective and appointive offices, serving in each with dignity and honor although not without controversy. He managed to win considerable respect in both parties as was demonstrated when he received a unanimous confirmation for the Supreme Court in 1941. Ironically, he is largely forgotten today except among foreign policy and cold war scholars. Yet in his time Sir Knight Byrnes ranked among the most significant figures of the twentieth century and deserved to be best remembered as one of the best-known Americans and Masons of his time.

**Note**: The principal source for the life of James F. Byrnes is the biography by David Robertson, Sly and Able, *A Political Biography of James F. Byrnes* (1994). It should be supplemented by his own memoirs, *Speaking Frankly* (1947) and *All in One Lifetime* (1958), and the essays in the Kendrick A. Clements edited volume, *James F. Byrnes and the Origins of the Cold War* (1982). Alonzo Hamby's *Man of the People: A Life of Harry S. Truman* (1995) is also relevant. His Masonic record is detailed in William R. Denslow, *10,000 Famous Freemasons I* (1957), p. 166.

January 2005; slightly revised 2011

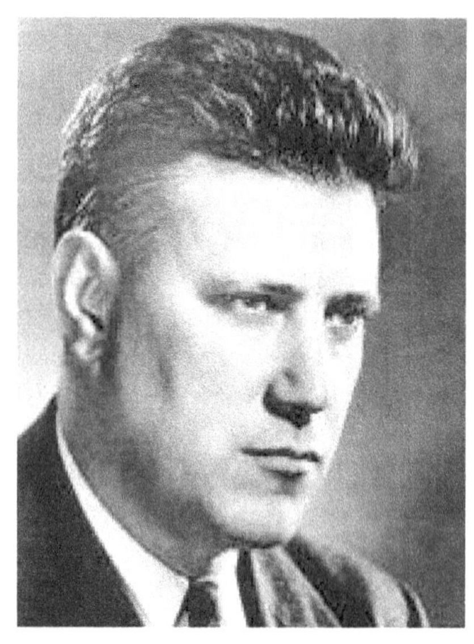

**Brother Jesse Hilton Stuart:**
*Appalachian Literary Giant*

Appalachia is that portion of the Eastern United States that some folks have characterized as "hillbilly country." It extends from southern New York to northeast Mississippi, but its heartland is eastern Kentucky and Tennessee, West Virginia, southwestern Virginia, and western North Carolina. Will Wallace Harney, one of the first to write about the area, referred to it and its inhabitants as "a strange land and a peculiar people." While the stereotypes of Appalachian backwardness created by Hollywood and cartoons are an exaggeration, there have been those who attempted realistic literary interpretations of the "Southern Highlands." One of the most astute of these writers, Brother Jesse Hilton Stuart of Greenup County, Kentucky, is the subject of this sketch.

The man who became Appalachia's leading literatus was born near Greenup on August 8, 1906 (or 1907). Like most people of eastern Kentucky, the Stuarts were poor. Jesse's father, Mitchell Stuart, worked occasionally at mining coal but usually as an impoverished tenant farmer. During World War I, he got a labor job on the railroad at four dollars a day. This enabled him to save enough to buy fifty acres of land. Jesse and his brother James labored with their dad to help scratch a living from the soil. Although Mitch Stuart was illiterate and his wife Martha had only a second grade education, both parents endeavored to inspire their children with a desire for schooling. Getting even a high school education in that part of Kentucky in those days took some real effort, but Jesse managed to graduate from Greenup High School several weeks before his 20th birthday. The most beneficial experience in those days came from the encouragement he received from an English teacher, Mrs. Hatton.

That September, Stuart enrolled in Lincoln Memorial University in Harrogate, Tennessee. He labored at various jobs in order to pay his way and keep eating. He continued receiving encouragement—this time from English professor H. H. Kroll—to continue developing his writing skills. While there, Jesse met James Still, another aspiring mountain author. Stuart also edited the school paper and began publishing poems in small magazines. He managed to earn a B.A. degree, graduating in 1929.

That fall, Stuart began his teaching career. Actually, he had a term in a one room school back when he was eighteen and had not yet finished high school. In that situation, he had to whip the school bully in order to gain respect. In his new assignment, Stuart found himself the sole high school teacher in a remote one-room high school that had only fourteen students at a salary of one hundred dollars monthly. The following year, he became principal at Greenup High School only four years after his own graduation from the same school. Although the school year went well, the board decided not to rehire him because he asked for a salary increase to $1,500 annually. Jesse spent the following year at Vanderbilt where he did graduate study with that group of writers known as the Fugitives, particularly Professor Donald Davidson. Although Stuart never finished his M.A. degree, a manuscript he prepared there was later published as the autobiographical work, *Beyond Dark Hills.*

Back in Greenup County, the local county board of education hired Jesse Stuart as county superintendent. There followed a year of controversy, as Stuart's ideas were somewhat ahead of their time. The twenty-six year old executive then decided to avoid another squabble by taking a position as principal at McKell High School in South Shore, opposite Portsmouth on the Ohio River. From 1933 to 1937, Jesse spent four years at South Shore, Kentucky. The big problems there involved such things as figuring out a way to keep the team's star football player on the field when he had a tendency to bite opposing players. He solved the problem by having the boy wear a catcher's mask during football games.

During those years in South Shore, Jesse Hilton Stuart also took his Masonic work. He received his Entered Apprentice degree in Harrison Fullerton Lodge No. 937 on October 28, 1935; was passed to Fellowcraft on January 13, 1936; and was raised as a Master Mason on March 4, 1936. After fifteen years he demitted to Greenup Lodge No. 89 where he retained membership for the rest of his life.

In that same period, Stuart also began to be taken seriously as a literary figure. In 1934 his short story "Kentucky Hill Dance" first appeared in *The New Republic* magazine. His poems had already appeared in such literary journals as *The Virginia Quarterly Review,* but after the publication of his book of poetry, *Man With a Bull-Tongue Plow,* his reputation as a serious man of verse soared. In 1936 his first book of short stories, *Head O' W-Hollow,* appeared, further enhancing his literary persona and enabling him to spend a year in Scotland on a Guggenheim Fellowship. Perhaps following the lead of American literary critic Mark Van Doren, the Scots often compared his poems to those of literary hero and fellow Mason, Robert Burns.

Returning to Greenup County in 1938, Stuart found school politics in more controversy than ever, but finally he stepped out of it by taking a position as a remedial English instructor at Portsmouth High School in Ohio. In 1939 he decided to leave teaching and attempt to earn his living by a combination of sheep farming and his literary endeavors, including touring and public speaking. He also married Naomi Dean Norris that October following a lengthy courtship. Over the next few years, he published his aforementioned autobiographical work, *Beyond Dark Hills*; another short story collection, *Men of the Mountains*; and two novels, *Trees of Heaven* in 1940 and his best-known work, *Taps for Private Tussie,* in 1943. The latter became a Book-of-the-Month selection and eventually a popular motion picture as well. The novel concerns a down-and-out mountain family who squanders the military insurance money of a soldier relative who was presumably killed in the war but who eventually turns up very much alive. Although satirical, the book's tone angered some people because of the way certain characters were portrayed. The success of the work ended Stuart's monetary concerns that had hitherto plagued his life.

Probably because of wartime shortages, Stuart came back to Greenup High School as superintendent in the fall of 1942 until March of 1944 when he was inducted into the United States Navy.

The writer spent the remainder of the conflict writing training manuals. Returning to Kentucky at the end of 1945, Brother Stuart continued his career of writing, turning out a number of short stories, poems, and novels. *The Thread That Runs So True* (1949) recounted his teaching experiences in detail with some name and place changes but thinly disguised. For instance Greenup County became Greenwood, McKell High became Maxwell, Portsmouth became Dartmouth, Ironton became Toniron, and Ashland became Auckland. Popular as reading for future teachers as well as its literary quality, the book has remained continuously in print for more than a half century.

Jesse Stuart spent his remaining years continuing to write and lecture. On occasion, he returned to teaching. Except for a year (1956-

1957) back at McKell High School as principal, most of his teaching now consisted of summer terms as a visiting professor at various colleges and universities. A heart attack slowed him down for a year after October of 1954. As his literary reputation grew, his recognition as a literary figure increased. In 1954, he was named Poet Laureate of Kentucky, and Governor Lawrence Weatherby designated October 15, 1958, as Jesse Stuart day. He was also honored on the Network TV show, *This Is Your Life,* and spent 1960-1961 teaching at the American University in Cairo, Egypt.

Back in the Bluegrass State, Stuart spent two years as Author in Residence at Eastern Kentucky University in Richmond. During the fifties and sixties, he turned out eight children's books as well as more novels, short stories, and poems. Two novels are unusual in that they had settings outside of Kentucky. *Daughter of the Legend* (1965) dealt with the Melungeons of East Tennessee, and *The Land Beyond the River* (1973) concerned food stamp and welfare fraud in Appalachian Ohio.

As Jesse began to age and his health became more precarious, he started to think about his legacy. In 1960 he donated his papers to Murray State University. In 1978, a stroke rendered him an invalid. In 1979 the Jesse Stuart Foundation was formed, and in 1980 it received the right to administer his literary works. That same year he also donated his farm to the Commonwealth of Kentucky as a nature preserve. These actions proved fortunate because another stroke in May of 1982 left him helpless. On February 17, 1984, the once powerful school teacher who had to initially win respect with his fists, passed to "the celestial lodge above," nearly forty-eight years after being raised a Master Mason.

As a literary figure, Jesse Stuart has been increasingly considered a major American author. Like all writers, he has been criticized; a major criticism being his unquestioning acceptance of most traditional values. While a strong advocate for increased education expenditures, he also wished to emphasize character development. One of his memorable quotes is: "I'd rather have a C student with an A character than to have an A student with a C character." One suspects that Brother Stuart would not be pleased with the value-free education that prevails in many, if not most, public schools today. While Jesse Stuart's busy career as a teacher and writer probably prevented him from being particularly active in Masonic Lodge work in his forty-eight years as a member, he nonetheless managed to exemplify in his chosen professions what our venerable fraternity is all about: to make good men better.

**Note**: A good critical study of Stuart as man and writer is Harold Richardson, *Jesse: The Biography of an American Writer, Jesse Hilton Stuart* (1984). A shorter work of value is Jerry Herndon and George Brosi, *Jesse Stuart: The Man and His Books* (1988). The photo is courtesy of the Jesse Stuart Foundation, P. O. Box 391, Ashland, Kentucky. For his Masonic record, I am indebted to the staff at the Grand Lodge of Kentucky.

September 1999, slightly revised 2011

## Brother Jimmie Davis:
*The Singing Governor*

In recent decades, show business and sports personalities have gone on to carve out successful careers in politics. For instance, the late Jack Kemp, a former Buffalo Bills quarterback and member of Fraternal Lodge No. 625 in Hamburg, New York, was a nominee for Vice President. Yet the phenomenon is hardly as new as it may appear. W. Lee O'Daniel, a flour salesman who led western swing bands such as the Light Crust Doughboys and Hillbilly Boys in the mid-thirties, was elected governor of Texas in 1938. However, O'Daniel, a member of Ninnescah Lodge No. 230 in Kingman, Kansas, was not really a musician but a businessman who had a band and served as their radio announcer. The first real musical figure to make it big on the political scene, country singer Jimmie Davis, won election as governor of Louisiana in 1944 and again in 1960. Along the way, Davis made several hundred recordings for such companies as Victor, Capitol, and Decca, including one of the popular standards of the twentieth century, "You Are My Sunshine."

Like many other Southerners of his generation, James Houston Davis grew up in poverty as the son of a near-impoverished sharecropper. The actual date of his birth remains a bit uncertain, but it is most likely September 11 (or September 19, 1900), although estimates of the year have ranged from 1899 to 1908. As Jimmie later said, keeping track of time could sometimes be a challenge in the country where there were no newspapers or radio. The place was a modest cabin in the Beech Springs community of Jackson Parish, halfway between Quitman and Jonesboro, Louisiana. The struggle to survive in those early years probably helped him gain the enduring strength that sustained him for a long life. Unlike many poor folks, the elder Davis, who had only a third grade education, insisted that his children get as much schooling as they could. Thus, about the time that Jimmie finished eighth grade, the residents of Beech Springs constructed a modest high school, and young Davis became one their first graduates. Continuing to make local history, he became the first to attend college and then the first to return and become a teacher.

In addition to hard work and striving for schooling, music filled an important gap in the Davis home. It helped sustain them through economic hardship and provided both home entertainment and spiritual comfort. "Amazing Grace" was the first song Jimmie remembered hearing. When his younger sister Elsie died at age four, that lyric and "How Firm a Foundation" gave hope to the unfortunate family and their neighbors at the funeral service prior to lowering the child's last remains into the ground. Music played a role in the happier moments as well, and Jimmie learned to love both secular and sacred songs both inside and outside of school and church. Davis learned to play guitar a little as he got older, but it would be as a vocalist that he made his mark in the world.

Jimmie Davis chose Louisiana College in Pineville as the place to further his education and managed to survive and pay for his schooling by doing a variety of odd jobs. Sometimes he would simply sing on street corners in nearby Alexandria and pass the hat to secure funds. His efforts eventually paid off and he obtained a four-year degree in 1924 after which he returned to Beech Springs as both a teacher and coach. He also went to Louisiana State University during summer terms and earned a Master's degree in 1927.

The same year that the young teacher obtained his M.A., he also began his Masonic labors. On March 21, 1927, Jimmie was initiated an Entered Apprentice in Jonesboro Lodge No. 280 in Jonesboro, Louisiana. Academic endeavors at L.S.U. may have slowed his progress in the order, but not for long, because on September 5 the Lodge Brethren passed him to the degree of Fellowcraft. Only eleven days elapsed until they raised him to the sublime degree of Master Mason. Some time later, Jimmie took the Scottish Rite degrees in the Valley of Shreveport.

Shortly after receiving his M.A., Jimmie Davis took a new position teaching history at Dodd College, a girls' school in Shreveport. During this time, he also began his singing career via KWKH radio in that same Red River city. This historic station at the time belonged to W. K. Henderson who became famous for his opposition to chain stores and the use of public highways by the trucking industry. Jimmie sang both the popular and country songs of the day as can be illustrated by the fact that his first recording session in the spring of 1928 included cover versions of Gene Austin's "Ramona" and the Jimmie Rodgers' hit "Away Out on the Mountain." Issued on Henderson's own Doggone label, the discs had limited distribution and are exceedingly rare today. A second attempt at recording on Columbia in December of 1928 resulted in two unreleased songs. Finally, beginning in September of 1929, Davis recorded for the Victor label and was a regular in the recording studios from that time.

By the time he began recording for Victor in 1929, Jimmie had dropped his work at Dodd College and taken a position as clerk of the Shreveport Criminal Court. This job paid $190.00 per month, provided Davis with a modest but steady income, and gave him sufficient time to continue his part-time musical career. Meanwhile, he kept cutting sessions for Victor, having a total of sixty-eight issued songs through 1933. While his discs chalked up only modest sales in this period—few buyers could be found in the depression-wracked economy—the music holds up as excellent examples of white blues music in the Jimmie Rodgers style, some of it with accompaniment by African-American guitarists Oscar "Buddy" Woods and Ed Schaffer. Jimmie's best seller in the early years was a humorous number titled "Bear Cat Mama from Horner's Corners," which was also covered by a Masonic cowboy singer named Gene Autry.

In 1934, Jimmie switched his recording allegiance to the new Decca label and immediately turned out a major hit with "Nobody's Darling But Mine," a number that became an all-time country standard. In his first decade with Decca, Davis had over 140 sides released. These included such major hits as "It Makes No Difference Now," "Sweethearts or Strangers," "Columbus Stockade Blues," "There's a New Moon Over My Shoulder" (also a hit for Brother Tex Ritter), and the prison ballad that became a bluegrass standard, "Shackles and Chains." An April 30, 1938 *Collier's* article "Thar's Gold in Them Hillbillies," ranked him in stature with Gene Autry and the Carter Family at the top of their musical field.

In the meantime, Davis had settled in at Shreveport as a home base. In 1936, he married Alvern Adams, a young school teacher, and in 1937, he moved his Blue Lodge membership to the local Joppa Lodge No. 362. In 1938, he sought and won the elective office of Public Service Commissioner which put him in charge of the city's police department. Four years later, Davis moved up the ladder by winning a four-year term on the Louisiana Public Service Commission. This office had earlier been a proven springboard to the governorship for Huey Long among others. In 1944, it did the same thing for the popular country singer.

While in public office in Shreveport, Davis had continued his musical endeavors as time permitted, traveling to recording sessions during vacations. On February 5, 1940, he waxed what would become the trademark song of his career, a song titled "You Are My Sunshine." Since Jimmie and his steel guitarist Charlie Mitchell, owned the song, it became one of the most noted copyrights in musical history. Its popularity led to quick cover versions by other artists including Gene Autry and Bing Crosby. "You Are My Sunshine" became one of the great commercial hits of that era and made the name of Jimmie Davis a household word. By May of 1942 when he went to Hollywood for another record session, Jimmie also got the opportunity to sing it in the motion picture, *Strictly in the Groove.* Later he appeared in other films such as *Riding Through Nevada* (1942) and *Frontier Fury* (1943), both Charles Starrett westerns. Still later he starred in two Monogram films, *Louisiana* (1947) and *Mississippi Rhythm* (1949), the former picture actually being his own life story.

In 1944, Jimmie successfully sought the Louisiana governorship. His four-year term was marked by a fairly harmonious period in a state noted for its turbulent politics. Davis continued the moderate reforms of his predecessor Sam Houston Jones, and benefited from a strong economy that war-time and post-war prosperity had brought to the Pelican State. One of his first actions as leader of his state's delegation to the 1944 Democratic Convention was to second the nomination of Brother Harry S. Truman for Vice President. This proved to be a fortunate move for Davis as it led to a close friendship with a man who would become President in less than a year. As governor, Davis gave Louisiana four years of balanced budgets and left the treasury in better shape than he found it. He also led the way to the establishment of a retirement system for teachers and state workers. One of his most courageous acts was to veto a right to work law which had sailed through the legislature. Although he curtailed his singing career, he did not stop it. As the governor, he gave numerous benefit concerts and managed to get away for a few recording sessions. Some critics complained when he was out of state for twelve days filming the movie *Louisiana* (1947) that told his life story and in which he played himself, but in the long run it brought favorable publicity to a state that needed it.

Ironically, Jimmie Davis never became a full-time entertainer until 1948 when he left the governor's chair. He went on a lengthy tour, visited President Truman in the White House, made another motion picture, and started a regional weekly radio program, *The Jimmie Davis Hour,* heard via syndication in thirteen states. He made a brief switch to Capitol Records in 1949, but soon returned to Decca. In fact, his long tenure with Decca/MCA may well have been second only to the late bluegrass legend Bill Monroe. After the popularity of the inspirational number "Suppertime," in 1953, followed by "Mansion Just Over the Hilltop" and "Someone to Care," he became increasingly although not exclusively associated with sacred music. For nearly twenty years from the mid-fifties, Jimmie turned out some thirty long-play albums, most of them filled with religious numbers both old and new.

In 1959, Davis decided to again seek the governorship. Louisiana had again been rocked with another wave of sensationalism during the Earl Long years (remember the movie *Blaze!),* and Jimmie hoped to restore some of the "peace and harmony" that had characterized his first term. Early in 1960, he cruised to a fairly easy runoff win, defeating New Orleans mayor deLesseps Morrison by some 70,000 votes to win a second term.

Putting the Earl Long-Blaze Starr scandal behind them was easy enough for Governor Davis, but calming the emotions aroused by the civil rights, school integration controversy proved more challenging. The Davis position of moderate segregationist hardly satisfied extremists at each end of the spectrum, although in retrospect Jimmie could later say that he managed to avoid the violent confrontations that took place in neighboring states. Critics also complained about some of his public works projects including the "Sunshine Bridge" and a newly constructed governor's mansion, but time has vindicated his support of the building programs. As in the first term, fiscal responsibility proved another hallmark of the second Davis era. Ironically, Davis had his last record hit midway through his term with a 1962 revival of one his early hits, the nostalgic favorite, "Where the Old Red River Flows," a lyric he had first made for Victor thirty years earlier. Also for a dozen years, Davis maintained a plural membership at A.U. Peterson Lodge No. 455 in Folsom, Louisiana but eventually demitted from there, retaining his membership in Joppa Lodge No. 362 in Shreveport all the while.

Following his second retirement from the statehouse, Jimmie continued his singing career. Tragedy struck in 1967 when his wife Alvern became a cancer victim. Two years later, Davis remarried, this time to Anna Carter Gordon, a longtime member of the legendary gospel singing Chuck Wagon Gang. After leaving Decca/MCA Records in 1974, he recorded for Paula, Plantation, and especially Canaan. Some of these discs were released as the Jimmie Davis Trio, which included Anna and guitarist James Wilson. Continuing to release albums up through the early eighties, he cut a pair of compact discs in 1993, making him perhaps the only vocalist in American musical history to make recordings in eight different decades.

Although a third quest for the statehouse in 1971-1972 proved unsuccessful, Jimmie Davis continued to be a popular figure on the gospel music circuit. Meanwhile, numerous honors came his way. In 1965, the Jimmie Davis Tabernacle was dedicated near his childhood home, a beautiful structure that seats some 750 persons. The childhood home was also restored. As a vocalist, he was honored by inclusion in the Songwriter's Hall of Fame, the Gospel Music Hall of Fame, and in 1972, the Country Music Hall of Fame. On October 18, 1985, he belatedly received his fifty-year pin from the Grand Lodge of Louisiana.

Jimmie Davis remained active in singing well into his nineties, among other things appearing in a CBS-TV special in the spring of 1992 and making a guest appearance at the *Grand Ole Opry* in September of 1995. Each year on the first Sunday in October, thousands gathered at the Jimmie Davis Tabernacle to pay their respects. The Singing Governor lived long enough to celebrate his 100$^{th}$ birthday and passed away on November 5, 2000, a unique figure in the annals of Christian Masons. As country music historian Ronnie Pugh has written, if someone had put his life story into a novel of Southern life, critics would no doubt call it unrealistic. Nonetheless, the story of the "Singing Governor" was as true as life could get.

**Note**: The book by Gus Weill, *You Are My Sunshine: The Jimmie Davis Story* (1977, 1987 & 1991) is the only biography to date, although a promised more definitive one by Kevin Fontenot has yet to appear. For his Masonic records, they were supplied by Jack Crouch, Grand Secretary of the Grand Lodge of Louisiana through the assistance of Ohio's Grand Secretary, David Dresser and my own blue lodge secretary, Roger E. VanDyke.

March 1997; slightly revised 2011

## Sir Knight Jimmy Wakely: *From Melody Kid to Movie Cowboy Hero*

"Dedicated to the Memory of Sir Knight George N. Barkhurst, KYCH, KCT, of Logan Commandery No 78, Logan, Ohio"

Prior articles in this journal have focused on the careers of Masonic movie cowboys, particularly those of the singing variety. Jimmy Wakely had a shorter career as a cowboy star than some of his contemporaries and never came close to attaining the stature of the late Sir Knights Gene Autry or Roy Rogers. Yet he starred in more pictures than Rex Allen, and some consensus exists that he was a better singer than the others. Sir Knight Wakely did not become a Mason until his movie career had ended, and except for Tex Ritter (who belonged to the same Blue Lodge), Jimmy died earlier than the others; nonetheless, he managed to sustain a respectable career as an entertainer on the Hollywood scene for more than four decades.

James Clarence Wakely was born in Mineola, Arkansas, on February 16, 1914. At the age of three, his farmer father moved his family to Octavia, Oklahoma, where he continued to scratch out a hard scrabble existence from the soil. Later, the Wakelys moved to Battiest and then Cowden, Oklahoma, still searching for prosperity. When the Great Depression hit, the family's economic condition went from bad to worse. Meanwhile, Jimmy had learned to play guitar and piano. He entertained the family and neighbors by playing the songs of Brother Jimmie Rodgers who had gained widespread popularity among rural folk. Later, when the Wakelys moved to Rosedale, Oklahoma, they all became devoted fans of western swing pioneer Milton Brown and His Musical Brownies who were earning great popularity via Fort Worth radio.

Their neighbors, the George Miner family, also admired Brown's music, and Jimmy developed strong feelings for daughter Inez. Jimmy Wakely married Inez Miner on December 13, 1935, and the couple subsequently had four children: Deanna, Carol, Linda, and John. At the time of his marriage, Jimmy operated a service station in Rosedale. The little family moved into Oklahoma City about 1937 where Jimmy began to pick up part-time musical jobs. Later that summer, Wakely went to work in a medicine show where he earned fourteen and then seventeen dollars per week. That fall he received an offer to sing in a trio on WKY radio in Oklahoma City. This was a good move, but not much happened until Jim convinced the owner of the sponsoring Bell Clothing Company to change the Bell Trio to a western-styled group. He then got his friends, Johnny Bond and Scotty Harrell, into the trio, and they became quite popular, making many personal appearances throughout the Sooner State.

In the summer of 1939, the Trio made a quick trip to Hollywood where they worked as musical support in a Roy Rogers film, *Saga of Death Valley*. However, their big break came when Gene Autry did a guest spot on their radio program and then hired them as regulars on his new CBS network show, *Melody Ranch*. As a result, the renamed Jimmy Wakely Trio came to California to stay. Jimmy himself later phrased the situation thusly: "Through the grace of God and [Brother, later Sir Knight] Gene Autry, I got a career."

In addition to his *Melody Ranch* position, Wakely landed a solo contract with Decca Records, and although he had no monumental hits, he did cut some thirty-four sides over the next five years. Two songs in particular did quite well: his 1943 cover version of Elton Britt's "There's a Star Spangled Banner Waving Somewhere" and a 1944 offering, "I'm Sending You Red Roses."

The Trio also appeared in many motion pictures with Charles Starrett and also with Johnny Mack Brown. Although they made only one film with Gene Autry, the two years that they worked as regulars on his *Melody Ranch* radio program gave them an association with this superstar and contributed to their popularity. The Jimmie Wakely Trio also appeared in a hillbilly-type variety comedy with Slim Summerville titled *I'm From Arkansas*. In 1944, Monogram Pictures decided to make four singing cowboys films with Wakely as the star. These movies did well enough with the public that studio executives opted to produce a regular series. They signed Jimmy to a five-year contract.

During that period, Jimmy Wakely starred in a total of twenty-eight musical westerns. Only Sir Knights Autry, Ritter, and Rogers made more singing cowboy films. In the first dozen pictures, another prominent show business Mason and Shriner, Lee "Lasses" White (1888-1949), a former minstrel man and *Grand Ole Opry* star, played his sidekick. When White's health declined in 1947, the late Dub "Cannonball" Taylor (also reputed to be a Mason) replaced him for the duration of the series. Leading ladies in Wakely films included Gail Davis who as "Annie Oakley" became the first female to star in her own western TV series; Polly Bergen [then Burgin] who went on to become a successful actress and songstress; and Christine Larson who was Ronald Reagan's girl friend prior to his courtship and marriage to Nancy Davis. Whip Wilson, who became a member of North Hollywood Lodge No. 542 and from 1949 starred in his own western series at Monogram, made his film debut in a Wakely picture. The better-known Wakely movies include such titles as *Song of the Sierras, Springtime in Texas, Song of the Range,* and *Six gun Serenade.*

As Jimmy Wakely's movie career picked up steam, so too did the success of his singing efforts. In 1947 he signed with Capitol which was then becoming a major label. Later that year, he recorded a composition, "One Has My Name, the Other Has My Heart," written by fellow singing cowboy Eddie Dean. In 1948 it spent eleven weeks at the top of the country charts and scored high in the pop field as well. This established Jimmy as a major singing star with crossover appeal. Over the next three years, Wakely turned out several more big solo hits for Capitol that included Floyd Tillman's "I Love You So Much It Hurts," "Mona Lisa," "My Heart Cries for You," and a revival of the old country song, "Beautiful Brown Eyes." Unlike Eddie Dean, who sang in a style that many thought did not seem sufficiently country, Jimmy Wakely managed to also hold his down-home audience with such numbers as "Oklahoma Blues," "I Wish I Had a Nickel," and his rendition of the Jack Guthrie classic, "Oklahoma Hills."

Jimmy scored his biggest musical success in a 1949 duet with pop songstress Margaret Whiting when their version of another Tillman composition, "Slipping Around," became a million-seller. It stayed at number one on the country charts for seventeen weeks and topped the pop listings for another three. They also had several good follow-up hits with "I'll Never Slip Around Again," "Let's Go to Church (Next Sunday Morning)," "A Bushel and a Peck," and a modernized version of that 1866 favorite "When You and I Were

Young, Maggie." Despite their commercial acumen, some tension and jealousy apparently existed between the two as some witnesses reported seeing them counting the solo words that each sang on their recording sessions. After 1953, Jimmy left Capitol for the Coral label and then returned to Decca. In the mid-sixties he started his own company, Shasta Records. National Periodical Publications (or DC) in 1949 initiated a Jimmy Wakely comic book series. Bi-monthly issues came until early 1952 when the series was terminated. Since DC specialized in "super heroes" such as Superman, Batman, and Wonder Woman, their western titles never sold as well, and as a result, the eighteen Wakely comics actually bring better prices in today's collector market than those of Allen, Autry, and Rogers which sold more widely at the time.

From 1952 until 1958, *The Jimmy Wakely Show* was a regular weekly musical feature on the CBS radio network. Even though big time network radio went into decline in this period, Jimmy's program lasted longer than most of them and kept his name in the public spotlight. Besides, since Jimmy came into ownership of the show's tapes, in later years it provided him with a considerable volume of material for Shasta Records. He made only one significant film in this period, *Arrow in the Dust* (1954), starring Sterling Hayden in which he played a supporting role and sang a song.

By the mid-fifties, Jimmy Wakely's motion picture stardom and big hit records were all behind him, but he still recorded for a major label, kept in fine voice, and remained a popular live show performer until the mid-seventies. In addition to appearances on the West Coast, the "Melody Kid" (as he had once been known) proved an appealing performer on the Nevada club circuit. In 1976 he told film historian David Rothel that he had played a total of 120 weeks at Harrah's over a period of seven years in addition to other locales and military bases. In later years, son John and daughter Linda joined his show which by all accounts rated as top-notch entertainment.

Jimmy became a Mason during those years, joining Metropolitan Lodge No. 646 in Los Angeles. Both Rod Cameron and Tex Ritter had taken their degrees in this lodge, but by that time, Tex had moved to Nashville and Rod would soon be dropped from the rolls. At any rate, James Clarence Wakely was initiated an Entered Apprentice on February 6, 1968; passed to the degree of Fellowcraft on February 20; and was raised a Master Mason on March 26, 1968. Some years later, Metropolitan Lodge merged with South Pasadena

No. 367, and Jimmy continued membership there until June 2, 1981, when he demitted and affiliated that same day with Old West Lodge No. 813 in Newhall, California where he retained his membership for the rest of his life.

Meanwhile, the cowboy vocalist had continued in his Masonic endeavors by petitioning the York Rite bodies. After completing them with his Knighting in Calvary Commandery No. 62, Knights Templar in Pasadena, Wakely became a Noble of Al Malaikah Temple, AAONMS, on November 29, 1969. The following fall, on December 5, 1970, when fellow cowpokes Rex Allen and John Wayne took their journey across the hot sands, Jimmy Wakely was present to give them moral support.

In later years, Wakely worked on the road less often and renewed interest in his first love—radio. For at least a decade from 1966, he taped a one-hour daily record and interview program for the Armed Forces Radio Network. For a time he even had a taped program on Radio Iran for the benefit of American residents there, which presumably stopped with the 1979 Revolution. These programs, together with occasional show dates and the growth of Shasta Records as a mail order business, kept the Melody Kid occupied in later years.

In 1976 Jimmy told David Rothel that he enjoyed good health, and he obviously remained in good voice. Rothel also noted that he coughed several times during the interview. Those coughs may have been an indication of future health problems, because a few years later, he was diagnosed as having emphysema. On September 23, 1982, Sir Knight James Clarence Wakely passed away at the age of sixty-eight. A Shrine emblem appears on his tombstone.

Jimmy Wakely has not been forgotten. A few years ago, Linda Lee Wakely authored an affectionate biography, *See Ya' Up There Daddy: The Jimmy Wakely Story*. In 1996 Capitol Records released a compact disc of his best musical efforts in their *Vintage Collections* series. Other compact discs have been issued in Europe. Western film buffs treasure his movies, collect them on video-cassettes and DVDs, and gather annually in such locales as Knoxville, Charlotte, and Memphis to watch motion pictures of Jimmy and other B-western stars of a not-so-long-ago but bygone era. Like Sir Knights Autry, Ritter, Rogers, and Wayne along with Brothers Rex Allen, Harry Carey, Hoot Gibson, Buck Jones, Tom Mix, and Whip Wilson, Sir Knight Wakely projected a virtuous on-screen image that America's youth could not only admire but also emulate.

**Note**: The best source for information on Jimmy Wakely is his daughter's aforementioned book together with the chapter on him in David Rothel, *The Singing Cowboys* (A. S. Barnes & Co., 1978). For his Masonic record, I am indebted to the staff of the Grand Lodge of California and to that of Al Malaikah Shrine Temple. I also appreciate the kindly information and counsel of Brother Bobby Copeland of Knoxville, Tennessee.

November 2000; slightly revised 2011

## Brother Joseph Warren Stilwell:
*The General Called "Vinegar Joe"*

The fact that numerous American military leaders in World War II were Masons is fairly well known. However, the list runs much deeper than those with five stars: Arnold, Bradley, King, and MacArthur. It also includes such nearly forgotten figures as Walter Krueger. In between those two extremes is one of the Masonic Generals who faced some of the most challenging tasks of the entire conflict who is the subject of this sketch, Joseph Warren Stilwell, commander of the China Burma India Theater.

The man who became known as "Vinegar Joe" Stilwell was born in Palatka, Florida, of an old New York family on March 19, 1883. However, he grew up in Yonkers, New York, where he displayed some degree of rebellion against the strict religious regimen that his parents, Dr. Benjamin and Mary Peene Stilwell, endeavored to impress upon him. Nonetheless, he still excelled in academics, football, and track. Then after some unruly behavior at a school dance, his father, thinking he need more discipline, changed his plan of sending him to Yale and used his political connections to secure a West Point appointment for young Joe.

At the United States Military Academy, Stilwell again did well in his studies, displaying a special aptitude for foreign languages. He also served as captain of the cross country team, introduced the new sport of basketball, and played on the football team. On the downside, he also earned some demerits, particularly in his senior year. Still his academic record held up sufficiently that when he graduated in 1904, he ranked 32nd in a class of 124.

Since the young Second Lieutenant finished in the top third of his class, he could choose his preference of assignments and picked the Philippines which the Americans had only had as a possession for six years. Placed in the 12th Infantry, Stilwell sailed for Manila in

October of 1904, making a stopover in Hawaii. The Philippine Revolt had in theory been suppressed in 1902, but in fact, the islands continued to be unstable in many rural areas. After fourteen months, the young officer was back at West Point as a Spanish instructor. During summers he traveled through Latin American countries including Guatemala and Mexico to hone his linguistic skills. While at West Point, he also coached the basketball team and assisted with other sports. In 1910, Stilwell married Winifred Smith of Syracuse, New York. The couple eventually had three children, Joe, Jr. who became an army officer like his dad and two daughters, both of whom married army officers. In 1911, Stilwell found himself on another field assignment in the Philippines but also made brief trips to Japan and for seventeen days to China.

China, at the time, was entering into a period of revolution. The Manchu Dynasty that had ruled since 1644 was collapsing. Sun Yat-sen, a western-educated Cantonese physician and the Provisional President, had in the words of historian Barbara Tuchman "a political philosophy but no power." Provincial dictators known as "war-lords" continued to wield strength for decades. A nationalist political party, the Kuomintang, endeavored to bring order out of chaos with limited results. This, in short, described the China that would be intertwined with the life of Joseph Warren Stilwell until his death.

First Lieutenant Stilwell was back in the states by 1912 and soon found himself at West Point again teaching English and History in 1913-1914 and then teaching Spanish for the next two years. It was about this time that he experienced Masonic light. Joining West Point Lodge No. 877 in the spring of 1916, Joseph Warren Stilwell took his degrees in a four-week span on May 4, May 18, and June 1, 1916. He remained a member of West Point Lodge until his death more than thirty years later.

With World War I underway in Europe, a "movement for preparedness" gained momentum, and Congress passed the *Army Act* in April of 1916, to double the number of personnel. That summer, Stilwell began a new assignment of training reserve officers at the camp in Plattsburg, New York. In September, he received a promotion to Captain and after the declaration of war was sent to France where his knowledge of French proved useful. Back in the United States in July of 1919, he soon found himself with a China assignment that required an intensive study of the Chinese language, both Mandarin and Cantonese. Over the next several years, he had three stints as a military attaché at the Chinese legation in Peking (now Beijing), eventually becoming the top attaché. These duties encompassed the years 1920-1923, 1926-1929, and 1935-1939. During those times, Chiang Kai-shek consolidated his position as head of the Kuomintang. Finally in Stilwell's last tour of duty, as historian Matk Boatner, III quipped, "he had a ringside seat." By the time he finished the third tour, Colonel Stilwell seemed likely to soon retire.

Between China assignments in 1931, Stilwell served as commanding officer at Fort Benning, Georgia where he made a positive impression on fellow officer George C. Marshall who would become Chief of Staff and play a key role in his later career. He also earned the nickname of "Vinegar Joe." Known for a sometime sour disposition, a subordinate drew a cartoon of Stilwell's face rising out of a bottle of vinegar. However, he took it in good grace and even had copies made to send to his friends.

After General Marshall became head of the Army and with another preparedness situation in progress as war clouds again began to gather, Brother Stilwell received a promotion to Brigadier General and then to Major General in fairly rapid order. He commanded the 7th Infantry Division from July 1940 until July 1941, and the 3rd Corps from July until December 1941. After Pearl Harbor, Stilwell initially was "earmarked for operations in North Africa." However, when General Hugh Drum did not take command of the China Burma India Theater, Stilwell received the assignment. His chief goal was to keep the beleaguered Chinese under Generalissimo Chiang Kai-shek in the war. This proved to be a frustrating challenge of the first magnitude.

"Vinegar Joe" had impressions of Chiang going back to the late twenties. While he generally viewed the Kuomintang leader as one of the strongest figures in China (especially in a political sense), he also witnessed what seemed like inexhaustible corruption and incompetence in his leadership in the struggle against the Japanese. Chiang had worries about the Communist faction of Mao Tse-tung (Mao Zedong in the modern spelling) who were readying to oppose him once the Japanese threat eased. Stilwell wanted Chiang to reform the army and get rid of the lackluster generals in his ranks. Yet these were the same individuals the Generalissimo had to depend on to keep him in power. Chiang felt that the air power furnished by General Claire Chennault could keep the Japanese at bay while Stilwell wanted greater use of Chinese ground troops. Furthermore, they quarreled over the use and allocation of Lend Lease supplies and funds. Finally, while Stilwell's theater of operation in theory was equal to that of Eisenhower in Europe or of MacArthur in the Pacific, in reality, these ranked higher in terms of priority. Stilwell often found himself and his army in a virtually impossible situation.

Brother Stilwell commanded the China Burma India Theater from February of 1942 until October of 1944. Initially his forces were driven out of Burma but eventually were able to recover much of their losses and reopen a truck road back into China by which Lend Lease material could be transported back into the oppressed country. Stilwell earned admiration from his troops because of his concern for their safety and his willingness to share in enduring their hardships. However, the differences between "Vinegar Joe" and Chiang Kai-shek brought the two increasingly to the breaking point.

In the opinion of Barbara Tuchman who authored the lengthy study, *Stilwell and the American Experience, 1911-45,* "Had it been within the Generalissimo's power or philosophy to adopt Stilwell's program for reform of the army, he would have had the combat efficiency to resist the Japanese offensive of 1944 and, quite possibly, to overcome the Communists in the clash that was to come." Despite his problems, Stilwell received a promotion to full General in August 1944. However, Chiang would not or could not do what the American commander wanted. Stilwell's dissatisfaction grew, and he increasingly in private and in his dispatches referred to Chiang, a man of fairly small physical stature, as "the Peanut." Chiang Kai-shek in turn began to demand that Stilwell be recalled. Finally, on October 19, 1944, Stilwell was relieved of his command and took a new domestic assignment.

Back in the states for a few months, Stilwell still hoped for a field command. At first it appeared that he might not get one. He was initially put in charge of Army ground forces. However, on June 18, 1945, General Simon Bolivar Buckner was killed by a shell in the invasion of Okinawa. Vinegar Joe now had command of the Tenth Army, taking over the reins on June 23. What remained on the island in the Ryukyus was described as largely a "mopping-up stage" preparing the way for the ultimate invasion of the Japanese home islands. Okinawa would be the major American base for this operation. Hiroshima and Nagasaki would make this massive operation unnecessary, but no one knew that in late June and early July. "SO IT IS OVER" Stilwell wrote in his diary when the Japanese surrendered on August 14.

With the conflict ended, Stilwell was given command of the Presidio at San Francisco. However, his career was drawing to a close. Physicians discovered that he had cancer of the stomach. On October 11, he was awarded the Combat Infantryman Badge, but it was not pinned on him at bedside, "lest Stilwell realize that he was dying." He did in fact die in his sleep the following day. According to his wishes, no public funeral was held and his ashes scattered. The China problem remained, and in 1949, the forces of Chiang Kai-shek fled to the recently reclaimed island of Formosa. Pundits would toss around blame for the loss of China for many years. Yet it is hard to disagree with historian Tuchman's conclusion that "China was a problem for which there was no American solution . . . In the end, China went her own way as if the Americans had never come." Nonetheless, Brother "Vinegar Joe" Stilwell did his best in a most difficult assignment. It would have been impossible to ask or demand a more valiant effort.

**Note:** the ultimate source for this article is the massive volume by Barbara Tuchman, *Stilwell and the American Experience in China, 1911-1945* (New York: Macmillan, 1970), supplemented by Mark M. Boatner III, *The Biographical Dictionary of World War II* (Novato, CA: Presidio Press, 1999). For his Masonic records I am indebted to Bro. Thomas Savini of the Livingston Library, Grand Lodge of New York.

Hitherto unpublished

## Sir Knight John W. Bricker: *Champion of Old Guard Conservation*

During the middle third of the 20th century, John William Bricker ranked among the more prominent Masonic political figures on the national scene. During his career, the one-time Ohio farm boy held the office of state attorney general, governor, United States senator, and candidate for vice president. Unlike some politicians who are merely joiners and members, Sir Knight Bricker took his Masonry seriously and remained active throughout his adult life, particularly in the Scottish Rite. In this sense, he bore a strong resemblance to one of his major philosophical adversaries, Brother Harry S. Truman. While the "Man from Missouri" carried the banner of liberalism throughout his career, Bricker championed a brand of conservatism that reflected the values of self-reliant Americans and that saw little or no virtue in the type of centralized government and welfare state associated with the New Deal and the Fair Deal.

John Bricker was born on a farm near the village of Mt. Sterling in central Ohio on September 6, 1893. His parents, Lemuel and Laura King Bricker, came from German and Scotch-Irish stock, and the future governor had a twin sister Ella. As a youngster, John learned about the hard work of farming from experience and received an early initiation in politics: his father took him to local Pleasant Township Republican meetings. As he grew to adolescence, John took strong interests in debate and basketball. When he attended Mt. Sterling High School, these activities would dominate his social life. One historian wrote that many of Bricker's friends from the time he was eighteen thought that he would someday be governor.

After finishing high school in 1911, young John turned his attention toward Ohio State University and the eventual study of law. First, however, he taught in a one-room rural school for a year in order to earn enough money to enter college. While Bricker was a good student, his star shone brightest in forensics and baseball. He became the Buckeyes' regular catcher, and there he earned a varsity letter and acquired a reputation as a good fielder but weak hitter. Showing his interest in politics, he and Paul Herbert (another future Mason who experienced a long career in Ohio government) formed a club to support Brother Frank Willis for governor and later Charles Evans Hughes for president. After his 1916 graduation, Bricker entered law school.

Shortly after John entered law school, the United States entered World War I, and the young law student tried desperately to enter military service. Rejected by the army, navy, and the marines because of a slow heartbeat, he did YMCA volunteer work at nearby Camp Sherman in Chillicothe. He also sought special appointment as a minister which the Central Ohio Christian Church body soon granted him. This enabled the young law student to enter the army as a chaplain.

While awaiting his commission, John Bricker sought membership in Mt. Sterling Lodge No. 269 in his hometown. Initiated on December 20, 1917; passed on January 17, 1918; and raised a master Mason on March 17, 1918, John would be a member of this lodge for 68 years. Finally, his orders came through, and Lieutenant Bricker was sent to Camp Eustis, Virginia, where he spent his military career providing aid and spiritual comfort to those suffering through the great influenza epidemic. The war ended before he could be sent to France, and in mid-December the young chaplain returned to Ohio.

Back in the Buckeye State, Bricker finished law school, married Harriet "Abbey" Day, chemistry major from Urbana, and joined a local law firm. Soon he and another young lawyer and Mason, John Vorys, became activist Republicans, an avocation that would eventually carry both men to the halls of Congress. When Charles C. Crabbe won the attorney general's post at the statehouse in November of 1922, he appointed John as legal counsel for the Public Utilities Commission. A conservative both by nature and inclination, Bricker nonetheless championed the cause of utility regulation and consumer protection. In four years at this job, he won wide praise for his fairness and honesty.

He also continued his Masonic endeavors in this period, completing the Scottish Rite in Scioto Consistory on April 21, 1922, and becoming a Noble of Aladdin Shrine Temple on May 6, 1923. He also became a Companion of Friendship Chapter No. 22, Royal Arch

Masons on May 23, 1927. John joined a number of other fraternal groups including the Odd Fellows, Moose, and Eagles in addition to being a Rotarian for some sixty years, but Masonry was always his "paramount" organizational interest.

Returning to private law practice in 1927, John's first attempt to run for state-wide office came in 1928 when he sought the GOP nomination for attorney general. He lost that primary by less than 9,000 votes, but he later accepted an appointment to the Public Utilities Commission, where he again amassed a record as the consumer's friend. In 1932, he won the attorney general position by a narrow 10,008-vote margin in what turned out to be an otherwise dismal year for Republicans. John served a pair of two-year terms as the state's top lawyer and once more earned an enviable record. Furthermore, as the New Deal was in its heyday, Democrats held most state offices. Bricker ranked as the leading Republican in Ohio. In 1936 he became the GOP standard bearer for governor but lost to incumbent Democrat, Martin L. Davey (a member of Rockton Lodge No. 316 in Kent) by 126,688 votes. However, he ran a half million votes ahead of presidential nominee, Sir Knight Alfred Landon (of St. Bernard Commandery No. 10, Independence, Kansas) in Ohio and retained stature among Republicans.

During the thirties, John Bricker continued his activity in Masonry. He completed the York Rite degrees in Mt. Vernon Commandery No. 1 in Columbus on March 27, 1934, and Columbus Council No. 8 on March 13, 1936. However, the Scottish Rite became his special forte. As Walter H. Kropp and John A. Eckler noted in his obituary: "An active ritualist, he was active in the 20° (Grand Master of Virginia) from 1925 to 1941; and the 29° (Sieur Dr Coucy) from 1927 through 1943. He was memorable as the Commander of the 32° from 1934 through 1970 though he seldom performed after 1962. He was crowned an honorary member of the Supreme Council, 33° at Milwaukee, Wisconsin, September 29, 1937, and was the senior ranking member in the Valley of Columbus. On September 24, 1942, he was made an active member of the Supreme Council, N.M.J., a post he held for 34 years. For many years he held the office of Grand Minister of State, the third ranking office in the Supreme Council, and in 1971 he became the 14th recipient of the Gourgas Medal, the highest honor in Scottish Rite Masonry."

In 1938 John Bricker made his second—and this time successful—run for governor. He benefited from an unseemly rivalry between the controversial Governor Davey and his primary opponent Brother Charles Sawyer (of Madisonville Lodge No. 419). The Roosevelt administration contributed to Davey's primary defeat, and the angry lame duck governor refused to endorse Sawyer. Furthermore, the Ohio electorate, growing weary of New Deal reforms, not only elected Bricker by some 118,000 votes but also sent Robert A. Taft to the United States Senate. John would win his next two terms by margins in excess of 300,000 votes.

John Bricker's three terms as governor of Ohio helped make him a national figure. Except for an unfortunate dispute with Cleveland mayor and fellow Republican, Harold Burton (of Pythagoras Lodge No. 682), late in 1939 over relief funding in that city, the governor managed to avoid major controversy and provided Ohio with six years of conservative but efficient government. Wartime prosperity restored vitality to the state economy, and while Bricker cooperated with the President on defense and war measures, he remained a firm critic of the New Deal. In 1940 he won a second term by defeating Davey by more than 346,000 votes and in 1942 bested John McSweeney by 377,000, making him a presidential hopeful for 1944.

In 1940, when Brother Wendell Willkie had received the GOP nomination, Bricker had initially backed Ohio's conservative Senator Bob Taft. In 1944 Taft opted not to run and threw his backing to Bricker. Because both men represented the conservative-isolationist wing of the party, delegates in the eastern and larger states remained wary of their electability. As my history professor at Ohio University, George Lobdell, phrased it many years ago, "The delegates loved Bricker but married [Thomas] Dewey." The Ohio governor ended up with the vice presidential nomination. In an election in which all major party national candidates were Masons, Roosevelt and Truman defeated Dewey and Bricker by an electoral count of 432 to 99. The 46% of the 1944 vote received by the Republicans, nonetheless, represented the Republicans' best showing against the nearly invincible Roosevelt.

John Bricker finished his governorship in January 1945 and returned to his private law practice but only for slightly more than a year. In 1946 he sought a seat in the United States Senate. Senator Harold Burton had been appointed to the United States Supreme Court by President Truman, and Bricker decided to seek the seat. He won a full six-year term, defeating his Democratic opponent, James Huffman, by 328,000 votes. That fall had been a good one for

Republicans as they took control of both houses of Congress for the first time since the days of Herbert Hoover. Senator Bricker quickly became ranked among the staunchest critics of New Deal-Fair Deal policies. As his biographer, Richard O. Davies, put it, he rapidly found himself "stereotyped as a stalwart leader of the Old Guard."

The new Senator had an especially difficult time reconciling his opposition to communism with his equally strong distaste for foreign aid programs designed to lessen the appeal of this radical ideology. Meanwhile, he found a means through a constitutional amendment that could weaken the role of the executive branch in foreign policy, and it came to be known as the "Bricker Amendment." In 1952 the Buckeye State lawmaker won a second term to the Senate by defeating former Toledo Mayor, Michael DiSalle. Dwight Eisenhower won the Presidency. Bricker had high hopes for his amendment, but while it won majority support in the Senate, it failed to garner a two-thirds majority. Modified by veteran Georgia Senator, Walter George (of Vienna Lodge No. 324), it still came out one vote short, 60-31, of the needed two-thirds. Failure of President Eisenhower to support the Bricker Amendment proved crucial in its defeat. Ironically, during the peak period of opposition to the Viet Nam War, much of the so-called "New Left" nostalgically looked back to the Bricker Amendment as a lost opportunity.

In 1958 John Bricker contemplated retirement but finally chose to seek a third term. Meanwhile, many Ohio business leaders began favoring a "right-to-work amendment." John began pleading with them in private to abandon the idea or at least to postpone it for a year. The veteran lawmaker correctly figured that it would arouse the ire of organized labor to a hitherto unprecedented opposition and quite likely cause the Republican Party to suffer a major defeat. His warnings proved prophetic. Bricker had never been in good standing with the Unions, but the right-to-work issue inflamed A.F.L.-C.I.O. leadership to a fever pitch. Bricker lost the election to the lackluster Democrat, Stephen M. Young, by 155,000 votes. At sixty-five, the "Defender of the Old Guard" had fought his last campaign.

Back in Ohio, the retired politician lived on for another twenty-eight years. He continued to head his prestigious law firm and served another decade on the Ohio State University Board of Trustees. He also remained active on behalf of Ohio Republicans. In both 1962 and 1968, this writer had the privilege of introducing him as main speaker at GOP rallies in his hometown of Albany, Ohio and can testify that the "old guardsman" could still inspire the faithful with the best of them. In Columbus, Bricker attended to the work of his law firm and met with old friends such as real estate tycoon-Pittsburgh Pirate owner, John Galbreath (of University Lodge No. 631) and Ohio State football coach Woody Hayes. He remained active into his mid-eighties. Bricker made his last public appearance with President Reagan on the O.S.U. campus at St. John's Arena in 1984. His wife, Harriet, died on June 1, 1985, and after that John "lost the will to live." On March 22, 1986, a few months before his 93rd birthday, John Bricker died of heart failure.

In death, the *Cincinnati Enquirer* eulogized the former governor and senator accurately and accordingly: "John Bricker had the good fortune to look precisely like what he was—a conservative Midwesterner who believed fervently in the American Dream, because he was one of its beneficiaries." In some respects, Bricker's brand of conservatism had become a bit dated by the time of his political retirement. Perhaps so, but one can hardly say that his reliance on honesty, self help, and individualism were wrong. Like others in American politics, John Bricker made his share of mistakes, but his reputation for honor and integrity has held up well. A Mason for 68 years and a Knight Templar for 52 years, John W. Bricker at his best exemplified the highest characteristics of the order.

**Note**: The best Bricker biography is Richard O. Davies', *Defender of the Old Guard: John W. Bricker and American Politics*, (Columbus: Ohio State University Press, 1993). For his Masonic Record I am indebted to David Dresser, Grand Secretary of the Grand Lodge of Ohio; Earl Gifford, Grand Secretary of the Grand Chapter of Ohio; Richard Palm, Grand Recorder of the Grand Commandery of Ohio; and Richard Frasher, Secretary of the Valley of Columbus, A.A.S.R., N.M.J.

February 2000; slightly revised 2011

**Brother John Elway:**
*Denver Bronco—Hall of Fame Quarterback*

During the first half of the twentieth century, the numbers of Masonry's famous figures from the world of athletics were many and numerous. With the passage of time and membership declines in recent decades, the number has dropped. In the realm of football, such names as Red Grange, Don Hutson, and Glenn "Pop" Warner highlighted Brother Jerry Erikson's list of "Fraternal Footballers." In the immediate past generation, one gridiron name that stands out is Denver Bronco quarterback, Brother John Elway, who earned his way into the National Football League Hall of Fame during a professional career that extended from 1983 through 1998.

John Albert Elway, Jr. was born in Port Angeles, Washington, on June 28, 1960, the son of a football coach. One could almost say that the game was in his blood. A grandfather had once played on a team that had opposed the Carlisle Indians and Jim Thorpe. His father had been a quarterback at Washington State until injuries curtailed his playing career. In addition to the senior Elway known as "Jack," the family included mother Janet and two sisters, Lee Ann who was older and Jana who was John's twin (deceased in 2002). The family lived at various locales in Washington and Montana as Jack Elway's coaching positions changed.

About the time that John entered high school, the father became head coach at Cal State Northridge (later at San Jose State), and the family settled in Granada Hills, California, which had become known for a stellar high school football program. As a quarterback at Granada Hills High, the teenage John compiled a record that included 5,711 yards passing for forty-nine touchdowns. In addition to being academically strong, John excelled in basketball and baseball and was drafted by the Kansas City Royals. Nonetheless he opted for college, choosing Stanford over both Southern California and his father's San

Jose State. Presumably he chose Stanford because of their passing game, and he could also play baseball there.

Leland Stanford, Jr. University was hardly a super team during John Elway's college days, but he nonetheless proved himself to be an outstanding competitor and a great quarterback. He moved into the starting position as a sophomore and showed his mettle by completing 248 passes for 2,884 yards and twenty-seven touchdowns, leading among other things to a Stanford upset over Oklahoma. Coaches of rival teams including those of U.C.L.A. and Southern Cal began comparing him to some of the game's all-time greats. His junior year came as something of a disappointment as the team had a 4-11 record. Still, Elway's individual statistics were such that most players would envy them: 214 completions for a total of 2,674 yards and twenty touchdowns.

John bounced back as a senior with 262 completions for 3,242 yards and twenty-four touchdowns. Stanford only won five games, but their quarterback managed to finish second in balloting for the Heisman Trophy behind Herschel Walker of Georgia. Stanford's mediocre 20-23 during Elway's college career may have kept him from winning the coveted award, but he still entered the NFL draft as a top prospect. As an economics major, he maintained a B average in the classroom and did well enough on the baseball diamond that he signed with the New York Yankee organization, having two good seasons with Oneonta in their minor league system.

Football had been John Elway's best sport and the game that attracted the most attention. The Baltimore Colts chose him as their number one draft choice. However, the Baltimore franchise had no appeal for either John or his advisor father, and he demanded to be traded or else he would simply opt for a baseball career. After a standoff, the Colt's management agreed to trade his contract rights to the Denver Broncos. With all the media attention that accompanied his arrival in Colorado, the press considered his performance less than spectacular. The rookie quarterback spent much of the season as understudy to regular, Steve DeBerg, starting on occasion. Playing roughly half the time, Elway completed 123 passes for 1,663 yards and seven touchdowns and carrying the ball twenty-eight times for 146 yards and a single TD. The next year he got more playing time and improved his record.

The third year with the Broncos, 1985, proved to be the one where the Elway charm came of age. He led the league in attempted and completed passes which gave his team 3,891 yards and twenty-two touchdowns. His rushing totals added 253 more yards. His team led the league in total passing and total offense. It would be the first of seven consecutive seasons in which the Stanford alumnus would pass for more than 3,000 yards and carry the ball for at least 230.

During this remarkable streak, one achievement eluded the star quarterback, and that was leading the Broncos to a victory in the Super Bowl. Three times the Denver team reached the pinnacle only to falter, losing to the New York Giants, the Washington Redskins, and finally the San Francisco 49ers. The latter loss proved especially humiliating as the 49ers rolled over the hapless Broncos by a score of fifty-five to ten. Although John Elway scored the only Denver touchdown, it hardly came as a consolation prize in which to take pride. Many years passed before another opportunity came to the Broncos.

John Elway did have some career downswings. One came in the first part of the 1989 season when he was somewhat off his game. The press launched a series of tasteless attacks, accusing him of being stingy with restaurant tips, and a Denver newspaper complained about the quality of Halloween candy passed out to trick-or-treaters. Later in the season, his records improved, and while his numbers were down somewhat, he still managed to surpass 3,000 yards in passing totals. The ungrateful critics then simply turned their venom on others.

John Elway had one of his best seasons in 1993 with 348 completions, total yards passing of 4,030, and twenty-five touchdowns. A Super Bowl trip eluded his team that year. Former Pittsburgh Steeler quarterback, Terry Bradshaw, charged that John had been excessively coddled, first by his supporting family and second by the Denver organization. Although stung by this criticism, Elway conceded that it would be hard to be rated a truly great quarterback until his team had posted a Super Bowl victory.

By 1997, the Bronco rebuilding program began to show significant results. Their running game led by Terrell Davis began to compete with their always strong passing attack, and the Denver eleven was strong at every position. Finally in Super Bowl XXXII, the time had come. In what was billed as a showdown between the John Elway-led Broncos and the Brett Favre-led Green Bay Packers, Denver finally came home a winner by a 31-24 score. As the bio section on the Elway web site reads, "The dark cloud of doubt that had followed from his first Super Bowl defeat onward evaporated in an unbridled celebration of vindication!" Just to prove that their Super Bowl "jinx" had vanished, the Broncos also took XXXIII in January of 1999 with a 34-19 victory over the Atlanta Falcons. John Elway was named the game's "Most Valuable Player."

A few weeks after that savored victory, John Elway announced his retirement. At thirty-nine he was ready to hang up his shoes. His career totals then included 51,475 yards passing and 300 TD passes in regular season play plus 3,407 yards rushing and thirty-three touchdowns scored. His playoff and Super Bowl statistics added 355 more completions, 4,964 yards, and twenty-seven touchdown passes. He scored six TDs in such competition. His formal retirement announcement came on May 2, 1999.

John Elway may have retired from the gridiron, but he continued in a variety of business endeavors. Some of those have included a couple of restaurants in the Denver area and principal ownership of the Arena League football franchise, the Colorado Crush. At one time he owned five auto dealerships in Colorado, but subsequently sold them while retaining one in Ontario, California. He has also partnered with Bassett Furniture in developing certain products. In 2006 when a Pennsylvania high school student was punished—somewhat foolishly—for wearing a John Elway Denver Bronco football jersey to class by a Steeler fan-teacher, Elway sent the youth a recliner chair (no mention of what he sent the teacher!). As a philanthropist, he started the John Elway Foundation which raises money for two charities that help abused children. Although mentioned as a possible candidate for the United States Senate in 2008, he chose not to run. He did, however, accept a position with the Broncos as Executive Vice President for Football Operations in January of 2011.

John Elway's Masonic membership dates from February 22 and 23, 2002, when he was part of a Grand Lodge of Colorado two-day class. He passed his proficiency on June 28, 2002, and is described as a "perpetual member" of South Denver Lodge No. 93, a status which is usually termed a life member in most grand jurisdictions. He has apparently not joined other Masonic bodies.

In his personal life, John Elway was married to Janet Buchan (who had been a member of the girl's swimming team at Stanford) until they divorced in late 2003. The couple had three daughters: Jessica and Jordan have graduated college while Juliana is still a college student. A son, John Albert Elway, III, completed high school in 2008 and played some college football. Elway married former Oakland Raiders cheerleader Paige Green in September of 2008.

John Elway's attainments on the football field speak for themselves. In 2007, he ranked third among all NFL quarterbacks in passes attempted and completed and fourth in touchdown passes. Elway entered the National Football Hall of Fame in Canton, Ohio in 2004. He is also a successful businessman and philanthropist. Masons should not only be proud of Brother Elway but be honored that he took the time to join our fraternity.

**Note**: Most of the data on Brother Elway comes from his 1990 entry in *Current Biography* and from his web site. His Masonic record came from the staff at the Grand Lodge of Colorado.

October 2007, slightly revised 2011.

## Brother John G. Tower: *The Lone Star Senate Conservative*

In May of 1961, a diminutive political science professor from Wichita Falls, Texas made national headlines when Lone Star State voters chose him to replace Vice President Lyndon Johnson in the United States Senate. The attention John Tower received stemmed from the fact that he was the first Republican elected to a major office in Texas since Brother Edmund J. Davis held the governor's office during Reconstruction.

Believed by some pundits to be little more than an anomaly at the time, Tower went on to serve nearly twenty-four years in the Senate, to become a key figure in the transformation of Texas into a two-party state, and to become a major person in the modern conservative movement. Hawkish on defense, Tower along with fellow Masonic Senators Barry Goldwater, Henry "Scoop" Jackson, John Stennis, and J. Strom Thurmond deserved much of the credit for the rebuilding of the American military establishment in the early 1980s.

John Goodwin Tower was born in Houston, Texas, on September 29, 1925, the son of Reverend Joe and Beryl Goodwin Tower. Both of his grandfathers served as Methodist clergymen as well, and John later served on the board of stewards at the First Methodist Church in Wichita Falls. Unlike his ancestors, however, John apparently had no call to preach. In his autobiography, *Consequences,* Tower recalled that his parents moved around from one east Texas parsonage to another during his childhood.

By the time John was in high school, the Towers supplemented their income by working a largely subsistence farm near Beaumont. When John was a high school junior, he failed geometry, and his father worked him atypically hard on the farm that summer at "chopping cotton." Thereafter, young John Tower devoted more time to his studies, and after graduating from Beaumont High School in 1942, he went on to Southwestern University in Georgetown, Texas for a year. However, by then the nation was deeply involved in World War II, and patriotic feeling in the Lone Star State ran high. Tower had often watched the shiploads of Japan-bound scrap iron departing from the Beaumont docks, and in June 1943, he enlisted as an aviation cadet in the United States Navy. He was not, however, "pilot material" so he spent the remainder of the war on a gunboat in the Pacific.

Back in Texas, Tower returned to Southwestern University, earning a political science degree in 1948. Tower apparently had an academic career in mind and took graduate courses in political science at Southern Methodist University while working as a radio announcer and in insurance. In 1951 he took a teaching position at Midwestern University in Wichita Falls. A year later, Tower took a year's leave to attend the London School of Economics in England, and while there he did research on his thesis, "the Conservative Worker in Britain." Receiving his M.A. in political science from S.M.U. in 1953, Tower continued his career as a professor at Midwestern until his initial Senate campaign.

Like most Texans, John Tower had been reared a Democrat, but he switched to become a Republican in 1948. The Texas GOP was quite small in those days, but it began to enjoy some growth during the Eisenhower era with the help of conservative Democrat Governor Allan Shrivers who crossed party lines to support the popular general in his successful bids for the White House. Tower became an active Republican, but the party's only significant success came with the election of Bruce Alger of Dallas to congress.

In 1960 Texas Republicans nominated Tower to challenge the powerful Senate leader, Lyndon Johnson. Although the little professor had no chance of beating the popular LBJ, he waged a spirited campaign and pulled a surprising 41% of the votes. Since Johnson moved into the vice presidency, Tower, who had earned high name recognition, again ran for the seat in a special election and on May 27, 1961, took it by about 10,000 votes. Tower, as much as anyone, realized that he had become the beneficiary of a feud in which many Texas liberals had either supported him or stayed home to spite the conservative wing of the Democrats and their candidate William Blakely. John Tower, they reasoned, would be an easy mark in 1966 when he ran for the full term. Their analysis proved that they underestimated the professor who went on to win election three more times.

For better or worse, John Tower quickly established himself as one of the Senate's most conservative members. He developed into one of the most popular GOP speakers, being cast in the mold of Arizona's Brother Barry Goldwater, but he enunciated his convictions with more intellectual authority. A strict constructionist on constitutional issues, about the only thing the Senator consistently supported on appropriations tended to be those that would "provide for the common defense." In 1966 Tower defeated Texas Attorney General Waggoner Carr to win a full six-year term.

Shortly after Senator Tower's successful 1966 bid for re-election, he began his Masonic career, receiving all three of his Blue Lodge degrees on October 19, 1967, in Iowa Park Lodge No. 713 in Iowa Park, Texas. Iowa Park is a suburb of Wichita Falls. Less than two years later, he took the Scottish Rite degrees in the Valley of Dallas on July 19, 1969. Some years later, the Scottish Rite recognized his efforts in public life by awarding him the KCCH on October 20, 1975, and the 33° on December 1, 1979. Senator Tower also became a Noble of the Ancient Arabic Order of Nobles of Mystic Shrine.

After Richard Nixon was elected president, Brother Tower became something of a spokesman for White House defense policy, a somewhat thankless task in those days of growing dissatisfaction with the Vietnam conflict. Nonetheless, the Senator had become a major figure on the Washington scene and was recognized in his home state where in his own words he "had finally become the candidate of the Texas political establishment." As such, Tower managed to win another term in 1972 by his largest margin, defeating H. Barefoot Sanders, an LBJ protégé, by some 310,000 votes.

Tower's third term witnessed a number of political and personal problems. On the first front, the Senator had to endure, along with other Republican leaders such as Brothers Barry Goldwater, Hugh Scott, and John Rhodes, the virtual downfall of the Nixon Administration as the traumas of Watergate unfolded. On a personal level, the Senator's longtime marriage—since 1952—to Lou Bullington deteriorated and eventually ended in divorce. This proved a source of discomfort to the couple's three grown daughters: Penelope, Marian, and Jeanne. A second Tower marriage to Lilla Cummings also failed. Ironically, the Senator and his wife eventually became close friends again and shortly before his death, he dedicated his memoirs to her.

In 1978 Tower won his fourth term in the Senate, squeaking out a narrow 12,227 vote victory over Congressman Bob Krueger.

During the early years of the Reagan Administration and the only years that Tower's party was in the majority, the Texan became Chairman of the Senate Armed Services Committee. The Texas Senator, in conjunction with such other pro-defense stalwarts from both sides of the aisle and from several and various positions on the political spectrum, included such Masons as Henry Jackson, John Stennis, and Strom Thurmond along with non–Masons like the current Secretary of Defense William Cohen. They worked together to help restore dignity and pride to the Armed Services. That paved the way for America's prevailing in the "Cold War." One might contend that their far-sighted policies made victory possible without having to fire a shot.

In 1984 John Tower chose not to seek re-election. After 23½ years in the Senate, he retired. When he left that august body on January 3, 1985, he took with him praiseworthy remarks of such colleagues as Brother Sam Nunn (D-Georgia) who said; "all...can attest to his skill, his leadership, and his successes in guiding a strong defense program through Congress." This testimony to Tower's talent would become ironic considering that Nunn later took the lead in opposing Tower's nomination as Secretary of Defense in 1989.

After retirement, John Tower again served his country as chairman of the commission that investigated the Iran-Contra affair. The central questions in this circumstance concerned the role of Col. Oliver North and Admiral John Poindexter in having Israel send arms to Iran and using the money to support the "Contra" rebels in Nicaragua. The participant Americans hoped that the Iranians might pressure those holding American citizens in Lebanon to release them. The Tower Commission concluded that whatever the intentions of the administration, it had the appearance of an arms for hostages deal.

In 1989 the newly-elected President, George H. W. Bush, nominated John Tower to be Secretary of Defense. However, Tower lost his bid for confirmation in a rather unsavory set of hearings that centered on charges that Tower had been something of a hard drinker and Senate playboy in the mid-seventies. Senator Nunn took the lead in opposition, and although Tower drew warm praise for his character from such staunch liberal Senators as Eugene McCarthy and Brother George McGovern along with pro-defense conservatives like John McCain, Tower lost on a close vote. In many respects it came as a sad end to a distinguished career in public service. Ironically, the former Texas senator had been a virtual teetotaler for several years. A few

Democrat solons rose above what had become a partisan battle, among them Brother Lloyd Bentsen, the other Senator from the Lone Star State.

John Tower went back to Texas, ran his consulting firm, and wrote his memoirs. In his early days as a senator, he had explained his philosophy in a volume entitled *A Program for Conservatives* (1962). In *Consequences: A Personal and Political Memoir* (1991), he related an account of his life with special emphasis on the battle concerning the rejection of his nomination to be Secretary of Defense. The memoir also served as Tower's swan song in more ways than one, for he died in a plane crash on April 5, 1991.

The best tribute to John Tower's career in public life, however, had probably been stated nearly thirty years earlier by fellow Senator Brother Barry Goldwater who described him as "a clear minded, articulate, and vigorous apostle of individual liberty and Constitutional government." For better or worse, Brother John Goodwin Tower spent the remainder of his life fulfilling that description.

**Note**: The source of information on Senator John Tower is his autobiography *Consequences* (1991). For his Masonic record, I am indebted to the staff at the Grand Lodge of Texas and to Mrs. Joan Sansbury, Librarian of the Ancient Accepted Scottish Rite, Southern Masonic Jurisdiction. The portrait photograph was obtained through the efforts of former Senator from Ohio, Mike DeWine.

June 2001; slightly revised 2011

## Brother John Llewellyn Lewis: *American Labor Leader*

The annals of American labor have produced a number of charismatic leaders, at least two of which were Masons. Samuel Gompers co-founded and long directed the American Federation of Labor during its early decades. Raised in Dawson Lodge No. 16 in Washington, D.C. on May 9, 1904, Gompers held the fraternity in high esteem. According to biographer Harold Livesay, Gompers died with his hand held in a Masonic grip by James Duncan, head of the Granite Cutters' Union. The other major figure, John L. Lewis, left no known record of his view of Masonry but joined at an earlier age and held membership longer. Lewis is remembered today as a co-founder of the CIO and especially for his forty years as President of the United Mine Workers' of America.

John Llewellyn Lewis was born in the small coal camp of Cleveland, Iowa on February 12, 1880. His parents Tom and Louisa Watkins Lewis had migrated to America only a few years earlier from their homeland in Wales. Like many other Welsh immigrants to America, the Lewis and Watkins clans gravitated toward mining communities, and the south central Iowa coalfields had opened only in 1876. The family lived a typical late 19$^{th}$ century working class existence, moving frequently as Tom Lewis shifted his labors from one mine to another, usually on the edge of poverty. To the degree that young John had a hometown, it would be the somewhat larger county seat town of Lucas. The eldest child in the family, young John had four younger siblings who survived infancy. For a time they lived in Lucas, Iowa, where Lewis got in three and one-half years of high school, an above average education for his day.

About 1897, the Lewis family moved back to Lucas. Young John divided his labors between farm and mine (his occupation is listed as "farm laborer" in the 1900 census) and apparently engaged in amateur theatrics. He also joined Good Shepherd Lodge No. 414, F. & A. M. in Lucas, being raised on September 19, 1902. Afterward, the young adult wandered about in the West for a time, being on the scene of a major mine disaster in 1903 at Hanna, Wyoming. By the end of 1905, Lewis returned to Lucas and went back to work in the mines.

John Lewis was an active member of Good Shepherd Lodge in this period and rose to the office of Junior Warden in 1907. On June 5th of that year, he married Myrta Bell, the daughter of a local physician and Worshipful Master of the aforementioned lodge. Prior to her marriage, Myrta had taught school and attended Drake University. Otherwise, 1907 was not a good year for Lewis as he ran for mayor of Lucas and lost. He also entered into a feed and grain business with a partner named Brown that failed. In the spring of 1908, John L. and Myrta Lewis left Iowa for Panama, Illinois, a new coal camp. A few weeks later, other family members also moved to the Illinois town.

In Panama, Union Local 1475 soon proved to be a vehicle for Lewis' advancement in the labor movement. Within a year of his moving to Illinois, he had become president of the local. In 1911, he accepted a position as an organizer for the A.F. of L. based in Santa Fe, New Mexico. Somewhat later, he was appointed statistician for the U.M.W. of A. and in July 1917 vice president of the union, enjoying the friendship of President John White. When White became a member and administrator of the Federal Fuel Board in October of 1917, the popular but ineffectual Frank Hayes became president and Lewis first vice president. As Hayes' health and drinking problems increased, Lewis took leadership responsibility from March of 1919 and became active president on January 1, 1920. Elected to the position later that year, John L. Lewis led the United Mine Workers until his retirement in mid-January 1960.

The U.M.W. union that John L. Lewis had inherited enjoyed unprecedented prosperity during World War I. As a result, union membership, normally about 200,000 to 250,000, soared to just over a half-million. The aftermath, however, led to declining demand for coal and a shrinking market. Union leaders struggled to maintain their wartime gains in a much weaker position. In addition, Lewis had to contend with numerous critics within his union's ranks and in the labor movement as a whole. Overall, one can conclude that John L. had more success at dealing with his rivals than in his efforts to stabilize market demands and the wage and price structure in the troubled coal industry.

The Lewis effort to maintain the position of miners was embodied in the February 1924 "Jacksonville Agreement" that called for retaining a $7.50 daily wage to union miners for the next three years. At the time, the bargain was hailed as a great advancement in the course of industrial democracy. Knowing it would be difficult for all mine operators to comply with this contract, Lewis apparently hoped that it would force marginal mines to close and their work force to seek employment elsewhere while the stronger players would continue to honor the agreement.

What happened, however, was an increasing shift of the coal business to non-union mines in the South. In addition, some Northern operators violated their contracts. By 1927, the U.M.W. was in serious trouble, and with the onset of the Great Depression conditions worsened. Union membership sank to a twentieth century low of 85,000 with 53,000 of those being in Illinois.

With the near collapse of the United Mine Workers, others attempted to fill the gap but with relatively little success. A Communist group, the National Miners' Union, attempted to organize workers and lead a strike, but in the long run about their only legacy came in the form of several noted protest songs. In Illinois, the Reorganized United Workers Union led by John Walker, Adolph Germer, and Frank Farrington flourished for a time. In the embattled Mountain State, Frank Keeney led the West Virginia Miner's Union, and in 1932, another Illinois group led the Progressive Miners' Union. However, none could create work where none existed and eventually the United Mine Workers and John L. Lewis outlasted them all.

The recovery of the U.M.W. tended to be closely linked to Franklin D. Roosevelt's New Deal and the National Industrial Recovery Act. Although Brother Lewis had given his political endorsements to Republican nominees through the twenties and to Herbert Hoover's failed reelection bid in 1932, he also generally welcomed New Deal initiatives in labor policy. The N. R. A. and the later Wagner Act gave a degree of shelter to the United Mine Workers that had not existed earlier. As a result, their membership climbed again in the middle and later thirties. In fact, Lewis was so elated with New Deal labor policies that he endorsed FDR for a second term in 1936, the only time he ever endorsed a Democratic presidential nominee.

During his years of service to the U.M.W., Lewis shifted his residence and his Masonic membership. In the period when the union headquarters was located in Indianapolis, John L. affiliated in 1919 with Ancient Landmarks Lodge No. 319. Ironically, the mine leader made his residence in Springfield, Illinois where he lived in a large brick home. In 1934, his union moved its headquarters to Washington, D.C., and Brother Lewis bought a home in suburban Alexandria, Virginia. By that time, the family included a daughter, Kathryn, born in 1911 and a son John, Jr. born in 1918. An older daughter, Mary Margaret, had died at the age of seven in 1917. In 1946, Lewis moved his lodge membership back to Lucas, Iowa. Good Shepherd Lodge no longer existed, so he affiliated with Paul Revere Lodge No. 638, retaining membership there until he died. Apparently, during his later years he also held a plural membership in a Virginia lodge.

Beginning in 1935, the charismatic leader led in the formation of the Committee for Industrial Organization (CIO) within the American Federation of Labor. This action sparked confrontation within the labor movement that included Lewis having an exchange of fisticuffs with William Hutcheson of the Carpenters' Union. Favoring the concept of industrial unionism over craft unionism, the CIO enjoyed success in organizing auto, rubber, and steel workers. In 1938, he led the CIO unions out of the A.F. of L., changing their name to the Congress of Industrial Organizations and also served as their president.

In 1940, John L. Lewis returned to the GOP fold, breaking with FDR over the third term issue and endorsing Republican Wendell Willkie. He experienced less success in getting rank and file union members to follow his lead. After Willkie's loss, Lewis resigned as president of the CIO while retaining mine union leadership for nearly twenty more years.

Lewis showed himself to be something of an isolationist in the immediate pre-World War II period. During the war, he led his union out on strike more than once and often displayed a strong degree of independence during the war and into the post-war years as well. In 1946, he clashed with the Truman Administration on several occasions, prompting the president to make his famous remark that "I wouldn't appoint John L. Lewis dog catcher." Lewis' equally famous reply (too long to be quoted here) suggests that Lewis was extremely wary of the growth of the federal bureaucracy.

By the fifties, Lewis was not only increasingly showing his age, but also he was leading a union that again faced a declining membership. Americans turned to natural gas and other sources of fuel, and many mines closed, never to reopen. As in the twenties, the

UMW experienced serious problems. Once flourishing coal camps that dotted the hillsides and valleys in West Virginia and other Appalachian states became centers of chronic poverty and unemployment. Nearly eighty, the old war horse of the American labor movement retired in January of 1960 from an organization he had led through good times and bad for some forty years. He continued, however, to oversee the union's retirement and welfare fund. Several weeks after his eighty-ninth birthday, Lewis died on June 11, 1969.

The Lewis legacy proved to be a mixed one. He had, of course, achieved a great deal for rank and file miners and provided able leadership of the early CIO, but also he had some failures and some victories such as the Jacksonville Agreement that in practice had more often than not proved hollow. Some of his efforts such as the 1942 plan to unionize the nation's three million dairy farmers got nowhere. Perhaps his greatest shortcoming was in not training an adequate future leadership in the UMW. His immediate successor, the aging Thomas Kennedy, soon died and the once proud union fell into the hands of the corrupt and incompetent W. A. "Tony" Boyle.

Still, at his death, few would have disagreed with the comment of steel workers' leader, David McDonald, "In the field of labor, he was the greatest Roman of them all." Since 1969, his image may be a bit more tarnished, but the sixty-seven year Mason with the big bushy eyebrows typified the labor movement in his era as did no other man.

**Note**: Two significant biographies on Lewis are by Melvyn Dubofsky and Warren Van Tine, *John L. Lewis: A Biography* (1977) and Robert H. Zieger's *John L. Lewis: Labor Leader* (1988). See also "Recent Death of John L. Lewis Recalls Exchange with Truman" by Jerry Marsengell in *The Royal Arch Mason,* IX: 11, Fall 1969, pp. 329-330. Thanks to Sir Knight Glenn McKee and the United Mine Workers of America for supplying the photographs. Much appreciation also goes to student aid Abby Goodnite Ehman for preparation of the original manuscript.

June 1998; slightly revised 2011

## Sir Knight John Wayne: *Hollywood's Symbol of Americanism*

Among twentieth century Americans, John Wayne ranks high on the list for name recognition. Through the nearly four decades that Wayne characterizations graced film screens, the man became a virtual symbol of the American spirit. Heroism, rugged individualism, intestinal fortitude, and unapologetic patriotism typified the persona that John Wayne portrayed on celluloid. In real life, of course, he was sometimes more and sometimes less than the image that Hollywood created for him. Although his Masonic membership stretched over only the last nine years of his life, he may well be the fraternity's best-known member other than presidents, kings, and prime ministers.

Like many motion picture stars, John Wayne was born with a much more ordinary-sounding name. Marion Robert Morrison entered life in Winterset, Iowa, on May 26, 1907, the son of Clyde and Mary Brown Morrison. The elder Morrison worked as a pharmacist but encountered financial difficulties. In 1911, his Rexall Drug Store in Earlham, Iowa went under, forcing the Morrisons into bankruptcy. Clyde Morrison also began to experience health problems. In 1914, the family moved to California, settling first near Lancaster and then permanently in the growing city of Glendale. By this time, another boy, Robert born in December of 1912, completed the Morrison family circle.

In Glendale, young Marion Morrison lived his adolescent years. He absorbed patriotic American values he would embrace throughout life in the Boy Scouts, YMCA, and Order of DeMolay. A strong student academically, he did even better in football where he distinguished himself as a left guard. He also acquired the nickname of Duke which he carried throughout life. Graduating from Glendale High School second in his class, the future movie star won a football scholarship to the University of Southern California.

At Southern Cal, Morrison joined the men of Sigma Chi, held a part-time job waiting on tables, and got in sufficient football playing time to earn a letter. The next year, however, he injured his shoulder which effectively ended his athletic career. Dropping out of school at the end of his sophomore year and having met people connected with the film industry, young Marion began to pick up work in the movie studios. He played a few bit parts, doubled, and worked as an extra. Marion also made friends with John Ford who was already on his way to becoming a legendary director. The latter hired Duke to be an assistant property man at $35.00 per week. Between 1927 and 1929, Morrison learned a great deal about the making of films. By 1930, he had been given his stage name of John Wayne and landed a choice part in a new major sound picture, *The Big Trail.*

*The Big Trail* had been intended by Fox Studio and director Raul Walsh as a monumental epic of the Westward Movement supplemented by Wayne's search for his father's killer. The film has some good moments, especially the outdoor scenery and action, and Wayne handled his role well for a newcomer. However, the stilted dialogue made *The Big Trail* a big 125-minute flop. For the next several years, John Wayne found himself relegated mostly to starring roles in low-budget westerns.

During these years, many of the characteristics associated with the later John Wayne persona began to appear. Much of his walk and talk, it was said, he learned from Brother and Sir Knight Yakima Canutt, a one-time champion rodeo cowboy who had starred in a few silent films but by the thirties usually played villainous roles while specializing in stunt work. Meanwhile, Wayne starred in numerous westerns with such forgettable titles as *The Trail Beyond, The Lawless Frontier, Riders of Destiny,* and *The Man From Utah.*

George (Gabby) Hayes often had supporting roles in these films. In one feature, *Born to the West,* Duke shared top billing with another cowboy star, Johnny Mack Brown (also reputed to be a Mason), and Marsha Hunt who subsequently became a major film actress in the forties. Occasionally he appeared in lesser roles in non-westerns such as *College Coach* and *Central Airport.*

In 1938, Herbert Yates of Republic Pictures contracted John Wayne to appear in the *Three Mesquiteers* Series replacing Robert Livingston in the role of Stoney Brooke. Other co-stars in the series included Ray "Crash" Corrigan and comic sidekick/ventriloquist Max Terhune. The Duke considered the series a bit too juvenile for his tastes despite its popularity and longed for the day when he could advance to major roles in big budget films. Fortunately, that time was not long in coming.

John Ford in 1939 cast John Wayne as the Ringo Kid in *Stagecoach*, the film that finally elevated him to the ranks of major stardom. His performance in the screen version of the Ernest Haycox short story, *The Stage to Lordsburg*, took him out of low budget pictures and made him the central figure in what most critics deem the most significant western ever made. It was filmed in Monument Valley on the Arizona-Utah border, and this locale subsequently reappeared in several later Wayne pictures. He followed up this performance with significant roles in other sagas such as *The Dark Command, Allegheny Uprising*, and the movie version of Harold Bell Wright's famous novel, *The Shepherd of the Hills.*

Although John Wayne continued to appear in westerns such as *The Spoilers* and *In Old California* and other adventure films like *Reap the Wild Wind*, the coming of World War II added another legendary persona to the Wayne image, that of the rugged heroic man in uniform, beginning with *Fighting Tigers* in 1942 and continuing with *Fighting Seabees, Back to Bataan, They Were Expendabl*e, and *Sands of Iwo Jima.* During later wars the Duke continued to make military films, many of them designed to lift morale and showcase patriotism including *Operation Pacific, Flying Leathernecks, Jet Pilot*, and finally in 1968, one of the few pro-Viet Nam War films, *The Green Berets.* Somewhat ironically, while Wayne became the ultimate war hero on the movie screen, he himself as the father of four children, was not conscripted during the war. He could have enlisted, but did not, choosing instead to maintain the morale on the home front with his masculine image.

The later forties saw John Wayne emerge as the ultimate star of big budget westerns just as Roy Rogers and Gene Autry dominated the singing cowboy "oaters." The John Ford-directed trilogy— *Fort Apache, She Wore a Yellow Ribbon* and *Rio Grande* —together with *Red River* set the image. Two other films, *Angel and the Badman* and *Three Godfathers*, ranked close behind. *Dakota* and *The Fighting Kentuckian* added little to the Duke's luster, being vehicles that Republic studio head Herbert Yates placed Wayne in to boost the career of his protégé and romantic interest Vera Ralston, but they did little harm to Wayne's career. He did much better in a pair of high adventure films, *Tycoon* and *Wake of the Red Witch* along with the comedy, *Without Reservations.*

The decade of the fifties saw the Duke continue to star in high profile pictures. Quality westerns included *Hondo, Rio Bravo* and *The Searchers*, the latter of which again reunited him with director John Ford. His other films from that period included the classic airplane drama, *The High and the Mighty, Blood Alley* with Lauren Bacall, and another John Ford vehicle, *The Quiet Man* which some critics rated among his best performances outside of his western roles.

For better or worse, during the Cold War John Wayne became almost as well known for his outspoken opposition to Communism as for his motion picture stardom. He eventually took a key role in the Motion Picture Alliance for the Preservation of American Ideals, serving as its president from March 1949 until June 1953. Some of his pictures in this period are staunchly anti-Communist such as *Big Jim McLain* and *Blood Alley*. Along the way he antagonized some Hollywood people on the liberal-left and paid something of a price for it. Some friends believed that he failed to garner an Oscar nomination for *The Quiet Man* because of his outspoken criticism of Communists.

The Duke also engaged in production and direction of films although with mixed success. His first production company, Wayne-Fellows, did well but dissolved when his partner Bob Fellows encountered domestic problems and Wayne bought him out, changing the firm's name to Batjac. The 1960 epic film *The Alamo* saw Wayne as star, producer, and director. He played the part of Davy Crockett. While the picture grossed a great deal of money, its costs were so huge that the film was judged a financial failure.

The fiscal problems of *The Alamo* to the contrary notwithstanding, John Wayne went on to make several quality westerns in the sixties. These included *The Man Who Shot Liberty Valance, The Sons of Katie Elder, The War Wagon* and at the decade's close, *True Grit*. This latter film finally won him his long overdue Academy Award. In the film, Wayne created another of his memorable characters—the hard-nosed, grizzled, one-eyed old lawman, Rooster Cogburn. Accepting the coveted Oscar on April 7, 1970, the Duke gave a brief and honorable acceptance speech.

With another major western *Chisum* completed and scheduled for release, John Wayne flew off to Tucson, Arizona, to make another film, *Rio Lobo*, at the Old Tucson movie set. During this stay in southern Arizona, Wayne, at the age of sixty-three, took the steps that would make him a Mason. Petitioning Marion McDaniel Lodge No. 56 in Tucson under the name the world knew him by, Marion Morrison received his Entered Apprentice degree on June 9, 1970; passed as a Fellowcraft on the following day; and was raised a Master Mason on July 11, 1970. Later that fall, he took the Scottish Rite degrees in the Valley of Pasadena, California, on November 21, 1970. Sir Knight Wayne completed his York Rite work that same fall in the appropriately named (for him) Golden West Commandery No. 43 in Los Angeles. On December 5, 1970, he became a Noble of Al Maliakah Shrine Temple. Rex Allen, another noted film cowboy, took the Scottish Rite and Shrine work at the same time with Allen becoming a Noble of Sabbar Temple in Tucson. For the next six years, the Duke served as an "ambassador-at-large" for Al Malaikah Temple.

Although age and declining health had begun to take their toll on John Wayne in the seventies, he continued to turn in some quality screen performances. These included *Big Jake, The Cowboys, Cahill, U.S. Marshal* and *The Train Robbers*. In a memorable line in the latter film, he tells a young Ann-Margret, "I've got a saddle older than you." But perhaps his best role in the later years came in *Rooster Cogburn,* a sequel to *True Grit* that co-starred Katherine Hepburn, another venerable Hollywood legend. Maybe in reaction to turning down the role made famous by Clint Eastwood in *Dirty Harry,* he did a pair of tough-cop pictures, *McQ* and *Brannigan,* the latter filmed largely in London.

The Duke made his last movie in 1976. Titled *The Shootist,* it tells of an aging and out-of-place gunfighter's last days and is one of the few pictures in which Wayne dies in the end. As such, it seemed a fitting end of a career that dated back to 1928 when young Marion Morrison made his first screen appearance as an uncredited extra in *Hangman's House.* Wayne had had an earlier battle with cancer in 1964 and had licked it, making his bout with the dread disease public in such a manner as to give hope to others. One critic argued that this action had been one of the most heroic things that he ever did in his private life.

Age and ill health were obviously slowing the aging legend down somewhat, but it came as something of a surprise on January 13, 1979, when what had been considered a relatively simple gall bladder surgery stretched into a nine-hour ordeal. The diagnosis of stomach cancer was bad enough, but further word came on the 17$^{th}$ that it had continued to spread. His last months were unpleasant as his condition declined rapidly. On May 21, his one-time leading lady, Maureen O'Hara, appeared before Congress urging passage of a bill to have a special medal titled "John Wayne, American" struck on his behalf. Brother and Senator Barry Goldwater (R-Arizona) introduced the bill. It passed and President Carter signed in time for the Duke to be notified on his birthday. Just a little over two weeks later, he died after receiving the last rites of the Roman Catholic Church. He had described himself in later years as a "'cardiac' Catholic." As his most adept biographers Randy Roberts, and James Olson state, "nothing better illustrates John Wayne's ecumenical personality better than the fact that he was simultaneously a loyal Mason and a "'cardiac' Catholic."

In some ways it seems ironic that John Wayne has come to symbolize America. While deeply patriotic, it has been pointed out that nearly all of his heroics were performed on the silver screen and not in real life. For all the military bravery the public saw him perform in pictures, he did not serve in World War II. Much of his private life could hardly be deemed that of the ideal role model. For much of his adult life, he drank heavily. His treatment of women, particularly his first wife, could hardly be described as anything but less than honorable. Although still married to his third wife at the time of his death, they had been separated for several years. Yet in the final analysis, his screen persona is not a false one. In many respects, that image of the rugged individual, warts and all, taking his stand for truth and justice represent what Sir Knight John Wayne was all about. In that sense, he exemplified many of the ideals of Christian Knighthood.

**Note**: There is an abundance of biographical data on John Wayne, but the source with the most depth is Randy Roberts and James S. Olson, *John Wayne, American* (New York: The Free Press, 1995) which puts his Masonic activity in proper context although some dates are inaccurate. For his Masonic record I am indebted to Robert Henderson, P.G.M. and Grand Secretary of the Grand Lodge of Arizona and the staff at Al Malaikah Shrine Temple in Los Angeles. Thanks also to student assistant Abby Goodnite Ehman for technical aid.

February 1998; slightly revised 2011

Larry Householder,
Speaker of the House of Representatives

**Sir Knight Larry Householder:**
*Former Buckeye State Speaker of the House*

In the American system of government, the position of Speaker of the House has traditionally been one of considerable power and prestige. This concept has held true at both the state and national levels. It should come as no surprise that numerous Masons have occupied the Speaker's Chair in both Washington D.C., and in many state capitals. In the nation's capital, Masonic Speakers of the House have included the first person to hold that title, Frederick A. C. Muhlenberg, as well as such luminaries as Henry Clay, Joseph Cannon, and Carl Albert.

Within the state of Ohio, these individuals have ranged from early occupants of the Chair typified by Elias Langham, Philemon Beecher, and Duncan McArthur to more recent figures such as C. William O'Neil, William Saxbe, and Roger Cloud. The late Vernal G. Riffe, Democrat of Scioto County (a member of Western Sun Lodge No. 91 and 33° Mason, Valley of Cincinnati), held the post for some twenty years (1975-1995). A more recent Masonic leader in the General Assembly, Sir Knight Larry Lee Householder of Perry County, held the post for three years in the early part of the new century.

Larry Lee Householder was born in Zanesville, Ohio on June 6, 1959, the son of Enos E. (Bud) and Barbara Haas Householder. He came from a Masonic family as his father had been a member of New Lexington Lodge No. 250 for more than forty years before his death in 1989. On the maternal side, both his grandfather and an uncle were lodge members. Some of Larry's ancestors had been in Perry County for six generations.

Householder grew up in northern Perry County and after completing high school, attended Ohio University in Athens. He majored in Political Science and completed an A.B. degree in 1982.

While in college, Larry served for a time on the student senate and held membership in Phi Delta Theta fraternity. Sir Knight Israel Foster, a three-term Congressman from Athens (1919-1925) is also remembered as a zealous Phi Delt.

It was during the summer prior to entering his senior year in college that Householder told his father that he was interested in becoming a Mason. He later told the editor of the *Beacon,* that "His face lit up. He was thrilled." Accordingly, Larry received his Entered Apprentice degree in New Lexington Lodge on August 20, 1981, and was passed to the degree of Fellowcraft on September 10. The fall quarter at Ohio University then intervened, and the youth was not raised a Master Mason until December 15, 1981. Nearly twenty years later, he was quoted in the *Beacon* thusly, "Freemasonry is an organization of great integrity, composed of very honorable people."

Brother Householder continued his search for further light in both the York and Scottish Rites. He took the former in New Lexington Chapter No. 149, R.A.M.; New Lexington Council No. 75, R.&S.M.; and New Lexington Commandery No. 57, receiving the Order of Red Cross and Order of Malta on April 30, 1982, and being Knighted on May 8, 1982. His father, Enos Householder, also took the York Rite work that spring. Larry completed the Scottish Rite at the Valley of Columbus on November 13, 1982, and become a Noble of Aladdin Shrine Temple on December 4, 1982. According to Companion Wilbur Barnes, Householder once took the part of Nebuzaradan in the Super Excellent Master degree. After he became Speaker of the House, he received the 33° on September 23, 2002.

After college, Larry Householder went into the insurance business as a State Farm agent and like many southeast Ohioans, also farmed on a part-time basis. From his high school days, he was active in the Future Farmers of America, and he holds a lifetime alumni status in that organization. It has been said in his part of the state that one needs a regular job in order to support his farming habit. Active in the Republican Party, he was elected a precinct committeeman in 1988 and also served on local boards and commissions.

In 1994, Householder made his first run for public office—a success when he won a race for Perry County Commissioner. This prompted him to challenge incumbent legislator Mary Abel for the legislature. Abel had survived largely on the basis of strength in her own heavily Democratic Athens County, the home of Ohio University with its large student votes. Republicans had long believed that a strong opponent who could unite the other counties in the district could win the seat. Householder proved to be that person.

The passage of a term limit amendment created a situation in which younger legislators could advance more rapidly in terms of gaining seniority than before. As a result, Sir Knight Householder rose more quickly through the ranks than would have been possible earlier. He also won second, third, and fourth terms without a great deal of difficulty and learned quickly how to exercise strong leadership. Early in his service, Larry set his sights on the Speaker's Chair.

In 2000, Ohio House Republicans had agreed to alternate the Speaker's position with Householder and William Harris of Ashland, each serving for a year. However, when Harris moved into the State Senate following a vacancy in the upper house, Householder moved into the Speaker's Chair serving more than three years until term limits ended his own tenure at the end of 2004.

Although he never held the Speaker's position as long as the two-decade tenure of Brother Vernal Riffe, he apparently studied the long-time lawmaker's tactics and learned a great deal from them. He was voted the most effective member of the Legislature in 2003. According to *Columbus Dispatch* reporter Joe Hallett, "A coup d'etat against Householder is unimaginable . . . loyalty [to him] will likely be strengthened because of Householder's strong first year leadership." Still attached to farming on a part-time basis, Hallett reported that Sir Knight Larry arose at 4:30 AM most mornings to feed the 25 sheep and 15 llamas on his Perry County farm before he helped wife, Taundra, get their five sons ready for school."

Term limited as his fourth term came to an end in 2004; an unexpected opportunity came up back in Perry County as the incumbent Democratic County Auditor died. Householder decided to run for the unexpired term. It seemed, in retrospect, to have been a politically unwise decision. Meanwhile, reckless charges against two of his close aides (while as Speaker) aroused controversy. While Householder won the election for county auditor for the remaining two years by a mere 270 votes, he spent a great deal of money in a narrow victory and chose not to seek a full term in 2006. He was eventually exonerated of any wrongdoing in his position as Speaker.

Larry Householder retired from politics after his term as auditor expired. He remains at his farm near Glenford, Ohio. As of 2011, he has kept a low profile, but his record as a strong Speaker of the Ohio General Assembly remains an honorable one.

**Note:** Basic data on Sir Knight Householder comes largely from the Ohio Masonic publication, *Beacon*, spring 2001 and a lengthy article in the *Columbus Dispatch*, December 23, 2001. The staffs at the Grand Lodge and Grand Commandery of Ohio supplied his Masonic Records along with the Valley of Columbus AASR and Aladdin Shrine.

June 2002; revised 2011

## Brother "Little" Jimmy Dickens:
*Music City Legend*

One of the truly legendary figures in country music is a four-foot eleven-inch vocalist from the mountains of southern West Virginia known as Little Jimmy Dickens. Known for his humorous novelty songs such as "Take an Old Cold Tater and Wait" and "May the Bird of Paradise Fly up Your Nose," Dickens first joined the *Grand Ole Opry* more than sixty years ago with the help and encouragement of Brother Roy Acuff. In 1983 Little Jimmy was inducted into the Country Music Hall of Fame. Some fifteen years later, on January 31, 1998, at the age of seventy-seven, this remarkable man was raised to the sublime degree of Master Mason.

James Cecil Dickens was born in Raleigh County, West Virginia, on December 19, 1920. Jim ranked as the oldest child in a rather large family, and his grandparents, Lewis and Edna Dickens, reared the boy. Music filled an important social role on both sides of Jim's family and in the community as well. The youth grew up hearing traditional ballads such as "John Henry," "Jesse James," "Barbara Allen," and "John Hardy." Dickens, too, began to sing and while in his early teens learned to play chords on his uncle's guitar.

Little Jim made his first public appearance at a talent contest in Pineville, West Virginia at age fifteen. He sang "Silver Haired Daddy of Mine," a number associated with Brother Gene Autry. To his surprise, Dickens won and subsequently entered other contests. When radio station WJLS Beckley went on the air in March 1939, Jim soon became a more or less regular performer. Surprisingly, several of the musicians at this small station enjoyed notable careers including Molly O'Day, the Lilly Brothers, Speedy Krise, and the Bailes Brothers (like Jimmy, two of this foursome, Homer and Kyle, later became Masons). Another brother, Walter Bailes, gave Dickens his initial nickname "Jimmy the Kid." He also worked with another musician, Mel Steele, and even quit school for a time and journeyed to WMMN Fairmont working for Steele. Later Jim came back home and resumed his education graduating from Trap Hill High School in Surveyor, West Virginia, in 1940. Although then only four feet, six inches in height and tipping the scales at eighty-five pounds, he still managed to play on the basketball team earning a letter.

Dickens entered West Virginia University at Morgantown and again played on WMMN radio in nearby Fairmont. In 1941, entertainment won out over academics and the pint-sized picker went into radio full time. He then teamed up with T. Texas Tyler at WIBC Indianapolis. Tyler dubbed his partner the "World's Smallest Cowboy Entertainer." Dickens remained in Indiana from 1941 until 1945. After Tyler entered military service in 1943, Jimmy performed solo. While there he grew five additional inches after turning twenty-one.

Beginning in 1945, Dickens spent roughly a year at each of three different stations. The first at WLW Cincinnati provided the singer with experience at the nation's most prestigious radio outlet. The second at WIBW Topeka took him to the Kansas plains. The third at WKNX Saginaw, Michigan, saw him at a daytime station in a northern locale. On October 21, 1947, Roy Acuff played a concert in the City Auditorium and renewed his acquaintance with Jim—the two had shared the stage at a concert in Cincinnati a couple of years earlier. The veteran *Grand Ole Opry* star promised to help Little Jimmy get a guest spot on the venerable show at WSM. His initial appearance on this famous show came on February 21, 1948. Returning to his regular program in Michigan, Dickens received another call to come to Nashville. In August 1948, he became a *Grand Ole Opry* regular. On September 16, he signed a contract with Columbia Records, but because the Petrillo ban was in effect at the time, did not have his initial recording session until January 16, 1949.

That first visit to the studio yielded what became the Dickens trademark song, "Take an Old Cold Tater and Wait." This number originally dated from 1921 and was composed by E. M. Bartlett, a hymn writer best known for "Victory in Jesus." Little Jimmy had learned it during his days in Indianapolis. It helped create an image of a little fellow who was something of a loser in the game of life. Later Dickens' songs reinforced this image: "Sleepin' at the Foot of the Bed," "(Plain Old) Country Boy," "I'm Little but I'm Loud," "Cold Feet," and "Out Behind the Barn." Ironically, he could also do more serious material with equal effectiveness such as the love ballad, "My Heart's Bouquet" and the tear-jerker, "Pennies for Papa," but the comic, novelty numbers generally became the big hits.

The early fifties were good ones for Little Jimmy Dickens, and he gained a reputation as one of America's most popular country singers. Fans listened to him zealously on the *Opry* and turned out to see him on road shows where he worked heavily in this period. In 1957 he left the *Opry* and WSM, touring nationwide for a year with the highly successful Philip Morris Caravan. Thereafter, Jim simply worked personal appearances on the strength of the reputation he had built up over the years. He continued to record for Columbia but had no hits from 1955 through late 1962.

In November 1962, a heart song titled "The Violet and a Rose" put Dickens back in the *Billboard* top ten. The following year he had a modest hit with "Another Bridge to Burn." In the mid-sixties Jim scored his biggest success with a new novelty song, "May the Bird of Paradise Fly up Your Nose," which not only topped the country charts but reached number fifteen in the pop listings. The little guy again reached major celebrity status, and through the rest of the decade, his songs appeared on the charts. In 1967, he switched from Columbia and signed with Decca for whom he did three albums and had three minor hits, the last of which, a heart-rending recitation titled "Raggedy Ann," became the number that he thereafter used to close his show.

In the early seventies, Little Jimmy signed with United Artists Records and had a couple of modest hits in "Everyday Family Man" and "Try It, You'll Like It." At various times he also recorded for Gusto and some smaller firms. In 1975, Dickens returned to the *Opry* with another assist from Roy Acuff and has been a regular there since that time. He also continued his touring schedule, although he relaxed it somewhat from the mid-nineties. Increasingly, he has made numerous on-stage quips about his own lack of height and in recent years about aging as he has joined the ranks of senior citizens.

By the 1980s, Dickens' stature as a pivotal figure in the industry began to grow. In 1982 when the Country Music Association chose Marty Robbins for the year's Hall of Fame inductee, Robbins lamented that older pioneers such as Little Jimmy Dickens had not yet been included. Marty's tragic death two months later made his acceptance speech a virtual campaign nomination oration for Dickens. Accordingly, in October 1983, Jimmy Dickens entered the Country Music

Hall of Fame. The man sometimes known to the world as "Ma Dickens' little tater eatin' boy" had reached the pinnacle of his profession.

Entry into his hallowed circle did not change Little Jimmy. Off stage he continued to be the same humble, polite person he had always been. He waxed a new album, and some of his recordings with a boogie and rockabilly flavor were reissued in Europe. Columbia released a new album containing some of his best-known hits in their *Columbia Historic Edition Series.* The German Company, Bear Family, released two boxed sets containing his entire Columbia output on compact disc.

After his first eleven-year marriage ended in divorce, Jim married Ernestine Jones, and the couple adopted a daughter, Pamela Jean. Ernestine died in a tragic car accident on January 1, 1968. On December 24, 1971, Dickens married a tall blonde named Mona Evans, and they made their home in the Nashville suburb of Brentwood.

Jimmy had long desired to become a Mason and petitioned Hiram Lodge No. 7 in Franklin, Tennessee. He received his Entered Apprentice degree on August 5, 1997, and was passed to the degree of Fellowcraft on December 2, 1997. In a special meeting on January 31, 1998, held in the auditorium of the Grand Lodge of Tennessee, a few blocks from the old Ryman Auditorium where he had debuted on the *Opry* nearly a half-century before, James Cecil Dickens was raised to the sublime degree of Master Mason. A crowd of some 1,400 Masons from six states witnessed the event. Sir Knight Jim Custer of Lookout Commandery No. 14 and Limestone Lodge No. 176 reported that Brother Dickens listened attentively to the degree work. Brother Custer also reported that the new Mason intended to seek "further light" in Masonry and apparently did so as the Order of the Purple Cross was bestowed on him a few years later. One cannot help but think that this honor may have resulted more from his celebrity status than from long years of toiling "in the quarries," so to speak.

Brother Dickens has continued to appear on the *Grand Ole Opry* as his health permits, still making quips about being mistaken for being "Mighty Mouse in his pajamas." With advancing age, he has been in and out of the hospital numerous times in the past decade, but as of late 2011 he was still taking his bows before the audience, a legendary figure in "Music City, USA."

**Note**: The principal biographical material on Jimmy Dickens comes from my prior article in the *JEMF Quarterly* (1984) and the booklets in the Bear Family boxed sets written by *Grand Ole Opry* announcer Eddie Stubbs. Sir

Knight Jim Custer provided his observation at the time of Dickens' raising. The late Brother Charlie Louvin of Phoenix Lodge No. 131 and Brother Joe Edwards of John B. Garrett Lodge No. 711 added perspectives, and the staff at the Grand Lodge of Tennessee provided degree dates. Student aid Abby Goodnite Ehman typed the original article.

April 1999; slightly revised 2011

## Charlie and Ira Louvin:
*Masonic Country Harmony Duet*

During the later 1930s and afterwards, harmony duets often featuring two brothers emerged as a major force in country music. Among the more creative of these early duets were the Delmore Brothers from Alabama, the Monroe Brothers of Kentucky, the Callahan Brothers from North Carolina, and the Blue Sky Boys (Bill and Earl Bolick) also from North Carolina. The popularity of these teams waned somewhat in the forties but new teams still gained renown. For instance, the four Bailes Brothers—Kyle, Johnnie, Walter, and Homer—came from West Virginia and often performed with two of them as a duet (two of the Bailes Brothers, Kyle and Homer, subsequently became Masons with Homer being quite active in the York Rite bodies in Louisiana). The ultimate of these duets, the Louvin Brothers, arrived somewhat later on the scene, and to date are the only ones other than the Delmores and one Monroe (Bill) to be enshrined in the Country Music Hall of Fame, being inducted in 2002.

The original surname of the Louvin Brothers had been Loudermilk and they were born near Section, Alabama in the Sand Mountain region; Ira Lonnie on April 21, 1924, and Charles Elzer on July 7, 1927. There were also five daughters in the family of C. M. and Georgeanne Loudermilk, and about 1929, they settled near the village of Henager, Alabama where the entire family survived through farming some twenty-three acres of cleared ground. It was tough living, but community folks made their own entertainment through playing music. The Loudermilks were part of this lifestyle as their father played the old-time banjo and sang a bit while their mother knew both old traditional ballads and nineteenth-century Tin Pan Alley survivals as well as the old church songs drawn from books like the *The Sacred Harp.* Ira and Charlie absorbed these musical traditions, and from the later thirties, the harmony styling of the duet acts, especially the Delmore Brothers and the Blue Sky Boys from their Bluebird Records. The vocal blend on many of the harmony duets was a high tenor and a lower-pitched lead voice, and the singers usually accompanied themselves on either two guitars or a mandolin and guitar. As Ira and Charlie developed their skills, the former usually sang the high tenor and played mandolin while the latter sang lead and played guitar.

By the time they reached adulthood, the Loudermilk boys had developed a pretty good duet. In the latter part of 1942, they had their own program at WDEF in Chattanooga as the "Radio Twins," but World War II soon caught up with them. Ira was drafted early in 1943, but injured his back in basic training and received a discharge after eighty-nine days. The brothers then worked for a time with fiddler Bob Douglas, another Chattanooga radio hillbilly. In July 1945, Charlie turned eighteen and soon afterward enlisted in the army where he remained until late in 1946. Ira went to Knoxville and not long afterward found a musical job with Charlie Monroe and his Kentucky Pardners. After Charlie got out of the service, the brothers reunited; it was about this time that they shortened their stage name to Louvin. They also made the acquaintance of a fellow musician who was a natural promoter, James Edward Hill, who was known to the entertainment world as "Smilin' Eddie Hill." The three soon went to Memphis and WMPS radio where Hill secured regular program work for them. With the exception of a year spent back in Knoxville and other spots and a period when Charlie was back in the service, Memphis would be the Louvin Brothers' main home until 1954. During this time, they made a record for the small Apollo label in 1947, a single for Decca in 1949, and the first of a dozen songs for MGM in 1951.

It was also during their Memphis years that the Louvin Brothers became Masons. Petitioning Algerona Lodge No. 168, both Ira and Charlie took their Entered Apprentice and Fellowcraft degrees on February 11, and March 17, 1952. Since Master Mason degrees take somewhat longer to confer, they were raised to that level on different dates. Ira received his on April 21, 1952 and Charlie on April 28, 1952. With the exception of a six-month period in 1955 and 1956 when Ira was in arrears for dues, he remained a member of Algerona Lodge until March 1, 1965 when he took a demit. Whether he intended to affiliate with another lodge will probably never be known as he met his tragic death not long afterward. Charlie eventually moved his membership to Phoenix Lodge No. 131 in Nashville where he became a fifty-year member in 2002. He also took the Scottish Rite degrees in the Valley of Nashville and became a noble of Al Menah Shrine. Their sometime radio associate Smilin' Eddie Hill also became a Mason although whether it was at this time or some other period is not currently known.

While the Louvin Brothers were gaining experience as vocalists on Memphis radio, they were also becoming known as songwriters. As early as mid-1949, other artists were putting Louvin compositions on disc and they were earning reputations as some of the best writers contracted to the Acuff-Rose Publishing Company. Their own recordings, while technically excellent, had met with only moderate success, with an inspirational Korean War song "The Weapon of Prayer" doing best. As a result they made a label change, going to Capitol Records in September of 1952. Their first session produced their best-known sacred effort "The Family Who Prays." At first the Louvin Brothers recorded only sacred songs for Capitol. After they had done eight sides for their new contract, Charlie was drafted again, but managed to get in ten more numbers—at sessions in September and November—before being sent to Korea. When he got back to Memphis in May of 1954, he and Ira decided to go to Birmingham, Alabama and play on WVOK radio. Things did not go well for them in Alabama, and they were on the edge of starving out when Ken Nelson, their Capitol producer, managed to get them on the *Grand Ole Opry* in late February of 1955.

Not only did "Opry" membership provide the Louvins with the break they needed, but Nelson finally yielded to their requests to also record secular material. In May of 1955, they recorded "When I Stop Dreaming," which became one of their biggest hits. They followed it up with "I Don't Believe You Met My Baby," which went all the way to number one. Ironically, it was one of the few Louvin hits that they did not compose themselves. By the end of 1956, they had added three more top ten country hits to their resumes: "Hoping that You're Hoping," "You're Running Wild," and "Cash on the Barrel Head." That year they also recorded one of the first and best country music concept albums, *Tragic Songs of Life,* made up of a combination of old traditional ballads such as "Knoxville Girl" and "Mary of the Wild Moor" and newer songs that sounded archaic such as "My Brother's Will" and "A Tiny Broken Heart." This album has become one of the true collector's items for those who treasure what true country music is all about. The Louvins also continued to record ample amounts of sacred songs.

After 1956, the Louvin hits came fewer and farther between. Part of the reason for this slackening resulted from the increasing impact of rock and roll music upon more traditional country sounds. Still, over the next five years the brothers experienced seven more *Billboard*-charted numbers with the most successful being "My Baby's Gone" in the latter part of 1958. They also continued to turn out classic Capitol albums such as the sacred offering *Satan Is Real* in 1958; a set of patriotic numbers, *Weapon of Prayer,* in 1961; and tribute albums to country greats of an earlier generation such as the Delmore Brothers and the Nashville country scene's most celebrated Mason, Sir Knight Roy Acuff.

However, tension began to build within the ranks. Ira, who was more the creative genius of the two, became increasingly temperamental, especially when drinking. Furthermore, his home life was unstable having been married four times in a total life span of forty-one years. Charlie was the more business like and steady of the brothers and had a peaceful domestic life (Charlie married Betty Harrison in 1949 and the pair reared three sons). The brothers finally split up in August 1963, recording a final album together that September, a sacred offering titled *Thank God for My Christian Home.* Ira, relieved of the pressure of constant touring, moved back to Alabama and with his fourth wife Anne Young, began to put his life back together. He also made a solo album for Capitol and he and Anne began to play a few show dates.

Charlie Louvin continued as a solo artist for Capitol and as a *Grand Ole Opry* performer. In August 1964, he had the first and most successful of some thirty-charted numbers with "I Don't Love You Anymore" which reached the number four spot. In 1965, he had another top-ten hit with "See the Big Man Cry." In fact, by the end of the sixties Charlie Louvin had made the *Billboard* listings more times than the Louvin Brothers had done as a team. In the early seventies Charlie made several duets with country girl singer Melba Montgomery (whose husband Jack Solomon is a member of Madison Lodge No. 762) of which "Something to Brag About" and "Did You Ever" did quite well. Charlie's last charted record in 1989 was a cover of Roy Acuff's old classic "The Precious Jewel" which included Roy helping out on the chorus and Donna Stoneman playing mandolin.

In some ways this seems ironic because Charlie's solo career has never attained quite the legendary status that the brothers did even though he had more hit records.

Ira Louvin's brief career as a solo artist consisted of one mid-level hit, "Yodel, Sweet Molly" in 1965, the year of his death. In June of 1965, Ira and Anne, while returning from a show date in Missouri, were both killed in an automobile crash on Interstate 70 when a car going the wrong way on the four lane struck them head-on the early morning of June 20. Bill Monroe, the legendary "Father of Bluegrass" who once said that country music had produced only two great tenor singers and that Ira was one of them, fulfilled a commitment to sing "Swing Low Sweet Chariot" at his funeral.

Charlie Louvin continued to record and make appearances on the "Grand Ole Opry." He also made some efforts to re-create the Louvin sound with the aid of Louisiana vocalist named Charles Whitstein. In October 2002, the Louvin Brothers were inducted into the Country Music Hall of Fame, an honor many persons believed was long overdue. Charlie continued his musical career on a limited basis until he died on January 26, 2011.

A visit and discussion by this writer with Charlie Louvin in 1997 revealed a man who took his Masonic vows and membership quite seriously. For instance, he discussed other Masonic country music figures as known brothers only if he had sat in lodge with them. He also demonstrated himself to be a gentleman of the highest order. His fraternal brothers the world over can take pride in the musical achievements of the Louvin Brothers in general and of Brother Charles E. Louvin as man and Mason in particular.

**Note**: To date the best available work on the Louvin Brothers is Charles K. Wolfe, *Close_Harmony: The Story of the Louvin Brothers* (Jackson: University Press of Mississippi, 1997), although Charlie Louvin insisted that a far superior book was in the works. An eight compact disc boxed set containing all 219 original Louvin Brothers recordings is available as Bear Family Records (BCD 15561). Many other Louvin Brothers and Charlie Louvin compact discs are also in print. For the Louvin Brothers Masonic records I am indebted to Ms. Stacy Sullivan of the staff at the Grand Lodge of Tennessee, to Joan Sansbury of the Scottish Rite Library in Washington, and lastly to Charlie Louvin himself.

May 2004; slightly revised 2011

**Brother Matthew B. Ridgway:** *Korean War General and NATO Commander*

A half-century ago when the Korean War was coming to an end and Cold War tensions remained high, Brother Matthew Bunker Ridgway stood at the top of the United States Army establishment. Appointed head of the U.S. Eighth Army on December 23, 1950, following the accidental death of Brother Walton H. Walker, Ridgway's name soon became a household word. Four months later he found himself elevated to the post of supreme commander of United Nations forces in the Far East when Brother and President Truman dismissed Brother and General Douglas MacArthur. After a year in this uncomfortable role, Truman then named Ridgway commander of the NATO forces in Europe. Finally in 1953, he became Army Chief of Staff. After leaving the service in mid-1955, the General enjoyed a long retirement during which time he wrote an excellent history of the Korean War. On top of all that, Brother Ridgway was a sixty-nine year Mason.

Matthew Bunker Ridgway was born at Fort Monroe, Virginia on March 3, 1895, the son of Colonel Thomas Ridgway, a career army officer. Young Matt was in a sense reared with the expectation of following in the family tradition and grew up on various military bases. After graduating from English High School in Boston in 1912, he entered the United States Military Academy at West Point, New York. He served as manager of the football team and upon graduation on May 15, 1917, became a lieutenant in the Third Infantry. With the United States entering World War I, the young junior officer hoped for an assignment in France, but to his chagrin spent the next fifteen months on the border at Eagle Pass, Texas. In September of 1918, he returned to West Point as an instructor. At the time, he felt he had missed the only opportunity he would ever have for a true war experience. Years later, he would revise this opinion.

During Ridgway's nearly six years back at the United States Military Academy, his duties were largely spent in athletic administration. He also petitioned West Point Lodge No. 877. Brother Ridgway received his first two degrees on April 3 and April 17, 1924. He was raised to the sublime degree of Master Mason on May 1, 1924. Many years later, he would seek additional light in Masonry, but soon after his raising, the junior officer was sent to Fort Benning, Georgia.

In Georgia, at Fort Benning, Ridgway prepared for his first overseas assignment. Beginning in June of 1925, he commanded a company of American infantrymen in Tientsin, China. For the next fifteen years, he alternated between foreign and domestic duties that took him to such locales as Nicaragua, the Canal Zone, and the Philippines abroad, and to Texas, Kansas, Illinois, California, and back to Fort Benning. Along the way, the career officer gained fluency in Spanish. This helps explain his service on the Commission of Inquiry and Conciliation concerned with the Paraguay-Bolivia boundary dispute (remember the 1932-1935 Chaco War?). In May of 1939, he accompanied General George C. Marshall on a "special mission" to Brazil. From then onward—if not before—he came to be considered something of a Marshall protégé.

In his personal life, Matthew Ridgway married Margaret Wilson in 1930. They subsequently became the parents of daughter, Virginia Ann. This marriage dissolved in June of 1947. The General remarried the following December to Mary Anthony. The couple had a son, Matthew Junior.

In September 1939, Major (soon to be Colonel) Ridgway became a part of the War Department General Staff where he worked in the War Plans division until January 1942. With the United States now actively engaged in World War II, he finally got the field command that had eluded him in the earlier conflict. In March 1942, as a Brigadier General, he became assistant division commander of the Eighty-Second Infantry; a few months later he became its commander.

In August of 1942, the Eighty-Second became one of the Army's first air-borne units. Sent to North Africa in April of 1943, Ridgway participated in the July invasion of Sicily and in the Italian campaign between September and November of that year. On D Day—June 6, 1944—he participated with his paratroopers on the

Cotentin Peninsula, doing his part to make the invasion of Normandy an allied victory. One of his citations read, "His personal bravery and heroism . . . were deciding factors in the success" of the operation.

Ridgway subsequently participated in the liberation of the Netherlands and Belgium, taking his men across the Rhine, Weser, and Elbe Rivers to a junction with Russian troops on May 2, 1945. By that time as commander of the Eighteenth Air-borne Corps, he had become recognized as "an outstanding authority on the use and command of air-borne troops." With fighting over in Europe, General Ridgway was transferred briefly to the Philippines. However, the war ended before he saw any action in the Far East. By October, the General had been ordered back to the Mediterranean where he spent three months on duty. In January of 1946, his superiors placed him on the "Military Staff Committee of the United Nations." This body advised the Security Council on military matters. Brother Ridgway remained in this capacity until 1948. At the end of 1947, he received permanent rank as a Major General, although he had been a temporary Lieutenant General since June of 1945. Cold War tensions remained high and Ridgway took charge of the Caribbean Command when his U. N. work ended. In 1949, he became Deputy Chief of Staff in the Pentagon. In June 1950, the Cold War suddenly turned hot with the North Korean invasion of South Korea.

On the evening of December 22, 1950, the General was preparing for a quiet evening at home with friends when he received an urgent call informing him that General Walton Walker had just died in a jeep accident and that he would immediately take charge of the Eighth Army on the ground in Korea. He would have to depart for the Far East before Christmas. Following a brief meeting with General MacArthur in Tokyo on the 26th, he took charge of an army that had been in retreat for a month. Chinese intervention in November had led to a reversal in what had once looked like a victory and an overly optimistic prediction that the troops would be "home for Christmas." Over the next three months, Ridgway's forces managed to not only stabilize the situation but recapture Seoul and make advances.

General Ridgway received another promotion in mid-April when President Truman dismissed MacArthur as overall Far East Commander. The Truman-MacArthur controversy placed Ridgway in a difficult situation, but he did as well as could be expected under the circumstances. While peace talks soon commenced, they initially made only minimal headway. Ridgway's troops kept up the pressure and after some hard fighting, took control of some strategic locales. The most famous of these battles, Heartbreak Ridge, came into allied hands in mid-October of 1951 after some thirty-seven days of bitter combat.

A brief lull in the action following the capture of Heartbreak Ridge enabled the Far East Commander to take a brief respite from work. On October 17, 18, 19, and 20, 1951, General Ridgway took the Scottish Rite degrees in the Valley of Tokyo, Japan. Many years later, on October 21, 1985, he would be made a K.C.C.H. and elected to receive the 33rd Degree.

Back in Korea, the military front remained relatively stable, although some fierce combat continued. After a year at the Far East Command, Ridgway was transferred to Europe where he replaced General Dwight Eisenhower as Commander of the NATO Forces. Although no military action took place in Europe, Cold War tensions remained high. France and Italy were somewhat unstable, and both had large, threatening Communist movements and they sometimes engaged in disruptions. The death of long-time Soviet strongman Joseph Stalin in March of 1953 initiated a new round of uncertainty.

Nonetheless, Matthew Ridgway acquitted himself well in this Command, and in the spring of 1953, President Dwight Eisenhower named him Army Chief of Staff. By this time, the peace talks in Korea had begun to move forward, and in July a truce was signed. Ridgway, a full General since 1952, remained in his post until mid-1955. Once it became apparent that the Panmunjom Truce appeared likely to hold, the inevitable calls for reductions in the military budget followed. After the midterm elections of 1954, downsizing announcements followed, far larger than Ridgway wished to accept, to wit a half-million men reduction in army strength. As a result, Ridgway felt compelled to resign and announced his retirement. Among his most prized possessions was a July 1, 1955 telegram from his mentor, Brother and General George C. Marshall, who wished him well and congratulated him on "a splendid military career of magnificent fighting leadership and great executive ability."

Upon his retirement from the military, Brother Ridgway took a position as Chairman of the Board of Trustees at the Mellon Institute of Industrial Research. In 1960, he retired from this position but continued to make his home in Pittsburgh. His memoir, *Soldier* was published by Harper and Brothers in 1956. A little more than a decade later, a second book by Ridgway, a well-received volume titled *The*

*Korean War,* appeared from Doubleday and Company. General Ridgway became one of the longest-lived high ranking officers in American History. He died on July 26, 1993, at his home in Fox Chapel, Pennsylvania, at the advanced age of ninety-eight. He had been a Mason for sixty-nine years and a Scottish Rite member for forty-two. As a man and as a Mason, Matthew Bunker Ridgway had served his country with honor and dignity. His fellow citizens could hardly have asked for more.

**Note**: The best sources for Ridgway are his own two books *Soldier* (1956) and *The Korean War* (1967). For his Masonic record, see William R. Denslow, *10,000 Famous Freemasons, IV,* p. 37. Additional information came from Brother Thomas M Savini, Director of the Chancellor Robert R. Livingston Masonic Library of the Grand Lodge of New York, and of the Scottish Rite, thanks to *Journal* editor Dr. John R. Boettjer.

June 2005; slightly revised 2011

## Sir Knight Norman Vincent Peale:
*A Powerful Positive Thinker*

When discussing influential Protestant clergy of the last half of the twentieth century, two names are likely to dominate the conversation—Billy Graham and Norman Vincent Peale. The Reverend Graham has, of course, been the leading evangelist. Peale is a more complex figure. An active minister for six decades, he also became known as a writer of self-help books, working "to consciously integrate psychological insights with religious beliefs." A Mason for sixty-seven years, he served rather proudly as both a Grand Chaplain and Grand Prelate in his ninety-five year lifespan.

The Peale story begins modestly in the small Greene County, Ohio town of Bowersville where a physician-turned-Methodist preacher, Charles Clifford Peale, delivered his firstborn son on May 31, 1898. Three years later the Peales had second son Robert, and much later, third son Leonard was born. Methodist ministers frequently shifted from church to church so young Norman lived at various times in Highland, Norwood, and eventually Bellefontaine where he finished high school in 1916. He then entered Ohio Wesleyan University in Delaware.

Norman Peale spent four years at O.W.U. graduating in 1920. Initially he worked as a newspaper reporter in Findlay, Ohio and Detroit, Michigan, but in 1921 he entered the Boston University School of Theology. The following September, being ordained, Peale pastored a small church in Berkeley, Rhode Island, for two years while completing his studies at Boston with both the M.A. and S.T.B. degrees. Moving to Brooklyn, New York, following graduation in May 1924, he became assistant pastor at St. Mark's Methodist Church in Brooklyn. A year later he took charge of the struggling Kings

Highway Church also in Brooklyn. During his three years there in the pulpit, church membership increased from forty to about nine hundred. This represents the kind of success that attracts wide attention.

While serving at Kings Highway Church, Reverend Mr. Peale became a Mason in Midwood Lodge No. 1062 in Brooklyn. In following this path, family tradition played a role as father and grandfather, Clifford and Samuel Peale, had Masonic histories dating back to 1869. Norman was initiated an Entered Apprentice on January 6, 1926; passed a Fellowcraft on January 20; and raised a Master Mason on March 3, 1926. Peale's membership in Midwood Lodge spanned sixty-seven years. Thanks to a pair of mergers, Midwood consolidated with Lexington Lodge No. 310 in 1970 and Brooklyn Lodge No. 288 in 1988, ultimately becoming Midwood No. 288 at the time of his passing.

In 1927, the Reverend got a call to the University Methodist Church in Syracuse where he spent the next five years. As a minister, he continued to be successful. Sunday morning attendance jumped upward, and he did well with outreach programs at the University of Syracuse. Perhaps the most significant aspect of his stay in upstate New York occurred when he met a young co-ed at Syracuse University named Loretta Ruth Stafford. A minister's daughter, she had earlier vowed that she would never marry a preacher. However, over the next few months, Ruth had a change of heart. The couple was married on June 20, 1930, and subsequently parented three children in a union that endured for sixty-three years.

In Syracuse, the Reverend Peale sought additional Masonic light when he joined the Valley of Syracuse, AASR, completing degrees on February 27, 1928. No specifics on how active Brother Peale was in his early years in the fraternity have been recorded, but the following statement made some years later suggests that he went to meetings frequently: "Attending Lodge and participating in Masonic activities gave me confidence. I learned to work with people. . . . All I had to do was bring it out."

A dramatic change occurred in Peale's life in the spring of 1932 when on a March Sunday he was asked to deliver a guest sermon at Marble Collegiate Church in New York City, a Dutch Reformed congregation. This church had encountered decline over the previous two years, and their board, impressed by Peale's preaching, hoped he could revive it. Accepting this pastorate required changing denominations, but he accepted the challenge and began his service there in October. Marble Collegiate would be Peale's ministerial home for the next fifty-two years. Those decades also saw his rise to national prominence and a vast expansion of his religious activity in new directions. For instance, he had done some radio programs in Syracuse, but in 1933 initiated a regular radio program, *The Art of Living*, which gave him a large new audience. Both in the pulpit and over the air, he aspired "to show" people "the practical advantages of Christianity." According to scholar Gardiner H. Shattuck, "rather than preaching in obtuse theological terms," Peale was "determined to talk in simple language that anyone could understand."

The Reverend Mr. Peale also became one of the earliest ministers to "consciously integrate psychological insights with religious concepts." Some hold that having a father who was both a physician and a preacher no doubt influenced his ideas in this area. By the later thirties, he worked with a psychiatrist, Dr. Smiley Blanton and they ultimately co-authored two books—*Faith Is the Answer* (1940) and *The Art of Real Happiness* (1950). In the summer of 1940, Peale spent a vacation in Hollywood as technical advisor on a Fredric March film, *One Foot in Heaven.*

As war clouds began to gather, Norman Vincent Peale found himself in an awkward situation. From the beginning, he had denounced such individuals as Hitler ("a maniac") and Mussolini ("a buzzard"), but reflecting his conservative rural Ohio background, had little use for the New Deal. When war came, he first wanted to enter the service as an army chaplain, but Ruth who was expecting their third child talked him out of it. So the Peales spent the war years on the "home front." In January of 1944 they purchased a place of their own in Pawling, New York, a twenty-acre small farm, for $25,000 which they paid for through lecture fees. Their neighbors included such Masonic notables as Governor Thomas Dewey and Lowell Thomas as well as noted newsman Edward R. Murrow. Pawling was the Peales' home for the remainder of their lives.

Right after the war, the Peales started another endeavor with the little inspirational magazine, *Guideposts* which grew from humble beginnings to a 2008 paid subscription of 2,195,000. Since several persons often read a single copy, one estimate gives it an approximate readership of about fifteen million. Within a decade, *Guideposts* had grown to a subscription list of 800,000. In that same positive period, Brother Peale also had his first best-seller with *A Guide to Confident Living* (1948).

The end of the decade also saw Norman Vincent Peale expand his Masonic activity. He had moved his Scottish Rite membership to the Valley of New York in 1934. In 1949 he was appointed Grand Chaplain of the Grand Lodge of New York, a position he held for three years. A life member of Crescent Shrine temple in Trenton, New Jersey, Noble Peale served as Imperial Chaplain in 1955. On September 23, 1959, the AASR, NMJ coroneted him as a 33° Mason, but this would not be the last of his fraternal activity.

In 1952, Brother Peale reached a new zenith of influence with the publication of what would become a multi-million selling volume, *The Power of Positive Thinking*. The book remained on the best-seller lists for more than three years and made the name Norman Vincent Peale household words. However, fame and success can often be accompanied by criticism and controversy. Such was the case with the now widely-acclaimed pastor of Marble Collegiate Church.

Critics of Brother Peale charged that his approach was intellectually shallow as well as too reliant on optimism. Others held, according to Gardiner Shattuck, that he was "converting belief in God into belief in human potential and distorting Christianity into a gospel of self-reliance." Hurt by these charges, Peale considered giving up his pastorate. At one point he even wrote a letter of resignation. On top of all that, his father was on his deathbed. Younger brother Leonard told him to continue, as "he owed his loyalty to the millions who believed in him, not to the handful who criticized." However, his decision to hold on came in a message his stepmother Mary told him after Charles Peale had passed on as quoted in Arthur Gordon's *Norman Vincent Peale: Minister to Missions* (1958). His father said, "Tell Norman I've read every word he's ever written . . . and . . . it's in harmony with the basic truths of Christianity and the teachings of Jesus. . . ." As for his critics, the dying father related, "tell Norman I said they were just a bunch of jackasses, and to pay them no heed . . . and never quit." That settled it. Peale handed his letter of resignation to his wife with the words "here, tear it up." Norman Vincent Peale kept on preaching and writing.

At Marble Collegiate Church, membership had grown from six hundred to three thousand. Crowds waited in line each Sunday morning to hear his sermons, thousands read his advice column in *Look* magazine, and millions heard his radio and television programs. His friends and admirers included President Eisenhower, F.B.I. Director J. Edgar Hoover, baseball executive Branch Rickey, publisher Frank Gannett, and western film star Roy Rogers. Well-known religious figures who befriended and defended him included Billy

Graham and his own predecessor at Marble Collegiate, Daniel A. Poling, who wrote a positive editorial in *The Christian Herald*. A Hollywood film, *One Man's Way* in 1964, starring Don Murray in the lead role, brought Peale's life to the silver screen.

Although Brother Peale avoided heavy participation in politics, he did not remain totally aloof from it, generally reflecting the views of his Midwestern Republican heritage. This brought some criticism from failed presidential nominee Adlai Stevenson who once said that he found St. Paul appealing and Peale appalling. Peale opposed the election of John Kennedy as a Catholic and did not criticize the Viet Nam War. Less partisan in performing marriage ceremonies, he officiated at the nuptials of both David Eisenhower and Julie Nixon and Kentucky Governor John Y. Brown and former Miss America Phyllis George.

As perhaps the best-known American Mason in the pulpit, Brother Peale spoke often of his membership and pride in the Fraternity, commenting at one point, "to me it means a personal relationship with great historical personalities . . . and also with the finest body of men with whom it is possible to assemble anywhere." In 1971, he again became General Chaplain in New York and so remained until awarded Chaplain Emeritus status in 1985. The Grand Lodge presented him the Distinguished Achievement Award in 1972. The Scottish Rite NMJ accorded him the Gourgas Medal in 1973 and the SMJ, the Grand Cross in 1987.

While continuing into his fourth decade as minister at Marble Collegiate, still another Masonic honor came to Reverend Peale in 1970 when G. Wilbur Bell of Illinois, Grand Master of the Grand Encampment of Knights Templar, appointed him Grand Prelate for the 1970-1973 triennium. Since he had not been a prior York Rite member, it necessitated that he be "knighted at sight" by a Grand Master before being appointed Grand Prelate." Following the fulfillment of his duties, he received the York Rite degrees in Evanston, Illinois in February 1974 with Sir Knight F. William Young, Grand Commander of New York, among those present. Shortly afterward, Companion and Sir Knight Peale affiliated with the bodies in upstate New York in which Young held membership: Excelsior Chapter No. 164, R.A.M., now in Shortville; Palmyra Council No. 26, R. & S. M., in Palmyra; and Red Jacket Commandery No. 81, K. T., in Canandaigua. In February of 1975, Peale was presented with a plaque certifying membership "in these bodies" by Sir Knight Alvin I. Crump, Past

Department Commander. Red Jacket Commandery No. 81 in 1996 merged with Jerusalem No. 17, Geneva No. 29 and Zenobia No. 41 to become Sagoyewatha Commandery No. 17 of Phelps, New York. Sir Knight David W. Taber, who currently serves as Recorder of both Palmyra Council and Sagoyewatha Commandery, recalls the above events and as the source of the preceding quotes concludes that "we were very proud to claim such a distinguished gentlemen and spiritual giant as a fellow Companion and Sir Knight."

Although Norman Vincent Peale continued to preach at Marble Collegiate well into his eighties, not retiring until 1984, he also still received numerous honors and endured criticism from some circles. As new waves of Mason-bashing gained support in the early 1990s, the sixty years-plus proud member remained unflinching. (For a typical bashing of Peale and Masonry, see www.letusreason.org.) In the February 1993 *Scottish Rite Journal*, he responded to criticism as follows: "To me, Freemasonry is one form of dedication to God and service to humanity. I am proud to walk in fraternal fellowship with my Brethren. Why am I a Freemason? Simply because I am proud to be near [a Brother] who wants to keep the moral standards of life at high level and leave something behind so others will benefit. Only as I personally become better can I help others to do the same."

These were the characteristics that defined Reverend Peale, striving for self-improvement, maintaining a positive outlook with a realization that man is fallible while holding to conservative social values, and urging mankind to do their best. He held to it until his death on December 24, 1993. Ruth Peale carried on with much of his work including *Guideposts* until her own passing in 2008. Brother Peale's ultimate achievement was explained by J. Harold Ellens, editor of the *Journal of Psychology and Christianity*. Ellens said: "Norman Peale saw psychology and Christian experience as very compatible . . . he had the courage to stand pat on this position in spite of the opposition of the entire Christian church for nearly half a century. His genius was that he . . . translated psycho-theology into the language of the people."

**Note**: Biographies of Rev. Peale are: Arthur Gordon, *Norman Vincent Peale: Minister to Millions* (1958) and Carol V. R. George, *God's Salesman: Norman Vincent Peale and the Power of Positive Thinking* (1993). His autobiography is the *True Joy of Positive Living* (1984). Shorter sketches can be found in American National Biography Online (www.anb.org); Ohioana Authors (www.ohioana-authors.org) and *Current Biography* 1946 and 1974. For his

Masonic records, I am indebted to Thomas Savini of the Livingston Library, William Holland of the Scottish Rite Museum, and David W. Taber, Recorder of Palmyra Council No. 26 and Sagoyewatha Commandery No. 17, both in New York.

May 2011; slightly revised 2011

## Brother Omar Nelson Bradley:
*The G. I.'s Five Star General*

When General Omar Bradley died in 1981, Alden Whitman, writing his obituary in the *New York Times*, reflected that only seven men up to that time had ever attained either the rank of "General of the Army" or "General of the Armies." The *Times* listed the men as Henry H. Arnold, Omar Bradley, Dwight Eisenhower, Douglas MacArthur, George Marshall, John Pershing, and George Washington. What the newspaper did not mention was that all of these men except Eisenhower were Masons.

Omar Nelson Bradley was born on February 12, 1893, in the small village of Clark, Missouri. According to one story, his mother, Sarah Hubbard Bradley, named him Omar because no other Bradley in that area had that sobriquet, and she wanted to avoid any confusion. His father, a schoolteacher, John S. Bradley, died when his son was thirteen. Growing up in Moberly, Missouri, the youth hunted, fished, studied, and applied to the United States Military Academy on the advice of his Sunday school teacher. The latter thought that West Point would be the best way for a "poor boy" to attain a first-class education. As a cadet, Bradley played both football and baseball, becoming especially known for his good throwing arm from the outfield. He graduated in 1915, ranking 44$^{th}$ in a class of 164. Another classmate, Dwight David Eisenhower, ranked 25$^{th}$ in the same group of graduates.

After commencement, Bradley spent a tour of duty on the turbulent Mexican border where the revolution had been going on since 1911. He was neither a part of the Pershing expedition that went in pursuit of Pancho Villa, nor did he get sent to France as part of the American Expeditionary Force. He did receive a temporary promotion to the rank of major. In December 1916, he was married to Mary

Quayle with whom he had attended high school back in Moberly. In the post-war period he spent more than twenty years as a peacetime officer, alternating between teaching duties and taking advanced courses in military science. Bradley began these duties teaching military science and tactics at South Dakota State College.

In 1920, the young officer began four years of service at West Point as instructor of mathematics. It was during those years that he petitioned West Point Lodge No. 877 in nearby Highland Falls, New York. Omar N. Bradley received his Entered Apprentice Degree on October 18, 1923; his Fellowcraft Degree on November 1; and his Master Mason degree on November 15, 1923. His rapid progress in the degrees at regular two-week intervals suggests the type of efficiency that he would become known for as an infantry commander in the next great war. He remained a member of West Point Lodge for fifty-seven years. A few years later, he took the Scottish Rite work in the Valley of Ft. Leavenworth, Kansas completing them in Army Consistory on April 11, 1929. He was twice suspended in the Scottish Rite, once for a few days in January 1937 and for a quarter century from the end of 1940 until August 1965. Thereafter he remained in good standing for the rest of his life eventually receiving the K. C. C. H. and thirty-third degree.

After his Military Academy stint, Bradley went to Fort Benning, Georgia for a year and then to Hawaii for three years where he divided his time between Schofield Barracks and Fort Shafter. Back in the states he spent a year at the Command and General Staff school at Fort Leavenworth, Kansas and then went back to Fort Benning to serve four years as an instructor at the Infantry School. Not long afterward, he returned to West Point for another round of teaching, this time in tactics. During this time, Bradley was promoted to Lieutenant Colonel in 1936.

In June of 1938, Omar Bradley received a new assignment on the War Department General Staff. According to Alden Whitman, "by 1940 he was an obscure lieutenant colonel in civilian clothes who rode a bus to work in the old Munitions Building in Washington." The next year, Bradley went to Fort Benning a third time as a commandant of the Infantry School and as a brand new Brigadier General, the first member of the class of 1915 to become a general. Eisenhower would soon catch up with and surpass his classmate. Soon after the declaration of war in December of 1941, the new general was sent first to Camp Claiborne, Louisiana and then in June of 1942 to Camp Livingston. At the latter training station, he impressed both his superiors and subordinates with his physical endurance. It was said that he could do anything that those half his age could handle and then some. Obstacle courses and swinging across ravines, streams, and swamps were all handled with prowess by the forty-nine year old Bradley.

In February of 1943, General Bradley joined the North Africa campaign. Over the next two and one-half years, his military reputation would be made. After a few weeks as a field aide to General Eisenhower, Bradley became commander of the Second United States Army Corps. On May 7, his troops captured the Tunisian city of Bizerte, and three days later he received the surrender of General Krause and 25,000 badly-beaten troops of the Africa Korps. As for Bradley, he was soon involved in plans for the Italian Campaign and the invasion of Sicily. Prior to the conclusion of this phase of the war, General Marshall transferred Bradley to England where he would command the First United States Army and prepare for the Normandy invasion.

From the time of the D-day invasion which began on June 6, 1944, until the surrender of the Germans the following May, Bradley again proved he had what it took. As subordinate only to Eisenhower in the chain of command (and Montgomery in theory at least for a time), he bore a heavy burden with quiet but efficient resolve. Although requiring a great deal of tough combat fighting, the allied advance was sure and steady, slowed only temporarily by the German counter-offensive at the Battle of the Bulge in December of 1944. The General conceded that he had "greatly underestimated the enemy's offensive capabilities" but added that Montgomery and Eisenhower had done the same. Like Eisenhower, Bradley also clashed with British Field Marshal, Sir Bernard Montgomery. At one point in the early weeks of 1945, the usually congenial Brother Bradley bluntly informed Eisenhower, "You must send me home, for if Montgomery goes in over me, I will have lost the confidence of my command." According to Alden Whitman, it took British Prime Minister Winston Churchill to pour "oil on the troubled waters" and smooth the ruffled feathers of wounded pride among the top commanders.

In March, Bradley's troops began crossing the Rhine via the now famous "bridge at Remagen" and in the remaining weeks took some 325,000 German prisoners. With combat coming to an end in May, the man who had earned the nickname "G. I.'s General" because of his concern for his infantrymen and the respect they conferred upon him, returned to Washington and became head of the Veteran's Administration, a post he held until 1947. Meanwhile, numerous honors began coming his way including honorary doctorates from several American universities and military decorations from many of the World War II allies. In 1948, he became Chief of Staff of the United States Army and in 1949, Chairman of the Joint Chiefs of Staff. In 1950, Omar Nelson Bradley was promoted to General of the Army, thus becoming one of the very few persons to attain the fifth star. In 1951, his widely admired memoirs, *Bradley: A Soldier's Story*, came off the presses. Reviewers generally praised the volume. According to John P. Marquand, some passages possessed "a stark, grave beauty that is close to being literary" and that it "is a book to be read and reread, and one to be kept indefinitely." Bradley retired early in 1954, but since five star generals "are always available for recall to active duty," he never fully retired in that sense.

No longer actively engaged in day-to-day military activity, Brother Bradley joined the Bulova Watch Company initially as head of the Research and Development Laboratories and later as Chairman of the Board. He also served on the Board of Directors for Food Fair Stores and for Metro-Goldwyn-Mayer, Inc. In December of 1965, Mary Quayle Bradley, the General's wife of forty-nine years, passed away. The couple had a grown daughter, Elizabeth. Later, he married Esther "Kitty" Buhler who survived him.

In 1974, the Valley of Cincinnati named their Fall Class after the general, and he planned to attend, but a last minute, illness prevented it. He did, however, send them a message outlining his views on Masonry, part of which is quoted herein: "I have served as a Mason since 1923 when I first joined the lodge at West Point, and I have always tried to live by the tenets for which Freemasonry stands. The goals of Freemasonry are to be diligently sought by men of good faith but can be achieved only by those who enjoy the privileges of freedom.... The fraternity of Freemasonry is aware that a democracy such as ours cannot be defeated. It can lose only through default.... Our Nation has not failed us. We shall not fail our Nation."

A few months later, representatives of the Supreme Council and the Valley of Cincinnati presented General Bradley with the Killian H. Van Rensselaer Gold Medal. In 1977, the octogenarian general settled at Fort Bliss, near El Paso, Texas. One of his last official duties was to attend the inauguration of President Ronald Reagan in

January of 1981. By this time, the old general was confined to a wheelchair, a condition credited to an injury dating back to his football days at West Point. Back in Texas, he celebrated his 88th birthday and a few weeks later went to New York in April to attend a dinner and meeting of the Association of the United States Army. He suffered a fatal cardiac arrest and died on April 8, 1981, thus passed one of the most revered Masons and military leaders in the annals of the American Republic. Bradley was a credit to his country and to his fraternity and an inspiration to those who can rise from modest circumstances to achieve greatness.

**Note**: The best account of Bradley's life is his own *Bradley: A Soldier's Story* (New York: Henry Holt & Co., 1951). However, for purposes of this sketch, I found his entry in *Current Biography* (1943) and the lengthy obituary by Alden Whitman, "Gen. Omar N. Bradley Dead at 88; Last of Army's Five-Star Generals," *New York Times,* April 9, 1981, pp. 1, D21 most useful. For his Masonic record I am indebted to V. W. Thomas M. Savini, Director of the Chancellor Robert R. Livingston Masonic Library of the Grand Lodge of New York.
For the Scottish Rite to Bro. John Boettjer of *The Scottish Rite Journal* and for the quote to Bro. Jack deVise in his excellent book, *A Magnificent Heritage* (2003), pp. 404-406.

January 2004; slightly revised 2011

## Brother "Pawnee Bill:"
*Frontiersman and Showman*

The American frontier produced a number of persons who achieved prominence, and some gained a legendary status. A surprising number of these individuals were Masons despite the fact that Masonry tends to be associated with a more settled society. Masonic figures on the frontier include men like explorers Meriwether Lewis, William Clark, Kit Carson, the leadership of the Montana Vigilantes, and a number of noted Texas Rangers. One of the most famed, William F. Cody, gained wide recognition as "Buffalo Bill," a frontier scout, dime novel hero, and developer of the Wild West Show. The subject of this sketch, Gordon William Lillie, gained only slightly less renown as "Pawnee Bill." While younger and having less frontier experience than Cody, Lillie nonetheless had his share of experiences in the Wild West. He was probably as good a showman, sometimes a rival, occasionally a partner, and certainly a better business man than Buffalo Bill.

Much of America's frontier experience had already happened when Gordon William Lillie was born near Bloomington, Illinois on February 14, 1860. As the eldest of four children of a flour mill operator, young Gordon was much influenced by stories of the Wild West, particularly those contained in dime novels about Buffalo Bill that began to appear in 1869. He persuaded his family to move to Sumner County, Kansas in 1873 and then in mid-1875 finally coaxed them to let him leave home. After visiting in the booming cow town of Wichita, he found a job at the Pawnee Indian Reservation, helping to build a house for the agent. Over the next several years, young Gordon Lillie spent a great deal of time among the Pawnees and learned their language and way of life. These experiences resulted in his gaining the nickname by which he would become known,

"Pawnee Bill," and also in 1878 another sobriquet bestowed upon him by his Native-American friends, "White Chief of the Pawnees."

During his years among the Pawnees, Lillie worked in a variety of jobs including interpreter and teacher in the agency school. He also became skilled in hunting, trapping, and the general knowledge needed for survival on the plains and prairies. He left the agency in August of 1881 and worked as a farm and ranch hand in the general vicinity of Caldwell, Kansas. Then in 1883, Buffalo Bill Cody, who had been working in a variety of stage plays, began organizing his fabled Wild West Show. A man named Charlie Burgess—whose father had known Gordon Lillie at the Pawnee Agency—was looking for Gordon on Cody's behalf. A group of Pawnees were to work in the show, but the Indian Commissioner would approve only if someone would be responsible for them and look out for their well-being. He was told that "there is a young man out there who was in the service for a time who talks Indian like a native, wears long hair, and is a great friend of the Pawnees." Having seen Cody in person back in 1873, just before his family moved to Kansas, young Gordon Lillie accepted the offer and went to work in the show. He found some personal disappointment, learning that his hero had human frailties including a periodic drinking problem and was financially irresponsible. Still, he also noted the man's positive qualities (Cody had also been a member of Platte Valley Lodge since January 10, 1871), and Lillie became a key member of his troupe.

As the show moved eastward attracting huge crowds, Gordon Lillie met the love of his life when the group reached Philadelphia. He met a girl named May Manning who was a student at Smith College. The two soon began to correspond and following her graduation, were married on August 31, 1886. Uncertain as to how she would adjust to life on the plains, May somewhat surprisingly became an expert rider and rifle shot. In December 1887, friends back in Philadelphia presented her a medal inscribed "Champion Girl Shot of the West," and her fame was almost equal to that of Annie Oakley. When Pawnee Bill established his own show, May Lillie became one of the star attractions.

At about the same time that May received her medal, Pawnee Bill who been thinking about starting his own show entered the fray. He launched Pawnee Bill's Wild West in the spring of 1888 and for the first few weeks drew large crowds with Bill and May as star attractions along with Annie Oakley who had a temporary rift with her normal employer, Buffalo Bill. After Cody returned from England and the weather turned bad, things went sour. In late October, Bill gave up, and the show folded. Gordon Lillie returned to Kansas in time to lead a party of "boomers [i.e. settlers]" into a section of the newly-opened Oklahoma Territory. He reorganized his show as Pawnee Bill's Historical Wild West, Indian Museum, and Encampment. Benefiting from his earlier mishaps, this time his production proved successful, and he gave his former employer, Buffalo Bill, real competition.

Lillie's show popularity undoubtedly was also buoyed by his own appearance as a dime novel hero. In 1888, the first of fourteen of these lurid pieces of fiction came off the presses of Beadle & Adams, Frank Tousey, and Street & Smith, written by such masters of the art as Colonel Prentiss Ingraham (who had written many of the Buffalo Bill stories), Paul Braddon, and Edward W. Wheeler. The stories had little basis in fact, but kids continued to devour them with gusto. One offering in 1891 even bore the title *Pawnee Bill's Shadow; or, May Lillie, the Girl Dead Shot.* Many years later (1917-1919), another series in which both Buffalo Bill and Pawnee appeared together resulted in twenty-seven additional titles.

Meanwhile, the Wild West Show continued to do well, and more lands in Oklahoma Territory opened for settlement including what would become the town of Pawnee. Not only did Gordon and May Lillie establish their home there in the off season, but Bill's parents and sisters also located there. In 1894, he took his Wild West show to Europe where the troupe performed for royalty including King Leopold of Belgium and Queen Wilhemina of the Netherlands. Back in Oklahoma, Gordon Lillie used his profits to become a stockholder in the Arkansas Valley Bank of which he eventually became vice president. Interested in preventing the American Bison from becoming extinct, he purchased 2,000 acres south of town and established his Buffalo Ranch.

It was during one of the Wild West show off-seasons that Pawnee Bill became a Mason in Pawnee Lodge No. 82. Gordon William Lillie was initiated an Entered Apprentice on January 7, 1899; passed to the degree of Fellowcraft on January 14, 1899; and raised to the sublime degree of Master Mason on February 2, 1899. He remained a faithful member until his death forty-three years later. He also joined the Scottish Rite bodies in Guthrie and became a noble of Akdar Temple, AAONMS in Tulsa. After his retirement from show business,

Bill and the Miller Brothers of 101 Ranch fame (who had the last wild west show), staged a rodeo for the Imperial Shrine session at Washington, D. C. in June 1923. Not exclusively Masonic, Bill joined Lodge No. 654 of the Benevolent and Protective Order of Elks and a number of old-time cowboy groups. He also proved to be a firm supporter of the Boy Scouts of America.

Pawnee Bill's Historic Wild West continued to prosper. In 1907, he expanded the show and added the Great Far East to his billing, including such features as elephants and exotic attractions associated with Asia, Australia, and Africa. In other words, it became more like a regular circus. Meanwhile, Lillie's chief rival experienced a series of problems including a wreck of his show train, injuries, and retirement of Annie Oakley, the death of his principal advisor, Nate Salisbury, heavy debts to James Bailey of Barnum & Bailey fame, and a personal scandal. In 1908, Pawnee Bill and Buffalo Bill came to an agreement to merge their shows. Cody's financial recklessness still troubled Lillie, but against his own better judgment and out of lingering respect for his long-time idol, he agreed to the union as "Buffalo Bill's Wild West and Pawnee Bill's Great Far East" for the 1909 season. In 1910 and 1911 the combination made money, partly because it was advertised as Buffalo Bill's "farewell tour." By 1912, however, this concept was beginning to wear thin, and business declined. As Lillie's biographer, Glenn Shirley put it, "there were profits, but hardly enough to keep Buffalo Bill ahead of creditors." Things went worse in 1913, and in July, legal entanglements caught up with the show. The last performance took place in Denver on July 21, 1913, as Pawnee Bill refused to spend any more of his personal funds to keep it afloat. To again quote Glenn Shirley, "thus, Buffalo Bill's Wild West and Pawnee's Far East died ingloriously." Cody went back to his home in North Platte, Nebraska, and Pawnee Bill returned to Oklahoma, having sufficient personal funds to survive in comfort. When the old scout died in 1917, Gordon Lillie wrote, "time smooths everything. Buffalo Bill died my friend" adding the conclusion, "he was just an irresponsible boy."

Back in Pawnee, Oklahoma, Gordon and May Lillie had their numerous business interests and friends. He supported the Boy Scouts and efforts to protect and enlarge the surviving bison herds. To accommodate numerous tourists, he built a facility known as Old Town and Indian Trading Post which was completed in 1930 and provided employment for many of his Pawnee Indian friends.

Generally speaking, one might say that he enjoyed his status that one person termed "being famous for being famous." In retirement he often spent part of each summer in Taos, New Mexico, where he and May celebrated their golden wedding anniversary on August 31, 1936.

Unfortunately, this gala would prove to be a last hurrah for the aging couple. Two weeks later on a return trip to Pawnee from Tulsa, they were involved in a serious auto crash, and May died from injuries on the morning of September 14. Bill's own health began to deteriorate in the following months, but he continued to drive about his properties in his old Pierce Arrow and made plans to donate some of his attractions to the Boys Scouts of America. Sadly, Old Town burned in 1939. As residents of his ranch prepared to arrange an 82nd birthday party, the old frontiersman died on February 3, 1942, one day after the 43rd anniversary of his raising in Pawnee Lodge. He was buried beside May in the family mausoleum in the local Highland Cemetery. One of the few remaining symbols of a vanished era had gone to his reward.

**Note**: The definitive work on Gordon Lillie is Glenn Shirley, *Pawnee Bill: A Biography of Major Gordon W. Lillie* (Lincoln: University of Nebraska Press, 1965). For his Masonic Record, I appreciate the rapid assistance of the staff at the Grand Lodge of Oklahoma, Garry Odom, P. G. M., Grand Secretary.

July 2007; slightly revised 2011

## Brother Powel Crosley, Jr.:
*Queen City Entrepreneur, Industrialist, Sportsman*

Some people are born innovators although it may take some time for them to find their proper niche, so to speak. The subject of this sketch made his mark in life as an inventor, a businessman, a radio pioneer, and as owner of a major league baseball team, all in the city of Cincinnati. Brother Powel Crosley wore a number of hats in his varied career, and while he had his share of disappointments, by and large, he demonstrated a considerable degree of success. Today, his name is probably best remembered for the ball park that bore his name during what many consider the Golden Age of the National Game, but he was much more than that.

Powel Crosley, Jr. was born in Cincinnati on September 18, 1886, the son of Charlotte Utz and Powel Crosley, Sr., an attorney who had moved his practice to the Queen City from Warren County. As a youth, he attended public schools in the College Hill section of the city and then the Ohio Military Institute from which he was graduated in 1905. From childhood, he demonstrated a great deal of energy in gadgets and new technological developments. At the age of twelve, he built a four-wheeled wagon powered with an electric motor and sold it to his father who promised him to buy it for ten dollars if it would work. To his father's surprise it did work! The proud youngster repaid his eight dollar expense, gave his investor brother, Lewis, a dollar, and "gloatingly pocketed" a ten per cent profit. Over the next sixty years, he would pocket several million more.

The youngster entered the University of Cincinnati's engineering school and then switched to law but was too restless to stick with either. Automobiles were his first love, and it was said that he dropped out of college to take a chauffeur's job just so he could drive one. He worked at a variety of other jobs and built his first car called the "Marathon Six" in 1907, but the financial Panic of 1907 ended his hopes to put it into production. Powel planned to enter a car in the Indianapolis 500 but had to drop out when he broke his arm. Starting a firm called the American Automobile Accessories Company, he made and marketed a number of by-products and accessories that included a gasoline fortifier called "gastronic," a radiator cap that doubled as a flag holder (very popular during World War I), and a device to help keep the car back in line after it had hit a rock in a bumpy road that he termed "the litl shofur." By 1920, the company was also making phonograph cabinets, canoes, and printed advertising. Meanwhile in 1910, Crosley married Gwendolyn Aiken on October 17, and the couple had two children, Powel III and Martha. Mrs. Crosley died in 1939, and the widower eventually married two more times and was widowed once more.

Powel Crosley began his Masonic journey in 1917 in College Hill Lodge, No. 641. He was initiated on September 27, passed on November 15, and raised to the Sublime degree of Master Mason on December 20, 1917. Powel Crosley, Sr. had previously been a member of Kilwinning Lodge No. 356 in Cincinnati but demitted and affiliated with College Hill Lodge about the same time the son was taking his degree work. The father remained a member until his death in 1932 and the son until his death in 1961. He also joined the Valley of Cincinnati AASR, completing his work on May 22, 1919, and became a member of Syrian Shrine Temple on May 24, 1919.

Meanwhile, Powel Crosley found a new interest, one that would provide him with his greatest fame, success, and wealth. Radio became a new fad, and young Powel III wanted one. The father shopped around a bit but found that they cost at least one hundred dollars. Thrifty by nature, he spent 25 cents on a booklet called "The ABCs of Radio" then bought some parts, and built one for less than twenty-five dollars. As Henry Ford was then doing for the automobile, Powel Crosley soon did the same for radio. He built and marketed a radio that the masses could afford and made himself a multi-millionaire in the process.

By the beginning of 1922, Crosley was selling many radios. In March of 1922, so that his buyers would have something to hear, he started station WLW. Within a decade, this station became known as "the Nation's Station," and with 500,000 watts of power, 700 on your AM radio dial had become the most powerful broadcasting outlet in the world. It was said that one could hear the station over barbed wire fences and the metal fillings in your teeth! While Crosley himself did the first broadcasts from his home, once the station really took off, Crosley left most of the day-to-day management to others. Many programs that originated from there eventually made it big on the networks including *Moon River*, *Midwestern Hayride* (first known as *Boone County Jamboree*), *Plantation Party*, and the long-running soap opera *Ma Perkins*. Under Crosley Broadcasting and its successor Avco Corporation (after 1945), such regional and national stars developed as Doris Day, Rosemary and Barbara Clooney, Red Skelton, Ruth Lyons, Paul Dixon, Bob Braun, and Phil Donohue.

In addition to radio manufacturing and broadcasting, Crosley's corporation turned out other products. Perhaps the most successful was the refrigerator known as the "Shelvador," the first to contain shelves on the inside of the door. Powel Crosley offered the inventor a twenty-five cent royalty for each one sold, but the man insisted on a $15,000 cash payment instead. Crosley paid the $15,000 and came out ahead on the deal. Other products in the Crosley line included the "Roamio," the first car radio in 1930; "Koolrest," an air conditioner; "Icyball," a portable refrigerator; "Tredkote," a tire patch; "Driklenit," an auto polish; and "X-er-vac," a scalp massage. Some of the products were a bit ahead of their time and not really successful until later, but they demonstrated the man's love for innovation and tinkering. Some of these products were his and some were bought from others.

In 1934, Powel Crosley purchased the controlling interest in the virtually bankrupt Cincinnati Baseball Club Company at the urging of General Manager Larry McPhail. He was not a dedicated fan but did want the franchise to remain in the Queen City. With McPhail's guidance, he made improvements to Redland Field, renaming it Crosley Field and installed lights. On May 24, 1935, more than 20,000 fans watched the Reds defeat the Phillies in the first major league night game. That contest and six others helped boost team attendance. Four more years elapsed before the Reds, under the management of Brother Bill McKechnie, brought home league pennants in 1939 and 1940 with a World Series win over Detroit in the latter year. The authors of the authoritative team history, *Redleg Journal*, described the club's long time owner; "a private man, Crosley preferred to remain behind the scenes as club owner and gave his general managers control of personnel decisions." He did, however, inaugurate Shrine Night at Crosley Field.

Brother Crosley still dreamed of bringing an inexpensive compact automobile to the masses. In 1939, he was ready to launch his Crosley car through department store outlets. His original plan for the Crosley auto was for it to sell for $325 and get fifty miles to a gallon of gasoline. World War II intervened before he could have much success. By September of 1944, it appeared that the War would soon be winding down, and as WLW historian Dick Perry phrased it, "Mr. Crosley dusted off his dream and started all over again." Accordingly, in 1945 he sold WLW for sixteen million dollars to Aviation Corporation (which ironically had once manufactured another legendary car, the Cord). In 1947, this company became Avco Broadcasting. Powel Crosley still owned the Reds, but for six years he turned over the presidency to Warren Giles. He then could concentrate virtually all of his efforts to Crosley Motors.

The auto manufacturing plant was located in Marion, Indiana. Initially, things started off well enough. To again quote Dick Perry's *Not Just a Sound,* "at the end of the first official sales year (July 31, 1947), more than sixteen thousand of the little cars had been sold at $888 each, and Crosley Motors showed a profit of $476,065. The next year, thirty thousand of the little things were sold." Crosley Motors had two more good years. Then the Korean War began, and a scarcity of material increased steel prices along with a sharp jump in labor costs. Sales dropped to 4,000 in 1951 and to just under 2,000 in 1952. After three straight years of annual million dollar losses, the Crosley auto died. The Marion plant closed and was sold to General Tire for $60,000. Ironically, before the fifties ended, the German import Volkswagen made a hit with American consumers, suggesting that the Crosley may have just been a decade ahead of its time.

After Warren Giles became National League president, Brother Powel Crosley resumed the executive position with the Cincinnati Baseball Club Company, a position he retained for the rest of his life. The Reds had dropped to the second division in 1945 where they remained for a decade although they did provide their fans with some exciting moments. One came in 1947 when long, lanky sidearm pitcher Ewell "the Whip" Blackwell (a Mason) had his phenomenal 22-8 season. In the mid-fifties, the team produced a number of powerful hitters typified by the muscular Ted Kluzewski and also included such long-ball hitters as Gus Bell, Wally Post, and future Hall of Famer, Frank Robinson. In 1956, the Reds proved to be not only a strong contender but also amassed a team record with 221 home runs. They also became the first Reds team to draw over a million fans at home. Crosley continued to remain in the background in that era with Gabe

Paul as General Manager and Birdie Tebbetts as the most successful field manager in that period.

One of Crosley's last acts as club president and principal owner was to hire William O. "Bill" DeWitt, 33° in the Valley of Cincinnati in 1972, as general manager on November 8, 1960. Brother Crosley died unexpectedly four months later, but the leadership of DeWitt and manager Fred Hutchison brought the Reds the league pennant in 1961, their first in twenty-one years. Crosley's daughter and heir, Mrs. Stanley Kess, subsequently sold her stock to DeWitt.

After Crosley Motors died in 1952, Powel Crosley lived on for another nine years. Although of retirement age, he remained active as Reds president and as a member of the board of directors of the Fifth Third Union Trust and of the *Cincinnati Enquirer*. Some years after Gwendolyn's death, he married again to Eva Brokaw, but she died in 1954. Two years later, at seventy, he wed a third time to Charlotte Wilson who would survive him. He also served on hospital boards and spent time on his two farms—in Indiana and Georgia—and owned other homes in Canada and South Carolina in addition to his residence on Kippling Avenue in the Queen City; he maintained an office in the Carew Tower. An avid yachtsman, he also kept close tabs on the Reds. Powel Crosley, III preceded his father in death, so daughter, Mrs. Stanley Kess, was his only surviving child when he passed on March 28, 1961, just as the team was ready to go north. Later, a mural was unveiled at Crosley Field, highlighting major events in the life of the forty-three year member of College Hill Lodge who had contributed so much to the Queen City of the West. Crosley Field was replaced by a new park in 1970, but forty-five years after his death, his legacy continues. WLW remains as a major radio station, and the Reds still take the field for 162 games each season.

**Note**: The major source for the life of Powel Crosley is Dick Perry, *Not Just a Sound: The Story of WLW* (Prentice-Hall, 1973) along with several books on the Cincinnati Reds. Ill. Bro. George Braatz, Grand Secretary of the Grand Lodge of Ohio supplied his blue lodge records, Harry Carpenter of the Valley of Cincinnati, his Scottish Rite, and the staff of Syrian Shrine Temple for the AAONMS. Thanks also to Sir Knight Norman Lincoln of Eaton, Ohio and S K Roger E. Van Dyke who proofread the manuscript. After this article was originally written, a definitive biography by Rusty McClure with David Stern and Michael A. Banks was published, *Crosley: Two Brothers and a Business Empire That Transformed the Nation* (Clerisy Press, 2006).

April 2007; slightly revised 2011

**Pee Wee King:**
*Tennessee Waltz King and Fifty-Year Mason*

Over the past two and one-half centuries, the entertainment world has been enriched by the contributions of numerous Masonic brethren. These range from great actors of past centuries such as David Garrick and Edwin Forrest to such twentieth century favorites as beloved comedian Red Skelton from the film and TV screen. In the country and western music field, Masons include such pioneer figures as Jimmie Rodgers and Harry "the Bum Song" McClintock as well as modern stars like Roy Clark and Mel Tillis.

The subject of this sketch, Pee Wee King, played a significant role in the modernization of the music, bringing it out of the hills and mountains to concert halls and network television. Along the way, band leader Pee Wee King and one of his Golden West Cowboys, vocalist Redd Stewart, created such memorable hit songs as "Slow Poke," "Silver and Gold," "Bonaparte's Retreat," "Changing Partners," and most especially "Tennessee Waltz," which became a huge hit and all-time classic in both the pop and country fields. In 1965, it became the fourth official song of the state.

A member of the Country Music Hall of Fame since 1974, Pee Wee King, like his friends Eddy Arnold and Roy Acuff, was a long-time member of East Nashville Lodge No. 560. He received his fifty-year pin in 1993.

King came from Polish stock, originally being named Julius Frank Anthony Kuczynski when born at Abrams, Wisconsin, on February 18, 1914. His dad knew how to play violin and concertina, and young Frankie took lessons on both, but the accordion became his favorite, and he mastered it. Having learned something about polka music through his father and having played in their family band, the youth was also attracted to western musical styles. For entertainment purposes, he shortened his name to Frankie King. He worked on local radio in Milwaukee and Racine until J. L. Frank (1900-1952) hired him to back rising WLS Chicago radio star, Gene Autry.

Frank, a pioneer booking agent and manager, would play a major role in King's life, not only becoming his manager but also his father-in-law and the man who would spur his interest in Masonry. Autry, a longtime member of Catoosa Lodge No. 185 in Oklahoma and eventual super star, gave King his nickname, Pee Wee, since at 5'7" he was the shortest person in the touring unit.

After some time, Autry went to Hollywood while King went to WHAS in Louisville. Pee Wee worked with Frankie Moore and his Log Cabin Boys until 1936 when he formed the Golden West Cowboys the same year he married Lydia Frank. The Golden West Cowboys then went to WNOX Knoxville for three months prior to joining the *Grand Ole Opry* at WSM Nashville on June 1, 1937.

During his eleven years at the Opry, Pee Wee King and the Golden West Cowboys contributed numerous innovations to radio's most venerable institution. His band ranked as the first to use electrical instruments on that stage, the first to use drums, and the first to use a horn ("Taps" when Franklin Roosevelt died in April 1945).

Henry (Redd) Stewart (1921-2003) had been the principal vocalist with the band, but during his time in military service during World War II, such fill-ins as Eddy Arnold and Lloyd (Cowboy) Copas later went on to launch careers as solo stars. Stewart, while in the service, wrote the classic sentimental war song, "The Soldier's Last Letter."

The Golden West Cowboys also made periodic junkets to Hollywood, beginning with the Gene Autry film, *Gold Mine in the Sky*, in 1938. Later, the band made four more films, two each with Johnny Mack Brown and Charles Starrett.

Pee Wee also became interested in Masonry during his Nashville years. He credits J. L. Frank (another Mason in the Country Music Hall of Fame as was long-time *Opry* manager Jim Denny) with spurring his interest in the Fraternity. King petitioned East Nashville Lodge No. 560, was accepted, initiated, passed, and ultimately raised to the sublime degree of Master Mason on December 20, 1943. Fellow Opry stars, Roy Acuff and Eddy Arnold, followed in Pee Wee's footsteps. The three took the Scottish Rite degrees together in the Valley of Nashville in May of 1944 and became nobles of Al Menah Shrine Temple on June 27, 1944.

Several other members of the Golden West Cowboys also joined the order. At one point in the early fifties, they were a one hundred percent Masonic band. These included key figures Redd Stewart, Gene Stewart, James "Shorty" Boyd, Charles Wiginton, and drummer Harold "Sticks" McDonald. An earlier member of the group, Curley Rhodes, was also a Mason and long active as a Shrine Clown. Opry comedians who sometimes toured with the band included known Mason, Rod Brasfield, and reputed Mason, Ben "Duke of Paducah" Ford.

In 1946, Pee Wee King and Redd Stewart composed "Tennessee Waltz," which would be their best-known song. They recorded it for RCA Victor in December of 1947, and while it did quite well for them, its peak came in 1950 when Patti Page's Mercury Record version topped the pop listings for thirteen weeks. Other top ten arrangements in the popular field included those by Jo Stafford, Guy Lombardo's Royal Canadians, and the team of Les Paul and Mary Ford. Both Roy Acuff and Cowboy Copas (a Fellowcraft Mason in John B. Garrett Lodge No. 711) had country hits with it as did Pee Wee's own version. One historian believed that "Tennessee Waltz" might well be the single most valuable copyright in country music history. It sold a reported six million records just during those early years. It still sells today.

Pee Wee King left Nashville and the *Opry* in 1948, returning to Louisville and WAVE-TV. Nonetheless, he continued turning out hit records for RCA Victor. In 1951, the country-western accordion player enjoyed his biggest personal hit, "Slow Poke," which spent fifteen weeks atop the *Billboard* country charts and three at number one on the pop listings. He even cut a separate version for the British market titled "Slow Bloke."

His versions of "Changing Partners," "You Belong to Me," "Silver and Gold," and "Busybody" all ranked as major hits between 1950 and 1955. The Golden West Cowboys also turned out many quality instrumentals which went a long way toward bridging the gap between pop and country sounds as they existed at the time.

In addition to Louisville, Pee Wee and his band also had television shows in Chicago, Cleveland, and Cincinnati. During the 1955 summer season, he had a prime time 9:00 PM ninety-minute program on the ABC network. Originating in Cleveland, the show was a replacement for that of comedian Sid Caesar.

In the mid-fifties, King adapted sound-wise to style changes better than one might have expected. The band even did a spirited cover version of "Blue Suede Shoes" for RCA. While neither he nor his band members ever became rock stars, one can say in retrospect that King did make notable contributions to some of the emerging new waves that were engulfing the musical world in the later fifties.

Through the 1960s, Pee Wee King and Redd Stewart with a smaller band continued to be popular figures on the county fair circuit throughout the Midwest. Their RCA Victor days were behind them, but they continued cutting discs for Starday and even smaller companies like Briar, Cuca, and Jaro. Many of their songs were newer recordings of their earlier hits. A pair of singer-dancers, the Collins Sisters, worked with them for many years, and in the mid-sixties, the band made a movie titled *Country-Western Hoedown.*

From the beginning, Pee Wee took an active part in the affairs of the Country Music Association. His long service included several years on their board of directors, including a term as president. He also took part in a variety of business affairs around Louisville.

Masonically, Brother King moved his Scottish Rite and Shrine memberships to Louisville. He retained his connection with East Nashville Lodge No. 560, where he received his fifty-year pin on August 2, 1993. In 1996, he wrote, "I still attend meetings," without specifying as to which body he referred.

Pee Wee and Lydia reared four children and continued to reside in Louisville where he was a much-respected leading citizen. He did much to elevate respect for his field of entertainment. While he experienced some health problems after reaching his eighties, he managed to turn out a virtual autobiography in collaboration with a Bellarmine College professor, Wade Hall. He could take considerable pride in his career and Masonic achievements prior to his death at eighty-six on March 7, 2000.

**Note:** Those who wish to learn more about Brother King could consult Charles K. Wolfe, *Kentucky Country: Folk and Country Music of* Kentucky (Lexington: University Press of Kentucky, 1982). After this article originally appeared, Wade Hall, *Hell-Bent for Music: The Life of Pee Wee King* (Lexington: University of Kentucky, 1996) came out which is essentially an autobiography. In preparing the original article, I had assistance from Sir Knight Ray Huffines who served as Secretary of East Nashville Lodge, Sir Knight Norman Lincoln of Eaton, Ohio, and Brother Frank "Pee Wee" King, himself who answered all of my questions to the best of his recollection.

October 1994; slightly revised 2011

**Brother Randolph Scott:**
*Riding the Trail Alone*

In 1973, the Statler Brothers recorded a nostalgic song about the Hollywood movie western that touched upon the decline of morality in films. The song was titled "Whatever Happened to Randolph Scott?" The Statlers viewed Scott as a symbol of the better quality cowboy films of an earlier era. As the song's composers, Donald and Harold Reid, well knew, Scott was at the time a hale and hearty 75-year old star who had been retired from the screen for just over a decade. Less known was the fact that the former star had been a Mason for more than fifty years. Unlike many of Hollywood's Masonic celebrities typified by Gene Autry, Ernest Borgnine, and Red Skelton, Scott apparently said little about his Masonic connections—both Blue Lodge and Scottish Rite—which pre-dated his acting career but extended until his death at the age of 89.

George Randolph Scott was born in Orange County, Virginia, on January 23, 1898 (Hollywood publicists would later give him a 1903 birth date). It was later reported that he was born in Virginia only because his mother was there at the time and that the Scott family's home was in Charlotte, North Carolina. His family had prospered in the textile industry. Scott-Charnley, and young George grew up with ideas of a career in textile engineering. He attended Georgia Tech and played football, but after sustaining an injury on the gridiron, he transferred to the University of North Carolina at Chapel Hill where he earned his degree.

Back in Charlotte, Scott petitioned the oldest Masonic lodge in the city, Phalanx No. 31, receiving his Entered Apprentice degree on November 23, 1920. He was subsequently passed to Fellowcraft on April 25, 1921, and was raised a Master Mason on May 3, 1921. Less than two years later, he joined the Scottish Rite bodies in Charlotte receiving his degrees on April 24, 25 and 26, 1923. At the time, he gave his occupation as "accountant" and his place of birth as Mecklenburg County, North Carolina (the locale of Charlotte). Scott's Blue Lodge membership continued uninterrupted for sixty-eight years until his death. He was suspended twice in the Scottish Rite: first from April 28, 1930, until March 10, 1931, and second from December 31, 1934, until January 10, 1940. Nonetheless, he received his 50-year pin in January 1979 and a 60-year Blue Lodge pin on July 31, 1982. Few other movie stars maintained Masonic memberships for a longer period. Only Gene Autry, with sixty-nine years of Masonic connections, comes to mind.

George R. Scott, the Charlotte accountant and textile engineer, apparently had aspirations to become an actor and at the age of thirty set out for Hollywood with a letter of introduction to Howard Hughes. The latter helped him get a role as an unbilled extra in a 1928 Fox film, *Sharp Shooters.* Small parts followed in other films by which time he had dropped his first name and become known simply as Randolph Scott.

The Virginia gentleman had his first starring role in a 1932 Paramount B feature, *Heritage of the Desert*, based on a Zane Grey novel. Over the next three years, he starred in eleven other features based on Zane Grey stories which established him as a solid performer in western roles. As biographer Jefferson Crow explained, "he looked the part" and "he sounded like you would expect a Grey hero to sound."

For Scott's first dozen years or so in the motion picture business, he was not confined to westerns but appeared in a wide variety of cinematic productions, although not usually in the lead role. A few of these included: *Hello Everybody* (1933) in which he plays an agent of a power company who is sent to romance Kate Smith but ends up falling in love with her sister; the Stark Young novel, *So Red the Rose* (1935); and a low-budget thriller, *Murders in the Zoo* (1933). One of his more memorable roles in this era was the Irving Berlin musical, *Follow the Fleet* (1936) in which Scott and Harriet Hilliard had the second leads behind Fred Astaire and Ginger Rogers. He also did two films with child superstar Shirley Temple, *Rebecca of Sunnybrook Farm* (1938) and *Susanna of the Mounties* (1939). Randolph Scott had the lead role in the film version of the frontier epic by James Fenimore Cooper, *Last of the Mohicans* (1936), although not exactly a western. Some critics argue that his role of Hawkeye—more than any other—made him a real star.

As Scott's motion picture career moved forward, his personal life took some twists and turns. After sharing a beach house with another rising star, Cary Grant, in his early years in Hollywood, Scott married Virginia Cherrill in February of 1934. The union soon deteriorated, and the couple divorced just thirteen months later. In 1936, Scott married second wife, Marianne DuPont Somerville. They too split in 1939. In 1944, Scott married for the third time to Marie Patricia Stillman. This marriage terminated only with the star's death forty-three years later. The happy couple subsequently adopted two children, Sandra and Christopher. After Scott's demise, the latter authored an affectionate biography, *Whatever Happened to Randolph Scott?* (1994).

In the later thirties, the actor's career was again dominated by significant roles in westerns. In Paramount's *The Texans* (1938), he starred with Joan Bennett, Walter Brennan, Robert Cummings, and Brother Raymond Hatton (Henry S. Orme Lodge No. 458 in L.A.), an adaptation of Emerson Hough's popular novel of a trail drive, *North of '36*. Hollywood had an era of encounters with historical nonfiction, including films on such real life characters as Jesse James, Wyatt Earp, Belle Starr, and the Dalton Gang. While much of the content was pure imagination, the central personages were real. Tyrone Power and Henry Fonda portrayed the outlaw brothers from Missouri while Scott had the third lead as a fictional sympathetic lawman. In *Frontier Marshal,* an adaptation of Stuart Lake's novel-like biography of Wyatt Earp. Scott had the title role. Opposite the beautiful Gene Tierney as *Belle Starr,* the Virginia-Carolina gentleman portrayed Belle's husband, Sam Starr, remade into a Confederate guerilla leader rather than the horse thief he actually was. *When the Dalton's Rode*, based on the autobiography of surviving ex-outlaw Emmett Dalton, featured Scott as a young lawyer.

During the war years, a string of patriotic films with military heroes dominated the silver screen. While Brother Scott's films never achieved the classic status of those of John Wayne, they remain commendable efforts. *To the Shores of Tripoli* (1942) contrasted Scott as a tough sergeant with a spoiled young recruit John Payne (reputed to be a Mason). *Bombardier, China Sky,* and *Gung Ho!* all supported the cause of saving the world from Fascists and Nazis. Finally, he made a guest appearance in the 1944 Universal musical *Follow the Boys*, about the USO. Scott did not leave westerns behind as he had one of his more memorable roles in the film version of the Rex Beach novel, *The Spoilers,* as the corrupt gold commissioner who loses a memorable knock-down, drag-out fist fight with John Wayne, one of the few major Scott roles as a villain.

After the war, nearly all of Randolph Scott's films were westerns, many of them in color. Unlike the series type B pictures which relied on a formulaic pattern with a low budget and a comic sidekick, Scott's films had bigger budgets in which the hero was often something of a "loner" with a "past." Several had Scott playing opposite some of Hollywood's main-stream leading ladies of the era such as *Trail Street* and *Return of the Badmen,* both in 1947 and with Anne Jeffreys; *Abilene Town* (1946) with Rhonda Fleming; *Hangman's Knot* (1952) with Donna Reed; *Man in the Saddle* (1951) with Joan Leslie; *Tall Man Riding* (1955) with Dorothy Malone; and *Decision at Sundown* (1957) with Karen Steele. While remembered as a comic sidekick for Hopalong Cassidy in the TV series, Brother Edgar Buchanan of Eugene, Oregon Lodge No. 11 did make appearances in five Scott pictures. Film critics have often suggested that much of the quality and success in Brother Scott's movies can be credited to the presence of Harry Joe Brown as either director or producer in many of them. Another veteran director who worked well with Scott, Budd Boetticher, also was in many of his films.

Randolph Scott's film career wound down in the early sixties. *Comanche Station* with Nancy Gates and Claude Akins was well-received, and Scott had intended to retire when it was finished early in 1960. Two year later, however, he chose to do one more picture, co-starring with another Hollywood veteran, Joel McCrea in *Ride the High Country.* The two play veteran law officers with Scott planning to steal the gold shipment the two are guarding. In the end, Randolph cannot turn his back on an old friend McCrea and ultimately survives and does his duty. Film historian, William Everson, called it "not only one of the best westerns of the sixties, but one of the best from any period."

After *Ride the High Country,* George Randolph Scott retired from the motion picture screen at the age of sixty-four. He lived on for another quarter century passing to the "celestial lodge above" on March 2, 1987. According to son, Chris, he enjoyed playing golf, spending time with his family, and tending his investments which apparently made him one of Hollywood's more affluent actors, attending the All-Saints Episcopal Church most Sundays, and making the most of a privacy that he had always treasured. Conservative in both philosophy and lifestyle, he made the acquaintance of politicians like Dwight Eisenhower and Richard Nixon, evangelist Billy Graham, and a few show business celebrities such as Fred Astaire, Freeman Gosden, Cary Grant, and Donna Reed.

Unlike many Masonic actors, he apparently did not join the Shrine, and seemingly few were aware of his long-time membership in the order which ultimately totaled sixty-eight years in Phalanx Lodge and fifty-eight years in the Valley of Charlotte.

In declining health in his last few months, he passed away after his 89th birthday. He was survived by wife, Patricia, and children, Sandra and Chris. His remains were returned to Charlotte and interred in Elmwood Cemetery.

As a motion picture star, Randolph Scott may not have quite attained the legendary status of either a John Wayne or a Clark Gable, but within the ranks of western movie stars, a work by film historian Boyd Magers, *Top 100 Cowboys of the Century*, rated Scott in eleventh place, behind such popular legends as John Wayne, Gene Autry, Roy Rogers, and Tom Mix but ahead of such figures as Audie Murphy, Johnny Mack Brown, and Hoot Gibson. According to Magers, "The Gentleman from Virginia personified the pioneer spirit of America." Another critic, Kalton C. Lahue, wrote in *Riders of the Range* (1973), "Randolph Scott was an accomplished actor" and "he brought a dimension to his roles [that the B-western stars] were unable to muster." As such, Scott ranks among the more accomplished Masons in his profession.

**Note**: The most accessible biographical material on Scott are Jefferson Brim Crow III, *Randolph Scott: A Film Biography* (1994) and the family memoir, C. H. Scott, *Whatever Happened to Randolph Scott?* (1994). For his Masonic records I am indebted to Walter J. Klein of Charlotte who first called attention to Randolph Scott's Masonic connection in "The Accountant on West Tenth Street" in *The Scottish Rite Journal*, October 2002, p. 55. Further data was supplied by the staff of the Grand Lodge of North Carolina in Raleigh and Managing Editor Dr. John Boettjer of *The Scottish Rite Journal.* I also appreciate the aid of Brother Bobby Copeland and Brother Jerry Douglass of the respective Valleys of Knoxville and Little Rock.

August 2003; slightly revised 2011

**Brother Rex Allen:**
*The Arizona Masonic Cowboy*

Several of the Hollywood western movie heroes were Masons including one of the younger ones. Rex Allen, nicknamed the "Arizona Cowboy," ranked as the youngest of the breed and had more of a ranching background than the others. Arriving on the scene more than a decade after the veterans Gene Autry, Tex Ritter, and Roy Rogers had become stars, he made fewer films than the others and had fewer hit records but nonetheless sustained a long career and had many successful songs on the Mercury and Decca labels.

Rex Allen was born in Willcox, Arizona, on December 31, 1920, with the name Elvie Allen. The "Rex" came a little later as Rex Bell, an early thirties cowboy star, became one of his mother's favorites. Besides, as Allen later put it, "Elvie is a lousy name for show business." The Arizona Cowboy spent his early years on a small ranch about forty miles from town. Hard work and tragedy were facts of life for the Allens. Rex's baby sister died from a childhood illness, and his older brother Wayne died from a rattlesnake bite. After that, the family moved into Willcox for a time and then to a ranch about four miles from town. Not long after, Rex's mother, Faye Clark Allen, died from blood poisoning. Horace Allen, with the help of his mother-in-law, managed to hold the family together. Later he remarried and had two additional daughters.

Horace Allen was an old-time fiddler, and he got Rex a guitar so he could provide accompaniment for him at the local dances. Rex learned to sing the songs he had heard on recordings by Jimmie Rodgers, Gene Autry, Carson Robison, and the Carter Family. Sometimes he could earn as much as $1.50 in tips at the Willcox barber shop on a Saturday. Rex also involved himself in musical activities at church and school but resisted efforts at the latter to convert him into a serious vocalist. Young Allen continued to prefer country and cowboy songs.

Rex's dad ran into problems with the cattle business about 1934 when drought and the Great Depression about finished him. After that, Horace entered the plastering trade. Rex went to Phoenix with him after high school and became a hod carrier. There he met another plasterer who eventually gained fame and wealth as New York Yankee owner Del Webb. On Saturdays, Allen obtained a little radio show on station KOY where he became friends with an announcer who later became Governor of Arizona, Jack Williams. Rex also had some ideas about becoming a rodeo cowboy but didn't have much success.

In 1939, Rex decided to bum around the country for a time, hoping to land a regular job in radio. Lynn Davis, an announcer at WHIS in Bluefield, West Virginia, recalls that he worked there for a few days. Finally he landed a regular spot at WTTM in Trenton, New Jersey. The pay was minimal, and with a war on, Allen worked in a rubber mill on the night shift. He later moved up north a bit by landing a spot at WCAU Philadelphia with the Sleepy Hollow Gang as a fiddler and harmony singer in their trio. This enabled him to become a full-time entertainer, but Rex wanted more. Roy Acuff helped him get an audition at the *Grand Ole Opry*, but they had just hired Eddy Arnold for their vacancy. An established star couple, Lulubelle and Scotty Wiseman, did better for him with the *National Barn Dance*, and in 1945 Rex moved to Chicago and station WLS. As Rex pointed out, the Windy City was home to many network radio shows, and when he got on those programs, his income shot upward.

Rex spent four and one-half years in Chicago and did very well there. He met his wife Bonnie Linder, and they married in 1946. The young singer also signed a contract with Mercury Records. During his years at WLS, Allen played shows throughout the five-state area blanketed by the station's powerful signal. The traveling was a grueling experience, but Rex was young and enjoying the fruits of musical stardom. He had an operation to correct the crossed vision that had troubled him from childhood, and his eldest son Rex, Jr., was born there on August 23, 1947.

The *National Barn Dance* had earlier provided Gene Autry with a steppingstone to Hollywood stardom, and in 1949, it did the same thing for Rex Allen. Both Gene Autry and Roy Rogers, whom he had met on tours, had mentioned this as a possibility; Autry in 1947 when he prepared to depart from Republic and Rogers when he began to look ahead to departing from that studio. Rex did not begin to think seriously about a film career until contacted by Republic executive, Herbert Yates. Since Rex had a rather substantial income from network radio, he managed to negotiate a better initial contract arrangement with Yates than either Gene or Roy who had come in during the Great Depression when a $75.00 weekly salary seemed good.

The Allen family moved to California in the latter part of 1949, and Rex began receiving a star buildup months before his first movie, *The Arizona Cowboy*, was even made, let alone released. By the end of 1950, he had a total of four pictures under his belt and had made a guest spot in a Rogers film. By the end of 1950, Monte Hale had made his last pictures for Republic, and in 1951, Roy Rogers made his final movie for the Yates-controlled studio. Only Rocky Lane of the action cowboys and Rex Allen remained at a studio that once had a half-dozen or more series stars in their stable at one time. Rex continued with his series until early 1954 as the star in nineteen singing cowboy features.

During the period from 1951 to 1959, Rex was enough of a household word among the youth of America that Dell published a *Rex Allen Comics*. After his motion picture series ended, Allen appeared in a few other films in later years, most notably *The Secret of Navajo Cave* in 1976.

Like the other motion pictures in the B Western class, a certain number of recurring figures appeared in the Rex Allen films. By the second picture, Rex had obtained a quality horse named Koko, nicknamed "the miracle horse of the movies." After some early fluctuations in sidekicks, the studio used Buddy Ebsen in five and then Slim Pickens in the last eleven. Mary Ellen Kay was leading lady in six of his features, the only girl to appear more than once. The Republic Rhythm Riders provided musical support in several of the Allen films.

Rex Allen's Masonic career got underway shortly after his life as a Republic film hero came to a close. His last starring feature, *The Phantom Stallion*, was copyrighted in February of 1954, and that August 6th he took his Entered Apprentice Degree in Hollywood Lodge No. 355. Subsequently passed to the degree of Fellowcraft on April 20, 1955, Rex Elvie Allen was raised a Master Mason on May 26, 1955. Recalling his entry into the fraternity some thirty-four years afterward, the Arizona Cowboy reminisced that fellow Masons Gene Autry, Tex Ritter, and Roy Rogers had signed his petition. Ritter, a fairly new Mason himself at the time, along with western singer Tex Williams, another member of Hollywood No. 355, had helped him learn his memory examinations. Ritter also took part in his "raising."

Rex's career as a movie cowboy may have been on the wane, but his singing career continued unabated. He had switched from Mercury to Decca in 1952 and the next year had a major hit with "Crying in the Chapel." He kept busy with a touring and rodeo schedule and remained a popular attraction. On his travels, Rex often used guitarist Speedy Haworth and fiddler Wade Ray (a Mason and Shriner) as support musicians.

In 1958, Allen filmed a syndicated television program titled *Frontier Doctor.* Rex played the lead role of Dr. Bill Baxter. The producers filmed thirty-nine of the half-hour dramas, and the series thrived for several years, keeping his name before the public.

In 1961, Rex returned to his original record label Mercury and in 1962 scored another major hit with "Don't Go Near the Indians." The story song concerned an Indian boy who had been stolen and reared by a white family and subsequently fell in love with his Indian maid sister. Later he had another contract with Decca, making the last of his seven appearances on the *Billboard* charts in 1968 with his rendition of "Tiny Bubbles." Rex also recorded extensively with Buena Vista as well as for smaller companies.

During the sixties, Allen did a good deal of narration work for Walt Disney in both nature films and for the Disney television programs. By his own estimate, Rex did about 150 TV programs for Disney. He also did narrations on the movies, *The Legend of Lobo* in 1962 and The *Incredible Journey* in 1963. Motion picture historian Leonard Mattin in his book, *The Disney Films* (1973) wrote "Allen . . . became a Disney favorite in the 1960s and with good reason. His friendly easygoing approach to the script brings a great deal of life to any subject, and the musical interpolations are a welcome change of pace."

Back in 1951 when Rex's career as a movie hero was really taking off, folks back in Willcox initiated Rex Allen Days as a community event and rodeo to honor their hometown hero. The event continues to attract numerous fans and is held each year in late September. There is also a Rex Allen Museum in Willcox which contains some Masonic mementos in addition to other Allen items.

Rex continued in Masonry. For a brief period (1964-1965), he held a dual membership in Conejo Valley Lodge No. 807 in Thousand Oaks. In November of 1970 he took the Scottish Rite degrees in the

Valley of Pasadena and the Shrine, December 5, 1970. John Wayne also took his degrees at the same time. A dozen residents of Willcox and Tucson journeyed to Los Angeles for the Al Malaikah Winter ceremonial degree work. Allen and the Arizonians became members of the Sabbar Shrine Temple in Tucson. Some years later, Rex along with Gene Autry, Roy Rogers, and Burl Ives were all honored for their efforts on behalf of Masonic and Shrine charities. Of his Lodge activity Rex wrote in his autobiography that "I think my association as a Mason has made a better man out of me." He concluded, "I'll be one 'til I die."

By the nineties, the Arizona Cowboy had pretty much retired. He made an occasional appearance at a Western Film Fair and in 1989 published his autobiography. In 1998, Rex Allen was living near Tucson, Arizona, and forty-three years after his raising he remained on the rolls of Hollywood Lodge No. 355. Rex Allen passed away on December 17, 1999, when his ranch caretaker accidentally ran over him, a sad end to a noteworthy career. The last of the Hollywood singing cowboys—like his forebears Gene, Roy, and Tex—had been a distinguished Mason in the world of American entertainment.

**Note**: The best source of information about Rex Allen is his autobiography, *The Arizona Cowboy: My Life, Sunrise to Sunset* (Scottsdale, AZ: RexGarRuss Press, 1989). For Allen's Masonic record I am indebted to John L. Cooper, III and Eileen M. Irby at the Grand Lodge of California and to Joan Sansbury, Librarian at the A.A.S.R., S.J. in Washington. Thanks also to Abby Gail Goodnite Ehman for student aid and word processing.

June 1999; slightly revised 2011

**Brother Robert C. Byrd:**
*Mountain State Senator and Fiddler*

In the past half century, few members of the United States Senate wielded more influence than West Virginia's Robert Byrd. At various times during the seventies and eighties, he held the positions of majority whip, majority leader, and minority leader. Described by both friends and foes as one of the hardest workers in the Senate, Byrd had also honed his musical skills in his spare moments and won sufficient acclaim as a traditional fiddler to record an album of old-time tunes and appear as a guest on the "Grand Ole Opry."

Byrd spent many of his early years in relative poverty. He was born Cornelius Calvin Sale, Jr. in North Wilkesboro, North Carolina, on November 20, 1917. The future Senator's mother died in the influenza epidemic a few months later. His father then sent the infant to live in West Virginia with his aunt and uncle, Vlurma and Titus Dalton Byrd. His adoptive parents renamed him Robert Carlyle Byrd. Oddly enough, until he was fifty-four, Byrd believed that his birth date had been January 15, 1918. This date appears on his Masonic records and early biographical sketches.

Life in the West Virginia coalfields—with a shrinking bituminous market—could be difficult in the twenties and even rougher in the Great Depression. Nonetheless, in those years, young Byrd managed to get through high school, graduating first in his class in 1934. During those bleak days, Byrd took up the fiddle, learning the instrument from listening to local mountain fiddlers and to records by the Kessinger Brothers. Charleston's Clark Kessinger (1896-1975) was already on his way to legendary status with his fiddle, and he set the standard by which other fiddlers would be judged. The fiddle and school work provided about the only pleasant moments in a youth otherwise dominated by hard times. Robert recalled that in some years no one in the family received anything for Christmas and that he had only one toy during his entire childhood.

With no money for college, Bob Byrd labored first in a gas station and then in a grocery store. Learning the meat cutter's trade, he obtained regular employment as a butcher, and by the end of the thirties, his earnings had climbed to $65.00 per month. Meanwhile, in 1936 he married Erma James, and they subsequently reared two daughters. Old timers in the Beckley area recalled that he might also fiddle at a local dance and do a tune or two with the musicians at local radio station WJLS.

When World War II broke out, Byrd went to Baltimore, Maryland, and worked in the shipyards as a welder. Returning to Raleigh County in 1945, Robert Byrd opened his own grocery in the town of Sophia and also taught a Bible class in the local Baptist church. The latter became so popular that a local radio station soon carried his lectures. In 1946 he ran for and was elected to the West Virginia House of Delegates. Later he won a seat in the state senate. Always interested in self-improvement, the young legislator took college classes at Morris Harvey (now the University of Charleston) and also at Marshall University in Huntington

In 1952, Bob Byrd moved up the political ladder and sought a seat in Congress. One of his primary opponents uncovered the fact that Byrd had briefly belonged to the Ku Klux Klan, but the candidate acknowledged his error as a "mistake of youth" and pressed forward with his campaign. That fall, the voters in the staunchly Democratic Sixth District sent the former grocer-meat cutter to Washington with a 57% vote majority. Fiddlin' Bob Byrd, as Mountain State newspapers sometimes called him in those days, went on to serve three terms in the House. A vocal critic of the Eisenhower Administration, the West Virginia Democrat generally took liberal positions on economics and labor issues but ranked more conservative on social and foreign policy questions. Still interested in self improvement, he took courses at both George Washington and American Universities, eventually obtaining his law degree from the latter institution in 1963.

Back home in West Virginia, Byrd who had already become a member of several fraternal organizations including the Elks, Moose, Knights of Pythias, and Odd Fellows, petitioned Mountain Lodge No. 156 in Coal City (Sophia had no blue lodge). He received his Entered Apprentice degree on July 6, 1957. Six months later on

December 5, he was passed to the degree of Fellowcraft and on January 2, 1958, the lodge brethren raised Robert Carlyle Byrd to the sublime degree of Master Mason. Four months later on April 24, 1958, he completed the Scottish Rite degrees in John W. Morris Consistory in Charleston. More Masonic honors would come his way in later years.

With three House terms under his belt, Robert Byrd in 1958 chose to seek a seat in the United States Senate. Long-time West Virginia Democratic Senators, Brother Harley M. Kilgore and Brother Matthew M. Neely, had died in 1956 and 1958 respectively. The generally-weak West Virginia GOP had experienced a good year in 1956 when Eisenhower carried the state and Brother Cecil Underwood won the governorship while old-guard isolationist conservative Chapman Revercomb, who had earlier served a term in the Senate (1943-1949), won the race to complete Kilgore's term. However, by 1958 Revercomb seemed especially vulnerable. Byrd defeated the aging Republican by a comfortable 118,000 vote margin and never faced serious opposition thereafter. At the time of his death, Byrd was midway through his ninth term.

In his early years as a Senator, Byrd initially became a protégé of Lyndon Johnson and then Georgia's Brother Richard Russell. By 1961, he had become Chairman of the Senate Appropriations subcommittee on the District of Columbia, where he took a strong stand on law and order issues and initially opposed self-government for the nation's capital, although he later shifted his position on the latter. A staunch anti-Communist on foreign policy questions, the Mountain State Senator supported the Viet Nam conflict and initially condemned anti-war demonstrators. By the end of the sixties, he had sufficient standing with the Nixon Administration to be seriously considered for a Supreme Court judgeship. In 1971, Byrd defeated Teddy Kennedy for the position of majority whip. After that, Byrd tended to follow the party line more than before but still displayed occasional streaks of independence.

Meanwhile more Masonic honors came Robert Byrd's way. On October 3, 1967, the Southern Jurisdiction of the Scottish Rite elected him to receive the KCCH, and on October 6, 1967, he also received the 33°. A decade later on October 13, 1977, he was chosen to receive the Grand Cross.

A full recap of Senator Byrd's career cannot be really be undertaken in a brief article of this nature, so the following does little more than hit the high points. After six years as majority whip, the

West Virginia solon succeeded Mike Mansfield as Senate majority leader, a post he retained throughout the Carter presidency. With the election of Ronald Reagan to the White House and a GOP Senate takeover after November of 1980, Byrd became minority leader for the next six years until the Democrats recovered control in January of 1987. After two more years as majority leader, the Mountain State Senator relinquished his position at age seventy-one but continued to hold his Senate seat. In terms of Senate service—if not in age—he eventually passed the record-setting J. Strom Thurmond as having sat in the Senate longer than anyone.

During the late seventies and early eighties, Byrd also gained new attention for his fiddling skills. County Records, a Floyd, Virginia-based company oriented toward traditional music, released an album entitled "Mountain Fiddler" in 1978 (re-released in 2010). Critics generally applauded the effort, and it allegedly became County's all-time best seller. The Senator made an appearance on the *Grand Ole Opry* where he was introduced by another fiddler (and lifelong Republican) Sir Knight Roy Acuff. Byrd also recorded seven reels of fiddle music for the Library of Congress and appeared at several public functions as a musician. In 1983 he spoke at the 50th anniversary of Wheeling, West Virginia's longtime show, "Jamboree, USA," where this writer met him and had an opportunity to thank the Senator for writing the forward for his book, *Mountaineer Jamboree: Country Music in West Virginia.* He spoke of recording another album but never did.

Even after Brother Byrd passed his ninetieth birthday, he remained a prominent and powerful figure in the Senate. Like all politicians, he had his critics, particularly outside of West Virginia. His channeling of large amounts of federal funds into his state has been a sore spot with those outside of the Mountain State. In West Virginia there are many bridges, highways, and buildings named for him. A zealous guardian of Senate privilege, he became a fierce critic of the line-item veto enacted by a GOP Congress and signed by President Clinton (later overturned by the Supreme Court).

Robert Byrd's political career ended with his death on June 28, 2010. As a man of humble origins who climbed high on the ladder of success, he had but few equals. Among prominent Masons in the second half of the twentieth century, Byrd is among the most significant. Like such noted past Masonic members of the Senate as Henry Clay, Stephen Douglas, Robert LaFollette, and Everett Dirksen, Robert Carlyle Byrd took his place among the giants of American politics.

**Note**: I wish to express my appreciation to the staff of the Grand Lodge of West Virginia and Ms. Joan Sansbury of the AASR Library in Washington, DC for Senator Byrd's Masonic Record. Biographical data comes from the two entries in *Current Biography*. The photo came from the Senator. The original typescript was by Shasta Amos Blankenship.

May 1999; slightly revised 2011

## Sir Knight Robert H. Jackson:
*Supreme Court Judge and Prosecutor at Nuremberg*

In 2003, William E. Leuchtenburg, a well-known historian of the New Deal Era, wrote "Robert Houghwout Jackson is the most important public figure of the twentieth century no one has ever heard of." This may be something of an exaggeration as he is a familiar name to legal scholars and mid-century historians, yet he is forgotten among the general populace. In his day Sir Knight Jackson served in a presidential cabinet, on the United States Supreme Court, and perhaps most significant of all, as United States Chief Prosecutor of Nazi war criminals.

Robert Jackson was born in Spring Creek, Pennsylvania, on February 13, 1892, to William E. and Angelina Jackson. As a child, the family moved to Frewsburg, New York. After high school, the youth went to work as a clerk for an attorney cousin and prominent Democrat in nearby Jamestown. Although he later attended law school in Albany for a year, Robert was essentially a product of a vanishing system whereby one studied law as an apprentice for another lawyer. During his time in Albany, he made the acquaintance of a young state senator and Mason named Franklin D. Roosevelt. After passing his bar exams in 1913, Jackson began to practice law and within a few years became one of Jamestown's, and indeed far western New York's, leading barristers. He also became somewhat active in Democratic politics and bar association activities. Throughout his law career, he kept a caption on his wall with a quote from Brother Rudyard Kipling that read, "He travels fastest who travels alone," a phrase he exemplified in the progress of his own life. In 1916, Robert married Irene Gerhardt and the couple subsequently had a son and a daughter.

During his years in Jamestown, Robert H. Jackson became a member of Mount Moriah Lodge No. 145. He received his degrees on September 17, October 1, and October 22, 1929. In November of 1930,

Jackson took the Scottish Rite degrees in the Valley of Jamestown, New York. He also joined the York Rite bodies in Jamestown, including Jamestown Commandery No. 61. In 2001, his framed Knight Templar sword had an honored spot in the Jamestown Masonic Temple. He ranks with cartoonist Brad Anderson, creator of the Great Dane with a human mind set, Marmaduke, as Jametown's most famous Mason to the outside world.

Brother Bob Jackson began his political life when Franklin Delano Roosevelt was elected Governor of the Empire State in November of 1928, becoming a key advisor to FDR. Nonetheless, he remained in western New York until FDR entered the White House. In February of 1934, he took a position as general counsel in the Treasury Department, a job that concerned litigation in tax collecting. It was in this circumstance that he led in a civil suit against Brother Andrew Mellon, a super-wealthy former Republican Secretary of the Treasury, on charges of underpayment of taxes. This high-profile case led to a March 1936 promotion and transfer to the Justice Department as an assistant attorney general in the Tax Division and still later in charge of the Antitrust Division. In these jobs, Jackson argued cases before the Supreme Court.

In March of 1938, Jackson was appointed Solicitor General. From that point on, he was often seen as on the fast track for higher rewards within the administration. Associate Justice Louis D. Brandeis observed that he should be made Solicitor General for life. Meanwhile, for a time, pundits saw the New Yorker as a possible future governor of New York and even as a potential president. The chief's top political advisor, Jim Farley, argued that Jackson was insufficiently known. Roosevelt himself eventually concluded that Jackson was too much of a gentleman to be a successful candidate, but he still remained in serious contention for higher appointments.

Three times Robert Jackson was rated as a serious candidate for Supreme Court consideration. Three times he was passed over for the Supreme Court, first by Felix Frankfurter, second by Brother William O. Douglas, and then by Attorney General Frank Murphy. The latter appointment, however, led to Jackson being named to the cabinet in January of 1940 as a replacement for Murphy. A little over a year later Chief Justice Hughes retired, and the President subsequently elevated Justice Harlan F. Stone as his replacement and then named Jackson as the new Associate Justice.

In his early years on the High Court, Jackson found himself having to make some challenging decisions, balancing the needs of national security and civil liberties. When the national interest was not at stake as in the famous case of "West Virginia State Board of Education v. Barnette" (1943), he came down forcefully on the side of liberty. For those who may have forgotten, this was the famous case that held that one could not be required to salute the flag if it conflicted with his or her religious views. Yet free speech should also have its limits. In a case that might be worth revisiting in more recent times, Jackson held in a dissenting opinion in the case of "Terminiello v. Chicago" (1949) that "if the court does not temper its doctrinaire logic with a little practical wisdom, it will convert the constitutional *Bill of Rights* into a suicide pact."

Although a staunch New Dealer, some court observers began to think that Judges Jackson and Felix Frankfurter had moved more toward the center of the legal philosophical spectrum while Hugo Black, William O. Douglas, and Franklin Murphy remained committed liberals. In fact, Black and Jackson had an uneasy relationship for a few years in the later forties although they remained outwardly civil. Perhaps it was because of this difference that Jackson jumped at the opportunity to take a leave of absence from the high court to serve as chief prosecutor at the Nuremberg trials. He subsequently described this duty as "infinitely more important than my work on the Supreme Court." In his closing speech in July of 1946, Jackson made the eloquent conclusion that if "you were to say of these men that they are not guilty, it would be as true to say that there has been no war, there are no slain, there has been no crime." While his overall performance was not without criticism, it did result in nineteen convictions and three acquittals.

Chief Justice Stone had died in April of 1946. Jackson apparently felt disappointed that President Truman named his Treasury Secretary, Brother Fred Vinson of Louisa, Kentucky, to lead the Court and probably thought that his quarrel with Black might have been responsible. Nonetheless, he returned to the fall term of the Court in October and generally maintained a discreet silence in his public pronouncements concerning his views on the Alabama judge. One might add that there were other Masons on the Court in those years besides Jackson and Vinson. They included Hugo Black, William O. Douglas, Sherman Minton, Harold Burton, Tom Clark, and after Vinson's death, Sir Knight Earl Warren.

Jackson's significant judicial decisions in those latter years included his upholding the 1949 conviction of Communist Party leaders in "Dennis v. United States" in 1951, coupled with his dissent in government efforts to inquire about private thoughts of suspected Communists in 1950 in "American Communications Ass'n v. Douds." Put simply, Jackson upheld the right of Communists (or anyone else) to think as they wished, but not to actually "advocate the overthrow of the government." In another important 1952 decision, he concurred with a Court majority in its invalidation of government seizure of private steel mills during the Korean War in "Youngstown Sheet & Tube Co. v. Sawyer."

In what may have been the most significant case of the mid-century, "Brown v. Board of Education" (1954), Jackson had some doubts but ultimately joined in the unanimous verdict. He had been hospitalized but was present when the Court reached the monumental decision on May 17 to overturn the old decision rendered in "Plessey v. Ferguson" (1896) and outlawed segregated public schools. Ironically, by that time Jackson had increasingly leaned toward what became termed the doctrine of "judicial restraint." Jackson himself realized that this may have seemed at variance with his earlier endorsement of FDR's 1937 court reform plan, but nearly two decades of experience had tested and altered his philosophy These later theories were exercised in practice by Jackson's law clerk in the early fifties, William H. Rehnquist, who as a protégé spent some thirty years on the Federal Bench including nearly two decades as Chief Justice.

Sir Knight and Justice Jackson died a few months later on October 9, 1954, after suffering a second heart attack. While his fame may not be as great as many of his fellow judges, his significance is no less a celebrated one. His court opinions have been cited as among the most eloquent and well-reasoned in court history. This alone would lend strong support to William Leuchtenberg's view expressed at the beginning of this article.

**Note**: A full-length biography of the judge is Eugene C. Gerhardt, *America's Advocate: Robert H. Jackson* (1958). More useful for this brief article is the sketch by Douglas P. Woodlock in *American National Biography* (2000), and the introduction by William Leuchtenberg to Jackson's *That Man: An Insider's View of Franklin Roosevelt* (2003), published nearly a half-century after his death. Jackson's blue lodge, Scottish Rite and Shrine record is found in William R. Denslow, "10,000 Famous Freemasons" (1958), II, p. 286. Jerome Erickson, Nicholas Andin, and Robert Cave have been helpful in their search for his still incomplete York Rite records.

September 2008; slightly revised 2011

## Rod Cameron:
*Silver Screen Cowboy and Once a Mason*

Someone once described Rod Cameron as "the poor man's John Wayne." Like the "Duke," Cameron was a rugged, handsome, and able actor who proved ideal for he-man type action films. While Rod became a star, his stature never approached that of Wayne's. Among the unusual twists that Rod's life took, none quite equaled the fact that he became one of the few men in history who also married his mother-in-law. Also Cameron's Masonic membership did not endure until his death for reasons that are now likely to remain unknown. Nonetheless, he was a well-known Mason in the entertainment world for nearly two decades.

Cameron was born Roderick Nathan Cox in Calgary, Alberta, Canada, on December 7, 1910. His father was a mechanical engineer and moved back east to Toronto two years later where the family lived until 1925 when Robert Cox passed away. The surviving Coxes then moved to New York, and Rod finished high school in White Plains where he participated in sports and amateur theatrics.

As a teenager, Rod Cox allegedly aspired to become a member of Canada's famed Northwest Mounted Police, but some type of injury kept him from qualifying. At any rate, he went to work chiefly as a construction laborer, an occupation he pursued for roughly a decade. Somewhere during this period he moved to California and began aspiring to break into pictures. After several tries, he landed a small part in a Bette Davis film at Warner Brothers called *The Old Maid*. Although Rod "Cameron," as he was now known, received a screen credit, his scenes were actually cut out of the film. Rod then spent three years at Paramount as a contractee, playing mostly bit parts.

In 1943, the Rod Cameron star began to rise when he landed the role of Rex Bennett in a pair of adventure serials at Republic, *G-*

*Men vs. The Black Dragon* and *Secret Service in Darkest Africa*. Both proved highly popular and Cameron started to get better roles and was soon signed to a long-term contract at Universal. At this studio he played the lead role in a series of six B westerns, typified by Boss of *Boomtown* and *Trigger Trail*, while playing support roles in other films.

Finally in 1945, Rod got his big break, starring opposite Yvonne DeCarlo in *Salome, Where She Danced*, in a big budget technicolor feature. This film elevated Rod to true star status and led to two more starring pictures with Miss DeCarlo, *Frontier Gal*, and *River Lady*. He also starred in *Pirates of Monterrey* with the late Maria Montez.

Over the next two decades, Rod Cameron's stock in trade became medium budget adventure films—mostly but not exclusively westerns. This placed him in a category with George Montgomery, Audie Murphy, and Randolph Scott. Discussion of all these films would encompass excessive space and only a few examples are included: *Stampede* with Gale Storm (1949), *Southwest Passage* with Joanne Dru (1954), *Hell's Outpost* with Joan Leslie (1954), and *Santa Fe Passage* with Faith Domergue (1955). Non-western adventures included *The Sea Hornet* with Adrian Booth (1951) and *The Jungle* with Marie Windsor (1952). In all, Cameron starred in about three dozen of these adventure films.

Rod also starred in three syndicated television series during the fifties. The first in 1953, *City Detective,* saw him in the title role as Bart Grant of the NYPD. Most successful was *State Trooper* from 1957 to 1959; its concern was the Nevada State Police, and it lasted through one hundred and forty half-hour segments. The last, *Coronado 9* in 1959, featured Rod as a private eye. He was also a guest on numerous TV shows over the years.

Rod Cameron's Masonic life began on April 4, 1949, in Metropolitan Lodge No. 646 in Los Angeles. He was passed a Fellowcraft on February 21, 1950, and was Raised a Master Mason on April 18, 1950. He took the Scottish Rite degrees in the Valley of Los Angeles on June 14-19, 1951. He subsequently became a Noble of Al Malaikai Shrine Temple. He remained a member of these bodies for the rest of the fifties and through most of the next decade. He was suspended NPD from the A.A.S.R. on March 1, 1968, and from Metropolitan Lodge on November 4, 1969. As usual, the record is silent as to why this happened. He apparently never sought reinstatement.

Regarding his personal life, Cameron married Doris Stanford, a church organist, about 1937. This marriage failed as did a second one to Angela Alves-Lico in 1950. This union produced a son named Anthony in 1954. Later in 1960, Rod married Angela's mother, Dorothy Alves-Lico. This marriage endured until Cameron died some twenty-three years later.

Rod Cameron made his last movie appearance in 1978 in a forgotten film with the unlikely title of *Love and the Midnight Auto Supply*. He later retired and moved to Georgia where his son was a baseball player. The one-time silver screen cowboy and former member of Metropolitan Lodge No. 646 died on December 21, 1983, a few months after a visit to the Charlotte, North Carolina Film Fair.

**Note**: The chapter on Rod Cameron in *Buck Rainey's Heroes of the Range* (Waynesville, NC: World of Yesterday 1987) contains a brief biography. For his Masonic history I am indebted to John Cooper, David Dresser, Eileen Irby, and Joan Sansbury. Abby Goodnite prepared the original manuscript.

May 2000; slightly revised 2011

## Sir Knight Roy Acuff:
*King of Country Music*

Articles in *Knight Templar* have focused on the careers of well-known figures from the entertainment world such as cowboy actor Tom Mix and band conductor John Philip Sousa. This narrative reviews the life and accomplishments of an east Tennessee mountain boy who also made good. Roy Claxton Acuff rose from humble beginnings to become known as the "King of Country Music." In a career that spanned some sixty years, Acuff performed on Nashville's *Grand Ole Opry* for more than half a century, sold millions of records, and starred in several motion pictures. Casual fans will remember him for popularizing songs like "The Great Speckled Bird," "Wabash Cannonball," "The Precious Jewel," and "Wreck on the Highway."

Born on September 15, 1903, near Maynardville, Tennessee, Roy Acuff's father was a struggling Missionary Baptist minister who later studied law and became a county judge. Grandfather Acuff had fought for the Union during the Civil War, and Roy would reflect his "mountain Yankee" and Southern mountain Republican values throughout his life. While Roy absorbed much of the rich Appalachian culture during his youth which would later be reflected in his own music, the young Acuff manifested more interest in baseball and other sports. When his father moved the family to the Knoxville suburb of Fountain City in 1919, Roy belatedly entered junior high and then high school, graduating from Knoxville Central High in 1924. Athletics constituted his principal interests in those days, and he lettered in baseball, basketball, and football.

After graduation, Roy worked as a callboy for the Louisville and Nashville Railroad and played semipro baseball until he was felled by sunstroke in 1929. He spent many months recovering his health and vigor, during which time he listened to early country phonograph records and learned to play the fiddle. By 1932, Acuff had emerged from convalescence and toured for several months with the Mocoton Medicine Show. When this valuable experience ended, he formed a band—the Crazy Tennesseans—which performed alternately over WNOX and WROL radio stations in Knoxville. The group played shows throughout the little towns and villages of East Tennessee but barely earned enough cash to survive in those Depression days.

In October of 1936, the Crazy Tennesseans journeyed to Chicago where they made their initial twenty recordings for the American Record Corporation (absorbed into Columbia in 1938). Among these numbers was a religious lyric of obscure origins, "The Great Speckle Bird," which would ultimately become his signature song. Although none of the tunes could be classed as immediate hits, they sold well enough for the band to be recalled for additional sessions in March of 1937 and November of 1938. Ironically, some of the material recorded was somewhat uptown country arrangements of pop songs with various band members doing the singing, but the numbers with Roy's lead vocal and the rough-edged hard country sound went over better.

In the meantime, Roy moved his band from Knoxville to Nashville where they joined the cast of the *Grand Ole Opry* at WSM radio. The shift would prove a wise move in terms of being in the right place at the right time. The *Opry* had been a popular radio show since it had started in November of 1925, but portions of it began to be carried via a regional network in 1939 and then nationally by NBC in 1941. Furthermore, the country music scene had increasingly shifted from an emphasis on string bands and vocal duets toward individual solo stars. Uncle Dave Macon, the reigning individual Opry star, continued as a popular and revered figure, but at age seventy in 1940, he was a bit elderly to capture the younger audience. Acuff, who looked younger than he actually was, could and did hold this group. Older country folk, however, found his sentimental mountain ballads such as "The Precious Jewel" and moralistic warnings like "Wreck on the Highway" to their liking as well as the numerous sacred songs in his repertoire. By the end of 1940, he stood at the top in his field and remained there for several years thereafter.

In 1940, Roy Acuff took his band—renamed the Smoky Mountain Boys when he came to Nashville—to Hollywood for their first film *Grand Ole Opry* for Republic Pictures. It also starred Uncle Dave Macon, *Opry* emcee George D. Hay, and vaudeville veterans, the Weaver Brothers and Elvira. Although generally classed as corny by most critics, light in plot, and intended primarily for rural audiences, it did quite well at the box office and further spread the fame of the man baseball pitcher Dizzy Dean termed the "King of Country Music." The same could also be said of the seven other films in which Acuff appeared during the decade of the forties. Some of the later efforts for Columbia Pictures such as *Smoky Mountain Melody* and *Night Train to Memphis* rank among the better of their type.

During this decade of his peak popularity, Roy Acuff petitioned East Nashville Lodge No. 560 to receive the degrees of Freemasonry. Accepted for membership, he was initiated an Entered Apprentice on November 29, 1943. Subsequently Acuff passed to the degree of Fellowcraft on January 10, 1944, and received the Master Mason degree on February 21, 1944. Three months later he completed the Scottish Rite degrees and was created a Noble of Al Menah Shrine Temple on June 27, 1944. Beecher R. Kirby, known on stage as "Bashful Brother Oswald" and a long-time member of the Acuff band, also became a Mason at Madison Lodge No. 762 and the Scottish Rite and Shrine in Nashville. More than eleven years after his raising, on the last three days of November of 1955, Roy took the York Rite degrees at Edward D. Corbitt Chapter No. 147, R. A. M.; Nashville Council No. 1, R. & S. M.; and Nashville Commandery No. 1 K.T., all in the Tennessee capital city.

In 1948, Roy, being a popular figure of Southern mountain Republican stock, was prevailed upon by Volunteer State GOP leaders to seek the governorship of Tennessee. Two persons of country music backgrounds (and also both Masons), W. Lee O'Daniel of Texas and Jimmie Davis of Louisiana, had already been elected to the top office in their respective states. While East Tennessee provided solid Republican majorities, the state as a whole remained Democratic, and neither Roy nor his senatorial running mate, B. Carroll Reece (long-time congressman, GOP National Chairman, and member of Roan Creek Lodge No. 679, Butler, Tennessee, and Wautauga Commandery No. 25, Johnson City, Tennessee) did as well as hoped. Nonetheless, the King did rack up a record that stood for some years as one for amassing the greatest number of votes, for a loser, in a Tennessee gubernatorial contest. Although primarily an entertainer, he did participate in political causes of his choosing mostly for moderate to conservative Republicans, but he never again sought public office. He did, however, win the friendship of several presidents from Dwight D. Eisenhower to George H. W. Bush.

The decade of the fifties saw Roy Acuff decline somewhat in popularity as newer and younger country stars began pushing him out of the limelight, yet he remained a revered figure in the business. After fifteen years and over 175 recordings, he left the Columbia label in 1951, switching to Capitol and later Decca, MGM, and Hickory. By the end of the decade, Acuff began approaching the legendary status that he would hold for the last three decades of his life. Like Bob Hope, Roy derived special satisfaction from touring foreign military bases during the holiday season and did so many times. In 1962, he became the first living member of the Country Music Hall of Fame. (By 2011, at least sixteen other entertaining Masons had been elevated to this honor: Eddy Arnold, Gene Autry, Rod Brasfield, Roy Clark, Jimmie Davis, Jimmy Dickens, Ferlin Huskey, Grandpa Jones, Pee Wee King, the Louvin Brothers, Tex Ritter, Jimmie Rodgers, Roy Rogers, Hank Thompson, and Mel Tillis.)

Life on the road tended to be a grueling experience, and Roy barely survived an auto crash in 1965. But he mended and continued onward, although he did not travel quite as much afterward. From the early 1970s he increasingly contented himself with Friday and Saturday night appearances at the *Opry* and on certain special occasions. Through wise investments—including Acuff-Rose song publishing—he no longer had to work at all, but he chose to do so because of his sheer love of performing and his fans' expectations. Acuff received numerous civic and Masonic honors through the years including the Knight Commander Court of Honor (KCCH) on October 15, 1979, and the 33° on October 21, 1985.

A little more than seven years after receiving this high Masonic honor, Ill. Brother, Companion, Sir Knight, and Noble Roy Claxton Acuff went to his reward on November 23, 1992. In order to prevent his funeral from being turned into a spectacle as sometimes happens with celebrities, he was buried within hours of his death. A memorial service was held several days later. His wife Mildred had passed on several years earlier. A son and daughter survived; the latter had managed his business affairs in later years. That many of Acuff's recordings remain available today on compact disc, some of them recorded more than seventy years ago, testify to the enduring quality of much of his music.

**Note**: Those wishing to learn more about Brother Acuff may consult the book by Elizabeth Schlappi, *Roy Acuff: The Smoky Mountain Boy* (Gretna, LA: Pelican Books, 1978 and 1993). For Masonic records, I am indebted to the Grand Secretaries of the Grand Lodges of Ohio and Tennessee, as well as to Sir Knights Roger E. Van Dyke and Roger Wiseman. December 1993; slightly revised 2011

## Sir Knight Roy Clark:
*Country Music Superstar*

One of the most familiar figures on the country music scene in the past forty years has been a multi-talented instrumentalist with an extroverted personality who exhibits a flair for both comedy and song. As a star of the popular television program, *Hee Haw,* for some twenty-three years (1969-1992), Roy Clark set a standard for quality entertainment that has been equaled by few others in his field. A previous winner of the Country Music Association's Entertainer of the Year Award (1973), Clark also won their Musician award twice, Comedian once, and shared the Instrumental award twice. Furthermore, Roy has been a member of the *Grand Ole Opry* since 1987 and also operated his own theater in Branson, Missouri, for fifteen years. While Clark's Masonic career has been of more recent vintage, he has distinguished himself within the Fraternity as well as in his chosen profession as entertainer-musician.

Roy Linwood Clark was born in Meherrin, Virginia, on April 15, 1933, the son of a tobacco farmer who subsequently became a government employee. Both his father, H. L. Clark and his mother Lillian, played musical instruments. Young Roy learned to play banjo at an early age but made his initial public appearance at a school program playing a homemade stringed instrument that his dad had fashioned from a cigar box with a ukulele neck attached.

Somewhat later, in 1942, the Clarks relocated to the Washington, D. C. area where the youngster carried the *Washington Star*, played baseball, and engaged in amateur boxing as a light-heavyweight. His musical career evolved from working in the elder Clark's square dance band. Roy recalls that he began to get serious about music when he was about thirteen. A year later, he made his first local television appearance when he and his dad sang the Eddie

Dean song, "One Has My Name, the Other Has My Heart," over WTTG in Washington.

Music ultimately won out over sports in young Clark's career. The St. Louis Browns offered him a tryout, but it involved paying his own expenses to their Florida training camp. His boxing interests declined sharply after he suffered a severe defeat in his sixteenth professional fight. Live music, however, flourished in the Washington area nightclubs, and a fellow with Roy's skills could earn a living there. Dropping out of high school several weeks before graduation, the teenager embarked upon a form of livelihood that would eventually make his name a household word.

Roy Clark spent more than a decade on the Washington club circuit with some brief stints elsewhere. In 1950, he won the banjo picking contest at the national competition in Warrenton, Virginia. The prize included a guest appearance on the *Grand Ole Opry* at WSM radio in Nashville. He also toured with some Opry acts including the comedy team of Lonzo and Oscar (Sullivan), reputed to be Masons. After about six months, Clark developed an ulcer and returned to Washington where his Nashville experience provided him with opportunity to get bookings in the better clubs such as the Famous, the Bob White, and the Dixie Pig.

During those years, Roy usually led his own bands, but he did work for a couple of years with Jimmy Dean and his Texas Wildcats, a country act that had some national exposure via network morning television. Roy also made his first recordings on the Four Star label in 1951, assisted other local musicians in their record sessions, and experienced a brief unhappy first marriage. Somewhat later on August 31, 1957, he was married to his second and present wife, Barbara Joyce Rupard.

Roy Clark's career took a significant turn for the better in 1960 when he joined Wanda Jackson's band, the Party Timers, for a series of shows at the Golden Nugget in Las Vegas, Nevada. Roy fronted the band and played lead guitar. He also supported Wanda on some of her Capitol discs which soon led to his own contract with that company. The highlight of his work with Capitol included an acclaimed guitar album, *The Lightning Fingers of Roy Clark,* and a hit recording, "The Tips of My Fingers," in 1963. As a client of the Kansas-based Jim Halsey Agency, Roy began to work out with his own band from 1961, playing shows all over the country but especially in the Midwest. In 1964 and 1965, he had a pair of lesser hits with "Through the Eyes of a Fool" and "When the Wind Blows in Chicago," respectively.

In 1968, Clark signed with Dot Records and had some of his biggest hits for that firm over the next five years. Those included "Yesterday, When I Was Young," "I Never Picked Cotton," "Thank God and Greyhound," "Somewhere Between Love and Tomorrow," "Honeymoon Feelin," and his number one hit, "Come Live With Me" in 1973. In addition to mainstream country songs and dazzling instrumentals, Roy recorded a pair of bluegrass albums which featured various family members and their neighbors.

In 1969, Roy Clark began his twenty-three-year career as co-host of the television program *Hee Haw.* Originally conceived as a country-western version of the hit comedy show *Laugh-In,* the sixty-minute extravaganza premiered on CBS-TV in mid-June. The combination of country music from both cast regulars such as Buck Owens and Grandpa Jones combined with rustic humor from such long-time masters of the art as Archie Campbell and Junior Samples, and beautiful girls typified by Gunilla Hutton and Misty Rowe struck a responsive chord with middle and working class Americans. Although much of the comedy harkened back to the nineteenth century minstrel and vaudeville stage, folks liked it, and *Hee Haw* became an instant hit. It sparked mostly negative attacks from elite critics, but remained among the top twenty programs during its two-year run on the networks. Top executives at CBS, stung by the harsh criticism, canceled the program in July of 1971, but it survived as a syndicated show for another generation, more popular than before. After 1992, no new segments were filmed although Roy made some introductions for a season of prime re-runs known as *Hee Haw Silver.* Roy remained the principal star through its entirety and played a major role in its enduring success. His musical and comedy skills, together with his pleasing personality, all contributed to the *Hee Haw* positive image.

Meanwhile, Roy moved from his long-time home base in Washington to Tulsa, Oklahoma. In 1974, he purchased what had been known as the Titus mansion, and he and Barbara soon made it their "dream home." In the more than three decades that the Clarks have resided in Tulsa, they have become prominent in a number of philanthropic endeavors, and the community has reciprocated in a variety of ways. For instance, in 1977, a Roy Clark Elementary School was named for him in Tulsa as was an airport in Skiatook, Oklahoma.

His charitable activities have also resulted in buildings—or parts thereof—being named for Roy in various locales in Tennessee and Virginia.

No doubt it was a combination of Clark's entertainment status and philanthropic work which resulted in the decision of the Grand Master of the Grand Lodge of Oklahoma to make him a Mason "at sight." This was done when he received his degrees on December 9, 1987. Afterward, Roy affiliated with Jenks Lodge No. 497 in suburban Jenks, Oklahoma, as a "perpetual member." He subsequently sought additional light in Masonry on his own. Clark completed the Scottish Rite degrees in Tulsa on July 16, 1988, and became a noble of Akdar Shrine Temple later that same day. Less than two years later, Roy Linwood Clark completed his York Rite work and was Knighted on February 24, 1990. He is a member of Trinity Commandery No. 20 in Tulsa, the latter a body that already counted Gene Autry as a member.

The genial country entertainer from rural Virginia by way of Washington, D. C., has hardly been content with simply resting on his laurels. Both in 1976 and again in 1988, Clark took "goodwill tours" of the Soviet Union, thus doing his bit to help melt the Iron Curtain. In 1987 he added *Grand Ole Opry* membership to his resume. Thus Roy became a part of the world's longest running radio show that has counted such Masons among its former members as Roy Acuff, Stoney Cooper, Charlie Walker, Little Jimmy Dickens, and Ralph Stanley. Somewhat earlier, Roy had opened his own Roy Clark Theater in Branson, Missouri, where he appeared for several years between touring to other show dates and periods of rest and relaxation.

Roy's name continued to be seen on the country and western charts through the seventies and eighties. His last really big hit was "If I Had It to Do All Over Again" in 1976, but he had several more modest ones including "Chain Gang of Love" for MCA in 1980, "The Last Word in Jesus Is Us" for Songbird in 1981, and an instrumental rendition of the ever popular "Wildwood Flower" for Churchill in 1983. Through 1989, Clark had placed fifty-two numbers on the *Billboard* country charts, ten of which had also crossed over onto the pop listings.

Although the career of Sir Knight Clark continues, it has been sufficient to have already made numerous contributions to the country music field. In 1993, he authored a popular autobiography *My Life—In Spite of Myself,* released in both hardcover and paperback. In 2009 Roy was enshrined in the Country Music Hall of Fame. Most recently in April of 2011, he was honored by the Oklahoma House of

Representatives, chosen for the Oklahoma Music Hall of Fame, and named by Governor Martha Fallin as Oklahoma Music Ambassador for Children. Not bad for a high school dropout from a small town in the Virginia Piedmont!

**Note**: Those who wish to learn more about Sir Knight Roy Clark may wish to consult his autobiography written with Marc Eliot, *My Life—In Spite of Myself* (1993 and 1994). Roy's Masonic record was first detailed in *The Masonic Hospital Visitor,* Fall-Winter 1992. Thanks also to the Clark publicist in Nashville who supplied the photograph.

June 1996; slightly revised 2011

## Sir Knight Roy Rogers: *King of the Cowboys*

One of the great advantages enjoyed by American children who grew up in the 1940-1955 era was being able to have Roy Rogers as a hero and role model. While most of us never got to ride the range on the back of the great palomino horse Trigger, have Dale Evans cook our breakfast, or sing with the Sons of the Pioneers, we did learn a great deal about honesty, facing up to adverse situations, and distinguishing right from wrong. Although there were other cowboy heroes who rode across the silver screen and exemplified many of these same virtues, including Gene Autry, Tex Ritter, Rex Allen, and Rod Cameron—all Masons—none had quite as much appeal as the former farm boy from Appalachian Ohio who left us each week with that pleasant farewell of "happy trails to you."

The man who became famous as the King of the Cowboys started out in life with the much less glamorous name of Leonard Franklin Slye in Cincinnati, Ohio, on November 5, 1911. At the time, Andrew and Mattie Slye lived at 412 Second Street, an area since occupied by a stadium. Len had two older sisters, Mary and Cleda, and later another girl Kathleen completed their family circle. Like many working class folk, life was often a struggle for the Slyes. With the help of his blind brother, Andy built a houseboat and took his brood back up the Ohio River to the city of Portsmouth in July of 1912. The family docked their boat at the landing in the latter river city for some time, later moving it on to dry land. Some of young Lennie's earliest recollections are of the great Ohio River flood of 1913. About 1917, the Slyes moved to a farm some twelve miles from town in the rural community of Duck Run.

Earning a living at farming in southern Ohio can be somewhere between difficult and impossible. Andy Slye soon returned to Portsmouth where he labored in a shoe factory and came home only on alternate weekends. Young Len had to do his share to keep food on the table by doing much of the farm work. The youth also attended a one-room school and had some of the best moments of his youth in a 4-H Club when his pig Evangeline took first prize at the Scioto County Fair. This won the boy a trip to the State Fair in Columbus where he spent much of a day riding the elevator in the Neil House. On another occasion, Len rode his horse to Portsmouth to visit his Dad and take in his first western movie, a silent one starring Hoot Gibson, a member of Truth Lodge No. 628 in Los Angeles.

In his youth, Len Slye had hopes of becoming a dentist, but that was not to be. After two years of high school in nearby McDermott, the youngster dropped out of the educational system to enter the school of hard knocks. The family returned to Cincinnati with both Andy and Lennie going to work in another shoe factory. Cleda had married and remained on the farm in Duck Run while Mary had also married and gone to California. The latter caused the male Slyes to come down with a mild case of "California Fever," which they alleviated by going west for a long four-month visit in the summer of 1930. Andrew and Leonard found jobs driving gravel trucks. Although they returned to Ohio that fall, the "California dream" had taken permanent hold, and they soon went west again to forever make it their home. Returning to their truck-driving jobs proved to be of short duration, because the company they worked for became bankrupt during the Great Depression. The young migrant soon found himself forced to become an itinerant fruit picker in order to survive.

The struggling Len Slye also began to do a little picking and singing with family and friends—primarily a cousin named Stan Slye. He also sang in a group called the Rocky Mountaineers whose membership included a young Canadian named Bob Nolan and an Oklahoman named Tim Spencer. While this group had little financial success, Slye, Nolan, and Spencer later formed a combination that did make it. In the meantime, Len also worked with some other musical teams such as the International Cowboys, the O-Bar-O Cowboys, and Jack and his Texas Outlaws. None of them did much more career-wise than to avoid starvation, but on one tour through New Mexico, Len met a girl in Roswell named Arlene Wilkins who became his wife on June 14, 1936

Meanwhile, Len Slye got together again with Bob Nolan and Tim Spencer forming another group called the Pioneer Trio that developed a fine harmony trio sound. They landed a regular radio spot at KFWB in Los Angeles. Within a few months, they obtained a sponsor who paid them each a $35.00 weekly salary. With the addition of the slick fiddle and guitar duo of Hugh and Karl Farr, the trio became the Sons of the Pioneers. On August 8, 1934, they began recording for Decca, a session that included the classic songs "Way Out There" and "Tumbling Tumbleweeds." The one-time farm boy from Duck Run had commenced his climb up the ladder of success.

Leonard Slye remained with the Sons of the Pioneers until the fall of 1937. The group recorded additional sessions for Decca and then switched to the American Record Corporation (later Columbia). That same fall, Republic Studios decided to hire another singing cowboy. The firm was experiencing contract problems at the time with Brother Gene Autry of Catoosa Lodge No. 185 in Oklahoma. After auditioning some seventeen hopefuls, they signed Leonard Slye for $75.00 per week on October 13, 1937. Within a few weeks, they also signed him to a solo contract with the American Record Corporation (Herbert Yates was a power in both ARC and Republic). Soon the boy from Duck Run who had begun to use the name Dick Weston in the bit parts he earlier played in films had been transformed into "Roy Rogers," an upcoming singing cowboy hero.

Roy's first starring role, *Under Western Stars*, saw the young actor championing the cause of dust bowl plagued ranchers. Before the end of 1938, he had starred in three more films. The following year saw him star in eight horse operas and make an additional guest appearance in a Weaver Brothers and Elvira feature. In 1939, *Motion Picture Herald*, ranked him third in popularity among B Western stars and through the next fifteen years, he never ranked any lower in these ratings. Only Gene Autry and William "Hopalong Cassidy" Boyd stood higher, and by 1942 when Leonard Slye legally changed his name to Roy Rogers, he had nudged Boyd out of the number two slot. The following year, with Gene Autry in military service, Rogers took over the top spot and never relinquished it through 1954 when the poll stopped being taken.

In August 1940, Roy Rogers switched his recording allegiance to Decca. He spent three years with this company, cutting twenty-eight songs plus another half-dozen square dance numbers. Although none of the releases classified as super-hits, Decca's PR people contended in 1943 that his disc sales averaged 6,000 per week. Not recording again until after the war, Roy began with RCA Victor in August of 1945 and remained with that firm through the fifties. Most of the title songs from his best-known films appeared on that label such as "Don't Fence Me In," "Home in Oklahoma," "The Gay Ranchero," and "Along the Navajo Trail."

Many film experts date Rogers' long ascendancy to the top of his field from his 1943 motion picture, *King of the Cowboys,* coupled with his photo on the July 12, 1943 cover of *Life* magazine. With his nearest competition in military service and with thirty-four starring roles behind him, Roy Rogers had reached the top of his profession. In this period, his movies became more elaborate, sometimes running more than seventy minutes in length rather than the fifty-five to sixty-two minutes usually allowed for B films. Some were also shot in "trucolor," the Republic watered-down version of Technicolor. From then until 1951 when his series ended with *Pals of the Golden West,* Roy remained at the top. In addition to his motion picture and recording career, the King of the Cowboys also began his own weekly radio program over the Mutual Broadcasting System on November 21, 1944. After a short hiatus, it moved to NBC in 1946 and remained on the air until 1955. Beginning in January of 1948, Dell initiated a regular comic book series which by year's end reportedly reached monthly sales of 1.3 million. Numerous product endorsements made Rogers' name a household word, especially in homes with children.

During Roy's peak period of popularity, he petitioned Hollywood Lodge No. 355 through the help of a friend named Joe Espalier. As quoted in Bobby J. Copeland's article, "Masonic Cowboys" from *Favorite Westerns and Serial World No. 40* (1993), Rogers said, "I visited a Shriners' Hospital and saw all the good that those folks did for kids. I made up my mind right then that I wanted to be a Mason." Accepted into the order, he was initiated an Entered Apprentice on April 15, 1946. A month and a half later in June, the Lodge Brethren passed him to the degree of Fellowcraft and raised him a Master Mason on June 27, 1946. Assuming that Roy also wanted to be a Shriner, four more years elapsed before that occurred; perhaps some events in his personal life caused the delay.

Roy and his wife Arlene had adopted a daughter, Cheryl, in 1941, and in 1943, the couple had a girl named Linda. On October 28, 1946, the proud pair had a son named Roy, Jr., known as Dusty in his childhood, but tragedy struck when Arlene died a few days later from an embolism. Suddenly left alone with three small children to rear, the King of the Cowboys had more than his share of burdens. In the months that followed, Roy turned increasingly to Dale Evans (born Francis Octavia Smith on October 31, 1912), who had been the leading lady in most of his Republic films since 1944. This circumstance soon blossomed into romance, and the couple married in Davis, Oklahoma, on December 31, 1947.

Although Republic pictures matched Roy with a new leading lady, Jane Frazee, for a time, Roy and Dale were soon reunited on the screen. A little later when Dale took time off to await a visit from the stork, Penny Edwards appeared in a half dozen of his films. Then Dale returned for the final two in 1951: *South of Caliente* and *Pals of the Golden West*. In all, Dale Evans appeared in twenty-eight of the eighty-two Roy Rogers Republic Westerns.

In the meantime, Roy continued his Masonic journey in June of 1950 when he joined the Scottish Rite (SJ) bodies in Los Angeles. He also became a Noble of Al Malaikah Shrine Temple in Los Angeles. Sometime later, Rogers became an honorary member of the DeMolay Legion of Honor. On August 5, 1988, he moved his Scottish Rite membership to Long Beach.

On August 26, 1950, Dale gave birth to the couple's only child, a girl named Robin. Sadly, Robin had Down's syndrome and lived for only two years. Nonetheless, the experience drew them closer to God and inspired Dale to write her book, *Angel Unaware.* The Rogers family subsequently adopted three additional children; Sandy, Debbie, and Dodie; as well as rearing another foster daughter, Marion. Unfortunately, two of these children died in accidents some years later.

Roy Rogers left Republic studios in the spring of 1951 to embark on a career move to television. The golden age of the B Western was winding downward, but Herbert Yates did not want Roy to do a television series. As a result he left Republic and over a six-year period filmed an even one hundred thirty-minute TV shows. While *The Roy Rogers Show* was designed for a juvenile audience, numerous adults watched it too. The program premiered in December of 1951 and continued until mid-1957. In addition to Roy and his faithful steed, Trigger, Dale Evans who ran a café, comedian Pat Brady with his temperamental jeep "Nellybelle," and Roy's wonder dog, Bullet, appeared on every program. Quite popular in the earlier years, the program seemed somewhat dated by the time it left the air as the trend toward more sophisticated adult westerns hit in the mid-fifties. After he left Republic, Roy starred in only one movie during his TV years, the highly popular spoof, *Son of Paleface* (Paramount, 1952), with Bob Hope and Jane Russell.

After twenty consecutive years in the public eye, Roy Rogers' career began to slow down a bit after 1957. He and Dale continued to make personal appearances and recordings, but their media exposure was increasingly limited to guest spots. In the fall of 1962, they hosted an ABC Network variety show and in 1975 he made another movie, *MacIntosh and T. J.* In this film Roy plays an aging modern cowboy who helps a troubled teenager. While not like his earlier heroics, he still played a good if unspectacular role model for youth. In the later sixties and early seventies, he recorded several albums for Capitol Records including some mid-level country hits such as "Money Can't Buy Love" and "Lovenworth." In the sixties Roy, together with the Marriott Corporation, started a chain of restaurants and in 1965 opened a museum in Apple Valley, California, the main attraction of which was Trigger who passed away at the age of thirty-three. Roy had him stuffed and mounted. In 1976, Roy and Dale relocated their museum to Victorville, California, where it remained until after their deaths, and the children moved it to Branson, Missouri (it has since closed). Among mementos, it contained numerous Masonic and Shrine memorabilia. In 1991 Roy recorded a new album for Warner Brothers called *Tribute* which contains Roy singing with several contemporary country stars.

Among other things, Roy Rogers continued Masonic activity. In 1975, he received the KCCH and in 1979 the 33°. On November 9, 1983, he received the York Rite degrees in a single day as part of a class that was named in his honor. He became a member of San Pedro Chapter No. 89, R.A.M.; Harbor Council No. 45, R. & S.M.; and San Pedro Commandery No. 60, K.T., all in San Pedro, California. On February 24, 1997, he received his fifty-year award from Hollywood Lodge No. 355.

The King of the Cowboys has been honored in many ways. In 1976 he was elected to the National Cowboy Hall of Fame in Oklahoma City. In 1982, he was elected to the Country Music Hall of Fame. For several years, his hometown of Portsmouth has held a Roy Rogers Festival in his honor. Sometimes Roy, Dale, or some of the children have put in appearances. Roy's mural with signature occupies a spot on the city's flood wall of murals. The fact that so many of his films are available on home video and that numerous of his recordings are on compact disc is a tribute to his enduring popularity.

By the time Roy Rogers reached his mid-eighties, he had pretty much retired except for occasional visits to his museum. According to various sources, he spent his last years watching such daytime TV dramas as *The Guiding Light* and tuning in to Rush Limbaugh on talk-radio. He and Dale celebrated their golden anniversary at the end of 1997, and six months later on July 6, 1998, he rode off into the sunset for the final time. Dale outlived him by two and one half years, passing on February 7, 2001. As one of the best-known Masons of the twentieth century, few people have set better examples for their fellow citizens than the man born as Leonard Slye, but known to the world as Roy Rogers.

**Note**: Roy Rogers, Jr., David Dresser, and Earl Gifford in Ohio along with Ms. Bonnie Johanson, staff member of the Grand Lodge of California, helped with compiling the Roy Rogers Masonic record. For additional biographical data one may wish to consult the autobiography *Happy Trails: Our Life Story with* Jane and Michael Stern (1994) and David Rothel, *The Roy Rogers Book,* (1987). Since the original publication of this sketch, these have been superceded by Raymond E. White, *King of the Cowboys, Queen of the West: Roy Rogers and Dale Evans* (2005).

September 1997; slightly revised 2011

## Sir Knight Samuel J. Ervin, Jr.:
*A "Plain Old Country Lawyer" and Senate Legend*

Nearly four decades ago, in 1973 and 1974, an aging conservative Democrat Senator from North Carolina became an American folk hero as the Watergate Investigation Committee's televised hearing led to the unraveling of the Nixon Administration and to the President's eventual resignation. Until that time, Sam Ervin had mostly been known as a staunch conservative Southerner opposed to Civil Rights legislation, for the limiting of federal power, and as a strict constructionist on constitutional issues. Although he soon retired from the Senate, Sir Knight Ervin, who frequently termed himself "a plain old country lawyer," became one of that august body's symbols of old fashioned integrity. His folksy wit and homespun mannerisms helped reassure a confused public through a difficult period of American history. Because of Ervin, they believed that at least some common sense could still be found in Washington.

Samuel James Ervin, Jr. was born in Morganton, North Carolina, on September 27, 1896, one of a family of several children. His father, a local attorney, had been described as a "fiery" and "flamboyant" man who believed that "the greatest threat to our liberties comes from government." After attending the public schools in his hometown, Ervin went to Chapel Hill where he attended the University of North Carolina, receiving his Bachelor of Arts degree in 1917.

With the United States having declared war on the German Empire in April of 1917, the college graduate enlisted as a private in the 28th Infantry Regiment and soon found himself in France. During eighteen months on the "western front," Ervin received two Purple Hearts, an Oak Leaf Cluster, a Silver Star, and the Distinguished

Service Cross. His combat experience included participation in the Battle of Cantigny and the Aisne-Marne offensive.

Back in North Carolina, Ervin passed the bar exams in 1919, but he did not enter practice immediately, engaging in further legal study at Harvard from which he took an LL.B. degree in 1922. Returning to Morganton, he commenced his law practice and also got into politics as a successful candidate for the North Carolina legislature from Burke County. He was returned as a member of the General Assembly for two additional terms (not consecutive).

Although a devout Presbyterian, Ervin displayed an early affinity for championing civil liberties and free speech. It was said that as a state legislator he played a key role in defeating a bill to ban the teaching of evolution. He argued that "such a resolution . . . serves no good purpose except to absolve monkeys of their responsibility for the human race." Since legislative sessions were of briefer duration in those days, Ervin also had ample opportunity to further his law practice. In 1924, he married Margaret Bell of Concord, and they subsequently had a son and two daughters.

Sam Ervin also took his initial steps into Masonry in those years as a member of Catawba Valley Lodge No. 217 in Morganton. He received his respective degrees on February 2, February 16, and February 23, 1922. Brother Ervin sought more light in the craft as a Companion of Catawba Chapter No. 60, Royal Arch Masons in Hickory and as a Sir Knight in Lenoir Commandery No. 33 in Lenoir. He completed his Scottish Rite degrees in the Valley of Charlotte on November 16, 1922. Nearly forty-one years later he received the 33° and also held membership in the Shrine and the Red Cross of Constantine. On October 11, 1973, Senator Ervin received the Grand Cross. Not exclusively Masonic in his fraternal connection, he also held membership in the Knights of Pythias.

In terms of political office, Sir Knight Ervin seems to have had a strong preference for the judicial branch of the government. He served as judge of the Burke County Criminal Court from 1935 to 1937 and of the North Carolina Superior Court from 1937 to 1943. The judge also served in a part-time role as a trustee of the University of North Carolina from 1932 to 1935 and again for a year in 1945.

Ervin's initial entry into the national legislative area came about somewhat because of an unfortunate tragedy in 1945. Sam's younger brother Joseph W. Ervin, a Charlotte lawyer, had been elected to Congress in 1944, but he died on Christmas Day of 1945. On January

22, 1946, older brother Sam was chosen without opposition to complete his brother's term. He did not seek re-election but retired on January 3, 1947. During his eleven months in Congress, he served on the Post Office Committee and opposed exempting teenagers from the draft. Ervin returned to his law practice in Morganton until appointed an Associate Justice of the North Carolina Supreme Court on February 3, 1948. He remained on the state's high court for more than six years.

When North Carolina's senior senator, Clyde R. Hoey, died on May 21, 1954, Governor William Umstead appointed Judge Ervin to fill the seat until the November election when the remaining two years of Hoey's term could be filled by a special election. Assigned to the Government Operations Committee, the junior senator from the Tar Heel State soon found himself in the middle of the controversy surrounding the actions of Wisconsin's flamboyant Joseph McCarthy. In November 1954, Ervin was elected to fill out the remainder of Hoey's term. He went on to win additional six-year terms in 1956, 1962, and 1968 in what had been heavily Democratic North Carolina (until the late sixties only a few mountain counties in the far west had been GOP dominated). As one political observer remarked of Brother Ervin, "He has no power base, no machine in North Carolina, they just reelect him.

During his nearly twenty-one years in the Senate, Ervin usually voted with the coalition of southern Democrats and Republicans on social issues. He supported a strong defense, including American military action in Vietnam throughout that controversial conflict. The Tar Heel solon generally took the state's rights point of view concerning civil rights legislation with his best-remembered quote on the subject being, "We will not fool history as we fool ourselves when we steal freedom from one man to confer it on another." When the feminist-supported Equal Rights Amendment first surfaced in 1970, Ervin remarked that he was opposed and "trying to save women from their fool friends and from themselves."

In 1969 he probably gained more national attention than since his role in the McCarthy censure for helping to force the resignation of Supreme Court Judge and one-time Lyndon Johnson crony, Abe Fortas, on conflict of interest charges. In his strict construction views on the *Constitution*, the Americans for *Constitution* Action generally gave him scores of ninety or higher while the liberal-oriented Americans for Democratic Action gave him ratings usually in the ten percent range. However, if Sir Knight Ervin generally cold-shouldered civil rights actions and legislation in the 1960s, he remained unyielding in his defense of civil liberties, especially in defending the rights of the individual from a "big brother" government.

Perhaps this characteristic best explains his later dogged pursuit of the Watergate burglars and their cohorts. In unsuccessfully opposing the District of Columbia crime bill of 1970, Ervin viewed the sophistication of computerized data-bank crime gathering information as a long-range threat to the republic for "short-term purposes." He called the plan "a mass surveillance system unprecedented in American history" and a "blueprint for a police state." Ironically, while adamant about defending the rights of individuals from an intrusive government, he also opposed the tendency of courts to free criminals on technicalities.

Some of the highlights of Senator Ervin's earlier years in the Senate included his service on the committee that investigated labor racketeering from 1957 to 1960. Robert Kennedy first came to prominence as an attorney for this committee headed by Sir Knight John McClellan of Arkansas. In his influential book, *The Enemy Within*, the future Attorney General wrote of Ervin's ability to take on hostile witnesses, saying among other things, "I heard [him] on several occasions destroy a witness by telling an appropriate story which made the point better than an hour-long speech or a day of questioning." Kennedy concluded that Ervin "could be particularly devastating when a witness was pompous or overbearing." He proved especially unyielding in his questioning of Jimmy Hoffa. Together with John Kennedy, the North Carolinian co-sponsored the Kennedy-Ervin Labor Reform Bill, but he ultimately preferred the House version which became known as the Landrum-Griffin Bill of 1959.

In the early seventies, Sir Knight Ervin became especially critical of the Equal Rights Amendment pushed by feminists. He also attacked the Nixon Administration policies that he viewed as government infringements on civil liberties. Perhaps this became a prologue to his service as Chair of the Committee investigating Watergate. The televised hearings made the North Carolinian a folk-hero to the same liberal press that sometimes earlier characterized him as a reactionary Southern conservative. Tee-shirts portraying his caricature appeared referring to the aging lawmaker as "Uncle Sam." Nixon defenders increasingly saw him as overly partisan. In the long run, the positive images prevailed as Nixon faced impeachment charges and an outraged public forced his resignation.

Ervin did not seek reelection in the fall of 1974, but retired back to Morganton at the age of seventy-eight to his alleged preference of being "just a country lawyer." By this time, his son, Sam J. Ervin III (also a Mason), was serving as a North Carolina Supreme Court Judge, but the old hero of the Watergate hearings sometimes ventured out of his office onto the lecture circuit.

When the old gentleman visited Rio Grande College in the 1979-1980 school year, my own interest in meeting Ervin was to hear his stories concerning Fiddling Bob Taylor, a legendary Tennessee Senator and musician (member of Dashiell Lodge No. 238 in Elizabethton), who passed away in 1912. One recalls a colleague—Brother Jake Bapst, later of Centerville Lodge No. 371—complimenting him on his resemblance to the drawings Garry Trudeau had made in the *Doonesbury* comic strip at the time his name became a household word.

In retirement he also wrote two books, *The Whole Truth* in 1980 and *Preserving the Constitution* in 1985. By the latter year, he had been a Mason in Catawba Valley Lodge for sixty-three years. Two months later, on April 23, 1985, Brother and Sir Knight Sam J. Ervin passed to the "celestial lodge above," one of the most distinguished men and Masons of his era.

**Note**: Biographical data on Sir Knight Ervin may be found in Paul R. Clancy, *Just a Country Lawyer: A Biography of Senator Sam Ervin* (1974). For his Masonic records, I am indebted to the staff at the Grand Lodge of North Carolina, Brother John Boettjer, former Managing Editor of the *Scottish Rite Journal*, and William R. Denslow, *10,000 Famous Freemasons, II* (1958). Brother Boettjer also permitted the use of the copy of the Ervin portrait in the Scottish Rite Hall of Honor.

April, 2003, slightly revised 2011

## Sir Knight J. Strom Thurmond: *The Ultimate Senior Senator!*

While there have been many persons who have sustained lengthy careers in American politics, none, with the possible exception of Robert Byrd, could match that of South Carolina's James Strom Thurmond for sheer longevity. Not only did the Southern lawmaker have a lengthy career but one that stretched to over a half-century in the national spotlight. From his first election as a county school superintendent through a succession of such offices as state senator, judge, governor, and being the second longest-serving United States Senator in history, Thurmond's public service has been distinguished. More than anything else, his life illustrates an ability to adjust to changing social conditions in the South while remaining firmly grounded in traditional values and conservative principles. Moreover, Sir Knight Thurmond's Masonic life was actually longer than his political one and ranked as equally distinguished.

James Strom Thurmond was born in Edgefield, South Carolina, on December 5, 1902. Although one of the Palmetto State's lesser counties in size and population, Edgefield County has had a disproportionately high share of prominent politicians. Sir Knight Johnnie Morris, Grand Recorder of the Grand Commandery of South Carolina, points out that nine governors have called Edgefield home and that the majority, like Thurmond, have belonged to Concordia Lodge No. 50. Thurmond's father was involved on the local political scene and was an associate of Pitchfork Ben Tillman, a colorful if somewhat demagogic populist-oriented governor and senator of the 1890-1918 period. According to one of Thurmond's biographers, Jack Bass, Strom's father never got far in quest for elective office because he had once killed a man in self defense; however, as a campaign manager for Tillman, he attained considerable success. The elder Thurmond is said to have stressed to young Strom that he should avoid killing anyone if he aspired to elective office.

At any rate, Strom grew up in a relatively comfortable, middle class family atmosphere in Edgefield as the son of a small-town lawyer and farmer. At the age of nine, so goes the story, the youngster made a silent vow to himself that he would someday be governor. Meanwhile he had to complete high school, which he did in 1918, after which he entered Clemson College. There the future senator studied agriculture and took a role in a wide variety of extracurricular activities. These included most sports, debate, literary, and dancing clubs. He also became a strong exemplar of physical fitness, a characteristic that distinguished Thurmond throughout his long life.

Graduating from Clemson in 1923, Strom Thurmond took a position that fall, teaching agriculture at McCormick High School and also coaching football and basketball. A year later he returned to Edgefield where for the next five years, according to biographer Nadine Cohodas, he "earned a reputation as both a dedicated instructor and a tough coach." In summer he taught English and other subjects at "a rural farm school."

During those years as a local teacher, J. Strom Thurmond took his plunge into Masonry by joining Concordia Lodge No. 50 in Edgefield. He received his Entered Apprentice degree on March 6, 1925, was passed to the degree of Fellowcraft on April 3, and raised a Master Mason on May 1, 1925. Some years elapsed before he sought and received additional Masonic "light."

In 1928 Thurmond made his initial run for public office when he successfully sought and won the position of Edgefield County School Superintendent. Taking office in mid-1929, the ever-active teacher began to study law with his father. Passing his bar exams in the fall of 1930, Brother Thurmond combined law and education until the fall of 1932 when he was elected state senator from his district, ironically defeating the son of Ben Tillman in the August primary by a vote of 2,350 to 538. Shortly after taking office, he attracted much attention and ruffled more than a few political feathers by proposing to cut legislator salaries in half in Depression-racked South Carolina. While the bill was tabled, it failed to hurt the young senator with his constituents who sent him back to Columbia for a second term unopposed.

In 1936, Strom attended his second Democratic National Convention where he was among the delegates from his home state who remained stationary when racist senior senator, "Cotton Ed" Smith (former Mason, NPD in 1933), walked out of the convention to protest an African-American minister giving the opening prayer. This illustrated Thurmond's position as a racial moderate—for his time and place—in that era when a segregated South was the accepted order of the day. When the legislature was not in session, the young state senator built a successful law practice back in Edgefield, working with both black and white clients.

In January of 1938 the South Carolina legislature chose Thurmond to fill a vacant state judgeship. This position provided the aspiring politician with an opportunity to gain a wider circle of acquaintances. General consensus has it that Thurmond proved himself to be fair and able on the bench. He also attracted wide attention in November of 1941 when he courageously faced down a man with a loaded shotgun and talked an accused murderess into giving herself up to the law. In April of 1942, the judge took a leave of absence and joined the United States Army. Distinguishing himself in combat, Strom returned to his judicial post, but he resigned in a matter of months to seek the governorship.

The 1946 gubernatorial contest in South Carolina featured a crowded field of ten candidates in the Democratic primary. Since nomination was equivalent to election in what was then a one-party state, a run-off took place between the top two vote getters in the initial contest in the event that no one had a majority. James McLeod, a conservative physician from Florence, and Thurmond survived the first contest. In the September 3, 1946 run-off, Thurmond defeated McLeod by some 35,000 votes, and his childhood dream soon became a reality.

In his inaugural address on January 21, 1947, the new governor sounded a progressive note. He denounced rule by political cliques or "rings," advocated more safety laws to protect textile workers, and strove for more money for education, especially for black schools which were woefully inadequate in that segregated era. While he had considerable success with his programs, other forces attracted considerable attention as well, including events that would soon challenge the social structure of the South, especially the system of racial segregation. One occurred in February of 1947 when Willie Earle, a Greenville African-American, was taken from jail and lynched. Thurmond condemned mob rule and pushed hard for bringing the perpetrators of the deed to trial. Unfortunately, an all-white jury acquitted them, but the governor's strong stand for justice ended lynching in South Carolina. In other respects, however, Thurmond generally adhered to the more traditional Southern states' rights position. This stand soon placed the governor in the national spotlight.

Although official duties kept the governor quite active, he managed to find time to pursue private matters as well. Always busy with politics, Thurmond had never pursued a serious romance until 1947 when he began courting Jean Crouch, a recent graduate of Winthrop College. The two were married that November and remained a happy couple until Jean's death from cancer in 1960. In April of 1948, the governor received further Masonic "light" when he took the Scottish Rite degrees in Columbia, completing them on the sixteenth.

In 1948 Thurmond, who had nearly always avoided direct use of racial issues in politics, became increasingly alienated from the mainstream of the Democratic Party. Ironically, he had once counted himself as firmly in the Truman camp. Increasing federal support for civil rights alienated not only him but many other white Southerners from their traditional moorings. After the Democratic Party adopted the strong civil rights plank introduced by delegate and Sir Knight Hubert H. Humphrey of Minnesota, the governor and others chose to vote with their feet. In mid-July, he accepted the presidential nomination of the States Rights Democrats (nicknamed "Dixiecrats"). In the subsequent contest in which all four main candidates were Masons (Truman, Dewey, Wallace, and Thurmond), the South Carolina governor carried four states and amassed thirty-nine electoral votes (one more than the combined totals of Landon, McGovern, and Mondale).

As his term for governor was expiring in 1950, Thurmond decided to challenge incumbent Democratic United States Senator, Olin Johnston (of Center Lodge No. 37 SC). However, he failed to defeat him in the primary (the only state race Thurmond ever lost). When his term expired in January of 1951, Brother Thurmond retired to practice law in Aiken. In November of 1952, the ex-governor joined his successor, Brother James Byrnes, in supporting GOP nominee, Dwight Eisenhower, for president in what one might term a forerunner of things to come.

On September 1, 1954, United States Senator and Brother Burnet Maybank (Landmark Lodge No. 76 SC) suffered a fatal heart attack. In an election to fill his unexpired term and with the support of Governor Byrnes, Strom Thurmond won in a write-in vote, the first of only two persons in modern history to win a Senate seat by a write-in vote (the other is Lisa Murkowski of Alaska in 2010). Ironically, Strom had promised to resign in 1956 and not run as an incumbent even though no one opposed him. With the exception of that period between April 4 and November 7, 1956, he served in the Senate continuously from December of 1954 until his retirement on January 7, 2003, making him the longest-serving senator in the nation's history—until his record was surpassed by Brother Robert Byrd in 2008.

In his early years in the Senate, Strom Thurmond tended to be most associated with the States' Rights Southern Democrat point of view. This generally took the form of opposition to federal civil rights bills, Southern lawmakers taking the position that such bills were prerogatives of individual states and quite unnecessary. While Thurmond clung to the traditional patterns of race relations during the fifties, it would be wrong to categorize him as a racist in the manner of such earlier Southern demagogues as Cole Blease, Cotton Ed Smith, and Theodore Bilbo. Back in 1948, he had gone out of his way to say, "We do invite and we do not need the support of Gerald L. K. Smith or any other rabble rousers who use race prejudice and class hatred to inflame the emotions of the people."

Still, Strom had yet to challenge the prevailing assumptions of his culture. Neither had he given in to the prevailing winds of change. The ultimate moment in this phase of his career came when he staged a futile one-man filibuster against a civil rights bill before the Senate. On August 28 and 29, 1957, he gave the longest single speech in Senate history (24 hours and 18 minutes), surpassing the earlier record of Brother Wayne Morse (McKenzie River Lodge No. 195 OR) by nearly two hours. South Carolina voters responded by sending him back to the Senate seven more times until he ultimately retired at the age of one-hundred.

The Kennedy and early Johnson years saw Strom Thurmond becoming increasingly alienated from the mainstream of the Democratic Party where New Frontier and Great Society liberalism held sway. On the other hand, GOP conservatives had taken control of their party and nominated Barry Goldwater for president. Thurmond felt quite compatible with the Arizona Senator, and on September 17, 1964, he not only announced his support for Goldwater but also switched parties and became a Republican. Thurmond knew Goldwater had little chance to win, but he correctly believed that he could make inroads into the South. With Thurmond's help, Goldwater carried five Southern states. First with the Dixiecrat movement and then with his dramatic switch of 1964, Strom Thurmond had helped remake the South into a two-party region. Also, rather than commit political suicide as some old friends suggested, the Senator seemed much more at ease and equally popular as a Republican. While he moderated his stand on racial issues over the years, adjusting to new realities, he remained a staunch conservative and supporter of limited government.

In 1968, Senator Thurmond favored Richard Nixon for president over more conservative possibilities because he believed that Nixon was preferable to the alternatives and that a vote for independent candidate George Wallace would be wasted. Accordingly, he campaigned heavily throughout the South on Nixon's behalf and helped him carry South Carolina and other parts of Dixie as well. Not long afterward, the eight-year widower married again to Nancy Moore, a much younger former Miss South Carolina. The couple went on to have four children over the next decade. For a man to father four children with the first born when he was sixty-eight and live to see them all reach adulthood was certainly a tribute to his physical fitness and lean living habits.

As a senator in later years, Thurmond fought hard for tougher penalties for federal crimes. He also worked to get more strict constructionists in the federal courts. Like West Virginia's Robert Byrd, Brother Thurmond labored strenuously to see that South Carolina got its share—and perhaps more—of federal money. He demonstrated as much zeal for his African-American constituents as he did for Caucasians which enabled him to get a respectable share of the black vote. As a long-time army reservist, Thurmond provided strong support for the defense buildup of the Reagan era (along with Masonic Senators Goldwater, Jackson, Stennis, and Tower). During the Bush presidency, the senator once accused of being a racist provided solid support for Justice Clarence Thomas although it was obvious at the televised hearing that his own auditory abilities had begun to erode.

More Masonic honors came to J. Strom Thurmond as the years passed. On October 23, 1969, he received the 33°. After *Knight Templar* magazine published an article in the October 1977 issue entitled "Our Templar Senators," it may well have indirectly led to prominent Masons who had not taken the York Rite degrees to do just that. In Arizona, a class headed by Senator Goldwater and Representative John Rhodes became Sir Knights on April 22, 1978. However, that group was small compared to what transpired in Columbia, South Carolina. To quote portions of a 1999 letter from then Grand Recorder

Morris, "J. Strom Thurmond was elected to receive his York Rite Degrees in Columbia Chapter No. 5, R.A.M.; Union Council No. 5, R.&S.M.; and Columbia Commandery No. 2, K.T. on . . . February 3, 1978. . . . Senator Thurmond along with over 200 other candidates received their degrees in a one day festival named the 'J. Strom Thurmond Class' on February 11, 1978. . . knighted a Knight Templar at approximately 5:30 P.M., Senator Thurmond being the active candidate in the Orders of the Temple."

On October 16, 1987, the AASR, SJ awarded him their highest honor, the Grand Cross. Earlier that year, ultra-liberal Senator Patrick Leahy of Vermont had leveled some very unfair attacks on Freemasonry in a Senate hearing. Thurmond not only defended the Fraternity in some articulate comments but also helped secure the confirmation of Federal Judge Brother David Santelle.

For the first six years of the Reagan Administration when Republicans had a Senate majority, J. Strom Thurmond served as chair of the Judiciary Committee. As the senior Senator of his party, being President Pro Tem of the Senate made him fourth in the presidential succession line. When he retired in January 2003, he was the longest-serving senator ever as well as the oldest senator ever. Robert Byrd in 2008 surpassed him for time spent in the Senate, but the age record seems likely to hold.

By the time, Sir Knight Thurmond died on June 26, 2003, he had lived through the horse and buggy era into the space age. He saw South Carolina progress from a bastion of segregation to a bi-racial society. When I called the Grand Lodge of South Carolina a dozen years ago to obtain his blue lodge record, the young lady who answered the phone reported that he had already received his seventy-year pin. When I asked if she thought he might seek another term, she replied without hesitation, "I sure hope so." By the time of his demise, he had been a Mason for seventy-eight years and a Knight Templar for twenty-five years. As his biographer, Nadine Cohodas concluded in 1993, if Thurmond had not always been in the forefront of change, he managed to adapt once the rules became different. As teacher, legislator, judge, soldier, and Mason, he served his constituents with honor and dignity.

**Note**: The best biographical sources for Sir Knight Thurmond are Nadine Cohodas *Strom Thurmond and the Politics of Change* (1993) and Jack Bass and Marilyn Thompson, *Ol' Strom: An Unauthorized Biography of Strom Thurmond* (1999). For his Masonic Records I am indebted to the staff at the Grand Lodge of South Carolina; Mrs. Joan Sansbury, Librarian of the AASR, SJ; and Johnnie Morris, Grand Recorder of the Grand Commandery of South Carolina. Thanks also to Shasta Amos Blankenship for original manuscript preparation.

December 1999, slightly revised 2011

## Sir Knight Tex Ritter:
*Hollywood's Singing Cowboy*

From the mid-thirties onward, Americans have been entertained on stage, screen, radio, and television by a host of what became known as singing cowboys. In their films, these folks championed truth, justice, and clean living while entertaining us with songs that painted pleasant word pictures of life on the frontier and the open ranges of the American West. While the West of the imagination that Hollywood created may have been more myth than reality, it was quite real and vivid to the millions of youth and numerous others who watched their films. Although most of these young viewers never became cowboys, they often adopted many of the values that these celluloid heroes exemplified as their own. Perhaps given these characteristics, it is little wonder that at least six of the eight major singing cowboys had Masonic affiliation. These six were Rex Allen, Gene Autry, Bob Baker, Roy Rogers, Jimmy Wakely, and the subject of this narrative, Tex Ritter. The latter won his way into the hearts of millions of fans atop his magnificent steed, White Flash.

Born Woodward Maurice Ritter on a farm near Murvaul in Panola County, Texas, on January 12, 1905, the youngster grew up in a family of fourth-generation Texans. After spending his early years in a rural environment, the Ritters moved to Nederland near Beaumont. The future cowboy star rode the interurban into the city where he had the lead role in the junior class play, *The Terrified Bridegroom,* and also played on the basketball team. Following graduation in 1922, he moved on to the University of Texas with intentions of studying law. Glee club, dramatics, and the study of cowboy lore with such professors as the noted J. Frank Dobie soon competed with legal studies for young Ritter's attention.

Tex remained in Austin until 1928 and while gaining a good education found himself one course short of a law degree. He drifted to New York, where New Yorkers began to call him "Tex" and landed a position in a Broadway production called *The New Moon.* In the fall of 1929, he went to Chicago and enrolled in law school at nearby Northwestern. However, in mid-January of 1930, the young Texan dropped out of law school and went back to *The New Moon* then playing in Milwaukee. Soon he was back in New York where he landed a part in another play titled *Green Grow the Lilacs*. It ran for eight weeks in New York and then went on the road for fifteen more. Tex also became a radio singer of cowboy songs on a program titled *Cowboy Tom's Roundup* and also via a show of his own called *Tex Ritter's Campfire*. Gaining something of a reputation as an authentic western singer, Ritter recorded four songs for the American Record Corporation in the early months of 1933. His best-known effort was the traditional song "Rye Whiskey." In January of 1935, he signed with Decca, a company for which he cut an additional thirty songs through 1939.

By the time Ritter cut his second session for Decca in December of 1936, he had shifted his base of operations to Hollywood. In 1935, Gene Autry had become the first singing movie cowboy to achieve national stardom with Republic Pictures. Other studios began searching for similar potential stars. Warner Brothers signed Dick Foran who possessed a rather sophisticated singing style, but who managed to star in a short-lived series. Producer Edward Finney signed Tex Ritter to appear in a singing western series for Grand National Pictures. His first film, *Song of the Gringo,* was released on November 22, 1936. Through July of 1938, Ritter starred in a dozen B Westerns for Grand National. Perhaps the most memorable, *Trouble in Texas,* matched Tex with an attractive nineteen-year-old leading lady named Rita Cansino who later became more famous as the international sex-symbol, Rita Hayworth. Other Ritter leading ladies included Eleanor Stewart and Iris Meredith. Horace Murphy often had the role of the comic sidekick. With his deep voice and Texas accent, the one-time Broadway actor probably ranked as the most authentic-sounding Hollywood singing cowpoke.

Authenticity and Tex's popularity, however, did not constitute enough stature to save Grand National from bankruptcy in mid-1938. With Edward Finney continuing to produce his films, Ritter moved over to a more solvent poverty-row studio, Monogram, where he starred in twenty more westerns through May of 1941. *Take Me Back to Oklahoma* with Bob Wills and His Texas Playboys probably constituted his most significant effort for that company. Arkansas Slim Andrews worked as a sidekick in many of the Monogram "oaters," often accompanied by his cantankerous mule Josephine. Dorothy Fay was Tex's leading lady in two of these films, and the pair became life partners when they married on June 14, 1941. They subsequently had two sons, Tom and John, the latter eventually becoming a TV sitcom star prior to his untimely death.

After the Monogram series ended, Tex Ritter became something of a journeyman singing cowpoke for the remainder of his motion picture career. At Columbia he shared top credit with Wild Bill Elliott in eight films and in one with Charles Starrett. Beginning in September of 1942, Ritter and Johnny Mack Brown did eight movies together for Universal. After Brown left that studio to do his own series for Monogram, Tex had three solo outings for Universal which many critics consider his best efforts: *Arizona Trail, Marshall of Gunsmoke,* and *Oklahoma Raiders.* All three featured Fuzzy Knight as sidekick and Johnny Bond's Red River Valley Boys as support musicians. Jennifer Holt, the sister of RKO action cowboy star Tim Holt, was the leading lady in two of them. Beginning in the fall of 1944, Tex co-starred with Dave O'Brien and Guy Wilkerson in the PRC low-budget Texas Ranger series. He made eight of these films through the end of 1945 which wound up his career as a movie cowboy. Thereafter his appearances in pictures came either in support roles or as a vocalist on sound tracks. Since many of his earlier films continued to be shown for some years in drive-in theaters and on Saturday matinees, many fans were unaware that his movie career had virtually terminated.

Meanwhile, Tex Ritter continued to be a recording star. In June 1942, he began an association with the new Capitol Record Company that would continue for the remainder of his life. Early releases included covers of Gene Autry's "Jingle, Jangle, Jingle" and Jimmie Davis' "There's a New Moon Over My Shoulder," the latter of which became one of Capitol's first major hits. In 1945, he had his biggest hit with "You Two-Timed Me Once too Often" which remained atop the *Billboard* country and western charts for eleven weeks. Some years later, he would make an even bigger impact with the theme from the award-winning film *High Noon* which scored high on the pop charts in the fall of 1952.

In 1952, a promoter named William Wagnon initiated a barn dance type program called *The Town Hall Party*. In order to get a major TV station to carry the program, Wagnon needed someone with star stature for a headliner. Tex Ritter filled this bill and not only starred but also emceed much of the program. *The Town Hall Party* became the major country and western music venue in the far West, running until January of 1961. For a time, as much as three hours of it was televised every Saturday night in the Los Angeles area, and tens of thousands of fans came to see Tex and their other favorites in person. In addition, thirty-nine syndicated half-hour programs were televised under the name *Ranch Party* and shown nationally on many local TV stations.

It was during the early days of *Town Hall Party* and right after the success of *High Noon* that Tex Ritter began his Masonic work in Metropolitan Lodge No. 646 in Los Angeles. He took his Entered Apprentice degree on March 31, 1953; passed to the degree of Fellowcraft on June 30; and was raised a Master Mason on August 18, 1953 (another Hollywood cowboy, Rod Cameron, already belonged to this lodge and Jimmy Wakely would later so become). Somewhat later, he completed his York Rite degrees in Hollywood Commandery No. 56. On March 19, 1955, Tex became a Noble of Al Malaikah Shrine Temple. He apparently treasured his Shrine connection and, like Hank Thompson, displayed his pin with considerable pride on his Capitol album covers. In 1972, he demitted from Al Malaikah and affiliated with Al Menah Temple in Nashville.

As *The Town Hall Party* faded in 1961, Tex needed a new hit song to sustain his career and got one with a revival of Eddie Dean's 1954 song-recitation "I Dreamed of a Hillbilly Heaven." With slightly updated lyrics, the song reached the fifth spot on the country charts and number twenty on the pop listings. In 1963 and 1964, he served as president of the fairly new Country Music Association and worked tirelessly to upgrade the music's image. As a result, he became the first western singer to be elected to the Country Music Hall of Fame in 1964. Ironically, while Ritter had never had as much motion picture success as either Gene Autry or Roy Rogers, he managed to be chosen for that Hall of Fame prior to either of them. With the musical scene in the West in a bit of recession (it would soon re-emerge with Bakersfield as its new center), Tex relocated to Nashville and joined the cast of the *Grand Ole Opry*, the longest running program in the history of radio.

Tex spent his latter years in Nashville as an *Opry* member and as something of an elder statesman in the field. In essence, he was someone who bridged the gap between the country tradition and the western tradition. Back in California for a visit on June 15, 1966, Metropolitan Lodge held a testimonial dinner in his honor. Biographer Johnny Bond described it as one of the "highlights of his life." Like other well-known Nashville artists, he toured a fair amount from time to time, including an appearance at The Plains, Ohio, in 1969 where this writer was fortunate enough to meet him in person and hear him relate a story of his first record session back in 1933. He also appeared in some country music motion pictures from that era such as *Nashville Rebel* and *The Girl from Tobacco Row* in which he played a major role as a Southern tobacco farmer who doubled as a lay preacher. Although he had no more big hit records, Tex had several smaller ones that kept his name on the charts regularly. These included numbers such as "Just Beyond the Moon" and "Comin' After Jenny." He also did some fine recitations including one about an incident where a plane in which he was riding got hijacked and flown to Cuba titled "A Funny Thing Happened on the Way to Miami" and "Dark Days in Dallas" which dealt with the Kennedy assassination. His last chart maker which appeared after his death was the Gordon Sinclair composition "The Americans (A Canadian's Opinion)."

Tex also dabbled in politics but without much real success. According to his first biographer, Johnny Bond, Ritter had been enthusiastic in his 1964 support of GOP conservative Brother Barry Goldwater, a long-time member of Arizona Lodge No. 2 in Phoenix. In 1970, he threw his hat into the Tennessee Republican U.S. Senate primary. Opposed by east Tennessee Congressman William Brock, Tex ran a distant second. Brock went on to win in November and later served the nation as Secretary of Labor. Tex not only lost the nomination, but also ran up a campaign debt which plagued his last years. Like Roy Acuff, Ritter found that being a beloved musical figure did not guarantee victory at the ballot box. Nonetheless, he continued to be much admired as a person and for his contributions to the entertainment world.

Although Brother Ritter's health had been a little shaky toward the end, his death came as a surprise. On January 2, 1974, he went to the Nashville jail to post bail for one of his band members when he suffered a fatal heart attack. Last rites were held at Nashville's First Presbyterian Church. Dorothy and the two sons, Tom and John, survived him. Today, over thirty-five years after his passing, Tex Ritter remains a fondly-remembered figure. Many of his movies are available on videocassette and DVD, and many of his songs are recorded on compact disc. Except for the tense, the inscription on his plaque at the Country Music Hall of Fame remains as relevant today as it was when placed there in 1964. It reads, "His devotion to his God, his family, and his country is a continuing inspiration to his countless friends throughout the world."

**Note:** The best source for information on Ritter is the out-of-print biography by Johnny Bond, *The Tex Ritter Story* (1976) and the newer book by Bill O'Neal, *Tex Ritter: America's Most Beloved Cowboy* (1998) as well as the chapters in David Rothel, *The Singing Cowboys* (1978) and Gary Yoggy, ed., *Back in the Saddle* (1998). His Masonic records were furnished through the help of Bonnie Johanson of the Grand Lodge of California and the staff of Al Malaikah Shrine Temple.

December 1997; slightly revised 2011

## Sir Knight "Tex" Williams:
*Capitol Records' First Million Seller*

Tex Williams is remembered as the first singer to have a gold record on the Capitol label in 1947. While his musical career was much more accomplished than that, his biggest claim to fame resulted from the novelty recording of "Smoke, Smoke, Smoke (that Cigarette)." Williams had other hit records, was an accomplished vocalist, and led a fine swing band, the "Western Caravan," for many years and also starred in a series of Universal-International motion picture "shorts."

Tex was born Sollie Paul Williams near Ramsey, Illinois, on August 23, 1917. His father, Thomas Williams, operated a blacksmith shop and grist mill. He also played fiddle for local dances and other social events which probably stimulated the numerous Williams children to take an interest in music. Sol and his older brother, Earl began playing music together about 1923 and were soon entertaining their neighbors. As a youth, he attended Prairie Mound Grade School and later went to Bigham High. About 1930, calling himself "Jack" Williams (the nickname Tex came along some years later), the aspiring musician made his first radio appearance over WJDL in Decatur, Illinois. About 1934, he joined a group called Peggy West and her Rocky Mountaineers, and they soon shifted from Decatur to WDZ in Tuscola. Making a living was next to impossible in the depression-racked Midwest, so in 1938 Williams went to Washington State where he and another older brother, Menifee Williams, worked as apple pickers. In his free moments he again worked with a variety of local musical groups. About 1939, he picked and sang on a regular basis for some months in a place called the Silver Dollar Tavern near the construction site of the Grand Coulee Dam.

Playing rhythm guitar and singing vocals in his deep bass voice, Williams first joined a band called the Reno Racketeers and then went to work with the Colorado Hillbillies headed by Walt Shrum. Soon he and Cal Shrum teamed up, and Tex had the opportunity to appear in a motion picture as a backup musician starring Tex Ritter, *Rollin' Home to Texas* (1940). Sol's biggest opportunity came in 1942 when he became a key figure in a new band being formed by Foreman Phillips and headed by Spade Cooley, a fiddler that Williams had initially met a couple of years earlier when he was part of the Reno Racketeers. When the Cooley band moved to the Venice Pier Ballroom in late 1942, they became the hottest attraction on the West Coast, drawing crowds of 3,000 to 5,000 per night. By that time, the wartime economy had lifted the country out of the Great Depression. The band boasted three lead vocalists (Smokey Rogers, Deuce Spriggins, and Sol Williams) who also performed as the trio of Oakie, Arkie, and Tex, the latter giving the Illinois-born vocalist the nickname that he would carry professionally for the rest of his life. During this period (1943), Tex met and married Dallas Orr who worked as a vocalist with the Happy Perryman band, a union that endured for forty-two years. Later she often worked with Tex's Western Caravan.

The Spade Cooley orchestra did not invent western swing, as bands like those of Milton Brown and Bob Wills had been playing it in Texas since the early to mid-thirties. However, Cooley soon became known as the "King of Western Swing," and his war-time California band was the first to use the name. With Williams on vocals, the band began recording in 1944, and by late March 1945 their song, "Shame on You," with Tex's singing had hit the top on the *Billboard* charts where it remained number one for nine weeks and on the listings for a total of thirty-one. Through mid-1946, they had five more top ten hits with four featuring Tex's lead voice and the other song, "Detour" being an Oakie-Arkie-Tex trio. Spade Cooley and his Orchestra were indeed riding high.

However, Spade Cooley found it difficult to live with success and became increasingly jealous and quarrelsome. When Capitol Records approached Tex about a solo contract, Cooley said no, so Tex either quit or was fired. About half of the Cooley band, including such key figures as Rogers, Spriggins, and fiddler Cactus Soldi also left Cooley and formed the nucleus of Tex Williams and his Western Caravan. The new band opened at the Redondo Barn on July 4, 1946, and cut their first session for Capitol on July 24. Their release of "The California Polka" made the charts on November 30, 1946.

Capitol executives had spent so much money promoting their pop artists that they were considering dropping their mid-level country-western contractees, but Tex came up with the signature song that gave both him and the label their first gold record. "Smoke! Smoke! Smoke! (That Cigarette)" which had been primarily composed by Merle Travis, stayed number one on the country charts from mid-July until the end of October of 1947 and spent six weeks on top of the pop listings as well. He followed it up with ten more hits on Capitol throughout the remainder of the decade. Many were novelty and talking blues numbers which often tended to obscure Tex's talents as a smooth, deep-voiced vocalist that had characterized his work with the Cooley band.

Tex Williams also entered motion pictures on a regular basis at the end of the forties. In addition to the first film appearance with Cal Shrum in the Ritter film, he had one Charles Starrett movie *Outlaws of the Rockies* (1945), as a member of the Cooley band. In 1949, Universal-International signed him to a series of musical shorts averaging twenty-five minutes in length. There were sixteen of these films which also featured Smokey Rogers and Deuce Spriggins. They usually had a light plot, three or four musical numbers, and an attractive starlet as leading lady, most notably Donna Martell (in six) or Barbara Payton. The series began with *Six Gun Music* in January 1949 and concluded with *Ready to Ride* in October of 1950. Eight of the films were pieced together to make four feature length pictures all entitled *Tales of the West.* Cowboy music historian Douglas Green believes that Tex might have had a bigger career as a film star but for the fact that a childhood bout with polio left him with a slight limp which impaired his image as an action star.

During his film career, Tex Williams also began his Masonic life becoming an Entered Apprentice in Hollywood Lodge No. 355 on December 8, 1949. Passed to the degree of Fellowcraft on January 26, 1950, he was raised a Master Mason on March 30, 1950. On June 7, 1977, he became a plural member of Old West Lodge No. 813 in Newhall, California, and held membership in both lodges at the time of his death. Tex took his York Rite work in Chapter No. 121 and Hollywood Commandery No. 56, becoming a Noble of Al Malaikah Shrine Temple on April 21, 1951. Tex took his Masonic and shrine memberships seriously, perhaps because of his childhood ailment. The 1952 edition of the *Scrapbook of Hillbilly & Western Stars* reads "A great deal of his time is taken up with charity work and benefits; his favorite project is entertaining crippled children, wherever they may be."

By 1951, Tex's Capitol recordings—despite their consistent high quality—were no longer achieving hit status. As a result he signed with RCA Victor, but the switch still didn't produce any hits although again they were fine products. The truth was that western swing no longer sold the way it had in the immediate post-war era. By 1953, Williams had gone to Decca where he remained for five years recording some thirty-eight single sides and an album in their *Dance-O-Rama* series. A return to Capitol and two years on Liberty had the same results. It would in fact be 1965 before Tex Williams was again on the charts.

Although Brother Williams went for more than a decade with no hit records, he continued to be a popular performer, particularly in the Western states. He had successful television shows on the West Coast including one broadcast from Knott's Berry Farm. Roberta Shore, who later became a teen-age heart throb and leading lady on *The Virginian* TV series, got her start in show business on this program and also entertained with Tex and his Western Caravan at shopping center and supermarket openings. Her fond memories of Williams include the following: "I . . . was lucky enough to be put on his weekly television shows that he had from Knott's Berry Farm . . . . I was ten and a half when I was on *The Tex Williams Show*. . . about 1954. I just loved him. He was just a kind, kind man. He was married [but] had no children. He had a limp. I think he had polio when he was younger." Ms. Shore, now a resident of Salt Lake City, repeated to me at the 2003 Charlotte Film Fair. "He was just a wonderful man," she reminisced.

In 1957, Tex disbanded the Western Caravan but continued to work as a solo artist. Finally in 1965, Tex signed with Boone Records and again returned to the *Billboard* listings. Over the next decade, he made the charts eleven more times, and while none were of the caliber of "Smoke, Smoke, Smoke," they kept his name before the public, and he kept working. His most notable numbers in the later years were "Too Many Tigers" (1965), "Bottom of a Mountain" (1966), and the tongue-in-cheek "The Night Miss Nancy Ann's Hotel for Single Girls Burned Down" on Monument in 1971. His last charted number on the Granite label came out in 1974.

By the early eighties, Tex Williams worked much less frequently as health problems began to slow him down. He passed away on October 11, 1985. Ironically, by the time of his death, interest in western swing music had begun to resurge. Capitol Records issued a compact disc of his best recordings in their *Vintage Collections* series, and two more are available on the British Archive of Country Music label. Associates remember him as one of the nicest guys in the entertainment business. He proved himself as a man and a Mason. One could hardly ask for more.

**Note:** Good articles on Tex Williams include Ken Griffis, "The Tex Williams Story," in the *JEMF Quarterly* (15:1, 1979), pp. 5-9; and Rich Kienzle, "Tex Williams: Talking His Way to Fame," in *The Journal of the American Academy for the Preservation of Old-Time Country Music* (16, August 1993), pp. 18-19. For his Masonic records I appreciate the assistance of Al Donnici of the Grand Lodge of California, Albert Lewis of the Grand York Rite of California, and the staff of Al Malaikah Shrine Temple.

March 2004; slightly revised 2011

## Brother Theodore Roosevelt, Jr.: *His Father's Son and Military Hero*

With rare exceptions, most sons of presidents of the United States do not reach the heights of success and achievement of their fathers. One who came closer than most was Brother Theodore Roosevelt, Jr. who managed not only to distinguish himself on the field of battle in two wars but also held a variety of public offices, serving honorably in all of them. Still, being in the shadow of his famous father proved challenging for the eldest boy in "The Lion's Pride."

Theodore Roosevelt, Jr. was born in the family hometown of Oyster Bay, New York, on September 13, 1887, the eldest child of Theodore and Edith Carow Roosevelt and the second child of the future president (TR had a daughter Alice by his first wife Alice Lee Hathaway who had died young). In the next decade, the Roosevelts had four additional children; Kermit, Ethel, Archibald, and Quentin. Under the father's direction, the Roosevelt boys received not only a serious education in book learning but also rigorous outdoor activity. The father was often away from home as he served on the United States Civil Service Commission under President Benjamin Harrison and then as president of the New York Police Board.

In 1897 when Sir Knight William McKinley became president, the elder Roosevelt became Assistant Secretary of the Navy, but he resigned when the Spanish American War broke out. The year 1898 was a busy one for the future president as he left the Navy Department for the Army, distinguishing himself in the Rough Riders, and by that fall he was a successful candidate for governor of New York. Eleven-year-old Ted was sent to the Albany Military Academy in the state capital. In youthful games, he often led his playmates in playing "Rough Riders." Two years later, Dad was elected vice president on the ticket with McKinley. As vice president-elect, Theodore Roosevelt took his first Masonic degree in Matinecock Lodge No. 806. By the time he was raised on April 27, 1901, he occupied the second highest office in the land. His oldest son, thirteen at the time, was a student at Groton.

When Theodore Roosevelt became president following McKinley's assassination in September, Ted remained at Groton most of the time, although he did come to the White House for special occasions. After Groton, the nation's first son went on to Harvard where his father worried that the press was excessively violating the youth's privacy. Although placed on academic probation at one point, the warning he received caused him to reverse himself and devote more attention to study. As a result, he worked harder and graduated in 1908, a year earlier than originally planned.

Ted Roosevelt then took a job with the Hartford Carpet Company in Connecticut. He soon began a romance with Eleanor Alexander, whom he married in June 1910. The couple eventually had four children. After the wedding, Ted and Eleanor moved to San Francisco where the young bridegroom went to work in the office of his company. Two years later Ted returned to New York, taking a position with Bertron Griscom Company, a banking firm. In Philadelphia, he secured an even better banking job which provided him with a good income, but when World War I broke out, he urged the country to prepare for the conflict even before his military-minded father did.

When Congress declared war in April of 1917, former President Roosevelt asked President Wilson for authority to "raise two divisions." However, Wilson, mindful of TR's frequent criticisms of him and not a little vindictive, refused. Realizing that he was too old for field duty, he then wrote his friend General and Sir Knight Pershing, requesting that he include sons, Ted and Archie, both in training in the reserves at Plattsburg, New York, in the first contingent of A.E.F. troops headed for France. Pershing honored his friend's desire, and the boys pulled out of New York on June 20, 1917. The Oyster Bay Lion's two other cubs, Kermit and Quentin, also entered the army where the latter died in an airplane crash in July of 1918.

Ted Roosevelt compiled a quality military record in France. In addition, his wife Eleanor volunteered for the National War Work Council and helped set up YMCA canteens for American soldiers in France. Ted was promoted from Major to Lieutenant Colonel and commanded the 26th Regiment of the First Division. Wounded in action twice, he participated in the battles of Soissons, Cantigny, St. Mihiel, and Argonne-Meuse. Shortly after the November 11, 1918 armistice, he ran into an old staff officer friend who told him that he had been recommended for several military honors, but he had not received them because "people might say that you were promoted or decorated because you're the son of your father, and might criticize us." Ted's reaction remains unknown, but he had already learned the challenges of being a presidential son.

Initially assigned to a staff position in the army of occupation in Germany where he was when news reached him of his father's death on January 6, 1919, Ted was called to Paris in mid-February for a special meeting. This conclave had been called to discuss formation of a new post-war veterans' organization which subsequently became the American Legion. He also met with his recently widowed mother who had journeyed to France to visit the grave of Quentin Roosevelt. Shortly afterward, he returned to the states to help with formation of the Legion but also announced that he would take no prominent office in the group as he had decided to go into politics. That November he was elected to the New York state legislature. Almost immediately after being seated, the new lawmaker found himself embroiled in controversy as a move arose to deny five duly-elected Socialists their seats. While denouncing Socialism and Marxism, the new legislator supported them on the grounds that they had been properly elected and by themselves could do little harm. He found himself on the losing side as they were expelled anyway by an overwhelming margin.

During his days as a New York freshman legislator, Ted Roosevelt joined his father's lodge, Matinecock No. 806 in Oyster Bay. He took his degrees on December 17, 1919; May 19, 1920; and was Raised a Master Mason on July 7, 1920. Later, he also joined the Scottish Rite bodies in Washington, D. C. and Kismet Shrine Temple in Brooklyn.

In 1920 Ted expressed a preference for his father's old comrade, retired General (and Sir Knight of Englewood Commandery No. 50 in Chicago) Leonard Wood for president, but he enthusiastically endorsed the Harding-Coolidge ticket once Wood's candidacy faltered. On the stump nationally for the GOP ticket, the younger Roosevelt handily won re-election to the legislature but resigned to become Assistant Secretary of the Navy. In his new role, Ted ironically found himself having to reduce the size of a branch of service that his father had labored to build up in 1897 and 1898. This reduction was the result of the Five Power Treaty on naval limitation adopted at the Washington Conference of 1922.

In 1923, President Harding died suddenly, elevating Calvin Coolidge to the presidency. Not long afterward, news broke concerning what became known as the Teapot Dome and Elk Hills oil lease scandals. The principal villains in the affair were Interior Secretary Albert Fall and petroleum tycoon Harry Sinclair. However, the Navy Department was indirectly involved, and Ted had known Harry Sinclair, so he feared that he might be linked to the sordid affair because he had once owned stock in Sinclair and his brother Archie had worked for that company. A Senate investigation committee chaired by Thomas Walsh of Montana cleared Roosevelt, and a few months later he tried for another public office, running for governor of New York. A hot contest with incumbent Democrat, Al Smith ensued. Much to Ted's chagrin, his first cousin Eleanor, wife of distant cousin Franklin D. Roosevelt, toured the state on Smith's behalf with a truck bearing a giant teapot labeled "Teapot Dome." The chasm between the Republican Roosevelts of Oyster Bay and the Democrat Roosevelts of Hyde Park widened. Ted Roosevelt was defeated by the fairly close margin of 108,589 votes out of more than three million cast. It was his last run for public office, although he later held significant appointed positions.

After Theodore Roosevelt's retirement from the White House in 1909 and his defeat as Bull Moose candidate in 1912, he had gone on respective safaris into the wilds of Africa and the Amazon Basin. Ted, following his loss of the governor's race, now did likewise, going with brother Kermit on a long scientific expedition into the hinterlands of Asia, a trip that saw them in deserts and jungles as well as the Himalayas. Following their return to the U.S., Ted wrote a book about his efforts and he and Kermit began planning another expedition in search of the giant panda. By the time they returned, Herbert Hoover had been elected president and had appointed Ted as the next governor of Puerto Rico. He assumed his duties on October 7, 1929.

Originally considered by some Americans as a Spanish-American War prize in 1898, Puerto Rico had more often "proved to be a headache" for the United States Poverty persisted, and the islanders suffered from frequent hurricanes. Nonetheless, Governor Roosevelt had high hopes that he could improve conditions, even though the onset of the Great Depression made his job more challenging. Still, some improvements came about. He succeeded in more than doubling the number of cruise ships to stop at the island, encouraged more vegetable growing, brought the colony's budget into balance for the first time in seventeen years, induced President Hoover to become the first United States president to visit Puerto Rico, and at one point even donated about a quarter of his own personal fortune ($100,000) to stave off a financial panic. In January of 1932, Hoover named him Governor-General of the Philippines. In a year on this job, Ted helped quell unrest by having more public meetings, but when distant cousin Franklin D. Roosevelt was elected president, he submitted his resignation which the new president immediately accepted.

Back in civilian and private life, Ted Roosevelt took a job with American Express and later in 1935 with the publishing firm of Doubleday, Doran, and Company which had published his own latest book. As war clouds gathered in Europe, Ted became an advocate of neutrality and initially affiliated with the America First Committee. But as conditions changed through 1940 he became increasingly disillusioned with the group and became an advocate of preparedness. He had retained his army reserve commission and by the spring of 1941, requested General George C. Marshall to again place him on active duty. Visiting the White House, he patched up the "family feud" with FDR. In April he returned to his old division as Colonel Roosevelt. On December 17, 1941, he was promoted to Brigadier General. At that time, military historian Mark Boatner described him as being "in advanced years [54], poor eyesight, fibrillating heart, and arthritis so bad he had to use a cane [but] otherwise a fit fighting man."

A month later, Roosevelt made a daring proposal that he parachute by himself "into the Philippines to bolster civilian morale as the former governor general." While Marshall thought the plan might have merit, General MacArthur vetoed it. As second in command to Major General Terry Allen, he went to England and then to North Africa. While the First Division fought well, complaints surfaced about the lack of discipline. In the summer of 1943, after underestimating enemy strength in the assault on the town of Troina, Allen's independence led to both his and Roosevelt's dismissal. Roosevelt was assigned elsewhere. Meanwhile his jeep driver had the words "Rough Rider" painted beneath the windshield of the general's vehicle.

In late February 1944, Ted was made Assistant Division Commander of the Fourth Infantry Division. Plans were being made for the invasion of Normandy which took place on June 6, 1944. When the invasion came, General Roosevelt at Utah Beach was the only person of rank that high to be in the first wave to land. Once the city of Cherbourg was secured, General Eisenhower made Ted military governor of the city. Six weeks after D-day, on July 11, the General visited briefly with his son Quentin who had been in the attack at Omaha Beach and told the boy that he had been experiencing heart problems. When the son got back to his unit at 2 A.M., he was told that his father had died of a heart attack just after midnight. Ironically, Eisenhower had just recommended his promotion to Major General. Days later he was awarded the Medal of Honor "for gallantry and intrepidity at the risk of his life and beyond the call of duty." President Roosevelt presented the medal to Ted's widow in a White House ceremony on September 22, 1944.

Brother Roosevelt's bravery at Utah Beach assured him a place in the history of World War II combat. Years later when Brother Omar Bradley was asked to name the bravest act of warfare he had ever known, he said it in four words, "Ted Roosevelt, Utah Beach." General George Patton, no shrinking violet, noted in his diary that Ted Roosevelt was the bravest soldier he ever knew. Journalist A. J. Leibling in the *New Yorker* termed him a peerless warrior. The representation of him by Henry Fonda in the film, *The Longest Day*, is said to be quite accurate as Hollywood history goes. While his achievements may not have been quite as significant as his namesake, Theodore Roosevelt, Jr. certainly measured with the best as a man and as a Mason.

**Note**: The ranking biography of Ted Roosevelt is H. Paul Jeffers' *Theodore Roosevelt, Jr.: The Life of a War Hero* (2002). Also useful is the book by Mark M. Boatner III, *Biographical Dictionary of World War II* (1996). For his Masonic record I am indebted to Thomas M. Savini of the Chancellor Robert R. Livingston Masonic Library of the Grand Lodge of New York.

February 2006; slightly revised 2011

## Brother Thomas A. Jenkins:
*Welsh-American Congressman*

In recent years, much has been written about the contributions of various ethnic groups to American culture and society. One of the most influential although least heralded are the Welsh, a Celtic people who hailed from the far western side of Great Britain. When the United States was industrializing in the late 19th century, the Welsh often mined the coal and fired the furnaces that made it possible. Many of these Welshmen joined Masonic lodges. During the 1960s, two Welsh-Americans from southern Ohio, Dan Jenkins and Ben Evans, served terms as Grand Master of the Grand Lodge while another, Jim Rhodes, spent much of the decade as the Buckeye State Governor. Across the American scene, noted Welsh-American Masons have ranged from farmer- businessman Bob Evans to mine union legend John L. Lewis.

Another major figure among Welsh-Americans is the subject of this sketch, Thomas Albert Jenkins, who spent a third of a century in the United States Congress. Although he never attained great fame outside of his southern Ohio district, Brother Jenkins had become a virtual legend there long before his period of national service ended.

Tom Jenkins was born in Oak Hill, Ohio, on October 28, 1880. His parents, Samuel and Ann Jenkins, had migrated to the heart of the southeastern Ohio Welsh settlements from their native land with their four older children in 1870. In Ohio, the family had nine more children of which Tom ranked third from the youngest. The elder Jenkins worked in the coal mines and took part in the affairs of the town's thriving Welsh Congregational Church (now a museum) and other local activities. It was said that Tom's mother never enjoyed life in America and continued to speak Welsh for the rest of her life. Oak Hill had a strong industrial base with numerous brick yards, nearby coal mines, and charcoal-fueled iron furnaces. Most of the male populace went to work in their teens. Sam Jenkins stressed education and temperance to his children. Seven of them became teachers, and two became lawyers.

After finishing high school in 1897, young Tom who had been reared on hard work, taught school and attended a local institution of higher learning, Providence University, which he hoped would prepare him for law school. Meanwhile, his father died in 1901. Tom continued to teach and did farm labor in the summer.

In the spring of 1902, Jenkins petitioned Portland Lodge No. 366 in Oak Hill and received his Entered Apprentice degree on June 26, 1902. He was passed on July 21 and raised on August 28, 1902. Many years later while riding through Oak Hill on a political trip accompanied by Sir Knight Earl Jenkins (no kin) of Ironton, the latter remembered the aging Tom pointing out a hay field and recalling that he labored all day on that particular farm the day he received his Master Mason degree.

Although Brother Tom had saved but little money, he entered law school at Ohio State University in 1903 but had to work part time as a bill collector. He was graduated in 1907 and opened a law practice in Ironton. Meanwhile he began a courtship with Miss Mabel Wynne of Columbus. They married in Oak Hill on January 19, 1909.

Newly married and settled in Ironton with a prospering law practice, Jenkins became more active in the community. On February 24, 1910, he affiliated with Lawrence Lodge No. 198, having applied for a demit the previous month. He also took the Capitular degrees in LaGrange Chapter No. 68, Royal Arch Masons, being exalted on October 16, 1914. The companion followed with the Cryptic degrees in Ohio Council No. 92 and remained a member of these bodies for the rest of his life. Some doubt exists as to whether he took the Chivalric orders or not, as the records of Ironton Commandery No. 45 are missing for 1916-1919 when he would likely have joined. However, the minutes of that body took no note of his passing as did the others. Jenkins also joined the Methodist Church and served as secretary of the Ironton Flood Relief Committee.

In 1916, he won an easy victory as a Republican to the office of prosecuting attorney. Two terms as a prosecutor enhanced the Welshman's reputation as a lawyer. Jenkins won the majority of some five hundred cases in those years and also worked hard in World War I bond sale drives and in Red Cross fund-raising.

After a year back in full-time private practice in 1921, Brother Jenkins soon sought and won a seat in the Ohio Senate. His main achievement, the Jenkins Act, "equalized educational institutions throughout the state." Southeastern Ohio school districts seem to have always been perpetually under-funded, and the Jenkins Act provided a corrective. Ironically, no "fix" ever lasts long as the Ohio Legislature continues to grapple with this problem in 2014.

In 1924, the ambitious Jenkins sought the local seat in Congress. Incumbent Republican, Israel M. Foster (a member of Athens Commandery No. 15 and the other Masonic bodies in Athens, Ohio), had served three terms and earned some fame as sponsor of a proposed constitutional amendment to ban child labor. Apparently little ideological difference existed between the two men, and both generally appealed to voters on the issue of party loyalty and the fact that Foster had held office for three terms. Jenkins campaigned heavily on the Washington-like slogan, "two terms are enough for any man." Tom won the primary and general elections and went on to serve for seventeen terms! Foster accepted defeat gracefully and went on to serve seventeen years in a federal judicial position.

During his years in Congress, Tom Jenkins built up an enviable record in constituent services that undoubtedly helped sustain him in office for so long. When visiting various public events in any locality in his district, he always made a point to have someone in the community nearby to supply first names of area residents. This enabled him to give the impression that he knew most of his constituents on a first-name basis.

Jenkins did much more than simple grandstanding for the folks back home. He also took an active part in Congressional actions. His early years were characterized by a concentration on immigration issues. Although the son of immigrants himself, Tom generally favored tighter restrictions. This position put him in frequent conflict with Sir Knight Fiorello LaGuardia of New York who opposed further restrictions on newcomers.

The coming of the Great Depression followed by the New Deal changed the focus of Congress during the thirties and placed Jenkins and the GOP in the minority. Like many Republicans, Tom supported some New Deal measures and opposed others. The Welsh-American voted yes for Social Security, the Civilian Conservation Corps, the National Recovery Administration, and the Agricultural Adjustment Act. However, he adamantly cast a no vote on the Tennessee Valley Authority, the W.P.A., and the tariff reciprocity treaties. Becoming disillusioned with the N.R.A. even before the Supreme Court declared it unconstitutional, he then strongly favored the Guffey-Snyder Act on behalf of coal miners. In fact, throughout his tenure in Congress, Jenkins enjoyed strong support from coal miners and their union.

How active Tom Jenkins remained in Masonic circles is hard to determine unless one checked registers throughout his area. Certainly he continued to be somewhat active. For instance, on April 22, 1932, he served as principal speaker at a special meeting of Paramuthia Lodge No. 25 in Athens, Ohio. The local Brethren held a program celebrating the 200$^{th}$ anniversary of George Washington's birth and took up a collection contributing to the George Washington Masonic Memorial.

The coming of World War II saw an increasing shift to foreign problems on the part of Congress. Companion Jenkins generally identified with the isolationist faction in the House, opposing Lend-Lease, revision of the Neutrality Acts, and Selective Service. After Pearl Harbor, however, he supported war efforts but continued to criticize domestic restrictions, especially in the area of food pricing and production.

The 1946 elections witnessed the first Republican-controlled Congress since Herbert Hoover's first two years. Jenkins became a candidate for Majority Leader but lost out to Representative Charles Halleck of Indiana. Jenkins continued as a critic of the Truman foreign policy and opposed his plans of aid to Greece and Turkey but favored the modified Taft-Hartley Act. Not wholly negative toward Fair Deal programs, he supported increases in the minimum wage and extending Social Security coverage. He also authored a bill enabling states to collect taxes on mail order cigarettes.

In his later years in Congress, Tom Jenkins became increasingly less active. He spoke out strongly in opposition to Communism and worked to secure projects for his district, one of which was the dam on Sunday Creek that resulted in the creation of Lake Burr Oak. *The Glouster Press* called their town the best locale "in the state by a dam site." As a result of his efforts, the completed dam bore his name. A wing of the hospital in his home town of Oak Hill was also named for the congressional veteran.

In 1952, Thomas A. Jenkins received his fifty-year pin from Lawrence Lodge and continued to serve in Congress for the first six years of the Eisenhower presidency. He favored most of Ike's fiscal and economic policies but continued in opposition to many of his foreign aid programs. Sir Knight Earl Jenkins, who accompanied the veteran lawmaker on many of his travels in the district, recalls that Tom showed increasing signs of old age and that the younger man often took over the driving chores in the interests of safety.

In 1956, Jenkins won his seventeenth term in Congress but had a primary opponent in the person of Athens Mayor, Peter B. Seel (a member of Paramuthia Lodge No. 25). Seel no doubt had a greater interest in positioning himself for a future run, but died the following year in an auto crash. In 1958, Companion Tom, in failing health, had another strong and younger primary challenger in Homer "Pete" Abele (of Delta Lodge No. 207 and Jackson Commandery No, 53). Jenkins withdrew from the race as he was unable to campaign.

That November proved to be a disaster for Republicans as Democrats captured the Congressional seat for the first time in the century. Sir Knight Abele did win a congressional term in 1962 and later served many years as an appellant court judge. As for the retired and undefeated Jenkins, he lived only for eleven months, passing away in a private nursing home in Worthington, Ohio, on December 21, 1959.

On January 11, 1960, many of his former colleagues paid verbal tributes to their deceased comrade. Brother Clarence Brown, a long-time Congressman himself and 33° Mason, summed up his Brother's legacy: "Tom Jenkins' life was one of accomplishment which again demonstrates the opportunity America and our system of government affords to all who wish to work hard and live an upright life." Increasingly forgotten by a younger generation and recalled primarily today by old-timers, Brother Tom Jenkins deserves to be remembered as one of the outstanding Welsh-Americans of his day, as one of the most durable Congressmen of the twentieth century, and as a distinguished Mason in public service.

**Note**: No biography of Tom Jenkins exists but the unpublished M. A. Thesis by Henry F. Tribe, "An Ohio Republican in Turbulent Times: The Political Career of Thomas A. Jenkins" (Ohio University, 1982) is an adequate account. In researching his Masonic records, I am indebted to Sir Knights Walter Butler, Earl Jenkins, and Lloyd Webb, all of Ironton Commandery No. 45 and J. Clayton Smith of Athens Commandery No. 15. Also thanks to Abby Goodnite Ehman for technical assistance.

April 1998, slightly revised 2011

**Brother Thomas Corwin:**
*From "Wagon Boy" to Grand Master and Buckeye Statesman*

In the Jacksonian era, one of America's leading statesmen was Brother Thomas Corwin. Of Kentucky birth, Tom came to Ohio with his parents at an early age and eventually became an acclaimed attorney and orator. Entering national politics as a Whig, he served in numerous elected and appointed offices, eventually becoming Secretary of the Treasury. Along the way, the one-time "Wagon Boy" served as Worshipful Master of his home Lodge, Grand Master of the Grand Lodge of Ohio, and was knighted in the oldest Commandery in the Buckeye State at that time.

Thomas Corwin was born in Bourbon County, Kentucky, on July 29, 1794. His parents, Matthias and Patience Corwin, had a total of nine children and moved to Warren County, Ohio in 1798. Young Tom worked on the family farm as a youngster. Matthias Corwin, more than just a man of the soil, served in the General Assembly twelve times, two of them as Speaker of the House. Son Tom eventually served three times. An older brother, Moses B. Corwin, eventually spent a couple of terms in the United States Congress. In 1812 when Tom was seventeen, the United States declared war on Great Britain. The youth worked as a wagon boy, moving military supplies for the army on the Ohio and Michigan frontier. This experience provided Corwin with the sobriquet "Wagon Boy" that he would carry throughout life. After the war, the young man studied law in Lebanon, Ohio, being apprenticed to Joshua Collett. His admittance to the bar came in 1817.

As a young barrister, Tom Corwin quickly gained a reputation for public speaking. In 1818, he became prosecuting attorney for Warren County, spending the next decade in this position representing the state in both petty and major criminal cases.

Simultaneously, the "Wagon Boy" gained a reputation for "stump speeches" second to none in the Buckeye State, becoming especially noted for his satire and biting wit. While still holding the office of prosecutor he also represented Warren County in the legislature for three one-year terms.

While building his name as a lawyer and orator, Thomas Corwin became a Mason in Lebanon Lodge No. 26, probably in 1819. According to the Grand Lodge of Ohio's website, he is reported to have served as Worshipful Master in 1820, 1821, 1824, and 1843. He was later exalted in Lebanon Chapter No. 5, Royal Arch Masons and knighted in Mount Vernon Commandery No. 1, Knights Templar in Columbus on January 13, 1826 (at a time when Ohio had only two Commanderies). After serving as Master of Lebanon Lodge, Brother Corwin held the office of Grand Orator in 1821 and 1826, Deputy Grand Master in 1823 and 1827, and ultimately M. W. Grand Master in 1828. According to Edwin Selby and Harvey Walker's *History of Royal Arch Masonry in Ohio, 1816-1966*, Companion Corwin also held offices in the Grand Chapter of Ohio, but they provide no details.

Meanwhile, during the decade he served as prosecutor and was active in Grand Lodge business, Brother Corwin courted and married Sarah Ross in 1822. The couple became the parents of five children. In later years, an oft-told story relates that Corwin, an active Baptist, sent a son to Denison College in Granville, Ohio, to attain higher education with instructions to diligently apply himself to his study. The son complained that the heavy academic work was taking a toll on his health to which the unsympathetic father replied: "I am informed that you are seriously injuring your health by study. Very few young men now-a-days are likely to be injured in this way, and if you should kill yourself by over study, it will give me great pleasure to attend your funeral." Apparently "tough love" has been around since the 1840s! Tom Corwin's biting wit was hardly confined solely to courtroom oratory and the speaking stump but was also found in his household.

In 1830, having completed three terms in the General Assembly and a decade as prosecutor, Brother Thomas Corwin began a national political career by seeking and winning a seat in the United States Congress from his southwest Ohio district. By that time, the country's political divisions had evolved into what had become known as the second party system consisting of the Jacksonian Democrats and the National Republicans who changed their name to

"Whigs" in 1833. Corwin identified with the latter party and usually closely allied himself with the ideas of Brother Henry Clay and his "American System," supporting a protective tariff to encourage industrialization, federally-funded internal improvements, and a national bank to insure economic stability. According to tradition, Clay, Corwin, and other prominent Whigs often held meetings to discuss political strategy at the famed Golden Lamb Tavern in the heart of downtown Lebanon, Ohio. During the decade of the 1830s, Tom Corwin won election to Congress five times, earning a reputation as one of the most capable Whig orators and succeeding on two issues major to Buckeye voters, securing continued funding for the National Road (later U. S. Route 40) and Ohio boundary claims in the "Toledo War," a dispute over the line between Ohio and Michigan Territory in 1836-1837.

With the country in economic depression following the Panic of 1837, Whig hopes for state and national victory in the 1840 election rose to an all-time high. The state convention nominated the "Wagon Boy" for governor. He campaigned tirelessly for himself and presidential candidate William Henry Harrison, earning not only a dual victory but also receiving acclaim as the "most successful stump speaker of his time." Unfortunately, the "great Whig hope" was short lived. Harrison died after a month in office and the new President John Tyler fell out with party leaders in Cabinet and Congress. In Ohio, Democrats ignored Corwin's proposed banking reforms "in a crisis of inaction," leaving the Governor, in his own words, with little to do but "appoint notaries public and pardon convicts in the penitentiary." This did, however, give Brother Corwin time to continue his lucrative law practice which provided a supplement to his $1,500 annual salary. In 1842 when Corwin sought a second term, defections from Whig ranks by the anti-slavery Liberty Party cost him some 5,000 votes, and he suffered his only political defeat by a margin of 1,872.

In 1844, Whig fortunes in Ohio turned in their favor with Henry Clay winning the state and legislature, sending Tom Corwin to the U. S. Senate once more, and giving the "Wagon Boy" a national base. During his five years in the Senate, Brother Corwin achieved both his greatest fame (and also infamy in some circles) by his strong opposition to the Mexican War. Large numbers of Americans—especially in the Northern states—viewed the conflict as a thinly-veiled effort on the part of the Polk Administration to add slave territory to the Union. In what Ohio historian Thomas H. Smith called "probably the greatest antiwar speech given in the Senate" (at least prior to 1975), Corwin denounced the war on February 11, 1847, in inflammatory terms that won him both strong friends and equally potent enemies. Many Northern Whigs hoped the Ohioan would be their presidential standard bearer in 1848, but it was not to be.

Tom Corwin knew that even with the war over, Southern Whigs could never bring themselves to support his candidacy for president. Therefore, in the final analysis, the Ohio Senator threw his support to General Zachary Taylor, one of the two major military heroes in a war he had just opposed. Realizing that he would be portrayed as a hypocrite and that the Free Soil Party had no chance to win, Corwin stuck with the Whigs, writing that "Consistently with my notions of duty . . . [and] believing the Mexican War as I do to be a great national sin, I shall vote for the man who fought it. Holding slavery to be a great evil, I shall vote for him who owns . . . 200 Negroes."

Corwin's instincts proved correct as Taylor showed himself to be no friend of slavery. Unfortunately, the new president died in July of 1850, and Millard Fillmore, although weaker in many respects, did sign the *Compromise of 1850* and placed Corwin in the cabinet. The "Wagon Boy" had initially been offered the position of Postmaster General and refused, but did accept Secretary of the Treasury. His service in the Fillmore cabinet has been described by historians as competent and honorable but in the words of Homer C. Hockett "without distinction." After the death of Henry Clay, he supported the unsuccessful campaign of General and Brother Winfield Scott in 1852. However, on a personal level, Corwin placed some of his own money in corporate shares and lost it "by an unfortunate investment in railroad stock."

After his tenure at the Treasury Department terminated in March of 1853, Brother Corwin returned to Lebanon and devoted more time to his law practice which proved wise considering the debt burden. More or less out of politics, he lamented the decline of the Whig Party which he believed to be the only reasonable alternative to the increasingly divisive sectional tensions. Although no supporter of slavery, Corwin was not an abolitionist either. In 1856, the aging "Wagon Boy" reluctantly endorsed John C. Fremont for president, rejecting the third party candidacy of his old boss Millard Fillmore. In 1858, local Republicans persuaded him to run for the United States Congress, and he won both that year and in 1860. As the secession crisis deepened, Corwin, along with other old Whigs in Congress such as Brother and Senator John Crittenden of Kentucky, endeavored to effect meaningful compromise to no avail. Following the inauguration of Abraham Lincoln, the new President appointed Tom Corwin to his last significant government post, Ambassador to Mexico.

Corwin's past opposition to the Mexican War made him a popular figure south of the border. His goal to prevent Mexican recognition of the Confederate States of America proved successful. His encouragement of support for the government of Brother Benito Juarez and resisting French imperialism also helped. At the age of seventy, the old Whig leader resigned his post effective September 1, 1864. He returned to Washington and practiced law for a year, dying on December 18, 1865.

Thomas Corwin's remains were returned to Lebanon, Ohio, where friends and family laid him to rest in the local cemetery with Masonic honors. The man himself once humorously suggested that his epitaph read, "Dearly beloved by his family; universally despised by Democrats, useful in life only to knaves and pretended friends." In reality, however, this was not the case. His name and reputation endured for generations in southern Ohio where male children often received the first name "Corwin," one of the best-known examples of these being Corwin M. Nixon, 33° who spent thirty years in the Ohio legislature representing Warren County. While the presidency eluded him, Brother Corwin served his state and nation with honor. As Professor J. Jeffrey Auer of the University of Virginia concluded in his study, "In one of the critical periods of American history, Ohio's Tom Corwin played a leading role."

**Note**: No adequate modern biography of Thomas Corwin exists but useful sketches may be found by H. C. Hockett in the *Dictionary of American Biography* (1930), J. Jeffrey Auer in *The Governors of Ohio* (1969), and Frederick Blue in *American National Biography Online* (www.anb.org). His Masonic records can be found in Allen Roberts, *Frontier Cornerstone* (1976), W. R. Denslow, *10,000 Famous Freemasons I* (1957), and W. A. Cunningham, *History of Freemasonry in Ohio I* (1909) and the Grand Lodge of Ohio's website (www.freemason.com).

September 2010; slightly revised 2011

**Brother Tommy G. Thompson:**
*Wisconsin's Welfare Reform Governor and Cabinet Member*

In American politics, Wisconsin has gained a reputation as a reform-oriented locale. This tradition dates back a century when Brother and Sir Knight Robert A. LaFollette became a political power in the Badger State. The LaFollette reforms evolved into what is known as the "Progressive Movement" in American history. Like "Fighting Bob" LaFollette of a century ago, Wisconsin's Governor (1987-2001), Tommy G. Thompson, has earned a reputation for reform.

Current observers vary in attitude from those who view Brother Thompson as following in the LaFollette tradition to others who see him as reversing the progressive's reform policy. To Thompson's way of thinking, his manner combines old-fashioned virtue and compassion in what has been termed "tough love." Whatever the long-range verdict may be, his reforms have been popular in the short run. If he had completed his fourth term, he would have been only the fourth governor in American history to have served sixteen years as chief executive of a state and only the second to have served them consecutively.

However, in late December of 2000, President-elect George W. Bush selected him to join his cabinet as Secretary of Health and Human Services. Thus continues a tradition—probably a coincidence—that every Presidential Cabinet has had at least one Mason in it. The Clinton Cabinet had Clinton's first Treasury Secretary Lloyd Bentsen and later Agriculture Secretary Dan Glickman.

Thomas George Thompson was born in Elroy, Wisconsin, on November 19, 1941. His father, Allan Thompson, was a school teacher turned grocery store owner-operator. His maternal grandfather had been a LaFollette socialist. LaFollette himself was a maverick Republican most of the time with occasional drift into the Progressive Party and did gain Socialist Party support in his 1924 Presidential run.

Above all else, the Thompson family practiced the virtues of hard work. According to an oft-repeated story, when little Tommy was four he wanted a tricycle, and his father gave him an opportunity to work at twenty-five cents an hour to earn the money. Speaking of his father in later years, the Governor said, "I had to pay for everything myself, but he always gave me the opportunity to work for what I needed."

Tommy Thompson finished high school at Elroy in 1959 and entered the University of Wisconsin. While he had considered himself a Democrat when he entered college, the strong (perhaps excessively so) liberalism he encountered in Madison began to turn him toward conservatism and the Republican Party. Campus conformity has turned many impressionable youth into flaming liberals, but it also works in reverse on some persons. Thompson ranks among the latter and retained the values with which he grew up, supplemented by Brother and Senator Barry Goldwater's book, *The Conscience of a Conservative.* Following his 1963 graduation with a Political Science major, Tommy entered law school and earned his J. D. Degree in June of 1966.

Several weeks after graduating from the University of Wisconsin Law School, Tommy G. Thompson initiated his political career by challenging a seven-term, incumbent Democrat for his seat in the lower house of the state legislature. Young Thompson, however, ran a vigorous people-oriented campaign and came out the winner. According to one story, Thompson's opponent took him so lightly that he took a vacation in the midst of the vote garnering season while the ambitious youngster attended virtually every public event where he could be heard or seen. Tommy's 1966 victory proved to be the first of many, and he went on to serve ten terms in the Wisconsin House and spent the last five of those twenty years as the GOP Minority Leader.

As a legislator, Thompson earned a reputation as both a staunch fiscal and social conservative. His frequent opposition to new and what he considered excessive spending bills led critics to dub him "Dr. No." By 1986 he had accumulated sufficient legislative experience to seek the governor's office. Despite the fact that incumbent Democrat Anthony Earl looked like an easy favorite to win a second term, Thompson did not let this deter his quest.

Tommy Thompson not only conducted a vigorous campaign but also took advantage of Democrat strategic blunders. For instance, the opposition attempted to portray Thompson in "dark Nixonian image" as one who had voted against numerous liberal programs. However, their tactics backfired against Tommy's upbeat brand of conservatism that emphasized economic growth, private sector job creation, personal responsibility, and the curtailing and also reforming of the ever-expanding welfare system.

His message struck a responsive note with voters, and the man from Elroy ended up with somewhat more than 800,000 votes to just over 701,000 for Earl, hardly a landslide but with a convincing 53% of the votes cast. In fact, in the next three contests for governor, none of Thompson's opponents chalked up as large a percentage as Anthony Earl.

Governor Thompson's welfare reform ideas have generally developed in a series of steps, beginning with a six percent reduction in benefits designed in part to discourage persons from adjacent states from moving to Wisconsin in order to obtain larger entitlements. Another early reform bore the title "Learnfare" and withheld AFDC payments to parents whose children were habitually truant from school. "Workfare" required recipients to either work or be enrolled in vocational education courses. As a result, somewhat more than half had signed up for job training programs by 1991.

In the spring of 1990, Wisconsin's chief executive became a member of Sun Prairie Lodge No. 143 in Sun Prairie. (There is no lodge in Elroy). He received all his degrees on June 9, 1990, as part of a one-day class. In becoming a Mason, Thompson has joined a select group of statesmen from the Badger State, ranging from Henry Dodge and Philatus Sawyer, John Spooner and Robert LaFollette, to more nearly contemporary figures such as Alexander Wiley and Melvin Laird. Some years later he took the Scottish Rite degrees in the Valley of Madison. He received the 33° on September 23, 2003.

That November, Governor Thompson's welfare reform programs proved sufficiently popular for him to win a second term by a relatively easy margin. He defeated Democrat Thomas Lofton by a vote of 802,219 to 576,292. These numbers gave the governor a comfortable 58% majority.

Phase two of the Thompson reforms began with the Parental and Family Responsibility Imitative in February 1991. Since under previous Wisconsin Law single parent families received more AFDC assistance than two parent ones, Thompson contended that the system provided a disincentive to marriage. He proposed bringing up the per-capita amount for two parent families to an equal amount but eliminating payments for single mothers who had more than one child. Critics termed this proposal "bride-fare" and argued that Thompson wanted to enforce his religious views upon others. (He, his wife, and three children are practicing Roman Catholics.) The governor denied the charge and replied to the scoffers, "I…certainly don't want to force anyone to get married but don't think that the welfare system should act as an impediment [to marriage]."

In 1993, Governor Thompson introduced his plan that not only required welfare recipients to work but limited payment to a maximum of two years (three years for food stamps and child care). Democrats toughened the bill thinking the governor would veto it, but to their surprise, he signed the plan in December of 1993. Critics also argued initially that the negative aspects of these programs would not take place until the governor had left office. Ironically, he was still in office, and many of the critics were retired by the Wisconsin electorate. Thompson remained in the state house, and even now many of his reforms are still in placel.

The governor won a third term in 1994, and in a banner year for the GOP nationally, he shone as one of their brightest stars. Tommy Thompson defeated opponent Chuck Chvola by more than two to one. He amassed 1,052,776 votes to 480,343 for the opposition, an amazing 68% of the total for one of the biggest victories in Wisconsin history.

Such success soon spurred rumors that Thompson might enter the presidential race in 1996. The Governor did make a few trips to New Hampshire and Iowa in 1995, but ultimately he opted not to enter the crowded field in either 1996 or 2000. He did continue his efforts in the field of welfare reform and also education reform. His work in the latter area found him in cooperation with what at first glance seemed like unlikely allies in Black Democratic legislator Polly Williams and Milwaukee Democrat Mayor John Norquist. Their program limited experimentation in the "voucher plan."

It is a little early to tell how this and some of the other Thompson reforms will work out in the long run. Some have been challenged in the courts; others will likely face challenges. Some may be overturned. Others may survive. However, the electorate continued to support the Governor and many of his programs. In 1998 he won an unprecedented fourth term, easily defeating Democrat Ed Garvey by nearly 370,000 votes and getting almost as many votes as he received in 1994.

After fourteen years as Governor, Tommy Thompson looked forward to a job change in January of 2001 when President-elect George W. Bush selected him to replace Donna Shalala as Secretary of Health and Human Services. The nomination generally drew praise from conservatives and some skepticism from liberals. The *New Republic,* in an article, took the position that Thompson's rhetoric was much more conservative than the reality of his reforms. However, the more conservative *Washington Times* in a reflective editorial wrote, "Repeatedly, Mr. Thompson has succeeded in first developing and then implementing Wisconsin-based, innovative, conservative solutions to some of the nation's most difficult social problems. Whether the issue has been welfare reform, the education of impoverished inner-city children, the provision of health insurance for poor children and their parents, or the long-term care of the elderly, Mr. Thompson has been in the political forefront offering new approaches, including school vouchers for poor children and work-based welfare reform to some of the most intractable problems. . . . Notwithstanding predictions to the contrary from liberal critics, the national poverty rate actually declined in 2000 to its lowest rate in 20 years. Under Mr. Thompson, Wisconsin has reduced its child poverty rate by half to one of the lowest rates in the country. The plunging Wisconsin welfare caseload and poverty rate have permitted the state to increase its assistance to the truly needy in the form of child care, transportation, and health insurance."

To turn back the tide of "big government" and reduce continued growth of the welfare state has become a monumental task. Many applauded Governor Thompson's actions and have emulated him in other state reform programs. Still others have been highly critical. Only time will tell whether "tough love," "compassionate conservatism," and the values learned in the smaller towns and cities (such as Elroy, Wisconsin; Albany, Ohio, etc.) will provide a ray of hope for Americans in the 21st century and help solve the nation's growing social problems. If they do, then Brother Tommy Thompson will rank with his long-ago predecessor, Brother "Fighting Bob" LaFollette. If they do not, the United States will likely face even greater crises in the future. Both men placed their states in the forefront of movements for change. For better or worse, both LaFollette and Thompson have been innovators in efforts to improve society as they knew it.

After President Bush won a second term in 2004, Brother Thompson chose to depart from his cabinet post and returned to Wisconsin. He joined a law firm but spent most of his time in firms associated with health care providers and health care insurance. He took time out from this to accept the 2007 Distinguished Service Award from the Grand Lodge of New York. Eschewing opportunities to run for office in 2006, 2008, and 2010, he announced in 2011 that he would seek the seat of the retiring Wisconsin senior Democratic Senator Herb Kohl, unsuccessfully as events would prove.

**Note**: The best source of data on Tommy G. Thompson is the 1995 entry in *Current Biography* supplemented by articles in contemporary news journals. For his Masonic Record, I am indebted to the staff at the Grand Lodge of Wisconsin. The governor's office supplied the photograph.

April 2001; revised 2011

## W. C. Fields:
*An American Comedy Original and once a Mason*

Although more than six decades have passed since his death, W. C. Fields remains a familiar name among show business personalities. New biographies appear with regularity, and his films continue to be shown on television. Known for his bulbous red nose and irreverent, cynical, ad-libbed one-liners, Fields ranks among the most original and distinct figures in the annals of the entertainment world. While often identified as a Mason, little detail has hitherto been provided beyond identification of his Lodge.

The man who became world famous as W. C. Fields was born William Claude Dukenfield in Philadelphia, Pennsylvania, on January 29, 1880. Some books give his birthdate as February 10 or April 9, 1879. His father, James Dukenfield, had come to Philadelphia from England several years earlier and married a local girl named Kate Felton. They settled in the Germantown area where James earned a marginal livelihood selling fruit and vegetables from a horse-drawn wagon. William was the eldest of five children; the family also included two other boys and two girls.

Since W. C. Fields as an adult told a wide variety of stories about his youth, separating truth from tall tales can be difficult. The Dukenfields had a tough time making ends meet, and the father was a stern disciplinarian. Young William seems to have acquired a fourth grade education (or less), but at the age of nine, he became fascinated by a juggler and soon set out to master the art of juggling. Unfortunately, his father viewed such action unfavorably, particularly his wasting of good lemons and other fruits that the boy was prone to use for props and learning tools. At the age of eleven, the pair had a serious fight, and Bill Dukenfield ran away from home. He claimed to have lived by his wits from then onward, eating what he could buy, beg, borrow, or even steal and sleeping wherever he could. However, more recent Fields scholars discount this tale as an exaggeration. He contended that eight years elapsed before he contacted his family, but the current view is that he more or less remained at home until he was about eighteen.

As he developed his juggling skills, W. C. Dukenfield slowly made his way into the world of show business, shortening his name somewhere along the way. He got it legally changed in 1908. By the end of the nineteenth century, he was earning $125 weekly in vaudeville and had left the hardscrabble days of his youth behind. Wearing the clothing of a hobo, he became known as the "tramp juggler," and he increasingly worked a degree of comedy into his act.

Fields also took a bride. On April 8, 1900, he married a New York showgirl named Harriet Hughes. Shortly afterward, he took Harriet to Philadelphia and became reacquainted with his parents and younger siblings. Bill and Harriet had a son, William Claude Fields, Jr. in 1904. However, the marriage unraveled, and the couple separated in 1905 but never divorced, perhaps because of Harriet's strong Catholicism. Mrs. Fields took the young boy back to New York where he eventually was graduated from Columbia and became a lawyer.

During the years between his marriage and World War I, W. C. Fields was quite active on the vaudeville circuits, and his popularity increased steadily. In addition to hitting the first class houses in the U.S. (including both Keith-Albee and Orpheum), he toured the British Isles, Europe, Australia, New Zealand, and South Africa. Playing for the crowned heads of Europe, he became a particular favorite of King Edward VII of England.

In that same period, Fields also became a Mason. He petitioned E. Coppee Mitchell Lodge No. 605 in Philadelphia. Because of his heavy touring schedule, a special dispensation was granted to confer all three degrees on the same day. He received all the Blue Lodge degrees on May 20, 1907, in the then relatively new Philadelphia Masonic Temple. According to former Pennsylvania Grand Lodge Secretary, Thomas Jackson, Fields visited his home lodge only once thereafter, but Jackson opines that Fields may have visited other lodges during his frequent tours. His interest in the fraternity apparently waned after a few years. He continued as a member of E. Coppee Mitchell Lodge until 1924 when he was suspended, N.P.D., and never sought reinstatement.

By 1914, Fields' popularity commanded a $500 weekly salary as "the tramp juggler" or "the eccentric juggler." While touring Australia that year, he received a cablegram in Melbourne from a New York producer, Charles Dillingham, offering him a part in the play, *Watch Your Step.* Taking some six weeks to get to New York, Fields found that he had gone halfway around the world for a one-night stand. Fortunately, an old friend named Gene Buck landed him a contract in the *Ziegfeld Follies of 1915.* In the meantime, he temporarily returned to vaudeville, working several weeks on the Orpheum circuit through April of 1915, and then he left for New York to prepare for the June 1 opening.

W. C. Fields appeared in every edition of the *Ziegfeld Follies* from 1915 through 1921. Several other prominent Masonic show business figures also appeared in the show through that period including Eddie Cantor, Leon Erroll, Will Rogers, Bert Williams, and Ed Wynn. Ironically, Fields did not get along particularly well with Brother Florenz Ziegfeld of Accordia Lodge No. 277 in Chicago, who apparently had little use for comedians. After his career with the *Follies* ended, the Philadelphia-born juggler-turned-comedian spent a year in George White's *Scandals.*

Fields now longed for success in a starring dramatic production and found it in *Poppy.* He portrayed the character, Eustace McGargle, described by Fields biographer, R. L. Lewis as "a preposterous fraud whose livelihood was gained by milking citizenry at small country fairs." The part fit the Fields' persona so well that many critics believed that his later stage and screen characterizations were simply variations of Eustace McGargle. It also started Fields on a career of creating odd pseudonyms for himself such as Otis Cribblecoblis, Ambrose Wolfinger, and the dentist, Dr. O. Hugh Hurt.

*Poppy* ran on Broadway for 346 performances and established Fields as a top comedian. He then went on to play the part in a silent film version renamed *Sally of the Sawdust* (1925). He made several more silent films including *So's Your Old Man* (1926) and *Tillie's Punctured Romance* (1928). He then returned to the stage for a season with Earl Carroll's *Vanities.* Finally in 1931, having lost a considerable sum in the stock market (but not nearly all of his money), he again went to Hollywood where sound films had taken over. In spite of a distinct voice that seemed made for sound, he experienced some initial difficulty getting back into films. He made several "shorts" for Mack Sennett, including *The Dentist* (1932) and now the classic *The Fatal*

*Glass of Beer* (1933), a satire on melodramas. He also made longer pictures beginning with *Million Dollar Legs* (1932). This farce has Fields portraying the president of the mythical country of Klopstokia. He also did another longer film, *If I Had a Million.*

Of the several Fields' motion pictures from the mid-thirties, his role as Mr. Wilkins Micawber in the M.G.M adaptation of Dickens' novel, *David Copperfield* (1935) is probably the most memorable. A sound remake of *Poppy* (1936) costarring a young Rochelle Hudson, *Mississippi* (1935) with Bing Crosby, and *Man on the Flying Trapeze* (1935) also rank high on the list of favorites. During the making of *Poppy,* Fields became so ill that a double had to be used in many of his scenes.

A heavy drinker ever since his Ziegfeld days, Fields had become notoriously so, although he bragged in all seriousness that he had never missed or been late for a performance. The comic suffered from several illnesses, but he preferred having his fans think he was drunk rather than sick. After completing the film, Fields spent several months recuperating at a private sanitarium.

He made a comeback of sorts, conquering the new medium of network radio as a regular on *The Chase and Sanborn Hour* beginning in May of 1937 with ventriloquist Edgar Bergen and his dummy, Charlie McCarthy. The insults that Fields and McCarthy traded still rank as radio comedy classics. Although Fields was a regular on the program for only a year, he continued as an occasional guest until well into the forties. From October of 1938, he became a regular on *Your Hit Parade,* doing a quarter-hour comedy each week. With a $6,500 weekly salary from Chase and Sanborn and $7,000 on the *Hit Parade,* Fields found a medium, in which he had little interest prior to his illness, to be quite lucrative.

Neither were his days as a motion picture star over yet. He did one last film for Paramount, *The Big Broadcast of 1938,* a variety show style movie. Then Fields moved to Universal where he starred in a series of four pictures with much of the scripts written by himself or ad-libbed as he went along. While many film critics do not rank these pictures as among his best, they do tend to be those most familiar to contemporary audiences since they have frequently been shown on television.

The series began with *You Can't Cheat an Honest Man* (1939) and has W. C. Fields playing another con-artist character named Larson E. Whipsnade. Another film legend, Mae West, costars with him in *My Little Chickadee* (1940), the title from a favorite Fields' euphemism for attractive young ladies. Most critics believe that the third film, *The Bank Dick* (1940), ranks as the best of his Universal offerings. In it the comedian created another of his legendary characters, Egbert Souse. *Never Give a Sucker an Even Break* (1941) costarred Fields with young songstress Gloria Jean who plays his niece, Margaret Dumont, and his Masonic pal from the Ziegfeld days, Leon Erroll. It closed out his stint with Universal.

Other than occasional guest spots on network radio and in a few films, the career of W. C. Fields had begun to fade. His health declined more rapidly as the years of heavy drinking began to take their toll. He went back to the sanitarium and died there on Christmas Day, 1946. Although often characterized as an atheist or as an agnostic, biographer Robert L. Taylor contends that Fields "had a sort of religion of his own, but that it was dissociated with the church." Caught reading the Bible at one point in his later years, he replied with his characteristic brand of cynical humor that he was "Looking for loopholes." Recent biographer, Simon Louvish, thinks that some of his negative attitude toward formal religion may date from his wife's strong—and perhaps to his way of thinking, fanatical—embrace of Catholicism after their separation. He notes that this attitude "had not been so apparent before." In his will, Fields left $10,000 each to his estranged wife and son with whom he had reconciled in later years. He also made allowances for other relatives and friends. However, the remainder of his estate, $771,000, was to found and endow an orphanage. Harriet and W. C. Fields, Jr. hired lawyers and broke the will. In 1954 the court awarded them most of the estate. In 1980, the Postal Service honored Fields' memory with a stamp.

In the final analysis, one suspects that in spite of the laughter he provided for millions, W.C. Fields was not a happy person. His grandson termed him "perhaps the most complex, confusing, and contradictory man who ever lived." However, as a figure in humorous entertainment, he has had few equals. One film historian concluded that his genius lay in his ability to unite the verbal and visual aspects of comedy. Like some other Masons of fame—ranging from Rod Cameron to Mark Twain, Fields' connection with the square and compass did not endure for his lifetime, but like them, the words and visual images he created remain with us.

**Note**: The following provide additional reading on Fields: Ronald J. Fields, ed., *W. C. Fields by Himself: His Intended Autobiography* (1973); Wes D. Gehrung,

*W. C. Fields: A Bio-Bibliography* (1984); Simon Louvish, "Man on the Flying Trapeze: the Life and Times of W. C. Fields" (1997); Carlotta Monti, *W. C. Fields & Me (As told to Cy Rice)* (1971); and Robert Lewis Taylor, *W. C. Fields: His Follies and Fortunes* (1949). In addition to these sources, I especially appreciate the efforts of Thomas Jackson who as Grand Secretary of the Grand Lodge of Pennsylvania not only furnished me with Fields' Masonic record but also copies of all the relevant documents.

January 2002; slightly revised 2011

**Waite Hoyt:**
*Hall-of-Fame Pitcher, Play-by-Play Announcer and Once a Mason*

In recent years, major league baseball players who went on to become play-by-play announcers have become fairly common, but such was not always the case. In recent decades, one can think of Jerry Coleman, Joe Nuxhall, Don Drysdale, Herb Score, and perhaps most obviously the late Dizzy Dean. Yet there were others who pioneered in the trade. One of the best who also earned his niche in the Hall of Fame at Cooperstown was Waite Hoyt who was the ace right hander of the New York Yankees at nearly the same time that Brother Herb Pennock was their southpaw hurling star. After two decades in the majors, Hoyt went into sportscasting and spent even longer in that field, putting in nearly a quarter century broadcasting Cincinnati Reds games.

Waite Charles Hoyt was born in Brooklyn, New York, on September 9, 1899. The Hoyts were in fact long-time residents of Brooklyn. Waite's father had been in the clothing business but switched his employment to Swift and Company when it appeared that there was little opportunity for advancement with the firm of L. Heller and Sons. Children growing up in Brooklyn in those days developed an early interest in baseball, and Waite was no exception. At first he wanted to be a second baseman (an early idol was Larry Doyle of the Giants) although soon afterward he became a pitcher because his original team lacked uniforms, but another unit that had them needed someone who could throw hard. On such mature judgment, great decisions are sometimes made!

Young Hoyt soon proved himself to be a hard thrower and soon attracted attention from professional scouts. The Baltimore Federal League team showed an interest in 1915. However, his parents objected to his leaving home at fifteen. He did not sign, although he did sign with the hometown New York Giants prior to his sixteenth birthday and ended the season pitching batting practice for John McGraw's National League team.

The next season as a sixteen-year-old, the youth divided his time between Mt. Carmel in the Penn State League and Hartford of the Eastern League, compiling impressive won-lost records of 5-1 and 4-5, respectively. Apparently his control could have been better in Connecticut as he walked forty-four batters while striking out only half that number. Two more years in the minors saw the still teenaged hurler dividing his time between the Southern League and the International. While his won-lost record appeared unfavorable, his earned run averages were quite good, being 3.23 during a stint at Memphis and a much stronger 2.51, 2.73 and 2.10 at the other locales. In between longer service at Nashville and Newark in 1918, the eighteen-year-old Hoyt made his major league debut on July 24, 1918, pitching one inning for the Giants, giving up no hits, and striking out two batters. The Giants subsequently traded Hoyt to Rochester of the International League, but he refused to report and not being under contract to them, instead started in 1919 pitching for the independent Baltimore Drydocks. This made him a virtual "free agent," and in mid-season, he signed with the Boston Red Sox with the stipulation that he be allowed to start a game within four days. Manager Ed Barrow thought this was a "fresh" demand for a teenager, but he honored it, and Hoyt soon started a game against Detroit and beat them 2-1 in twelve innings. Waite went 4-6 that year and 6-6 in 1920. On December 15, 1920, the now twenty-one-year-old hurler was traded to the New York Yankees as part of an eight-player deal and his climb to baseball greatness really began.

Waite Hoyt spent nearly a full decade with the Bronx Bombers and made most of his major achievements with that club. Having the advantage of a strong team behind him, Hoyt, along with such noted figures as Herb Pennock and Carl Mays (both Masons), managed to be on six pennant winning teams in that period, compiled an enviable Word Series record of 6-3, and pitched 27 innings in the 1921 post-season game without giving up an earned run (he did give up two unearned runs in the final game, suffering a heartbreaking loss). He also had several strong seasons in this period as well, winning an excess of twenty games in two seasons (1927 and 1928) and nineteen in two other seasons (1921 and 1922). Over his nine full seasons with the club, he averaged seventeen wins per season. Should anyone be surprised that he once quipped, "The secret of success is to play for the New York Yankees?"

During the course of his 1927 season when the Yankees had perhaps the greatest team in the game's history, Waite Hoyt also became a Mason in Kings County Lodge No. 511 in his native Brooklyn. Taking his degrees over the course of the season, he was initiated an Entered Apprentice on April 19, 1927 (a day when Bob Shawkey took a 1-0 loss to the Red Sox); passed a Fellowcraft on June 29, 1927 (George Pipgras that day pitched his team to an 8-2 victory over the Red Sox); and raised a Master Mason on September 27, 1927 (the Yanks took Washington 15-5 behind the pitching of Urban Shocker). Other Masons on that team included center fielder, Earl Combs, and left-handed pitcher, Herb Pennock. Brother Hoyt apparently became a member of the Tall Cedars of Lebanon, as he was so pictured in a charity game they sponsored. On October 18, 1929, Hoyt affiliated with Larchmont Lodge No. 1030 and demitted from Kings County eleven days later.

After going 22-7 in that fabulous year, Hoyt did as well in 1928, going 23-7. In three World Series appearances in those great seasons, he won three games. In 1929, however, he experienced an off-year going 10-9 while the Yankees lost the pennant to a resurging Philadelphia team. In addition, Miller Huggins died near the season's end, and on May 30, 1930, Waite Hoyt and shortstop Mark Koenig were traded to the Detroit Tigers. In the Motor City, he recovered some of his older skills, going 9-8 for the remainder of the season, but his ERA jumped to 4.73. After starting off even worse in 1931, the once superb hurler compiled a 3-8 record, and the Tigers placed him on waivers in June. Connie Mack hoped that the one time "Schoolboy" could help the Athletics who were in the thick of another pennant race and his hunch proved correct. Waite went 10-5 in the remainder of 1931 but lost the fifth game of the World Series 5-1 for his final appearance in the fall Classic.

Mack would have signed Hoyt again in 1932 but agreed instead to give the veteran pitcher his release so he could sign with his hometown team, the Dodgers. That proved to be a mistake; in mid-season he went to the Giants. Overall, his 1932 record was 6-10, and his ERA was 4.35. In many respects, it was the low point of his career, as he had posted at least ten victories in every season since first coming to the Yankees in December of 1920. In a retrospective interview in 1976, the Hall of Fame pitcher credited this weak performance to domestic difficulties. In the summer of 1931, Hoyt testified in a divorce case on behalf of his former Yankee team mate "Jumping Joe" Dugan. Waite's wife Dorothy Pyle Hoyt, testified for Mrs. Dugan and not long after went to Reno to establish a Nevada residence herself. On May 12, 1933, Waite, who had signed with the Pittsburgh Pirates a few months earlier, married again to Ellen Burbank. It may have been a more stable home life that did it, but whatever, Hoyt found himself again in Pittsburgh. In four full seasons and part of another with the Bucs, Brother Hoyt recovered part of his old form and proved himself an effective spot-starter and reliever. His best year with the Pirates was 1934 when he went 15-6 with a 2.92 ERA. In all, his days in Pittsburgh show his win-loss totals at 35-31, hardly up to his old form but respectable. Released by the Pirates in June of 1937, the Dodgers again signed him, and he went 7-7 in thirty-eight appearances, posting a 3.23 ERA. However, after a half dozen ineffective appearances in 1938 with three losses and no victories, the now thirty-eight-year-old aging "Schoolboy" hung up his glove for major league play but pitched in several games for the semi-pro Brooklyn Bushwicks. In all, his major league pitching record was 237-182 with a 3.59 ERA. In addition, he went 6-4 in World Series play with a 1.81 ERA.

Waite Hoyt had several experiences with show business having once toured with a vaudeville act in the off-season and had also hosted a short-term radio program as early as 1937. He decided to opt for a future in radio. He hosted a variety of pre-and-post game shows in New York until January of 1942 when the Burger Brewing Company of Cincinnati hired him to be a play-by-play announcer for Reds games. From 1948 through 1954, those Reds games that were televised also had the advantage of Hoyt's announcing work. He remained at this position for twenty-four years, becoming a favorite with fans. In addition to his fine coverage of the games he was virtually unparalleled in being able to draw on his years of experience and discuss them during rain delays. In the winter months, Hoyt often had a television sports program, *The Waite Hoyt Hall of Fame*, where he interviewed various celebrity athletes.

In the early sixties, a long play album of his stories titled *The Best of Waite Hoyt in the Rain* was released and eagerly sold to his many fans. Hoyt was especially in prime form in discussing his many experiences with the legendary Babe Ruth, his teammate on the great Yankee assemblages of the roaring twenties. In fact, he also proved a valuable oral resource to both amateur and professional baseball historians. Frank Graham, who wrote *The New York Yankees* in 1943, is supposed to have shared his royalties with Hoyt who contributed most of the information on the 1921-1930 era. He also contributed to other works of baseball history as a source of information including the lengthy introduction to G. H. Fleming's *Murderer's Row: The 1927 New York Yankees* (1985), which he completed only a few months before his own death in 1984.

Waite Hoyt retired after the 1965 season, because Burger Brewing lost the radio broadcasting franchise. In those days, the broadcasters were employed by the sponsors; today they are employed by the ball club. However, in 1972 he came back as co-announcer on the telecasts and then retired for good. He continued to be well known in the Cincinnati area. According to Sir Knight Norman Lincoln of Eaton, Ohio, he never charged for his services when he spoke to Masonic groups, which is ironic because according to the records of the Grand Lodge of New York, he had been suspended for non-payment of dues on November 19, 1935. Elected to the Baseball Hall of Fame in 1969, Hoyt later served on the Veteran's Committee for Hall of Fame selection. He remained an honored statesman of the game until his death in Cincinnati on August 25, 1984. The Brooklyn-ite had been a resident of the Queen City for half of his life.

**Note**: The best sources of information on Waite Hoyt are William A. Cook, *Waite Hoyt: A Biography of the Yankees' Schoolboy Wonder*, (McFarland, 2004) and the interview in Eugene C. Murdock, *Baseball Between the Wars* (Meckler, 1992), pp. 23-62 as well as Frank Graham, *The New York Yankees* (Putnam, 1943) and G. H. Fleming, *Murderers' Row* (Morrow, 1985). Thanks also to the staff at the Grand Lodge of New York and to Sir Knight Norman Lincoln of Eaton, Ohio and Sir Knight Peter Westbere of Guelph, Ontario for pictures.

August 2008; slightly revised 2011

## Sir Knight Walton H. Walker: *The Korean War's "Stand or Die" General*

The Korean War ended nearly sixty years ago. This conflict might give Masons, including those who are veterans of that conflict, a moment to reflect on the fact that in addition to Brother Harry S. Truman, as commander-in-chief, at least four prominent generals in that "police action" were among their brothers. General and Brother Douglas MacArthur is one of the most prominent military leaders in the nation's history. General and Brother Matthew B. Ridgway will be recalled as the man who took MacArthur's place in April of 1951. General and Brother Mark Clark was in overall command at the time the truce was signed in July of 1953. The fourth man, General and Sir Knight Walton "Johnny" Walker, is largely forgotten today. Yet in the first six months of this war, Walker as commanding general of the Eighth Army and in charge of the ground forces, played a role second in significance only to that of MacArthur.

Walton Harris Walker was born in Belton, Texas, on December 3, 1889. Both of his grandfathers had fought for the Confederacy, but Walton's father followed the more peaceful profession of operating a dry-goods store. Interested in a military career from youth, he attended a local military school in Texas, Virginia Military Institute, and eventually the United States Military Academy in West Point, New York, graduating in 1912.

Back home that summer, young Walker made his entrance into Masonry, joining Belton Lodge No. 166. The young officer received his blue lodge degrees on June 27, July 25, and August 23, 1912. Four days later, he petitioned Belton Chapter No. 76, Royal Arch Masons receiving the Mark and Past Master degrees that same night, August 27, 1912. Moving rapidly, he received the Most Excellent Master Degree on September 3 and the Royal Arch on September 5,

1912. His Commandery record is somewhat vague, but a Walter Harris Walker took all three degrees in Belton Commandery No. 23 on December 26, 1912. Since there is no birth date given in the Grand Commandery of Texas records, we can only guess that it is the same person. He demitted from both the Belton Chapter and Commandery in the early 1930s, and it is not known at this time where or even if he affiliated. However, three standard reference books all identify him as a Knight Templar. In the spring of 1913, he took the Scottish Rite, completing them in the Valley of Galveston, Texas on March 20. In 1949, he received the K.C.C.H. He also belonged to the Shrine in Galveston.

Meanwhile as a young lieutenant, Walker was assigned briefly to Fort Sheridan, Illinois, and then to Fort Sill, Oklahoma (several times). With the unrest that resulted from the Mexican Revolution, numerous army units were stationed at various points in Texas, including that of Walker who participated in the American occupation of Vera Cruz. However, American entry into World War I in April of 1917 caused the American Army to focus more attention on events in Europe. A month after that conflict began, Walton Walker was promoted to Captain on May 15, 1917.

Captain Walker received assignment to the Second Battalion of the 57th Infantry. A few months later, the War Department transferred him to the Thirteenth Machine Gun Battalion and sent him to France in April of 1918. Over the next several months, the young Captain saw plenty of action at St. Miheil and in the Meuse-Argonne campaign where he was temporarily promoted to Major. He was also awarded the Silver Star with Oak Leaf Cluster for "gallantry under fire." After the November 11, 1918 armistice, Walker remained in Europe with the army of occupation until July of 1919.

Back in the United States, Walker received permanent rank of Major on July 1, 1920, and a promotion to Lieutenant Colonel on August 1, 1935. His duties in this peacetime era took him to numerous domestic bases including Fort Benning, Georgia; West Point, New York; Fort Leavenworth, Kansas; Fort Monroe, Virginia; and Vancouver Barracks, Washington. During that period, on March 18, 1924, Major Walker courted and married Caroline Victoria Emerson of Baltimore, Maryland. The couple had one son, Sam S. Walker, who followed his father into a military career, graduating from West Point in 1946.

During the inter-war period, Walker had received only one overseas assignment, serving in China with the Fifteenth Infantry Regiment on international railroad patrol. However, with World War

II on the horizon, Colonel Walker would soon see more than his share of foreign soil. He spent much of 1940 and the early part of 1941 in the War Plans Division of the War Department, becoming Executive Officer in December 1940. Four months later, he became commanding officer of the 36th Infantry at Camp Polk, Louisiana, and then commander of the Third Armored Brigade in the same locale. Placed in charge of Desert Training at Camp Young, California, in 1942, preparing soldiers for the North Africa campaign, *Time* magazine quoted a colleague that Walker's concept of readying the troops was to "make training so damned hard that combat would seem easy." In April of 1943, the now General Walker went with the Third Armored Division to Fort Campbell, Kentucky, and shortly thereafter to Europe.

Walton Walker's command was re-designated the Twentieth Corps in October of 1943 as part of General George S. Patton's Third Army. For nine months following D-day, Walker's corps pushed relentlessly against the Axis, crossing the Moselle in November of 1944, penetrating the Siegfried Line in February of 1945, liberating the prisoners at Buchenwald, and reaching the outskirts of Chemnitz in April. On April 27, General Patton presented him with the same three stars of a temporary Lieutenant General that he had earlier received from General Eisenhower. This must have been a proud moment for Walton Walker, because according to many observers, Patton had been his role model.

In June of 1945, General Walker received a year-long assignment in Dallas, Texas, in charge of the Eighth Service Command and then the Fifth Army Area with headquarters in Chicago. In September of 1948, he took command of the Eighth Army, the principal ground force of the United States in the Far East. He remained in this station for the rest of his life.

In this command and with the Far East a potential powder keg, particularly with the Communist forces in control of mainland China from early 1949, Walker wanted his troops to be in a state of "combat readiness." He believed they had been "softened" by the relatively light occupation duties they were then encountering in Japan and South Korea. The General delivered a major address on this subject on June 10, 1950.

Some two weeks later, Walker's warnings proved prophetic when the North Koreans mounted a major surprise invasion of the South. General Douglas MacArthur was overall Far East Commander, and Walker was in charge of the forces on the ground. Outmanned and outgunned, the South Koreans and their United Nations allies (mostly Americans) fell back to what became known as the Pusan Perimeter. It was at this point that Walker issued his famous "stand or die" order, maintaining that a Dunkirk-style withdrawal could not be achieved. More American and Australian reinforcements poured in, and Pusan held, "saved by a miracle."

A little later, MacArthur initiated the Inchon landings, and it suddenly became the enemy's time to retreat. Walker's Eighth Army took the offensive and advanced rapidly northward until the Chinese intervention forced them southward again. South of the 38th parallel, Walker's career ended suddenly as he died in a jeep wreck on December 23, 1950 (December 22 in the United States). Within hours, Brother and General Matthew Ridgway of West Point Lodge No. 877 in New York was appointed to replace him.

Meanwhile, General Walker's remains were brought to Japan and taken to Yokohama where Mrs. Walker had been living. According to William R. Denslow, "at the request of his widow, the Star in the East Lodge No. 640 . . . conducted Masonic services." Brother and President Truman issued the following statement: "Our country has suffered a tremendous loss. . . . General Walker had a great talent for generalship. He was a true leader of his men and suffered with them the hardships of his campaigns. He was a soldier—a real soldier. To you and me there is no higher compliment." Brother and General Douglas MacArthur wrote complimentary remarks about the late general in his memoirs. Back home in Belton, Texas, the *Times* reported that "Walker's death was a severe blow to folks in this central Texas town who had watched him grow to manhood and had pridefully followed his Army career." The General's aged and frail mother, Mrs. S. S. Walker, took his death well all things considered, saying it just "something I have to bear." As for the decision to bury him in Arlington National Cemetery, she agreed that he belonged to the entire country as much as to his family and to Belton. Congress posthumously awarded him a fourth star. Walker's son, Sam S. Walker, remained in the service and eventually earned a fourth star himself.

While General Walker is fondly remembered in some circles, he is not as well known among the general public as his achievements merited. Nonetheless, he served his country well in three wars. As a man and Mason, Walton Harris Walker exemplified the highest tenets of his profession.

**Note**: The main source of data on Walton Walker is the sketch in the 1950 edition of *Current Biography*. For his Masonic records I am indebted to Bro. Bruce Mercer of the Grand Lodge of Texas, Loyd Chance of the Grand Commandery of Texas, and Dr. John Boettjer of *The Scottish Rite Journal*. Thanks also to Sir Knight Paschal King of Kenton Commandery No. 58 and Oak Hill, Ohio for the material he obtained from the Internet. Also thanks to Sir Knight Roger Van Dyke for his careful proofreading.

June 2004; slightly revised 2011

## Sir Knight Whip Wilson:
*A Different Kind of Western Hero*

In the annals of Masonic movie cowboy stars, Sir Knight Whip Wilson ranks as one of the lesser-known figures. While his level of fame and success never reached that of early-day figures such as Harry Carey, Buck Jones, and Tom Mix; the singers typified by Gene Autry, Tex Ritter, and Roy Rogers; or the big budget stars represented by Glenn Ford, Audie Murphy, and John Wayne, Wilson managed to carve out his niche in film history by being a bit different from all of the above. Like the late and somewhat better remembered Lash LaRue, Brother Wilson achieved his near uniqueness by complementing his six-gun prowess with a wielding of a bullwhip to capture the bad guys.

The man who gained fleeting fame as Whip Wilson began life with a name neither alliterative nor exotic. Roland Charles Meyers was born in Granite City, Illinois, on June 16, 1911. There were a total of nine children in the Meyers family, and as Roland grew older, he and his father expressed divergent views on a variety of issues. While his parents encouraged his musical interests, the youth preferred piano while his dad wanted him to become a violinist. Since he cared for neither school nor his violin teacher, the independent thinking fourteen-year-old ran away from home and landed a laboring job on a dairy farm. He soon found that milking cows held even less appeal, and he swallowed his pride and returned home. His stern father then gave him a choice between returning to school and getting a job in the local steel mill. Young Meyers opted for the latter.

Roland Meyers held a variety of jobs in locations extending from Missouri to Texas over the next twenty years as he struggled to find his place in life. These included diverse positions ranging from being a singing waiter to that of working in the border patrol at El

Paso. At seventeen he joined the army, and while he was stationed at Fort Bliss, Texas, he met and subsequently briefly married a woman named Ann. When his army duty ended and the couple moved to the St. Louis area, Ann became homesick for Texas, and their marriage ended.

Roland Meyers found a job as a singing waiter (he allegedly sang with a strong baritone voice) at the Bismark Café in St. Louis. He met an older woman named Madeline who had a background in opera. She decided to provide him with additional voice training. They, too, married briefly and unsuccessfully. Roland landed some part-time and temporary work in local operas and stage productions, but it was never enough to sustain him.

In 1937 while still employed as a singing waiter, he met Monica Lane. They became life partners on July 2, 1938. Later, when Meyers had become famous as Whip Wilson, the diminutive 4 feet, 10-inch Monica toured with her husband singing such country songs as "I'm Little But I'm Loud," initially made famous by Little (and later Brother) Jimmy Dickens. After this marriage, our subject's personal life stabilized, but together he and Monica continued their pursuit of the elusive American dream for another decade.

R. Charles Meyers (more and more going by his middle name) returned to El Paso, Texas, and joined the Border Patrol, but increasingly sang on a part-time basis at night clubs in nearby Juarez. The World War II years found the couple operating a combination service station-truck stop café at Davis Mountain Station, a remote west Texas locale.

Shortly after the war ended, an agent called him with the news that he thought he could get Meyers a major part in the musical "Oklahoma" if he would come to Hollywood. The couple then moved to California, but the big role never materialized, and the pair had to make ends meet by operating a boarding house.

For a time, Meyers even took a job as a garage mechanic in Huntington Park while awaiting his big break. Finally, he was offered a lead part in the London Company's rendition of the hit musical, *Annie Get Your Gun*, but he refused because a new agent thought he could land him major roles in western movies. Monica relates the following story: the agent felt sure that a contract was about to come through with Monogram Pictures, and she was determined to get her husband a stylish western suit that he had spotted in a clothing store window. Although she had no money, the store manager let her take the suit home in return for holding her jewelry in his safe until she produced the cash. That very afternoon, the call came to sign the contract with Monogram, and the agent advanced the funds to pay for the suit and to retrieve the watch and wedding ring. Roland Charles Meyers not only wore the suit when he signed the contract but would later wear it to the grave.

At this time, R. Meyers received the stage name "Whip Wilson." However, a contract with Monogram hardly ranked as a guarantee to fame and fortune. One of the "poverty-row" film studios, Monogram, was one jump behind Republic and only a jump ahead of P.R.C. on the ladder of movie corporations. The company thrived on low-budget comedies such as their Bowery Boys series and such western films that starred Johnny Mack Brown in the action line and Jimmy Wakely in the musical genre. According to Wakely, Scott Dunlap, a Monogram producer (and a Mason) who had been associated with Buck Jones, hoped that in Roland Meyers he had not only found a second Buck Jones but also a competitor to the bullwhip wielding Lash LaRue who had been building a following since the inauguration of his film series at P.R.C. in 1947.

In mid-1948, Monogram introduced Wilson to movie audiences by casting him in a Wakely film, *Silver Trails.* He received a "star" buildup and for four years from the beginning of 1949 through the end of 1952 had his own series of twenty-two pictures. His first lead role was in *Crashing Thru.* Other titles in the Wilson series included *Arizona Territory* (1950), *Stage to Blue River* (1951), and his final effort, *Wyoming Roundup,* (1952). In the first twelve episodes, veteran character actor Andy Clyde (a member of Cahuenga Lodge No. 513 since 1943) who had been "California Carlson" in the Hopalong Cassidy series had the sidekick role of "Winks." Clyde also ranked as one of the most active Masons in the movie community. According to non-member Rand Brooks, Andy spent three or four nights a week in lodge activity of some type. By all accounts, it was the Scottish-born Andy Clyde who kindled the spark of Masonic interest in Whip Wilson.

Other significant support actors also appeared in Whip's films. After the departure of Andy Clyde, Fuzzy Knight, another veteran sidekick, took his place. Wilson also had some of the most appealing leading ladies in the B-Western genre. The late Reno Browne, an excellent horsewoman, appeared in six of his films. In fact, the pair was sufficiently popular that their pictures appeared four times on the covers of western romance magazines. Phyllis Coates also had the lead female role in six Wilson pictures and is best remembered as the original Lois Lane in the *Superman* TV series. Ms. Coates was also the female lead in one of the last movie serials, *Panther Girl of The Congo*. Other Wilson leading ladies included Lois Hall and Noel Neill (also a TV Lois Lane) in two more films each. Others who appeared more than once in Wilson movies included Myron Healy, Iron Eyes Cody, Tommy Farrell, Jim Bannon, Terry Frost, John Merton, and a noted movie villain who has his own significant Masonic career, the late Pierce Lyden.

Ironically, by the time Whip became a Mason, he and Andy Clyde no longer worked together, although Andy apparently helped out in all the degree work. Roland Charles Meyers was elected by ballot to receive his degrees in North Hollywood Lodge No. 542 on December 6, 1951. He was initiated an Entered Apprentice the following week on December 13, 1951, passed to the degree of Fellowcraft on the following March 3, and was Raised a Master Mason on March 27, 1952. Monica thought he took the Scottish Rite, but that is an error. He did take the York Rite degrees, exalted on March 27, 1954, in what became North Hollywood Chapter No. 151, R.A.M.

At the end of 1952, Monogram Pictures cancelled the B-Western series of Whip Wilson and their long running action hero, Johnny Mack Brown. That type of film had been dying slowly because of the competition of television. Rex Allen and Rocky Lane held on for a little longer at Republic, and Gene Autry continued making pictures for Columbia into 1953. Bill Elliott and Wayne Morris made a few more so-called high grade B pictures for the Monogram parent company, Allied Artists. Actually, since Monogram only paid their stars a $250.00 weekly salary, Wilson had derived much of his income from heavy touring between pictures anyway. He and Monica had organized a road show called the Flying W Roundup and worked a heavy schedule of theater appearances which included a combination of musical numbers, whip tricks, and horse tricks performed by Whip's horse Rocket (originally named Bullet). They continued this for a couple of years after the movie making had stopped, but with no new pictures coming out, their days on the traveling theater and rodeo circuit would be numbered. In 1955, Wilson performed the whip tricks in a Burt Lancaster film, *The Kentuckian,* which proved to be his Hollywood and show business swan song.

During his days in St. Louis, Charles Meyers had taken some courses in drafting and engineering, and they proved to be useful once Hollywood no longer had use for a whip-wielding cowboy. He soon landed a job at North American Aviation and moved to Anaheim. In this period, he completed his York Rite work when he was knighted in Long Beach Commandery No. 40, K.T. on May 21, 1960. He became a Noble of El Bekal Shrine Temple on May 28, 1960. On June 10, 1960, he affiliated with Fullerton Chapter No. 90, R. A. M. but retained his Blue Lodge in North Hollywood.

After seven years, Whip and Monica purchased some rental property on the shore of Lake Tahoe and hoped to settle down to a quiet semi-retirement. However, it was not to be. Beginning in January 1964, the one-time cowboy star experienced three heart attacks. Late that summer, he and Monica moved to San Rafael where the altitude was lower, and Whip would be able to receive better medical care. Tragedy struck again when a fourth heart attack on October 22, 1964, proved fatal. Monica took Roland Charles Meyers back to Illinois where he was buried in the blue western suit she had obtained for him when he signed his movie contract.

In 1981, Monica Meyers who had returned to the St. Louis area published a booklet entitled, *Crashing Thru: My Life with Whip Wilson.* In 1998, Brother Bobby Copeland of Oak Ridge, Tennessee, a dedicated western film fan, self-published *The Whip Wilson Story,* a somewhat longer work that contains additional information gleaned largely from persons who worked in the man's films. Copeland probably wrote the definitive conclusion on the subject—while "Wilson never attained outstanding star status... fans agree that [he] has his place and made his mark, just not as indelibly as some others." Masons can remember that Sir Knight Wilson was for a time a distinguished member of the motion picture community in his chosen occupation.

**Note:** The aforementioned booklets constitute the best available sources of information on Roland Charles Meyers, a.k.a. Whip Wilson. As for his Masonic record, Brother Richard Duenckel obtained it from the records of North Hollywood Lodge. It was supplemented by additional data from the staff of the Orange County, California York Rite Bodies and El Bekal Shrine Temple in Anaheim. I also appreciate the help of Brother Copeland.

January 2000; slightly revised 2011

**Sir Knight William Saxbe:**
*Attorney General, Diplomat, Senator*

Among prominent Masons in government service in the last six decades, few have served their country in as many diverse positions as William B. Saxbe. Known to his friends as "the squire of Mechanicsburg," Saxbe has been a state legislator, a United States Senator, a state and national Attorney General, and finally an Ambassador to India. On top of all this, Saxbe was a member of his Blue Lodge and Scottish Rite Valley for more than sixty years, a Chapter member for more than a half-century, and a Council and Commandery member for nearly as long.

William Bart Saxbe was born on June 24, 1916, the son of Bart R. and Faye Carey Saxbe in Mechanicsburg, Champaign County, Ohio, where his ancestors had settled in 1825. On his mother's side, Saxbe claimed descent from Patrick Henry. Bill's father practiced the occupation of a cattle buyer. As a youth, Saxbe attended Mechanicsburg High School where he played football. After finishing high school, he went to Ohio State University where he majored in political science.

During his college days, young William Bart Saxbe petitioned Mechanicsburg Lodge No. 113 in his hometown. After receiving his Entered Apprentice degree on November 2, 1937, he became a Fellowcraft on December 7, 1937. On January 18, 1938, William Saxbe was raised to the sublime degree of Master Mason. That spring he took the Scottish Rite degrees in the Valley of Dayton, receiving the 32° on April 23, 1938. On December 3, 1938, Bill was created a noble of Antioch Shrine Temple in Dayton. Two years later he received a Bachelor of Arts degree from Ohio State University. A member of the Ohio National Guard, he soon found himself called to active duty and spent the next five years in the Army Air Force.

Although Saxbe had given serious thought to becoming an Episcopal minister after the war, he ultimately decided on law school instead and returned to Ohio State University. In the fall of 1946, he also found himself a successful candidate for the Ohio General Assembly (otherwise known as the legislature) as a Republican. Bill ultimately served four consecutive terms in the House. During his third term, he served as majority floor leader and in the fourth as Speaker of the House. Meanwhile in 1948, he graduated from the Ohio State University law school.

As a law school senior, Brother Saxbe took his capitular degrees in Mechanicsburg Chapter No. 168, R.A.M., being exalted on December 9, 1947 (this Chapter later merged with Urbana Chapter No. 34). More than five years elapsed before the busy legislator completed his York Rite work, but he eventually received both the Royal and Select Master degrees on October 15, 1952, in Urbana Council No. 59, R. & S. M. The following spring, he received the Order of Red Cross on April 24, 1953, and both the Order of Malta and the Order of the Temple on May 16, 1953, all in Raper Commandery No. 19 in Urbana, Ohio.

It has been said that Sir Knight Saxbe's ultimate goal in life was a seat in the United States Senate. He made a somewhat premature effort to achieve that objective in 1954 when he entered the primary election to fill the unexpired term of the deceased Robert A. Taft. However, he had s stiff opponent in Brother George H. Bender who had previously been on the statewide ballot as a congressman-at-large. The younger man put up a good fight but lost to the better-known Bender by a vote of 254,390 to 188,783.

After two years in private law practice, Bill Saxbe again entered the political arena when he sought the post of attorney general in the Buckeye State. This time, he benefited from ballot name recognition and nosed out his closest rival by 3,356 votes in a four-way primary race. Saxbe had an easy win in the fall as he defeated Democrat Steven Young by nearly 160,000 votes as GOP gubernatorial candidate, Sir Knight C. William O'Neill of Marietta Commandery No. 50, ran up a 426,000 vote majority. The Mechanicsburg lawyer described the post of state attorney general as "one job [I] really liked." One associate described him as a "tough, capable crime fighter."

In 1958, however, Saxbe fell victim to a Democrat landslide that engulfed the GOP. Republican support of a "right to work" amendment dragged the entire party down to defeat except for Secretary of State Ted Brown. Saxbe opposed right-to-work legislation and distanced himself from his running mates, but he still lost the race by some 94,000 votes. As with his first defeat, Bill returned to his law practice. In 1962 and again in 1966, he recaptured the attorney general office, defeating Robert Sweeney of Cleveland by respective majorities of 108,406 and 287,233.

Halfway into his third term as state attorney general, William Saxbe finally got his opportunity to achieve his life-long goal of a United States Senate seat. Conservative Democrat incumbent Frank J. Lausche had alienated enough liberals within his own party that they ran a strong candidate, John J. Gilligan, against him in the primary thus defeating him. By contrast, Saxbe cruised to an easy primary victory and went on to defeat Gilligan in November by 114,812 votes in a hard-fought contest. At the age of fifty-two, the Squire of Mechanicsburg "had achieved his lifelong ambition."

Once in the Senate, only a few months passed before Saxbe began to sound disillusioned. He viewed the Washington establishment, including his own party's Nixon administration, as out of touch with reality. Confessing boredom, he doubted that he would serve a second term. The slow pace of Congress in transacting business seems to have been the principal reason for his dissatisfaction, and he began seeking ways to speed up the process with an unlikely ally in the person of California liberal Democrat Alan Cranston. After two years, he made one of his by then familiar blunt remarks: "The first six months I kept wondering how I got there. . . After that I started wondering how all of them did."

Like another blunt spoken Senator, Sir Knight Barry Goldwater of Arizona, Sir Knight Saxbe also became increasingly unhappy with the Nixon Administration. Even before Watergate, he once referred to top Nixon staff members H. R. Haldeman and John Ehrlichman as "a couple of Nazis." Given these and other remarks, it came as something of a surprise when President Nixon chose the maverick lame duck Senator from Ohio to become Attorney General following the resignation of Brother Elliott Richardson and the sacking of Special Watergate Prosecutor Archibald Cox. William Saxbe's independent stance through the seventies and the reputation for integrity he had on both sides of the aisle not only put him in a good position to maintain the honor of the Justice Department but also to win confirmation from an increasingly hostile Senate. Sworn into office on January 4, 1974, the year Bill Saxbe spent at the helm of the Justice Department is given credit for maintaining confidence in the department during the closing months of the Nixon administration and the early months of Gerald Ford's time in the White House.

In early 1975, President Ford appointed William Saxbe to be Ambassador to India. During his Senate days, Saxbe had traveled extensively and in 1971 had been a critic of Pakistan. Given the Senator's often quoted bluntness, he might seem an unlikely choice for a sensitive diplomatic post, yet his criticism of India's long-standing rival on the Indian sub-continent made him a natural for this position. He spent two years as an Ambassador, serving until the advent of the Carter Presidency.

His government service behind him, Bill Saxbe became a member of the Columbus law firm of Chester, Saxbe, Hoffman & Wilcox. Later he worked with other law partnerships. More Masonic honors came to him as well. On October 19, 1979, the Grand Lodge of Ohio presented him with the Rufus Putnam Distinguished Service Award, and on September 30, 1982, he received the 33° in St. Louis. Over the years, various Ohio colleges awarded him honorary degrees including Wilmington, Central State, Findlay, Walsh, Ohio Wesleyan, Capital, Ohio State, and Bowling Green. In 1982 he became special counsel for the Central States Teamsters' Union Pension Fund.

In retirement, the former Senator divided his time between his Mechanicsburg farm and a winter home in Boynton Beach, Florida. Bill and his wife, Dolly, had two sons and a daughter. Both of the sons followed their father into Masonry. In due time, he received sixty-year pins from Mechanicsburg Lodge and the Valley of Dayton, and fifty-year awards in all of the York Rite bodies. Sir Knight Saxbe, the Squire of Mechanicsburg, passed away on August 24, 2010. He left behind a record of having served his state and nation with dignity, honor, and integrity.

**Note**: In researching Sir Knight Saxbe's Masonic career, I am indebted to Grand Secretary of the Grand Lodge of Ohio, David Dresser, and the late Earl Gifford, Grand Secretary of the Grand Chapter of Ohio and to the recorders of Urbana Council and Raper Commandery. Staff members at the Valley of Dayton, AASR, and Antioch Shrine Temple were also helpful. Saxbe's memoir, *I've Seen the Elephant: an Autobiography* (2000) is a good account of his life and opinions. A former attorney who served as a deputy Attorney General, the late Sir Knight Walter J. Howdyshell, also shared some of his recollections of "the Squire of Mechanicsburg." Abby Gail Goodnite Ehman typed the original article.

July 1999, slightly revised 2011

## Sir Knight Yakima Canutt: *King of the Hollywood Stunt Men*

In the development of the motion picture, the stunt men (and women) are the ones who most often flirt with real danger. They are the ones who fall off the cliffs, crash the automobiles, and make the flying leaps for life that the heroic-looking lead stars often get the credit for doing. While the death-defying stunts are never quite as heroic in reality as they appear to be on the screen, they do involve considerable risk, and many stunt people have incurred broken bones and experienced serious accidents. While stunt men, unlike stars, have never become household names, within the film industry, many have gained considerable renown and respect. However, none in this era seem to have achieved as much recognition as the subject of this sketch, Yakima Canutt.

Enos Edward Canutt was born on November 29, 1895, in a little ranch house on Peniwawa Creek in the eastern part of the state of Washington. Contrary to rumors, partly spread by Yakima himself, Canutt did not have any Indian blood in his veins. Except for a brief period when his father worked for the state, Canutt grew up on the family ranch. As a result, he learned a lot about horses and cattle. Fascinated in particular with bronco riding, young Enos Canutt began to engage in that activity in his mid-teens. His parents expressed reluctance to having their son engage in such risky business. By 1912, however, they had begun to relent.

Canutt's first entry in rodeo competition came in the fall of 1912 at the Whitman County Fair in Colfax. After that, the youth drifted about for a time in various jobs but came back to ranch work and rodeo competition. In 1914, he added steer bulldogging to his talents. Canutt met and mingled with the legendary figures on the rodeo circuits such as Tex McCloud, Buffalo Vernon, Bill Pickett, and

Jackson Sundown who was a full-blooded Nez Perce. In 1916, he acquired his nickname, "Yakima," at the Pendleton Roundup in Oregon. At the time he was running around with some cowboys from Yakima, Washington. A newspaper photo of him being thrown from a horse bore the caption, "Yakima Canutt leaving the deck of a Pendleton bronc." Although Enos was not really from Yakima, the misidentification stuck with him as a nickname.

Over the next several years, Canutt found considerable fame as a rodeo cowboy. He won first place in saddle bronc riding at Pendleton three times (1917, 1919 and 1920). He also took first in bulldogging in both 1920 and 1921. From Texas rodeos as far south as Wichita Falls and Fort Worth to trips eastward to Chicago and New York, Yakima Canutt had become a big name in rodeo circles. In 1917, 1919, 1920, and 1923, he won the Police Gazette award for all-around cowboy. In the latter part of World War I, Yakima served in the United States Navy, spending virtually all of his service stint in Bremerton, Washington. After discharge, he went back to the rodeo.

During his bronc riding years, Yakima also became a Mason. He was raised to the sublime degree of Master Mason on September 8, 1921, in LaCrosse Lodge No. 155 in LaCrosse, Washington. His younger brother, John Maceo Canutt, conferred the degree. He subsequently completed his York Rite work in Colfax Commandery No. 12, Knights Templar in Colfax, Washington. Years later, after he had settled in Hollywood, Yakima became a member of Al Malaikah Shrine Temple and the 233 Club made up of Masonic actors.

Western movies were becoming quite popular and many rodeo cowboys found work in Hollywood in the off-season. Their skills in handling horses and cattle created a demand for their services. Canutt had his first motion picture experiences in 1919. As Canutt became older, he looked more and more to them for a livelihood. Although he made his first films with Tom Mix in 1919, Yakima went on to star in a number of low-budget silent westerns. He did not have the right type of voice to be a hero in talking pictures; in his own words, he said that he "sounded like a hillbilly in a well." Canutt turned to smaller parts and stunt work. Although one can often catch his bit part acting in mid-thirties reruns of John Wayne films in which he often played a villain, Yak also doubled and did the stunts for Wayne in the same movies. As events developed, it would be the stunts that made Canutt a Hollywood legend in his own lifetime.

The most famous of Canutt's stunts involved falling or jumping from a stagecoach among the running horses, and as the coach or wagon passed over him, then grabbing the back of the vehicle and climbing up onto the coach from the rear. In his 1979 autobiography, Yakima wrote, "to this day, it has never been duplicated in its entirety by anyone else." He first did it with a freight wagon in the Jack Randall film, *Riders of the Dawn* in 1937, but most famously in the John Wayne classic *Stagecoach* in 1939. Canutt added, "I was paid a thousand dollars each time I did it, and in those days, that was really big money."

To catalog all of Yakima Canutt's creative efforts as a double-stunt man would require a great deal more space than is available here. However, one might just note that many of them involved films in which the stars were fellow Masonic actors. For instance, in *The Devil Horse* (1932), doubling for Brother Harry Carey, he held onto a wild horse's neck with his legs and his head hanging down. In *Man of Conquest,* a film about the life of Sam Houston who was portrayed by Brother Rickard Dix, he took a number of spectacular horse falls and created some realistic wagon crashes. And of course his work with John Wayne who later became a Mason has already been discussed. Finally, in 1941 while doing a stunt in a relatively routine Roy Rogers (who also became a Mason) film, *Idaho,* Yakima sustained two broken ankles. After that he took more care in his stunt work and began looking for other ways to sustain himself in the motion picture business.

One skill that Canutt attained was the ability "to handle animal sequences." This skill included not only horses but other animals as well dating back at least to *Darkest Africa,* a 1936 serial with famed lion tamer and Brother Clyde Beatty. Canutt's most interesting work on a jungle film came in 1953 on location in French Equatorial Africa where he assisted in the making of *Mogambo* which starred Brother Clark Gable along with Grace Kelly and Ava Gardner. Interestingly enough, Canutt had earlier doubled for Gable in the scene from *Gone With the Wind* in which Rhett Butler drives the wagon through the burning city of Atlanta.

By the time Yakima helped with the gorilla scenes in *Mogambo,* he had already found his next calling as a second unit or action scene director. He achieved this with a pair of lavish medieval costume dramas filmed in England, *Ivanhoe* and *Knights of the Round Table.* Thereafter, Yakima continued to direct stunt and action scenes in such westerns as *The Naked Spur, The Lawless Rider,* and *Far Horizons* as well as a pair of Disney classics with Brother Fess Parker, *Westward Ho, the Wagons,* and *Old Yeller.* His later fame would come from his work in big budget spectaculars filmed in Europe.

The first of these efforts, *Ben Hur* in 1959, featured the spectacular chariot race where Charlton Heston in the title role bested Stephen Boyd. *Spartacus* in 1960 starred Kirk Douglas and Jean Simmons and told of the great slave revolt in ancient Rome. Canutt staged the magnificent battle scenes. *El Cid,* the epic of medieval Spain, again starred Heston and also Sophia Loren and featured more spectacular battle scenes. Heston also starred in *Khartoum* (1966) and Canutt re-created the action scenes that typified the conflict between the British and Arabs in the 1880s Sudan. *Helen of Troy* (1956) and *The Fall of the Roman Empire* (1964) were hardly considered outstanding films but not because of Canutt's direction of the action scenes.

As Yakima became older, he slowed down somewhat but still did some work on action scene direction. He had some successes with another Disney classic *Swiss Family Robinson* (1964), *Cat Ballou* (1965), *Where Eagles Dare* (1967), and *A Man Called Horse* (1969). Canutt did his final film with John Wayne, *Rio Lobo,* in 1970 and his final western in *Equus* three years later with Richard Burton.

In his later years in the movie business, Yakima Canutt received a great deal of recognition for his decades of hard work. In 1966, he received a special Oscar recognizing his achievements as a great stunt man and also for the various devices he had developed in the interests of safety. A decade later he was inducted into both the National Cowboy Hall of Fame and the National Rodeo Hall of Fame. Both of his sons went on to become acclaimed stunt men in their own right. In 1978, the Academy of Motion Picture Arts and Sciences honored Sir Knight Canutt with a dinner where his friend Charlton Heston introduced him as "simply the best that ever was at what he does."

In 1979, Yakima's autobiography, *Stunt Man,* was published. Charlton Heston contributed the "Foreword" and Brother John Wayne a brief "Afterword." The man who had taken so many risks and defied death more than anyone in film industry lived to celebrate his 90$^{th}$ birthday. When he died on May 24, 1986, Sir Knight Enos E. "Yakima" Canutt had been a Mason for nearly sixty-five years. Even more time had elapsed since his first 1919 appearance before a movie camera. During the ensuing decades, Brother and Sir Knight Canutt built an enviable reputation for being the best in his trade.

**Note**: The best source for Canutt is his modestly told autobiography, *Stunt Man* (1979). For his Masonic record see Jerry Erikson, "Freemasons in the Entertainment World, Part V," in *The Royal Arch Mason*, IX: 11, Fall 1969, pp. 343-344. Thanks also to Abby Goodnite Ehman for technical assistance.

July 1998; slightly revised 2011

## The Author – Ivan M. Tribe

Ivan M. Tribe was born in Albany, Ohio, on May 1, 1940. He grew up there and was graduated from Albany High School in 1958. He attended Ohio University, obtaining a B.S. Ed. in 1962, majoring in History and Government, and an M.A. in 1967 in American History. After teaching high school in Vinton and Meigs Counties for six years, he entered the doctoral program at the University of Toledo completing his Ph.D. in 1976.

Tribe joined the history faculty at Rio Grande College (later the University of Rio Grande) in Ohio in 1976, obtaining the rank of Professor in 1990 and retiring as Emeritus Professor in 2007. During his academic career, he published numerous articles in professional history journals and popular periodicals. His main areas of specialization were in the areas of Appalachian communities and in popular culture, especially bluegrass and country music history. The latter included three books: *Mountaineer Jamboree: Country Music in West Virginia* (University of Kentucky Press, 1984), *The Stonemans: An Appalachian Family and the Music that Shaped Their Lives* (University of Illinois Press, 1993), and *Country: A Regional Exploration* (Greenwood Press, 2006). In addition, he co-authored *Rio Grande: From Baptists and Bevo to the Bell Tower, 1876-2001* (Jesse Stuart Foundation, 2002), and four volumes of a local history nature.

Bro. Tribe began his Masonic career at age twenty-one, being raised in Albany Lodge No. 723 on August 17, 1961, where he served as Master in 1967 and was Education Officer for ten years. Continuing in the York Rite, he was Exalted in Athens Chapter No. 39 on May 2, 1962, served as High Priest in 1966-1967, was greeted in Athens Council No. 15, R. & S. M. on November 28, 1962, and served as Illustrious Master in 1969-1970. Knighted in Athens Commandery

No. 15 on January 4, 1963, he served as Commander in 1990-1991 and in 1999-2000. He currently serves Athens Commandery as Sentinel.

In other Masonic bodies, Brother Tribe holds Scottish Rite membership in the Valley of Cambridge, Ohio (33° on September 26, 2000). Other memberships include Ohio Priory No. 18, K.Y.C.H.; past Sovereign Master, William J. Rees Council No. 141, A.M.D. (plural member of) Ohio River Valley Council No. 104); Ohio Valley College No. 196, Y.R.S.C.; Tecumseh Council No. 81, Knight Masons; Past Worthy Patron of Albany Chapter No. 558, O.E.S.; Lafayette Conclave, Red Cross of Constantine; and Royal Order of Scotland. For forty-six years he has been a member of Aladdin Shrine and the Hillbilly Degree for thirty-six. Tribe also holds membership in Phi Alpha Theta (history honorary), Patrons of Husbandry (Grange), and Knights of Pythias.

In public service, Tribe was Mayor of Albany, 1962-1965; member of the Athens County Board of Elections, 1964-1968; and Alexander Board of Education, 1970-1971.

He and his wife of forty-eight years, the former Deanna Tripp, a retired Community Development Specialist with Ohio State University Extension, live in McArthur Ohio. Since 1983, they have hosted a weekly educational country music radio program for Ohio University Public Media. They are both die-hard Cincinnati Reds fans.

www.ingramcontent.com/pod-product-compliance
Lightning Source LLC
Chambersburg PA
CBHW020600270326
41927CB00005B/109

*9781613421697*